Justice Without Borders

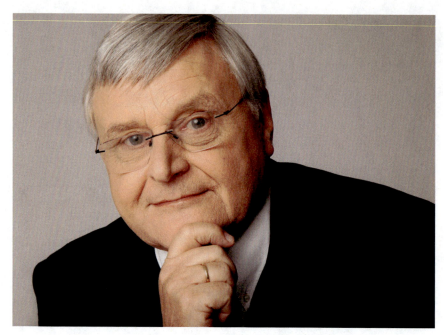

Wolfgang Schomburg

Justice Without Borders

Essays in Honour of Wolfgang Schomburg

Edited by

Martin Böse
Michael Bohlander
André Klip
Otto Lagodny

BRILL
NIJHOFF

LEIDEN | BOSTON

Library of Congress Cataloging-in-Publication Data

Names: Schomburg, Wolfgang, honouree. | Böse, Martin, editor. | Bohlander,
  Michael, 1962- editor. | Klip, Andre, editor. | Lagodny, Otto, 1958-
  editor.
Title: Justice without borders : essays in honour of Wolfgang Schomburg /
  edited by Martin Böse, Michael Bohlander, Andre Klip, Otto Lagodny.
Description: Leiden ; Boston : Brill, 2018. | Includes bibliographical
  references.
Identifiers: LCCN 2017055942 (print) | LCCN 2017057134 (ebook) | ISBN
  9789004352063 (E-book) | ISBN 9789004352049 (hardback : alk. paper)
Subjects: LCSH: Criminal law--European Union countries. | Criminal
  jurisdiction--European Union countries. | Double jeopardy--European Union
  countries. | Res judicata--European Union countries. | International
  criminal law--European Union countries. | Criminal justice, Administration
  of--International cooperation. | Schomburg, Wolfgang.
Classification: LCC KJE7975 (ebook) | LCC KJE7975 .J87 2017 (print) | DDC
  345.24--dc23
LC record available at https://lccn.loc.gov/2017055942

Typeface for the Latin, Greek, and Cyrillic scripts: "Brill". See and download: brill.com/brill-typeface.

ISBN 978-90-04-35204-9 (hardback)
ISBN 978-90-04-35206-3 (e-book)

Copyright 2018 by Koninklijke Brill NV, Leiden, The Netherlands.
Koninklijke Brill NV incorporates the imprints Brill, Brill Hes & De Graaf, Brill Nijhoff, Brill Rodopi,
Brill Sense and Hotei Publishing.
All rights reserved. No part of this publication may be reproduced, translated, stored in a retrieval system,
or transmitted in any form or by any means, electronic, mechanical, photocopying, recording or otherwise,
without prior written permission from the publisher.
Authorization to photocopy items for internal or personal use is granted by Koninklijke Brill NV provided
that the appropriate fees are paid directly to The Copyright Clearance Center, 222 Rosewood Drive, Suite
910, Danvers, MA 01923, USA. Fees are subject to change.

This book is printed on acid-free paper and produced in a sustainable manner.

Contents

Preface   VII
List of Abbreviations   X
Academic Writings of Wolfgang Schomburg   XIII
Decisions as Judge of UN-ICTY and UN-ICTR   XXIII

1 European Criminal Law and Brexit   1
   Kai Ambos

2 Energising the Law's Response to Terrorism: The Decision of the Appeals Chamber of the Special Tribunal of Lebanon and the Need for Further Action   23
   David Baragwanath

3 The Transnational Dimension of the *ne bis in idem* Principle and the Notion of *res iudicata* in the European Union   49
   Martin Böse

4 "The Global Panopticon": Mass Surveillance and Data Privacy Intrusion as a Crime against Humanity?   73
   Michael Bohlander

5 Environmental and Cultural Heritage Crimes: The Possibilities under the Rome Statute   103
   Helen Brady and David Re

6 The Role of Comparative Law in Transnational Criminal Justice   137
   Albin Eser

7 Protecting Human Rights through Exclusionary Rules? Highlights on a Conflict in Criminal Proceedings from a Comparative Perspective   159
   Sabine Gless

8 Implementing Kampala: The New Crime of Aggression under the German Code of Crimes against International Law   180
   Florian Jeßberger

9   The Serendipitous Nature of the ICC Trial Proceedings Risks the ICC's Credibility   202
    Michael G. Karnavas

10 Vom eingeschränkten Nutzen strafrechtlicher Urteile für die Historiographie: Ein Beitrag zum Zustandekommen des ersten deutschen Urteils wegen Völkermordes in Ruanda   248
    Stefan Kirsch

11 Fundamentally Dissenting Judge Schomburg   266
    André Klip

12 Combatting Terrorism without Secret Services?   283
    Otto Lagodny

13 Judging in International Criminal Cases: Challenges, Aspirations and Duties   299
    Howard Morrison

14 25 Years of International Criminal Justice: Ebb and Flow or Rise and Fall?   317
    Jan Christoph Nemitz

15 International Criminal Liability for Incitement and Hate Speech   335
    Ines Peterson

16 Die Konfliktregion Südosteuropa und das internationale und nationale Strafrecht   359
    Herwig Roggemann

17 International Prosecution of Sexual and Gender-Based Crimes Perpetrated during the First World War   395
    William A. Schabas

18 The ICTY's *Šešelj* Trial: Taking Stock of a Disaster   411
    Matthias Schuster

19 *Aut iustitia aut pax?* Enforcement of International Prison Sentences in (Former) Conflict Areas   436
    Michael Stiel and Carl-Friedrich Stuckenberg

Preface

Justice without borders: During his entire career, Wolfgang Schomburg sought, and was a, Justice without borders. National borders were never relevant to him. The more transnational a case was, the more it presented an incentive to employ his creativity on the basis of his firmly held principles. We think it is apposite to describe his person and career with words taken from the *laudatio* on the occasion of the award of the honorary degree of Doctor of Civil Law at Durham University on 26 June 2013:[1]

Wolfgang Schomburg is a man of principles, which is always a good thing in a judge. He is also a political man and has held high political office in Germany, which some may say is not such a good thing for a judge. Yet, during his entire illustrious career he has striven to curb the influence of politics over justice and to maintain the independence of the judiciary. This finally led him to sit in judgment over people accused of exerting the ultimate influence of politics over justice: The use of violence to oppress, expel and sometimes even exterminate whole sections of society in the former Yugoslavia and Rwanda. His experience has caused him to doubt that there will ever be full equality before the law, or that judges will ever find absolute truth or justice. Yet, he has dedicated himself to fighting for these fundamental values.

Wolfgang was born in Spandau in 1948, which at the time was part of the British sector of Berlin. His grandfather was an ardent Social Democrat and a member of the resistance under the Nazi regime. After the war, when the Americans took control of the town where he lived, he was made its mayor. The town was ceded to the Soviets in 1948. Because his grandfather refused to cooperate politically with the Communist Party, he was sent to one of the former Nazi concentration camps then used by the Soviets. He died while imprisoned there. Wolfgang and his mother were evacuated from Berlin to West Germany by the British Royal Air Force in 1949.

His family history had instilled him with the desire to make the pursuit of justice his profession. After obtaining his law degrees he was given the opportunity to prove his mettle, when he became a prosecutor in the white-collar crime unit in West Berlin in 1974. It was the practice at the time that any intended search of suspects' premises had to be notified to the Senator for Justice; frequently after such notice had been given, certain suspects would miraculously receive advance warning of the impending visit. Wolfgang and some of his colleagues – who were eventually given the moniker "The Upright Seven"

---

1 Professor Michael Bohlander, Durham University.

by some of the press – decided that the practice had to stop and conducted one search without such prior notice, which was then crowned by success – and led to the practice being abandoned.

In the 1980s Wolfgang became the leader of the Social Democratic Lawyers in Berlin for eight years and was eventually himself proposed by the Mayor of Berlin to be Justice Senator – however, he ultimately lost out on gender diversity grounds and instead became under-secretary of state to the new Senator, Jutta Limbach.

Wolfgang Schomburg is one of the fathers of the German Law on International Cooperation in Criminal Matters, and has been one of its foremost commentators ever since. He was also one of the main promoters of the creation of Eurojust, an EU-wide clearing-house for judicial cooperation in criminal matters, which was eventually established in The Hague. Together with British and other lawyers, most prominently Dame Audrey Glover, he was instrumental in abolishing the post-war occupation relict of the death penalty in West Berlin in 1987/88.

In 1995 he was appointed to the bench at the German Federal Court of Justice. During his time there, he was the first federal judge to take paternity leave because his Danish wife's career in the EU required her to move to Greece for a time, and he looked after their two children for 18 months.

In 2001 he was elected judge of the International Criminal Tribunal for the Former Yugoslavia and in 2003 became a member of its Appeals Chamber, and that of the sister tribunal for Rwanda. He retired from the international bench in 2008; he has since worked in private practice and remained active in promoting the rule of law, especially in transitional countries. Because he had, in addition to his "daytime job", authored many substantive and often leading scholarly publications, had lectured globally at scores of universities, had for many years assisted the Council of Europe in promoting the Rule of Law in countries of the former Soviet Union, had accepted the Chair of Durham Law School's Centre for Criminal Law and Criminal Justice and has since taught pro bono on its LLM programme, Durham University conferred an Honorary Professorship on him in 2009.

In 2008, the German Federal President awarded him one of Germany's highest honours, the Great Cross of Merit, for his services to international justice. Wolfgang Schomburg, to borrow without the original sarcasm from a writer who gained some prominence on British shores, is an honourable man. It is therefore right that we honour him with this *liber amicorum*.

We owe a great debt of acknowledgment to a number of people who have contributed to the publication of this *liber amicorum*. We would like to thank Brill Publishers for their great interest in the book, and we are particularly grateful to Ms. Verity Adams who was in charge of the English proofreading and to Mr. Nick Ertural (Bonn) for his support throughout the editorial process.

Martin Böse, Michael Bohlander, André Klip, Otto Lagodny
Bonn, Phnom Penh, Maastricht, Salzburg,
October 2017

List of Abbreviations

AIDP	Association Internationale de Droit Pénal
	International Association of Penal Law
AQIM	al-Qaeda in the Islamic Maghreb
BezG	Bezirksgericht
	District Court
BGH	Bundesgerichtshof
	Federal Court of Justice (Germany)
BKA	Bundeskriminalamt
	Federal Criminal Police Office (Germany)
BVerfG	Bundesverfassungsgericht
	Federal Constitutional Court (Germany)
CAH	Crime against Humanity
CAR	Central African Republic
CAT	UN Convention against Torture
CCD	UN Conference of the Committee on Disarmament
CCTV	Closed Circuit Television
CDDH	Diplomatic Conference on the Reaffirmation and Development of International Humanitarian Law
CFR	EU Charter of Fundamental Rights
CH-CPC	Swiss Criminal Procedure Code
CISA	Convention implementing Schengen agreement
CJEU	Court of Justice of the European Union
CSCE	Commission on Security and Cooperation in Europe
DRC	Democratic Republic of the Congo
EAW	European Arrest Warrant
ECCC	Extraordinary Chambers (Courts of Cambodia)
ECHR	European Convention of Human Right
ECJ	European Court of Justice
ECRIS	European Criminal Records Information System
ECtHR	European Court of Human Rights
EGMR	Europäischer Gerichtshof für Menschenrechte
	European Court of Human Rights
ENMOD	Convention on the Prohibition of Military or Any Hostile Use of Environmental Modification Techniques
EPPO	European Public Prosecutor Office
EU	European Union
EuHB	Europäischer Haftbefehl
	European Arrest Warrant

LIST OF ABBREVIATIONS

GCC	German Criminal Code
	Strafgesetzbuch (StGB)
GCCIL	German Code of Crimes against International Law
	Völkerstrafgesetzbuch (VStGB)
GCHQ	Government Communications Headquarters (UK)
GenStA	Generalstaatsanwaltschaft
IBA	International Bar Association
ICC	International Criminal Court
ICCPR	International Covenant on Civil and Political Rights
ICJ	International Court of Justice
ICRC	International Committee of the Red Cross
ICTR	International Criminal Tribunal for Rwanda
ICTY	International Criminal Tribunal for Yugoslavia
ILC	International Law Commission
IMT	International Military Tribunal at Nuremberg
IMTFE	International Military Tribunal for the Far East
IRG	Gesetz über die internationale Rechtshilfe in Strafsachen
	Act on International Cooperation in Criminal Matters
IS	Islamic State (militant group)
ISIS	Islamic State of Iraq and Syria (see IS)
ISISC	International Institute of Higher Studies in Criminal Sciences
IStGH	Internationaler Strafgerichtshof
	International Criminal Court
JCE	Joint Criminal Enterprise
JIT	Joint Investigation Team
MICT	Mechanism for International Criminal Tribunals
NGO	Non-governmental Organization
NSA	National Security Agency (USA)
OLG	Oberlandesgericht
	Higher Regional Court
OTP	Office of the Prosecutor
PJCCM	Police and Judicial Co-operation in Criminal Matters
PNR	Passenger Name Records
PRC	People's Republic of China
RAF	Rote Arme Fraktion
	Red Army Faction (militant group)
RPE	Rules of Procedure and Evidence
RSCSL	Residual Special Court for Sierra Leone
RTLM	Radio télévision libre des mille collines
SCAP	Supreme Commander for the Allied Powers
SČP	Serbian Chetnik Movement

SCSL	Special Court for Sierra Leone
SFRJ	Sozialistische Föderative Republik Jugoslawien
	Socialist Federal Republic of Yugoslavia (YSFR)
SIS	Schengen Information System
SRS	Srpska radikalna stranka
	Serbian Radical Party
StGB	Strafgesetzbuch
	German Criminal Code
STL	Special Tribunal for Lebanon
StPO	Strafprozessordnung
	German Code of Criminal Procedure
TEEC	Treaty of the European Economic Community
TEU	Treaty on European Union
TFEU	Treaty on the Functioning of the European Union
UIDHR	Universal Islamic Declaration of Human Rights
UK	United Kingdom
UN	United Nations
UNSC	United Nations Security Council
UNSG	United Nations Secretary General
UNESCO	United Nations Educational, Scientific and Cultural Organization
UNTOC	United Nations Convention Against Transnational Organized Crime
USA	United States of America
VCLT	Vienna Convention on the Law of Treaties

Academic Writings of Wolfgang Schomburg

1. Der Beitrag der Justiz zum Frieden in Ekkehard Griep (ed), *Wir sind UNO* (Herder 2016) 200–201.
2. Ne bis in idem. Vom Auslieferungshindernis zum internationalen strafrechtlichen Doppelverfolgungsverbot als EU-Grundrecht. Eine Einführung anhand von Texten in Gudrun Hochmayr (ed), *„Ne bis in idem" in Europa* (Nomos 2015) 9–26.
3. Europastrafrecht und Europäischer Haftbefehl – Mogelpackungen zum Nachteil europäischer Bürger in Stephan Breitenmoser, Sabine Gless and Otto Lagodny (eds), *Schengen und Dublin in der Praxis* (Dike 2015) 221–246.
4. About responsibility in Philipp Ambach, Frédéric Bostedt, Grant Dawson and Steve Kostas (eds), *The Protection of Non-Combatants During Armed Conflict and Safeguarding the Rights of Victims in Post-Conflict Society* (Brill 2015) 34–52.
5. *Der Friedensbeitrag des UN-Tribunals für Ruanda: Strafgerichtsbarkeit kann auch transnational erfolgreich sein* (2014) 62 Vereinte Nationen 59–64.
6. IRG – AICCM / Gesetz über die internationale Rechtshilfe in Strafsachen – Act on international cooperation in criminal matters with Michael Bohlander (Beck 2013).
7. Grundlagen der Zusammenarbeit with Otto Lagodny and Nina Marlene Schallmoser in Martin Böse (ed), *Europäisches Strafrecht* (Nomos 2013) 495–536.
8. Responsibility to Protect against Genocide and other Crimes against Humanity – The role of the judiciary in Ekkehard Griep (ed), *Des Friedens General* (Herder 2013) 360–374.
9. *International Cooperation in Criminal Matters* with Otto Lagodny, Sabine Gless and Thomas Hackner (eds), (5th edn, Beck 2012).
10. Zur Notwendigkeit effektiver internationaler Strategien gegen Hochseepiraterie und für den Schutz der Menschenrechte auf hoher See with Irene Suominen-Picht (2012) 124 Zeitschrift für die gesamte Strafrechtswissenschaft 578–590.
11. *Criminal matters: transnational ne bis in idem in Europe* (2012) 13 ERA Forum 311–324.
12. Verbot der mehrfachen Strafverfolgung, Kompetenzkonflikte und Verfahrenstransfer with Irene Suominen-Picht (2012) Neue Juristische Wochenschrift 1190–1194.
13. Verteidigung im international-arbeitsteiligen Strafverfahren with Otto Lagodny (2012) Neue Juristische Wochenschrift 348–353.
14. Jurisprudence on JCE – Revisiting a Never Ending Story. About a Judge Made Mode of Criminal Liability Before Some International Tribunals (2012) 3/1 Godišnjak Akademije pravnih znanosti Hrvatske 59–92.

15. Sudska praksa oujedinjenom zločinačkom poduhvatu (UZP) (2012) Nova pravna revija 12–31.
16. The Jurisprudence on JCE – Criminal Law v. Public International Law? in Olivier de Frouville (ed), *Punir les crimes de masse: entreprise criminelle ou co-action?* (Anthemis 2012) 165–200.
17. Gewaltenteilung in Europa and „Das Beste, was in Menschenhand liegt" in Reinhard Müller (ed), *Staat und Recht* (2011) 24–26, 312–318.
18. Überblick über die strafrechtlichen Konventionen des Europarates in Ulrich Sieber, Franz-Hermann Brüner, Helmut Satzger and Bernd von Heintschel-Heinegg (eds), *Europäisches Strafrecht* (2nd edn, Nomos 2011) 134–140.
19. Überblick über die Aktivitäten des Europarates auf strafrechtlichem Gebiet in Ulrich Sieber, Franz-Hermann Brüner, Helmut Satzger and Bernd von Heintschel-Heinegg (eds), *Europäisches Strafrecht* (2nd edn, Nomos 2011) 127–133.
20. *Some reflections on the right to self-representation before International Tribunals* (2011) 12 ERA Forum 189–195.
21. Sur le rôle des procédures dans l'établissement de la vérité in Isabelle Delpla and Magali Bessone (eds), *Peines de guerre* (Éditions EHESS 2010) 171.
22. The Jurisprudence on JCE III (2010) Journal für Strafrecht 131.
23. International Criminal Courts and Tribunals, Procedure with Jan Christoph Nemitz in Rüdiger Wolfrum (ed), *Max Planck Encyclopedia of Public International Law* (Oxford University Press 2010).
24. Development of Human Rights before International Tribunals (2010) Hvratski Ljetopis za Kazneno Pravo I Praksu 909–940.
25. *Common Law versus Civil Law – Die Ad-hoc-Strafgerichtshöfe für das ehemalige Jugoslawien und Ruanda – Ihre immanenten Grenzen auf der Suche nach der Wahrheit* (2009) 99 Betrifft Justiz 108.
26. The Role of International Criminal Tribunals in Promoting Respect for Fair Trial Rights (2009) 8 Northwestern University Journal of International Human Rights 1–29.
27. *Wahrheitsfindung im internationalen Gerichtssaal* (2009) 1 Vereinte Nationen 3–9.
28. *Kein Frieden ohne Gerechtigkeit, keine Gerechtigkeit ohne Wahrheit* in 50 Jahre Zentrale Stelle Ludwigsburg (Stuttgart 2009).
29. Kämpferin gegen die Gummiwand, book review, Carla Del Ponte, *Im Namen der Anklage* (2009) 5 Vereinte Nationen 235–236.
30. Human Rights in Proceedings before the International Criminal Tribunals in Chile Eboe-Osuji (ed), *Protecting Humanity, Essays in International Law and Policy in Honour of Navanethem Pillay* (Brill 2009) 707–726.
31. Extradition and Referral/Transferral for International Criminal Courts (Lecture b) in International Surrender of Persons: A Transcontinental Approach, Centro de Estudas Judiciários and Academy of European Law, Lisbon, November 2008.

32. Unterlassene Informationen nach Artikel 36 WÜK – Anmerkungen zur aktuellen Rechtsprechung with Matthias Schuster (2008) Neue Zeitschrift für Strafrecht 593–597.
33. Transnationales „ne bis in idem", book review, with Ines Peterson and Matthias Schuster (2008) 19 Criminal Law Forum 287–298.
34. *Extradition and Mutual Assistance*, book review, with Ines Peterson and Matthias Schuster (2008) 19 Criminal Law Forum 287–298.
35. *The ad-hoc Tribunals for the Former Yugoslavia (ICTY) and Rwanda (ICTR)* (2008) 2 VN Forum (Nederlands Vereniging voor de Verenigde Naties) 10–19.
36. *Development of international Criminal Jurisdiction* in Nürnberg 60 Jahre danach, Nürnberg 2007.
37. Genuine Consent to Sexual Violence under International Criminal Law with Ines Peterson (2007) 101 American Journal of International Law 121–140.
38. The Legal Foundation of the Concept and Role of Public Prosecution in Criminal Procedures in: *Ministry of Justice of the Hashemite Kingdom of Jordan / United Nations Development Programme – Programme on Governance in the Arab Region (UNDP-POGAR)*, Legal Organization of Public Prosecution, Amman 2007, 19–28.
39. International Experiences Concerning the Role of Public Prosecutor in: *Ministry of Justice of the Hashemite Kingdom of Jordan / United Nations Development Programme- Programme on Governance in the Arab Region (UNDP-POGAR)*, Legal Organization of Public Prosecution, Amman 2007, 81–87.
40. In Honour of Vespasian Pella, Development of International Criminal Law – With special emphasis on the procedural challenges of the ad hoc Tribunals (2007) Romanian International Law Review 256.
41. The Protection of Human Rights of the Accused before the International Criminal Tribunal for Rwanda with Jan Christoph Nemitz in Emmanuel Decaux, Adama Dieng and Malick Sow (eds), *From Human Rights to International Criminal Law / Des droits de l'homme au droit international pénal* (Brill, Nijhoff 2007) 89–108.
42. Streugedanken zu Herwig Roggemann – Jurist, Rechtspolitiker, Internationalist in Dirk Fischer (ed), *Transformation des Rechts in Ost und West, Festschrift zum 70. Geburtstag von Herwig Roggemann* (BWV 2006) 635–640.
43. Das 2. Europäische Haftbefehlsgesetz with Thomas Hackner, Otto Lagodny and Sabine Gless (2006) Neue Zeitschrift für Strafrecht 663–669.
44. Internationale Rechtshilfe in Strafsachen with Otto Lagodny in Bertold Huber (ed), *Handbuch des Ausländer- und Asylrechts* (Beck 2006).
45. Some Thoughts about the Role of the ICTY in Establishing Truth (2006) University of Durham Student Law Journal 73–76.
46. *International Cooperation in Criminal Matters* with Otto Lagodny, Sabine Gless and Thomas Hackner (eds), (4th edn, Beck 2006).

47. Konkurrierende nationale und internationale Strafgerichtsbarkeit und der Grundsatz „Ne bis in idem" in Jörg Arnold, Björn Burkhardt, Walter Gropp, Günter Heine, Hans-Georg Koch, Otto Lagodny, Walter Perron, Susanne Walther (eds), *Menschengerechtes Strafrecht – Festschrift für Albin Eser* (Beck 2005) 829–846.
48. Internationale vertragliche Rechtshilfe in Strafsachen (2005) Neue Juristische Wochenschrift 3262–3266.
49. Die Zusammenarbeit mit den Internationalen Strafgerichtshöfen in Stefan Kirsch (ed), *Internationale Strafgerichtshöfe* (Nomos 2005) 129–138.
50. *Fragwürdige Abmachungen* (interview) (2005) 3 Der Spiegel 97–98.
51. The Protection of Human Rights of the Accused before the International Criminal Tribunals for the former Yugoslavia (ICTY) and Rwanda (ICTR) in Károly Bárd and Richard Soyer (eds), *Internationale Strafgerichtsbarkeit* (NWV 2005) 71–96.
52. *The defence rights in the practice of the international criminal tribunals* with Tobias Wild (2004) 5 ERA Forum 533–544.
53. Christoph Safferling, Towards an International Criminal Procedure; Kai Ambos, Der Allgemeine Teil des Völkerstrafrechts: Ansätze einer Dogmatisierung, book review, with Nina H.B. Jørgensen (2003) 14 European Journal of International Law 205–207.
54. *Internationale Rechtshilfe in Strafsachen: Ein Leitfaden für die Praxis* with Thomas Hackner, Otto Lagodny and Norbert Wolf (Beck 2003).
55. National Report Germany with Otto Lagodny in Albin Eser, Otto Lagodny and Christopher L. Blakesley (eds), *The Individual as Subject of International Cooperation in Criminal Matters* (Nomos 2002) 205–290.
56. Germany, Concurrent National and International Criminal Jurisdiction and the Principle "ne bis in idem" (2002) Revue Internationale de droit pénal 941–964.
57. Internationale Rechtshilfe in Strafsachen (2002) Neue Juristische Wochenschrift 1629–1632.
58. Ein neuer Start! Internationale vertragliche Rechtshilfe in Strafsachen – Kurzübersicht zur aktuellen Rechtsentwicklung (2001) Neue Juristische Wochenschrift 801–806.
59. Internationale vertragliche Rechtshilfe in Strafsachen – Kurzübersicht zur aktuellen Rechtsentwicklung (2000) Neue Juristische Wochenschrift 340–343.
60. *Kriminalitätsbekämpfung im zusammenwachsenden Europa*, Bundeskriminalamt (ed) (Luchterhand 2000).
61. EUROJUST neben EUROPOL (2000) Kriminalistik 13–21.
62. *The Public Prosecutor's office – child of the revolution – motor of the international co-operation in criminal matters*, CoE Doc.: ADACS – DAJ-PR (2000) 04, Strasburg 2000.

63. Report on the Draft Code of Criminal Procedure of the Republic of Moldova in: Comments on the Draft Criminal Procedure Code of the Republic of Moldova, CoE Doc.: ADACS – DAJ-EXP (2000) 14, 3, Strasbourg 2000.
64. Draft law on the State Court of Bosnia Herzegovina of 19 May 2000 (enforced 20 November), co-operation in a working group of the Venice Commission (responsible for the part on Criminal Procedure), consolidated working paper (Strasbourg, 19 May 2000).
65. Are we on the Road to a European Law-Enforcement Area? International Cooperation in Criminal Matters. What Place for Justice, European Journal of Crime? (2000) 8 Criminal Law and Criminal Justice 51–60.
66. *Auf dem Wege zu einem Europäischen Rechtsraum!* (2000) Deutsche Richterzeitung 341–344.
67. Comment lutter efficacement contre la criminalité organisée dans l'Union européenne? et Le rôle de la justice: nécessité et attributions d'eurojust: Protéger Le Citoyen Contre Le Crime International in Jacques Delors (ed), Comité Européen d'Orientation Notre Europe (Paris 2000) 26.
68. Greater Efficiency in combating organised crime within the European Union and The role of the judiciary: necessity and tasks of Eurojust, in Jacques Delors (ed) *Protecting European Citizens against international crime European Steering*, Comité Européen d'Orientation Notre Europe (Paris 2000) 23.
69. Größere Effizienz bei der Bekämpfung der organisierten Kriminalität in der Europäischen Union in Jacques Delors (ed), *Schutz des Europäischen Bürgers vor internationaler Kriminalität*, Comité Européen d'Orientation Notre Europe (Paris 2000) 4.
70. Die Rolle der Justiz: Notwendigkeit auf Aufgaben von EUROJUST in Jacques Delors (ed.), *Schutz des Europäischen Bürgers vor internationaler Kriminalität*, Comité Européen d'Orientation Notre Europe (Paris 2000) 4.
71. Die Europäisierung des Verbots doppelter Strafverfolgung – Ein Zwischenbericht (2000) Neue Juristische Wochenschrift 1833–1840.
72. Internationale Rechtshilfe aus der Sicht der Justiz, Polizei-Führungsakademie (Münster 1999) 245.
73. Internationale Rechtshilfe in Strafsachen in *Handbuch des Ausländer-und Asylrechts* (Beck 1999).
74. Schengen II in *Handbuch des Ausländer-und Asylrechts* (Beck 1999).
75. Steuerstrafverfahren wegen Hinterziehung von belgischen Eingangsabgaben: Strafklageverbrauch durch ein belgisches transactie-Verfahren – Anmerkung zu BGH, Urteil vom 2. 2. 1999 – 5 StR 596/96 (1999) Strafverteidiger 246–249.
76. Erweiterte Anmerkung zu Fürstlich Liechtensteinischer Gerichtshof – 8 Rs 35/98-75 (1999) Jus and News 266.

77. Auslieferungsrecht: Familiäre Interessen des Betroffenen als Auslieferungshindernis (1999) Neue Zeitschrift für Strafrecht 358–359.
78. *Auf dem Wege zu einem europäischen Rechtsraum?* (1999) Deutsche Richterzeitung 107–1113.
79. Internationale vertragliche Rechtshilfe in Strafsachen (1999) Neue Juristische Wochenschrift 550–551.
80. Strafsachen in der Europäischen Union (1999) Neue Juristische Wochenschrift 540–543.
81. Justizielle Zusammenarbeit im Bereich des Strafrechts in Europa: EUROJUST neben Europol! (1999) 32 Zeitschrift für Rechtspolitik 237–240.
82. Überstellung eines Strafgefangenen in die Türkei (1999) Neue Zeitschrift für Strafrecht 198–200.
83. Internationale Polizeiliche Zusammenarbeit aus der Sicht der Justiz in Manfred Baldus and Michael Soiné (eds), *Rechtsprobleme der internationalen polizeilichen Zusammenarbeit* (Nomos 1999) 186.
84. Datenschutz im Internationalen Rechtshilfeverkehr in Alfred Büllesbach (ed), *Datenverkehr ohne Datenschutz? Eine globale Herausforderung* (Otto Schmidt Verlag 1999) 131–155.
85. Zum Stand der Vollstreckungshilfe durch Überstellung in das Heimatland (1998) Neue Zeitschrift für Strafrecht 142–144.
86. Das Europäische Netzwerk der Rechtshilfe in Strafsachen in: Rechtsprobleme der Internationalen Zusammenarbeit in Strafsachen, Polizei-Führungsakademie (Münster 1998) 249.
87. Impact of Human Rights Aspects from a German Point of View in *Les systèmes comparés de justice penal* (Eres 1998).
88. Europarat und Strafrecht in *Lexikon des Rechts* (Luchterhand 1998).
89. Schengener Durchführungsübereinkommen und Strafrecht in *Lexikon des Rechts* (Luchterhand 1998).
90. Vereinte Nationen und Strafrecht in Lexikon des Rechts (Luchterhand 1998).
91. *A new Start for European Legal Co-operation in Criminal Matters*, DAJ/DOC (99) 26 (EN) (Strasbourg 1999).
92. Aspects from A German/European Perspective (1998) Nouvelles Etudes Pénales 175–177.
93. *Zur Eintragung eines belgischen Abwesenheitsurteils in das deutsche Bundeszentralregister* (1998) Juristische Rundschau 347–349.
94. *Die Rolle des Individuums in der Internationalen Kooperation in Strafsachen* (1998) Strafverteidiger 153–158.
95. Internationale vertragliche Rechtshilfe in Strafsachen (1998) Neue Juristische Wochenschrift 1044–1045.

96. *International Cooperation in Criminal Matters* (zuvor: *Gesetz über die Internationale Rechtshilfe in Strafsachen*) with Otto Lagodny (eds) (3rd edn, Beck 1998).
97. Das Schengener Durchführungsabkommen und Strafrecht in Gerhard Ulsamer (ed), Ergänzbares Lexikon des Rechts, Neuwied (loose-leaf collection), 8/1315 (February 1998).
98. Internationale vertragliche Rchtshilfe in Strafsachen (1997) Neue Juristische Wochenschrift 3328–3330.
99. *Aus der Rechtsprechung des BGH zu verdeckten Ermittlungen, in Reform oder Roll-Back? Weichenstellung für das Straf- und Strafprozessrecht*, 21. Strafverteidigertag (Kassel 1997).
100. Position and Role of the Judiciary within the context of the principle of the separation of powers in Judicial Systems in a Period of Transition (Council of Europe Publishers, Strasbourg 1997) 19.
101. *Stephan Weber, Überstellung in den Heimatstaat* (Peter Lang 1997), book review.
102. *Internationales "ne bis in idem" nach Art 54 SDÜ* (1997) Strafverteidiger 383–385.
103. Das Schengener Durchführungsübereinkommen: Anmerkungen und Bewertungen zu Titel III (Polizei und Sicherheit) aus einer deutschen justiziellen Sicht (1997) 119 Juristische Blätter 553–562.
104. Karl Würz, Das Schengener Durchführungsübereinkommen (Boorberg 1996), book review.
105. Die Regionalisierung des internationalen Strafrechts und der Schutz der Menschenrechte bei der internationalen Zusammenarbeit in Strafsachen (1996) 108 Zeitschrift für die gesamte Strafrechtswissenschaft 685–687.
106. Strafrecht und Rechtshilfe im Geltungsbereich des Schengener Durchführungsübereinkommens in Polizeiführungsakademie Münster-Hiltrup, Grenzüberschreitende Zusammenarbeit der Schengener Staaten – Internationales Seminar vom 17. bis 19. September 1996 (Münster 1996) 45.
107. Draft Statute for an International Court (Siracusa Draft) prepared by a (and as a member of) a Committee of Experts, International Association of Penal Law, Istituto Superiore Internazionale di Szienze Criminali, Max Planck Institute for Foreign and International Criminal Law (Siracusa/Freiburg July 1995).
108. The Regionalization of International Criminal Law and the Protection of Human Rights in International Cooperation in Criminal Proceedings Section IV of the XV Congress of the International Association of Penal Law (1995) 3/1 European Journal of Crime, Criminal Law and Criminal Justice 98–105.
109. Jugoslawien-Strafgerichtshof-Gesetz (1995) Neue Zeitschrift für Strafrecht 428–430.
110. Strafrecht und Rechtshilfe im Geltungsbereich von Schengen II (1995) Neue Juristische Wochenschrift 1931–1936.

111. Internationale vertragliche Rechtshilfe in Strafsachen (1995) Neue Juristische Wochenschrift 243–244.
112. *Internationale samenwerking in strafzaken en rechtsbeschwermin: pleidooi voor een geintegreerde nationale en internationale benadering* with Tom Vander Beken and Patrick Zanders (Bruxelles 1995).
113. International Assistance in Criminal Matters, National Report: Federal Republic of Germany, to the X. *International Congress of the International Association of Procedural Law (Taormina/Sao Paulo* 1995).
114. Internationale Rechtshilfe in Strafsachen: Bundesrepublik Deutschland with Otto Lagodny in Peter Gilles (ed), *Transnationales Prozeßrecht* (Nomos 1995) 43–76.
115. International Cooperation in Criminal Matters and Rights of the Individual from a German Perspective with Otto Lagodny (1994) 2 European Journal of Crime, Criminal Law and Criminal Justice 379–405.
116. The Regionalization of International Criminal Law and the Protection of Human Rights – xvth International Congress of Penal Law, Rio de Janeiro – Section IV, Report (1994) 4 Revue International de droit pénale (RIDP).
117. Neuere Entwicklungen im Recht der internationalen Rechtshilfe in Strafsachen with Otto Lagodny (1994) Strafverteidiger 393–402.
118. *Vollstreckungshilfe und europäische Integration, Dokumentation* (1993) Europäische Akademie 85.
119. *"Entlastung der Rechtspflege" durch weniger Auslandszeugen?* with André Klip (1993) Strafverteidiger 208–212.
120. Die neue Weltordnung braucht einen internationalen Strafgerichtshof (1993) Zeitschrift für Rechtspolitik 308–309.
121. Justiz, Aliierte und Sonderstatus in Berlin Handbuch – Das Lexikon der Bundeshauptstadt, Geschichte und Zeitgeschichte (FAB 1992).
122. *Internationale Rechtshilfe in Verkehrsstrafsachen – insbesondere – Das neue Überstellungsrecht und die Vollstreckungshilfe im Verhältnis zu Österreich* with Otto Lagodny (1992) Deutsches Autorecht 445–448.
123. Neuere Entwicklungen der internationalen Rechtshilfe in Strafsachen with Otto Lagodny (1992) Neue Zeitschrift für Strafrecht 353–360.
124. *Richtlinien für den Strafverteidiger in Strafverfahren mit Auslandsbezug – Neueste Entwicklungen im internationalen Rechtshilfeverkehr* with Otto Lagodny (1992) Strafverteidiger 239–244.
125. *Gesetz über die Internationale Rechtshilfe in Strafsachen* with Otto Lagodny (eds), (2nd edn, Beck 1992).
126. *Hans Wrobel, Hans Verurteilt zur Demokratie: Justiz und Justizpolitik in Deutschland 1945–1949*, book review (Decker & Müller 1989).

127. Rudolf Wassermann (ed), *Strafprozessordnung: Alternativkommentar* (Luchterhand 1988), book review.
128. *Bereinigung des alliierten Rechts in Berlin* (1987) 6 Politik und Kultur 30.
129. Otto Lagodny, *Die Rechtsstellung des Auszuliefernden in der Bundesrepublik Deutschland* (Max-Planck-Institut fur Auslandisches und Internationales Strafrecht 1987), book review.
130. Zur Zulässigkeit einer Strafvollstreckung von in der Bundesrepublik Deutschland erkannten Strafen in der Türkei im Wege der internationalen Vollstreckungshilfe (1986) Neue Zeitschrift für Strafrecht 78–79.
131. *Die öffentliche Bekanntmachung einer strafrechtlichen Verurteilung* (1986) Zeitschrift für Rechtspolitik 65–68.
132. Zur Entschädigung für ungerechtfertigte Auslieferungshaft (1985) Neue Zeitschrift für Strafrecht 223–224.
133. *Herbert Stern, ein Richter für Berlin* (München 1985); Judgement in Berlin (New York 1984), book review.
134. *Presse – Polizei – Justiz, Bildberichterstattung im Spannungsverhältnis von Pressefreiheit und staatlichem Strafverfolgungsanspruch* (1984) Archiv für Presserecht 80–84.
135. Treupflicht iSd § 266 StGB Abs 1 bei Sicherungszession (1984) Zeitschrift für Wirtschafts- und Steuerstrafrecht 143–144.
136. *Zum Spannungsverhältnis zwischen dem Verbot der wörtlichen Mitteilung von Schriftstücken aus staatsanwaltschaftlichen Ermittlungsakten und dem presserechtlichen Auskunftsanspruch* (1984) Strafverteidiger 337–339.
137. Steuerhinterziehung auch bei vorläufiger Steuerfestsetzung (1984) Zeitschrift für Wirtschafts- und Steuerstrafrecht 183.
138. *Beiordnung eines Rechtsanwalts als Beistand im Auslieferungsverfahren* (1983) Strafverteidiger 454.
139. *Das neue Weinstrafrecht: Nicht der Weisheit letzter Schluss* (1982) Die Weinwirtschaft 779.
140. Das neue Weinstrafrecht with Gernot Fischer (1983) Neue Zeitschrift für Strafrecht 11–13.
141. *Internationale Rechtshilfe in Strafsachen aus der Sicht des Strafverteidigers und des Beistandes* (1983) Strafverteidiger 38–43.
142. *Gesetz über die Internationale Rechtshilfe in Strafsachen* with Sigmar Uhlig (eds) (1st edn, Beck 1983).
143. Ausgewählte Probleme des Bundeszentralregistergesetzes with Ulrich Sawade (1982) Neue Juristische Wochenschrift 551–558.
144. Das strafrechtliche Verbot vorzeitiger Veröffentlichung von Anklageschriften und anderen amtlichen Schriftstücken (1982) Zeitschrift für Rechtspolitik 142–145.

145. Internationale Rechtshilfe in Strafsachen (1982) Recht und Politik 203.
146. Bekämpfung der Wirtschaftskriminalität – Theorie und Praxis (1980) Recht und Politik 206.
147. Zur Strafbarkeit der Vortäuschung von Anzahlungen mit dem Ziel der Erlangung von Präferenzen nach dem Berlinförderungsgesetz (1979) Betriebs-Berater 1765–1766.
148. Das Steuergeheimnis im Strafverfahren (1979) Neue Juristische Wochenschrift 526–527.
149. Kriminalpolitisches Programm – Eine Stellungnahme (1977) Recht und Politik 79.
150. Bevölkerungsbefragung zur Strafrechtsreform 1969 (1969) Juristische Arbeitsblätter 701.
151. *Juni und danach nichts mehr*, in Baum vor dem Frühling (self-published, Darmstadt 1966), 43.

Decisions as Judge of UN-ICTY and UN-ICTR November 2001–November 2008

ICTY Trial Chamber II (Presiding Judge as of 23 November 2001)

Judgements of First Instance
   Presiding

- Prosecutor v. Miroslav Deronjić,[2] Sentencing Judgement 30 March 2004
- Prosecutor v. Dragan Nikolić, Sentencing Judgement 18 December 2003
- Prosecutor v. Milomir Stakić, Judgement 31 July 2003
- Prosecutor v. Milomir Stakić, Decision on Rule 98*bis* Motion for Judgement on Acquittal 31 October 2002

Other Cases Presiding/Pre-trial Judge

- Prosecutor v. Vidoje Blagojević *et al.*
- Prosecutor v. Janko Bobetko
- Prosecutor v. Radoslav Brđanin and Momir Talić
- Prosecutor v. Enver Hadžihasanović *et al.*
- Prosecutor v. Darko Mrđa
- Prosecutor v. Mile Mrkšić *et al.*
- Prosecutor v. Mitar Rašević

Confirmation of Indictments pursuant to Rule 47 RPE (ICTY)

- Prosecutor v. Ljubiša Beara
- Prosecutor v. Ljubomir Borovčanin
- Prosecutor v. Momir Nikolić

Selected Important Decisions

- Prosecutor v. Vojislav Šešelj – Decision on Prosecution's Motion for Order Appointing Counsel to Assist Vojislav Šešelj in his Defence of 9 May 2003
- Prosecutor v. Enver Hadžihasanović *et al.* – Decision on Joint Challenge to Jurisdiction [Command Responsibility pursuant to Article 7(3) of the Statute] of 12 November 2002

---

2   Dissenting Opinion on Deronjić's sentence.

- Prosecutor v. Dragan Nikolić – Decision on Defence Motion Challenging the Exercise of Jurisdiction by the Tribunal [Legality of Arrest] of 9 October 2002
- Prosecutor v. Radislav Brđanin and Momir Talić – Decision on Defence Motion to Disqualify the Trial Chamber hearing the Radoslav Brđanin-Momir Talić Trial of 3 May 2002
- Prosecutor v. Enver Hadžihasanović *et al.* – Decision on Prosecution's Motion for Review of the Decision of the Registrar to Assign Mr. Rodney Dixon as Co-Counsel to the Accused Amir Kubura of 26 March 2002

Appeals Chamber (ICTY) (1 October 2003–17 November 2008)

Appeal Judgements
Presiding

- Prosecutor v. Baton Haxhiu
- Decision Rejecting Notice of Appeal[3] 4 September 2008
- Prosecutor v. Naser Orić,[4] Judgement 3 July 2008
- Prosecutor v. Dario Kordić and Mario Čerkez,[5] Judgement 17 December 2004

Member of the Bench

- Prosecutor v. Milan Martić[6] (Pre-Appeal Judge), Judgement 8 October 2008
- Prosecutor v. Momčilo Krajišnik (Pre-Appeal Judge)[7]
- Prosecutor v. Pavle Strugar[8]
- Prosecutor v. Dragan Zelenović, Judgement on Sentencing Appeal 31 October 2007

---

3 Decision on Admissibility of Notice of Appeal Against Trial Judgement.
4 Separate and Partially Dissenting Opinion on scope of command responsibility (Art. 7(3) of the Statute).
5 Joint Dissenting Opinion (with Judge Güney) on cumulative convictions.
6 Separate Opinion on joint criminal enterprise.
7 Self-recused according to Fundamentally Dissenting Opinion on the right to self-representation appended to Decision on Krajišnik's Self-Representation of 11 May 2007.
8 Pre-Appeal Judge until 20 September 2006 (Final Decision on "Defence Notice of Withdrawing Appeal" and "Withdrawal of Prosecution's Appeal against the Judgement of Trial Chamber II dated 31 January 2005.") Exchange from bench per 21 February 2008 against Orić case.

- Prosecutor v. Sefer Halilović,[9] Judgement 16 October 2007
- Prosecutor v. Fatmir Limaj et al.,[10] Judgement 27 September 2007
- Prosecutor v. Miroslav Bralo, Judgement on Sentencing Appeal 2 April 2007
- Prosecutor v. Josip Jović, Judgement (Contempt) 15 March 2007
- Prosecutor v. Stanislav Galić,[11] Judgement 30 November 2006
- Prosecutor v. Blagoje Simić,[12] Judgement 28 November 2006
- Prosecutor v. Ivica Marjiačić and Markica Rebić, Judgement (Contempt) 27 September 2006
- Prosecutor v. Mladen Naletilić and Vinko Martinović,[13] Judgement 3 May 2006
- Prosecutor v. Miodrag Jokić, Judgement on Sentencing Appeal 30 August 2005
- Prosecutor v. Milan Babić, Judgement on Sentencing Appeal 18 July 2005
- Prosecutor v. Tihomir Blaškić,[14] Judgement 29 July 2004
- Prosecutor v. Radislav Krstić, Judgement 19 April 2004
- Prosecutor v. Mitomir Vasiljević, Judgement 25 February 2004
- Prosecutor v. Milorad Krnojelac,[15] Judgement 17 September 2003
- Prosecutor v. Dragoljub Kunarac et al., Judgement 12 June 2002

Appeal on Decisions by the Referral Bench (Rule 11bis of the Rules, ICTY)
Presiding

- Prosecutor v. Gojko Janković, referred to Bosnia-Herzegovina, 15 November 2005

---

9   Separate Opinion on the applicability of Rules 42 and 43 of the Rules of Procedure and Evidence.
10 Partially Dissenting and Separate Opinion and Declaration on the standard for appellate review, the responsibility of Haradin Bala and Isak Musliu, and the principle of in dubio pro reo.
11 Separate and Partially Dissenting Opinion on the increase of Galić's sentence and the "crime of terrorization."
12 Dissenting Opinion on the correct pleading of the mode of liability and joint criminal enterprise.
13 Joint Dissenting Opinion (with Judge Güney) on cumulative convictions and Separate and Partly Dissenting Opinion on the definition of the crime of deportation.
14 Separate Opinion on Blaškić's sentence.
15 Separate Opinion on the definition of the crime of deportation.

Member of the Bench

- Prosecutor v. Vladimir Kovačević, Serbia, 28 March 2007
- Prosecutor v. Mitar Rašević and Savo Todović, Bosnia-Herzegovina, 4 September 2006
- Prosecutor v. Paško Ljubičić, Bosnia-Herzegovina, 4 July 2006
- Prosecutor v. Željko Mejakić *et al.*, Bosnia-Herzegovina, 7 April 2006
- Prosecutor v. Radovan Stanković, Bosnia-Herzegovina, 1 September 2005

Interlocutory Appeals
Presiding / Member of the Bench

- Prosecutor v. Ljube Boškoski and Johan Tarčulovski
- Prosecutor v. Rasim Delić
- Prosecutor v. Ante Gotovina and Ivan Čermak
- Prosecutor v. Sefer Halilović
- Prosecutor v. Ramush Haradinaj *et al.*
- Prosecutor v. Gojko Janković
- Prosecutor v. Josip Jović
- Prosecutor v. Momčilo Krajišnik
- Prosecutor v. Marijan Krizić
- Prosecutor v. Fatmir Limaj *et al.*
- Prosecutor v. Milan Lukić and Sredoje Lukić
- Prosecutor v. Milan Martić
- Prosecutor v. Željko Mejakić
- Prosecutor v. Slobodan Milošević
- Prosecutor v. Milan Milutinović *et al.*
- Prosecutor v. Ratko Mladić
- Prosecutor v. Vujadin Popović *et al.*
- Prosecutor v. Jadranko Prlić *et al.*
- Prosecutor v. Ivica Rajić
- Prosecutor v. Mićo Stanišić
- Prosecutor v. Savo Todović
- Prosecutor v. Zdravko Tolimir

Selected Important Decisions

- Prosecutor v. Milan Milutinović *et al.* – Decision on Prosecution's Appeal from Decision on Lazarević Motion for Temporary Provisional Release dated 26 September 2008

- Prosecutor v. Milan Lukić and Sredoje Lukić – Decision on the Prosecution's Appeal against the Trial Chamber's Order to Call Alibi Rebuttal Evidence during the Prosecution's Case In Chief of 16 October 2008.
- Prosecutor v. Jadranko Prlić *et al.* – Decision on Slobodan Praljak's Appeal of the Trial Chamber's Decision on the Direct Examination of Witnesses Dated 26 June 2008 of 11 September 2008
- Prosecutor v. Jadranko Prlić *et al.* – Decision on Prosecution's Appeal Against Trial Chamber's Order on Contact Between the Accused and Counsel During an Accused's Testimony Pursuant to Rule 85(C) of 5 September 2008
- Prosecutor v. Jadranko Prlić *et al.* – Reasons for Decision on Prosecution's Urgent Appeal Against „Décision relative à la demande de mise en liberté provisoire de l'accusé Pušić" Issued on 14 April 2008 (with Dissenting Opinion on the scope of a Trial Chamber's discretion as regards the provisional release of an accused) of 23 April 2008
- Prosecutor v. Jadranko Prlić *et al.* – Decision on Appeals Against Decision Admitting Transcript Jadranko Prlić's Questioning Into Evidence of 23 November 2007
- Prosecutor v. Pavle Strugar – Decision on Strugar's Request to Reopen Appeal Proceedings (with Dissenting Opinion on possibility of post-conviction transfer of a person to the territory of the former Yugoslavia) of 7 June 2007
- Prosecutor v. Momčilo Krajišnik – Decision on Momčilo Krajišnik's Request to Self-Represent, on Counsel's Motion on Appointment of *Amicus Curiae*, and on the Prosecution Motion of 16 February 2007 (with Fundamentally Dissenting Opinion on the right to self-representation) of 11 May 2007
- Prosecutor v. Momčilo Krajišnik – Decision on "Motion by Mićo Stanišić for Access to all Confidential Materials in the Krajišnik Case" (with Partially Dissenting Opinion on the applicability of Rule 69 vis-à-vis Rule 75 of the Rules) of 21 February 2007
- Prosecutor v. Momčilo Krajišnik – Decision on Krajišnik's Appeal against the Trial Chamber's Decision Dismissing the Defense Motion for a Ruling that Judge Canivell is Unable to Continue Sitting in this Case of 15 September 2006
- Prosecutor v. Dario Kordić and Mario Čerkez – Decision on „Mario Čerkez's Motion for Review of the Registrar's Decision in Relation to the Financial Status of the Accused" (Confidential and *ex parte*) of 26 February 2004 on the question of indigence before the Tribunal and whether family members of an accused are liable for the costs incurred by defence counsel.

Appeals Chamber (ICTR) (1 October 2003–17 November 2008)

Appeal Judgements
Presiding

– Emmanuel Ndindabahizi v. The Prosecutor, Judgement 16 January 2007

Member of the Bench

– The Prosecutor v. Siméon Nchamihigo[16]
– François Karera v. The Prosecutor[17]
– Tharcisse Muvunyi v. The Prosecutor, Judgement 29 August 2008
– The Prosecutor v. Athanase Seromba, Judgement 12 March 2008
– Aloys Simba v. The Prosecutor,[18] Judgement 27 November 2007
– Mikaeli Muhimana v. The Prosecutor,[19] Judgement 21 May 2007
– Sylvestre Gacumbitsi v. The Prosecutor,[20] Judgement 7 July 2006
– Jean de Dieu Kamuhanda v. The Prosecutor,[21] Judgement 19 September 2005
– The Prosecutor v. André Ntagerura et al,[22] Judgement 7 July 2006
– Juvénal Kajelijeli v. The Prosecutor, Judgement 23 May 2005
– Laurent Semanza v. The Prosecutor, Judgement 20 May 2005
– The Prosecutor v. Elizaphan Ntakirutimana and Gérard Ntakirutimana, Judgement 13 December 2004
– Eliézer Niyitegeka v. The Prosecutor, Judgement 9 July 2004

---

16 Replaced November 2008.
17 Replaced on 19 June 2008.
18 Partially Dissenting Opinion on Simba's sentence.
19 Joint Partly Dissenting Opinion (with Judge Shahabuddeen) on the rape of two girls by the Appellant, and Partly Dissenting Opinion on the right to be informed.
20 Separate Opinion on Gacumbitsi's responsibility for committing genocide (pleading of the indictment, "committing").
21 Separate Opinion on aiding and abetting and cumulative convictions.
22 Dissenting Opinion on the indictment and the principle of *nullum crimen sine lege*.

CHAPTER 1

European Criminal Law and Brexit

Kai Ambos

Abstract

Brexit will not only affect the trade relations between the UK and the EU but also vast areas of criminal law and procedure influenced and largely formed by EU law. This is especially true in the area of police and judicial cooperation – take for example the European Arrest Warrant – where the UK has always actively participated in the drafting and implementation of the relevant legal instruments and the actual cooperation. The paper will inquire how Brexit will affect the future relationship between the UK and the EU in these areas.

The Brexit vote of 23 June 2016[1] entails a lot of uncertainty with regard to the future relationship of the UK with the EU, not least in the field of criminal justice cooperation. With the adoption of the (Notification of Withdrawal) Bill[2] and Prime Minister May's actual triggering of Art. 50 Treaty of the European Union ('TEU') on 29 March 2017[3] formal withdrawal negotiations have in the meantime started. This little essay will first describe the area concerned, i.e., European Criminal Law in the narrow sense (1), then we will look at the current relationship of the UK with the EU in the criminal justice area (2), and, last

---

* This contribution is an elaborated version of an article published in German in the Juristenzeitung (JZ) under the title *Brexit und Europäisches Strafrecht*, JZ 72 (2017) 707–713.
** Professor of Criminal Law, Criminal Procedure, Comparative Law and International Criminal Law at the Georg-August Universität Göttingen (GAU); Judge Kosovo Specialist Chambers, The Hague; Director Centro de Estudios de Derecho Penal y Procesal Penal Latinoamericano (CEDPAL), GAU. – I thank my student research assistant Tjorven Vogt for editorial assistance.
1 The turnout was 72,2%, 51,9% voted to leave and 48,1% to remain, cf <http://www.bbc.co.uk/news/politics/eu_referendum/results>, last accessed 21 November 2017.
2 Bill 2016–17, cf <http://services.parliament.uk/bills/2016-17/europeanunionnotificationofwithdrawal.html>, last accessed 21 November 2017.
3 PM May sent a six page letter to Council President Tusk, *inter alia*, emphasizing the UK's interest in a 'deep and special partnership', cf. http://news.bbc.co.uk/2/shared/bsp/hi/pdfs/29_03_17_article50.pdf, last accessed 21 November 2017.

but not least, sketch out possible options of the UK's post-Brexit relationship with the EU in the criminal justice area (3).

The piece is dedicated to *Wolfgang Schomburg* who did not only have a formative influence of the case law of the ICTY where he served as the first German judge from November 2001 to November 2008 but also edited the perhaps most important German commentary on mutual assistance in criminal matters.[4] In this commentary, European Criminal Law plays a prominent role. In addition, Schomburg was appointed honorary professor in Durham Law School, UK, in March 2009. For both reasons I am confident that this paper will find his interest.

1   EU Criminal Law and Justice (European Criminal Law in the Narrow Sense)

Taken at face value, the term 'European criminal law' refers to a genuinely supranational criminal law, that is, to provisions by which the citizens of the Union are directly confronted with the sovereign punitive force – the *ius puniendi* – of the Union as immediately applicable criminal law. However, genuine criminal law legislation by the Union is restricted to a few explicitly defined areas – above all, the protection of the Union's financial interests.[5] Only to this extent is it possible to speak of European criminal law in a true, supranational sense, and, arguably, of a European criminal law or justice *system* in a narrow sense, that is, a limited subject matter area where the Union itself is the sole creator of criminal law norms (albeit depending on the Member States with regard to their enforcement).[6]

Otherwise, 'European Criminal Law' is a kind of *umbrella term* covering 'all those norms and practices of criminal and criminal procedural law' based on the law and activities of the EU (European law in the *narrower* sense) and the Council of Europe (European law in the *wider* sense), leading (or aiming to lead) to widespread *harmonisation*[7] of national criminal (procedural)

---

[4] W Schomburg, O Lagodny, S Gless and T Hackner, *Internationale Rechtshilfe in Strafsachen*, 5th edn (München: C.H. Beck 2012).

[5] Cf K Ambos, *European Criminal Law* (Cambridge: CUP 2018) Ch. 1 mn. 22 ff.

[6] See for such a limited concept of 'system' also P Asp, *Procedural Criminal Law Cooperation of the EU* (Stockholm: University of Stockholm 2016) 211–213 (with general considerations of the concept of 'system' at 207–208, 213).

[7] On harmonisation and the related concepts ,assimilation', 'standardisation' and 'approximation', Ambos ... (n 5) Ch. 1 mn. 28.

law.[8] While Brexit refers to the Union, having a supranational nature, there are no signs that the UK wants to leave the Council of Europe, a regional organisation of 47 States,[9] although there has been quite severe criticism against the Council's human rights system – part of the UK's domestic law by way of the 1998 Human Rights Act[10] – and against the UK-related case law of the European Court of Human Rights.[11] At any rate, this is not (yet) relevant in the Brexit context.

The Union's *authority to legislate* criminal law has to flow from its primary law, that is, the Lisbon Treaty (principle of conferral).[12] The respective authorisation has to be explicit or at least possible to establish – with reasonable certainty – through interpretation. In this regard, Art. 5(2) TEU, replacing

---

8   In a similar vein, D Flore, *Droit pénal européen* (Brussels: Larcier 2009) 11–19; C Safferling, *Internationales Strafrecht* (Berlin et al.: Springer 2011) § 2 mn. 7, § 9 mn. 5 ff; H Satzger, *International and European Criminal Law* (Oxford: Hart 2012) § 5 mn. 2–3; M Böse, in Sieber et al., *Europäisches Strafrecht* 2nd edn (Baden-Baden: Nomos 2013) 55 ff; U Sieber, in ibid., 36–37; H Satzger, in ibid., 251–252; R Esser, *Europäisches und Internationales Strafrecht* 3rd edn (Heidelberg: C.F. Müller 2014) § 1 mn. 3; A Klip, *European Criminal Law* 3rd edn (Cambridge et al.: Intersentia 2016) 1–2; H Satzger, *Internationales und Europäisches Strafrecht* 7th edn (Baden-Baden: Nomos 2016) § 7 mn. 2–3. On European law in the narrower and broader sense, see e.g. Hefendehl, *ZIS*, 1 (2006) 229; M Herdegen, *Europarecht* 18th edn (München: C.H. Beck 2016) § 1 mn. 2–11. On the historical development of European criminal law, cf P Asp, *Substantive Criminal Law Competence* (Stockholm: Jure Bokhandel 2012) 24 ff; H G Nilsson, *EuCLR*, 2 (2012) 106 ff; Kainer, *EuR-Bei*, 48 (2013) 88 ff; Böse, in Sieber et al., *Europäisches Strafrecht* 2nd edn (Baden-Baden: Nomos 2013) 49 ff.
9   <http://www.coe.int/en/web/portal/home>, last visited 21 November 2017.
10 UK Human Rights Act 1998, 9 November 1998 (HRA), preamble, available at <http://www.legislation.gov.uk/ukpga/1998/42/pdfs/ukpga_19980042_en.pdf>, last accessed 21 November 2017. On the genesis of the ECHR from a British perspective, see A W B Simpson, *Human Rights* (Oxford: Oxford University Press 2004) 91 ff (offering a detailed account of the negotiations and the ratification process [649 ff, 711 ff, 808 ff] as well as of the previous attempts of rights protection [91 ff, 157 ff, 221 ff, 390 ff 597 ff]).
11 Cf K Ambos (n 5) Ch. 2 mn. 3.
12 Cf Art. 5(1), (2) TEU; also C Schröder, *Europäische Richtlinien und deutsches Strafrecht* (Berlin et al.: de Gruyter 2002) 118; H Satzger, *International and European Criminal Law* (n 8) § 6 mn. 18; H Satzger, *Internationales und Europäisches Strafrecht* (n 8) § 8 mn. 18; B Hecker, *Europäisches Strafrecht* 5th edn (Berlin: Springer 2016) § 4 mn. 43; C Safferling (n 8) § 9 mn. 51 ff; R Esser, *Europäisches und Internationales Strafrecht* (München: C.H. Beck 2014) § 2 mn. 121; Husemann, *wistra*, 23 (2004) 449; Braum, *wistra*, 25 (2006) 123; Zieschang, in Sieber et al., FS Tiedemann (Cologne et al.: Carl Heymanns 2008) 1313; Rosenau, *ZIS*, 3 (2008) 12; A Klip (n 8) 37 ('principle of conferral'); F Meyer, *Strafrechtsgenese* (Baden-Baden: Nomos 2012) 338, on the threat that competences become watered down, which exists nonetheless, 340 ff.

the earlier Art. 5(1) Treaty of the European Economic Community ('TEEC'), envisages that the Union 'shall act only within the limits of the competences conferred upon it by the Member States in the Treaties'. The precedence of Member State competence is confirmed by the principles of *subsidiarity* and *proportionality*.[13] The former principle represents a legally binding and justiciable rule for the exercise of competences, forcing the Union to review the necessity and (higher) efficiency of its activities ex ante in order to be able to justify them ex post.[14] The principle of proportionality entails that action taken on the basis of Union law against the Member States – corresponding to the relationship between state/citizen in national constitutional law – can only then appear legitimate if it is a suitable, necessary and appropriate means to achieving a Union aim;[15] the measures taken by the Union may not go beyond the minimum intervention necessary to achieve the goal in question.[16] If criminal law is understood correctly as the expression of a specific legal culture and history and thus of State sovereignty, then subsidiarity and proportionality become condensed in this area, forming an *imperative to use criminal law in the most restrictive form possible* in line with the general principle of *ultima ratio* ('strafrechtsspezifisches Schonungsgebot').[17] For this reason alone, the 'fundamental aspects' of the criminal justice systems of the Member States represent an insurmountable hurdle for Union law[18] and set the '*emergency brake procedure*'[19] in motion.[20]

---

13 Cf Art. 5(1), (3), and (4) TEU; Art. 69 TFEU; cf also Draft Council conclusions (2009) 4; P Asp, *EuCLR*, 1 (2011) 44 ff; P Asp (n 6) 190–191; Zöller, in Baumeister et al., *FS Schenke* (Berlin: Duncker & Humblot 2011) 596–597; Safferling (n 8) § 9 mn. 58 ff; Turner, *AmJCompL*, 60 (2012) 562–563; Böse (n 8) 49–50.

14 Cf B Hecker (n 12) § 8 mn. 49; cf also A Klip (n 8) 37–38; Meyer (n 12) 352 ff. On the component of the principle of subsidiarity that protects freedoms, cf Kubiciel, *ZIS*, 5 (2010) 745; cf also Bernardi, *RP*, 27 (2011) 23 ff.

15 Generally on a specific model of 'legal reserve' (in the sense of *réserve legal* or *Gesetzesvorbehalt*) for the EU Muñoz de Morales R., *EuCLR*, 2 (2012) 252–253, 274–275 (advocating a model based on discursive deliberation [input legitimacy] and accountability [output legitimacy] to be achieved by a transparent, participative and rational legislative process; unfortunately, the paper is written in poor English).

16 B Hecker (n 12) § 8 mn. 52 ff; cf also A Klip (n 8) 38, 176 ff; in greater detail, P Asp (n 8) 188 ff.

17 On this, cf K Ambos (n 5), Ch. 3 mn. 37 ff. On the particular demands with regard to subsidiarity in this context, cf also A Klip (n 8) 40.

18 For a similar view of this matter, cf A Klip (n 8) 178–180; for a principled approach Silva Sánchez, *RP*, 13 (2004) 138 ff.

19 Arts. 82(3), 83(3) TFEU.

20 On this, cf K Ambos (n 5) Ch. 3 mn. 5 ff and 11–12.

While European criminal law in the narrow sense is no comprehensive, self-contained European criminal law or justice system of its own,[21] there is a system of sorts, that is, 'some sort' of an *'umbrella-like' system* that 'connects' the specific areas (which we may call 'micro systems', e.g. the harmonised criminal law, the mutual recognition instruments, the human rights system)[22] and which may, on the operational level, be more aptly characterized as a 'Verbund' (compound network / aggregate association) of the different entities and organs in charge of the investigation and prosecution of transnational crimes.[23] Insofar the European criminal justice institutions, especially Europol and Eurojust, play an increasingly important, albeit hidden and intransparent, role in the shaping of European criminal justice policy in practice.[24] At any rate, no independent, new (supranational) European criminal law is created beyond the Union's (limited) competence in the area of financial crime; rather, as a rule, national criminal law (either existing laws or those yet to be created) is influenced by European law.

Strictly speaking, we are dealing with *Europeanised* criminal law, which is why any comparison with federal legislation such as that of the USA is necessarily flawed.[25] Besides the (limited) supranational criminal law regarding the

---

21 For the relevant arguments against cf P Asp (n 6) 209–211.
22 Cf P Asp (n 8) 216–217.
23 For a ground-breaking analysis cf F Meyer, in Herzog et al., *GS Weßlau* (Berlin: Duncker & Humblot 2016) 194 ff (understanding the concept of 'Verbund', originating in European administrative law [196–198], in a descriptive-analytical and at the same time critical sense [198] and applying it to the area of European criminal prosecution [the 'EU-Strafverfolgungsverbund', 199] by way of a functional and impact-oriented approach ['funktions- und wirkungsorientierte Herangehensweise', 200], thereby distinguishing between three sorts of 'Verbünde' (compound networks): one regarding execution/enforcement ['Vollstreckung- und Substitutionsverbund'], characterised by mutual recognition and the increasing overlapping of criminal procedure and legal assistance (201–202), another one regarding collection and storage of information/data ['Informationsverbund', 202–204] and a third one regarding investigation/prosecution *stricto sensu* ['Verbundverfolgung im engeren Sinne', 204–210], at 201–210).
24 F Meyer (n 23) 204 ff (identifying a 'surprising' transformation and an increasing influence of the said EU criminal justice agencies [207] with critical implications democratic accountability and rights protection [210–214]).
25 For such a (flawed) comparison, see Gómez-Jara, in Bacigalupo and Meliá, *Derecho penal y política transnacional* (Barcelona: Atelier 2005) 153 ff, 166 ff; Gómez-Jara, *EuCLR,* 3 (2013), 170; Gómez-Jara, *European Federal Criminal Law* (2015) 15 ff; contra, S Sánchez, in Fernández, *Constitución Europea y derecho penal económico* (Madrid: Ed. universitaria Ramón Areces 2006) 258–259. Cf also the comparison between the USA, Switzerland and the EU in J Ouwerkerk, *Quid pro Quo?* (Cambridge et al.: Intersentia 2011) 242 ff, 264 ff.

protection of the financial interests mentioned above we can distinguish *three forms of Europeanisation* of criminal law: through the implementation of treaties and other normative guidelines of the Council of Europe,[26] through the principle of mutual recognition (thereto in a moment) and through forms and techniques of influence that are specific to European law.[27] In substance, the Europeanisation of the Member States' criminal law occurs mainly through the harmonisation of substantive and procedural law and through legislative acts on the mutual recognition of decisions in criminal law. Previously, the regulation of Member State cooperation in criminal law was only possible on an intergovernmental basis in the area of the Third Pillar of Police and Judicial Cooperation in Criminal Matters ('PJCCM').[28] Through the communitisation of the Third Pillar by the Lisbon Treaty, the regulation of PJCCM now occurs in the area of freedom, security and justice at Union level,[29] which enables the European Council to define 'strategic guidelines'.[30] The normative Europeanisation goes hand in hand with and is complemented by an *institutionalisation* entailing the creation of different European criminal justice institutions already referred to above.

Distinguishing between *substantive* and procedural law[31] one can further say that in the former there is the option of harmonising legislation through

---

26 See K Ambos (n 5) Ch. 2 mn. 25.

27 See on the latter K Ambos (n 5) Ch. 2 mn. 29.

28 Cf thereon Ambos (n 5) Ch. 4 mn. 1 ff.

29 Art. 67 TFEU. On the EU's aims in this area, cf Sieber, *ZStW,* 121 (2009) 3 ff. For a critical view on the relationship between those three components in European security policy, cf Kaiafa-Gbandi, *EuCLR,* 1 (2011) 10. For a linguistic-judicial perspective Tiberi, in Ruggieri *Criminal Proceedings, Languages and the European Union* (Berlin, Heidelberg: Springer 2014) 9 ff; Spiezia, in Ruggieri (n 29) 23 ff (stressing both the importance of several languages for the Union's identity but also the ensuing problems for cooperation).

30 Art. 68 TFEU. On the (difficult) implementation of Art. 68 TFEU giving the Council a kind of prerogative (crit. S Toscani and O Suhr, in Meng et al., *Europäische Integration und Globalisierung* (Baden-Baden: Nomos 2011) 584–585) and possible new 'post-Stockholm' guidelines, see Salazar, *eucrim,* 9 (2014) 22 ff; on key points for a future post-Stockholm programme, Herlin-Karnell, *eucrim,* 9 (2014) 28 ff; on the need for a framework of principles for European criminal policy, Parisi and Rinoldi, *eucrim,* 10 (2015) 111 ff; on the need of evidence-based criminal policy but lack of reliable empirical data cf Pérez Cepeda, Benito Sánchez and Gorjón Barranco, *EuCLR,* 3 (2013) 125 ff. In fact, Council and Commission have, long before the Lisbon Treaty, adopted 5-year programmes (Tampere (1999), The Hague (2004) and Stockholm (2009)) and respective action plans implementing those programmes.

31 For a detailed treatment see K Ambos (n 5) Ch. 3 vs Ch. 4.

passing of minimum requirements defining criminal offences and sanctions in areas of 'particularly serious crime' with a cross-border dimension (so-called 'eurocrimes').[32] In the field of *procedural* law, judicial cooperation is based on the principle of *mutual recognition*.[33] This means that 'judgments and judicial decisions'[34] made in one Member State also have to be recognised in another Member State, that is, ultimately, these decisions have to be directly enforceable and actually enforced in all Member States.[35] Of course, mutual recognition in turn presupposes *mutual trust* which cannot be imposed by legislative fiat but is premised upon mutual respect, rights observance and common values.[36]

---

32 Art. 83(1) TFEU.

33 Art. 82(1) first subparagraph TFEU. For a detailed examination, cf P Nalewajko, *Grundsatz: either leave it together or separate like that: Grund-satz der gegenseitigen Anerkennung* (Berlin: Duncker & Humblot 2010) 64 ff; A Suominen, *The Principle of Mutual Recognition in Cooperation in Criminal Matters* (Cambridge, Portland: Intersentia 2011), 17–18, 23 ff, 42 ff, 66 ff, 343 ff; M Mavany, *Die europäische Beweisanordnung* (Heidelberg et al.: C.F. Müller 2012) 3 ff (history), 33 ff (concept); S D Hüttemann, *Principles and Perspectives of European Criminal Procedure* (Florence: European University Institute 2012) 37 ff; see also de Hoyos, *RDCE*, 9 (2005) 808 ff (drawing a distinction between mutual recognition in a narrower and wider sense, 812 ff, 820 ff); Jégouzo, *RIDP*, 77 (2006) 97 ff; Bernardi, *RSC*, 72 (2007) 725; Manacorda, *RSC*, 72 (2007) 899 ff, 909; H G Nilsson, *RIDP*, 77 (2006) 53 ff; T M Krüßmann, *Transnationales Strafprozessrecht* (Baden-Baden: Nomos 2009) 574 ff, 589 ff; Fichera, *European Arrest Warrant in the EU* (Cambridge, Antwerp, Portland: Intersentia 2011) 48 ff, 59 ff; Taupiac-Nouvel, *EuCLR*, 2 (2012) 239 ff; H Satzger (n 8) § 8 mn. 23 ff; P Asp (n 6) 42–44, 46 ff, 59 ff, 76–77; calling for more mutual recognition Valdés, *ERA Forum*, 16 (2015) 291 ff.

34 Art. 82(1) TFEU.

35 H G Nilsson, *eucrim*, 9 (2014) 21; on enforcement as the most important but not the only function of mutual recognition cf P Asp (n 6) 48–50, 60–61; on mutual recognition as the expression of a system of 'global legal pluralism' cf V Mitsilegas, *EU Criminal Law after Lisbon* (Oxford, Portland: Hart Publishing 2016) 125 ff (128).

36 On mutual trust and rights observance as basis for mutual recognition Mitsilegas (n 35) 125 ff (explaining a lack of trust with 'moral distance' [at 129, 151] and concluding that '[T]his deification of mutual trust ... poses, however, significant challenges on the effective protection of fundamental rights, which seems to be subordinated to the requirement to respect presumed and uncritically accepted trust'. [at 151]); Ronsfeld, *Rechtshilfe, Anerkennung und Vertrauen* (2015) 211 ff (217 ff) (listing a joint reference system, mutual sympathy and coordination, transparency and integrity as trust-founding measures); on the relationship between mutual recognition and trust also Ostropolski, *NJECL*, 6 (2015) 167; on trust resulting from harmonisation P Asp (n 6) 54; on the indicators for mutual trust P Albers, in Albers et al., *Evaluation Framework* (2013) 315; Böse, in Albers et al., *Evaluation Framework* (2013) 357–361; on the weakening of mutual trust by rights violations, BVerfG, No. 2 BvR 2735/14, Decision (15 December 2015), in *NJW*, 69 (2016), 1149,

Perhaps, the lack of this trust is one of the main reasons for the limited mutual recognition in judicial practice.[37]

Apart from the (traditional) *EU law* stricto sensu, that is the primary law of the Treaties (TEU and Treaty of the Functioning of the EU [TFEU]) including annexes and protocols, the secondary instruments (regulations, directives, decisions, recommendations/opinions)[38] and several unwritten principles[39], there is the so-called *Schengen acquis* as a further important source for European criminal law. It consists of the first Schengen agreement on the gradual abolition of border checks of 14 June 1985 (Schengen I),[40] the Convention Implementing the Schengen Agreement (CISA, Schengen II, including the Schengen Information System ['SIS']) of 19 June 1990,[41] possible accession protocols and other legal acts.[42] The CISA was incorporated into Union law with the Amsterdam Treaty of 1997,[43] through which the CJEU gained jurisdiction over

---

paras. 73–75, English translation available at <https://www.bundesverfassungsgericht.de/SharedDocs/Entscheidungen/EN/2015/12/rs20151215_2bvr273514en.html>, last accessed 21 November 2017; calling for more mutual trust Herlin-Karnell, *eucrim*, 9 (2014) 30.

37 For a discussion with further references cf K Ambos (n 5) Ch. 1 mn. 26–27.
38 Art. 288 TFEU.
39 See thereto and generally on the sources K Ambos (n 5) Ch. 1 mn. 30–33.
40 Agreement between the Governments of the States of the Benelux Economic Union, the Federal Republic of Germany and the French Republic on the Gradual Abolition of Checks at their Common Borders, OJEU L 239 of 22 September 2000, 13–18. On the origin in a blockade by French truck drivers and the bilateral French-German agreement of Saarbrücken of 13 July 1984, cf E de Capitani, *ERA Forum*, 15 (2014) 104.
41 Convention Implementing the Schengen Agreement of 14 June 1985 between the Governments of the States of the Benelux Economic Union, the Federal Republic of Germany and the French Republic on the Gradual Abolition of Checks at Their Common Border, OJEU L 239 of 22 September 2000, 19 ff. On Schengen II specifically, cf K Würz, *Das Schengener Durchführungsübereinkommen* (Stuttgart et al.: Richard Boorberg 1997).
42 Cf Gless, in Schomburg et al. (n 4) 1637–1638; C Safferling (n 8) § 12 mn. 71; for a good overview of all changes G Huybreghts, *ERA Forum*, 16 (2015) 380 ff (with a table on 403 ff); summarising also E de Capitani *ERA Forum*, 15 (2014) 107–109 (with a very positive assessment focusing on the border regime, 101, 117–118 and *passim*).
43 Protocol (No 2) Integrating the Schengen *Acquis* into the Framework of the European Union (1997), OJEC C 340 of 10 November 1997, 93 = OJEU C 321E of 29 December 2006, 191–195; cf also Council Decision of 20 May 1999 (1999/435/EC) concerning the definition of the Schengen acquis for the purpose of determining, in conformity with the relevant provisions of the Treaty establishing the European Community and the Treaty on European Union, the legal basis for each of the provisions or decisions which constitute the acquis, OJEC L 176, 10 July 1999, 1–16; Council Decision of 20 May 1999 (1999/436/EC) determining, in conformity with the relevant provisions of the Treaty establishing the

the interpretation of the Schengen Convention.[44] Through the above mentioned 'communitisation' of the Third Pillar, the Court's jurisdiction results from Arts. 267, 67 TFEU.[45] *Protocol 19* to the Lisbon Treaty[46] upholds this legal situation. According to this Protocol, the Schengen acquis now applies to 30 States, namely 26 EU States[47] and four non-EU States (Iceland, Liechtenstein, Norway and Switzerland).[48] The CISA consists of eight titles and 142 articles.

European Community and the Treaty on European Union, the legal basis for each of the provisions or decisions which constitute the Schengen acquis, OJEC L 176 of 10 July 1999, 17–30.

[44] Art. 35(1) TEU, earlier version.

[45] Generally on the Court's jurisdiction see Art. 19(3) TEU.

[46] Lisbon Treaty, Protocol (No. 19) on the Schengen Acquis Integrated into the Framework of the EU, OJEU C 326, 26 October 2012, 290–292.

[47] Pursuant to Art. 2 in conjunction with Art. 1 Protocol 19 (n 46) these States are: Austria, Belgium, Bulgaria, Croatia, Cyprus, Denmark, Estonia, Finland, France, Germany, Greece, Hungary, Italy, Latvia, Lithuania, Luxembourg, Malta, Poland, Portugal, Romania, Slovenia, Slovakia, Spain, Sweden, the Czech Republic and the Netherlands. Although *Denmark* has opted out regarding the free movement of persons (cf Protocol (No 5) on the Position of Denmark (1997), OJEU C 321 E of 29 December 2006, 201–202 [to the Amsterdam Treaty] and Protocol (No 22) on the Position of Denmark, OJEU C 326 of 26 October 2012, 299–303 [to the Lisbon Treaty]), (unamended) Schengen acquis measures adopted before the Amsterdam Treaty are still binding and applicable upon it (Art. 3 Protocol (No 2) Integrating the Schengen *Acquis* into the Framework of the European Union (1997), OJEC C 340 of 10 November 1997, 93 = OJEU C 321E of 29 December 2006, 191–195); it can opt into measures which build upon the Schengen acquis (Art 3 Protocol 19, n. 46, in conjunction with Art. 4 Protocol 22 to the Lisbon Treaty).

[48] These States are associated members: For *Iceland* and *Norway* see Art. 6 Protocol 19 (n 46); see also Council Decision 2000/777/EC (1.12.2000) applying the Schengen acquis to the countries of the Nordic Passport Union (Denmark, Finland, Iceland, Norway, Sweden). For *Liechtenstein* see Protocol between the European Union, the European Community, the Swiss Confederation and the Principality of Liechtenstein on the accession of the Principality of Liechtenstein to the Agreement between the European Union, the European Community and the Swiss Confederation on the Swiss Confederation's association with the implementation, application and development of the Schengen acquis, OJEU L 160 of 18 June 2011, 21, and the associated Council decision of 13 December 2011, on the full application of the provisions of the Schengen acquis in the Principality of Liechtenstein (2011/842/EU), OJEU L 334 of 16 December 2011, 27–28. For *Switzerland* see Agreement between the European Union, the European Community and the Swiss Confederation on the Swiss Confederation's association with the implementation, application and development of the Schengen acquis, OJEU L 53 of 27 February 2008, 52–59 and the Final Act of 26 October 2004, OJEU L 53 of 27 February 2008, 71–73. On these third, non-EU States

Regulations particularly relevance to police and judicial cooperation are to be found in Title III ('Police and Security'), particularly in Chapters 1 to 5.[49] From a fundamental rights perspective, the prohibition of double jeopardy legally enshrined in Art. 54 CISA[50] is of particular significance.[51]

2 The UK's Special Status vis-à-vis the EU Criminal Justice System

During the pre-Brexit campaign the UK's very special relationship with the EU in the criminal justice area was hardly ever mentioned in public debates[52] except in some specialist academic fora.[53] Yet, it is important to acknowledge that the UK never fully embraced the Union's attempts to bring Member States closer together in the criminal justice area, especially as regards forms of co-operation which may infringe upon British sovereignty.[54] In general terms, it is worthwhile to recall that David Cameron's Brexit referendum was by no means the first UK referendum on the EU. In fact, the 1974 Labour government renegotiated the terms of the UK's accession to the then European Economic

---

see also Schröder and Stiegel, in Sieber et al., *Europäisches Strafrecht* (2014), 623–625 (Iceland and Norway), 625–626 (Switzerland), 631–632 (Liechtenstein); on Switzerland, cf also Meyer, *Criminal Law Forum* (*CLF*), 28 (2017), 275, at 281 ff.; on the practical work with the associated States cf G Huybreghts, *ERA Forum*, 16 (2015), 400–401. – *Monaco, San Marino, Andorra* and *Vatican City* have not joined the Schengen agreement, but they do not undertake controls of their borders with neighbouring countries (<http://www.schengenvisainfo.com/schengen-visa-countries-list/>, last accessed 21 November 2017).

49 For more detail, cf K Ambos (n 5) Ch. 4 mn. 5.
50 On the difficult relationship with Art. 50 of the Charter of the Fundamental Rights of the European Union (CFREU) cf K Ambos (n 5) Ch. 2 mn. 165 ff.
51 For a detailed analysis cf K Ambos (n 5) Ch. 2 mn. 161 ff.
52 Crit. also House of Lords, EU Home Affairs Sub-Committee, Future UK-EU Security and Policing Cooperation, HL Paper 77, 16 December 2016, 5 ('… this subject did not attract a commensurate level of attention in the referendum campaign, from either side.').
53 Thus, this author participated for example in an event organized by the European Criminal Law Association (UK), cf <http://www.eucriminallaw.com/> last visited 21 November 2017.
54 See e.g. see also Walker, *GLJ*, 17 (2016) 126 ('With its opt-outs from the Euro and Schengen, and also from some wider aspects of criminal justice and immigration policy under the Area of Freedom, Security and Justice, the UK was already a major beneficiary – probably *the* major beneficiary – of the EU's variable geometry even before it cut a new "customised membership" deal in February that would have allowed exemption even from the founding Treaty commitment to "ever closer Union."'). For a historical account cf House of Lords (n 52) 7–9.

Community (EEC) in 1973 and put the new agreement to a referendum on 5 June 1975 where it was endorsed.[55]

Concerning the above mentioned *Schengen acquis*, the UK (and Ireland) negotiated special regimes: It opted out of the policies regarding visas, asylum, immigration and others related to the free movement of persons (Title IV of Part Three TEC),[56] including with regard to the measures necessary to progressively establish the internal market pursuant to Art. 14 TEC.[57] As to the Schengen acquis the UK (and Ireland) reserved the right to decide on a case-by-case basis whether to participate in certain measures.[58] According to Art. 4 of Protocol 19 to the Lisbon Treaty the UK (and Ireland) 'may at any time request to take part in some or all provisions' with the (unanimous) approval of the Council; at the same time, they are entitled to opt out within three months.[59]

Under the *Lisbon Treaty* the UK negotiated, (again) together with Ireland, a separate *Protocol (21)*,[60] which gave it, on the one hand, the right to fully abstain from any future measures in the area of Freedom, Security and Justice, and, on the other hand, allowed it to selectively opt-in regarding individual measures.[61] This, in fact, amounted to a reintroduction of the veto – actually abolished by the Lisbon qualified majority voting – through the backdoor.

---

55 Cf A Dashwood et al., *EU Law* 6th edn (Oxford, Portland: Hart 2011) 10–11.
56 Protocol (No 4) on the Position of the UK and Ireland (1997), OJEU C 321 E, 29 December 2006, 198–200.
57 Protocol (No 3) on the Application of Certain Aspects of Article 14 of the Treaty Establishing the European Community to the United Kingdom and to Ireland (1997), OJEU C 321 E of 29 December 2006, 196–197.
58 Art. 4 Protocol 2 (n 43).
59 Art. 5(2) Protocol 19 (n 43); for a summary cf G Huybreghts, *ERA Forum*, 16 (2015), 402; House of Commons, Brexit: implications for policing and criminal justice cooperation, Briefing Paper No. 7650, 24 February 2017, 5.
60 Lisbon Treaty, Protocol (No 21) on the Position of the United Kingdom and Ireland in Respect of the Area of Freedom, Security and Justice, OJEU C 326 of 26 October 2012, 295–298.
61 Cf Protocol 21, Art. 2–4; de Busser, *ERA Forum*, 16 (2015), 286; J R Spencer, *Archbold Rev*, issue 7 (2012) 7; E Herlin-Karnell, *ALF*, 5 (2013) 100; M Fletcher, in Mitsilegas, Bergström, and Konstadinides, *Handbook EU Criminal Law* (Cheltenham (UK), Northampton (MA): Edward Elgar Publishing 2016) 82; V Mitsilegas (n 35) 44 ff; id., *CLR*, 63 (2016), 518–519; House of Commons (n 59) 4–5. Thus, Ireland opted-in regarding the instruments of the Security, Freedom and Justice Area, cf Ryan and Hamilton, in Healy et al., *Handbook of Irish Criminology* (Oxon, New York: Routledge 2016) 469 ff.

In addition, Protocol 36[62] gave the UK – as the only Member State[63] – a full *opt-out* option from all (135) police and criminal justice measures adopted under the pre-Lisbon 'third pillar' with effect from 1 December 2014,[64] unless they have been amended ('lisbonised').[65] As to the envisaged European Public Prosecutor Office (EPPO), the UK already made clear at the outset that it will not participate in this project unless there is a national referendum in favour ('referendum lock').[66] The UK would then have had the possibility of a subsequent selective *opt-in*.[67] On 24 July 2013, the UK made use of the opt-out and the 135 acts ceased to apply to it on 1 December 2014.[68] Nevertheless, the most relevant acts have still been applicable to the UK since, on the one hand, the opt-out does not apply to the amended ('Lisbonised') and the new (post-Lisbon) acts[69] and, on the other hand, the UK opted back in into thirty-five ('magic') measures, including some of the most important ones for

---

62   Protocol (No. 36) on Transitional Provisions, OJEU C 326 of 26 October 2012, 326.

63   Protocol 36 (n 62) applies only to the UK. Interestingly, Ireland, this time, did not express any concerns regarding the extended powers of the Commission and the ECJ regarding PJCCM; cf de Busser, *ERA Forum*, 16 (2015) 286.

64   Art. 10 (4) Protocol 36 (n 62) (allowing the UK not to accept the extended powers of the Commission and the CJEU as well as stipulating that acts re police/justice cooperation in criminal matters, 'shall cease to apply'); see also Council of the EU, 'UK notification according to Article 10(4) of Protocol No 36 to TEU and TFEU', 12750/13, Brussels, 26 July 2013; House of Commons (n 59) 5. On the relevant instruments included, see J R Spencer *Archbold Rev*, issue 7 (2012) 7–9; criticizing the UK's opt-out J R Spencer, *Archbold Rev*, issue 8 (2013) 6–7; crit. on the UK's pick-and-choose approach as incompatible with a consistent approach to EU law V Mitsilegas *CLR*, 63 (2016), 522–526 (discussing the EAW, confiscation measures and fraud).

65   Protocol 36 (n 62), Art. 10 (4) in fine with (2) (the former excluding the application of the opt-out to 'the amended acts which are applicable to the UK as referred to in paragraph 2'.).

66   EU Act 2011, Part 1 Sect. 6; thereto J R Spencer, in V Mitsilegas et al., *Globalisation, Criminal Law and Criminal Justice* (2015), 142–143; V Mitsilegas *CLR*, 63 (2016), 518.

67   Protocol 36 (n 62), Art. 10(5) (allowing the UK to 'notify the Council of its wish to participate in acts which have ceased to apply' pursuant to the previous opt-out). This selective (re-)opt-in will need the authorisation of the Commission or Council, i.e., the UK may only request re-admission but has no right to be readmitted; see also J R Spencer *Archbold Rev*, issue 7 (2012), 6; crit. of Prot. 36, Fletcher, in Mitsilegas, Bergström, and Konstadinides (n 61) 79 ff.

68   For the UK's letter and the respective notification of 24 July 2013, see UK notification (n 64); for a discussion of the measures see HM Government, Decision pursuant to Article 10 of Protocol 36 to the TFEU, July 2013, Command Paper 8671, available at <https://www.gov.uk/government/uploads/system/uploads/attachment_data/file/235912/8671.pdf>, last accessed 21 November 2017. On the process and the rhetoric in the UK leading to the opt-out, see J R Spencer *Archbold Rev*, issue 8 (2013) 7–8; M Fletcher, in Mitsilegas, Bergström, and Konstadinides (n 61) 86 ff, 94 ff; briefly J Blackstock and A Tinsley, *Archbold Rev*, issue 8 (2015) 5.

69   Protocol 36 (n 62) Art. 10(4) last clause in conjunction with Art. 10(2).

police and criminal justice cooperation,[70] including the respective jurisdiction of the CJEU.[71] Thus, in sum, the whole opt-out-opt-in-exercise turned out to be largely 'a purely paper one' and as 'gesture politics' with the practical consequences amounting to 'nil',[72] although, of course, the UK's selective approach to a supranational legal system like the EU constitutes a challenge to the coherence of the whole system.[73] The said 35 measures as such have been described as 'part of a very complex network of arrangements, agreements, understandings and controls' which could not be dismantled without affecting the structure as a whole and at the same time all individual measures.[74] At any rate, the Government then committed to publish annual reports in the 'form of an updated document describing JHA opt-in and Schengen opt-out decisions taken between 1 December 2009 and the present.'[75]

Similarly, the UK always struggled to accept the *jurisdiction of the ECJ* (now CJEU). When, under the Amsterdam treaty, its jurisdiction was expanded to

---

70 The measures, in total 35, are listed in HM Government (n 68) at 8–12 (e.g. EAW, ECRIS, Europol, Eurojust, ESO, Naples II, JITS, cooperation in international crimes via contact points, execution of orders regarding freezing property or evidence, mutual recognition of financial penalties, confiscation orders, criminal judgments entailing deprivation of liberty and supervision measures, exchange of information and intelligence, cooperation regarding asset recovery, Schengen, SIS II, Art. 54 CISA). See also HM Government, Decision pursuant to Article 10(5) of Protocol 36 to the Treaty on the Functioning of the European Union, July 2014 Cm 8897, available at www.gov.uk/government/publications, last accessed 6 March 2017.

71 See also Council Decision of 1 December 2014, concerning the Notification of the United Kingdom of Great Britain and Northern Ireland of its wish to Take Part in Some of the Provisions of the Schengen Acquis which are Contained in acts of the Union in the Field of Police Cooperation and Judicial Cooperation in Criminal Matters and Amending Decisions 2000/365/EC and 2004/926/EC, OJ EU L 345 of 1 December 2014, 1–5; House of Lords (n 52) 9; House of Commons (n 59) 5–6. See also de Busser, *ERA Forum*, 16 (2015), 287; Blackstock and Tinsley, *Archbold Rev,* issue 8 (2015) 5–6; M Fletcher, in Mitsilegas, Bergström, and Konstadinides (n 64) 90–94; V Mitsilegas *CLR*, 63 (2016), 520–522.

72 Cf J R Spencer *Archbold Rev,* issue 8 (*2013*) 9. In a similar vein Yvette Cooper, Shadow Home Secretary, commented on Cameron's claim to have 'clawed back 100 powers from Brussels': 'We have the power not to do a whole series of things we plan to carry on doing anyway, the power not to follow guidance we already follow, the power not to take action we already take, the power not to meet standards we already meet, the power not to do things that everyone else has already stopped doing and the power not to do a whole series of things we want to do anyway'. (Hansard, House of Commons, 7 April 2015, Column 363).

73 For a fundamental critique, especially with regard to the negative impact on rights protection, cf V Mitsilegas, (n 35) 49–50, 180–181, 266.

74 Cf House of Lords (n 52) 38 (quoting Lord Kirkhope).

75 House of Commons (n 59) 7.

the second and third pillar,[76] the UK did not submit the declaration necessary[77] to consent to this jurisdictional expansion.[78] Under the Lisbon treaty, the UK first opted out of the CJEU's jurisdiction with regard to police and criminal justice measures but then joined again with regard to the above mentioned 35 measures.[79]

3 Post-Brexit Options

3.1 *The Starting Point*

Given this anyway highly selective acceptance of EU criminal justice by the UK Brexit will only have limited consequences for the future cooperation between the Union of the 27 and the UK. In fact, the criminal justice measures which the UK decided to join (by an opt-in), in particular the 35 'magic' ones re-joined in July 2013, indicate where the UK's core interest in the criminal justice area lies. In terms of the negotiations, these measures constitute the starting point of the UK's negotiating position given that its continuing participation in these measures, one way or the other, 'will remain in the UK's national interest post-Brexit'.[80] Indeed, then Home Secretary Theresa made clear at the time that the UK pursues its core security interests with the opt-in into these measures since 'bilateral agreements would simply not work as effectively and our co-operation would suffer …'[81] Later she insisted that these measures 'make a positive difference in fighting crime and preventing terrorism.'[82] In a recent House of Commons report it is stated that '[T]he reasons for opting into these

---

76   Cf Art. 46 TEU (Amsterdam version).
77   Cf Art. 35(2) TEU Amsterdam (declaraction to accept jurisdiction).
78   The UK was joined by Ireland and Denmark; cf CJEU Research and Documentation Service, 'Jurisdiction of the Court of Justice to give preliminary rulings on police and judicial cooperation in criminal matters', March 2008 (<http://curia.europa.eu/jcms/upload/docs/application/pdf/2008-09/art35_2008-09-25_17-37-4_434.pdf>, last accessed 21 November 2017).
79   (n 70).
80   House of Lords (n 52) 6.
81   HC Deb 7 April 2014, columns 31–32, available at <https://www.publications.parliament.uk/pa/cm201314/cmhansrd/cm140407/debtext/140407-0001.htm>, last visited 21 November 2017.
82   Home Secretary's speech on the UK, the EU and our place in the world, 25 April 2016, available at <https://www.gov.uk/government/speeches/home-secretarys-speech-on-the-uk-eu-and-our-place-in-the-world>, last visited 21 November 2017.

measures were well rehearsed at the time, and the decision was subject to scrutiny by several parliamentary Committees.'[83]

The government is still of the view that criminal justice cooperation with the EU is of fundamental importance for the UK's overall security structure. The Secretary of State for Exiting the EU stressed that a strong cooperation in the criminal justice area should be one of the top overarching objectives in the negotiations.[84] In a White Paper the cooperation in the fight against crime and terrorism is listed as one of the 12 principles guiding the exit negotiations.[85] Similarly, in the House of Lords' view the UK 'benefits greatly from close and interdependent police and security cooperation with EU institutions and member states.'[86] In her letter triggering Art. 50 TEU PM May reaffirmed once more the UK's continuing interest – apart from close economic cooperation – in a bold security cooperation with the EU.[87] As top priorities for UK law enforcement agencies in the future cooperation with the EU the just mentioned House of Lords' report lists Europol, Eurojust, SIS II, the European Arrest Warrant (EAW), the European Criminal Records Information System (ECRIS), the Prüm Decisions (cross border cooperation)[88] and the Passenger Name Records (PNR)[89] showing a clear preference for data-access and -sharing;[90] the list largely corresponds to the 35 measures re-joined in July 2013.[91]

---

[83] House of Commons (n 59) 6.

[84] HC Deb, 12 October 2016, col 328; conc. House of Lords (n 52) 2, 5, 12–13, 42.

[85] HM Government, The UK's exit from and new partnership with the EU, February 2017, Cm 9417, 61 ff, available at <https://www.gov.uk/government/uploads/system/uploads/attachment_data/file/589191/The_United_Kingdoms_exit_from_and_partnership_with_the_EU_Web.pdf>, last visited 21 November 2017. See also the various government statements summarized in House of Commons, (n 59) 27–30.

[86] House of Lords (n 52) 5.

[87] (n 3).

[88] Council Decision 2008/615/JHA, 23 June 2008 on the stepping up of cross-border cooperation, particularly in combating terrorism and cross-border crime, OJ L 210/1 (6 August 2008) and Council Decision 2008/616/JHA, 23 June 2008 on the implementation of Decision 2008/615/JHA on the stepping up of cross-border cooperation, particularly in combating terrorism and cross-border crime, OJ L 210/12 (6 August 2008). On the UK's position cf House of Lords (n 52) 29–30.

[89] House of Lords (n 52) 2, 10, 27–28.

[90] See also House of Lords (n 52) 25–33, 44–45.

[91] See (n 70). The Prüm decisions have been re-joined by the UK in May 2016, cf Commission Decision (EU) 2016/809, 20 May 2016 on the notification by the United Kingdom of Great Britain and Northern Ireland of its wish to participate in certain acts of the Union in the field of police cooperation adopted before the entry into force of the Treaty of Lisbon and which are not part of the Schengen acquis, OJ L 132/105 (21 May 2016).

The Government believes that it has a strong negotiating position, being 'uniquely placed to develop and sustain a mutually beneficial model of cooperation ... from outside the Union', to get 'the best deal ... to cooperate in the fight against crime and terrorism' and to 'seek a strong and close future relationship with the EU, with a focus on operational and practical cross-border cooperation.'[92] In fact, the UK is still participating in all the mentioned 35 measures[93] and recently also opted in into the new 2016 Europol Regulation.[94] Thus, it is clear that the question is not whether but how the UK could most effectively participate in EU criminal justice cooperation after having left the EU.

3.2 Possible Agreements

As to possible treaty relations between the UK and the EU criminal justice area one may distinguish between the institutional level, represented especially by Europol and Eurojust, and secondary acts (mainly the previous framework decisions). Apart from that, the UK could also – following in particular the Swiss approach – autonomously adapt its national law to EU developments, thereby facilitating cooperation with EU Member States.[95]

3.2.1 Institutional Level

As to the institutional level, it is perfectly possible to have bilateral cooperation agreements[96] as in fact other States do.[97] Of course, the bilateral agreement

---

92 HM Government (n 85) 61–62.
93 Cf House of Commons (n 59) 8–13.
94 Regulation (EU) 2016/794 of the EP and of the Council of 11 May 2016 on the European Union Agency for Law Enforcement Cooperation (Europol) and replacing and repealing Council Decision 2009/371/JHA, 2009/934/JHA, 2009/935/JHA, 2009/936/JHA and 2009/968/JHA (OJ L 135 of 24 May 2016, 53); thereto K Ambos (n 5) Ch. 5 mn. 8 ff On the UK's position cf House of Commons (n 59) 10; welcoming the opting-in House of Lords (n 52) 17–18, 43.
95 On the Swiss model ('autonomer Nachvollzug') in this regard cf Meyer, *CLF*, 28 (2017), 275, at 281; see also on Norway cf Suominen, *CLF*, 28 (2017), 251, at 252, 265 ff.
96 For agreements with the agencies see also V Mitsilegas *CLR*, 63 (2016), 533–534; House of Commons (n 59) 16.
97 *Europol* has several 'operational agreements' with third States (e.g. Australia, Canada, Colombia, Liechtenstein, Norway, Switzerland and the USA) and also a few 'strategic agreements' (Bosnia and Herzegovina, Russia, Turkey, Ukraine), cf <https://www.europol.europa.eu/partners-agreements>. *Eurojust* has several agreements with third States (e.g. Liechtenstein, Norway, Switzerland, Ukraine and the USA) and organisations, cf <http://eurojust.europa.eu/about/Partners/Pages/third-states.aspx>, both last visited. On Norway

approach has its limits as we will see below. At any rate, UK security agencies and official have always stressed that ongoing tight cooperation with these two agencies is a number one priority.[98] The UK uses Europol more than any other country[99] and participates in most Joint Investigation Teams (JITS).[100]

3.2.2 Secondary Acts

As to the participation in secondary (mutual recognition) acts, the UK may also conclude agreements on specific areas of criminal justice cooperation such as the post Prüm framework and the EAW – whose importance for the UK is beyond any controversy[101] – following earlier practice.[102] Yet, being not

---

and Switzerland in particular see also House of Commons (n 59) 14–15; on Switzerland see also Meyer, CLF, 28 (2017), 285–286; on Norway Suominen, CLF, 28 (2017), 262.

[98] Cf House of Lords (n 52) 17, 22; House of Commons (n 59) 18, 21 (quoting Europol Director Rob Wainwright and the National Crime Agency re Europol and DPP Director Alison Saunders re Eurojust).

[99] HM Government, The UK's cooperation with the EU on justice and home affairs, and on foreign policy and security issues, Background Note, without date, para. 1.16, available at <https://www.gov.uk/government/brexit/uploads/system/uploads/attachment_data/file/521926/The_UK_s_cooperation_with_the_EU_on_justice_and_home_affairs__and_on_foreign_policy_and_security_issues.pdf>, last visited 21 November 2017.

[100] Cf House of Lords (n 52) 22 (where this is discussed in relation to Eurojust). JITS may be set up by Eurojust (Art. 6(1)(a)(iv) and 7(1)(a)(iv) Council Decision 2009/426/JHA of 16 December 2008, OJ L 138 of 4 June 2009, 14) or Europol (Art. 4(1)(d), 5(5) Europol Regulation 2016 (n 94). The original legal basis of EU law was Art. 13 of the EU Mutual Assistance Convention (OJEU C 197 of 12 July 2000, 1) and Framework Decision 2002/465/JHA; within the Council of Europe it is also provided for by Art. 20 Add.Prot. II to the European Convention on Mutual Assistance in Criminal Matters of 8 Nov. 2001. JITS are also provided for in Art. 19 UN Convention Against Transnational Organized Crime (Palermo Convention) of 15 November 2000 and Art. 49 UN Convention Against Corruption of 31 October 2003.

[101] Cf House of Lords (n 52) 34–35; House of Commons (n 59) 23–25 (inter alia quoting, at 24, the National Crime Agency [NCA] which posits that "leaving the EAW would ... pose a huge public protection risk to the UK"). In 2015, the UK received 13.797 EAWs, <http://www.nationalcrimeagency.gov.uk/publications/european-arrest-warrant-statistics/wanted-from-the-uk-european-arrest-warrant-statistics/829-eaw-part-1-master-calendar-year-v1-0-final-2009-2017>, /829-eaw-part-1-master-calendar-year-v1-0-final-2009-2017 last visited 21 November 2017.

[102] See e.g. Council Decision of 27 June 2006 on the signing of the Agreement between the European Union and the Republic of Iceland and the Kingdom of Norway on the surrender procedure between the Member States of the European Union and Iceland and Norway [2006] OJ L 292/1; thereto also V Mitsilegas CLR, 63 (2016), 533; House of Commons (n 61) 16.

a Schengen member, the UK would hardly get the privileged access of Norway and Iceland (being Schengen members), regarding the EAW and information sharing (Prüm, SIS II).[103] ECRIS access is even so far only given to EU Member States.[104] Only the PNR allows explicitly for bilateral agreements between the EU and third States, as for example the EU-Canada agreement shows.[105] Practitioners and security experts have especially stressed the importance of SIS II – joined by the UK in April 2015[106] – in tracking suspects and enforcing EAWs and other mutual recognition measures.[107] It is not least for this reason that the UK would have to negotiate an association agreement regarding the Schengen Acquis along the lines of the ones of the four non-Member States Iceland, Liechtenstein, Norway and Switzerland.[108] Looking beyond surrender of persons the UK must agree some form of cooperation in general investigative measures modelled after the European Investigation Order.[109] Of course, if UK-EU 27 agreements are not feasible, the UK may conclude bilateral agreements with individual Member States.[110] The setback of such an approach is that it would multiply the number of agreements – adding to the ones with the EU or one of its agencies various State to State agreements – which makes the handling ever more difficult.[111]

---

103 Cf House of Lords (n 52) 30–31, 35–36; House of Commons (n 59) 23, 25–26; on the importance of the ECRIS and the PNR in particular House of Lords (n 52) 26–28.

104 Cf House of Lords (n 52) 31.

105 The new agreement was signed on 25 June 2014 (12657/1/13 REV 1) but challenged before the CJEU (which declared it incompatible with Art. 7, 8, 21 and Art. 52(1) of the Charter of Fundamental Rights, cf. Opinion (Grand Chamber) of 26 July 2017, < http://curia.europa.eu/juris/document/document.jsf?text=fluggastdaten&docid=193216&pageIndex=0&doclang=EN&mode=req&dir=&occ=first&part=1&cid=277410#ctx1>, last visited 20 November 2017). See also House of Lords (n 52) 31.

106 House of Lords (n 52) 25 (pointing out that between April 2015 and 31 March 2016 6,400 alerts issued by other countries received hits in the UK).

107 Cf House of Lords (n 52) 25–26 (quoting the NCA considering SIS II 'an absolute game changer for the UK'); House of Commons (n 59) 22, 25 (quoting, at 22, the DPP, inter alia stating: 'That helps us because, when we issue a European arrest warrant, we do not just issue it to a particular country; it can go to all 27'.).

108 (n 48).

109 Directive 2014/41/EU, OJ EU L 130, 1 May 2014, 1; thereto K Ambos, (n 5), Ch. 4 mn. 88 ff. On the UK's position cf House of Lords (n 52) 40.

110 Thereto also V Mitsilegas CLR, 63 (2016), 534; House of Commons (n 59) 16.

111 Crit. insofar with regard to the approx. 120 bilateral EU-Switzerland agreements Meyer, CLF, 28 (2017), 289 ff.

3.2.3 New Forms of Cooperation

One should also note that, given the UK's special status and importance in the Union's criminal justice and security architecture, some unprecedented 'alternative arrangements'[112] may be possible. There is a mutual interest of both the EU and the UK to have the closest criminal justice cooperation possible since both sides benefit from this cooperation and the UK has certainly more to offer than just any third country.[113] At any rate, it is difficult to conceive that negotiations on all these options can be finished within two years (as envisaged by Art. 50 TEU).[114] More importantly, even if the current situation would be fully replaced by new agreements or 'alternative arrangements', cooperation would still not be the same as from within the EU. In other words, alternative approaches, as for example demonstrated by Switzerland,[115] have their limits. As rightly argued by Mitsilegas none of the post-Brexit options will be 'capable of providing to the UK a level of co-operation which is equivalent to the current level of co-operation as a member of the EU …'[116] In a similar vein, the already mentioned House of Commons report finds that 'it appears unlikely that any of these options would provide an equivalent level of co-operation as that currently enjoyed by the UK.'[117] The House of Lords even sees 'a real risk that any new arrangements the Government and EU-27 put in place by way of replacement when the UK leaves the EU will be sub-optimal relative to present arrangements, leaving the people of the UK less safe.'[118]

3.2.4 Consequences

Indeed, both on a political and operational level the UK will be worse off after Brexit. On the political level it will have no more influence on the development of EU law in this area; on the operational level, UK requests from outside the EU would not have the same priority as from within and mutual recognition

---

112 House of Commons (n 59) 3.
113 This point has been repeatedly made by UK officials and experts, see e.g. House of Lords (n 52) 31–32, 33.
114 See also House of Lords (n 52) 2 ('many years to negotiate'), 23, 24 (time to negotiate Eurojust agreement), 38 (length to negotiate EAW agreement). The Norway-EU agreement (n 102) has still not entered into force, cf Suominen, *CLF*, 28 (2017), 259.
115 Cf Meyer, *CLF*, 28 (2017), 289 ff. (concluding that 'the bilateral approach provides no viable institutional framework to cope with the demands of significantly increased cooperation. It no longer fits the level of actual cooperation and intertwinement. It is ill-prepared to foster a dynamic and cooperative evolution of common standards'.).
116 V Mitsilegas *CLR*, 63 (2016), 534.
117 House of Commons (n 59) 16.
118 House of Lords (n 52) 13, also 42.

would in fact be replaced or fall back to traditional mutual assistance.[119] As to Europol, the UK's status would depend on the nature of the agreement (only strategic or also operational);[120] even in the latter case the UK would not have the same access to the Europol databases, would not sit on the agency's management board[121] and could only send liaison officers to Europol Headquarters if agreed by the management board.[122] The UK would also lose its seat in the recently created Joint Parliamentary Scrutiny Group overseeing Europol's work since it is composed of members of the national parliaments and the European Parliament.[123] As to Eurojust, the UK would no longer participate in the On-Call Coordination[124] and would not have access to its case management system enabling cross checking of cases.[125] Also, it is not clear how an UK liaison prosecutor, pursuant to a bilateral agreement, would link up with Eurojust, especially whether s/he would be able to participate in transnational coordination in the same way as prosecutors from EU Member States.[126] In both cases, it would be difficult to get around the jurisdiction of the CJEU so disliked by the UK.[127] The continuing participation in JITs could be ensured by a bilateral agreement[128] or through participation in relevant multilateral treaties.[129] An EAW-like surrender procedure would require, as already pointed out

---

119   House of Commons (n 59) 16, 21–22; on the loss of political and strategic influence see also House of Lords (n 52) 10 (with quotes of security officials) 13, 23.

120   See on this distinction already (n 97) and the discussion re the UK in House of Lords (n 52) 17–18.

121   On its composition see Art. 10 Europol Regulation 2016 (n 94) (representatives of MS and Commission).

122   Cf Art. 8 Europol Regulation 2016 (n 94) (liaison officers to be sent by MS). See also House of Commons (n 59) 17–20, 26 (quoting, at 19, S. Peers and drawing a comparison with Denmark having opted out of all post-Lisbon measures and therefore not participating in the new Europol Regulation).

123   Cf Art. 51 Europol Regulation 2016 (n 94); see also House of Commons (n 59) 19–20.

124   Art. 5a (2) Eurojust Decision 2008 (n 100).

125   Cf. Art. 16 Eurojust Decision 2008 (n 100); see also House of Commons (n 59) 21.

126   Cf Art. 2 Eurojust Decision 2008 (n 100) (national members come from MS and only those participate in coordination/investigation activities); for a discussion House of Lords (n 52) 23 (especially quoting the DPP).

127   Cf re Europol House of Lords (n 52) 19.

128   See e.g. Art. 20(1) of the Swiss-German Police treaty of 27 April 1999, available (in German, French and Italian) at <https://www.admin.ch/opc/de/classified-compilation/19995927/index.html>, last visited 21 November 2017; but see Meyer, CLF, 28 (2017), 292 for the problems of Switzerland in this regard; generally also House of Lords (n 52) 24.

129   The UK is already a party, on the CoE level, to the AP II to the European Conv. on Mutual Assistance in Criminal Matters and, on an international level, to both the Palermo Con-

above, a Norway/Island-like agreement which in turn would require Schengen membership; otherwise, the UK would fall back on the burdensome 1957 Council of Europe Extradition Convention.[130] Even if the UK reached a Norway/Island-like agreement, it would have to get rid of the nationality exception (contained therein in Article 6) which would be hard to swallow for some of the EU Member States which have, like Germany, a prohibition to extradite nationals.[131]

Also, one must not overlook that any post-EU cooperation does not – contrary to the clearly expressed interest by the UK aiming at 'bespoke' adjudication arrangements[132] – entail 'complete independence from EU law'[133] since this law will still be applicable by way of the EU and its Member States (as the UK's partners). Thus, any agreement between the UK and the EU would have to be interpreted by the CJEU.[134] While this interpretation would not be directly binding on the UK (being no longer an EU member), it would indirectly affect it via the respective agreement (as interpreted by the CJEU). Similarly, a dispute resolution mechanism would have to be established which may involve the CJEU (whose jurisdiction has never been fully embraced by the UK).[135]

4   Conclusion

The UK's special status vis-à-vis the EU criminal justice area and its great influence in shaping and developing this area[136] may justify the Government's confidence in getting a special deal and achieving tailor made solutions which

---

vention and the UN Corruption Convention (entry into force for both 9 February 2006), all already mentioned above (n 100).

130   For a critique rightly House of Lords (n 52) 36–38.
131   The exception introduced in clause 2 of Art. 16(2) GG only refers to EU Member States and International Tribunals. For similar prohibitions see Ambos (n 5) Ch. 4 mn. 55.
132   Cf House of Lords (n 52) 11 (quoting the government's position that laws are to be made in Westminster, not in Brussels, and that those laws would be interpreted by British courts, not the CJEU) 13, 42.
133   House of Commons (n 59) 16.
134   Cf Art. 218 TFEU on agreements with third countries and the Court's competence in para. 11 regarding the compatibility of such agreements with the EU Treaties. See also House of Lords (n 52) 11–12.
135   See also House of Commons (n 59) 16–17.
136   See also Valsamis Mitsilegas, 'European Criminal Law After Brexit' (2017) 28 *Criminal Law Forum* 219, at 246 ff. (stressing the UK's contribution to EU criminal law on four levels: operational, strategic, legislation, implementation).

reconcile the UK's sovereignty and public security interests. Yet, the UK's selective approach to criminal justice, characterized by a mixture of opt-out, opt-in and neither/nor decisions, will make negotiations more complex than with a 'normal' Member State and may also generate resistance among certain Member States which never felt at ease with the UK's privileged treatment by the EU. At any rate, as we have seen, there are possible options on the table which may bring the UK as close as possible to the EU in terms of police and criminal justice cooperation if both parties have sufficient political will and are prepared to think out of the box taking recourse to unprecedented arrangements.

CHAPTER 2

Energising the Law's Response to Terrorism: The Decision of the Appeals Chamber of the Special Tribunal of Lebanon and the Need for Further Action

David Baragwanath

Abstract

Statistics of people forced from their homes and their country provide a troubling measure of social malaise. Among its causes is terrorism. This week, from a figure of 20m just over a decade ago, the number of internal and external refugees reached 65.3m. In a recent Address Professor Keith Hayward stated: "Terrorism, civil unrest, seemingly unstoppable immigration, cyber-activism, a growing 'precariat' [people living a precarious existence, without security or predictability, especially job security], the rise of 'theistic violence': these, and other portents, suggest a gathering storm of global discontent and rancorousness". In his report last year to the British Government its Independent Reviewer of Terrorism Legislation, David Anderson QC, advised: The highest priority risks are in summary: terrorism ..." In its Government Report On Counter-terrorism Efforts the Danish Government stated: "The Government's objective is to protect the population against terrorist acts in Denmark, to prevent terrorism by addressing its root causes, to ensure that the counterterrorism efforts are carried out in full in accordance with international law ... This report mainly focuses on counterterrorism developments over the past year, both nationally and in international cooperation." In Le Monde on 1 April 2016 « Le Caractère global du terrorisme appelle une justice globale » Mireille Delmas-Marty wrote: « Clearly a merely national response, however secure, cannot by itself deal with the entire threat." Having left Nazi Austria in 1937, Karl Popper concluded in The Open Society and its Enemies "... progress rests with us, with our efforts, with the clarity of our conception of our ends, and with the realism of their choice". In 2015 there were 11,774 terrorist attacks that killed 28,300 people. Yet the authoritative report by the International Bar Association's Task Force Terrorism and International Law advises there is no internationally agreed definition of what legal elements a definition of terrorism should possess.

---

* KNZM Appellate Judge and former President, The Special Tribunal for Lebanon.

The attempt at such definition by the 1937 International Convention for the Prevention and Punishment of Terrorism adopted under the auspices of the League of Nations was never implemented. Throughout the subsequent eight decades those responsible at international level for agreeing and enforcing such definition have failed to achieve agreement. They have now reached a point of inertia. This paper will address these issues.

Judge Schomburg's courage and independence are nowhere better seen than in the unhappily ever more topical sphere of terrorism. His partly dissenting judgment in the ICTY *The Prosecutor v Galić* AC Case No. IT-98-29-A 30 November 2006 gives classic emphasis to the need for strict application of the principle of legality, particularly in the struggle against terrorism of which the fundamental wrong is infringement of the rule of law whose function is to protect every person. I therefore offer in his honour the following revision of a public lecture delivered at the University of Copenhagen on 30 June 2016.

1 Prelude

Statistics of people forced from their homes and their country provide a troubling measure of social malaise. Among its causes is terrorism. In June 2016, from a figure of 20m just over a decade ago, the number of internal and external refugees reached 65.3m.[1]

In his recent Inaugural Address Professor Keith Hayward stated:

> Terrorism, civil unrest, seemingly unstoppable immigration, cyber-activism, a growing 'precariat' [people living a precarious existence, without security or predictability, especially job security], the rise of 'theistic violence': these, and other portents, suggest a gathering storm of global discontent and rancorousness.[2]

In his report last year to the British Government its Independent Reviewer of Terrorism Legislation, David Anderson QC, advised:

---

[1] http://www.unhcr.org/uk/news/latest/2016/6/5763b65a4/global-forced-displacement-hits-record-high.html. Website last visited 19 July 2017.
[2] 13 May 2016.

> The highest priority risks are in summary:
> terrorism ...[3]

In its *Government Report On Counter-terrorism Efforts* the Danish Government stated:

> The Government's objective is to protect the population against terrorist acts in Denmark, to prevent terrorism by addressing its root causes, to ensure that the counterterrorism efforts are carried out in full in accordance with international law ... This report mainly focuses on counterterrorism developments over the past year, both nationally and in international cooperation.[4]

In *Le Monde* on 1 April 2016 « Le Caractère global du terrorisme appelle une justice globale » Mireille Delmas-Marty wrote:

> Clearly a merely national response, however secure, cannot by itself deal with the entire threat.[5]

Having left Nazi Austria in 1937, Karl Popper concluded in *The Open Society and its Enemies*

> ... progress rests with us, with our watchfulness, with our efforts, with the clarity of our conception of our ends, and with the realism of their choice.[6]
>
> In 2015 there were 11,774 terrorist attacks that killed 28,300 people.[7]

Yet the authoritative report by the International Bar Association's Task Force *Terrorism and International Law* advises there is:

---

[3] 'A Question of Trust: Report of the Investigatory Powers' Review' (June 2015), para 3.10 citing UK Government, *2010 National Security Strategy*, updated annually.

[4] May 2012, Foreword by Danish Minister for Foreign Affairs Villy Søvndal.

[5] « Il est donc clair qu'une réponse purement nationale, aussi sécuritaire soit-elle, ne peut à elle seule supprimer toute menace. »

[6] Popper, Karl, The Open Society and its Enemies, The High Tide of Prophecy, Vol 2 (New York: Routledge 1999), at 280.

[7] Data compiled by the University of Maryland, reported by the US State Department: Foreign Policy, 3 June 2016.

no internationally agreed definition of what legal elements a definition of terrorism should possess.[8]

The attempt at such definition by the 1937 *International Convention for the Prevention and Punishment of Terrorism* adopted under the auspices of the League of Nations, in terms followed closely by a modern decision of the Appeals Chamber of the Special Tribunal for Lebanon, was never implemented. Throughout the subsequent eight decades those responsible at international level for agreeing and enforcing such definition have failed to achieve agreement. They have now reached a point of inertia.

2 Introduction

The current *impasse* over making terrorism a crime at international law is intelligible but intolerable.

Piracy has for centuries been a crime at international law.[9] A leading authority on the interpretation and application of piracy law can see no good reason not to treat terrorism the same: the crimes complement one another and require comparable treatment.[10] For reasons that follow I have reached the same conclusion.

Ten days after the 9/11 attacks in New York and Washington, President George W Bush proclaimed

> Our war on terror begins with Al Quaeda, but it does not end there. It will not end until every terrorist group of global reach has been found, stopped and defeated.[11]

And three days after the Paris attacks of 13 November 2015 President Hollande declared

---

8 Elizabeth Stubbins Bates, Richard Goldstone, Eugene Cotran, Gijs de Vries, Julia A. Hall, Juan E. Méndez and Javaid Rehman (eds) (Oxford 2011).

9 The Iliad and Odyssey describe raids by pirates on coastal communities; Julius Caesar was captured by Sicilian pirates whom he later captured and executed. The international law of piracy is now codified by Articles 100–107 of the United Nations Convention on the Law of the Sea, defining piracy and requiring all States to cooperate to the fullest extent in its repression.

10 Personal communication.

11 <http://edition.cnn.com/2001/US/09/20/gen.bush.transcript/> visited 13 May 2016.

> France is at war. The acts committed on Friday evening and near the Stade de France, are acts of war.[12]

Each President was using a powerful metaphor to express a determined response to aggressive and violent action against their people and institutions. But how can the metaphor of war be translated into an effective plan of action to meet the combination of events identified by Professor Hayward and David Anderson?

The problems are immense and demand optimum response from all relevant disciplines. There have been many initiatives proposed in various spheres.[13] My focus is confined to the law and its potential to do more. Specifically, what can it contribute to the objective of the Government of Denmark? How can the international community be persuaded to meet the challenge of Professor Delmas-Marty? And, ultimately, what can we scholars, lawyers and judges do, by way of clarification of our goals, making realistic choices, and effort, if we are to help the law play its part in achieving the progress demanded by Sir Karl Popper?

Currently the law's response to terrorism is incoherent. ISIS is said to have attracted recruits from some 125 different States and has committed or influenced attacks in 17 States, ten in the past six months.[14] On 8 June 2016 the UN Under-Secretary-General for Political Affairs, Jeffrey Feltman, briefed the

---

12 « La France est en guerre. Les actes commis vendredi soir à Paris et près du Stade de France, sont des actes de guerre. » <http://www.elysee.fr/declarations/article/discours-du-president-de-la-republique-devant-le-parlement-reuni-en-congres-3/> 16 November 2015. Speech by M François Hollande. Website last visited 19 July 2017.

13 A recent example is Rachida Dati's plea following the Nice outrage:

> 'To begin with, we must acknowledge that across France, there are a number of neighbourhoods that have become hotbeds of dysfunction and crime; these districts lack the resources at community level that are needed to provide for and support its citizens. Radicalisation draws its strength from the sense that young people living in these communities feel abandoned; in our cities today, a growing number of them have no training or qualifications. This has gone unnoticed for far too long. We must enable young people. We must break the cycle of despondency.
>
> How do we do this? Apprenticeship programmes: practical, community-based training courses followed by funding for viable work experience placements which are assured at the end of the successful completion of the course. We must activate a renewed sense of civic service, which would involve supporting a voluntary military service and would require a positive discrimination policy for students with learning difficulties.
>
> https://www.theguardian.com/commentisfree/2016/jul/19/nice-france-action-terrorism-radicalisation. Website last visited 19 July 2017.'

14 Personal communication by informed sources.

Security Council on the *Report of the Secretary-General on the threat posed by ISIL (Da'esh) to international peace and security and the range of United Nations efforts in support of Member States in countering the threat.*[15] It recounts that:

> The global threat emanating from ISIL remains high and continues to diversify ... recent international attacks perpetrated by members of ISIL demonstrate that the terrorist group is now moving into a new phase, with the increased risk that well-prepared and centrally directed attacks on international civilian targets may become a more frequent occurrence. In the past six months alone, ISIL has carried out, inspired, or claimed responsibility for, terrorist attacks in Bangladesh, Belgium, Egypt, France, Germany, Indonesia, Lebanon, Pakistan, the Russian Federation, Turkey and the United States of America. The attacks have killed over 500 individuals and injured hundreds more. The list does not include attacks and fighting in conflict zones inside Afghanistan, Iraq, Libya, the Syrian Arab Republic or Yemen. ISIL thus continues to pose a significant global terrorist threat ...
>
> The attacks in Paris in November 2015 and in Brussels in March 2016 demonstrate the ability of ISIL to mount complex, multi-wave attacks. National law enforcement agencies continue to investigate those attacks, but it is already clear that they were coordinated by foreign terrorist fighters who had returned to Europe from ISIL-held territory in the Syrian Arab Republic. To some extent, these cells received direction from the ISIL leadership and were supported and facilitated by a range of individuals and groups with pre-existing records of involvement in criminality (including Al-Qaida-affiliated terrorist groups). This demonstrates the ability of ISIL returnees to quickly link up and draw on the support of established radical networks and supporters of Al-Qaida and thereby enhance their newly acquired terrorism skills with local knowledge and support ...
>
> A worrying factor is that no Member State has reported that ISIL is short on, or lacks, arms or ammunition. Thus, in addition to risks connected with the outflow of returnees and funds from ISIL through Member States of the region, the potential inflow of arms and ammunition directly or indirectly to ISIL remains a serious concern.

The need for a concerted international response is overwhelming. Yet ISIL's ability to operate across State borders mocks the law's failure to provide the

---

15   S/2016/501, 31 May 2016.

obvious cross-border response of an international crime of terrorism. So my first focus is on how to achieve such definition and give coherence to the law.

The second focus is upon the application of such definition which must, I suggest, recognize the need to respond both to specific criminality and to its causes. There is also need to appreciate that the murder or other criminal act that forms one element of terrorism assumes another dimension when coupled with an intent to cause fear plus a transnational element.

3   Achieving Coherence in the Law

'Terrorism' is a word with a multitude of inconsistent senses: *The Routledge Handbook of Terrorism Research*[16] identifies some 250 different definitions of the term.[17] A fundamental problem may be the assumption that there is some identifiable thing called "terrorism" and what must be done is simply identify what it is and call it a crime. But at least for legal purposes, that is unattainable. On the contrary:

> … it is impossible to *define* a legal concept, and […] the task of legal writers should be rather to *describe* the use of a word like '[terrorism]' in the particular legal rules in which it occurs. '[Terrorism]' in the legal sense has no meaning at all apart from the rules of law in which it is used as a tool of legal thought.[18]

I have modified this passage from a celebrated essay by Professor Donald Harris of Oxford, which concerned the concept not of terrorism but of possession. His insight however, building on writings of Jeremy Bentham and Herbert Hart,[19] identifies the problem of using the word 'terrorism' as if it were a legal term of art. What is needed is to turn the process around: instead of peering minutely at what implications the word "terrorism" can have, identify and adopt what are the essential elements of a definition that meets the need for a crime which, starting with murder, kidnapping and the like, adds the intent to spread fear that extends the crime, together with a transnational perspective.

---

16   Alex P. Schmid (ed) (Routledge 2013).
17   Anthony Richards, 'Conceptualising Terrorism' (March 2014) 37/3 *Studies in Conflict and Terrorism* 213, at p. 226, text fn 95.
18   'The Concept of Possession in English Law' in Anthony Gordon Guest, *Oxford Essays in Jurisprudence* (Oxford 1961), 69, at 70.
19   'Definition and Theory in Jurisprudence' (1954) 70 LQR 37.

The need is indisputable in principle and in practice.

Hans Christian Andersen's *The Snow Queen, The Tinder Box* and *A Mother's Dream* described the horror of uncertainty. Their theme was picked up in Marina Warner's *No Go the Bogeyman: Scaring, Lulling and Making Mock*.[20] Whereas we can cope with and adapt to actual reality, uncertainty plays on the power of human imagination to magnify what usually turns out to be a less daunting reality.

So instead of allowing ourselves to be frightened by the shadowy abstractions "terrorism" and "terrorist" we need to focus on specifics: what conduct, by what people, for what reason? That allows us to turn to practice: to specific targets we can make specific responses. The problem becomes manageable.

The International Bar Association's Task Force's report identified aspects of international law obliging States to prevent and repress various aspects of "terrorism". It describes "a patchwork of 15 subject-specific multilateral conventions or protocols, seven regional treaties, and a range of UN Security Council and General Assembly resolutions" proscribing specific acts classified as terrorism, and imposes duties on States to criminalize and investigate those acts under their domestic law.[21] It reports that, in seeking agreement upon a counter-terrorism convention that would be enforceable under international law, there are particular sticking points:

- whether such convention should adopt a military (armed conflict) or police (law enforcement) approach to counter-terrorism;
- whether a definition of "terrorism" should include State terrorism and conduct by State armed forces;
- whether armed resistance to an occupying regime or to colonial or alien domination should be included or excluded.[22]

How should these points be dealt with? The answer in the immediate term is that there is plenty of work for a narrow definition that ignores them.

The Special Tribunal for Lebanon is the first international Criminal Tribunal mandated (inter alia) to investigate and try terrorist conduct.[23] Its terrorism

---

20   Chatto 1998.
21   At pp. 1–2.
22   At p. 2.
23   *Compare* ICTY, *Prosecutor v Galić*, AC, IT-98-29-A, 30 November 2006, para. 77, where for a charge of "unlawfully inflicting terror upon civilians as set forth in Article 51 of Additional Protocol I and Article 13 of Additional Protocol II to the Geneva Conventions of 1949 [as a violation of the laws or customs of war pursuant to] Article 3 of the Statute" it was held that actual infliction of terror is not an element of the crime of acts or threats of

jurisdiction is confined to interpretation and application of the terrorism provisions of the Lebanese domestic Criminal Code. But in view of:

> the well established principle that the courts will so far as possible construe domestic law so as to avoid creating a breach of the State's international obligations[24]

the Appeals Chamber preceded its discussion of the domestic law with analysis of international law. In its *Interlocutory Decision on the Applicable Law: Terrorism et al.*[25] that Chamber considered:

---

violence the primary purpose of which is to spread terror among the civilian population as charged under Count 1 of the Indictment".

24 *Boyce v R (Barbados)* [2005] AC 400, [2004] 4 LRC 749, [2004] UKPC 32 at [25] per Lord Hoffmann. There is an unhappy inconsistency between (1) that application to Barbados criminal law by the UK Privy Council of a principle cited by the leading text Robert Jennings and Arthur Watts (eds), *Oppenheim's International Law* , Volume 1 Peace (9th edn, Oxford 2008), para 19(1) as an established rule of English law – William Blackstone's assertion that the law of nations is part of the law of England, and (2) the UK Supreme Court's refusal to treat the principle as applicable to UK domestic public law: *R (Wang Yam) v Central Criminal Court* [2015] UKSC 76, [2016] AC 771. There a seven member panel stated: 'In accordance with *R v Secretary of State for the Home Department, Ex parte Brind* [1991] 1 AC 696, *R v Lyons* [2002] UKHL 44; [2003] 1 AC 976, para 13 and *R (Hurst) v London Northern District Coroner* [2007] UKHL 13; [2007] 2 AC 189, para 56, per Lord Brown of Eaton-under-Heywood with whose reasons Lord Bingham of Cornhill and Lord Rodger of Earlsferry agreed at paras 1, 9 and 15, a domestic decision-maker exercising a general discretion (i) is neither bound to have regard to this country's purely international obligations nor bound to give effect to them, but (ii) may have regard to the United Kingdom's international obligations, if he or she decides this to be appropriate.'

Lord Mance, who delivered the judgment, had however dissented in *Hurst*, stating: '78 ... I find unattractive the proposition that it is entirely a matter for a discretionary decision-maker whether or not the values engaged by this country's international obligations, however fundamental they may be, have any relevance or operate as any sort of guide ....'

Perhaps resolution can be achieved via *R (Keyu) v Secretary of State for Foreign and Commonwealth Affairs* [2015] UKSC 59, [2016] AC 1355 where Lord Mance delivered a sensitive and sophisticated speech, including: '150 Speaking generally, in my opinion the principle is that [Customary International Law], once established, should shape the common law, whenever it can do so consistently with domestic constitutional principles, statutory law and common law rules which the courts can themselves sensibly adapt without it being, for example, necessary to invite Parliamentary intervention or consideration.'

25 STL AC Interlocutory Decision on the Applicable Law: Terrorism *et al.* (16 February 2011) STL Casebook 2011, p. 27.

85... a customary rule of international law regarding the international crime of terrorism, at least in time of peace, has indeed emerged. This customary rule requires the following three key elements:

[1] the perpetration of a criminal act (such as murder, kidnapping, hostage-taking, arson, and so on), or threatening such an act;
[2] the intent to spread fear among the population (which would generally entail the creation of public danger) or directly or indirectly coerce a national or international authority to take some action, or to refrain from taking it;
[3] when the act involves a transnational element.

The Appeals Chamber did not attempt to deal with the IBA Task Force's three "sticking points", which did not arise in the case before it. We took the view that trying to deal with all points would guarantee failure to agree a definition; it is better to reach agreement on a narrower definition that deals with essentials. In simple English, half a loaf is better than none.

The decision encountered heavy criticism, largely on the basis that there was no existing crime of terrorism at international law and so the STL had no authority to define one. The criticism overlooked two points:

- the need, when interpreting the Lebanese statute, to consider whether there was an international crime of terrorism with which Lebanese legislation is presumed to conform (the Appeals Chamber held there was);
- that, as the STL Appeals Chamber put it: "[j]udges are not permitted to resort to a *non liquet*"[26]

that is, to say the case is too hard and we cannot give an answer. If we were bound to give an answer, the remaining question is whether we gave the right one.

As a member of the Appeals Chamber it is not my business either to defend or indeed acknowledge error in the decision, which must be left to speak for itself. It may however be noted that, given the critical mass of terrorism laws and practices documented both before and since we wrote, one of the critics, the leading authority on terrorism in international law Professor Ben Saul, has

---

26 *Interlocutory Decision on the Applicable Law* (n 22 above), at para 23. See also J Stone, 'Non liquet and the Function of Law in the International Community' (1959) 35 BYIL 124 and Baragwanath, "The interpretative challenges of international adjudication across the common law/civil law divide" (2014) 3/2 *Cambridge Journal of International and Comparative Law*, pp. 450–488.

modified his former opinion that it was too soon to speak of a specialised regime of 'international counter-terrorism law'. He now concludes:

> ... it is no longer unreasonable to speak of a discernible body of 'counter-terrorism law', even if such regime may not be as unified, centralized or coherent as some others. [There has been] a solid and irrepressible accretion of international norms and practices on terrorism, parented or serviced by competent institutions, and *recognized as a regime* by relevant actors in the system (including UN bodies, national institutions, NGOs, practitioners, and scholars. ... [It] is distinctively normative (not a purely political project), systemic, and institutionalised. It is ... here to stay ... – and builds on much older experiences of terrorism in international law.[27]

So it may be asked whether any of the Appeal Chamber's three simple elements falls outside the 1937 *International Convention for the Prevention and Punishment of Terrorism*, any part of the IBA Report's "patchwork" of subject-specific multilateral conventions or protocols, regional treaties, and resolutions, or Professor Saul's "discernible body of 'counter-terrorism law'"; and whether, if the 250 definitions of "terrorism" were plotted on a graph, any of the three elements would escape the consensus zone where the elements overlap.

Certainly the Appeals Chamber definition is skeletal, omitting elements that authors of the various other definitions would like to add. But however slender, a single common definition (whether that of the STL or a better one) is imperative to inject coherence into international criminal law. Until that is achieved the increasingly coherent forces of cross-border terrorism will continue to be immune from the most important element of counter-terrorism – an international criminal law that sets standards of behaviour, provides an agenda for international action, and gives general effect to the advice of Mr Nicolas Michel, Under-Secretary-General for Legal Affairs in support of the creation of the STL:

> ... Today, Lebanon needs the help of the international community to lay the foundation for lasting peace in the country and to become a force for peace in the region. As a precondition for this, steps must be taken to end the impunity of the perpetrators of odious crimes such as the

---

27   Ben Saul (ed), Research Handbook on International Law and Terrorism (Edward Elgar 2014), x–xi.

assassination of former Prime Minister Hariri. To that end, the truth must be revealed and justice must be done.[28]

4   Application of the Law

To respond to terrorism good law is essential. But the law must be given practical effect. How is that to be done? The STL has received evidence of meticulous preparation not only of the explosion that killed and injured its victims but of evading detection. While the killing of 22 people and injuring 226 others occurred in a bombing on 14 March 2005, it was not until 1 March 2009 that the STL came into being, receiving the files of the International Independent Investigation Commission that had preceded it. Most of the judges took up their duties full-time in The Hague only on 1 September 2011. The trial did not begin until 16 January 2014. The current mandate of the STL is until 28 February 2018.

The reason for such interval between the attack and the commencement of the trial was the difficulty and complexity of the investigation. While aspects of the Nazi crimes and their planning, as at the Wannseekonferenz of 20 January 1942, were conducted in secrecy even that was minuted and 30 copies of the plan for annihilation of the Jews were circulated. The Nuremberg prosecutors were so well equipped with evidence that the first trial, of the 23 major political and military leaders, was able to begin on 20 November 1945 and concluded on 1 October 1946. The current STL trial, by contrast, has presented major challenges for the investigators.

That was illustrated to us in an issue before the Appeals Chamber that is currently of topical interest in most if not all States: the tension between the general prohibition of access to telephone metadata without judicial approval and the value of such metadata for criminal investigation – because of the very information the law generally seeks to protect. The Prosecution claimed that, to conceal their identity, those responsible for preparing and carrying out the bombing had secured and used five different groups of mobile telephones obtained anonymously. We were required to evaluate:

(i)   the Prosecutor's claim that the Trial Chamber could admit evidence drawn from metadata records of *all* telephone and text messages in Lebanon over a period of no less than 7 ½ *years*, to establish the whereabouts

---

28   Addendum of 21 November 2006, S/2006/893/Add.1 to Report of the Secretary-General on the establishment of a special tribunal for Lebanon.

of particular mobile telephones relative to the movements of former Prime Minister Hariri prior to and immediately preceding and including his assassination;

(ii) a Defence claim that since the metadata had been obtained without judicial authority, privacy interests of the persons whose calls gave rise to the metadata were entitled to protection and its provision to the UNIIIC and the Prosecutor was unlawful and arbitrary.[29]

I dissented from the majority's dismissal of the Defence appeal, considering that further evidence and submissions were needed as to how and why the metadata were secured, by what process it was examined, and whether and to what extent privacy interests were protected or affected by the UNIIIC and the Prosecution. But the present point is the immense complexity of this part of the evidence required to try to identify the persons responsible not only for a crime but for the attempts to conceal its perpetrators.

So counter-terrorism requires not only sound law but the skills and resources required to meet the terrorists' efforts to hide their tracks. That comes at a cost. The STL has a budget of 60m Euros a year, required to fund among other costs the salaries of some 450 staff of a wide variety of skills, most in The Hague and 60 in Beirut.

5 Terrorist Sentencing: How to Respond to Both the Criminality and the Community's Need for Reconciliation

The criminal law has two functions. The first, already mentioned, is the important, yet essential *responsive* function: to bring to trial those who commit an offence. The second, more important, and more difficult, is *normative* and concerns addressing the causes of crime, altering behaviour so offending does not occur and achieving reconciliation within the community. While both involve other members of society, the judges have a major responsibility for each.

5.1 *The Responsive Function in the Case of Terrorism*
Terrorism is of a different quality from the criminal acts, such as murder, that are among its elements. That is because, to repeat the Appeal Chamber's version, the mental element is not only to kill but, in doing so:

---

[29] *The Prosecutor v Ayyash et al.*, STL-11-01/T/AC/AR126.9 (28 July 2015). See now Tele2Svererige AB v Post-och telestyrelsen and Secretary of State for the Home Department v Watson ECJ (Grand Chamber) C-203/15 and C-698/15 21 December 2016.

... to spread fear among the population (which would generally entail the creation of public danger) or directly or indirectly coerce a national or international authority to take some action, or to refrain from taking it.

While it is possible for an individual acting alone to possess such intent, more commonly terrorism is committed by persons acting in concert to attack a population or its institutions.

At sentencing sight regard must be had to the purposes and sentencing relevant to the particular offender. But the total context of the crime must also be considered.

The purposes and principles of sentencing differ among different communities. See for examples the ABA's *Handbook of International Standards on Sentencing Procedure 2010*[30] and the list contained in the New Zealand Sentencing Act 2002.[31]

Sitting in an international tribunal one must use a metaphorical periscope to look above one's own predilections. Michel Foucault's *Discipline and Punish* (1977)[32] argues:

> To find the suitable punishment for a crime is to find the disadvantage whose idea is such that it robs for ever the idea of a crime of any attraction ... But [the arsenal of penalties] must obey several conditions.

---

30 <http://www.americanbar.org/content/dam/aba/directories/roli/misc/handbook_of_international_standards_on_sentencing_procedure_2010_eng.authcheckdam.pdf>. Website last visited 19 July 2017.

31 The purposes of sentencing may include:
    'denounce the conduct
    hold the offender accountable
    protect the community
    provide for the interests of the victim
    promote sense of responsibility in the offender
    deter him
    assist his rehabilitation.'
And relevant factors of principle may be:
    'the seriousness of the offence
    the gravity of the offending
    its relationship to the maximum penalty
    its effect on the victim(s)
    the desirability of consistency of sentences
    the need to impose the least restrictive appropriate sentence.'

32 (Penguin 1991), 104–105.

[These include:] They must be as unarbitrary as possible .... The penalty must be made to conform as closely as possible to the nature of the offence ... The ideal punishment would be transparent to the crime that it punishes; thus for him who contemplates [the crime], it will be infallibly the sign of the crime that it punishes ... To derive the offence from the punishment is the best means of proportioning punishment to crime. If this is the triumph of justice, it is also the triumph of liberty, for then penalties no longer proceed from the will of the legislator, but from the nature of things; one no longer sees man committing violence on man.

But the terrorist is a zealot, devoted to (usually) his cause. One must take a large view of the court processes, beginning with the scrupulous fairness demanded of the STL by Article 16 of its Statute and reflecting the reality that the sentencer of a terrorist is presumed by the offender and his community to be a judge in the sentencer's own cause.

With all horrific crimes, among them terrorism, the sentencer must try to dissociate personally from the enormity of the events and sentence intellectually rather than from passion. The crime may well require a substantial response; grave offending is not to be trivialized in the eye of the community and, importantly, the victim(s).

Yet to respond to even an outrageous crime by an excessive sentence does harm rather than good. It does not help the victim, whose loss is likely to be irreparable. It demeans the community in whose name it is pronounced. It can indeed breed sympathy and by creating a martyr promote the objective that motivated his crime. That is destructive of the second – normative – function of sentencing.

5.2 *The Normative Function*

Because the sentencer of a terrorist can be seen by the offender and his supporters as biased a special effort must be made to lift the process above the personal and look to the big picture.

The task is the familiar one for judges in other contexts – en route to a decision, getting inside the head of each affected party and looking out through their eyes. It is very rare that the offender is irredeemably evil. Comparing notes after some 30 years as an advocate and twenty as a judge with a police officer of similar experience, our totals were closely similar; I identified six and he, with his greater insight, five. I excluded those I had prosecuted, defended, tried or dealt with on appeal who, despite appalling conduct, had some insight into notions of decency.

One must keep in mind the long-term goal: even the ultimate crime of unjustified war can be followed by reconciliation. The memorial to Aristide Briand, French Nobel laureate, appears in front of the Quai d'Orsay in Paris[33] and may be translated:

> It is not enough to be appalled by war; we must know how to organize against it the elements vital to defence ... It is about founding world peace on a legal base; achieving the rule of law by the common international effort which as a physical reality already exists.

But more important than anything judges can achieve individually is what the law may be able to do to assist the major player, the Security Council.

6   The Security Council

There is need for diffidence on the part of an outsider. Informed insiders speak of the achievements of the Security Council, often accomplished in private in the atmosphere of mutual respect that can develop among the diplomatic and political leaders called upon to discharge its immense task. One needs only to reflect on what the global situation would be if the Council did not exist.

So the following thoughts are presented not as offering solutions but as proposals from a legal perspective for consideration by others, among them the insiders who understand the practicalities.

Much good work is being done at a number of levels and by a range of UN agencies, of which the Security Council warrants particular analysis.

By Article 24 of the Charter of the United Nations its 193 State Members confer on the Council "primary responsibility for the maintenance of international peace and security". It speaks in two places of the Council's "duties".[34] By Article 39 the Council is required to decide what measures shall be taken to

---

33 Il ne suffit pas d'avoir horreur de la guerre. Il faut savoir organiser contre elle les éléments de défense indispensables. ... Il s'agit de fonder la paix du monde sur un ordre légal de faire une réalité de droit de cette solidarité internationale qui apparait déjà dans les faits comme une réalité physique.

34 Article 24:
   1. In order to ensure prompt and effective action by the United Nations, its Members confer on the Security Council primary responsibility for the maintenance of international peace and security, and agree that in carrying out its duties under this responsibility the Security Council acts on their behalf.

perform those duties. And by Articles 41–2 it may decide what measures are to be employed to give effect to its decisions.

Recent developments in other spheres of law have been towards recognizing the need, in the context of making and applying law, for sustained application of what a French scholar calls "a new vision for security".[35] For example, French Nobel laureate René Amalberti and his co-authors have commented on the Chernobyl disaster:

> ... it is stupefying to learn that certain of the factors that caused the ... disaster are rampantly present in other countries.[36]

It may be thought that the imposition on the Council under Article 24 of "duties" in respect of the Council's own primary responsibility – to determine the existence of any threat and to decide what measures shall be taken to maintain or restore international peace and security – must impose positive obligations on the Council itself. A domestic institution with such responsibilities would be subject to mandamus to perform them in a timely and effective manner.[37]

Should not international law similarly require the Council to concern itself with *processes* to ensure the maintenance of international peace and security stipulated by Article 24(1) and Chapter 7 of the UN Charter?

The most effective means to perform such duties – of ensuring prompt and effective action for the maintenance of international peace and security – is both to have in place well-prepared *systems* to monitor potential sources of trouble; and to act *immediately* in response to any real threat rather than waiting for it to manifest itself. While Article 99 empowers the Secretary-General to bring to the attention of the Security Council any matter which in his

---

2. In discharging these duties the Security Council shall act in accordance with the Purposes and Principles of the United Nations. The specific powers granted to the Security Council for the discharge of these duties are laid down in Chapters 6, 7, 8, and 12.

35 René Amalberti, *La conduit de systèmes à risques* (PUF 1996), p. 192 « une nouvelle vision pour la sécurité ». See also text at nn 44 ff below.

36 « ... il est stupéfiant de découvrir que certains des facteurs qui causèrent la catastrophe de Tchernobyl existent de façon rampante dans les autres pays » The Nobel laureate Georges Charpak, Richard L. Garwin and Venance Journé, *De Tchernobyl en tchernobyls* (Odile Jacob 2005), p. 8.

37 *Padfield v Minister of Agriculture and Fisheries* [1968] UKHL1, [1968] AC 997 (Minister *empowered* to respond to report of a committee of investigation concerning *inter alia* prices to be charged for milk did not have an unfettered discretion, so he did not even have to make a decision, but, in order to give effect to the policy of the legislation, was obliged to *exercise* the discretion.

opinion may threaten the maintenance of international peace and security, "Historically, this mandate has been invoked very rarely in country-specific situations."[38]

The Council itself is specifically empowered by Article 34 to investigate any situation which might lead to international friction in order to determine whether the continuance of the situation is likely to endanger international peace and security.

Yet a Security Council Research Report of May 2016[39] acknowledges that while:

> [c]onflict prevention is an issue for which all Council members have expressed their support. However, the Council's recent track record ... does not seem to match the rhetorical support. The indecisiveness of the Council in prevention stems from the resistance of member states to early international engagement and to political divisions, in particular among the P5, which tend to impede action by the Council, even in cases where national interests are not obviously at stake.

Article 34 does not specifically require that the Council must investigate situations of potential danger. But to be able to decide whether to investigate, the Council must cause itself to be *continuously* informed as to what situations may warrant investigation. Its obligation to take action must be proportionate to the threat, in the sense of evaluating and responding in timely fashion to the competing interests, harms and options.[40]

In summary, the Security Council is charged:

(1) with primary responsibility for the primary purpose of the United Nations – maintenance of international peace and security – and to that end, to take effective collective measures for the prevention and removal of threats to the peace;
(2) to perform on behalf of the United Nations its part of ensuring prompt and effective action;
(3) to be able for that purpose to function continuously with the assistance of appropriate staff appointed by the Secretary-General;

---

38   The Security Council Research Report of May 2016 next mentioned.
39   <Securitycouncilreport.org> p. 5, left column.
40   See Stephen Breyer, The Court and the World: American Law and the New Global Realities (2015), at p. 262.

(4) to determine the existence of any threat to the peace, breach of the peace, or act of aggression;
(5) to decide what measures not involving the use of armed force are to be employed to give effect to its decisions;
(6) to take such action by air, sea, or land forces as may be necessary to maintain or restore international peace and security.

The duties of the Security Council referred to in Article 24(1) and (2) are in part stated specifically, in part to be inferred:

> from the context, from the particular provisions, or from the general scope and objects, of the enactment conferring the power.[41]

Compared with State domestic constitutions, the Security Council as policy-maker for the United Nations is disadvantaged; not only has it no legislature to assist it but receives little input from any judiciary.[42] Yet the latter is a vital element of States' systems. Jeremy Bentham is celebrated for his advocacy that legislation be codified. But he observed:

> ... The legislator, who cannot pass judgment in particular cases, will give directions to the Tribunal in the form of general rules, and leave them with a certain amount of latitude in order that they may adjust their decision to the special circumstances.[43]

Perhaps this may be what the open-textured language of the Charter requires – input from judges. As *The Charter of the United Nations A Commentary*[44] acknowledges, the "duties" of the Security Council under the Charter are *legal* duties susceptible of consideration by the International Court of Justice, itself created by Chapter 14 of the same Charter, under Article 96:

---

[41] Julius v Lord Bishop of Oxford cited in Padfield v Minister of Agriculture, Fisheries and Food [1968] UKHL 1, [1968] AC 997 by Lord Pearce, at 20.

[42] David Baragwanath, 'Law and Peace The Role of the Hague Institutions in Promoting International Justice: a View from the Special Tribunal for Lebanon' (23 September 2015) to be published in Waikato Law Review. Steven R. Ratner speaks of The Thin Justice of International Law (Oxford 2015) and the desirability of achieving a thicker standard of global justice (p. 424). I agree.

[43] In his 'Theory of Legislation' (Etienne Dumont ed, Charles Milner Atkinson tr, Oxford 1914), at 62.

[44] Bruno Simma, Daniel-Erasmus Khan, Georg Nolte and Andreas Paulus (3rd edn, Oxford 2013).

a. The General Assembly or the Security Council may request the International Court of Justice to give an advisory opinion on any legal question.

While the opinion is advisory the obligation, stated in the Charter, is not.

Dame Roslyn Higgins QC, the former President of the International Court of Justice, advises:

> The Court has ... emphasiz[ed] ... that a UN organ needed legal advice in order to know how to conduct its business ...[45]
>
> the greatest role for Advisory Opinions is where there are uncertainties about the institutional arrangements within the UN ...[46]
>
> If organs are reluctant to seek advice on the development of their own competencies, except when forced to do so by the behaviour of occasional recalcitrant states, the Court's role as the supreme in-house counsel' to the UN will remain limited.[47]

What arguments might be made to the ICJ in support of such request? Recourse to existing jurisprudence, even if domestic, may be considered by the ICJ under Article 38(1)(c) of its Statute:

> 1. The Court, whose function is to decide in accordance with international law such disputes as are submitted to it, shall apply:
>
> ...
>
> d. ... judicial decisions and the teachings of the most highly qualified publicists of the various nations, as subsidiary means for the determination of rules of law.

Recent addresses have ventured to suggest use of Article 96 of the Charter to obtain an advisory opinion from the International Court of Justice on vital topics. One concerns climate change;[48] others have considered the present topic.[49] Most recently the Security Council has issued its own Research Report

---

[45] 'A Comment on the Current Health of Advisory Opinions' in Dame Rosalyn Higgins, Themes and Theories, vol 2 (Oxford 2009), 1043, 1047.

[46] At p. 1050.

[47] At p. 1052.

[48] Philippe Sands QC "Climate Change and the Rule of Law" UK Supreme Court 17 September 2015 <https://www.youtube.com/watch?v=eefitK8mtEI>. Website last visited 19 July 2017.

[49] David Baragwanath, School of Political Science and International Relations, Tongji University (Shanghai), 3 April 2015; Grotius Centre for International Legal Studies, University

"The Rule of Law: Can the Security Council make better use of the International Court of Justice".[50] It notes:

> The UN Charter envisioned a symbiotic relationship between the Security Council and the ICJ, the principal judicial organ of the UN. However, the Council has rarely taken advantage of this potential and, for the most part, the role of the Court has been neglected by Council members and by the Secretariat.
>
> ...
>
> Overall, the report concludes that, at a time when the demands on the Council are higher than ever in its history, strengthening the relationship between the Council and the Court could further promote international peace and security.[51]

It recognises:

> [A] more prominent role for the Court, within the confines set by the Council itself in this context, would likely strengthen the effectiveness and legitimacy of the Council as an institution.[52]

Such argument receives support from the domestic law analogy, brought into sharp focus by the Brexit case. It is fundamental to the rule of law that both State and citizen comply with the law which it is the function of the judiciary to interpret. The Constitution Reform Act 2005 (UK) had taken care to emphasise:

> 1 The rule of law
> This Act does not adversely affect –
> (a) the existing constitutional principle of the rule of law,
> (b) ...

Yet following the determination of the Divisional Court that Parliament's consent was required before the Executive Government could lawfully trigger the procedures for the United Kingdom's withdrawal from the European Union, certain media attacked the judges as "enemies of the people", the

---

of Leiden (The Hague), 2 June 2016. See General Assembly request 29 June 2017 for advisory opinion on legal consequences of separation of Chagos Archipelago from Mauritius in 1965.
50 Security Council Report 2016 No. 5 (20 December 2016).
51 At p. 1.
52 At p. 9.

expression used by Hitler's Nazis as an expression of anti-Semitic hatred.[53] The constitutional course, in fact taken by the United Kingdom Government, was to appeal the decision and, if necessary, invite Parliament to amend the law. By accepting the legal validity of the decision (now sustained on appeal) it demonstrated the strength of the rule of law in the UK – setting an example to others that all conduct, including that of the Government, must be performed within the law.

The Council has already taken notable steps including, following 9/11, a virtual mandamus, by Resolution 1373 of 28 September 2001 requiring States to enact appropriate domestic legislation to respond to terrorism. Many more resolutions have followed. There have been notable and valuable political and diplomatic efforts. But it is respectfully suggested that the International Court of Justice, created by the same Charter as the Security Council, is the *forum conveniens* to advise as to the nature of the Council's "duties" and could add legal power to the Council's political might.

Among topics on which the ICJ could advise are whether in discharge of its duties the Council might:

(1) exercise its legislative powers to create an international crime of terrorism, either along the lines of the STL Appeals Chamber's decision or with whatever improvement it considers appropriate;

(2) establish complementary to CTED a Counter-Terrorism institution that in close liaison with States will:
   (a) establish and maintain systems to perform the following functions;
   (b) identify emerging terrorist threats to international peace and security;
   (c) ensure that such threats receive prompt and adequate response under State(s) or Security Council direction;

(3) propose to the Assembly of States Parties amendment of the Rome Statute, and alternatively create an international counter-terrorism tribunal, to enable investigation and either reference to State courts or trial before itself of infringements of the international crime of terrorism;

(4) note that study of systems deficiencies and human error as their cause has now extended beyond the sphere of employment[54] where there is

---

53 Ian Kershaw, *Hitler* (Penguin 2008), 416.
54 James Reason, *Human Error* (Cambridge 1990), p. 1.

"Just over 60 years ago Spearman (1928) grumbled that 'crammed as psychological writings are, and must needs be, with allusions to errors in an incidental manner, they hardly ever arrive at considering these profoundly, or even systematically'. Even at the applied the private law principle that an employer must ensure a safe system of work.[55] The need for it to meet threat to international peace and security interests engages that principle *a fortiori*. The duties of the Council should include an obligation to devise, lay down, maintain, monitor and enforce effective *systems* to ensure the duties are performed. An element of that is making a proper assessment of potential risks. The following principle stated by an English judge has received endorsement by the highest UK court:

> Risk assessments are meant to be an exercise by which the employer examines and evaluates all the risks entailed in his operations and takes steps to remove or minimise those risks. They should be a blueprint for action. I do not think that [the trial judge] was alone in underestimating the importance of risk assessment. It seems to me that insufficient judicial attention has been given to risk assessments in the years since the duty to conduct them was first introduced. I think this is because judges recognise that a failure to carry out a sufficient and suitable risk assessment is never the direct cause of an injury. The inadequacy of a risk assessment can only ever be an indirect cause. Understandably judicial decisions have tended to focus on the breach of duty which has led directly to the injury.[56]

A pronouncement by the International Court of Justice as to the nature of the "duties" of its sister organization, created by the same Charter as itself, could be expected to be received with the respect to which that World Court is entitled.

---

time Spearman was not altogether justified ...; but if he were alive today, he would find less cause for complaint. The past decade has seen a rapid increase in what might loosely be called 'studies of errors for their own sake.'

The most obvious impetus for this renewed interest has been a growing public concern and the terrible cost of human error [referring to the Tenerife, Three Mile Island, Bhopal, *Challenger*, Chernobyl, *Herald of Free Enterprise*, King's Cross and Piper Alpha disasters] ...

Aside from these world events, from the mid-1970s onwards theoretical and methodological developments within cognitive psychology have also acted to make errors a proper study in their own right."

55 "the provision of a competent staff ..., adequate material, and a proper system and effective supervision": *Wilsons and Clyde Coal Company v English* [1937] UKHL 2, [1938] AC 57 per Lord Wright.

56 *Allison v London Underground Ltd* [2008] EWCA Civ 71 ; [2008] ICR 719 per Smith LJ at para 58 endorsed in *Kennedy v Cordia (Services) LLP* [2016] UKSC 6 para 89 per Lords Reed and Hodge.

If such duties were stated by the ICJ they would provide a valuable datum against which there could be regular appraisal of the Council's performance. For example if, as is in my view should be declared to be the position, the veto exercise does not relieve the holder of the *continuing* obligation to perform the Art 24 duties, breach of that obligation, if necessary by other means, would be a source of legitimate and continuing objective public criticism, which can matter to political entities.

Such approach could meet Dr Kissinger's twin concerns – that the international system is in constant flux and there can be a tendency to treat foreign policy as a series of human challenges rather than as a permanent enterprise.[57]

7   Conclusion

Subject only to the rule of law itself, the Security Council is simply the most important of *all* our resources we must activate and energise – among them the United Nations and its agencies, State governments, NGO, individual skills and effort – in a well-planned, systematic and vigorous programme carried out in accordance with that law.

The UN General Assembly and Security Council bicameral Resolutions on Peacebuilding (2016 and 2282) of 27 April 2016 display a visionary approach by both institutions. If the law can contribute in a similar spirit we can help provide alterative opportunities to the young people who have lost hope of a decent peaceful life and are induced to pursue the extreme ideas and conduct, including large scale suicide bombing, that converts others into refugees. Lacking other skills and experience, my focus is on what the law can be made to do to assist.

As to how it might be developed in future, the STL decision of the Security Council, to limit the criminal jurisdiction of an international tribunal to that of the existing domestic Criminal Code of a State, was innovative. First and vitally, it ensured compliance with the principle of legality with which this tribute began. The criminal law should express the fundamental norms of decency; the overarching requirement of fairness requires that criminal law must not be given retrospective effect. So no judge-made conclusion that terrorism is a crime against international law should impose criminal liability in the instant ooooj ot most it can, as in the STL decision, bear upon the interpretation of existing legislation; or, as in the case of a decision of the ICJ or of a final domestic court, have declaratory effect in respect of future conduct.

---

57   Henry Kissinger, *World Order* (Penguin 2014), p. 248, n. 31.

Secondly, by its explicit recognition of one of the possible concepts of terrorism as fit for an international court, the Security Council recognized the need to respond to alleged conduct as being more than simply murder (which is a further crime against the Lebanese Criminal Code over which the STL has explicit jurisdiction).

Thirdly, the Security Council appreciated that its intervention under Chapter 7 of the Charter of the United Nations was required in fulfilment of its duties under Article 24 – to respond to threats to international peace and security. On a fundamental challenge by defence counsel to the *vires* of the decision to create the STL I considered that the decision constituted a lawful response to the events that gave rise to it.[58] Since STL proceedings are current I make no further comment upon them. In other cases, where circumstances permit the Security Council to exercise its Chapter 7 powers, which extend to the use of armed force, there is no obvious impediment to its requiring a tribunal to apply whatever existing criminal law – either established at international law or previously enacted domestically by a State – it considers best fits the particular case.

There should in my opinion be created an international crime of terrorism justiciable before both all State domestic courts and, in appropriate cases, as proposed by Antonio Cassese, before a permanent international court with jurisdiction over such crime. That could be achieved to some extent by amendment of the Rome Statute of the International Criminal Court. But since its jurisdiction is limited by Article 5 to the most serious crimes of concern to the international community as a whole, that court lacks the flexibility provided by an alternative which I prefer. That is, for the Security Council by Resolution under Chapter 7 to create[59] a permanent skeletal court linked to UNCTED – the United Nations Counter-Terrorism Directorate, which reports to the five Permanent Members of the Security Council. Such court would be equipped to monitor actual and potential terrorist threats to international peace and security world-wide. In order to meet threats with cross-border implications, it would primarily serve the function of securing and employing information in liaison with the States which must continue to provide the major defence to terrorism. But it should also have, like the STL, capacity pursuant to a Security Council resolution itself by different organs to investigate, prosecute, defend

---

58 STL, *Prosecutor v. Ayyash et al.*, STL-11-01/PT/AC/AR90.1, 24 October 2012, Separate and Partially Dissenting Opinion of Judge Baragwanath, para. 95. My colleagues reached the same result on the basis that the STL lacked authority to pronounce on the topic.

59 Comparable to that adopted post September 11 to require all States to enact domestic counter-terrorism legislation: SC Res. 1373, S/RES/1373 (2001), 28 September 2001.

and try cases: ones that, because the terrorist activities operate across State borders or because of lack of sufficient State capacity, cannot be managed by domestic courts.

The challenge of definition that has resulted in the 80 year failure of States to agree could be met gradually, beginning with whatever narrow definition – whether the 1937 version or that of the STL or some third option – commands Security Council consensus as an appropriate means to assist the struggle with Al Qaeda, ISIS and their like, while in the interim excluding or leaving to *ad hoc* decision of the Security Council such current sticking points as the three noted by the IBA.[60] That would allow the Council, when required to make yet another resolution responding to "terrorism", to have a specific forum to employ either for liaison purposes or itself to receive jurisdiction over the problem.

---

60 (n. 22 above).

whether there should be adopted a military (armed conflict) or police (law enforcement) approach to counter-terrorism;

whether a definition of "terrorism" should include State terrorism and conduct by State armed forces;

whether armed resistance to an occupying regime or to colonial or alien domination should be included or excluded.

CHAPTER 3

The Transnational Dimension of the *ne bis in idem* Principle and the Notion of *res iudicata* in the European Union

Martin Böse

Abstract

Stating that no one must be subject to criminal proceedings for an offence for which he has already been finally acquitted or convicted within the European Union, Article 54 of the Convention Implementing the Schengen Agreement and Article 50 of the EU Charter of Fundamental Rights have provided the *ne bis in idem* principle with a transnational effect. This protection from double criminal punishment throughout the Union crucially depends upon whether criminal proceedings in a Member State have resulted in a "final" decision (acquittal or conviction). According to well-established case-law of the Court of Justice of the European Union, the *ne bis in idem* principle does not require the judgment of a court, but may also be triggered by the decision of a public prosecutor (e.g. a transaction). The Court, however, has recently held that the requirement of a final acquittal or conviction is not met if the decision has not been given after a determination as to the merits of the case (judgment of 29 June 2016, C-486/14, Kossowski). This paper will argue that the notion of *res iudicata* should not be defined by Union law alone, but has to rely on national procedural law of the Member State where the decision has been adopted; the key criterion should be whether or not the decision is "final" under national law. Thereby, the transnational effect of the *ne bis in idem* principle depends upon the scope and limits of *res iudicata* under national law.

1   Introduction

When I first met *Wolfgang Schomburg* he was chairman of the Law Examination Board in front of which I completed my second state examination. Despite its

---

*   Chair in Criminal Law and Criminal Procedural Law, International and European Criminal Law, Bonn University. – The author would like to thank *André Klip* and *Anne Schneider* for comments on an earlier draft and *George Ochieng Adipo* for English proofreading of the final version. All remaining errors are the author's.

formal purpose, the preliminary meeting before the final oral exam took place in a nice and friendly atmosphere. I remember that we touched upon recent developments in European criminal law and *Wolfgang Schomburg* mentioned a case pending before the German Federal Court of Justice (*Bundesgerichtshof*) where, for the first time, the Court had to rule on art 54 of the Convention Implementing the Schengen Agreement (CISA).[1] Nearly twenty years later, we met again at a conference on the *ne bis in idem* principle where he gave the opening Keynote Address.[2] Inspired by these personal encounters with *Wolfgang Schomburg* and by the fact that, as a reknown expert in the area of international cooperation in criminal matters, he actively took part in the discussion on the interpretation of art 54 CISA right from the beginning,[3] my contribution to his Festschrift will address the transnational dimension of the *ne bis in idem* principle.

The *ne bis in idem* principle protects the accused from double punishment, or more precisely: from double prosecution. According to the traditional understanding, this protection is limited to the criminal justice system in which the final decision (conviction or acquittal) was rendered (ie the sentencing state). Art 54 CISA takes the *ne bis in idem* principle a step further, stating that a person whose trial has been finally disposed of in one Contracting Party may not be prosecuted in another Contracting Party for the same acts. Barring proceedings in a state other than the sentencing state, art 54 CISA has provided the *ne bis in idem* principle with a transnational effect. The protection from double criminal prosecution throughout the Schengen area crucially depends upon whether criminal proceedings in the first state have resulted in a "final" decision. This article shall examine the criteria for a final decision in criminal proceedings that trigger the transnational effect of *res iudicata*. In that respect, the evolution of the *ne bis in idem* principle and its legal foundations from an international treaty to a fundamental right in the European Union has favoured an extensive understanding of *res iudicata* in a transnational context. As the most recent judgment of the Court of Justice of the European Union has applied a stricter interpretation of the *ne bis in idem* principle, the notion of

---

1 BGH Neue Zeitschrift für Strafrecht (NStZ) 1998, 149.
2 Wolfgang Schomburg, 'Ne bis in idem. Vom Auslieferungshindernis zum internationalen strafrechtlichen Doppelverfolgungsverbot als EU-Grundrecht. Eine Einführung anhand von Texten' in: Gudrun Hochmayr (ed), „*Ne bis in idem*" in Europa (Nomos 2015) 9 ff.
3 Wolfgang Schomburg, 'Strafrecht und Rechtshilfe im Geltungsbereich von Schengen II' [1995] 48 Neue Juristische Wochenschrift (NJW) 1931, 1933; Wolfgang Schomburg, 'Internationales "ne bis in idem" nach Art. 54 SDÜ', [1997] 17 Strafverteidiger 383 ff.

res iudicata shall be elaborated in the light of the rationale of the *ne bis in idem* principle and its transnational dimension.

2 The *ne bis in idem* Principle and the Requirement of a Final Judgment (Decision)

2.1 *The Origins of Art 54 CISA in International Treaty Law*

Art 54 CISA was not designed from scratch, but has originated from previous international treaties.[4] The transnational dimension of the *ne bis in idem* principle was firstly recognized in art 9 of the European Convention on Extradition (1957).[5] According to that provision, extradition shall not be granted if a court of the requested state has passed final judgment upon the person in respect of the offence for which extradition is requested (art 9 cl 1). If the competent authorities have terminated proceedings in respect of the same offence by a decision other than a judgment, the requested state "may" refuse extradition (art 9 cl 2). So, the mandatory extradition obstacle requires a "final judgment", ie a decision having the authority of *res iudicata* in the requested state whereas a decision merely terminating criminal proceedings because there are no grounds for prosecution (e.g. an *ordonnance de non-lieu*) is only considered an optional ground for refusal.[6] Furthermore, even if a "final judgment" was rendered in the requested state, the protection of the convicted or acquitted person is limited to extradition proceedings: art 9 of the European Convention on Extradition does not bar criminal proceedings in another state when the sentenced person has been arrested in that state and there is no need for an extradition request.[7]

The apparent *lacuna* in the protection from double prosecution has been addressed by subsequent treaties containing self-standing provisions on the *ne bis in idem* principle. In 1970, the European Convention on the International Validity of Criminal Judgments[8] provided this principle with a transnational effect by stating that "a person in respect of whom a European criminal

---

4 Wolfgang Schomburg, 'Internationales "ne bis in idem" nach Art 54 SDÜ' (n 1) 383; John Vervaele 'Ne bis in idem: Towards a Transnational Constitutional Principle in the EU?' [2013] 9 (4) Utrecht Law Review 211, 213 ff.
5 European Convention on Extradition of 13 December 1957 (ETS No. 24).
6 Explanatory Report to the European Convention on Extradition 8, 9.
7 John Vervaele (n 4) 217.
8 European Convention on the International Validity of Criminal Judgments of 28 May 1970 (ETS No. 70).

judgment has been rendered may for the same act neither be prosecuted nor sentenced nor subjected to enforcement of a sanction in another Contracting State" (art 53(1) of the Convention). The term "European criminal judgment" is defined as any "final decision delivered by a criminal court of a Contracting State as a result of criminal proceedings" (art 1(a) of the Convention), irrespective of whether the accused person is convicted or acquitted (art 53(1) (a), (b), (c) of the Convention). As follows from the distinct rules on judgments rendered *in absentia* and penal orders (*ordonnances pénales*) the protection by the *ne bis in idem* principle is not triggered by decisions adopted by a criminal court without a hearing of the accused person and solely on the basis of the file (see art 1(g) and art 21 of the Convention).[9] This applies all the more to penal orders issued by the public prosecutor's office.[10]

Since the European Convention on the International Validity of Criminal Judgments was ratified by a few states only,[11] the Member States of the European Communities drafted a new treaty, namely the Convention on Double Jeopardy (1987).[12] Art 1 of the Convention shaped the *ne bis in idem* principle in wording almost identical to art 54 CISA (1990).[13] Since the Convention on Double Jeopardy was based upon the rules on the *ne bis in idem* principle in the European Convention on the International Validity of Criminal Judgments, the *ne bis in idem* principle was considered inapplicable to decisions of the public prosecutor's office to discontinue criminal proceedings once the accused had fulfilled certain obligations (e.g. payment of a certain amount of money).[14]

---

9   Explanatory Report to the European Convention on the International Validity of Criminal Judgments (n 8) 12, 14, 32.
10 Ibid 32. See e.g. Swiss Code of Criminal Procedure (*Strafprozessordnung*), art 352 (*Strafbefehl*). A list of *ordonnances pénales* is provided in Appendix III of the Convention on the International Validity of Criminal Judgments (n 8).
11 In 1985, only six states had ratified the Convention (Austria, Cyprus, Denmark, Norway, Sweden and Turkey); in the meantime the Convention has been ratified and entered into force in 23 states.
12 Convention between the Member States of the European Communities on Double Jeopardy of 25 May 1987 (*Übereinkommen zwischen den Mitgliedstaaten der Europäischen Gemeinschaften über das Verbot der doppelten Strafverfolgung*), BGBl 1998 II 2227.
13 Explanatory memorandum of the German government to the Convention on Double Jeopardy (n 12), Bundestags-Drucksache 13/8195 (10 July 1997) 9; Michael Grotz, 'Das Schengener Durchführungsübereinkommen und der Grundsatz Ne bis in idem', [1995] 1 Strafverteidiger Forum 102.
14 Explanatory memorandum of the German government to the Convention Implementing the Schengen Agreement, Bundestags-Drucksache 12/2453, 9, 10.

The origins of art 54 CISA in international treaties and the underlying concept of final judgments resulting from a full trial formed the interpretation of the term "finally disposed of" in art 54 CISA. In the explanatory memorandum to art 54 CISA, the German government took the view that this term only applied to "foreign judgments" ("*ausländische Urteile*").[15] Accordingly, the German *Bundesgerichtshof* favoured an interpretation of art 54 CISA that covered court decisions only, but did not apply to out-of-court settlements such as an agreement between the Belgian customs authorities and the accused person whereby criminal proceedings were discontinued after the accused had paid the evaded customs and a financial penalty (*transactie*).[16,17] In another case, the *Bundesgerichtshof* held that the *ordonnance de non-lieu*[18] did not meet the requirements set out in art 54 CISA because it did not have the effect of *res iudicata* in the sentencing state (France), but allowed for the proceedings to be continued if new facts or evidence were provided.[19] In the eyes of the court, art 54 CISA required a final decision on the merits of the case, ie a conviction or acquittal.[20]

2.2 *The Transformation of Art 54 CISA into EU Law*

By the Treaty of Amsterdam, the Schengen acquis was integrated into the legal framework of the European Union.[21] Thereby, art 54 CISA became part of secondary EU law[22] and subject to the jurisdiction of the Court of Justice of the European Union (ex-art 35 TEU). In the first case on the interpretation of art 54 CISA, the Court of Justice had to deal with out-of-court settlements,

---

15 Ibid 91, 93.
16 Belgian Code of Criminal Procedure (*Code d'Instruction Criminelle*) 1808, art 216bis.
17 BGH NStZ 1998, 149, 151–152; NJW 1999, 1270, 1271; see also Christine van den Wijngaert [1998] 18 NStZ 152–153 (note).
18 French Code of Criminal Procedure (*Code de procédure pénale*) 1957, art 212.
19 BGHSt 45, 123, 127–128.
20 BGHSt 45, 123, 128; see also Michael Grotz (n 13) 102.
21 Protocol integrating the Schengen acquis into the framework of the European Union [1997] OJ C 340/93.
22 Council Decision 1999/435/EC of 20 May 1999 concerning the definition of the Schengen acquis for the purpose of determining, in conformity with the relevant provisions of the Treaty establishing the European Community and the Treaty on European Union, the legal basis for each of the provisions or decisions which constitute the acquis OJ L 176/1; Council Decision 1999/436/EC of 20 May 1999 determining, in conformity with the relevant provisions of the Treaty establishing the European Community and the Treaty on European Union, the legal basis for each of the provisions or decisions which constitute the Schengen acquis OJ L 176/17, 21.

namely the decision of the public prosecutor's office to discontinue proceedings once the accused had paid a certain amount of money (*Einstellung unter Auflagen*,[23] *transactie*[24]). In its preliminary ruling, the Court went far beyond the traditional interpretation of the *ne bis in idem* principle in international treaties (*supra* 2.1) and held that the term "finally disposed of" did not require a court decision but applied to any decision of the public prosecutor's office whereby criminal proceedings were discontinued and further prosecution was barred.[25] So, the reasoning of the court was based on the effect of the relevant decisions under national law: Once the accused had paid the amount of money determined by the prosecutor, he enjoyed protection from further prosecution.[26] The Court argued that restricting the scope of application to court decisions (judgments) would result in an interpretation of the *ne bis in idem* principle that would benefit perpetrators of serious crimes only, but not defendants having committed minor offences who were prosecuted in the framework of simplified procedures.[27] Placing a criminal judgment (conviction or acquittal) and the aforementioned decisions of the public prosecutor's office on the same footing, the Court did not pay attention to the fact that the latter do not have full effect of *res iudicata* as national law allows criminal proceedings to be continued if certain conditions are met, e.g. new facts reveal that the accused did not commit a misdemeanor (*Vergehen*), but a felony (*Verbrechen*).[28] These rules reflect that a judgment after full trial is less prone to error than decisions resulting from simplified procedures that are based on a summary examination of the charges. Accordingly, the threshold to revise a decision of the public prosecutor's office to discontinue criminal proceedings should be lower than that for a revision of criminal judgments.[29] Therefore, a restrictive interpretation of art 54 CISA would not only be in accordance with the origins of that provision in an international treaty, but also correspond to the national rules on *res iudicata*.

The Court, however, refused to take the intentions of the Contracting Parties into consideration because art 54 CISA had been integrated into the legal

---

23   German Code of Criminal Procedure (*Strafprozessordnung*) 1987, s 153a.
24   Dutch Criminal Code (*wetboek van strafrecht*) 1881, art 74.
25   Joined Cases C-187/01 and C-385/01 *Gözütok and Brügge* [2003] ECR I-1345 para 48.
26   German Code of Criminal Procedure (*Strafprozessordnung*) 1987, s 153a(1)5; Dutch Criminal Code (*wetboek van strafrecht*) 1881, art 74(1)2.
27   Joined Cases C-187/01 and C-385/01 *Gözütok and Brügge* [2003] ECR I-1345 para 40.
28   German Code of Criminal Procedure (*Strafprozessordnung*) 1987, s 153a(1)5; see also Dutch Criminal Code (*wetboek van strafrecht*) 1881, art 74b(1).
29   For a detailed analysis of the concept of *res iudicata* in the German criminal justice system see Henning Radtke, *Zur Systematik des Strafklageverbrauchs verfahrenserledigender Entscheidungen im Strafprozess* (Lang 1994) 342 ff.

framework of the Union.[30] Since the integration of the Schengen acquis was aimed at enhancing European integration and developing the Union as an area of freedom, security and justice in which the citizens of the Union enjoy the right to free movement, the *ne bis in idem* principle should also apply to final decisions of the public prosecutor's office barring further prosecution. The exercise of the right to free movement (art 21 TFEU) would be significantly hampered if persons having fulfilled the obligations for a discontinuation of proceedings were still facing the risk of being prosecuted in another Member State.[31]

In addition, the Court argued that the *ne bis in idem* principle is not conditional upon a harmonisation of the Member States' criminal laws, but is based upon mutual trust in their criminal justice systems even when the outcome of proceedings would differ from Member State to Member State (ie depend upon the criminal law to be applied).[32] In sum, the transformation of art 54 CISA into EU law resulted in an extensive interpretation of the *ne bis in idem* principle and the term "finally disposed of".

This extensive understanding, however, reached its limits when the second case on art 54 CISA came up. In *Miraglia*, a Dutch prosecutor had decided not to pursue prosecution, but to close the case.[33] Even though the decision was final under Dutch law and criminal proceedings could only be continued if new evidence were produced,[34] the Court held that art 54 CISA was not applicable because the Dutch authorities had closed the case on the sole ground that the competent authorities of another Member State (Italy) had initiated criminal proceedings against the accused person for the same conduct.[35] In the eyes of the Court, it would clearly run counter the objective to maintain and develop the Union as an area of freedom, security and justice if the decision to close a case in order to give priority to criminal proceedings in a Member State better placed for prosecution would, by itself, prohibit the competent authorities of that Member State from initiating or continuing a criminal investigation.[36] For that reason, the Court ruled that art 54 CISA was inapplicable to decisions where no determination had been made as to the merits of the case.[37]

---

30 Joined Cases C-187/01 and C-385/01 *Gözütok and Brügge* [2003] ECR I-1345 para 46.
31 Joined Cases C-187/01 and C-385/01 *Gözütok and Brügge* [2003] ECR I-1345 paras 35–38.
32 Joined Cases C-187/01 and C-385/01 *Gözütok and Brügge* [2003] ECR I-1345 paras 32–33.
33 Case C-469/03 *Miraglia* [2005] ECR I-2009 para 18.
34 Dutch Code of Criminal Procedure (*wetboek van strafvordering*) 1921, art 255.
35 Case C-469/03 *Miraglia* [2005] ECR I-2009 para 35.
36 Case C-469/03 *Miraglia* [2005] ECR I-2009 paras 33–34.
37 Case C-469/03 *Miraglia* [2005] ECR I-2009 paras 30, 35.

In its following judgments, the Court further developed the new criterion: Whereas the final acquittal for lack of evidence is based on such a determination and, thus, falls within the scope of art 54 CISA (*van Straaten*),[38] it was far from clear whether the same should apply to a court decision that prosecution was time-barred (*Gasparini*).[39] Referring to *Miraglia*, the Advocate General suggested to answer that question in the negative if the decision had been taken without any consideration to the merits of the case.[40] The scope of art 54 CISA should be limited to proceedings where the defendant had *de facto* been placed in jeopardy (ie the risk of being tried and convicted) because the court had examined the merits of the case albeit that the case was finally dismissed because prosecution was time-barred.[41] There is much to suggest that these conditions were met in *Gasparini* as the final decision in the sentencing state had been adopted by the Portuguese Supreme Court.[42] The Court of Justice, however, did not at all refer to *Miraglia* and the requirement of a determination as to the merits of the case and held that art 54 CISA applied to any court decision by which the accused was acquitted because the prosecution was time-barred.[43] In its essence, the reasoning of the Court was based on the very same arguments as in *Gözütok* and *Brügge* (ie the right to free movement in an area of freedom, security and justice, and the principle of mutual recognition).[44]

In subsequent judgments, the Court re-affirmed the broad interpretation of art 54 CISA and made its application solely dependant upon whether or not the decision adopted in the sentencing Member State was to be considered final. Accordingly, the *ne bis in idem* principle was held to apply to convictions resulting from trials *in absentia* (*Bourquain*).[45] In contrast, the scope of art 54 CISA did not cover a decision that does not definitively bar further prosecution and preclude new criminal proceedings in the Member State which instituted criminal proceedings (*Turanský*).[46] Thereby, the term "finally disposed of" is construed by reference to the procedural law of the sentencing state: The

---

38   Case C-150/05 *van Straaten* [2006] ECR I-9327 paras 60–61.
39   Case C-467/04 *Gasparini* [2006] ECR I-9199.
40   Opinion of Advocate General Sharpston of 15 June 2006, Case C-467/04 *Gasparini* [2006] ECR I-9199, paras 96, 99, 120.
41   Ibid paras 96, 120.
42   Case C-467/04 *Gasparini* [2006] ECR I-9199 para 18; see for the application of art 54 CISA to court proceedings in general Advocate General Sharpston (n 39) para 96 (note 78).
43   Case C-467/04 *Gasparini* [2006] ECR I-9199 paras 25, 33.
44   Ibid paras 27–30.
45   Case C-297/07 *Bourquain* [2008] ECR I-9425 paras 34, 52.
46   Case C-491/07 *Turanský* EU:C:2008:768 paras 36, 40, 45.

application of art 54 CISA requires a decision triggering the effect of *res iudicata* within the national criminal justice system. It must be noted, however, that the Court's case-law is based on a broad understanding of *res iudicata* that even covers judicial decisions subject to revision if new evidence is produced (e.g. *Einstellung unter Auflagen*).[47]

In the light of these judgments, it was hardly surprising that the Court ruled in *criminal proceedings against M* that a court decision to discontinue criminal proceedings (*ordonnance de non-lieu*[48]) fell within the scope of application of art 54 CISA.[49] In its reasoning, the Court referred to the national law of the Member State where the decision had been taken (Belgium) and stated that the *ordonnance de non-lieu* triggered the effect of *res iudicata* in that state because it precluded new criminal proceedings on the basis of the same facts and evidence.[50] In addition, the Court based its ruling on a second line of reasoning and argued that art 54 CISA had to be interpreted in the light of art 50 of the EU Charter of Fundamental Rights (CFR) and art 4 of Protocol No 7 to the European Convention on Human Rights (ECHR).[51] The Court referred to the case-law of the European Court of Human Rights according to which the *ne bis in idem* principle applied to judicial decisions irrespective of whether criminal proceedings can be reopened if there is evidence of new or newly discovered facts,[52] and argued that the final nature of the *ordonnonance de non-lieu* under art 54 CISA had to be qualified accordingly.[53] Thereby, the Court expressly recognized the transnational dimension of the *ne bis in idem* principle as a fundamental right in order to justify its broad interpretation of art 54 CISA.

In contrast, the most recent judgment (*Kossowski*) returned to the more restrictive approach in *Miraglia* that required a decision on the merits of the case.[54] In that case, the defendant was arrested in Poland and charged with extortion. As the crime had been committed in Germany, the Polish authorities requested copies of the investigation file from the competent German authorities but were not able to verify the statements by the victim and a hearsay witness because both of them were living in Germany and the defendant refused to give a statement. As a consequence, the Polish public prosecutor's office

---

47 See *supra* 2.2 at the beginning.
48 Belgian Code of Criminal Procedure (*Code d'Instruction Criminelle*) 1808, art 128.
49 Case C-398/12 *criminal proceedings against M* EU:C:2014:1057 para 41.
50 Ibid para 33, referring tot he Belgian Code of Criminal Procedure (*Code d'Instruction Criminelle*) 1808, art 246.
51 Ibid paras 35, 37.
52 *Sergey Zolutukhin v Russia* [GC] ECHR 2009-I 291, para 108.
53 Case C-398/12 *criminal proceedings against M* EU:C:2014:1057 para 39–40.
54 Case C-486/14 *Kossowski* [GC] EU:C:2016:483.

terminated proceedings for lack of sufficient evidence.[55] According to Polish law, the reopening of the investigation was only permitted where new facts or evidence were revealed.[56] Referring to the case-law of the Court of Justice, the competent court in Germany held that the decision of the Polish public prosecutor's office had the effect of *res iudicata* and criminal proceedings in Germany were precluded by art 54 CISA, and the appeals court referred the matter to the Court of Justice.[57]

The Court expressly acknowledged that the decision of the Polish public prosecutor's office precluded any further prosecution in Poland and, thus, had the effect of *res iudicata* according to the national law of the Member State in which the decision had been taken.[58] The Court, however, made the application of art 54 CISA (ie the term "finally disposed of") subject to two conditions, namely *res iudicata* in the domestic criminal justice system and, secondly, a determination as to the merits of the case.[59] The second condition that had been mentioned only incidentally in *Turanský*[60] and *criminal proceedings against M*,[61] was not met because the Polish authorities were not able to verify the victim's statements and, thus, to examine the merits of the case.[62] Like in *Miraglia*,[63] the Court argued that the application of art 54 CISA to such a decision would render the prosecution of crimes more difficult, if not impossible, because further prosecution would be barred throughout the Union without a detailed assessment of the unlawful conduct being necessary.[64] In contrast to its former judgments where the principle of mutual recognition had been given particular weight, the Court held that mutual trust could prosper only if the second Member State was able to satisfy itself that the final decision taken in the first Member State met the criteria set out in art 54 CISA (including a determination as to the merits of the case).[65]

In sum, according to the case-law of the Court of Justice, a decision finally disposing of a case must meet two conditions, namely (i) the effect of *res*

---

55 Ibid paras 13–16.
56 Ibid para 10, referring to Polish Court of Criminal Procedure (*Kodeks postępowania karnego*) 1997, art 327(2).
57 Ibid paras 19–23.
58 Ibid para 36–37.
59 Ibid 42.
60 Case C-491/07 *Turanský* EU:C:2008:768 para 45.
61 Case C-398/12 *criminal proceedings against M* EU:C:2014:1057 paras 28, 30.
62 Case C-486/14 *Kossowski* [GC] EU:C:2016:483 para 48.
63 Case C-469/03 *Miraglia* [2005] ECR I-2009 paras 30, 35.
64 Ibid para 49.
65 Ibid paras 52–53.

iudicata in the domestic criminal justice system (ie barring further prosecution on the basis of the same facts and evidence) and (ii) a determination as to the merits of the case.

3 Res iudicata and the Determination as to the Merits of the Case

As the analysis of the Court's case-law has shown, the transformation of the *ne bis in idem* principle from international treaty law into a supranational setting has brought about significant changes in content and scope of this principle. The Court's interpretation of art 54 CISA is based on a twofold reasoning, namely the establishment of a transnational fundamental right in EU law (art 50 CFR) and the emergence of an area of freedom, security and justice that transcends the fragmentation into various national criminal justice systems. These two aspects are mirrored in the double function of the *ne bis in idem* principle in a transnational context: On the one hand, art 54 CISA shall protect the accused from double prosecution within the Union (a transnational fundamental right), on the other hand, it shall enhance effective transnational law enforcement by coordinating criminal proceedings in the Member States.[66] A closer examination of the *ne bis in idem* principle will reveal that the restrictive approach taken in *Kossowski* and the requirement of a decision on the merits of the case do not fit with either of these two rationales.

3.1 The ne bis in idem *Principle as a Fundamental Right*

The *ne bis in idem* principle is a fundamental right enshrined in art 50 CFR. Its main purpose is to protect the individual from double prosecution and, thereby, to establish legal certainty for the acquitted or convicted person that he is not under the sword of Damocles of further criminal prosecution for the same acts.[67] Furthermore, the rationale is linked to the principle of proportionality because the institution of new criminal proceedings is considered an excessive (disproportionate) use of the state's *ius puniendi*.[68]

---

66   Martin Böse 'Der Grundsatz „ne bis in idem" in der Europäischen Union (Art. 54 SDÜ)' [2003] 150 Goltdammer's Archive für Strafrecht 744, 751–752.

67   Bas van Bockel *The* Ne bis in idem *Principle in EU Law* (Kluwer 2010) 25–27; Juliette Lelieur 'Transnationalising Ne Bis In Idem: How the Rule of Ne Bis In Idem Reveals the Principle of Personal Legal Certainty', [2013] 9 (4) Utrecht Law Review 198, 210.

68   Bas van Bockel (n 67) 27.

As the Charter forms part of primary EU law (art 6(1) TEU), art 54 CISA must be interpreted in line with its guarantees, art 50 CFR in particular.[69] Thus, a broad understanding of the term "finally acquitted or convicted" in art 50 CFR will apply to art 54 CISA as well. Art 50 CFR was drafted on the basis of art 4 of Protocol No 7 to the ECHR.[70] Therefore, art 50 CFR shall not be interpreted in a manner that its scope falls below the minimum standard established by the ECHR (art 52(3) CFR) and the corresponding case-law of the Court of Human Rights.[71] In art 4 of Protocol No 7, a final acquittal or conviction is linked to the authority of *res iudicata*, ie if the decision is irrevocable and not subject to further ordinary remedies.[72] According to the case-law of the Court of Human Rights, the decision of a public prosecutor to discontinue criminal proceedings is not considered a final acquittal because the decision can be revoked by the prosecutor general and, thus, does not have the authority of *res iudicata*.[73] This reasoning, however, implies e *contrario* that the decision of a public prosecutor to close a case must be considered "final" if further prosecution on the basis of the same facts and evidence is barred under domestic law. In the *Kossowski* case, the decision of the Polish authorities to discontinue criminal proceedings had this effect and, thus, qualified as final under this interpretation of art 4 of Protocol No 7 to the ECHR. This conclusion is not affected by the fact that the Polish Code of Criminal Procedure allows for the proceedings to be continued if new evidence is produced. As can be inferred from art 4(2) of Protocol No 7 to the ECHR, extraordinary remedies (e.g. the request for reopening the proceedings) are not taken into account for the purpose of determining whether or not a final decision has been taken.[74]

Even if a decision of a public prosecutor is irrevocable and, thus, "final" in a formal sense (not subject to further remedies), the authority of *res iudicata* might still require a determination as to the merits of the case. In *Marguš v. Croatia*, the issue was raised before the Court of Human Rights with respect to a court decision to terminate criminal proceedings because the charges against the accused were covered by an amnesty act.[75] The Grand Chamber

---

69   Case C-398/12 criminal proceedings against M EU:C:2014:1057 para 35.
70   Explanations relating to the Charter of Fundamental Rights [2007] OJ C 303/17, 31.
71   This applies to the Protocols to the ECHR as well, see the Explanations (n 70), 33.
72   Explanatory Report to Protocol No 7 to the European Convention on Human Rights 6, 7 (paras 22, 29).
73   *Horciag v Romania* App no 70982/01 (ECtHR, 14 March 2005); *Sundqvist v Finland* App no 75602/01 (ECtHR, 22 November 2005); see also *Smirnova v Russia* App no 46133/99 (ECtHR, 3 October 2004); *Marguš v Croatia* [GC] ECHR 2014-III 1 para 120.
74   *Sergey Zolutukhin v Russia* [GC] ECHR 2009-I 291, para 108.
75   *Marguš v Croatia* [GC] ECHR 2014-III 1.

did not rule on the question of whether a decision that had been taken without assessment of the accused person's guilt could be regarded as a final acquittal but held that the amnesty act was in breach with art 2 and 3 ECHR and, for that reason, art 4 of Protocol No 7 did not apply to a decision that had been based on that act.[76] In their concurring opinion, three judges argued that the notions "acquitted" and "convicted" implied that an assessment of the circumstances of the case had been made and that either the guilt or the innocence of the accused had been established.[77] This understanding corresponds to the substance-based approach of the Advocate General in *Gasparini* according to which a court decision that prosecution was time-barred does not qualify as a final decision under art 54 CISA.[78] According to this approach, art 54 CISA does not apply to any decision that is based upon a procedural obstacle that eliminates the state's jurisdiction and, thereby, hinders the court from ruling on the merits of the case.[79]

This understanding of the *ne bis in idem principle* originates from the concept of *res iudicata* in national criminal justice systems (*materielle Rechtskraft, autorité de la chose jugée*). This concept is based upon the presumption that the final judgment is true and, thus, bars a new investigation of the same facts (*res iudicata pro veritate habetur*).[80] As a consequence, the authority of *res iudicata* requires a determination of the guilt or the innocence of the accused. In Germany, the authority of *res iudicata* (*materielle Rechtskraft*) is triggered by judgments on the merits of the case (*Sachurteil*) whereas the decision to close the case for reasons of procedural law (*Prozessurteil*) does not have this effect[81]

---

76 Ibid paras 139–141; see also *Marguš v Croatia* App no 4455/10 (ECtHR, 13 November 2012), paras 67–68.

77 Joint concurring opinion of judges Spielmann, Power-Forde and Nussberger ibid para 8.

78 Opinion of Advocate General Sharpston of 15 June 2006, Case C-467/04 *Gasparini* [2006] ECR I-9199, paras 96, 120.

79 André Klip, *European Criminal Law* 3rd edition (Intersentia 2016) 289–290.

80 Juliette Lelieur (n 67) 200–201; see e.g. Bernard Bouloc, *Procédure Pénal* 25th edition (Dalloz 2016) 1035 (France); Paolo Tonini *Manuale di Procedura Penale* 14th edition (Giuffre 2013) 946 (Italy). According to the prevailing opinion in Germany, the final judgment by itself determines the guilt or innocence of the accused ("prozessuale Gestaltungstheorie"), see Claus Roxin and Bernd Schünemann *Strafverfahrensrecht* 28th edition (Beck 2014) 437 with further references.

81 BGHSt 18, 1, 5; Carl-Friedrich Stuckenberg '§ 260 StPO' in Löwe-Rosenberg *die Strafprozessordnung und das Gerichtsverfassungsgesetz* 26th edition, vol. 6/2 (de Gruyter 2013), para 123.

and, thus, does not fall within the scope of the *ne bis in idem* principle.[82] The same holds true for the *ne bis in idem* principle in the Dutch criminal justice system.[83] In France, however, the scope of *res iudicata* (*autorité de la chose jugée*) extends to court decisions stating that prosecution is time-barred or excluded by an amnesty law.[84] Likewise, it is well-established in the German criminal justice system that a final judgment for reasons of procedural law (*Prozessurteil*) has only limited effect of *res iudicata* (*eingeschränkte Rechtskraft*) that the decision must not be revoked for grounds of law, but proceedings may only be continued if the procedural obstacle has been eliminated.[85] Thus, if the court closes the case because prosecution is time-barred, the decision has *de facto* the same effect as a judgment on the merits of the case.[86]

Despite their divergence, the national concepts of *res iudicata* illustrate that the protection from double prosecution does not necessarily require an assessment of the merits of the case. Whether or not the *ne bis in idem* principle should be subject to this requirement depends upon whether the interpretation of this principle adheres to the traditional understanding of *res iudicata* in the strict sense or to a broader concept that extends to decisions that do not have full, but only limited authority of *res iudicata*. The rationale of the *ne bis in idem* principle to protect the individual from double prosecution favours the latter approach: Even if the final and irrevocable decision to discontinue criminal proceedings is based upon procedural law only, it may give rise to legitimate expectations that criminal proceedings will not be continued unless new facts are revealed by which the procedural obstacle is eliminated. If such a decision were excluded from the scope of the *ne bis in idem* principle, the defendant would be left in a situation of legal uncertainty and under the sword of Damocles of criminal proceedings to be continued for whatever reason. Furthermore, a broad interpretation of art 54 CISA perfectly fits with the Court's ruling in *Gasparini*,[87] but can also build upon *Gözütok* and *Brügge* where the Court applied the *ne bis in idem* principle to decisions that do not have full,

---

82   Eberhard Schmidt-Aßmann 'Art. 103 Abs 3 GG' in Theodor Maunz and Günter Dürig (eds), *Grundgesetz-Kommentar* (30th instalment – December 1992), para 295; Helmut Schulze-Fielitz 'Art 103 III GG' in Horst Dreier (ed), Grundgesetz-Kommentar, Vol. 3 (Mohr Siebeck 2008) para 29.

83   G.J.M. Corstens and M.J. Borgers *Het Nederlands Strafprocessrecht* 7th edition (Kluwer 2011) 190–191 (the Netherlands).

84   Bernard Bouloc (n 80) 1038–1039 and 1040.

85   BGHSt 18, 1, 5; Stuckenberg (n 81).

86   BayObLG VRS 77 (1989) 136; Stuckenberg (n 81); see also with regard to the Netherlands: Corstens and Borgers (n 83) 191.

87   Case C-467/04 *Gasparini* [2006] ECR I-9199 paras 25, 33.

but only limited authority of *res iudicata*.[88] According to German law, the decision of the public prosecutor's office to discontinue criminal proceedings once a certain amount of money has been paid implies neither a guilty verdict nor innocence of the accused person.[89] Accordingly, the prevailing opinion in Germany is that the scope of the *ne bis in idem* principle is limited to court decisions.[90] Nevertheless, it is generally accepted that the payment gives rise to the legitimate expectation that further prosecution of the same conduct is barred.[91] Accordingly, some authors refer to *Gözütok* and *Brügge* and argue that the traditional interpretation is obsolete and the *ne bis in idem* principle applies to final decisions of the public prosecutor's office that have (albeit limited) effect of *res iudicata*.[92]

But even if it were assumed that art 54 CISA required a determination as to the merits of the case, the Court's reasoning in *Kossowski* is not beyond doubt. According to the Court's case-law, an acquittal for lack of evidence is a decision on the merits of the case (*van Straaten*).[93] In *criminal proceedings against M*, art 54 CISA was applied to a court decision terminating criminal proceedings on the ground that there were insufficient facts and evidence (*ordonnance de non-lieu*).[94] In *Kossowski*, the public prosecutor's office discontinued proceedings for the very same reason, but the Court held nonetheless that there was no determination as to the merits of the case.[95] The Court's assessment was essentially based upon the fact that the public prosecutor's office failed to undertake a more detailed investigation but simply relied on the lack of available evidence.[96] At first glance, the distinction of the Court appears to

---

88   Joined Cases C-187/01 and C-385/01 *Gözütok and Brügge* [2003] ECR I-1345 para 48; see in this regard Juliette Lelieur (n 67) 206.

89   BVerfG NJW 1991, 1530, 1531; Werner Beulke '§ 153a StPO' in Löwe-Rosenberg *Die Strafprozessordnung und das Gerichtsverfassungsgesetz* 26th edition, vol. 5 (de Gruyter 2008), para 39.

90   Eberhard Schmidt-Aßmann (n 82) para 296; Helmut Schulze-Fielitz (n 78) para 29.

91   Eberhard Schmidt-Aßmann (n 82) para 296.

92   See with regard to art 4 Protocol No 7 to the ECHR: Robert Esser 'Das Doppelverfolgungsverbot in der Rechtsprechung des EGMR' in Gudrun Hochmayr (ed) „*Ne bis in idem*" *in Europa* (Nomos 2015) 27, 33, 38; Robert Esser 'Art. 6 EMRK/Art. 14 IPBPR' in Löwe-Rosenberg *Die Strafprozessordnung und das Gerichtsverfassungsgesetz* 26th edition, vol. 11 (de Gruyter 2012), para 1032; see also Stefanie Schmahl ,'Art. 103' in Bruno Schmidt-Bleibtreu, Hans Hofmann and Hans-Günter Henneke (eds) *Kommentar zum Grundgesetz* 13th edition (Heymanns 2014) para 85.

93   Case C-150/05 *van Straaten* [2006] ECR I-9327 paras 60–61.

94   Case C-398/12 *criminal proceedings against M* EU:C:2014:1057 para 17, 41.

95   Case C-486/14 *Kossowski* [GC] EU:C:2016:483 para 10, 48.

96   Ibid paras 48–49.

be reasonable, but it inevitably raises the issue of how "detailed" an investigation must be to qualify as an examination of the merits of the case.[97] In this regard, a corresponding concept in the national criminal justice systems can barely be identified since it would be considered a flagrant breach with the *ne bis in idem* principle to start new proceedings just because the final decision was not based upon a proper and detailed examination of the merits of the case.[98] Even if the Court's ruling in *Kossowski* were interpreted in a manner to eliminate extreme cases where almost no investigative efforts had been undertaken, the assessment would not only rely on an unclear and vague criterion, but also on factual circumstances related to the course of the investigation that are completely unknown to the defendant.[99] Such interpretation would leave the individual in limbo and, thereby, disregard his legitimate interest in legal certainty on whether (and to which extent) he enjoyed protection from further prosecution. The protective purpose of the *ne bis in idem* principle suggests an interpretation that does not refer to the assessment in the single case (*in concreto*), but to the formal qualification of the decision as "final" under domestic law (*in abstracto*).[100]

In sum, the foundations of the *ne bis in idem* principle in art 50 CFR and the principle of legal certainty support an interpretation of art 54 CISA that covers final decisions that do not have full, but only limited force of *res iudicata*. The notion of *res iudicata* implies that further prosecution on the basis of the same facts and evidence is barred. Whether or not this requirement is fulfilled must be assessed on the basis of the national law of criminal procedure on which the decision was based. The traditional concept of *res iudicata* that requires a judgment on the merits of the case does not fit with the protective purpose of the *ne bis in idem* principle because it ignores the interest in legal certainty and legitimate expectations arising from other judicial decisions terminating criminal proceedings. This understanding corresponds to the broad interpretation

---

97 Kilian Wegner 'Entscheidungen zur Verfahrenserledigung im Strafverfahren und ihre transnationale Rechtkraftwirkung gem. Art. 54 SDÜ, Art. 50 GRC' 17 (2016) Onlinezeitschrift für Höchstrichterliche Rechtsprechung zum Strafrecht 396, 401.

98 In a vertical setting, there is a standard for the assessment of a state's unwillingness or inability to effectively investigate and to prosecute (art 17(2) and 3, art 20(3) of the Rome Statute on the International Criminal Court), but art 54 CISA lacks a corresponding provision, and it must be doubted whether the mechanism in the ICC statute is appropriate in a horizontal setting, see Henning Radtke '§ 12 Der Grundsatz „Ne bis in idem" und Jurisdiktionskonflikte' in Martin Böse (ed) *Europäisches Strafrecht mit polizeilicher Zusammenarbeit* (Nomos 2013) para 7.

99 Kilian Wegner (n 97) 400.

100 See also Kilian Wegner ibid.

of art 54 CISA that has been developed in *Gözütok* and *Brügge* and which has been further elaborated in *criminal proceedings against M*.

3.2 *The* ne bis in idem *Principle and Effective Transnational Law Enforcement*

The protection from double prosecution and the individual interest in legal certainty is not absolute, but must be balanced with the public interest in effective law enforcement. The latter aspect was particularly highlighted in *Kossowski* when the Court argued that art 54 CISA had to be interpreted in the light of the need to promote the combating of crime within the area of freedom, security and justice.[101] Unlike in a purely domestic concept, the public interest in effective transnational prosecution is not only a limiting factor, but also an aspect enhancing the transnational dimension of the *ne bis in idem* principle. Right from the outset, the Court has based its interpretation of art 54 CISA on the principle of mutual recognition and the emergence of a single area of freedom, security and justice.[102] Being part of the EU framework of cooperation in criminal matters, art 54 CISA prevents a duplication of criminal proceedings and a waste of resources. Thereby, the transnational dimension of the *ne bis in idem* principle serves a coordinating function and contributes to a more effective transnational law enforcement.[103] Therefore, the application of art 54 CISA is not only a potential obstacle to the enforcement of criminal law in the Member States, but at the same time an instrument to enhance the coordination of criminal proceedings in the Union. When determining the scope of art 54 CISA, both aspects have to be taken into due consideration.

When the Court established that art 54 CISA required a determination as to the merits of the case, its reasoning was essentially based on the coordinating function of art 54 CISA when it stated that the *ne bis in idem* principle does not apply where a case had been closed on the sole ground that criminal proceedings in another Member State should be given priority (*Miraglia*).[104] In this case, the decision to close the case resolved a conflict of jurisdiction and, thereby, served a coordinating function. An application of art 54 CISA for coordination purposes would be superfluous, even dysfunctional because the *ne bis in idem* principle would bar criminal proceedings in the Member State

---

101 Case C-486/14 *Kossowski* [GC] EU:C:2016:483 para 47.
102 Joined Cases C-187/01 and C-385/01 *Gözütok and Brügge* [2003] ECR I-1345 paras 333, 36–37.
103 Martin Böse (n 66) 751–752.
104 Case C-469/03 *Miraglia* [2005] ECR I-2009 paras 33–34.

that was considered to be better placed for prosecution.[105] The Court rightly pointed out that such an interpretation would make it almost impossible to prosecute the crime with which the defendant had been charged.[106]

On the other hand, the application of art 54 CISA to out-of-court settlements (*Gözütok* and *Brügge*) had pathed the way to a broad interpretation of art 54 CISA that was not confined to judgments on the merits of the case having the authority of *res iudicata* in the strict sense. Giving the coordinating function priority over the Member State's interest in maintaining its *ius puniendi*, the Court extended the scope of art 54 CISA to decisions whereby prosecution is time-barred (*Gasparini*). The Advocate General argued that in the absence of harmonised rules on time bars to prosecution, the application of the *ne bis in idem* principle would result in a race to the bottom where the law of the Member State providing for the shortest limitation period would prevail.[107] The Court rejected this approach and re-affirmed its reasoning in *Gözütok* and *Brügge* that the application of art 54 CISA was neither conditional upon a harmonisation of the Member States' criminal laws nor dependant upon whether the outcome of criminal proceedings in the second Member State would be different.[108] If we accept the Court's assumption that the Union's interest in coordinating criminal proceedings in an area of freedom, security and justice outweighs the single Member State's interest to apply its own criminal law, it does not matter in that respect whether the final decision is based upon substantive law or procedural law. If a Member State has to recognize the criminal law of the Member State in which the final decision on the case was taken, even when the outcome would be different if its own national law were to be applied, the same holds true for mutual recognition of the laws of criminal procedure.[109] Accordingly, the distinction between a final decision on the merits of the case and a decision for reasons of procedural law must be rejected.

Instead, the rationale of the requirement of a determination as to the merits of the case must be related to the effective prosecution of crimes in a

---

105   Gudrun Hochmayr 'Europäische Rechtskraft oder gegenseitige Anerkennung. Anforderungen an die Bestandskraft der Erledigung' in Gudrun Hochmayr (ed) „*Ne bis in idem*" in Europa (Nomos 2015) 89, 110–111.
106   Case C-469/03 *Miraglia* [2005] ECR I-2009 para 33.
107   Opinion of Advocate General Sharpston of 15 June 2006, Case C-467/04 *Gasparini* [2006] ECR I-9199, paras 109, 113–114; see also André Klip (n 79) 290.
108   Case C-467/04 *Gasparini* [2006] ECR I-9199 paras 29–30.
109   See *vice versa* the Opinion of Advocate General Sharpston of 15 June 2006, Case C-467/04 *Gasparini* [2006] ECR I-9199, paras 112, 114 who pointed to the lack of harmonizing measures on the age of criminal responsibility and argued that the application of art 54 CISA required a certain degree of approximation of substantive criminal law, too.

transnational context. This reasoning became obvious in *Kossowski* where the Court refused to apply art 54 CISA to a final decision that had resulted from a failure to properly investigate the case.[110] According to this understanding, a determination of the merits requires the gathering and examination of facts and evidence and, if necessary, requests for mutual legal assistance (e.g. for the examination of witnesses).[111] In addition, the Advocate General argued that the decision to discontinue criminal proceedings had manifestly violated the rights of the victim (the right to be heard and the rights to information and compensation) and, therefore, did not fall within the scope of art 54 CISA.[112] In general, the reasoning in *Kossowski* was based on the concern that the decision to discontinue criminal proceedings often might turn out to be wrong if it had been taken without detailed examination of the facts and evidence and, in that case, the application of art 54 CISA would result in the impunity of the offender.

Obviously, the risk that the final decision is wrong is inherent to the *ne bis in idem* principle. Nevertheless, it must be acknowledged that, generally speaking, the risk decreases in the course of criminal proceedings. As it has been mentioned in the context of *Gözütok* and *Brügge* (*supra* 2.2), a judgment after full trial is less error prone than decisions in an early stage of proceedings (e.g. out-of-court settlements).[113] For this reason, the scope of the *ne bis in idem* principle in international treaties had been limited to judgments (*supra* 2.1). As a consequence of its transformation into EU law, however, art 54 CISA was interpreted in a broader sense that covered decisions with only limited authority of *res iudicata* (*supra* 2.2), namely the out-of-court-settlement (*Gözütok* and *Brügge*) and the *ordonnance de non-lieu* (*criminal proceedings against M*). The risk that such decisions turn out to be ill-founded and give rise to situations of impunity, is addressed by two limitations: First, the decision must have limited authority of *res iudicata* in the domestic criminal justice system. If the decision cannot be revoked unless new facts or evidence are revealed, the national criminal justice system implicitly requires the judicial authority to base its decision on the available facts and evidence. Second, since the decision has only limited authority of *res iudicata* it can be revised insofar as national law allows for continuing or reopening of criminal proceedings, e.g. where new facts and evidence reveal that the conduct under investigation qualifies as a

---

110 Case C-486/14 *Kossowski* [GC] EU:C:2016:483 para 48.
111 Opinion of Advocate General Yves Bot of 15 December 2015, Case C-486/14 *Kossowski* [GC] EU:C:2016:483 para 79.
112 Ibid paras 80–83.
113 For a detailed analysis of the German criminal justice system see Henning Radtke (n 29).

felony.[114] Any new proceedings, however, can be brought only in the Member State in which the decision to discontinue proceedings was taken.[115] The latter aspect clearly reflects the coordinating function of art 54 CISA as the *ne bis in idem* principle concentrates jurisdiction over the case in the Member States where the decision was taken and relieves the other Member States of their competence to prosecute.[116] The underlying rationale is that criminal proceedings shall be continued in the Member State where proceedings have already resulted in a final decision, and therefore new criminal proceedings will not have to start from the very beginning, but can build upon the findings of the previous investigation.[117] The rights of the victim do not preclude a concentration of proceedings: If the decision to close the case violates the rights of the victim, it is up to the victim to challenge the decision in the Member State where it has been adopted.[118] Thus, the application of art 54 CISA to decisions that have only limited authority of *res iudicata* does not give rise to massive impunity, but still leaves open the possibility to revise the decision and to bring the perpetrator to justice. On the contrary, art 54 CISA enhances the coordination of proceedings and, thereby, contributes to a more efficient transnational law enforcement.

However, the coordination mechanism under art 54 CISA can lead to accidental or arbitrary results because the *ne bis in idem* principle is based upon one criterion only: priority ('first come, first served').[119] In *Kossowski*, this became obvious as the crime had been committed in Germany and, thus, German courts were to be considered best placed for prosecution and trial. Instead, the Polish authorities were the first to take a final decision in criminal proceedings and, according to art 54 CISA, to assume exclusive jurisdiction over the case. Not surprisingly, the Court refused to apply art 54 CISA in order to maintain jurisdiction of the German courts. Like in *Miraglia*, the real reason for not applying the *ne bis in idem* principle was to avoid a dysfunctional case allocation that relieves the Member State which is better placed for prosecution of its

---

114 German Code of Criminal Procedure (*Strafprozessordnung*) 1987, s 153a(1)5.
115 Case C-398/12 *criminal proceedings against M* EU:C:2014:1057 para 40.
116 Martin Böse (n 66) 755.
117 Sibyl Stein Zum europäischen ne bis in idem nach Artikel 54 des Schengener Durchführungsübereinkommens (Lang 2004) 190.
118 As regards the right to compensation, art 54 CISA does not preclude the victim from bringing a civil action to seek compensation for the damage suffered in another Member State, see Joined Cases C-187/01 and C-385/01 *Gözütok and Brügge* [2003] ECR I-1345 para 47.
119 Commission 'Green paper on Conflicts of Jurisdiction and the Principle of ne bis in idem in Criminal Proceedings', COM (2005) 696 final 3; John Vervaele (n 4) 222.

competence to investigate the case. In such a constellation, the coordinating function of art 54 CISA favours an interpretation according to which the *ne bis in idem* principle does not apply. The requirement of a determination as to the merits of the case, however, does not address the particular problem, but goes far beyond the issue of coordination. Instead, the coordinating function of art 54 CISA has to be taken into consideration in a more specific manner.

The first option is not to apply art 54 CISA to any decision that terminates criminal proceedings on the sole ground that prosecution in another Member State is given priority (*Miraglia*).[120] This exception covers both unilateral decisions to close a case[121] and a request to take criminal proceedings.[122] Sometimes, such a decision will not have the authority of *res iudicata*, either.[123] Since the termination of proceedings serves the purpose of coordinating criminal proceedings in the Union, it does not give rise to legitimate expectations that there will be no further prosecution in another Member State. This assumption, however, is only valid if the decision contains sufficient reasoning on the grounds for terminating proceeding. Nevertheless, if it appears that criminal proceedings are discontinued because the available facts and evidence are insufficient (*Kossowski*), art 54 CISA will apply.

The second option is to exclude the application of art 54 CISA by recourse to the reservations under art 55 CISA. According to art 55(1)(a) CISA, a Contracting Party may declare that it is not bound by art 54 CISA where the crime was committed in its own territory. In *Kossowski*, the German criminal court referred to the corresponding declaration that had been issued by the German government and asked for a preliminary ruling on whether the exceptions under art 55 CISA were still applicable and in conformity with art 50 CFR.[124] In its preliminary ruling, the Court did not elaborate on the issue because it took the view that the conditions set out in art 54 CISA were not met.[125] According to the Advocate General, the reservation under art 55(1)(a) CISA did not become obsolete by the transformation of the CISA into EU law, but invalid

---

120   Gudrun Hochmayr (n 105).
121   See e.g. German Code of Criminal Procedure (*Strafprozessordnung*) 1987, ss 153c, 154b.
122   Art 6 of the European Convention on the Transfer of Proceedings in Criminal Matters of 15 May 1972 (ETS No 73).
123   Werner Beulke '§ 153c StPO' in Löwe-Rosenberg *Die Strafprozessordnung und das Gerichtsverfassungsgesetz* 26th edition, vol. 5 (de Gruyter 2008), para 35; see also art 21(2) of the Convention on the Transfer of Proceedings (n 122).
124   Case C-486/14 *Kossowski* [GC] EU:C:2016:483 paras 21, 23.
125   Ibid. para 55.

because it did not comply with art 50 CFR.[126] The German government had argued that the Member State in which a crime has been committed had legitimate interest in adjudicating the criminal conduct under its own criminal law if the legal assessment by the court of another Member State might be incomplete, e.g. when it convicted the perpetrator of a violent crime, but did not consider that the offender acted with the intention of glorifying nazism.[127] The Advocate General rejected this argument and held that such a case fell not within the scope of art 54 CISA because the crime adjudicated in the first Member State substantially differed from the crime to be prosecuted in the second Member State.[128] This interpretation of art 54 CISA, however, is not in line with the well-established case-law on art 54 CISA under which the *ne bis in idem* principle bars further prosecution of the same acts, "in the sense of a set of inextricably linked circumstances, independently of the legal classification of the acts and the interests protected by the criminal offences".[129] If the *idem* is determined in this manner, it cannot be denied that there might be a need for the exception under art 55(1)(a) CISA because the Member State where the judgment has been passed might not have full jurisdiction to adjudicate the criminal conduct in a comprehensive manner.[130] In a judgment that is based upon extraterritorial jurisdiction (e.g. the protective principle or universal jurisdiction), the assessment of the court is limited to certain offences (e.g. offences against the international community or the state claiming jurisdiction). In such a case, the Member State where the crime was committed might still have legitimate interest in initiating new criminal proceedings if the first judgment did not consider other protected legal interests that had been affected by the crime.[131] Irrespective of whether or not art 55(1)(a) CISA is held to be in conformity with art 50 CFR, the issue raised by the German court illustrates that concerns about the application of art 54 CISA were originating

---

126 Opinion of Advocate General Yves Bot of 15 December 2015, Case C-486/14 *Kossowski* [GC] EU:C:2016:483 paras 33–34, 48–68.

127 Ibid. para 59.

128 Ibid. paras 64, 66.

129 Case C-436/04 *van Esbroeck* [2006] ECR I-2333 paras 35–36, 42; confirmed in Case C-150/05 *van Straaten* [2006] ECR I-9327 para 53; Case C-467/04 *Gasparini* [2006] ECR I-9199 para 54; C-288/05 *Kretzinger* [2007] ECR I-6441 paras 29, 37; C-367/05 *Kraaijenbrink* [2007] ECR I-6619 para 36.

130 Since national criminal law provisions usually do not protect the interests of foreign states, similar problems arise with crimes against the state, see art 55(1)(b) and (c) CISA.

131 For a detailed analysis see Martin Böse in Martin Böse, Frank Meyer and Anne Schneider *Conflicts of Jurisdiction in Criminal Matters in the European Union. Volume II: Rights, Principles and Model Rules* (Nomos 2014) 131 ff, 140–141.

from a dysfunctional coordination of criminal proceedings because the "final" decision had not been taken in the Member State where the crime was committed (Germany). On the other hand, it is telling that the Court did not further elaborate on the requirement of a determination as to the merits of the case in *criminal proceedings against M* where the final decision (*ordonnance de non-lieu*) had been taken in the Member State where the criminal conduct had occurred (Belgium).[132]

In conclusion, neither the interest in effective transnational criminal law enforcement nor the coordinating function of art 54 CISA require a decision that was based upon a determination as to the merits of the case. This condition has originated from a strict concept of *res iudicata* that is limited to criminal judgments (ie convictions and acquittals in the strict sense). After the Court had rejected this approach (*Gözütok* and *Brügge*), the requirement of a decision on the merits lost its material basis and became an empty shell that was reactivated for the sole purpose to avoid an application of art 54 CISA where it would result in a dysfunctional coordination of criminal proceedings (*Miraglia*). Except for these cases, there is no valid reason not to apply art 54 CISA to decisions that have been taken without a determination as to the merits of the case.

4 Conclusion

According to art 54 CISA, the transnational effect of the *ne bis in idem* principle requires a decision finally disposing of a case. It is well-established case-law that this decision must have the effect of *res iudicata* in the domestic criminal justice system (ie barring further prosecution on the basis of the same facts and evidence). However, the second requirement established by the Court (ie a determination as to the merits of the case) does not comply with the character of art 54 CISA as a fundamental right (art 50 CFR) on the one hand, and its coordinating function on the other. A decision, however, is not "final" in terms of art 54 CISA if criminal proceedings were discontinued for the sole reason that criminal proceedings in another Member State would be given priority. Apart from that exception, the coordinating function of art 54 CISA and the requirement of legal certainty support an interpretation that a final decision to discontinue proceedings shall bar further prosecution in other Member States irrespective of whether the decision has been taken with or without assessment of the merits of the case. This interpretation of art 54 CISA does not ignore the

---

132   Case C-398/12 *criminal proceedings against M* EU:C:2014:1057 para 16.

Member States' interest in effective criminal law enforcement, but relies on the assumption that this interest is served best by an effective coordination of criminal proceedings.[133] *Wolfgang Schomburg* has repeatedly stressed the need for coordination of parallel proceedings and its repercussions on the transnational dimension of the *ne bis in idem* principle.[134] If, however, Member States fail to perform their coordination tasks,[135] it seems neither appropriate nor legitimate to let the individual bear the consequences and to subject him to the burden of new criminal proceedings.[136]

---

133 See also Case C-129/14 *Spasic* EU:C:2014:586 para 66.

134 Wolfgang Schomburg 'Konkurrierende nationale und internationale Strafgerichtsbarkeit' in Jörg Arnold, Björn Burkhardt, Walter Gropp, Günter Heine, Hans-Georg Koch, Otto Lagodny, Walter Perron, Susanne Walther (eds) *Menschengerechtes Strafrecht – Festschrift für Albin Eser zum 70. Geburtstag* (Beck 2005) 829, 843; 'Criminal matters: transnational ne bis in idem in Europe – conflict of jurisdictions – transfer of proceedings' [2012] 13 ERA-Forum 311, 320 ff.

135 See in this regard art 5 ff Framework Decision 2009/948/JHA of 30 November 2009 on prevention and settlement of conflicts of exercise of jurisdiction in criminal proceedings OJ L 328/42.

136 See also with regard to the "execution condition" in art 54 CISA ("provided that, if a penalty has been imposed, it has been enforced, is actually in the process of being enforced or can no longer be enforced under the laws of the sentencing Contracting Party."): Wolfgang Schomburg, Irene Suominen-Picht 'Verbot der mehrfachen Strafverfolgung, Kompetenzkonflikte und Verfahrenstransfer' 65 [2012] Neue Juristische Wochenschrift 1190, 1191; see, however, Case C-129/14 *Spasic* EU:C:2014:586 para 51 ff, 74; for a critical assessment of the Court's reasoning see Martin Böse 'Einschränkungen des transnationalen ne bis in idem – notwendiges Korrektiv oder Anachronismus?' in Gudrun Hochmayr (n 2) 171, 173 ff; Frank Meyer 'Transnationaler ne-bis-in-idem-Schutz nach der GRC – zum Fortbestand des Vollstreckungselements aus Sicht des EuGH' 15 [2014] Höchstrichterliche Rechtsprechung zum Strafrecht 269, 270 ff.

CHAPTER 4

"The Global Panopticon": Mass Surveillance and Data Privacy Intrusion as a Crime against Humanity?

Michael Bohlander

Abstract

This paper will argue that data collection and (ab-)use these days are endemic and occur in a widespread and systematic manner and more often than not based on the policy of governments or – increasingly – of big multinational IT companies and networks such as Google, Facebook etc. It will posit that they affect mainly civilians on a grand scale, whether for discriminatory reasons or simply indiscriminately, and have the potential for seriously violating some fundamental human rights, namely the rights to privacy and as a knock-on effect, the rights to freedom of speech and freedom of belief. The practice of such wholesale data gathering has thus all the hallmarks for being a contender to a new category of crime against humanity (CAH). Traditionally, CAH and other international crimes have been focussing either on, firstly, distinct violations of certain rules applicable to the conduct of armed hostilities, or, secondly, on physical or mental harm or damage, i.e. violations of the body, the mind or of property in the wider sense, as the basis for criminal liability, even if the means used to bring about such consequences are situated in cyber space, i.e. through cyber warfare. Most often, those two categories overlap to a large extent but not necessarily, since some of the rules of warfare are intended to provide for a degree of control over the conduct of military actions purely in the interest of allowing for the chance of a resumption of peaceful relations between the parties after a conflict has ended, and

---

* International Co-Investigating Judge, Extraordinary Chambers in the Courts of Cambodia (ECCC); Judge, Kosovo Specialist Chambers; Chair in Comparative and International Criminal Law, Durham Law School (UK). The views expressed are solely those of the author and do not represent the opinion of the United Nations, the ECCC, the Royal Government of the Kingdom of Cambodia, EULEX or the Kosovo Specialist Chambers. – The author would like to thank Otto Lagodny, Phillip Louis Weiner, and Caroline Fournet for comments on an earlier draft. All remaining errors are the author's. All webpages cited were last accessed on 12 April 2017, the date this chapter was finished.

hence of maintaining a minimum standard of humane conditions during such conflicts, if that can be said to be a realistic option at all. The protection of the symbols of the Red Cross and Red Crescent is one example. However, with the rapid development of information technology and its virtually unchecked use for unilateral or multilateral intelligence gathering purposes by many governments and major corporations, a new victim may finally have appeared on the scene, namely the above-mentioned bundle of fundamental political rights, the free exercise of which is a non-negotiable and crucial component of the democratic process. In other words, the violation of these rights may no longer be a mere tool in order to violate the traditional target rights related to physical and mental well-being, but represent a violation of a distinct new target right in and of itself.

∴

> And do not fear those who kill the body but cannot kill the soul. Rather fear him who can destroy both soul and body in hell.
> MATTHEW 10:28[1]

∴

> Visibility is a trap.
> MICHEL FOUCAULT, Discipline and Punish, 1975

∴

> The Court, being aware of the danger such a law poses of undermining or even destroying democracy on the ground of defending it, affirms that the Contracting States may not, in the name of the struggle against espionage and terrorism, adopt whatever measures they deem appropriate.
> European Court of Human Rights, Klass & others v Germany, para. 49, 1978

∴

---

[1] English Standard Version.

"Fear Eats the Soul"[2]

The Gospel of St Matthew warned people not to get their priorities wrong: The soul was considered more important than the body and hence they should fear God more than men, for he was the only one who could also destroy man's soul. However, about two millennia later it seems God is facing serious competition in that department. George Orwell's "1984" and many similar accounts published since the last century, as well as state regimes based on the exploitation of such ideas, have shown that Man is capable of destroying, or at the very least seriously crippling, the soul of his fellow human beings by making them afraid of the consequences of saying what they think. If such a regime of fear goes on long enough and is supported by sufficiently negative stimuli in the case of non-compliance, the vast majority of us will begin to suffer from a Pavlov reflex and become conditioned to not even think what we think.[3] One powerful negative stimulus is provided by making sure that any and all relevant data about each and every one of us are known to those who (a) have a major political or economic stake in what we think, as well as (b) the political or economic power to enforce their own position.

In the early years of this century, the activities of the American NSA and its British sister organisation GCHQ – like those of their counterparts of every ideological shade across the globe – in their "war on terror" have made it amply evident that they are capable of creating a culture of fear even among those who do not engage in any sort of terrorism-related activities. The 2016 UK Tory Government's Investigatory Powers Act, also called a "Snooper's Charter",[4] is an expression of the lengths conservative governments in particular will go to in order to acquire a blanket power of bulk data acquisition unrelated to any specific allegations against the individuals whose data are being syphoned off, and their intention to do away with encryption protections.[5] Coupled with

---

[2] English translation of the title of the film *Angst essen Seele auf* by Rainer Werner Fassbinder, from 1974; see http://www.imdb.com/title/tt0071141/.

[3] On the self-censoring effect on our understanding of privacy in the new digital age, see my Blood Music on Darwin's Radio – Musings on social network data transparency, cyborg technology, science fiction and the future perception of human rights, 2013 Global Community Yearbook of International Law and Jurisprudence, 2014, 45–64.

[4] Text at www.legislation.gov.uk/ukpga/2016/25/contents/enacted.

[5] See for the UK the criticism by Apple CEO Tim Cook in The Guardian, 21 December 2015, *Apple calls on UK government to scale back snooper's charter* at www.theguardian.com/technology/2015/dec/21/apple-uk-government-snoopers-charter-investigatory-powers-bill;

their ability to deploy real-world instruments such as, for example, drones, the same powers who preach the water of the sacrosanct nature of human rights, democracy and the rule of law to others, drink the wine of the torture or extrajudicial killings of those they deem outside the sphere of effective human rights protection, by creating new or previously unknown classes of adversaries, for example, "enemy combatants",[6] or by considering a separate criminal law for them, the so-called *Feindstrafrecht* or "criminal law of the enemy".[7]

The ancient ideal of open democracy is increasingly in danger of succumbing to the stifling overgrowth of executive control of sensitive knowledge about the very foundations of our society, something the Germans call *Herrschaftswissen*, a concept that has been translated as "hegemonic knowledge",[8] and which is seen as unfit for undiluted consumption by the wider body politic, mostly on the basis that such knowledge would harm the national security and endanger public peace.[9] The report of 23 September 2014 of the UN Special Rapporteur on the promotion and protection of human rights and fundamental freedoms while countering terrorism states:

> The States engaging in mass surveillance have so far failed to provide a detailed and evidence-based public justification for its necessity [...]. Viewed from the perspective of article 17 of the Covenant, this comes close to derogating from the right to privacy altogether in relation to digital communications. For all these reasons, mass surveillance of digital content and communications data presents a serious challenge to an established norm of international law. [...] [T]he very existence of mass

---

and www.computerworlduk.com/news/security/tim-cook-says-there-isnt-a-trade-off-bet ween-security-and-privacy-3632367/ and for the US the recent dispute between the FBI and Apple the references at www.computerworlduk.com/galleries/security/apple -vs-fbi-in-quotes-bill-gates-google-microsoft-edward-snowden-3635572/#2.

6   See www.cfr.org/international-law/enemy-combatants/p5312.
7   In Germany, for example, the main proponent of this concept is Günther Jakobs; see his "Zur Theorie des Feindstrafrechts" in Henning Rosenau/Sanyun Kim (eds), *Straftheorie und Strafgerechtigkeit*, Augsburger Studien zum Internationalen Recht, 2010, vol. 7, 167–182; an English translation is available online at www.lawlib.utoronto.ca/bclc/crim web/foundation/Dubber%20Appendix%20D.PDF.
8   Translation suggested at www.passagen.at/cms/index.php?id=94&L=1.
9   The German Home Secretary de Maizière stated in November 2015 that making public some of the reasons for cancelling an international football game in Hannover due to an alleged terrorist threat would "disturb" (*verunsichern*) the public; see Stefan Kuzmany, Der Spiegel, 18 November 2015, *Was wir nicht wissen wollen*, at www.spiegel.de/politik/ deutschland/de-maiziere-zu-laenderspiel-absage-wuerde-die-bevoelkerung-verunsi chern-a-1063439.html.

surveillance programmes constitutes a potentially disproportionate interference with the right to privacy. Shortly put, it is incompatible with existing concepts of privacy for States to collect all communications or metadata all the time indiscriminately.[10]

Democracy as a principle ceases to function as soon and inasmuch as the same information is not available to all participants to the discussion – not mentioning their ability to properly digest information of varying degrees of complexity. That was in principle always the case and to that extent, the democratic ideal was always a fragile concept tinged with a *soupçon* of also being an illusion. However, in our age of globalisation the interconnectedness of geopolitical interests, whether parallel or antagonistic, and the unprecedented and steadily increasing power of data processing systems together with the ensuing potential for the widespread and systematic repression, distortion or for any other form of abuse of information concentrated in the hands of a very few people, the ideal is in danger of being absorbed by the *real-politik* cynicism of the powerful on the one hand, and by the increasing aggressiveness in the reactions of the powerless[11] borne of the realisation that all the "democracy-speak" may just have been another "opium for the masses", on the other. The rise since 2010 of unabashedly public populist right-wing politics in Europe, the USA, Russia, Turkey etc. are a symptom of that danger. As I pointed out elsewhere,[12] however, the vast majority of individual data owners are increasingly guilty of contributory negligence by making a mass of sometimes intimate data available freely on social media platforms etc. The combined impact of the above-mentioned data "feeding frenzy", the smorgasbord of data often voluntarily offered by the users of social networks and the apparent increasing disinterest in political engagement and activism among the general population have yet to be fully studied.

This paper will argue that data collection and (ab-)use these days[13] are endemic and occur in a widespread and systematic manner and more often than not based on the policy of governments or – increasingly – of big multinational IT companies and networks such as Google, Facebook etc.[14] It will posit that

---

10   UN Doc. No. A/69/397 at para 18.
11   See the rise of activist groups such as Occupy, ATTAC, or PEGIDA.
12   See above (n. 3).
13   In fact, latest data show that the practice had already been well established in the 1990s at least for the GCHQ; see The Guardian, 21 April 2016, *UK spy agencies have collected bulk personal data since 1990s, files show* at http://gu.com/p/4tfde?CMP=Share_iOSApp_Other.
14   See on the interplay between data gathering by Facebook and governmental intrusion through the lens of a spiral of silence, Elizabeth Stoycheff, *Under Surveillance: Examining*

they affect mainly civilians on a grand scale, whether for discriminatory reasons or simply indiscriminately, and have the potential for seriously violating some fundamental human rights, namely the rights to privacy and as a knock-on effect, the rights to freedom of speech and freedom of belief.[15] The practice of such wholesale data gathering should thus have all the hallmarks for being a contender to a new category of crime against humanity (CAH). Traditionally, CAH and other international crimes have been focussing either on, firstly, distinct violations of certain rules applicable to the conduct of armed hostilities, or, secondly, on physical or mental harm or damage, i.e. violations of the body, the mind or of property in the wider sense, as the basis for criminal liability, even if the means used to bring about such consequences are situated in cyber space, i.e. through cyber warfare.

Most often, those two categories overlap to a large extent but not necessarily, since some of the rules of warfare are intended to provide for a degree of control over the conduct of military actions purely in the interest of allowing for the chance of a resumption of peaceful relations between the parties after a conflict has ended. Hence there is a need of maintaining a minimum standard of humane conditions during such conflicts, if that can be said to be a realistic option at all. The protection of the symbols of the Red Cross and Red Crescent may be seen as one example. However, with the rapid development of information technology and its virtually unchecked use for unilateral or multilateral intelligence gathering purposes by many governments and major corporations, a new victim may finally have appeared on the scene, namely the above-mentioned bundle of fundamental political rights, the free exercise of which is a non-negotiable and crucial component of the democratic process.

In other words, the violation of these rights may no longer be a mere tool in order to violate the traditional target rights related to physical and mental well-being, but represent a violation of a distinct new target right in and of itself. It is apposite to state at this point that the effects on the traditional and the new target rights do not exclude each other: It may still be feasible to construct a violation of physical or mental well-being as an unavoidable and/or foreseeable consequence of rampant intelligence gathering and use of

---

Facebook's Spiral of Silence Effects in the Wake of NSA Internet Monitoring, (2016) 93 Journalism and Mass Communication Quarterly, 296–311.

15 See for the worsening trend the article by Timothy Garton Ash in The Guardian, 12 May 2016, *Free speech is under attack, from Beijing to Istanbul*, http://gu.com/p/4j6xq?CMP=Share_iOSApp_Other.

information obtained in that way. Analysed through the Foucauldian lens of hidden technologies of governmentality, their seriousness will be exposed.

The Development of Government and Business Information Politics on Data Collection, Storage, Use and Sharing

The recent NSA and GCHQ scandals and the related Snowden affair have brought it to the wider public's attention that for years a data gathering campaign by national intelligence services on an unprecedented scale has been progressing in the shadows. The report by Ben Emmerson, the UN Special Rapporteur on the promotion and protection of human rights and fundamental freedoms while countering terrorism sets out in detail the nature and magnitude of these mass surveillance efforts.[16] They are well-known thanks to the efforts of a few insider whistle-blowers such as Snowden and dedicated fearless journalists, and thus need no closer description here. The justification for all of these intrusions into individuals' privacy is the war against terror and organised crime and the professed need to have such sweeping powers to counter the IT capacities of the terrorists and organised criminals.

There is little doubt that there is a conflict on the national and the international stages between the proponents of a judicially protected rights-based approach versus the parliamentary and governmental supporters of an executive-effectiveness-driven stance. The problem increases in states with a strong conservative governing party and a weak or non-existing liberal opposition; in this context, the recent rise in nationalistic and right-wing parties and governments in Europe and the United States must cause more than political unease. The UN Human Rights Council in its Resolution 28/16 of 24 March 2015,[17] which established the office of the UN Special Rapporteur on the right to privacy, and guided by General Assembly Resolution 69/166,[18] expressed its deep concerns over the threats caused by modern data technology and the largely uncontrolled uses it can be put to, and it chose to lay down a few policy ground rules for the way forward. The Council stated that it

> [r]eaffirms the right to privacy, according to which no one shall be subjected to arbitrary or unlawful interference with his or her privacy, family,

---

16   UN Doc. No. A/69/397 at paras 20 ff.
17   UN Doc. No. A/HRC/28/L.27, p. 3.
18   UN Doc. No. A/69/166.

> home or correspondence, and the right to the protection of the law against such interference, as set out in article 12 of the Universal Declaration of Human Rights and article 17 of the International Covenant on Civil and Political Rights;
> *Recognizes* the global and open nature of the Internet and the rapid advancement in information and communications technology as a driving force in accelerating progress towards development in its various forms;
> *Affirms* that the same rights that people have offline must also be protected online, including the right to privacy [...][19]

The first report by the newly installed Special Rapporteur of 8 March 2016[20] contained the following conclusions:[21]

> The tensions between security, corporate business models and privacy continue to take centre stage but the last twelve months have been marked by contradictory indicators: some governments have continued [...] to take privacy-hostile attitudes while courts world-wide [...] have struck clear blows in favour of privacy and especially against disproportionate, privacy-intrusive measures such as mass surveillance or breaking of encryption.
> There are strong indicators that Privacy has become an important commercial consideration with some major vendors adopting it as a selling point. If there is a market for privacy, market forces will provide for that market. [...] [C]onsumers world-wide are increasingly aware of risks to their privacy and the fact that they will increasingly choose privacy-friendly products and services over ones which are privacy-neutral or privacy-unfriendly;
> While some governments continue with ill-conceived, ill-advised, ill-judged, ill-timed and occasionally ill-mannered attempts to legitimise or otherwise hang on to disproportionate, unjustifiable privacy-intrusive measures such as bulk collection, bulk hacking, warrantless interception etc. other governments led, in this case by the Netherlands and the USA have moved more openly towards a policy of no back doors to encryption. [...]

---

19 UN Doc. No. A/HRC/28/L.27, 3.
20 Report of the Special Rapporteur on the right to privacy, Joseph A. Cannataci, UN Doc. No. A/HRC/31/64 (advance unedited version).
21 Ibid., at paras 48–52.

However, the 2016 litigation[22] in the United States based on the 1789 *All Writs Act*[23] concerning the FBI's request that Apple provide it with a backdoor software for its iPhone, and President Obama's remarks[24] about the justifiability of that request in principle – which he evidently even extended to the question of mere tax evasion[25] – puts a question mark over the practical implementation of this policy, at least by the US.

Government Intrusion

Government intrusion has reached international courts several times in recent decades. Data surveillance issues are not merely a matter for the domain of

---

22 Judge Orenstein, US District Court, Eastern District of New York, *In re Order Requiring Apple, Inc. to Assist in the Execution of a Search Warrant Issued by this Court*, Memorandum and Order of 29 February 2016, Docket no. 15-MC-1902 (JO) – available online at www.eff.org/.../applebrooklyn-2.29.16order.pdf. – Judge Orenstein denied the FBI's motion and held at p. 49 of the order: "How best to balance those interests is a matter of critical importance to our society, and the need for an answer becomes more pressing daily, as the tide of technological advance flows ever farther past the boundaries of what seemed possible even a few decades ago. But that debate must happen today, and it must take place among legislators who are equipped to consider the technological and cultural realities of a world their predecessors could not begin to conceive. It would betray our constitutional heritage and our people's claim to democratic governance for a judge to pretend that our Founders already had that debate, and ended it, in 1789." Judge Orenstein had already rejected an *ex parte* application by the FBI earlier in 2015; see *In re Order Requiring Apple, Inc. to Assist in the Execution of a Search Warrant Issued by this Court*, 2015 WL 5920207 (E.D.N.Y. Oct. 9, 2015). – The Central District Court of California had, however, entered an *ex parte* order against Apple on 16 February 2016 "to perform even more burdensome and involved engineering than that sought in the case currently before this Court – *i.e.*, to create and load Apple-signed software onto the subject iPhone device to circumvent the security and anti-tampering features of the device in order to enable the government to hack the passcode to obtain access to the protected data contained therein". See *In the Matter of the Search of an Apple iPhone Seized During the Execution of a Search Warrant on a Black Lexus IS300, California License Plate 35KGD203*, No. ED 15–0451M) (the "*California*" action), Order Compelling Apple, Inc. to Assist Agents in Search (C.D. Cal. Feb. 16, 2016).
23 28 U.S.C. § 1651(a) as amended on 24 May 1949 reads: "The Supreme Court and all courts established by Act of Congress may issue all writs necessary or appropriate in aid of their respective jurisdictions and agreeable to the usages and principles of law."
24 See Philip Elmer-DeWitt, *Here's What Obama Said at SXSW About Apple vs. FBI*, 12 March 2016, at http://fortune.com/2016/03/12/obama-sxsw-apple-vs-fbi/.
25 He said: "What mechanisms do we have available that even do simple things like tax enforcement? Because if in fact you can't crack that at all, and government can't get in, then everybody's walking around with a Swiss bank account in their pocket. So there has to be some concession to the need to be able to get to that information somehow." – ibid.

human rights courts proper, but have found their way into the wider application of EU law, for example. We will look only at some of the most recent cases to illustrate the problem for our purposes. Though not mainly a human rights court, the Court of Justice of the European Union (CJEU) in the case of *Digital Rights Ireland* declared an EU Directive on data retention to be in violation of EU law on 8 April 2014 (see also below on the domestic fate of the German law implementing the Directive).[26] Referring to the related CJEU case of *Schrems*[27] and the ECtHR case of *Zakharov*,[28] UN Special Rapporteur Cannataci, in addition to the statements from his report excerpted above, pointed out[29] two fundamental passages of their holdings, namely that in *Schrems* the CJEU stated, at para. 94,

> [i]n particular, legislation permitting the public authorities to have access on a generalised basis to the content of electronic communications must be regarded as *compromising the essence* of the fundamental right to respect for private life, as guaranteed by Article 7 of the Charter" [emphasis added],

and in *Zakharov,* at para. 270, the ECtHR opined that

> [t]he Court considers that the manner in which the system of secret surveillance operates in Russia gives the security services and the police technical means to circumvent the authorisation procedure and to intercept any communications without obtaining prior judicial authorisation. Although the possibility of improper action by a dishonest, negligent or over-zealous official can never be completely ruled out whatever the system [...], the Court considers that a system, such as the Russian one, which enables the secret services and the police to intercept directly the communications of each and every citizen without requiring them to show an interception authorisation to the communications service provider, or to anyone else, is particularly prone to abuse. The *need for*

---

26   Cases C-293/12 and C-594/12 – online at http://curia.europa.eu/juris/documents.jsf?num=C-293/12.

27   Case C-362/14 – online at http://eur-lex.europa.eu/legal-content/EN/TXT/?uri=CELEX:62014CJ0362.

28   Application 47143/06 – online at http://hudoc.ECHR.coe.int/eng?i=001-159324.

29   A/HRC/31/64 at paras 32 and 37.

safeguards against arbitrariness and abuse appears therefore to be particularly great [emphasis added].[30]

On 12 January 2016, the ECtHR consolidated its stance in *Szabó and Vissy v Hungary*[31] and criticised the absence of meaningful[32] judicial control of the intelligence operations, and especially the fact that a politically appointed government minister as the head of the relevant branch of the executive made the decision permitting the surveillance measures. The Court said – at para. 53 – that the mere existence of the relevant domestic legislation involved a menace which struck at the freedom of communication between users of the postal and telecommunication services. Citing the technological advances since the *Klass and Others* case[33] from 1978, it held that "the potential interferences with email, mobile phone and Internet services as well as those of mass surveillance attract the Convention protection of private life even more acutely". It added that "[i]n the face of this progress the Court must scrutinise the question as to whether the development of surveillance methods ... has been accompanied by a simultaneous development of legal safeguards...".[34] It was clearly not impressed by the Hungarian government's arguments, stating that "the possibility occurring on the side of Governments to acquire a detailed profile ... of the most intimate aspects of citizens' lives may result in particularly invasive interferences with private life. ... The guarantees required by the extant

---

30   In this context it is revealing that the former head of the German Intelligence Service, the *Bundesnachrichtendienst* (BND), Gerhard Schindler, told a parliamentary commission of inquiry that the BND's division for "technical intelligence" (*technische Aufklärung*) had used the NSA selectors provided to them with almost no effort at scrutiny as to their lawfulness under German law, and that the division had moved "beyond control". He had, before his dismissal, taken the unprecedented step of tasking a private consultants firm, Roland Berger, with examining the processes in the division and making recommendations for their improvement. See Tagesschau, 12 May 2016, *BND engagiert Beraterfirma Roland Berger* at www.tagesschau.de/inland/bnd-307.html. The Federal Data Protection Ombudsperson, Andrea Voßhoff, had declared the BND's surveillance practices as unconstitutional in February 2016. See Georg Mascolo, Tagesschau, 24 February 2016, *Abhörpraxis des BND "nicht verfassungskonform"* at www.tagesschau.de/inland/datenschutz-bnd-abhoerpraxis-101.html.

31   Application no. 37138/14, Judgment of 12 January 2016 – A request for referral to the Grand Chamber was pending at the time of writing.

32   The question is, of course, whether there can ever be any meaningful judicial control when the only source of information is the very same over which the control is to be exercised.

33   *Klass and Others v. Germany*, 6 September 1978, Series A no. 28.

34   See above (n 31), at para 68.

Convention case-law on interceptions need to be enhanced [...]. However, it is not warranted to embark on this matter in the present case, *since the Hungarian system of safeguards appears to fall short even of the previously existing principles*" [emphasis added].[35] Referring to the standards required for allowing such highly intrusive measures, the ECtHR reminded Hungary of the need for a strict interpretation of the principle of necessity.[36] The Court made very plain its disdain for the political executive option that had been chosen.[37] It held as a conclusion, that a violation of Article 8 ECHR had occurred, "[g]iven that the scope of the measures could include virtually anyone, that the ordering is taking place entirely within the realm of the executive and without an assessment of strict necessity, that new technologies enable the Government to intercept masses of data easily concerning even persons outside the original range of operation, and given the absence of any effective remedial measures, let alone judicial ones."[38]

---

35 ibid. at para 70.
36 ibid. at paras 73 to 75: "[...] given the particular character of the interference in question and the potential of cutting-edge surveillance technologies to invade citizens' privacy, [...] the requirement "necessary in a democratic society" must be interpreted in this context as requiring "strict necessity" in two aspects. A measure of secret surveillance can be found as being in compliance with the Convention only if it is strictly necessary [...] for the safeguarding the democratic institutions and, moreover, [...] for the obtaining of vital intelligence in an individual operation. ... A central issue common to both the stage of authorisation of surveillance measures and the one of their application is the absence of judicial supervision. The measures are authorised by the Minister in charge of justice upon a proposal from the executives of the relevant security services ... [*scil.* the TEK] ... which for its part, is a dedicated tactical department within the police force .... For the Court, this supervision, eminently political ... but carried out by the Minister of Justice who appears to be formally independent of both the TEK and of the Minister of Home Affairs ... is inherently incapable of ensuring the requisite assessment of strict necessity with regard to the aims and the means at stake."
37 ibid. at paras 76–77: "[Although] the Government's argument according to which a government minister is better positioned than a judge to authorise or supervise measures of secret surveillance [...] might be arguable from an operational standpoint, the Court is not convinced [...] when it comes to an analysis of the aims and means in terms of strict necessity. [T]he political nature of the authorisation and supervision increases the risk of abusive measures. ... For the Court, supervision by a politically responsible member of the executive, such as the Minister of Justice, does not provide the necessary guarantees."
38 ibid. at para 89. – Strong as that language may sound, the majority's final practical application of its principles was not enough for Judge Pinto de Albuquerque, who criticised his brethren in a separate but concurring opinion for departing from the supposedly greater stringency of the *Zakharov* test of the Grand Chamber regarding the degree of suspicion required before measures are authorised, and declared at its para. 35: "Yet while the tone

The Advocate General at the CJEU in his opinion of 19 July 2016 in a joint follow-up case on bulk data collection and retention to *Digital Rights Ireland*, namely *Tele2 Sverige AB et al.*,[39] while accepting that bulk collections and data retention regimes are in principle not incompatible with EU law, nonetheless argued that they needed to adhere to a closely circumscribed set of protective criteria. In particular he took the standard set by *Digital Rights Ireland* on the serious level of infringement caused by data retention obligations on online service providers as self-evident and no longer in need of further elucidation[40] and any intrusion was not justified by "[...] the combating of ordinary offences and the smooth conduct of proceedings other than criminal proceedings [...]. The considerable risks that such obligations entail outweigh the benefits they offer in combating ordinary offences and in the conduct of proceedings other than criminal proceedings".[41]

Applying the principles of proportionality and strict necessity, he exhorted the national courts not to "simply verify the mere utility of general data retention obligations, but rigorously verify that no other measure or combination of measures, such as a targeted data retention obligation accompanied by other investigatory tools, can be as effectiveness [sic!] in the fight against serious crime."[42]

---

is right, the substance of the judgment risks failing to allay entirely the serious dangers for citizens' privacy, the rule of law and democracy resulting from such a legal framework. Worse still, the choices made by the Chamber introduce a strong dissonant note in the Court's case-law. Paragraph 71 of the judgment departs clearly from paragraphs 260, 262 and 263 of *Roman Zakharov* and paragraph 51 of *Iordachi and Others v. Moldova*, since the Chamber uses a vague, anodyne, unqualified "individual suspicion" to apply the secret intelligence gathering measure, while the Grand Chamber uses the precise, demanding, qualified criterion of "reasonable suspicion". Judicial authorisation and review is watered down if coupled with the Chamber's ubiquitous criterion, because any kind of "suspicion" will suffice to launch the heavy artillery of State mass surveillance on citizens, with the evident risk of the judge becoming a mere rubber-stamper of the governmental social-control strategy. A ubiquitous "individual suspicion" equates to overall suspicion, i.e., to the irrelevance of the suspicion test at all. In practice, the Chamber condones *volenti nolenti* widespread, non-(reasonable) suspicion-based, "strategic surveillance" for the purposes of national security, in spite of the straightforward rebuke that this method of covert intelligence gathering for "national, military, economic or ecological security" purposes received from the Grand Chamber in *Roman Zakharov*. Only the intervention of the Grand Chamber will put things right again."

39   Cases C-203/15 and C 698/15, Opinion of 19 July 2016 – online at http://curia.europa.eu/juris/document/document.jsf?docid=181841&doclang=EN.
40   ibid at para 128.
41   ibid at para 172.
42   ibid at para 209.

He emphasised that empirical research had shown that the ubiquitous invocation of necessity in this context was far from justified.[43] He rejected the argument advanced by some parties, among them Germany, that a lack in protection under one part of the criteria could be made up for by a higher level of protection under others, the so-called "communicating vessels" approach; in his view, *all* criteria were mandatory minimum thresholds and could not be traded off against each other.[44] He was rather outspoken in his observations on the dangers of bulk data collection and data retention.[45]

The CJEU in its related judgment of 21 December 2016[46] affirmed its previous stance and followed the Advocate-General's critical view.[47] Under the

---

43   ibid.
44   ibid at para 244.
45   "The disadvantages of general data retention obligations arise from the fact that the vast majority of the data retained will relate to persons who will never be connected in any way with serious crime. [...] [I]n an individual context, a general data retention obligation will facilitate equally serious interference as targeted surveillance measures, including those which intercept the content of communications. Whilst the severity of such individual interference should not be underestimated [...] the specific risks engendered by a general data retention obligation become apparent in the context of 'mass' interference. [B]y contrast with targeted surveillance measures, a general data retention obligation is liable to facilitate [...] interference affecting a substantial portion, or even all of the relevant population. [T]he risks associated with access to communications data (or 'metadata') may be as great or even greater than those arising from access to the content of communications [...] 'metadata' facilitate the almost instantaneous cataloguing of entire populations, something which the content of communications does not. [T]here is nothing theoretical about the risks of abusive or illegal access to retained data. The risk of abusive access on the part of competent authorities must be put in the context of the extremely high number of requests for access [...] Tele2 Sverige has stated that it was receiving approximately 10,000 requests monthly, a figure that does not include requests received by other service providers operating in Sweden. In so far as the United Kingdom [...] is concerned, [...] an official report [...] records 517,236 authorisations and 55,346 urgent oral authorisations for 2014 alone. The risk of illegal access, on the part of any person, is as substantial as the existence of computerised databases is extensive." – Ibid., paras 252, 254–256, 259–260.
46   Joined Cases C-203/15 and C-698/15, Judgment of 21 December 2016 – online at http://eur-lex.europa.eu/legal-content/EN/TXT/?uri=CELEX:62015CJ0203.
47   Ibid. disposition after para. 134: "Article 15(1) of Directive 2002/58/EC [...], read in the light of Articles 7, 8 and 11 and Article 52(1) of the Charter of Fundamental Rights of the European Union, must be interpreted as precluding national legislation which, for the purpose of fighting crime, provides for general and indiscriminate retention of all traffic and location data of all subscribers and registered users relating to all means of electronic communication [and] [...] as precluding national legislation governing the protection and

regimes of the ECHR, arguably the most developed and sophisticated international human rights framework these days, and under the almost equally advanced CJEU jurisprudence, two systems that may be taken as indicative of the judicial attitude on the international level, major concerns exist about the current state of affairs and have, for example, been taken up as representative of the wider picture under general international law by the UN Special Rapporteur.

Non-state Actor Intrusion

The state sector is not the only actor in the massive use of data. The private sector is almost as voracious as the authorities in not only accumulating, but also commercialising data for private profit. Sometimes it acts on behalf of the government, sometimes for purely private purposes.[48] The actors range from internet companies and social media networks such as Google, Facebook and Twitter, to insurance companies, medical services and employers, who all desire access to the private data of their customers.

The Special Rapporteur, Ben Emmerson, had this to say in his 2014 report regarding the former:

> States increasingly rely on the private sector to facilitate digital surveillance. This is not confined to the enactment of mandatory data retention legislation. Corporates have also been directly complicit in operationalizing bulk access technology through the design of communications infrastructure that facilitates mass surveillance. Telecommunications and Internet service providers have been required to incorporate vulnerabilities into their technologies to ensure that they are wiretap-ready. The High Commissioner for Human Rights has characterized these practices

---

security of traffic and location data and, in particular, access of the competent national authorities to the retained data, where the objective pursued by that access, in the context of fighting crime, is not restricted solely to fighting serious crime, where access is not subject to prior review by a court or an independent administrative authority, and where there is no requirement that the data concerned should be retained within the European Union."

48   See, for example, The Guardian, 18 January 2017, *Home Office refuses to enforce privacy code on NHS staff using video* at www.theguardian.com/society/2017/jan/18/home-office-refuses-to-enforce-privacy-code-on-nhs-staff-using-video?CMP=Share_iOSApp_Other; and John Harris, The Guardian, 20 January 2017, *They call it fun, but the digital giants are turning workers into robots,* at www.theguardian.com/commentisfree/2017/jan/20/digital-giants-workers-robots-film-employee-monitoring-the-circle?CMP=Share_iOSApp_Other.

as "a delegation of law enforcement and quasi-judicial responsibilities to Internet intermediaries under the guise of self-regulation and cooperation" (see A/HRC/27/37, para. 42). The Special Rapporteur concurs with this assessment. In order to ensure that they do not become complicit in human rights violations, service providers should ensure that their operations comply with the Guiding Principles on Business and Human Rights, endorsed by the Human Rights Council in 2011[...].[49]

Special Rapporteur Cannataci in his three reports to the Human Rights Council[50] and the UN General Assembly[51] also addressed this matter, although he has so far put more of an emphasis on government-sponsored surveillance, where incidentally, he still held serious concerns and saw signs of evasiveness by some states and even attempts at dissuading him from looking into the matter too deeply.[52]

Microsoft in particular has an agenda of enabling the maximum amount of data sharing, as Mic Wright has described in a post[53] on MS Windows 10 of 29

---

[49] ibid at para 57. His more recent report of 22 February 2016 to the Human Rights Council – A/HRC/31/65 – primarily focussed on data issues in the context of the prevention of extremist violence, although at para. 39 he did voice a warning that the regulation of the internet discourse in the context of suppressing extremist propaganda may entail separate restrictions on the free debate of this vital agenda that may lead to researchers, journalists etc. being monitored for bona fide work and included in an overly broad definition of the topic.

[50] A/HRC/31/64 of 8 March 2016 and A/HRC/34/60 of 24 February 2017.

[51] A/71/368 of 30 August 2016.

[52] See A/HRC/34/60, for example, at paras 13, 19–29, 42.

[53] Mic Wright, The Next Web, 29 July 2015, *The Windows 10 privacy issues you should know about*, 29 July 2015, at https://thenextweb.com/microsoft/2015/07/29/wind-nos/#.tnw_SvgDxb9G: "[T]here are a few unsettling things nestling in there. [...] Microsoft has grabbed some very broad powers to collect things you do, say and create while using its software. Your data won't be staying on your computer, that much is for sure. [...] Sign into Windows with your Microsoft account and the operating system immediately syncs settings and data to the company's servers. That includes your browser history, favorites and the websites you currently have open as well as saved app, website and mobile hotspot passwords and Wi-Fi network names and passwords. You can deactivate that by hopping into the settings of Windows, but I'd argue that it should be opt-in rather than on by default. Many users won't get round to turning it off, even though they would probably want to. [...] Turn on Cortana, the virtual assistant, and you're also turning on a whole host of data sharing: To enable Cortana to provide personalized experiences and relevant suggestions, Microsoft collects and uses various types of data, such as your device location, data from your calendar, the apps you use, data from your emails and text messages, who

July 2015 in an illustration of what the individual average end user is up against. Anca Chirita, who advocates the innovative use of competition law to tackle private actors' handling of data, has recently tracked the privacy regimes of a number of providers and social media networks and found a wide variety of more or less unobtrusive mechanisms aimed at collecting data and sharing them as freely as possible with third parties.[54]

In essence, the use of data by non-state actors for commercial interests poses a similar, if not in the long run worse, threat as that conducted by the government. How do we move from the description of the overall situation to a legal characterisation as a CAH? We shall attempt to carve out some main criteria in the next section.

Transposing the Data Abuse Scenario into the International Law of Crimes against Humanity (CAH)

Finding a Violated Right

In the light of the grave and well-documented concerns held by both international courts and experts set out above, it should not be subject to serious debate that there is a – so far somewhat admittedly ill-defined – red line which is regularly being crossed by state and non-state actors when it comes to collecting private data. Traditionally, arising out of the historical development of

---

you call, your contacts and how often you interact with them on your device. Cortana also learns about you by collecting data about how you use your device and other Microsoft services, such as your music, alarm settings, whether the lock screen is on, what you view and purchase, your browse and Bing search history, and more." Lots of things can live in those two words "and more." Also note that because Cortana analyzes speech data, Microsoft collects "your voice input, as well as your name and nickname, your recent calendar events and the names of people in your appointments, and information about your contacts including names and nicknames." [...] Microsoft will collect information "from you and your devices, including for example 'app use data for apps that run on Windows' and 'data about the networks you connect to.'" [...] Windows 10 generates a unique advertising ID for each user on each device. That can be used by developers and ad networks to profile you. Again, you can turn this off in settings, but you need to know where to look: [...] Microsoft can disclose your data when it feels like it. This is the part you should be most concerned about: Microsoft's new privacy policy [...] is very loose when it comes to when it will or won't access and disclose your personal data."

54 Anca Chirita, The Rise of Big Data and the Loss of Privacy, in Mor Bakhoum, Beatriz Gallego Conde, Mark-Oliver Mackenordt & Gintare Surblyte. (eds.). *Personal Data in Competition, Consumer Protection and IP Law – Towards a Holistic Approach?* (Berlin/Heidelberg, Springer, 2017) – pre-publication pdf available at https://ssrn.com/abstract=2795992.

CAH and the related laws of armed conflict, the primary aim of the law on CAH had always been the protection against direct physical attacks on life and limb, personal liberty and property in one way or another. CAH, much like war crimes, attach liability to individuals and not to states. However, especially in the context of the CAH of persecution and other inhumane acts, inroads have over time been made into a wider understanding of rights that may be violated, including serious psychological harm.[55] Not least in the context of cyber warfare, it is not difficult to imagine that data abuse can also be used as an instrument for the purpose of violating any of the above-mentioned rights and interests. Given the international customary law's progressively disjunctive view of CAH and the need for them to be factually embedded in an armed conflict, it has long been recognised that they may be committed in peacetime as well; in fact, that is one of the major distinguishing features of CAH as opposed to the historically preceding concept of war crimes. That characteristic is what makes the idea of CAH such an appealing lens through which to interrogate the question of individual criminal responsibility for abuse of powers of or opportunities for data collection from private citizens and, again, possibly legal entities. These abuses happen often, or even mainly, in the absence of an armed conflict, although they may, of course, occur in the context of hostilities, too. However, the instrumental role of data abuse in the context of CAH is not what interests us here: The much more conceptually interesting question is whether the right to privacy as expounded in the above-mentioned decisions of international courts and reports of international experts can or should give rise to liability as a violation of a direct target right itself. When we are pursuing the question of whether privacy can be conceptualised as a new target right for CAH, this may take two forms: Firstly, inclusion as a target right in existing CAH such as persecution and other inhumane acts, secondly as a new category of CAH altogether.

It is immediately apparent that the inclusion into persecution seriously limits the reach of privacy as the target right, because persecution requires a discriminatory element, something which is almost by definition – albeit not necessarily – absent in the scenarios of indiscriminate surveillance and data collection. Other inhumane acts do not require this discriminatory element, yet their concept might seem too closely bound to – often subconsciously – emotionally charged equations to same-degree violations of the traditional protected interests of life and limb, personal liberty and mental harm; indeed,

---

[55] For an overview of the case law see Otto Triffterer/Kai Ambos, The Rome Statute of the International Criminal Court – A Commentary, 3rd ed., (C.H. Beck et al., Munich et al., 2016) (hereinafter Triffterer/Ambos), Art. 7 mn. 142.

as far as the law of the ICC is concerned, Art. 7(1)(k) ICC-Statute restricts the effect to an impact equating to serious physical or mental injury. Concerns have also been voiced about the specificity of the definition under customary international law from the point of view of the *nullum crimen* principle.[56]

Despite these limitations, it is nonetheless useful to look at the rights and protected interests that have so far been included under persecution in particular, because that CAH explicitly addresses an open-ended category of "fundamental rights". Persecution requires the intentional and severe deprivation of fundamental rights contrary to international law. The General Comment No. 24 of the UN Human Rights Committee from 1994[57] would seem to allow the conclusion that this category is certainly triggered when it comes to peremptory norms in the context of the ICCPR.[58] What is interesting for our discussion is the nature of the highlighted rights as civil and political rights, rather than rights to personal inviolability of body, mind or liberty. And while they are not listed in General Comment No. 24 because it deals with reservations to the ICCPR especially in the face of peremptory norms, Articles 17(1) and (2), 18(1) and (2) and 19(1) and (2) ICCPR would naturally qualify as foundations for a protection against mass surveillance practices, because their mention in the ICCPR squarely puts them in the bracket of fundamental rights under

---

56 See Kai Ambos, Treatise on International Criminal Law, vol. II, (OUP, 2014), (hereinafter Ambos, Treatise) 115 f. – There remains the added problem that in the exercise of charging or convicting for multiple legal characterisations based on the same facts, other inhumane acts may routinely be considered as a prime candidate for exclusion under the different-element test traditionally espoused by international criminal courts.

57 CCPR General Comment No. 24: Issues Relating to Reservations Made upon Ratification or Accession to the Covenant or the Optional Protocols thereto, or in Relation to Declarations under Article 41 of the Covenant *Adopted at the Fifty-second Session of the Human Rights Committee, on 4 November 1994, CCPR/C/21/Rev.1/Add.6, General Comment No. 24. (General Comments).*

58 ibid para 8: "Accordingly, provisions in the Covenant that represent customary international law (and a fortiori when they have the character of peremptory norms) may not be the subject of reservations. Accordingly, a State may not reserve the right to engage in slavery, to torture, to subject persons to cruel, inhuman or degrading treatment or punishment, to arbitrarily deprive persons of their lives, to arbitrarily arrest and detain persons, *to deny freedom of thought, conscience and religion,* to presume a person guilty unless he proves his innocence, to execute pregnant women or children, to permit the advocacy of national, racial or religious hatred, to deny to persons of marriageable age the right to marry, *or to deny to minorities the right to enjoy their own culture, profess their own religion, or use their own language.* And while reservations to particular clauses of article 14 may be acceptable, a general reservation to the right to a fair trial would not be [my emphasis]". – In the same sense Triffterer/Ambos, Art. 7 mn 142.

international law. All of those rights naturally are subject to a qualifying clause that allows encroachments for the sake of overriding public interests. Yet, the link between privacy, freedom of opinion and expression as well as freedom of thought, conscience and religion is strikingly obvious. Instances of recognition by international tribunals include social annex aspects to personal freedom such as freedom to exercise a profession, right to citizenship, participation in national life, or family life.[59] From there it is but a small step to think about the privacy rights as equating those already in the existing catalogue.

Demonstrating Equal Severity – A Foucauldian Perspective

One criterion that needs to be borne in mind when creating a new target right either within persecution or as a distinct CAH, is the equal severity element, i.e. that the new target right violation must be considered as equally serious as the classic ones, regarding life, limb, freedom and property, all of which are more or less directly linked to the body and the connected physical world. To many, this may not appear immediately obvious when talking about an abstract right such as privacy, which can be seen as a cluster of different aspects, of which data privacy seems even more abstract from the body than the traditional privacy aspects such as family life, (intimate) social interaction including sexual preferences, protection of one's home etc. It is helpful in this regard to analyse the issue of equal severity through the lens of Foucauldian discourse, and in particular his views on the hidden technologies of governmentality inherent in surveillance as an instrument of not merely collecting data as an end in itself, but of collecting them as a means to an end, a mere precursor to controlling the behaviour of their source, human beings, and thus their body (and soul), with the means of control being either external application in the guise of law enforcement, or worse, full internalisation by triggering a course of seemingly voluntary self-subjection by the very person from whose individual sphere the data are being culled, either by knowing alignment with the underlying political agenda ("I have nothing to hide") or through the subconscious acceptance of the hidden framework's agenda. The latter can be, and often is, hidden, for example, in workplace procedures based on state-sponsored policies or private commercial environments utilising the neo-liberal aim of objectification of the human, achieved through the adoption, as morally valuable, by the individual of the idea of self-responsibility for competitive striving to produce objectively measurable outputs.[60]

---

59   Triffterer/Ambos, ibid.
60   See for the developments in UK academia, with reference to the underyling general literature Rosalind Gill, Breaking the silence: The hidden injuries of neo-liberal academia, in

In his seminal work, *Discipline and Punish* – in its original French and in our context much more tellingly entitled *Surveiller et Punir* –, Michel Foucault argues that the corporal punishments of old have been replaced by a system which instead of physically afflicting the body subjects it to continuous and total monitoring, in order to control it and prevent deviant behaviour, and he takes as his prime example the rise of the prison system. In the chapter entitled "Panopticism"[61] in particular, he picks up on Bentham's[62] concept of the panopticon, i.e. a form of prison architecture consisting of individual cells assembled in an annular shape around a central tower from which each cell's inhabitant can be monitored at any given time without noticing himself that he is being watched. He traces the state's desire to monitor everyone as closely as possible back to states of public emergency, at the example of the plague:

> In order to make rights and laws function according to pure theory, the jurists place themselves in imagination in the state of nature; in order to see perfect disciplines functioning, rulers dreamt of the state of plague. Underlying disciplinary projects the image of the plague stands for all forms of confusion and disorder; just as the image of the leper, cut off from all human contact, underlies projects of exclusion.[63]

In essence, as is borne out by the current rhetoric of the counter-terrorism debate, Foucault posits that the public authorities are operating as much as possible on the basis of a continuous state of emergency, or "state of exception", as Giorgio Agamben would put it.[64] The ultimate aim of the Panopticon, just as

---

Róisin Ryan-Flood/Rosalind Gil. (eds.), *Secrecy and Silence in the Research Process: Feminist Reflections.* (London, Routledge, 2009). 228–244.

61 The chapter is available online in Race/Ethnicity: Multidisciplinary Global Contexts, Vol. 2, No. 1, The Dynamics of Race and Incarceration: Social Integration, Social Welfare, and Social Control, 1–12, Indiana University Press, at www.jstor.org/stable/25594995.

62 John Bowring (ed.), *The Works of Jeremy Bentham,* vol. 4 (Panopticon, Constitution, Colonies, Codification) [1843], available online at http://oll.libertyfund.org/titles/bentham-the-works-of-jeremy-bentham-vol-4.

63 ibid 4.

64 Giorgio Agamben, *State of Exception.* (Chicago, University of Chicago Press, 2005); for a critique see Stephen Humphreys, Legalizing Lawlessness: On Giorgio Agamben's State of Exception, EJIL (2006) 677–687. Malcolm Bull in his review *"States don't really mind their citizens dying (provided they don't all do it at once): they just don't like anyone else to kill them"* in the London Review of Books, vol. 26 no. 24, of 16 December 2014, 3–6, had this to say about Agamben's analysis: "We have moved from Athens to Auschwitz: the West's political model is now the concentration camp rather than the city state; we are no longer

much as that of data privacy intrusion, is the impression of constant visibility and flowing from that, the creation of self-monitoring by and a consequential adaptation of the person's behaviour:

> Hence the major effect of the Panopticon: to induce in the inmate a state of conscious and permanent visibility that assures the automatic functioning of power. So to arrange things that the surveillance is permanent in its effects, even if it is discontinuous in its action; that the perfection of power should tend to render its actual exercise unnecessary; [...], that the inmates should be caught up in a power situation of which they are themselves the bearers. To achieve this, it is at once too much and too little that the prisoner should be constantly observed by an inspector: too little, for what matters is that he knows himself to be observed; too much, because has no need in fact of being so. In view of this, Bentham laid down the principle that power should be visible and unverifiable. Visible: the inmate will constantly have before his eyes the tall outline of the central tower from which he is spied upon. Unverifiable: the inmate must never know whether he is being looked at at any one moment; but he must be sure that he may always be so.[65]

This behavioural adaptation, in Foucault's view, leads to a state of affairs where the object of the surveillance simultaneously becomes the subject of their own submission:

> He who is subjected to a field of visibility, and who knows it, assumes responsibility for the constraints of power; he makes them play spontaneously upon himself; he inscribes in himself the power relation in which he simultaneously plays both roles; he becomes the principle [*sic!*] of his own subjection. By this very fact, the external power may throw off its physical weight; it tends to the non-corporal; and, the more it approaches

---

citizens but detainees, distinguishable from the inmates of Guantanamo not by any difference in legal status, but only by the fact that we have not yet had the misfortune to be incarcerated – or unexpectedly executed by a missile from an unmanned aircraft....But although his recent examples come from the war on terror, the political development they represent is [...] part of a wider range in governance in which the rule of law is routinely displaced by the state of exception, or emergency, and people are increasingly subject to extra-judicial state violence."

65 ibid, 6.

this limit, the more constant, profound and permanent are its effects: it is a perpetual victory that avoids any physical confrontation and which is always decided in advance.[66]

Thomas McMullan, also based on Bentham's Panopticon, has succinctly explained the effect of present-day data intrusion.[67] Much more than the

---

[66] ibid, 7. – However, in the context of massive data privacy intrusion, a phenomenon he was unable to foresee in all its complexity in 1975, Foucault may have been somewhat too optimistic or theoretical in his views that the panopticon could also be opened up to scrutiny by the public and democratic control, when he said: "Furthermore, the arrangement of this machine is such that its enclosed nature does not preclude a permanent presence from the outside: we have seen that anyone may come and exercise in the central tower the functions of surveillance, that, this being the case, he can gain a clear idea of the way which the surveillance is practised. In fact, any panoptic institution, even if it is as rigorously closed as a penitentiary, can without difficulty be subjected to such irregular and constant inspections: and not only by the appointed inspectors, but by the public; any member of society will have the right to come and see with his own eyes how the schools, hospitals, factories, prisons function. There is no risk, therefore, that the increase of power created by the panoptic machine may degenerate into tyranny; the disciplinary mechanism will be democratically controlled, since it will be constantly accessible 'to the great tribunal committee of the world'. This Panopticon, subtly arranged so that an observer may observe, at a glance, so many different individuals, also enables everyone to come and observe any of the observers. The seeing machine was once a sort of dark room into which individuals spied; it has become a transparent building in which the exercise of power may be supervised by society as a whole." – ibid, 11. There is and always has been every indication that governments will not allow any meaningful outside interference or even scrutiny of the intelligence apparatus. Even ostensibly democratically established control mechanisms will have to rely on the assumption that the intelligence community will serve them with the full facts in any given case; they have no independent way of verifying the truthfulness of the intelligence actors nor of the truth of the information, and are unable to subject the security evaluations based on it and which they are being given to proper and independent scrutiny, because that requires expertise which only the intelligence service has and which it is unwilling to share. The societal othering scenario, which essentially underlies Foucault's writing in *Discipline and Punish*, is largely absent in the data privacy intrusion debate as such, where everyone is under surveillance by a very few, as opposed to the use of allegedly objectively gathered and reliable intelligence for the purpose of othering certain sections of society.

[67] See Thomas McMullan, The Guardian, 23 July 2015, *What does the panopticon mean in the age of digital surveillance?* at www.theguardian.com/technology/2015/jul/23/panopticon-digital-surveillance-jeremy-bentham, 23 July 2015: "In the private space of my personal browsing I do not feel exposed – I do not feel that my body of data is under surveillance because I do not know where that body begins or ends. We live so much of our lives online

references by McMullan to the line "[m]orals reformed – health preserved – industry invigorated", the following line from the preface written by Bentham is even more instructive for our purposes: "A new mode of obtaining power of mind over mind, in a quantity hitherto without example".[68] This hidden, in essence neo-liberal, *active* governmentality agenda is amplified in many instances by the *passive* response of the population, namely apathy or lack of awareness. For the UK environment, to take but one example, David Davis – who had actually been one of the persons challenging the previous UK intelligence law before the CJEU in the above-mentioned Case C-698/15 but had then removed himself from the case when he became a government minister under Theresa May – said, with maybe some exaggeration as to the unique position of the UK, "[i]n every other country in the world, post-Snowden, people are holding their government's feet to the fire on these issues, but in Britain we idly let this happen [...] Because for the past 200 years we haven't had a Stasi or a Gestapo, we are intellectually lazy about it, so it's an uphill battle",[69] while journalist Heather Brooke asserted that "[t]he spies have gone further than [George Orwell] could have imagined, creating in secret and without democratic authorisation the ultimate panopticon. Now they hope the British public

> [...] but feel nowhere near as much attachment for our data as we do for our bodies. Without physical ownership and without an explicit sense of exposure I do not normalise my actions. [...] My data, however, is under surveillance, not only by my government but also by corporations that make enormous amounts of money capitalising on it. [...][T]he amount of data on offer to governments and corporations is about to go through the roof, and as it does the panopticon may emerge as a model once more. Why? Because our bodies are about to be brought back into the mix. The [...] internet of things [...] will change digital surveillance substantially. With the advent of wider networked systems [...] everything [...] will soon be able to communicate, creating a [...] deluge of data [...] [which] won't only be passed back and forth between objects but will most likely wind its way towards corporate and government reservoirs. With everything from heart-rate monitors in smartwatches to GPS footwear, a bright light is once again being thrown on our bodies. [...] Much of the justification of this is the alleged benefits to health and wellbeing. "Morals reformed – health preserved – industry invigorated" – not Apple marketing material but Bentham's words on the panopticon. There may not be a central tower, but there will be communicating sensors in our most intimate objects."

68   John Bowring (ed.), The Works of Jeremy Bentham, vol. 4 (Panopticon, Constitution, Colonies, Codification) [1843], p. 39.

69   Andrew Sparrows, The Guardian, 8 November 2015, *David Davis: British 'intellectually lazy' about defending liberty*, at www.theguardian.com/politics/2015/nov/08/david-davis-liberty-draft-investigatory-powers-bill-holes.

will make it legitimate."[70] Telling in the context of the UK public's apparent lack of resistance and the above-mentioned allegation of being "intellectually lazy" with regard to governmental privacy intrusion is a survey published on 9 February 2015 on yougov.co.uk with the following questions and answers:[71]

The UK Investigatory Powers Tribunal (IPT) has just ruled that the UK intelligene agency GCHQ sharing information about UK citizens with America's National Security Agency did not comply with human rights and was unlawful Whatever your views about rights and wrongs, do you think it helped reduce terrorism?	
yes	49 %
no	27 %
don't know	24 %

a) Does it bother you that intelligence services could, if they wanted to, be spying on you right now? b) Do you think they are in fact spying on you personally in any way?	
a) Y b) Y	13 %
a) Y b) N	32 %
a) N b) Y	9 %
a) N b) N	44 %
Don't know	2 %

Would you allow a reality TV show to track you 24-hours a day for one month in return for £ 1,000?	
Yes	10 %
No	90 %

There are two things to be said about these questions, regardless of their statistical significance and reliability: Firstly, they are *vox populi* opinion questions on the lowest intellectual level, in fact almost relating more to moods or general feelings rather than the application of critical thinking, which may be indicative of the corresponding level of intellectual acumen expected and/or displayed of the respondent cohort, something especially highlighted by the Reality TV question, which disingenuously seems to suggest a similarity

---

70 Heather Brooke, The Guardian, 8 November 2015, *This snooper's charter makes George Orwell look lacking in vision*, at www.theguardian.com/commentisfree/2015/nov/08/surveillance-bill-snoopers-charter-george-orwell.

71 https://yougov.co.uk/news/2015/02/09/investigatory-powers-tribunal-intelligence-service/.

between such a scenario and mass surveillance by the state.[72] Secondly, the question in the top table cannot be answered without detailed knowledge of the actual threat scenario, which none of the respondents will have had; the only correct answer would have been "don't know"; furthermore it has a subliminal message that seems to say that human rights must take a backseat to security concerns. The fact that 49% of the respondents answered with "yes" shows a worrying tendency to believe the official narrative about the effectiveness of counter-terrorism measures more or less unquestioningly. Similarly, the fact that 53% of the respondents in the second table are simply not "bothered" by the prospect of being spied upon by intelligence services, regardless of whether they believe they are being spied upon now, does not bode well for the likelihood of any principled resistance to government intrusion into the personal data sphere. Here again, the neo-liberal incentive to make people adopt a seemingly self-chosen subservient attitude is demonstrated, exposing the governmental[73] technology of the "objective" public survey as a tool to reinforce a hidden governmentality aim, in that, firstly, the answer can be orchestrated to a large extent by the choice and wording of the questions. Secondly, the ostensibly "automatic" and non-manipulated – because merely mathematically calculated – survey result can then be deployed again as a supposedly objective means of verification of commonly shared societal morals and as an instrument of self-reassurance by the neo-liberal subject that she herself is conforming to expected and majority-validated patterns of thought and behaviour.

In sum, the violation of the right to data privacy is to all intents and purposes invariably intentional and, since it has all the potential for not only creating a passively suffered infringement of a protective shield of the person as a data subject, but much more for using the – mostly nebulous – awareness that the privacy veil is liable to be pierced at any given time as a mainly sub-conscious motivational driver to conform to hidden – and thus at best equally nebulously experienced – expectations transmitted by the governmentality frameworks of the day. Since these frameworks are multi-layered and can range from local city councils' petty use of CCTV cameras as a means of tracking people who discard litter in public spaces, over seemingly innocent commercial applications such as automatic number-plate recognition in car parks, to the more

---

72 It is open to question how the answers would have changed if the sum had been £ 10,000.
73 One of the founders and former Chief Executive Officer of YouGov is the Conservative MP Nadhim Zahawi; see Chris Tryhorn, The Guardian, 22 February 2010, *YouGov chief executive Nadhim Zahawi to stand down to run as Tory MP*, at www.theguardian.com/media/2010/feb/22/nadhim-zahawi-yougov-election-mp.

sinister technologies of counter-terrorism and immigration control as well as health-related commercial and employment applications, they produce an effect on the privacy subject that leads to a variated choice of mental and physical responses to actual situations in real life, and an overall wary reluctance to be a fully independent and actively contributing member of society. In other words, they create a fear that eats the soul. It should thus be accepted that massive data privacy intrusion has all the hallmarks of an equally severe violation of a fundamental right.

The Chapeau Elements

As with any CAH, there is the need for compliance with the chapeau elements of a widespread or systematic attack on a civilian population, of which the CAH would need to be a part. A nexus to an armed conflict is not necessary under customary international law. The attack need not be of a military character. Most of these elements would seem to be rather straightforward. Given the global, indiscriminate, intentional, planned and deliberate use by state and non-state actors, the attack – which can consist of the very act itself[74] – is both widespread and systematic, even if the framework of reference is reduced to one country or geo-political region. Regardless of whether a policy element is required or not under customary law,[75] the kind of data intrusion this paper is concerned with is hardly imaginable without such a policy – these are not isolated acts. The attack of mass data intrusion is almost in its entirety – apart from specific military espionage – directed against civilians. Considerably more thought needs to be spent on the nature of the acts underlying the attack. The ICC Statute's definition of attack refers to any of the acts mentioned under Art. 7(1), under customary law any multiplicity of acts of unlawful i.e. criminal interference with protected interests can suffice, and violence is not required.[76] Unless the discriminatory criteria for persecution are fulfilled and the violation of data privacy were to be interpreted as an infringement of a fundamental right of sufficiently equal severity, the ICC Statute, for example, would not appear to be able to accommodate violations of the fundamental right to data privacy as an underlying act that could be, or be connected to, an attack.

Whether under general international law the violation of data privacy is sufficiently criminalised at this time, is at best unclear. There is no convention-based international crime of violation of data privacy, and it is questionable

---

[74] Triffterer/Ambos, Art 7 mn 14.
[75] Triffterer/Ambos, Art 7 mn 109.
[76] Ambos, Treatise, vol. II, 58 f.

whether general customary law doctrine would allow the creation of a new category based on general principles in the criminal laws of individual states related to data protection – precisely because the states' laws will contain often rather broad-ranging public interest exception clauses. Even the *Proposed International Convention on the Prevention and Punishment of Crimes Against Humanity*[77] which might be seen as indicative of such an emerging consensus, does not foresee a residual clause that would make such a conclusion an easy one to draw. Its Art. 3 on the definition of the crime more or less tracks Art. 7 of the ICC Statute, hardly surprising given the need to find a platform on which most states would find it easy to support a Convention aimed at implementation in domestic law. Instead, the last paragraph of the Preamble makes a veiled reference to the idea of the Martens Clause.[78] That, of course, is not sufficient for establishing a fully-fledged CAH. As a matter of fact, the attitudes expressed over several sessions of the Sixth Committee by states to the ILC's Project on CAH[79] and collected by the proponents of the Convention, do not support a more hopeful picture. However, this finding – after what was said above in the context of the Foucauldian discussion – is hardly surprising: States prize the ability to monitor their citizens and other persons within their spheres if interest or influence, whether in the domestic or wider geo-political sense, to the largest degree possible; it is therefore unrealistic at best to expect them to subscribe to the creation of a basis of state practice that could reasonably be interpreted as giving rise to an individual liability of their chief agents under international criminal law, with penalties being almost exclusively long custodial sentences.

An example of the cautious approach even in developed international legal systems such as the EU is the recent *Regulation 2016/679 of 27 April 2016 on the protection of natural persons with regard to the processing of personal data and on the free movement of such data, and repealing Directive 95/46/EC (General Data Protection Regulation)*,[80] scheduled to apply from 25 May 2018,[81] which, to begin with, is not applicable to

---

[77] Text at http://law.wustl.edu/harris/cah/docs/EnglishTreatyFinal.pdf.

[78] ibid, 2. – see explanatory note 8 on p.3: "[...] that in cases not covered by the present Convention or by other international agreements, the human person remains under the protection and authority of the principles of international law derived from established customs, from the laws of humanity, and from the dictates of the public conscience, and continues to enjoy the fundamental rights that are recognized by international law [...]."

[79] http://law.wustl.edu/harris/crimesagainsthumanity/?p=1944.

[80] http://eur-lex.europa.eu/legal-content/EN/TXT/PDF/?uri=CELEX:32016R0679&from=EN.

[81] ibid, Article 99(2).

[...] competent authorities for the purposes of the prevention, investigation, detection or prosecution of criminal offences or the execution of criminal penalties, *including the safeguarding against and the prevention of threats to public security* [my emphasis],[82]

which eliminates the entire counter-terrorism and public policing aspect from its reach. After proscribing "administrative fines" of up to 20 million € or 4 % of the total worldwide turnover of the offending entity in Article 83, it states in Article 84 on penalties:

1. Member States shall lay down the rules on other penalties applicable to infringements of this Regulation in particular for infringements which are not subject to administrative fines pursuant to Article 83, and shall take all measures necessary to ensure that they are implemented. Such penalties shall be effective, proportionate and dissuasive.
2. Each Member State shall notify to the Commission the provisions of its law which it adopts pursuant to paragraph 1, by 25 May 2018 and, without delay, any subsequent amendment affecting them.

The central introductory recitals underlying Article 84 are at paras. 148–152. The latter states:

Where this Regulation does not harmonise administrative penalties or where necessary in other cases, for example in cases of serious infringements of this Regulation, *Member States should implement a system which provides for effective, proportionate and dissuasive penalties. The nature of such penalties, criminal or administrative, should be determined by Member State law* [my emphasis].

The Regulation in theory allows but does not explicitly mention imprisonment; the preference appears to be for financial sanctions. The financial penalties seem harsh but depending on the basis of the actual offence may not see the application of their maximum amounts very often; their financial impact may also be easily absorbed by the offending institution. In any event, it is a far cry between classification as a CAH and the imposition of mainly financial penalties, with a mere discretion of the EU Member States to use harsher means that attach to the person's body, i.e. imprisonment, and not their financial assets.

---

82   ibid, Article 2(1)(d).

Conclusion – Per Aspera ad Astra

In this paper, I have tried to interrogate the premise that we may need to move from a traditional understanding of the protected rights under international criminal law, especially in the context of CAH, to a 21st century paradigm. ICL still puts too much emphasis on the kind of harm that everyone can see and immediately relate to – threats to life, limb, liberty and property, with an emerging focus on sexual and gender-based violence.

However, there are rights which are in essence non-corporeal but the violation of which may cause equally tangible damage. The practice by governments and private actors of collecting vast amounts of data almost indiscriminately has, as the Foucauldian analysis in particular has shown, the potential for suppressing freedom of speech and belief, but also the distinct right to privacy, with a potency which equals that of the traditional target rights. The right to privacy has increasingly come to the forefront of public attention in law reform debates, centred mostly on the tropes of crime fighting and counter-terrorism efforts. This supposedly antagonistic relationship between individual freedom and control for the public – greater? – good makes for a formidable obstacle to finding a straightforward and timely solution.

Based on the assumption that despite a certain lack of sharp contours in the conceptual and terminological context, I posited that there has to be a "red line" on the level of international law when it comes to triggering the protection of (international) criminal law, all things being equal. An analysis of the current case law, however, has shown that any hope of an easy classification as a CAH – with the possible exception of the already existing crime of persecution – would seem to be unfounded. The sufficient degree of awareness that these days privacy may have become a right on a par with the traditional ones underlying CAH and war crimes has so far not materialised. Like any other law on the international level, international criminal law is made by states – that is, by those who, it might be said, are more part of the problem than of the solution. Yet, even in such an environment it is necessary to continue to speak truth to power and hope that, sometimes, the power of truth will eventually prevail.

CHAPTER 5

Environmental and Cultural Heritage Crimes: The Possibilities under the Rome Statute

Helen Brady and David Re

Abstract

This chapter examines the possibilities for prosecuting environmental and cultural heritage crimes under the Rome Statute. The ICC Prosecutor's 2016 Policy on Case Selection and Prioritisation refers to destruction of the environment as a factor the Prosecutor will consider in assessing the gravity of crimes when deciding whether to commence a prosecution. The chapter briefly traces the historical path from Nuremberg to the ICC of prosecuting environmental and cultural heritage crimes, including highlighting some missed opportunities. It outlines how cultural property and the environment have been legally protected under international humanitarian law and in international criminal law to date. It explores how such crimes could be prosecuted as war crimes, crimes against humanity, genocide and aggression (once the ICC has jurisdiction over that crime). For example, environmental crimes in international armed conflicts could be prosecuted as intentionally launching an attack knowing that it will cause widespread, long-term and severe damage to the environment. Other possibilities exist for charging damage to or destruction of the environment as war crimes in non-international and international armed conflicts. For crimes against humanity, destruction of the environment or cultural heritage could be a precursor to or the result of crimes against humanity such as forced transfer, persecution and inhumane acts. For genocide, environmental or cultural heritage damage could, in certain circumstances, be considered as acts in destroying a group in whole or in part. The chapter concludes that the ICC's jurisdiction over war crimes, crimes against humanity, genocide and, in the future, aggression offers potential to prosecute not only cultural property crimes but also environmentally-damaging or destructive crimes, and the Prosecutor's recent Case Selection Policy provides indications that this could transpire. It remains to be seen how and when, and in what circumstances.

---

* Helen Brady is the Senior Appeals Counsel and Head of the Appeals Section of the Office of the Prosecutor at the International Criminal Court. David Re is the Presiding Judge of the Trial Chamber at the Special Tribunal for Lebanon. The views expressed in this chapter are solely the co-authors' and should not be attributed to the Office of the Prosecutor or the International Criminal Court.

Introduction

Our cultural heritage and property has a special place in humanity's heart; it helps us to define who we are. Its protection has thus been recognised in international treaties and conventions for well over a century. This, however, has never stopped its targeting, damage and destruction in armed conflict, which of course continues to this day. If cultural property requires international criminal proscription against its damage and destruction, so too should the environment and other natural property. The former may indeed be vital for the mind and soul; but the latter is essential for our very physical integrity and survival. Both require protection.

Virtually all cultures have a connection with the natural environment that helps to define the cultural group. Our natural physical surroundings – hot or cold, dry or wet, mountainous, hilly or flat, coastal or inland, forest-covered or desert, icy or sandy, riverine, swampy or lake-filled, wilderness or farmland – all help define how we live and who we are. Many cultures have deep spiritual connections with specific environmental features. The natural or human influenced environment may be as culturally significant as objects of cultural property protected by international humanitarian law.[1] And yet, throughout the history of armed conflict the natural environment has suffered significant damage or destruction – either as an intended target or as an incidental quarry. Its targeting has been used as a weapon of war.

The principles of international humanitarian law evolved over many years, yet during this time there were countless missed opportunities to prosecute cultural heritage crimes. But the scarcity of international prosecutions for crimes against the environment is more striking.

The Rome Statute of the International Criminal Court (ICC) – regarded by many as the most up-to-date codification of international crimes – presents concrete opportunities to prosecute crimes against cultural property and crimes which damage or destroy the environment. The verdict and sentence in 2016 in the *Al Mahdi* case is the first example of a prosecution at the ICC related specifically to cultural property. The International Criminal Tribunal for the Former Yugoslavia (ICTY) tried similar charges. But apart from a

---

1   For example, it has been observed, "cultural monuments ... represent a common and irreplaceable heritage of all humankind. They serve as a defining link between us and our ancestry, and are essential to our identity." Further, "[w]ithout the protection of our cultural or religious patrimony the link with our heritage is severed, and with it is severed our ability to define our identity." Theodor Meron, 'The Protection of Cultural Property in the Event of Armed Conflict within the Case-Law of the International Criminal Tribunal for the Former Yugoslavia' (2005) 57/4 Museum International 41–60 at 56.

handful of post-World War II prosecutions, no cases have been brought before the modern international criminal courts or tribunals for environmental damage or destruction. The Rome Statute presents unique opportunities to rectify this. The rapid development of case-law on the principles of damage to cultural property at the ICTY, for example, shows how quickly the law can advance.

Crimes caused by or causing damage or destruction to the environment, the illegal exploitation of natural resources or illegal dispossession of land should attain a similar status in international criminal law to crimes against cultural property. However, until recently, the rapid evolution of international criminal law has not featured any real focus on environmental crimes.[2] This is despite the environmental degradation caused by instruments and methods of war such as landmines, cluster munitions, atomic bombs, chemical weapons, defoliation and deforestation. The ICC Prosecutor's 2016 case selection and prioritisation policy,[3] however, provides indications as to how charges involving environmental damage or destruction could be brought before the Court.

The ICC's mandate is limited to the crimes in the Rome Statute, which contains only one *express* reference to environmental crimes – as a war crime in an international armed conflict.[4] Despite this, damage to or destruction of the environment could potentially be prosecuted at the ICC as other war crimes or within genocide or crimes against humanity. This chapter explains how.

The Legal Protection of Cultural Property in War – A Brief Overview

A brief overview of the development, over more than a century, of the legal principles relating to the protection of cultural property demonstrates the slow but steady progression to their acceptance. The natural and human made environment are often inextricably linked, so the acceptance of principles protecting cultural property gives cause for optimism that protection of the environment will become an international norm within a much shorter period.

---

2 Steven Freeland, Addressing the Intentional Destruction of the Environment during Warfare under the Rome Statute of the International Criminal Court (Intersentia 2015), p. 35.
3 Case Selection and Prioritisation Policy, ICC Office of the Prosecutor, issued 15 September 2016, para 41. https://www.icc-cpi.int/itemsdocuments/20160915_otp-policy_case-selection_eng.pdf.
4 Rome Statute, Article 8 (2) (b) (iv). Similar provisions are in the Statute of the Iraqi Special Tribunal for Crimes against Humanity, 10 December 2003, art. 13 (b) (5) and the UN Transitional Administration in East Timor, Establishment of Panels with Exclusive Jurisdiction over Serious Criminal Offences, UNTAET Reg. 2000/15, 6 June 2000, s. 6 (1) (b) (iv).

The legal protection of cultural property during armed conflict has long been part of international humanitarian law. The 1863 Lieber Code, issued by President Abraham Lincoln and applicable to the United States military, specified that "Classical works of art, libraries, scientific collections, or precious instruments, such as astronomical telescopes, as well as hospitals, must be secured against all avoidable injury, even when they are contained in fortified places whilst besieged or bombarded".[5] The 1874 Brussels Declaration contained a similar provision.[6] The natural environment was not mentioned.

The 1907 Hague Regulations thereafter gave special protection to "buildings dedicated to religion, art, science, or charitable purposes, historic monuments, hospitals, and places where the sick and wounded are collected" and not used for military purposes.[7] But this did not spare such buildings during the military conflict that followed, especially in the First and Second World Wars. In fact,

---

5   General Orders No. 100: The Lieber Code, Instructions for the Government of Armies of the United States in the Field, (prepared by Francis Lieber, promulgated as General Orders No. 100 by President Lincoln, 24 April 1863), Article 35. Article 36 provides, "If such works of art, libraries, collections, or instruments belonging to a hostile nation or government, can be removed without injury, the ruler of the conquering state or nation may order them to be seized and removed for the benefit of the said nation. The ultimate ownership is to be settled by the ensuing treaty of peace. In no case shall they be sold or given away, if captured by the armies of the United States, nor shall they ever be privately appropriated, or wantonly destroyed or injured".

6   Project of an International Declaration concerning the Law and Customs of War (Brussels, 27 August 1874), Article 8 provides, "The property of municipalities, that of institutions dedicated to religion, charity and education, the arts and sciences even when State property, shall be treated as private property. All seizure or destruction of, or wilful damage to, institutions of this character, historic monuments, works of art and science should be made the subject of legal proceedings by the competent authorities". Under the heading: "Sieges and bombardments", Article 17 provides, "In such cases all necessary steps must be taken to spare, as far as possible, buildings dedicated to art, science, or charitable purposes, hospitals, and places where the sick and wounded are collected provided they are not being used at the time for military purposes. It is the duty of the besieged to indicate the presence of such buildings by distinctive and visible signs to be communicated to the enemy beforehand". The Declaration, a project of the Russian Czar, involving a conference of 15 European nations, was never ratified.

7   Convention (IV) respecting the Laws and Customs of War on Land and its annex: Regulations concerning the Laws and Customs of War on Land (The Hague, 18 October 1907). Article 27 provides, "In sieges and bombardments all necessary steps must be taken to spare, as far as possible, buildings dedicated to religion, art, science, or charitable purposes, historic monuments, hospitals, and places where the sick and wounded are collected, provided they are not being used at the time for military purposes. It is the duty of the besieged to indicate the presence of such buildings or places by distinctive and visible signs, which shall be notified to the enemy beforehand." Article 56. Provides, "The property of municipalities, that of

the Commission on Responsibility established at the 1919 Paris Peace Conference defined the "Wanton destruction of religious, charitable, educational, and historic buildings and monuments" as a war crime.[8] Between the wars, the 1935 Inter-American Washington (or Roerich Pact) also gave specific protection, stating that "historic monuments, museums, scientific, artistic, educational and cultural institutions shall be considered as neutral".[9] Some post World War II prosecutions reflected these protections.

The defendants in the 1946 Nuremberg International Military Tribunal (IMT) trial were charged with the plunder of public or private property under Article 6 (b) of the London Charter for crimes. The IMT's judgement detailed how the Nazis had looted private and public cultural property in the occupied Soviet Union and Poland, explaining how the policy was established with special emphasis on seizing material from Jews.[10] One defendant, Alfred Rosenberg, was found "responsible for a system of organized plunder of both public and private property throughout the invaded countries of Europe," found guilty of this as a war crime, and sentenced to death.[11] The judgement also referred to article 56 of the 1907 Hague Convention as a basis for the conviction.[12] In the *Hostages Trial*, General Lothar Rendulic was acquitted of causing

---

institutions dedicated to religion, charity and education, the arts and sciences, even when State property, shall be treated as private property. All seizure of, destruction or wilful damage done to institutions of this character, historic monuments, works of art and science, is forbidden, and should be made the subject of legal proceedings."

8   Commission on the Responsibility of the Authors of the War and on Enforcement of Penalties, Report presented to the Preliminary Peace Conference, March 29, 1919, Chapter II Violations of the laws and customs of war, category 20, reprinted in (1920) 14(1/2) American Journal of International Law 95–154 at 115.

9   Treaty on the Protection of Artistic and Scientific Institutions and Historic Monuments (Washington, April 15, 1935), Article 1.

10 Trial of the Major War Criminals before the International Military Tribunal Nuremberg 14 October 1945 to 1 October 1946, 1947, pp. 241–243; 22 IMT 203, 13 ILR 203.

11 He was also found guilty of committing crimes against the peace, and crimes against humanity. The judgement explained, at p. 241, "The Defendant Rosenberg was designated by Hitler on 29 January 1940 Head of the Center for National Socialist Ideological and Educational Research, and thereafter the organization known as the 'Einsatzstab Rosenberg' conducted its operations on a very great scale. Originally designed for the establishment of a research library, it developed into a project for the seizure of cultural treasures. On 1 March 1942 Hitler issued a further decree, authorizing Rosenberg to search libraries, lodges, and cultural establishments, to seize material from these establishments, as well as cultural treasures owned by Jews".

12 Trial of the Major War Criminals before the International Military Tribunal Nuremberg 14 October 1945 to 1 October 1946, 1947, p. 239; 22 IMT 203, 13 ILR 203.

damage to property, based on the Hague Convention, for pursuing a "scorched earth" policy in Norway.[13]

In 1954, following UNESCO's establishment, the Hague Convention for the Protection of Cultural Property in the Event of Armed Conflict, the main treaty regulating the protection of cultural property, was adopted.[14] The Convention defined cultural property well beyond buildings, obliged States to refrain from acts of hostility directed against cultural property and to abstain from using such property for military purposes, and urged State parties to criminalise breaches.[15] Its 1999 Second Protocol adds provisions to safeguard cultural property including preparatory measures in peacetime, fostering respect for cultural property, and employing precautionary measures in conflict.[16] But it too does not specifically mention the natural environment.

The two 1977 Additional Protocols to the Geneva Conventions of 1949 provided further protection to cultural property in wartime. Article 53 of Additional Protocol I, applicable in international armed conflicts – and headed "Protection of cultural objects and of places of worship" – prohibits acts of hostility directed against "the historic monuments, works of art or places of worship which constitute the cultural or spiritual heritage of peoples", using these objects in support of military effort and making such objects the object of reprisal.[17] Article 16 of Additional Protocol II, applicable in non-international armed conflict, contains a similar, although more limited prohibition and protection.[18] Additional Protocol I has some specific protections for protecting the "natural environment" that are not replicated in Additional Protocol II.

---

13   *Trial of Wilhelm List and Others (The Hostage Case)*, Judgment, US Military Tribunal, Nuremberg, (1949) VIII Law Reports of Trials of War Criminals, Case No. 47.
14   The Hague Convention for the Protection of Cultural Property in the Event of Armed Conflict (opened for signature 14 May 1954, 249 UNTS 240, entered into force 7 August 1956).
15   Article 28 stipulates that "the High Contracting Parties undertake to take, within the framework of their ordinary criminal jurisdiction, all necessary steps to prosecute and impose penal or disciplinary sanctions upon those persons, of whatever nationality, who commit or order to be committed a breach of the Convention."
16   Second Protocol to the Hague Convention for the Protection of Cultural Property in the Event of Armed Conflict (opened for signature 26 March 1999, 38 ILM 769, entered into force 9 March 2004). It also established a Committee for the Protection of Cultural Property in the Event of Armed Conflict to develop guidelines to implement, grant or rescind enhanced protection status, and established a fund for the Protection of Cultural Property in the Event of Armed Conflict.
17   Article 53, Protocol Additional to the Geneva Conventions of 12 August 1949, and relating to the Protection of Victims of International Armed Conflicts (Protocol I), 8 June 1977.
18   Article 16, Protection of cultural objects and of places of worship, "Without prejudice to the provisions of the Hague Convention for the Protection of Cultural Property in the

The preamble to the 2003 UNESCO Declaration concerning the Intentional Destruction of Cultural Heritage, refers to a notorious act of cultural destruction, "the tragic destruction of the Buddhas of Bamiyan that affected the international community as a whole"[19] and recommends measures to protect cultural property in peacetime and conflict.

In 1993, the United Nations Security Council established the ICTY to try serious violations of international humanitarian law committed in the former Yugoslavia. Article 3 (d) of the ICTY Statute proscribes crimes against cultural property, providing jurisdiction to prosecute as violations of the laws and customs of war, "seizure of, destruction or wilful damage done to institutions dedicated to religion, charity and education, the arts and sciences, historic monuments and works of art and science". This applies in international and non-international armed conflicts.[20] The 1994 Statute of the International Criminal Tribunal for Rwanda had no equivalent provision.[21]

The ICRC's Study on Customary International Humanitarian Law Rules published in 2005 identified rules on cultural property that had attained the status of customary international law applicable in both international and non-international armed conflicts.[22] Rule 38 provides, "A. Special care must be taken in military operations to avoid damage to buildings dedicated to religion, art, science, education or charitable purposes and historic monuments unless they are military objectives" and "B. Property of great importance to the cultural heritage of every people must not be the object of attack unless imperatively required by military necessity." Rule 39 prohibits the use of such property for purposes likely to expose it to destruction or damage, unless imperatively required by military necessity. Rule 40 prohibits seizure, destruction or wilful

---

Event of Armed Conflict of 14 May 1954, it is prohibited to commit any acts of hostility directed against historic monuments, works of art or places of worship which constitute the cultural or spiritual heritage of peoples, and to use them in support of the military effort", Protocol Additional to the Geneva Conventions of 12 August 1949, and relating to the Protection of Victims of Non-International Armed Conflicts (Protocol II), 8 June 1977.

19   These were 4th and 5th century monumental statues of standing Buddhas carved into a cliff-side in the Bamyan Valley in Afghanistan, destroyed by the Taliban in March 2001. The "Cultural Landscape and Archaeological Remains of the Bamiyan Valley" was inscribed on the UNESCO World Heritage List in 2003.

20   The ICTY Statute is annexed to Security Council Resolution 827 of 1993, passed under Chapter VII of the Charter of the United Nations.

21   Neither did the 2002 Statute of the Special Court for Sierra Leone. Article 1, "Competence of the Special Court" provided jurisdiction with respect to "serious violations of international humanitarian law" generally, but Article 4 "Other serious violations of international humanitarian law" set out only three specified crimes.

22   Jean-Marie Henckaerts and Louise Doswald-Beck (eds), *Customary International Humanitarian Law, Volume I: Rules* and *Volume II: Practice* (Cambridge University Press 2005).

damage to institutions dedicated to religion, charity, education, the arts and sciences, historic monuments and works of art and science, and pillage and vandalism directed against property of great importance to the cultural heritage of every people.

The principles relating to the protection of cultural property in armed conflict – and the obligation to prosecute breaches – are therefore quite clear.[23] Both the ICTY and the ICC have convicted persons for destroying cultural property as crimes under their Statutes which are based on these principles.

During the 1992–1995 war in Bosnia and Herzegovina, significant cultural structures, objects and documents were destroyed. An estimated 1200 mosques, 150 churches, four synagogues and more than 1000 other cultural monuments, works of art, and cultural institutions such as museums, libraries, archives and manuscript collections, were systematically targeted and destroyed.[24] Kosovo's cultural property also suffered during the 1998–1999 conflict, with a similar pattern of the forcible transfer of populations from villages and towns, followed by the removal or destruction of their cultural monuments and buildings. An estimated one third (around 225) of the mosques in Kosovo were damaged or destroyed by Serbian forces.[25] Thereafter, returning Kosovar Albanians destroyed or damaged more than 70 Serbian Orthodox sites.[26]

Damage to or destruction of cultural and religious property was prosecuted at the ICTY both as a war crime and a crime against humanity. Most charges and convictions were under the war crime in Article 3 (d) (as described above),

---

23   In 2004, the International Court of Justice confirmed the customary law status of the Hague Regulations, stating that "The Court considers that the provisions of the Hague Regulations have become part of customary law, as is in fact recognized by all the participants in the proceedings before the Court." Advisory Opinion on the "Legal Consequences of the Construction of a Wall in the Occupied Palestinian Territory", No. 131, 9 July 2004, para 89.

24   András Riedlmayer, 'Libraries are Not for Burning: International Librarianship and the Recovery of the Destroyed Heritage of Bosnia and Herzegovina' (1996) 21/2 Art Libraries Journal 19–23. The shelling of Sarajevo by Serb forces destroyed and damaged libraries, museums and religious monuments, such as Bosnia's National and University Library and its collection of rare books, manuscripts, periodicals and books. Another significant monument was the Old Bridge of Mostar, a beautiful 16th century Ottoman pedestrian bridge over the Neretva River, destroyed by Bosnian Croat and Croatian shelling in 1993.

25   Andrew Herscher and András Riedlmayer, 'Monument and Crime: The Destruction of Historic Architecture in Kosovo' (2000) Grey Room 108–122 at 112. Islamic religious schools and libraries, traditional stone houses (kullas) and three out of four Ottoman historic centres were damaged, Prishtina and Prizen suffered burning and destruction in their old parts.

26   Andrew Herscher and András Riedlmayer, 'Monument and Crime: The Destruction of Historic Architecture in Kosovo' (2000) Grey Room 108–122 at 112.

but Article 5, crimes against humanity, was also used, in particular the crimes of persecution, deportation and forcible transfer as an inhumane act.[27] The war crime in Article 3 (e) of "plunder of public or private property" was also used to prosecute and convict such conduct. This demonstrates, by analogy, how the ICC could prosecute environmental crimes, where appropriate, as both war crimes and crimes against humanity.

A few ICTY cases focused mainly on cultural property crimes, for example, one general was convicted for command responsibility for a shelling attack on the UNESCO World Heritage listed Old Town of Dubrovnik.[28] He was convicted of destruction or wilful damage to institutions dedicated to religion, charity and education, the arts and sciences, historic monuments and works of art or science as a war crime under Article 3 (d) of the ICTY Statute.[29]

Others were convicted for destroying cultural property including mosques and Catholic churches under both Article 3 (d) and Article 5 (h) as persecution as a crime against humanity.[30] Persecution could "take the form of confiscation or destruction of private dwellings or businesses, symbolic buildings or means of subsistence belonging to the Muslim population of Bosnia-Herzegovina."[31] Others were convicted for persecution as a crime against humanity, which

---

27 Article 5 (h) persecution, Article 5 (d), deportation, and Article 5 (i) forcible transfer as an inhumane act.

28 *Prosecutor v Pavle Strugar*, IT-01-42-T, ICTY Trial Judgement, 31 January 2005. Several civilians were killed and injured, and numerous buildings were damaged; six were completely destroyed. Monasteries, churches, a mosque and a synagogue were damaged.

29 *Prosecutor v Pavle Strugar*, IT-01-42-T, ICTY Trial Judgement, 31 January 2005, para 478. He was also convicted of attacks on civilians. The Appeals Chamber upheld his convictions and entered further convictions for devastation not justified by military necessity and unlawful attacks on civilian objects under Article 3: *Prosecutor v Pavle Strugar* IT-01-42-A, ICTY Appeals Judgement, 17 July 2008, para 332 and Disposition. His co-accused Miodrag Jokić pleaded guilty and was also convicted for destruction and damage to cultural property for his role in the attack against the old town of Dubrovnik, *Prosecutor v Miodrag Jokić*, IT-01-42/1-S, ICTY Sentencing Judgement, 18 March 2004.

30 *Prosecutor v Blaškić* IT-95-14-T, ICTY Trial Judgement, 3 March 2000, Disposition. The Appeals Chamber overturned most of his convictions because it was not satisfied that he ordered the attack on Ahmici or that he had the material ability to prevent or punish the crimes so as to establish his command responsibility: *Prosecutor v Blaškić* IT-95-14-A, ICTY Appeals Judgement, 29 July 2004, Disposition. Radoslav Brđanin was likewise convicted of aiding and abetting both crimes for the destruction of a large number of mosques and Catholic churches by Bosnian Serb forces in a number of municipalities in north west Bosnia: *Prosecutor v Radoslav Brđanin*, IT-99-36-T, ICTY Trial Judgement, 1 September 2004, paras 658, 677–678, 1050, 1054.

31 *Prosecutor v Blaškić* IT-95-14-T, ICTY Trial Judgement, 3 March 2000, para 227.

included cultural destruction;[32] with one Trial Chamber noting that "all of humanity is indeed injured by the destruction of a unique religious culture and its concomitant cultural objects."[33]

In Kosovo, high ranking Serbian government, army and ministry of interior officials were convicted, as members of a joint criminal enterprise to expel hundreds of thousands of Albanians from Kosovo, or as aiders and abettors – including for burning and destroying cultural monuments and religious sites. The destruction of cultural heritage and plunder was used to underlie criminal responsibility for deportation, forced transfer and persecution as a crime against humanity.[34] High-ranking military and civilian Bosnian Croats were also convicted for the destruction of cultural property, including mosques in several municipalities and the Old Bridge in Mostar, as the war crimes of destruction or devastation not justified by military necessity, destruction or wilful damage to institutions dedicated to religion or education, plunder and persecution in the Croat mini-state of Herceg-Bosna.[35] These judgements show international case law has rapidly developed in relation to cultural property and provide

---

32 For example, Milomir Stakić, Biljana Plavšić, Momčilo Krajišnik, Mićo Stanišić and Stojan Župljanin. Stakić was convicted of persecution for the destruction or damage to several mosques and Catholic churches in Prijedor: *Prosecutor v Stakić*, IT-97-24-T, ICTY Trial Judgement, 31 July 2003, paras 811, 826, Disposition; Biljana Plavšić pleaded guilty to persecution including destruction of cultural and sacred objects, and plunder in various towns and villages in Bosnia-Herzegovina: *Prosecutor v Plavšić*, IT-00-39&40/1-S, ICTY Sentencing Judgement, paras 15–16. Her fellow BiH Presidency member Momčilo Krajišnik was also convicted for persecution based, *inter alia*, on cultural destruction. The Trial Chamber found that more than 200 cultural and religious sites including mosques and Catholic churches were damaged or destroyed by Serb forces in 26 municipalities: *Prosecutor v Krajišnik*, IT-00-39-T, ICTY Trial Judgement, 27 September 2006, paras 836–840, However the Appeals Chamber overturned this part of his persecution conviction as it was not satisfied that such crimes were part of the common objective of the joint criminal enterprise: *Prosecutor v Krajišnik*, IT-00-39-A, ICTY Appeals Judgement, 17 March 2009, paras 177–178. Stanišić and Župljanin were each convicted of persecution for the destruction of a large number of cultural monuments by having participated in a JCE to permanently remove Bosnian Muslims, Bosnian Croats and other non-Serbs from the territory: *Prosecutor v* Stanišić and Župljanin, IT-08-91-T, ICTY Trial Judgement, 27 March 2013, Vol II, para 527.

33 *Prosecutor v Dario Kordić and Mario Čerkez*, IT-95-14/2-T, 26 February 2001, para 207.

34 *Prosecutor v Milutinović et al*, IT-05-87-1, ICTY Trial Judgement, 26 February 2009 and *Prosecutor v Đorđević*, IT-05-87/1-T, ICTY Trial Judgement, 23 February 2011.

35 *Prosecutor v Prlić et al*, IT-04-74-T, ICTY Trial Judgement, 29 May 2013, Vol III, see for example, paras 1584–1587. The Chamber inferred the large scale character of the destruction from the immense cultural, historic and symbolic value of the Old Bridge in Mostar in particular for the Muslim community.

precedents, by analogy, as to how similar developments could occur in relation to environmental prosecutions as war crimes or crimes against humanity.

ICTY cases also linked the destruction of religious and cultural institutions to genocide. In a Srebrenica case, a Trial Chamber noted that the physical or biological destruction of a group is often combined with "simultaneous attacks on the cultural and religious property and symbols of the targeted group," and that such attacks may be considered as evidence of intent to destroy the group.[36] This too illustrates, again by analogy, a possible route the ICC could take in addressing environmental crimes in the context of genocide.

At the same time, however, widespread environmental destruction and damage also occurred in Bosnia and Herzegovina. The longest lasting and most destructive in that conflict was the use of landmines. These have rendered large areas of Bosnia and Herzegovina's landscape unusable.[37] No prosecution resulted from the damage caused by laying landmines, although arguably it could have been prosecuted at least as a war crime.

Articles 8 (2) (b) (ix) and 8 (2) (e) (iv) of the Rome Statute provide the ICC with jurisdiction to try as a war crime in international and non-international armed conflicts respectively, "intentionally directing attacks against buildings dedicated to religion, education, art, science or charitable purposes, historic monuments, hospitals and places where the sick and wounded are collected, provided they are not military objectives". One case, that of Ahmed Al Faqi Al Mahdi, has been tried to completion. It concerned a single charge – to which the Accused pleaded guilty – under Article 8 (2) (e) (iv) of intentionally directing attacks against 10 buildings of religious and historical character (mausoleums and a mosque) in Timbuktu, Mali in 2012.[38] He was sentenced to nine years' imprisonment.

Both the Pre-Trial Chamber and the Trial Chamber emphasised the gravity of the crimes, with the Pre-Trial Chamber pointing to the "unanimous outcry of the international community and individuals."[39]

---

36   *Prosecutor v Krstić*, IT-98-33-T, ICTY Trial Judgement, 2 August 2001, para 5880. The Trial Chamber inferred the intent to physically destroy the group from such attacks including those against mosques and homes.

37   For example, in April 2017, more than 21 years after the Dayton Peace Accords ended the conflict, the Bosnia and Herzegovina Mine Action Centre estimated that 1091 km2 or 2.2% of the country was still affected by landmines, "Press Release April the 4th – International Mine Action Day". An estimated 80,000 mines remained.

38   *Prosecutor v. Al Faqi Al Mahdi*, Judgment and Sentence, ICC-01/12-01/15-171, 27 September 2016, para 11.

39   It highlighted that "[T]he Buildings/Structures played an important role in the life of the inhabitants of Timbuktu and that their destruction was considered as a serious matter and regarded by the local population as an aggression towards their faith. Some of the

The Trial Chamber found that the mausoleums and mosques qualified as both religious buildings and historic monuments, as evidenced by their role in the cultural life in Timbuktu and the status of nine of these buildings as UNESCO World Heritage sites. It held that "UNESCO's designation of these buildings reflects their special importance to international cultural heritage, noting that 'the wide diffusion of culture, and the education of humanity for justice and liberty and peace are indispensable to the dignity of man and constitute a sacred duty which all the nations must fulfil in a spirit of mutual assistance and concern'. Attacking these mausoleums and mosques was clearly an affront to these values [...]."[40]

The protected cultural values referred to in this case may be considered analogous to values which underlie the protection of the natural environment.

Damage or Destruction to the Environment in International Humanitarian Law

The discussion above illustrates the special protection given to cultural property in international humanitarian law and its increasing attention in international criminal law. At the same time, however, parties to armed conflicts have engaged in wilful environmental damage and destruction, not necessarily justified by military necessity. This has included manipulating or modifying the environment as a weapon of warfare, and subjecting the environment to attacks as the intended or incidental target – both of which have caused long-term and severe consequences. As referred to above, in the Bosnian context, the use of landmines in conflicts is one of the most insidious forms of environmental damage.

The detonation of atomic bombs over Hiroshima and Nagasaki by the United States of America in August 1945 caused massive civilian deaths, casualties and colossal environmental destruction. Another notorious attack on the environment was the use by the United States in Vietnam, Laos and Cambodia in the 1960s and 1970s of defoliants such as Agent Orange to destroy vegetation the enemy was using for cover and sustenance. Another was the burning of Kuwaiti oil fields by retreating Iraqi forces at the end of the Gulf War in 1991.

Buildings/structures have since been reconstructed, while in other instances something symbolic was built." *Prosecutor v. Al Faqi Al Mahdi*, Decision on the confirmation of charges against Ahmad Al Faqi Al Mahdi, ICC-01/12-01/15-84-Red, 24 March 2016, para 39.

40   *Prosecutor v. Al Faqi Al Mahdi*, Judgment and Sentence, ICC-01/12-01/15-171, 27 September 2016, para 46.

The retaliatory draining of the Mesopotamian marshes in Southern Iraq by Saddam Hussein's regime at the end of same war was another.

Obtaining access to natural resources can simultaneously trigger and fuel conflict. Three well-known examples of this are of the Democratic Republic of the Congo, Liberia and Sierra Leone where the fight for diamonds and other natural resources has had devastating human and environmental consequences.[41]

There are few international examples of prosecutions for intentionally damaging or destroying the environment during armed conflict. Yet, over the past few decades – in particular since the mid-1970s – international humanitarian law has made some progress in addressing this.

Several international humanitarian law treaties refer, indirectly or directly, to intentional environmental destruction during warfare. The most important are the Hague Conventions of 1899 and 1907,[42] the four Geneva Conventions of 1949, the 1976 Convention on the Prohibition of Military or Any Other Hostile Use of Environmental Modification Techniques,[43] and the 1977 Additional Protocols I and II to the Geneva Conventions.

The 1899 and 1907 Hague Conventions do not expressly protect the environment or prohibit intentional environmental destruction during hostilities. Rather, they contain general provisions limiting the means and methods of warfare that may also apply to environmental damage and destruction.

Article 23 (g) of the 1907 Hague Convention, prohibiting the destruction of "the enemy's property" unless "imperatively demanded by the necessities of war", was the basis of a charge against General Lothar Rendulic, who

---

41 See, e.g., Letter dated 10 November 2001 from the Secretary-General to the President of the Security Council and Addendum to the Report of Panel of Experts on the Illegal Exploitation of Natural Resources and Other Forms of Wealth of the Democratic Republic of the Congo, S/2001/1072, 13 November 2001; Letter dated 12 April 2001 from the Secretary-General to the President of the Security Council and the Report of Panel of Experts on the Illegal Exploitation of Natural Resources and Other Forms of Wealth of the Democratic Republic of the Congo, S/2001/357, 12 April 2001; Global Witness, 'The Truth About Diamonds', November 2006; 'Diamonds and the Civil War in Sierra Leone', the Courier ACP-EU, July-August 2001, 73; 'Natural Resources, Conflict and Conflict Resolution', United States Institute of Peace, Washington DC, 14 September 2007.

42 Hague Convention II with Respect to the Laws and Customs of War on Land, opened for signature 29 July 1899, 26 Martens (2nd) 949 (entered into force 4 September 1900); Hague Convention IV Respecting the Laws and Customs of War on Land, opened for signature 18 October 1907, 3 Martens (3rd) 461 (entered into force 26 January 1910).

43 Opened for signature 10 December 1976, 1108 UNTS 151; 16 ILM 88 (entered into force 5 October 1978).

commanded the German forces in Norway and Finland in 1944. He was tried before a US Military Tribunal at Nuremberg under Allied Control Council Law No. 10, in the *Hostages* trial, for using a "scorched earth" policy to attempt to hinder Russian forces in Norway.[44] The Tribunal, however, dismissed the charges, concluding that his actions were justified by military necessity based on his "honest judgment on the basis of the conditions prevailing at the time."[45]

The IMT at Nuremberg convicted General Alfred Jodl, the Chief of the Operations Staff of the High Command of the German Armed Forces, partly based on the Nazi regime's scorched earth policies. In October 1944, he ordered the evacuation of everyone in northern Norway and the burning of their houses, to prevent them helping the Russians.[46] In 1948, an investigation by a UN War Crimes Commission Committee found that nine German civil servants could be listed as war criminals for "wholesale cutting of Polish timber far in excess of what was needed to preserve the timber resources of the country" during the Second World War – *prima facie* a war crime under Article 55 of the 1907 Hague Convention.[47] The post Second World War cases thus provide some historical basis for prosecutions based upon environmental destruction as a war crime.

The Fourth Geneva Convention of 1949 contains important safeguards against intentional environmental destruction in armed conflict. Article 33 prohibits pillage – which may have environmental aspects – while Article 53 prohibits destruction by an occupying power of real or personal property belonging to private persons, or to the State, or to other public authorities, or to social or cooperative organisations, except where such destruction is rendered "absolutely necessary by military operations." Significantly too, article 147 proscribes as a "grave breach" of the Geneva Conventions "extensive destruction

---

44   *Trial of Wilhelm List and Others (The Hostage Case)*, Judgment, US Military Tribunal, Nuremberg, (1949) VIII Law Reports of Trials of War Criminals, Case No. 47, 34. Count two of the indictment alleged that he ordered the destruction "of all shelter and means of existence" which included the destruction of homes, public buildings, bridges, barn and "natural resources of an area".

45   *Trial of Wilhelm List and Others (The Hostage Case)*, Judgment, US Military Tribunal, Nuremberg, (1949) VIII Law Reports of Trials of War Criminals, Case No. 47, 69.

46   *Trial of Alfred Jodl*, Judgment of the International Military Tribunal, Trial of the Major War Criminals, 1 October 1946, pp. 324–325, reprinted in (1947) 41 American Journal of International Law 172–333 at 316.

47   United Nations War Crimes Commission, Case No. 7150 (Polish Forestry Case), History of the UN War Crimes Commission and the Development of the Laws of War, 1948, HMSO, London, 485 at 496.

and appropriation of property, not justified by military necessity and carried out unlawfully and wantonly". This too can have an environmental aspect.

The widespread use of defoliants by the United States of America during the Vietnam War to destroy vegetation, and attempts by the United States, as deliberate military strategies, to manipulate weather patterns in Indo-China to flood strategic routes, prompted negotiations on a treaty to prohibit environmental modification as a method of warfare. These included the United Nations Conference of the Committee on Disarmament (CCD) and the Diplomatic Conference on the Reaffirmation and Development of International Humanitarian Law (CDDH, Geneva, 1974–1977).[48] In 1976 the CCD adopted the Convention on the Prohibition of Military or Any Hostile Use of Environmental Modification Techniques (ENMOD),[49] a treaty intended to prohibit the manipulation of the environment as a weapon of warfare.

Article I (1) of ENMOD obliges State Parties to undertake "not to engage in military or any other hostile use of environmental modification techniques having widespread, long-lasting or severe effects as the means of destruction, damage or injury to any other State Party." Article II defines the term "environmental modification techniques" as "any technique for changing – through the deliberate manipulation of natural processes – the dynamics, composition or structure of the Earth, including its biota, lithosphere, hydrosphere and atmosphere, or of outer space." The prohibition is broad, and not subject to the defence of military necessity. The Convention, however, makes no reference to criminal or civil liability for a breach.

The 1977 Additional Protocol I significantly expanded the protections in the 1949 Geneva Conventions. First, general provisions expressly protect various environmental targets: Article 54 sets out a non-exhaustive list of "objects indispensable to the survival of the civilian population" – such as "foodstuffs, agricultural areas for the production of foodstuffs, crops, livestock, drinking water installations and supplies and irrigation works" – that cannot be "attack[ed], destroy[ed], remove[d] or render[ed] useless", subject to "imperative military necessity" in a situation where a State Party is defending its national territory against invasion. Further, Article 56 (1) prohibits attacks against "[w]orks and installations containing dangerous forces" – namely "dams, dykes and nuclear electrical generating stations" – unless they are used in regular, significant and

---

48   Michael Bothe, Carl Bruch, Jordan Diamond and David Jensen, 'International law protecting the environment during armed conflict: gaps and opportunities' (2010) 92/879 International Review of the Red Cross 569–592.

49   Opened for signature 18 May 1977, 1108 UNTS 151; 16 ILM 88 (entered into force 5 October 1978). As at May 2017, ENMOD had 77 State Parties.

direct support of military operations and such attack is the only feasible way to terminate such support.[50]

Second, Additional Protocol I is particularly significant as the first international treaty to directly refer to environmental damage in an international armed conflict. Articles 35 (3) and 55 expressly apply to damage caused to the natural environment. The term "natural environment" is not defined, but the ICRC Commentary on the Additional Protocols states that it should be understood:

> in the widest sense to cover the biological environment in which a population is living. It does not consist merely of the objects indispensable to survival mentioned in Article 54 ... but also includes forests and other vegetation ... as well as fauna, flora and other biological or climatic elements.[51]

Article 35 (3) prohibits the use of "methods or means of warfare which are intended, or may be expected, to cause widespread, long-term and severe damage to the natural environment." Article 55 states that:

1. Care shall be taken in warfare to protect the natural environment against widespread, long-term and severe damage. This protection includes a prohibition of the use of methods or means of warfare which are intended or may be expected to cause such damage to the natural environment and thereby to prejudice the health or survival of the population.
2. Attacks against the natural environment by way of reprisals are prohibited.

Significantly, neither provision is expressed to be subject to any notion of military necessity. One commentator has observed that Article 35 (3) seeks to limit the methods and means of warfare, while Article 55 is more like a "Geneva law" by creating a protected object, namely, the environment.[52] However, their

---

50   Article 56 (1) and (2) (a), (b), (c) of Additional Protocol I.
51   Protocol Additional to the Geneva Conventions of 12 August 1949, and relating to the Protection of Victims of International Armed Conflicts (Protocol I), 8 June 1977, ICRC Protocol I Commentary of 1987, para 2126.
52   Steven Freeland, Addressing the Intentional Destruction of the Environment during Warfare under the Rome Statute of the International Criminal Court (Intersentia 2015), pp. 85–86, citing Michael N. Schmitt, 'Humanitarian Law and the Environment' (2000) 28 Denver Journal of International Law and Policy 265–323 at 275.

utility has been questioned given their very high and unclear damage thresholds of widespread, long term *and* severe damage to the environment.[53]

The 1981 Certain Conventional Weapons Convention and its three Protocols, has an impact on environmental damage and destruction.[54] Its preamble affirms, "it is prohibited to employ methods or means of warfare which are intended, or may be expected, to cause widespread, long-term and severe damage to the natural environment." Protocol III, relating to the use of incendiary weapons (e.g. napalm and white phosphorus), provides incidental protection for the environment.[55] Three other conventions – the 1972 Biological Weapons Convention, which prohibits the development, production and stockpiling of biological and toxin weapons, the 1993 Chemical Weapons Convention, which comprehensively prohibits the development, production, acquisition, stockpiling, retention or use of chemicals likely to harm the environment, and the 1997 Anti-Personnel Mines Convention,[56] which bans anti-personnel mines

---

53   Steven Freeland, Addressing the Intentional Destruction of the Environment during Warfare under the Rome Statute of the International Criminal Court (Intersentia 2015), pp. 91–92. See also Michael Bothe, Carl Bruch, Jordan Diamond, and David Jensen, 'International law protecting the environment during armed conflict: gaps and opportunities' (2010) 92/879 International Review of the Red Cross 569–592 at 573. A committee established by the ICTY Prosecutor in 1999 to examine NATO's conduct in a bombing campaign against the former Federal Republic of Yugoslavia from 24 March to 9 June 1999 and to advise the Prosecutor whether to begin an investigation into allegations of violations of IHL by NATO personnel, considered the application of articles 35 (3) and 55 to the environmental damage caused by the bombing campaign, in particular relating to the use of deleted uranium projectiles and cluster bombs. The report concluded that the provisions had a "very high threshold of application" and that it would be "extremely difficult to develop a prima facie case upon the basis of these provisions, even assuming they were applicable" (para 15). The Committee found that while there was an obligation to avoid excessive long-term damage to the natural environment even when bombing legitimate military targets, what was "excessive" in this context could not be clearly defined (para 23).

54   Convention on Prohibitions or Restrictions on the Use of Certain Conventional Weapons which may be Deemed to be Excessively Injurious or to Have Indiscriminate Effects (and its Protocols I, II and III), in particular, Protocol III on Prohibitions or Restrictions on the Use of Incendiary Weapons, opened for signature 10 April 1981, 1342 UNTS 137 (entered into force 2 December 1983).

55   Article 2 (4) provides, "It is prohibited to make forests or other kinds of plant cover the object of attack by incendiary weapons except when such natural elements are used to cover, conceal or camouflage combatants or other military objectives, or are themselves military objectives."

56   Convention on the Prohibition of the Development, Production and Stockpiling of Bacteriological (Biological) and Toxin Weapons and on their Destruction, opened for signature

and similar weapons – likewise have an impact (at least indirect) on environmental damage and destruction.

In addition to this *jus in bello*[57] and disarmament treaties and conventions, several environmental law treaties were adopted in the last decades of the 20th Century. The non-binding or "soft law" instruments include the Stockholm Declaration of 1972,[58] and the Rio Declaration of 1992.[59] These are most significant in providing guidelines or standards of conduct that may influence States to protect the environment during armed conflict. Dozens of international agreements and treaties are also directed towards protecting the environment – many negotiated under the UN Environmental Programme (UNEP) – such as the 1998 Kyoto Protocol to the UN Framework Convention on Climate Change.[60] But very few multilateral international environmental law treaties specifically relate to environmental protection during armed conflict. Many are silent as to their applicability after the outbreak of hostilities, meaning that a treaty's express terms will generally determine whether it applies during armed conflict.[61]

---

10 April 1972, entered into force 26 March 1975; Convention on the Prohibition of the Development, Production, Stockpiling and Use of Chemical Weapons and on their Destruction, opened for signature 13 January 1993, entered into force 29 April 1997; Convention on the Prohibition of the Use, Stockpiling, Production and Transfer of Anti-Personnel Mines and on their Destruction, opened for signature 3 December 1997, 36 ILM 1507 (entered into force 1 March 1999).

57 Law that applies in war.

58 Declaration of the United Nations Conference on the Human Environment (16 June 1972) UN Doc A/CONF.48/14/Rev.1 (1973), principle 21 (States have ... the responsibility to ensure that activities within their jurisdiction or control do not cause damage to the environment of other States or areas beyond the limits of national jurisdiction.).

59 Declaration of the UN Conference on Environment and Development (14 June 1992) UN Doc A/CONF.151/26 (Volume 1), 31 ILM 874, principle 23 (The environment and natural resources of people under oppression, domination and occupation shall be protected) and principle 24 (Warfare is inherently destructive of sustainable development. States shall therefore respect international law providing protection for the environment in times of armed conflict and cooperate in its further development, as necessary.) See also World Charter for Nature, GA Re.37/7 (1982), principle 5 (Nature shall be secured against degradation caused by warfare or other hostile activities.).

60 Kyoto Protocol to the United Nations Framework Convention on Climate Change, opened for signature 16 March 1998, entered into force 16 February 2005.

61 Steven Freeland, Addressing the Intentional Destruction of the Environment during Warfare under the Rome Statute of the International Criminal Court (Intersentia 2015), pp. 106–107; Philippe Sands, Principles of International Environmental Law (2nd ed, Cambridge University Press 2003), p. 309; Michael Bothe, Carl Bruch, Jordan Diamond, and

But in any event, the international environmental law regime is generally one of State liability based on traditional principles of State responsibility rather than one of individual criminal responsibility.

Some customary international law principles also impact on damage or destruction of the environment in armed conflict, even if only indirectly. The key principle of military necessity prohibits acts during armed conflict that are unnecessary to achieve a military advantage. However, where an act is militarily necessary, collateral damage is permitted to the extent that prevailing military circumstances require. This is based on the circumstances as determined by the military commander at the time.[62]

Several of the most important *jus in bello* treaties, including the 1907 Hague Convention IV, the 1949 Geneva Convention IV, the 1954 Hague Convention on Cultural Property, the 1977 Additional Protocol I, and Protocol III to the 1981 Certain Conventional Weapons Convention, specifically refer to military necessity. The ICRC's draft Guidelines for Military Manuals and Instructions for the Protection of the Environment in Times of Armed Conflict – a model for national military manuals – likewise refers to "destruction of the environment not justified by military necessity" as a violation of humanitarian law and notes that the prohibition on destroying civilian objects, unless justified by military necessity, also protects the environment.[63]

The balancing test between military advantage and environment concerns, however, is "stacked heavily against the environment."[64] An obvious example was the United States' use of atomic bombs on Hiroshima and Nagasaki as a means of ending the war in the Pacific in 1945. The *Rendulic* case discussed above also shows military necessity as a defence to environmental crimes. There, a US Military Tribunal concluded that the destruction of the enemy's property by retreating military forces fell within the "necessities of war" exception

---

David Jensen, 'International law protecting the environment during armed conflict: gaps and opportunities' (2010) 92/879 International Review of the Red Cross 569–592 at 580, 590–591.

62 See generally, Francoise Hampson, 'Military Necessity' in Roy Gutman, David Rieff and Anthony Dworkin (eds), *Crimes of War, What the Public Should Know* (2nd ed, W W Norton 2007); Michael N. Schmitt, 'Military Necessity and Humanity in International Humanitarian Law: Preserving the Delicate Balance' (2010) 50 Virginia Journal of International Law 795–839.

63 ICRC, Guidelines for Military Manuals and Instructions on the Protection of the Environment in Times of Armed Conflict (30 April 1996) 311 International Review of the Red Cross 230–7, guidelines 8 and 9.

64 Peter Sharp 'Prospects for Liability for Environmental Crimes in the International Criminal Court' (1999) 18(2) Virginia Environmental Law Journal 217–243 at 241.

in article 23 (g) of the 1907 Hague Convention IV and thus acquitted the accused of these crimes.[65] But this was in 1948, in a trial before American judges and in circumstances in which the United States had arguably inflicted far worse environmental damage in Japan than Rendulic's forces had in Norway.

Two other fundamental humanitarian law norms provide protections for the environment in armed conflicts. Under the principle of distinction, the warring parties must always distinguish between the civilian population and combatants, and between civilian objects and military objectives, and accordingly must direct their operations only against military objectives.[66] This means that parties may only use weapons capable of distinguishing between civilian and civilian objects and military objectives. The related principle of proportionality stipulates that even when a legitimate military objective is attacked, the extent of military force used and any injury and damage inflicted upon civilians and civilian property must not be disproportionate to the expected military advantage.[67]

These principles, however, are limited in their application to the environment.[68] For the principle of distinction, it is unclear whether the environment is a civilian object. Furthermore, the proportionality principle can be difficult to apply given that it depends on an assessment of the military advantage *vis-à-vis* the civilian injury and damage, assessed from the position of a reasonably informed person in the circumstances of the actual perpetrator. These issues are exacerbated when environmental damage occurs.

A significant International Court of Justice (ICJ) case highlights the difficulty in applying the principle of proportionality to environmental damage in armed conflicts. In its *Advisory Opinion on the Legality of the Threat or Use of Nuclear Weapons* the ICJ confirmed that environmental factors must be considered

---

65 *Trial of Wilhelm List and Others (The Hostages Trial)*, Judgment, US Military Tribunal, Nuremberg, (1949) VIII Law Reports of Trials of War Criminals, Case No. 47, 69. Rendulic was convicted for other crimes not related to environmental destruction and sentenced to 20 years imprisonment, later reduced to 10 years.

66 *Prosecutor v Stanislav Galić*, IT-98-29-T, ICTY Trial Chamber, 5 December 2003, para 45, citing Article 48 of Additional Protocol I. See also Article 52 (2) Additional Protocol I and Article 13 (1) Additional Protocol II. See also *Legality of the Threat or Use of Nuclear Weapons (Advisory Opinion)* ICJ Reports 1996, 226 at 257 (para 78).

67 See generally, Horst Fischer, 'Principle of Proportionality' in Roy Gutman, David Rieff and Anthony Dworkin (eds), *Crimes of War, What the Public Should Know* (2nd ed, W W Norton 2007). See also Article 51 (5) (b) Additional Protocol I.

68 Steven Freeland, Addressing the Intentional Destruction of the Environment during Warfare under the Rome Statute of the International Criminal Court (Intersentia 2015), pp. 148–149, 153.

when examining proportionality and determining the legality of acts in warfare.[69] But while confirming that threatening or using nuclear weapons – and using them will inevitably cause severe environmental damage – should comply with the principles of international humanitarian law,[70] the Court could not categorically state that this would always violate international law.[71]

The ICRC's 2005 study on customary international humanitarian law contains three rules relating specifically to the natural environment.[72] These largely reflect, and in some respects go further than, the humanitarian law treaty provisions and the customary principles of military necessity, distinction and proportionality.[73]

Significantly, the study concluded that the environment is a civilian object and as such, protected by the same fundamental rules that protect other civilian objects, namely the general humanitarian law principles and those of distinction and proportionality. Rule 43, a norm of customary international law applicable in international and non-international armed conflicts, states:

> The general principles on the conduct of hostilities apply to the natural environment: A. No part of the natural environment may be attacked, unless it is a military objective. B. Destruction of any part of the natural environment is prohibited, unless required by imperative military necessity. C. Launching an attack against a military objective which may be

---

69   Legality of the Threat or Use of Nuclear Weapons (Advisory Opinion) ICJ Reports 1996, 226 at 242 (para 30).
70   *Legality of the Threat or Use of Nuclear Weapons (Advisory Opinion)* ICJ Reports 1996, 226 at 243 (para 33). ("while existing international law relating to the protection and safeguarding of the environment does not specifically prohibit the use of nuclear weapons, it indicates important environmental factors that are properly to be taken into account in the context of the implementation of the principles and rules of law applicable in armed conflict.") See also International Institute of Humanitarian Law, 'San Remo Manual on International Law Applicable to Armed Conflicts at Sea' (1995) 309 International Review of the Red Cross 595, para 44 ("methods and means of warfare should be employed with due regard for the natural environment taking into account the relevant rules of international law.").
71   Legality of the Threat or Use of Nuclear Weapons (Advisory Opinion) ICJ Reports 1996, 226 at 266 (para 105).
72   Jean-Marie Henckaerts and Louise Doswald-Beck (eds), *Customary International Humanitarian Law, Volume I: Rules* and *Volume II: Practice* (2005). While considered an important and influential study in IHL, some of the rules expressed in the study are not yet considered a true reflection of the status of customary law.
73   Steven Freeland, Addressing the Intentional Destruction of the Environment during Warfare under the Rome Statute of the International Criminal Court (Intersentia 2015), p. 170.

expected to cause incidental damage to the environment which would be excessive in relation to the concrete and direct military advantage anticipated is prohibited.

Rule 44, a norm of customary international law applicable in international and "arguably" also in non-international armed conflicts, states that:

> Methods and means of warfare must be employed with due regard to the protection and preservation of the natural environment. In the conduct of military operations, all feasible precautions must be taken to avoid, and in any event to minimise, incidental damage to the environment. Lack of scientific certainty as to the effects on the environment of certain military operations does not absolve a party to the conflict from taking such precautions.

Finally, Rule 45, a norm of customary international law applicable in international and "arguably" also in non-international armed conflicts is similar to the prohibitions in articles 35 (3) and 55 of Additional Protocol I, providing:

> The use of methods or means of warfare that are intended, or may be expected, to cause widespread, long-term and severe damage to the natural environment is prohibited. Destruction of the natural environment may not be used as a weapon.[74]

As this discussion shows, the principles relating to the protection of environmental property in armed conflict have steadily evolved, and most significantly, in the past few decades.

Prosecuting Environmental Damage and Destruction in International Criminal Law

The treaties and principles of customary international law referred to above demonstrate that international humanitarian law, and international

---

[74] Jean-Marie Henckaerts and Louise Doswald-Beck (eds), *Customary International Humanitarian Law, Volume I: Rules* (2005), p. 191. The summary notes that the US is a persistent objector to the first part of the rule, while France, the UK and the US (all nuclear powers) are persistent objectors with regard to the application of the first part of the rule on using nuclear weapons.

environmental law provide important legal protections for limiting the conduct of armed conflict that could intentionally or incidentally damage the environment.

Structural limitations and uncertainties, however, limit their use in addressing environmental damage and destruction in armed conflicts. These include a narrow and unclear definition of impermissible environmental damage. In wartime, commanders can also easily classify the natural environment as a military objective, if only because the enemy is using it. Moreover, the practical application of the principle of proportionality is uncertain when environmental destruction is "collateral damage" from military attacks.[75] But, most unfortunately, these treaties and principles do not provide a comprehensive regime to address environmental damage and destruction during armed conflict, let alone establish an effective system of individual criminal accountability for environmental damage.

This is a gap, but not an insurmountable one, and is where international criminal law may come in. The ICC has jurisdiction over the core crimes in the Rome Statute[76] – war crimes, crimes against humanity, genocide and, when it enters into force, the crime of aggression. This multilateral treaty, adopted in 1998 and entering into force in 2002, is considered to represent the most complete codification of international criminal law. It also largely reflects the status of customary international (criminal) law.[77]

The Rome Statute has just one express reference to damaging the natural environment, in article 8 (2) (b) (iv). This gives the ICC jurisdiction over the war crime of "intentionally launching an attack" knowing that it will cause "widespread, long-term and severe damage to the natural environment which would be clearly excessive in relation to the concrete and direct overall military advantage anticipated." This applies only in international armed conflicts.

This provision is historical as the first express reference to the environment in the constitutive document of an international criminal court or tribunal.[78]

---

[75] Michael Bothe, Carl Bruch, Jordan Diamond and David Jensen, 'International law protecting the environment during armed conflict: gaps and opportunities' (2010) 92/879 International Review of the Red Cross 569–592 at 578–579, 591.

[76] Opened for signature 17 July 1998, 2187 UNTS 3; 37 ILM 999 (entered into force 1 July 2002). As at May 2017, the Rome Statute had 123 State parties.

[77] *Prosecutor v Furundžija*, Case No. IT-95-17/1, ICTY Trial Chamber, 10 December 1998, para 227. In some respects the Rome Statute is considered more progressive than customary international law and in other respects it is considered more regressive than customary international law.

[78] It was later included in the Statutes of the Iraqi Special Tribunal and the East Timor Tribunal, see footnote 4 above. The Iraqi court was not an international court, and the East Timor one was a United Nations court.

As an "ecocentric" crime, requiring no direct harm to humans to trigger liability,[79] it thus has real and symbolic value.

In her 2016 "Case Selection and Prioritisation Policy", the ICC Prosecutor Ms Fatou Bensouda confirmed that when assessing gravity for the purpose of selecting cases for prosecution, within and across situations, she would assess, among other factors, the manner of commission of the crimes, including crimes committed by means of, or resulting in the destruction of the environment, and the impact of the crimes, including the social, economic and environmental damage inflicted on the affected communities.[80]

In the latter context, particular consideration will be given by the ICC Office of the Prosecutor to "Rome Statute crimes committed by means of, or that result in, the destruction of the environment, the illegal exploitation of natural resources or the illegal dispossession of land".[81] While this does not add new crimes to the ICC's mandate, the Office of the Prosecutor will consider these facts when looking at crimes within its mandate and deciding on whom to prosecute and for which incidents and conduct.[82]

---

79 Mark A. Drumbl, 'Accountability for Property Crimes and Environmental War Crimes: Prosecution, Litigation, and Development', International Center for Transitional Justice (November 2009) at p. 8. See also Kevin Jon Heller and Jessica C Lawrence, 'The First Ecocentric Environmental War Crime: The Limits of Article 8 (2) (b) (iv) of the Rome Statute' (2007) Georgetown International Environmental Law Review 61–96.

80 Office of the Prosecutor, Case Selection and Prioritisation Policy, 2016, paras 40 and 41. This builds upon the ICC Office of the Prosecutor's 2013 Policy Paper on Preliminary Examinations, which provided that environmental damage is a factor to be considered by the Office in the conduct of a preliminary examination of a situation that might warrant an investigation.

81 Office of the Prosecutor, Case Selection and Prioritisation Policy, 2016, para 41. See also para 7 stating that "[t]he Office will also seek to cooperate and provide assistance to States, upon request, with respect to conduct which constitutes a serious crime under national law, such as the illegal exploitation of natural resources, ... land grabbing or the destruction of the environment."

82 Helen Brady and Fabricio Guariglia, American Bar Association's ICC Project Arguendo Blog, 'The ICC OTP's Case Selection and Prioritisation Policy: An Insider's View: Consistency and Transparency while Preserving Prosecutorial Discretion', 15 December 2016. https://www.international-criminal-justice-today.org/arguendo/an-insiders-view/. Co-author Helen Brady in her capacity as ICC OTP Senior Appeals Counsel and Chair of the Working Group on the ICC OTP's Case Selection and Prioritisation Policy observed in a media interview that the added focus on the environment is "highly important and it's not just symbolic – it means something": see Phoebe Brathwaite, 'Environmental Crimes Could Warrant International Criminal Court Prosecutions', Inter Press service, Oct 1, 2016.

Several possibilities exist for prosecuting crimes against the environment under the Rome Statute, for example as war crimes in article 8. The Rome Statute's provisions on crimes against humanity in article 7 and genocide in article 6 – which require no nexus to armed conflict – do not expressly refer to environmental crimes as crimes against humanity, or as means to commit genocide. However, several article 7 crimes against humanity – namely extermination, persecution, inhumane acts, deportation and forcible transfer of population – and certain acts which can amount to genocide if committed with the requisite intent to destroy a national, ethnical, racial or religious group, namely deliberately inflicting on the group conditions of life calculated to bring about its destruction in whole or in part, are broad enough to capture – in certain circumstances – environmental crimes. In other words, environmental damage is the tool by which the atrocity in article 6 or article 7 is perpetrated and "[environmental] destruction becomes a crime because of its humanitarian consequences".[83]

Once the Court exercises its jurisdiction over the crime of aggression in article 8 *bis* of the Statute, environmental damage and destruction could possibly form part of the acts of aggression.

War Crimes

Article 8 (2) (b) (iv) provides express jurisdiction over the crime of intentionally launching an attack knowing that it will cause widespread, long-term and severe damage to the natural environment which would be clearly excessive

---

http://www.ipsnews.net/2016/10/environmental-crimes-could-warrant-international-criminal-court-prosecutions. See also, Tara Smith, 'Why the International Criminal Court is Right to Focus on the Environment', The Conversation, 23 September 2016, and Donald Anton, 'Adding a Green Focus: The Office of the Prosecutor of the International Criminal Court Highlights the "Environment" in Case Selection and Prioritisation' (2016) 31 Australian Environment Review (Forthcoming); Griffith University Law School Research Paper No. 17–03. Available at SSRN: https://ssrn.com/abstract=2879775.

83 Tara Smith, 'Creating a Framework for the Prosecution of Environmental Crimes in International Criminal Law' in William Schabas, Yvonne McDermott and Niamh Hayes (eds), *The Ashgate Research Companion to International Criminal Law, Critical Perspectives* (Routledge 2013), pp. 45–62 at 46 https://www.routledgehandbooks.com/doi/10.4324/9781315613062.ch2, citing Tara Weinstein, 'Prosecuting Attacks that Destroy the Environment: Environmental Crimes or Humanitarian Atrocities?' (2005) 17(4) Georgetown Int'l Environmental L. Rev 697–722 at 720.

vis-à-vis the concrete and direct overall military advantage anticipated. This war crime requires a nexus to an international armed conflict.

Its inclusion in the Rome Statute was a compromise.[84] The draft Statute, the basis of the negotiations at the 1998 Rome Conference, contained four potential options: one prohibiting launching an attack knowing it will cause widespread, long-term and severe damage to the natural environment not justified by military necessity; a second option prohibiting launching an attack knowing it will cause widespread, long-term and severe damage to the natural environment which would be excessive to the concrete and direct overall military advantage anticipated; a third option prohibiting launching such an attack but without an express reference to military necessity or military advantage; and a fourth one containing no such prohibition.[85] No provision was made for individual criminal liability for environmental damage in non-international armed conflict.

The article requires a balancing of the expected damage to the environment against the concrete and direct overall military advantage anticipated. To make it a crime, the former must be clearly excessive to the latter. As one commentator has noted, the practical effect is that environmental issues are "made secondary" to national security interests.[86]

Article 8 (2) (b) (iv) derives from provisions such as articles 35 (3) and 55 (1) of Geneva Conventions Additional Protocol I, and Article I (1) of ENMOD. Despite this, its terms are more stringent than those, requiring that the environmental damage satisfy all three types of injury – widespread, long-term *and* severe, *and additionally*, the damage must be *clearly* excessive. The ICC Prosecutor, and the Court itself, have not yet had to interpret "widespread", "long-term" and "severe".[87]

---

84   Herman von Hebel and Darryl Robinson, 'Crimes within the Jurisdiction of the Court' in Roy Lee (ed), *The International Criminal Court, The Making of the Rome Statute* (Kluwer Law International 1999), p. 111.

85   Report of the Preparatory Committee on the Establishment of an International Criminal Court, Draft Statute for the International Criminal Court (14 April 1998) UN Doc A/CONF.183/2/Add.1, Part 2 "War Crimes", Section B (b).

86   Mark A. Drumbl, 'Waging War against the World: The Need to Move from War Crimes to Environmental Crimes' (1998) 22/1 Fordham International Law Journal 122–153 at 126.

87   These terms, which are disjunctive in the ENMOD convention, were defined for that convention as (a) 'widespread'. encompassing an area on the scale of several hundred square kilometres; (b) 'long-lasting': lasting for a period of months, or approximately a season; (c) 'severe': involving serious or significant disruption or harm to human life, natural and economic resources or other assets: 1976 CCD Understanding Relating to Article I of ENMOD, 31 United Nations General Assembly Official Records Supp. No. 27 (A/31/27),

As for proportionality, the ICC's Elements of Crimes emphasises that the military considerations that decide the proportionality of the act must be determined on a subjective basis: "the expression 'concrete and direct overall military advantage' refers to a military advantage that is foreseeable by the perpetrator at the relevant time. Such advantage may or may not be temporally or geographically related to the object of the attack..."[88] Further, "this knowledge element requires that the perpetrator make the value judgement as described therein. An evaluation of that value judgement must be based on the requisite information available to the perpetrator at the time."[89]

This has caused some pessimism. One commentator describes the crime's inclusion in the Rome Statute as "cause for limited celebration, considerable disappointment, and some concern."[90] Another describes "the very considerable – perhaps insurmountable – legal hurdles that, for all practical purposes, will serve to curtail any effective prosecution."[91] However, despite the high damage threshold and the proportionality test – both posing evidentiary challenges for future prosecutions – a war crime expressly referring to environmental damage is a major advance in international criminal law.[92] One successful prosecution may overcome any such gloom.

An example of such an attack could be the deliberate targeting of a nuclear power station, causing environmental damage and human displacement, such as on a scale of that of Chernobyl in Ukraine, in 1986, and Fukushima in Japan, in 2011. Another example could be a large-scale cyber-attack on dams and waterways which causes massive flooding and ecological disturbance.

Annex I. These terms are conjunctive in article 55 (1) Additional Protocol I. In a 1993 report to the UN General Assembly the Secretary General stated, "there are substantial grounds, including from *travaux preparatoires* ... for interpreting 'long-term' to refer to decades rather than months. On the other hand, it is not easy to know in advance exactly what the scope and duration of some environmentally damaging acts will be."

88 ICC Elements of Crimes, article 8 (2) (b) (iv), footnote 36.
89 ICC Elements of Crimes, article 8 (2) (b) (iv), footnote 37.
90 Mark A. Drumbl, 'Waging War against the World: The Need to Move from War Crimes to Environmental Crimes' (1998) 22/1 Fordham International Law Journal 122–153 at 135.
91 Steven Freeland, Addressing the Intentional Destruction of the Environment during Warfare under the Rome Statute of the International Criminal Court (Intersentia 2015), p. 213. Donald Anton, 'Adding a Green Focus: The Office of the Prosecutor of the International Criminal Court Highlights the Environment in Case Selection and Prioritisation' (2016) 31 Australian Environment Review (Forthcoming); Griffith University Law School Research Paper No. 17–03 at p. 3.
92 See Knut Dörmann, 'War Crimes in the Elements of Crimes', in Horst Fisher, Claus Kreß and Sasha Rolf Luder (eds), *International and National Prosecutions of Crimes under International Law: Current Developments* (Arno Spitz 2001), 95–139 at 127.

Other war crimes in the Rome Statute, although not expressly referring to the environment, are also potentially broad enough to capture conduct which causes environmental damage or destruction. One example is the war crime in article 8 (2) (a) (iv) of extensive destruction and appropriation of property not justified by military necessity and carried out unlawfully and wantonly. As a grave breach of the Geneva Conventions it requires a nexus to an international armed conflict. Also within the context of international armed conflict, article 8 (2) (b) (xiii), destroying or seizing the enemy's property unless imperatively demanded by the necessities of war, article 8 (2) (b) (xvi), pillaging, article 8 (2) (b) (xvii), employing poisons or poisoned weapons, and article 8 (2) (b) (xviii), employing asphyxiating, poisonous or other gases, and all analogous liquids, material or devices, may also apply if such acts have environmentally-damaging consequences.

The scope for prosecuting environmental damage as a war crime in non-international armed conflicts is more limited. States at the Rome Conference chose not to include an express provision referring to damage to the environment such as that in article 8 (2) (b) (iv). This is despite insurgents in civil wars using forests as home bases and hiding grounds, and counter-insurgency forces responding by slashing and burning forests and by polluting rivers.[93]

Nor is the more "generic" crime of extensive, unlawful and wanton destruction and appropriation of property not justified by military necessity a war crime in non-international armed conflicts. However, other provisions could potentially be used to prosecute environmental damage or destruction in internal armed conflicts.

These include: article 8 (2) (e) (v), pillaging; article 8 (2) (e) (xii), destroying or seizing the property of an adversary unless imperatively demanded by the necessities of the conflict; article 8 (2) (e) (xiii), employing poisons or poisoned weapons; and article 8 (2) (e) (xiv), employing asphyxiating, poisonous or other gases, and all analogous liquids, material or devices.

Further, forcibly displacing a civilian population – article 8 (2) (b) (viii) in international armed conflicts, and article 8 (2) (e) (viii) in non-international armed conflicts – may also apply if such acts have environmentally-destructive consequences.

---

[93] Mark A. Drumbl, 'Waging War against the World: The Need to Move from War Crimes to Environmental Crimes' (1998) 22/1 Fordham International Law Journal 122–153 at 137, footnote 43.

Crimes against Humanity

The Rome Statute's article 7 crimes against humanity are "anthropocentric", focused on injury or harm to humans. This may explain why the definition contains no express reference to the environment, including its potential damage or destruction. Nevertheless, in certain circumstances, conduct with environmentally-damaging or destructive consequences could be prosecuted as a crime against humanity. In particular, this could be as extermination, persecution, inhumane acts, or even deportation and forced transfer. This of course requires establishing the elements of these crimes.

Article 7 (1) (b) criminalises extermination, which is defined in article 7 (2) (b) to include the mass killing of civilians through "the intentional infliction of conditions of life ... calculated to bring about the destruction of part of a population." The perpetrator must know that the act was or was intended as part of a widespread or systematic attack against the civilian population. Extermination is easier to prove than genocide, which requires proof of specific genocidal intention. The mass killing of civilians by intentionally inflicting conditions of life calculated to bring about their destruction could potentially occur by poisoning or draining water wells, destroying agricultural lands or wiping out forests or jungle habitats of indigenous groups.

Article 7 (1) (h) criminalises "persecution against any identifiable group or collectivity on political, ethnic, cultural, religious, gender ... or other grounds that are universally recognised as impermissible under international law, in connection with any act referred to in [article 7 (1)] or any crime within the jurisdiction of the Court." Persecution is defined in article 7 (2) (g) as "the intentional and severe deprivation of fundamental rights contrary to international law by reason of the identity of the group or collectivity". The deliberate destruction of a group's natural habitat, or damage to the group's natural environment, which impedes access to clean and safe food and water – if it reaches a significant enough magnitude – could amount to a breach of the group's fundamental rights. The Prosecution must therefore prove that the perpetrators acted with intent to discriminate on one of the identified grounds.

Article 7 (1) (k) provides another possibility for prosecuting acts that damage or destroy the environment. 'Inhumane acts' as a crime against humanity are those intentionally causing great suffering, or serious injury to body or to mental or physical health. These could be based upon environmental factors. For example, if a perpetrator intentionally damaged or destroyed vital elements of the natural habitat or environment that a population lives in or depends upon, thereby causing great suffering or serious injury to the population's physical or mental health, this could amount to inhumane acts as a crime against humanity. The Chernobyl and Fukushima examples apply equally here.

Article 7 (1) (d), deportation or forcible transfer of the population, is another possibility. Article 7 (2) (d) defines the crime as the "forced displacement of the persons concerned by expulsion or other coercive acts from the area in which they are lawfully present, without grounds permitted under international law." This could be when a government or organisation forces a group to leave its home in an inhabited forest or jungle by completely destroying it. The forcible displacement of the Marsh Arabs in Southern Iraq by the flooding of their habitat is a cogent example. Another example can be seen in the Prosecutor's Arrest Warrant against Omar Al Bashir which alleges that President Bashir targeted the land of rural communities, thereby forcing the displacement of the civilian population to allow oil companies to take advantage of the natural resources.[94]

Unlike war crimes, crimes against humanity can be committed in peacetime; a nexus to an armed conflict is not required. This widens their potential application to environmental crimes. However, they have rigorous threshold or contextual requirements. They require proof that the crimes were committed as part of a widespread or systematic attack directed against a civilian population, pursuant to or in furtherance of a State or organisational policy to commit the attack.

One commentator has argued that these contextual requirements greatly reduce, if not completely nullify, using crimes against humanity to pursue environmental crimes.[95] This, however, overlooks that it is only the *attack* that must be primarily directed at the civilian population, and that must be widespread or systematic, and pursuant to a State or organisational policy – rather than the acts themselves. Acts that intentionally damage or destroy the environment, such as deforestation, 'land grabbing' and exploiting the land of its natural resources could be prosecuted, where appropriate, if they result in inhumane acts, persecution, extermination or forcible transfer of a population. Their proscription as crimes against humanity will depend upon those underlying acts forming part of a wider attack against the civilian population, or part of a pattern of similar acts directed towards the civilian population, pursuant

---

94   *Situation in Darfur, Sudan: Prosecutor v al Bashir*, Decision on the Prosecution's Application for a warrant of arrest against Omar Hassan Ahmad Al Bashir, ICC-02/05-01/09-3, 4 March 2009, paras 99–100.

95   See Steven Freeland, Addressing the Intentional Destruction of the Environment during Warfare under the Rome Statute of the International Criminal Court (Intersentia 2015), pp. 203–204.

to a State or organisational policy to commit such an attack. For example, civilians could be targeted and dispossessed or forcibly transferred by making their land uninhabitable for them, but useful for say, a mining company.

This analysis of how crimes against humanity could be used to prosecute environmental crimes accords with the ICC Office of the Prosecutor's 2016 Case Selection and Prioritisation Policy. As noted above, this policy provides that the environmental impact of the crimes on the affected communities is a factor to be considered in selecting cases for prosecution, and that in this context, Rome Statute crimes committed by means of, or that result in, the destruction of the environment, illegal exploitation of natural resources or illegal dispossession of land will be given particular consideration.

Genocide

Acts designed to destroy a national, ethnical, racial or religious group (in whole or in part) could involve intentionally destroying the group's environment, as a way of trying to render impossible the group's ability to continue to exist. A potential avenue for criminalising such conduct as genocide exists under article 6 (c) of the Rome Statute. This provides that "[d]eliberately inflicting on the group conditions of life calculated to bring about its physical destruction in whole or in part" can amount to genocide. To constitute genocide, the acts must be done with the intent to destroy the national, ethnical, racial or religious group, as such – groups based on their social or cultural identity are not included in the definition.[96] The Elements of Crimes further stipulates that the genocidal acts must have taken place "in the context of a manifest pattern of similar conduct directed against that group or was conduct that could itself effect such destruction [of the group]."[97]

A footnote to article 6 (c) in the Elements of Crimes provides that "[t]he 'conditions of life' may include, but is not necessarily restricted to, deliberate deprivation of resources indispensable for survival, such as food or medical services, or systematic expulsion from homes."[98] This is a non-exhaustive list. Other examples could potentially include poisoning or draining water wells,

---

[96] The group can be defined using both objective and subjective criteria (*i.e.* that of the perpetrator and the victims): see *Prosecutor v Goran Jelisić*, IT-95-10-1, ICTY Trial Chamber, 14 December 1999, para 70, *Prosecutor v Georges Rutaganda*, ICTR-96-3, ICTY Trial Chamber I, 6 December 1999, para 57.
[97] ICC Elements of Crimes, Article 6 (c), element 5.
[98] ICC Elements of Crimes, Article 6 (c), footnote 4.

burning agricultural lands and destroying forests or jungles in which indigenous groups live or depend upon. A nuclear attack could be another. The Prosecution would need to prove that such acts were done with the intent to destroy the group's physical destruction (in whole or in part) and not merely their lifestyle.

One commentator has observed that the *dolus specialis*, or the required special intent, of genocide, and the restrictive nature of the groups that may be targeted for genocide, effectively means that the crime could rarely address the intentional destruction of the environment.[99] But others see more potential. For example, referring to the brutal targeting of the Ache Indians in Paraguay in the 1970s and the destruction of their forested habitation area to remove them from the land, to encourage mining and cattle-raising in the forests, one commentator has expressed her view that:

> No stretch of the imagination is required to foresee how environmental conditions, or the calculated and intentional destruction thereof, could be used as a means of effecting the destruction of a specific population, thereby amounting to an act of genocide.[100]

The scenario there could, however, present difficulties for proving genocidal intent. The perpetrators alleged that their intent was to clear and develop the land, and not to destroy the Indian group. Likewise, even though the Iraqi Government significantly drained the Mesopotamian Marshes (by 93%), leading to the deaths of large numbers of Marsh Arabs and the dispersal of many more, proving genocidal intent is problematic. The Iraqi Government's stated policy was of dam and canal building on the Tigris and Euphrates rivers for development purposes rather than to destroy an ethnic group.[101]

Prosecuting for genocide when (part of) the underlying criminal acts include the intentional destruction or damage to the environment of a group

---

99 See, e.g., Steven Freeland, Addressing the Intentional Destruction of the Environment during Warfare under the Rome Statute of the International Criminal Court (Intersentia 2015), pp. 197–198.

100 Tara Smith, 'Creating a Framework for the Prosecution of Environmental Crimes in International Criminal Law' in William Schabas, Yvonne McDermott and Niamh Hayes (eds), *The Ashgate Research Companion to International Criminal Law, Critical Perspectives* (Routledge 2013), pp. 45–62 at 47–48.

101 Tara Smith, 'Creating a Framework for the Prosecution of Environmental Crimes in International Criminal Law' in William Schabas, Yvonne McDermott and Niamh Hayes (eds), *The Ashgate Research Companion to International Criminal Law, Critical Perspectives* (Routledge 2013), pp. 45–62 at 49.

could present significant evidentiary challenges. Proof, however, should not be confused with the *legal* possibility of prosecuting such acts as genocidal acts under the Rome Statute.

Aggression

The crime of aggression in article 8 *bis* of the Rome Statute has not yet entered into force.[102] Yet, the invasion, attack or bombardment of one State by the armed forces of another could potentially lead to environmental damage or destruction – for example, where nuclear weapons or extreme biological or chemical weapons are used. It is not inconceivable that article 8 *bis* could be a possible route to prosecute environmental damage and destruction when one country wages aggressive war against another.

Conclusion

The principles relating to the protection of cultural property developed slowly, over many years. But those protecting the environment are crystalising comparatively far more rapidly.

We have always been socially aware of attacks on our cultural objects, and in particular, on our religious objects and symbols such as churches, mosques, synagogues and temples and their contents. But we are now far more environmentally aware than ever before; as is easily demonstrated by the numerous legal national and international environmental protection regimes that have developed over the last 40 or so years.

Added to this contemporary environmental awareness, and backed by legal protections, are the ICTY's prosecutions for cultural property crimes, under the heads of war crimes and crimes against humanity, and the ICC's 2016 conviction of an accused for intentionally attacking religious and historical buildings as a war crime. This shows how international case law can quickly develop where virtually none existed before.

At the ICTY, however, significant environmental crimes, some causing long-lasting, widespread and severe damage, could have been, but were not prosecuted. This is probably explicable in the context of the ICTY Prosecutor's focus on bringing to justice the perpetrators of the mass atrocity crimes of genocide,

---

102 Rome Statute, Article 15 *bis* sets out when the ICC may exercise jurisdiction over this crime.

extermination, persecution, deportation and forcible transfer based on killings, injury and harm suffered by individuals.

But we are moving into a different era, and the ICC's jurisdiction over war crimes, crimes against humanity, genocide and, in the future, aggression offers potential to prosecute environmentally-damaging or destructive crimes. Part of the ICTY's legacy shows how an area previously lacking in prosecutions, and hence judgements and case law, such as crimes against cultural property, can flourish legally. By analogy, the same could occur at the ICC with environmental crimes. The ICC Prosecutor's Case Selection Policy provides indications that this could transpire. But how and when, and in what circumstances, are the big questions.

CHAPTER 6

The Role of Comparative Law in Transnational Criminal Justice

Albin Eser

Abstract

The chapter explores the different paths and levels on which domestic and international criminal law may influence each other, what purpose might be served by such a conversation, and which methods are appropriate. In order to study these issues, two different epistemological categories appear useful. As far as the aim is concerned, recourse to foreign law is advisable, and potentially necessary, for two reasons: For the application of domestic or international criminal law in the context of judicial, or for the advancement of national or international law by means of legislative, comparative research. As far as the transnational context is concerned, foreign criminal law may play a role on three different levels: In the mutual dependence between national and foreign law and the administration of criminal justice, in international legal cooperation in criminal matters and, lastly, on the level of supranational criminal justice.

If one wanted to find out to what degree references to national criminal law play a role in the reasoning of international criminal tribunals, appropriate guidance may be found by looking for proceedings in which *Wolfgang Schomburg* served as a judge at the international tribunals for Rwanda (ICTR) and the former Yugoslavia (ICTY). Even without a thorough search simply relying on impressions received from browsing judgments of these courts, I dare to guess that Judge *Schomburg,* in whose honour this paper is prepared, is in the the upper class of the judges who do not shy away from supporting their reasoning through comparisons with national criminal law. Beside other instances later be referred to, as particularly significant examples two comparative expert opinions obtained from the Max Planck Institute for Foreign and International Criminal Law may be mentioned here: one requested by an ICTY

---

* Professor Dr. Dr. h.c. mult., M.C.J, Director Emeritus at the Max Planck Institute for Foreign and International Criminal Law Freiburg/Germany, former Ad-litem Judge at the International Tribunal for the former Yugoslavia at The Hague/The Netherlands.

Trial Chamber, presided by *Schomburg,* regarding information on the range of sentences the crimes concerned may be punished with according to penal laws of the former Yugoslavian States, of member States of the Council of Europe and of other major legal systems, as well as according to the jurisprudence of international criminal courts;[1] and the other expert report introduced by *Schomburg* in a dissenting opinion to an Appeals Chamber judgment, regarding the modes of participation in crime.[2]

So, when invited to make a contribution to his 70th birthday, I felt inspired – assuming that he also will find it worthwhile – to describe the various ways and levels on which national and international criminal law and practice can interact and influence each other, for what purpose such comparisons can serve and what methods they would require. This inquiry is best approached by making use of two categorical distinctions. First, with regard to purpose, taking foreign law into consideration may be advisable, if not even necessary, in two respects: for the application of domestic or international law in terms of judicative comparative criminal law or for the further development of national or international criminal law in terms of legislative comparative criminal law.[3] Second, with regard to its transnational scope, foreign law and justice may play a role in three areas and levels: in the interdependence of national criminal justice and foreign law (1), in international co-operation (2) and in supranational criminal justice (3).[4] Some of this will be considered in more detail in the following discussion.

---

1 Cf. *Prosecutor v Dragan Nikolić,* ICTY-IT-94-2-S, Trial Chamber II, Sentencing Judgement of 18 December 2003, paras. 38, 149 ss. Cf. also below 3.2.1 to n 57.

2 Cf. *Prosecutor v Blagoje Simić,* IT-95-9-A, Appeals Chamber, Judgment of 28 November 2006, Dissenting opinion of Judge Schomburg, paras. 19 ss. Cf. also below 3.2.1 to n 47.

3 For details of this differentiation between two – judicative and legislative – types of comparative criminal law, apart from the theoretical and evaluative-competitive categories within the foursome "tetrade" of comparative law, see Albin Eser, *Comparative Criminal Law. Development – Aims – Methods* (C.H. Beck/Hart/Nomos 2017), margin numbers 32 f., 50 ff.

4 As to these three levels of comparative criminal law, by distinguishing between the *trans*national application of domestic law on extraterritorial crimes, the *inter*national cooperation in criminal matters, and the *supra*national criminal justice – like it was already reflected in the three-stage set-up of an international workshop on transnational criminal law in Albin Eser and Otto Lagodny (eds.), *Principles and Procedures for a New Transnational Criminal Law* (edition iuscrim 1992) – cf. Albin Eser, 'Basic Issues of Transnational Cooperation in Criminal Cases', in Günter Heine, Björn Burkhardt and Walter Gropp (eds.), *Transnationales Strafrecht/Transnational Criminal Law. Gesammelte Beiträge/Collected Publications* (BWV 2011), pp. 305–325 (307 ff.) = www.freidok.uni-freiburg.de/data/3454. – By the way, the aforementioned international workshop on transnational criminal law had also been attended by *Wolfgang Schomburg* (cf. p. 875).

1 On the Horizontal Transnational Level

On this level, there are mainly three – partly overlapping – forms in which a comparative view beyond national borders can be required or at least helpful: when domestic criminal justice is dependent on foreign law (1.1), when advice from, or even import of, foreign law can enhance the administration of criminal justice (1.2), or when foreign criminal law can serve as a benchmark for the further development of national criminal law (1.3).

1.1 *Dependence of Domestic Criminal Justice on Foreign Law*
1.1.1 The Requirement of "dual criminality" for the Domestic Prosecution of Extraterritorial Crimes

This is nowadays probably the strongest case of dependence on foreign law: when domestic criminal law shall be applied to offences committed abroad. While for a long time on the European continent it was thought possible to extend one's own criminal law without reservation to extraterritorial crimes – despite the risk of transnational overlapping and international conflicts over interference –, one now tries to respect the sovereignty of the foreign country through the requirement of usually so-called "dual criminality". According to this – and with the exception of crimes governed by the principle of universality – the alleged offence must be criminally prohibited both at the domestic place where it is prosecuted and at the place of its commission.[5] Taking Germany as an example, there an "identical norm at the place of crime" is in particular required for the application of German criminal law to offences committed abroad under § 7 German Penal Code (StGB) for cases of the principles of "active" and "passive personality" (by which the extraterritorial application of domestic criminal law is based on the citizenship of the perpetrator or victim respectively, also known as "active" and "passive nationality" principles) as well as of the principle of "representative administration of criminal justice" (by acting on behalf of the jurisdiction of the place of commission, also known as "principle of complementary jurisdiction"). In all these cases it would not suffice simply to identify superficially similar criminal provisions,

---

5 For details to such a necessary link of the domestic jurisdiction trying the case and the extraterritorial place of the crime – with partly different requirements regarding the "identical norm at the place of crime" – see Albin Eser, '§ 7 Geltung für Auslandstaten in anderen Fällen', in Adolf Schönke and Horst Schröder, *Strafgesetzbuch Kommentar* (29th edn, C.H. Beck 2014), margin numbers 7 ff., 17, 23; Karin Cornils, *Die Fremdrechtsanwendung im Strafrecht* (De Gruyter 1978), pp. 217 ff., and from a more general European perspective André Klip, *European Criminal Law. An integrative Approach* (3rd edn, Intersentia Publishers 2016), pp. 175 ff.

rather their identical substance would have to be proven.[6] This, however, can hardly be investigated other than by way of comparison[7] – regardless whether the requirement of "dual criminality" is considered an element of substantive criminal law[8] or a procedural issue of jurisdiction.[9]

1.1.2 Filling of a Penal Provision with a Foreign Norm

In a similar way, the administration of criminal justice can also depend on the existence of a foreign provision. This in particular concerns the "blanket-type" application of foreign law as it can be observed especially at the European level.[10] As is characteristic for criminal laws of the blanket-type, the national criminal norm only establishes the sanctions and connects these to the elements of an offence, which is defined further by another act of law – usually called the "completing norm".[11] If this legal act is issued by an extra- or supranational authority, its consequence for the performance of domestic criminal justice is that foreign law has to be applied. This, however, can hardly be accomplished without a view beyond national borders.

1.2 *Import of Foreign Law into Domestic Criminal Law*

1.2.1 Incorporation of Foreign Criminal Provisions

This is probably the most intensive form of foreign law import. An example thereof can already be seen in the aforementioned filling of a "blanket" penal provision by a foreign "completing norm", particularly so when the foreign

---

6   For an in-depth analysis of this requirement of an "identische Tatortnorm" see Hans-Joseph Scholten, *Das Erfordernis der Tatortstrafbarkeit in § 7 StGB* (edition iuscrim 1995), pp. 27 ff.; cf. – also in a comparative manner – Karin Cornils, *Die Fremdrechtsanwendung im Strafrecht* (De Gruyter 1978), pp. 212 ff.

7   As to the method to be used for this comparison cf. Albin Eser, *Comparative Criminal Law. Development – Aims – Methods* (C.H. Beck/Hart/Nomos 2017), margin numbers 295 ff.

8   As in German doctrine: cf. Karin Cornils, *Die Fremdrechtsanwendung im Strafrecht* (De Gruyter 1978), p. 213.

9   As it seems to be the prevailing opinion in other countries: cf. Christine Van den Wyngaert, 'Double Criminality as a Requirement to Jurisdiction', in Nils Jareborg (ed.), *Double Criminality. Studies in International Criminal Law* (Iustus Förlag 1989), pp. 43–56.

10 With examples thereto cf. Ulrich Sieber, 'Strafrechtsvergleichung im Wandel', in Ulrich Sieber and Hans-Jörg Albrecht (eds.), *Strafrecht und Kriminologie unter einem Dach* (Duncker & Humblot 2006), pp. 78–151 (101).

11 So-called "Ausfüllungsnorm": cf. Albin Eser and Bernd Hecker, 'Vorbemerkungen vor § 1', in Adolf Schönke and Horst Schröder, *Strafgesetzbuch Kommentar* (29th edn, C.H. Beck 2014), margin number 3 with further references.

norm has been transformed into national law. This applies even more to the so-called "incorporated international crimes" that in various ways have been implemented into national penal codes along the Rome Statute. Whether this is done in a more or less direct or indirect way, such as by adoption, reference or creation of an equivalent national code,[12] in any case comparative expertise can be a helpful in finding the appropriate way for such an import of foreign law and its adjustment to national peculiarities.[13]

1.2.2 Implementing, Complementing and Limiting Functions of Foreign Law

Although less integratively than in the cases before, foreign law can also find the way into the domestic law by implementing, complementing or limiting it.

A classic and frequently cited example of the implementing function could be found in the Swiss Penal Code of 1937; according to its Art. 6 para. 1 sentence 2, if a Swiss citizen committed an offence outside Switzerland, then "the law of the place where the crime had been committed, was to be applied if it was the more lenient one".[14]

Of more topical importance are cases in which the application of the offence description (in terms if the German "Straftatbestand")[15] – or possible grounds for excluding criminal responsibility – may depend on so-called "incidental questions" of private or administrative law as, for instance, in the case of theft where the question of ownership of the chattel taken away from another has

---

12 For details to the various ways in which the provisions of the Rome Statute have been implemented into national codes see the findings of a comparative project concerning the national criminal prosecution of violations of international law, conducted by the Max Planck Institute for Foreign and International Criminal Law, summarized by Helmut Kreicker in Albin Eser, Ulrich Sieber and Helmut Kreicker (eds.), *Völkerstrafrecht im Ländervergleich* vol. 7 (Duncker & Humblot 2006), pp. 24 ff.

13 To such imports and transformations of foreign law see also Olympia Bekou, 'Crimes at Crossroads. Incorporating International Crimes at the National Level' (2012) 10/3 Journal of International Criminal Justice 677–691.

14 Even in view of this explicit obligation to implement foreign law, however, there was argument as to whether the judge was applying the more lenient foreign law as such (as assunmed by the Swiss Federal Court: cf. BGE 104 IV 77, 87 (1978), 118 IV 305, 308 (1992)), or whether the foreign law was turned into domestic law as "remitted federal criminal law" („verwiesenes Bundesstrafrecht": thus the prevailing opinion in the literature); cf. Peter Popp, 'Vor Art. 3', in Marcel Alexander Niggli and Hans Wiprächtiger (eds.), *Basler Kommentar Strafgesetzbuch* vol. I (Helbing & Lichtenhahn 2003), mn. 31.

15 Cf. Albin Eser, *Comparative Criminal Law. Development – Aims – Methods* (C.H. Beck 2017), margin number 106 n 249.

to be decided according to private (and not criminal) law.[16] When offences of this sort have been committed abroad but are to be prosecuted domestically, the question may arise whether and to what extent open elements of wrongdoing (such as the duty of care in the case of negligence or the obligation to avert a prohibited result in the case of an omission) or extra-criminal elements of the offence description (such as rules of proper accounting in insolvency crimes) should be determined according to the law of the domestic place of jurisdiction or the foreign place where the crime was committed.[17] Even this decision requires a comparative look beyond national borders, and this even more, when the elements of an offence description are to be complemented according to foreign law. This applies respectively in the case where foreign grounds for excluding criminal responsibility are to be considered, or when for determining the punishment cultural differences are to be taken into account, as it has recently been the subject of intense discussion, especially under the key word of "cultural defence".[18]

In contrast to these complementary functions, foreign law can also have a limiting effect. Here again the Swiss Penal Code with its reformed Art. 6 para. 2 of 2007 provides an example with regard to the sentencing of a crime committed abroad and prosecuted in the context of "representative administration of justice". In this case, "the court has to decide on sanctions that, overall, do not weigh more heavily on the perpetrator than those that would be applied according to the law of the place where the crime was committed". Although according to this rule – which is known in similar forms as transnational *lex mitior* from other legal systems as well[19] – both the evaluation of alleviating factors and the power of determining the sentence remain in the hands of the domestic judiciary, this task cannot be accomplished without transnational comparison of the relevant penal provisions.

1.3 *Improvement of the Criminal Law through Comparative Law*

Foreign law as a benchmark for the evaluation and further development of the domestic criminal law can play a role both on the judicative and the legislative

---

16   For more to such "incidental questions" cf. Albin Eser, 'Vorbemerkungen vor § 3', in Adolf Schönke and Horst Schröder, *Strafgesetzbuch Kommentar* (29th edn, C.H. Beck 2014), margin number 41.

17   For details see Albin Eser, ibidem, and fundamentally to such accessorial issues Karin Cornils, *Die Fremdrechtsanwendung im Strafrecht* (De Gruyter 1978), espec. pp. 16 ff.

18   Cf. – inter alia – the expert report to the 70th Deutsche Juristentag (German Lawyers Day) of 2014 by Tatjana Hörnle, *Kultur, Religion, Strafrecht – Neue Herausforderungen in einer pluralistischen Gesellschaft* (C.H. Beck 2014).

19   See – inter alia – § 10 para. 2 Danish Penal Code of 1930, Art. 19 para. 1 Turkish Penal Code of 2004.

level as well as it works in two directions: By learning from good as well as bad experiences made by other criminal jurisdictions, one can avoid the worse and adopt the the better ones.

1.3.1 Comparative Criminal Law as an "interpretation aid"

Even if – at least with regard to criminal law because of its especially distinct national character – it might be over the top to speak of comparative law as the "fifth" or even a "universal method of interpretation"[20], one cannot ignore that judges can learn a better understanding of their own law when they consult and take into account the jurisdiction and doctrine of another legal system – particularly within the same language and legal family.[21] Thus, when considering terms or elements of similar meaning, such as intent or negligence, commission of the offence or participation in it, a judge can hope to gain insights for the interpretation from their meaning in a related foreign legal system.[22]

This is even more obvious when – for the interpretation of one's own law – one can go back to its roots in a foreign "parent law".[23] For example, this can be

---

20 As postulated by Edward Schramm, 'Die Verwendung strafrechtsvergleichender Erkenntnisse in der Rechtsprechung des BVerfG [Bundesverfassungsgericht] und des BGH [Federal Supreme Court]', in Susanne Beck, Christoph Burchard and Bijan Fateh-Moghadam (eds.), *Strafrechtsvergleichung als Problem und Lösung* (Nomos 2011), pp. 155–178, 177 with reference to Peter Häberle and – focusing on private law – made explicit by Konrad Zweigert in the title of his 'Rechtsvergleichung als universale Interpretationsmethode' (1949/50) 15 Rabels Zeitschrift für ausländisches und internationales Privatrecht 677–691.

21 As demonstrated in an exemplary way by Robert Hauser, 'Die Rechtsvergleichung als Auslegungshilfe in der höchstrichterlichen Rechtsprechung im materiellen Strafrecht', in Theo Vogler (ed.), *Festschrift für Hans-Heinrich Jescheck* (Duncker & Humblot 1985) vol 2, pp. 1215–1232. Cf. also the comparative case material collected from the jurisprudence of the German Federal Constitutional Court and the Federal Supreme Court by Edward Schramm, 'Die Verwendung strafrechtsvergleichender Erkenntnisse in der Rechtsprechung des BVerfG [Bundesverfassungsgericht] und des BGH [Federal Supreme Court]' in Susanne Beck, Christoph Burchard and Bijan Fateh-Moghadam (eds.), *Strafrechtsvergleichung als Problem und Lösung* (Nomos 2011), pp. 160 ff. and 169 ff. respectively. With regard to similar references to foreign decisions by supreme courts in common law environments see Mads Andenas and Duncan Fairgrieve, 'Intent on making mischief: seven ways of using comparative law', in Pier Giuseppe Monateri (ed.), *Methods of Comparative Law* (Edward Elgar Publishing 2012), pp. 25–60, 31 ff.

22 As to the even more important interpretive function of comparative law on the supranational level cf. 2. 3. below.

23 Cf. Albin Eser, 'The Importance of Comparative Legal Research for the Development of Criminal Sciences', in International Association of Penal Law (ed.), *Les systèmes comparés de justice pénale: Comparative Criminal Justice Systems: From Diversity to Rapprochment* (Éditions érès 1998), pp. 77–108, 87 f. = www.freidok.uni-freiburg.de/data/3759; Hans-Heinrich Jescheck, 'Die Bedeutung der Rechtsvergleichung für die Strafrechtsreform',

the case when prohibitions or the rights of the accused are at issue in a type of criminal procedure that was taken over from another legal system – as, for example, the Turkish procedure was adopted from the German Code of Criminal Procedure. In such a case, the judge, when in doubt about the interpretation of taken-over law, may be well-advised to get clarification from the criminal jurisprudence of the country from which the rule in question originates.

1.3.2 Judge-made Development of the Law

More than mere interpretation is asked for when references to foreign law are made for adjusting current criminal law to new social developments. This borderline to legal policy might not yet have been transgressed when the German Federal Supreme Court (Bundesgerichtshof) – in the context of narrowing the meaning of the homosexual "committing an act of indecency" (according to the former § 175 German Penal Code) – found support in the foreign development of law.[24] In contrast, the step towards filling gaps for the further development of the law ("rechtsfortbildende Lückenfüllung") is certainly done when – by taking foreign legal development into account – the violation of a policeman's duty to inform a suspect about his right of silence is developed to an exclusionary rule with regard to the evidence illegally obtained.[25] In the same sense, it meant more than mere interpretation when the US Supreme Court excluded juvenile offenders from the death penalty – in a controversial majority decision[26] – and, thus, brought domestic backward law closer to more humane developments in foreign legal systems.[27]

---

in Arthur Kaufmann et al. (eds.), *Festschrift für Paul Bockelmann* (C.H. Beck 1979), pp. 133–154, 147 f.

24   BGH (German Federal Supreme Court), No. 2 StR 275/51, in *BGHSt* ('Entscheidungen des Bundesgerichtsthofs in Strafsachen') 1, pp. 293–298, 297 (13 July 1951). For further references to foreign criminal law in German court decisions cf. Albin Eser, *Comparative Criminal Law. Development – Aims – Methods* (C.H. Beck 2017), margin number 118.

25   Cf. BGH, No. 5 StR 190/91, in *BGHSt* 38, pp. 214–231, 228 ff. (27 February 1992); Edward Schramm, 'Die Verwendung strafrechtsvergleichender Erkenntnisse in der Rechtsprechung des BVerfG [Bundesverfassungsgericht] und des BGH [Federal Supreme Court]' in Susanne Beck, Christoph Burchard and Bijan Fateh-Moghadam (eds.), *Strafrechtsvergleichung als Problem und Lösung* (Nomos 2011), pp. 169 ff.

26   Cf. *Roper v. Simons*, 543 U.S. 551 (2005).

27   As to the ensuing controversy see the statement by Ruth Bader Ginsburg, '"Gebührender Respekt vor den Meinungen der Menschheit": Der Wert einer vergleichenden Perspektive in der Verfassungsrechtsprechung' (2005) Europäische GRUNDRECHTE-Zeitschrift (EuGRZ) 341–346.

1.3.3 Comparative Criminal Law as Aid for Legislative Law Reforms

If "law develops mainly by borrowing",[28] then – even more than by selective judicial ad-hoc amendments – further developments of the law will usually take place on the legislative way. This can be done for optimizing and modernizing the domestic criminal law by drawing attention to possibly better rules in foreign legal systems and – in search for the best possible standard of law in international "benchmarking" – to set reform processes in motion. While this may still be voluntary, in certain cases national lawmakers can be even bound by transnational agreements to adapt their law, as it is in particular the case with assimilations and harmonizations on the European level. As – due to space limitations here – described in more detail elsewhere,[29] it may be sufficient to note that – according to my experience in this field – there is almost no major criminal reform any more without making use of comparative law.

2 With Regard to International Cooperation

While on the transnational level dealt with before the employment of comparative law was one-sided in that a national jurisdiction would take notice of foreign law without necessarily getting in touch with the country concerned, on the international level of cooperation in criminal matters it is a sort of mutual affair in which both countries are more or less involved. On this truly *in-ter*national level between different criminal jurisdictions, there are mainly two instances where comparative law plays a role: in cases of extradition (2.1) and when multiple prosecution is at stake (2.2).

2.1 *The Requirement of "mutual criminality"*

In a certain parallel to the substantive-legal requirement of "dual criminality", according to which extraterritorial crimes can be prosecuted only if they are punishable both at the domestic place of the court and the foreign place of the crime,[30] a similar "mutual criminality" is also required at the level of international cooperation in criminal matters. According to this principle which plays an important role in international legal assistance, above all in the context

---

28   As is claimed in a frequently quoted dictum by Alan Watson, *The Making of the Civil Law* (Harvard University Press 1981), p. 181: though looking at the development of civil law, this may also apply to criminal law.
29   Albin Eser, *Comparative Criminal Law. Development – Aims – Methods* (C.H. Beck/Hart/Nomos 2017), margin numbers 133–148, 157–166.
30   Cf. 1.1.1 above.

of extradition, the conduct of the person concerned must be criminal under both the law of the country requesting extradition and the law of the country requested.[31] Whether this is the case in an individual instance, is – in a two-phase procedure of legal assistance sub-divided into a judicial admissibility and an executive approval procedure – usually to be examined during the first phase.[32] In order to do this, legal comparative work is necessary.

However, the comparison of norms which has to be made for the determination of "mutual criminality" is not exactly the same as that necessary for "dual criminality": while for the latter the greatest possible "identity" of the norm of the place of the commission is important, for the extradition out of Germany, for example, the focus in the relevant § 3 para 1 International Legal Assistance Act (IRG) is in principle merely on the fulfilment of the definitional elements of the offence (Tatbestandsmäßigkeit) according to German law; for that, however, a mere "adjustment in the general sense of the facts" is sufficient.[33]

2.2 Transnational Prohibition of Multiple Prosecutions

In a certain contrast to the need of cooperation in the case of extradition dealt with before, the issue of a transnational "ne bis in idem" at stake here is directed against possible international conflicts that can result from prosecutions of the same offense by different national jurisdictions. This can easily occur when, for example, a crime is committed in country A by a citizen of country B against a citizen of country C: in such a case each of the countries concerned may claim jurisdiction based on the principle(s) of territoriality, active personality or passive personality, respectively.[34] Whereas so far within

---

31 As, for instance, regarding the German extradition law, cf. § 3 International Legal Assistance Act (IRG); as to other proceedings of international legal assistance, in which mutual criminality can play a role, cf. the numerous references in Wolfgang Schomburg, Otto Lagodny et al. (eds.), *Internationale Rechtshilfe in Strafsachen* (5th edn, C.H. Beck 2012), p. 3205.

32 For details see Thomas Hackner, 'Einleitung', in Wolfgang Schomburg, Otto Lagodny et al. (eds.), *Internationale Rechtshilfe in Strafsachen* (5th edn, C.H. Beck 2012), margin numbers 58 ff.

33 The only really important aspect is that the conduct as such is punishable according to German law without necessarily requiring full punitive power of the German authorities. For details see Otto Lagodny, '§ 3', in Wolfgang Schomburg, Otto Lagodny et al. (eds.), *Internationale Rechtshilfe in Strafsachen* (5th edn, C.H. Beck 2012), margin numbers 3, 5 ff.

34 In addition to these links already referred to above at 1.1.1 as to further reasons why overlappings of various national criminal juirsdictions can occur at all, and why they should be avoided as much as possible, cf. Albin Eser, 'Konkurrierende nationale und transnationale Strafverfolgung – Zur Sicherung von "ne bis in idem" und zur Vermeidung von positiven

the same national jurisdiction a second prosecution would be barred by the internal "prohibition of double jeopardy", on the transnational level such a bar is not yet – or, at the most, only partly – recognized. On this area, countries could so far mostly only bring themselves to agree on a "principle of accounting" ("Anrechnungsprinzip"). This means that, when a crime has been adjudicated abroad, further prosecution and punishment domestically is not totally blocked, but rather the punishment imposed abroad must be credited against the new domestic punishment. However, because the national jurisdiction is only limited in this way, and not totally excluded, the domestic justice system is not spared further efforts of investigation and trial, nor is the already sentenced person – be he or she convicted or even acquitted – spared from further proceedings.

Meanwhile one tries to fend off such disadvantages with the "principle of recognition" ("Erledigungsprinzip") by which a sentence abroad is meant to stand in the way of a further domestic prosecution right from the start.[35] Even if the future lies with this principle – with the hoped-for increase in interstate trust in the rule of law within foreign criminal justice systems –,[36] so far it has only been able to prevail as transnational *ne bis in idem* in regions that are politically on an equal wave length, particularly in the European Union.[37]

Kompetenzkonflikten', in Ulrich Sieber, Helmut Satzger and Bernd v. Heintschel-Heinegg, *Europäisches Strafrecht* (2nd edn, Nomos 2014), pp. 636–660 = www.freidok.uni-freiburg. de/data/9724. For a comparative survey and analysis see Martin Böse, Frank Meyer and Anne Schneider (eds.), *Conflicts of Jurisdiction in Criminal Matters in the European Union* (Nomos 2013), and Walter Gropp, 'Kollision nationaler Strafgewalten – nulla prosecutio sine lege', in Arndt Sinn (ed.), *Jurisdiktionskonflikte bei grenzüberschreitender Kriminalität* (V&R 2012), pp. 41–63, 45 ff.

35 For details to these principles and their respective advantages and disadvantages see Albin Eser, 'Konkurrierende nationale und transnationale Strafverfolgung – Zur Sicherung von "ne bis in idem" und zur Vermeidung von positiven Kompetenzkonflikten', in Ulrich Sieber, Helmut Satzger and Bernd v. Heintschel-Heinegg, *Europäisches Strafrecht* (2nd edn, Nomos 2014), pp. 643 ff.

36 As to some further-reaching and some less far-reaching model drafts of a mechanism to avoid conflicts between criminal jurisdictions see Anke Biehler et al. (eds.), 'Freiburg Proposal on Concurrent Jurisdictions and the Prohibition of Multiple Prosecutions in the European Union' (2002) 73/3–4 Revue Internationale de Droit Pénal (ridp) 1195–1225, and Arndt Sinn (ed.), *Jurisdiktionskonflikte bei grenzüberschreitender Kriminalität* (V&R 2012), pp. 575–595 ff.

37 See *Albin Eser*, 'Justizielle Rechte', in Jürgen Meyer (ed.), *Charta der Grundrechte der Europäischen Union* (4th edn, Nomos 2014), pp. 652–717, 714 f. = www.freidok.uni-freiburg. de/data/9723.

However, whichever principle and procedure one may follow, without judicative criminal law one cannot get by: be it, to find out if, and to what extent, an offence tried abroad is identical to the offence under suspicion domestically, or be it, that – in the case of a simple crediting – the type and extent of the foreign sentence has to be balanced out against the domestic law.

3   In Relation to the Supranational Level

On this level, comparisons of law can – with fluid transitions – be helpful in three respects: in so far as the exercise of supranational criminal justice can depend on national law or jurisdiction (3.1), with regard to mutual inferences between national and supranational law (3.2), or in connection with the development of universal principles and supranational criminal law (3.3).

3.1   *Dependence of Supranational on National Criminal Justice*
3.1.1   The Principle of "complementarity"

This probably constitutes the strongest case in which the exercise of supranational criminal jurisdiction depends on national law and justice. According to this principle – first introduced by the Rome Statute in Art. 17 para 1 (a) and (b) regarding the relationship between national and supranational jurisdictions[38] – the International Criminal Court (ICC) is, amongst other things, authorized to prosecute when the primarily responsible national criminal justice system is either "unwilling or unable genuinely to carry out the investigation or prosecution".

For comparative criminal law this is important in two ways: On the one hand, for the ICC which could take on a suspected international crime when the primarily responsible national justice system cannot prosecute because there are – domestically – no corresponding crime descriptions; this requires the ICC both to determine the primarily responsible national jurisdictions and the examination of the relevant elements constituting an offence. On the other hand, a state affected by this – if it wants to ward off the politically embarrassing finding of its incompetence – would be well advised to incorporate

---

38 For details see William A. Schabas and Mohamd M. El Zeidy, 'Art. 17: Issues of admissibility', in Otto Triffterer and Kai Ambos (eds.), *The Rome Statute of the International Criminal Court. A Commentary*, (3rd edn, C.H. Beck/Hatt/Nomos 2016), pp. 781–831.

international crimes into its national criminal law system[39] – by way of the above mentioned "import of foreign law".[40]

3.1.2 Subsidiary Application of National Criminal Law

An even explicit dependence of supranational criminal justice on national criminal law – and thus requiring comparison – can result from provisions according to which national law has to be taken into consideration. Regarding such "subsidiary" application of national criminal law, the Rome Statute of the ICC has gone furthest so far with its step-by-step approach to "applicable law". Although according to Art. 21 para 1 national law is not first in line but to be considered only after the law of prior ranks – namely the Statute itself, treatise and principles of customary international law – provides no solution, the criminal law of certain individual countries (that would normally have jurisdiction) may come into play as part of the principles of law that are to be established by way of comparative law.

In a similar way, in Art. 24 para.1 s. 2 of the Statute of the ICTY it is envisaged that the Trial Chamber "shall have recourse to the general practice regarding prison sentences in the courts of the former Yugoslavia". This does not mean that the national statutory provisions would be declared to be directly applicable. At least, however, if not reaching further, through this reference to the legal practice there is the expectation that the court should give more intensive attention to the national law.[41]

3.2 *Mutual Influences between National and Supranational Criminal Law*

As is apparent already in the previous instances, when in the exercise of supranational justice national law has to be taken into account, if not even applied, this is a kind of foreign law import. This, however, is not the only way in

---

39   As to an international obligation to that effect see Albin Eser, 'Das Rom-Statut des Internationalen Strafgerichtshofs als Herausforderung für die nationale Strafrechtspflege', in Christian Grafl and Ursula Medigovic (eds.), *Festschrift für Manfred Burgstaller* (NWV 2004), pp. 355–373, 365 ff. = www.freidok.uni-freiburg.de/data/3675.

40   Cf. 1.2.1 above.

41   Another question is to what degree these demands are in fact made use of. Apart from the *Nikolić* Case (n 1), presided by Judge Schomburg, in which the court availed itself of a comparative expert opinion on the range of sentences in the former Yugoslavia, information of this sort seems to be scarcely collected, as may be concluded from a thorough case analysis by Silvia D'Ascoli, *Sentencing in International Criminal Law. The un ad hoc Tribunals and Future Perspectives for the ICC* (Hart 2011), espec. pp. 111 ff.

which elements of national criminal law can find entrance into the administration of supranational justice. Not less important are inferences by way of interpretation or recourse to general principles of law. This is not a one-way street though, but can run both bottom-up and top down between national and supranational law and justice in criminal matters.

3.2.1 National Law as Interpretation and Decision Aid for Supranational Criminal Law

In a similar way as domestic criminal law can draw support from other national law,[42] supranational criminal law can also look for interpretation aid in national law for words and terms that are not definitely unequivocal, or it may find support there for its reasoning. And this is indeed the main field in which – apart from recourses to international instruments – comparisons with national criminal law play a major role in the judicial application of supranational criminal law. To illustrate this with some examples, particular attention may be given to judgements in ICTY-proceedings in which *Wolfgang Schomburg*, this contribution is devoted to, served as a judge.

One of his main comparative battlefields concerned questions of perpetration and participation. Although the concept of "joint criminal enterprise", introduced as a mode of criminal responsibility already in the early *Tadić* appeals judgement[43], was already well established in the ICTY case law when he entered the court, as presiding judge in the *Stakić* trial Schomburg dared to challenge this concept by giving the modes of (direct or indirect) "co-perpetration", as it was particularly developed in German law, priority in the interpretation of the term "commission" of a crime.[44] After this alternative had been rejected in harshly – and anything but convincing – words by the appeals chamber,[45] Judge Schomburg – to the extent evident – did not miss any opportunity to demonstrate the various forms of co-perpetration as preferable over joint criminal enterprise: so first on a broad scale in a separate opinion to the appeals judgement in *Gacumbitsi*[46] and, additionally based on a comparative

---

42 Cf. 1.3.1 above.
43 *Prosecutor v. Duško Tadić*, IT-94-1-A; Appeals Judgement of 15 July 1999, paras. 185 ff.
44 *Prosecutor v. Milomir Stakić*, IT-97-24-T, Judgement 31 July 2003, paras. 439 ff. But cf. also the Dissenting Opinion of Judge Shahabudden in *Prosecutor v. Mitar Vasiljević*, IT-98-32-A; Appeals Judgement of 25 February 2004, paras. 3, 27 ff. with regard to the level of repsonsibility required for joint criminal enterprise and co- perpetratorship, respectively.
45 *Prosecutor v. Milomir Stakić*, IT-97-24-A, Appeals Judgement of 22 March 2006, para. 59.
46 *Prosecutor v. Silvestre Gacumbitsi*, ICTR-2001-64-A, Appeals Judgment of 7 July 2006, Separate Opinion of Judge Schomburg, paras. 5 ff., 16 ff.; cf. also the comparative considerations to co-perpetration in the Separate Opinion of Judge Shahabudden.

expert report on "Participation in Crime" by the Max Planck Institute for Foreign and International Criminal Law, in a dissenting opinion to the appeals judgement in *Simić*,[47] and further on reiterated in separate opinions to the appeals judgements in *Limaj*[48] and *Martić*[49] – without forgetting to emphasize that meanwhile the concepts of co-perpetratorship and control over the act have been recognized – with comparative references – by the ICC in the cases *Lubanga*[50] and *Katanga*.[51]

There are, of course, also decisions on other areas in which Judge Schomburg was involved and where recourse to national criminal law as well as to public international law has proven helpful. Regarding general elements of criminal responsibility, mention may be made of psychological assistance as sufficient for aiding and abetting in *Kamuhanda*[52], of the principal requirements of *mens rea* in *Blaškić*[53] and with special regard to aiding and abetting in *Krstić*,.[54] Further comparative instances of more general nature are the penalization of prohibitions in customary international law (concerning terror against the civilian population) in *Galić*[55] or the application of the principle of *lex mitior* in former Yugoslavia in *Deronjić*.[56]

Since sentencing is also a rewarding field of comparison, it was probably on the initiative of the presiding judge Schomburg that in the *Nikolić* case the Max

---

47   *Prosecutor v. Blagoje Simić*, IT-95-9-A, Appeals Chamber, Judgement of 28 November 2006, Dissenting opinion of Judge Schomburg, paras. 19 ss.
48   *Prosecutor v. Fatmir Limaj*, IT-03-66-A, Appeals Judgement of 27 September 2007, paras. 8 ff.
49   *Prosecutor v. Milan Martić*, IT-95-11-A, Appeals Judgement of 8 October 2008, Separate Opinion of Judge Schomburg, paras. 2 ff.; as to the sentencing in this case also referring (in para. 1) to the comparative expert report of the Max Planck Institute in the *Nikolić* case (n 1, 57).
50   *Prosecutor v. Thomas Lubanga Dyilo*, ICC-01/04-01/06, Decision on the confirmation of charges of 29. January 2007, paras. 317 ff.
51   *Prosecutor v. Germain Katanga and Mathieu Ngudjolo Chui*, ICC-01/04-01/ Decision on the confirmation of charges of 30. September 2008, especially concerning indirect perpetration by virtue of an organisational power apparatus, paras. 480 ff.
52   *Prosecutor v. Jean de Dieu Kamuhanda*, ICTR-99-54A-A, Appeals Judgement of 19 September 2005, Separate Opinion by Judge Schomburg, paras. 384 f.
53   *Prosecutor v. Tihomir Blaškić*, IT-95-14-A, Appeals Judgement of 29 July 2004, Separate Opinion by Judge Schomburg, paras. 34 ff.
54   *Prosecutor v. Radislav Krstić*, IT-98-33-A, Appeals Judgement of 19 April 2004, paras. 141 ff.
55   *Prosecutor v. Stanislav Galić*, IT-98-29-A, Appeals Judgement of 30 November 2006, Dissenting Opinion of Judge Schomburg, paras. 7 ff., 24.
56   *Prosecutor v. Miroslav Deronjić*, IT-02-61-S, Sentencing Judgement of 13 March 2004, paras. 162 ff.

Planck Institute for Foreign and International Criminal Law was requested to submit an almost worldwide comparative survey on the ranges of sentences.[57] By frequently being referred to, this also proved as informative in *Deronjić* with regard to the determination of the punishment in the case of a guilty plea.[58] The same applies to taking into account the impact of a crime on a victim's relatives when determining the appropriate punishment in *Krnojelac*.[59]

Regarding special crimes, references to national law played a role for the interpretation of "deportation" concerning the disputed "cross-border" transfer requirement in *Krnojelac*[60] and *Naletilić*,[61] as well as for the definition of "rape" in *Kunarac*.[62]

In the range of procedural law, national criminal law found attention with regard to the accused's right to appear as witness in his own defense in *Galić*,[63] to the point at which a person's status changes to being a suspect in *Halilović*,[64] to the principle of *in dubio pro reo* in terms of only relating to the establishment of facts and not the questions of law in *Limaj*,[65] and to the requirements for presenting an appeal in *Kunarac*.[66]

Apart from the ICTY-judgements in which Judge *Schomburg* was involved, merely some of those decsions in which national criminal law and/or public international law is paid special attention may be mentioned. This applies already to the establishment of the international tribunal in *Tadić*[67] and the

---

57 As to the broad scope to be covered by this "Sentencing Report" see the *Nikolić* decision (n 1) para. 38, presented by Ulrich Sieber (ed.), *The Punishment of Serious Crimes – A comparative analysis of sentencing law and practice* (Max-Planck-Institut 2004) vol 1 (*Expert Report*) and vol 2 (*Country Reports*).

58 *Deronjić* (n 56), Dissenting Opinion of Judge Schomburg, para. 14.

59 *Prosecutor v. Milorad Krnojelac*, IT-97-25-A, Appeals Judgment of 17 September 2003, paras. 259 f.

60 *Krnojelac* (n 59), where Judge Schomburg in his Dissenting Opinion went even back to the Roman law: para. 13.

61 *Prosecutor v. Miladen Naletilić and Vinko Marinović*, IT-98-34-A, Appeals Judgement of 3 May 2006, Dissenting Opinion of Judge Schomburg, with particular attention to customary international law and international principles of interpretation: paras. 10 ff.

62 *Prosecutor v. Dragoljub Kunarac et al.*, IT-96-23 & IT-96-23/!-A, Appeals Judgement of 12 June 2002, paras. 127 ff.

63 *Galić* (n 55), paras. 19 ff.

64 *Prosecutor v. Sefere Halilović*, IT-01-48-A, Appeals Judgement of 16 October 2007, Separate Opinion of Judge Schomburg, para. 4.

65 *Limaj* (n 48), Separate Declaration of Judge Schomburg, paras. 15 ff.

66 *Kunarac* (n 62), paras. 42 ff.

67 *Prosecutor v. Duško Tadić*, IT-94-1-AR72, Decision on the defence motion for interlocutory appeal on jurisdiction of 2 October 1995, espec. paras. 54 ff.

highly disputed rejection of "duress" as not affording complete defense to a soldier in *Erdemović*.[68] Broad comparative discussions can also be found to the already cited introduction of "joint criminal enterprise" in *Tadić*[69], as well as there to the motives required for crimes against humanity[70] and, in procedural respect, to the necessary "equality of arms".[71]

3.2.2 Supranational Influences on National Criminal Law

In the reverse direction to the bottom-up grounding of supranational on national criminal law, there can also be top-down influences from supra- or international law on domestic criminal law. This can result from the fact that, as described by Heinz Neumayer, "comparative law (delivers) valuable indications for the interpretation of laws which are around in ever increasing numbers, have grown on supranational legal soil and rise above the doctrinal structures of individual legal systems."[72] In this way influenced from above will become the more compelling, the more judges in the exercise of criminal justice are bound by concrete supranational prescriptions.

This is of growing importance, especially in the European area where national criminal law can be subjected to primary and secondary Union Law of the EU: primarily, by the fact that there might be upper and lower limits concerning the offence descriptions, or that sanctions that are adverse to Union Law may even be forbidden;[73] and secondarily, by the way that certain preconditions are set for the national criminal law, as particularly through directives according to Art. 83 of the Treaty on the Functioning of the European Union (TFEU).[74]

But even where there are no binding directives, the supranational influence on national criminal law – because of the rule of interpretation in conformity

---

68   *Dražen Erdemović*, IT-96-22-A, Appeals Judgment of 7 October 1997, with controversial separate and dissenting opinions by all judges.
69   *Tadić* (n 43).
70   *Tadić* (n 43), paras. 253 ff.
71   *Tadić* (n 43), paras. 43 ff, with special attention to this to the jurisprudence of the European Court of Human Rights.
72   This supply of components, emphasized by Heinz Neumayer, 'Grundriß der Rechtsvergleichung', in Rene David and Günther Grasmann, *Einführung in die großen Rechtssysteme der Gegenwart* (2nd German edn, C.H. Beck 1988), pp. 1–77, 31 as essential for the development of public international law, is no less significant for criminal law.
73   For details to the case law of the various European courts see André Klip (ed.), *Materials on European Criminal Law* (2nd edn, Intersentia Publishers 2014).
74   Thoroughly thereto see Kai Ambos, *Internationales Strafrecht* (4th edn, C.H. Beck 2014), pp. 566 ff.

with Union Law ('unionsrechtskonforme Auslegung') – should not be underestimated. According to this, the court – similar to domestic interpretation in conformity with the constitution ('verfassungskonforme Auslegung') – has to favour, out of a group of several variants of interpretation of a criminal norm all tenable according to national understanding, the one that best complies with Union Law, or at least does not contradict it.[75] In doing this, not only directives but also decrees and framework decisions of European institutions and bodies are to be taken into account.[76]

Going further than this, according to the rule of interpretation favourable to international law ('völkerrechtsfreundliche Auslegung'), supranational criminal law might find entry into national criminal law not only by incorporating international crimes via the importation of foreign law,[77] but also through the demand that, for example, the borderline of the wording of the (former) § 220a German Penal Code for genocide was to be "determined in the light of the international normative directive".[78] In the sense of the idea of interpretation in conformity with international law, even solely national crime definitions are to be interpreted and applied in accord with the development of international criminal law and the judicature of supranational courts.

3.3 Development of Supranational and Universal Criminal Law

While the previous instances take place mainly in the area of judicative comparative law, the following ones have essentially to do with legislative comparative law, with the focus on the creation of universal criminal law and the furtherance of supranational criminal justice.

3.3.1 Identification of the Highest Legal Principles and Preparation of International Conventions

First steps can be made through the identification of topmost legal principles through comparative law, that is to say, principles which have found extensive acceptance on a national level and thus can deliver national as well as transnational standards for further legal development.[79] This model function is of importance both on the substantive-legal level – for example, for the recognition

---

75 Cf. Klaus Gärditz, 'Europäisierung des Strafrechts und nationales Verfassungsrecht', in Martin Böse (ed.), *Europäisches Strafrecht* (Nomos 2013), pp. 227–268, 258 f.

76 For further details and references to court decisions see Kai Ambos, *Internationales Strafrecht* (4th edn, C.H. Beck 2014), pp. 582 ff.

77 As described above 1.2.1.

78 According to the German Federal Constitutional Court ('BVerfG'), No. 2 BvR 1290/99, (2001) Neue Juristische Wochenschrift 1848–1853, 1850 (12 December 2000).

79 This supply of components, emphasized by Heinz Neumayer, 'Grundriß der Rechtsvergleichung', in Rene David and Günther Grasmann, *Einführung in die großen Rechtssysteme*

of the principles of legality and personal guilt – and in the procedural area – for instance, for the development of rules of fairness established in general declarations of human rights.[80]

Such an establishment of topmost principles of law can at the same time serve as important preliminary work for the expansion and strengthening of international conventions and agreements. Renowned examples for this are the prohibition of genocide,[81] and the prohibition of cruel, inhumane and degrading punishment.[82] Not only do such world-wide elevations of more humane criminal justice need concrete comparative law based coordination with respect to the already achieved legal level, as well as some encouragement to progress together, but there is also the need to find – with regard to terminology and legal-technical matters – a transnationally operational set of instruments. In this sense, although not without pathos, the special responsibility of comparative law has been particularly invoked for the development of international criminal law.[83]

3.3.2 Optimizing International Criminal Justice

Such efforts may find their crowning conclusion in the establishment and promotion of international criminal justice. After this had happened initially in

---

der Gegenwart (2nd German edn, C.H. Beck 1988), pp. 1–77, 31 as essential for the development of public international law, is no less significant for criminal law.

80   Cf. Hans-Heinrich Jescheck, 'Die Bedeutung der Rechtsvergleichung für die Strafrechtsreform', in Arthur Kaufmann et al. (eds.), *Festschrift für Paul Bockelmann* (C.H. Beck 1979), pp. 133–154, 137 f.

81   Convention on the Prevention and Punishment of the Crime of Genocide of 9 December 1948.

82   As worldwide proclaimed in the prohibition of torture in Art. 5 of the Universal Declaration of Human Rights of 1948 and expanded by Art. 7 of the International Covenant on Civil and Political Rights of 1966 and supplemented in Arts. 3 and 5 of the European Convention on Human Rights of 1950 for the European area. With regard to these and other international agreements, designed to provide both improved legal protection and humanization of those inhumane punishments still existing in some places, cf. the comprehensive documentation by Christine Van den Wyngaert (ed.), *International Criminal Law. A Collection of International and European Instruments* (3rd edn, Martinus Nijhoff Publishers 2005).

83   Thus Hans-Heinrich Jescheck, *Entwicklung, Aufgaben und Methoden der Strafrechtsvergleichung* (Mohr 1955), p. 31, who, possibly remembering the outrageous abuses of criminal law in war time Germany, sees comparative law "as the objective conscience of mankind, called upon to secure justice through its great postulates of impartiality of the courts, equality of perpetrators before the law and proportionality of guilt and punishment, against the repercussions of "unconditional hatred" [with reference to Russell Grenfell] during the time of war: partisanship, unilateralism and excessiveness".

the form of geographically limited, temporary international Ad hoc tribunals for the prosecution and sentencing of crimes against international law in the former Yugoslavia (ICTY) and Rwanda (ICTR) – to which were added other similarly limited, nationally-internationally mixed courts for other regions also marked by the most horrendous violations of international law –, the establishment of a permanent international criminal court, as was achieved by the Rome Statute for the ICC, was basically only a question of time.[84]

What important role comparative law can play here, could hardly be demonstrated better than by having a look at the different conditions of emergence of the Ad hoc ICTY and ICTR compared with the ICC. While the urgency with which the Yugoslavia and Rwanda Tribunals had to be established left little time for sound preparation, the ICC could afford a longer lead-in time. Accordingly, the Statute that is authoritative for the work of the ICTY – and is almost the same in content for the ICTR – is, with 34 articles, extremely short; it contains – over and above jurisdictional provisions – very little in regard to the general requirements of criminal liability and not much more in regard to procedure. In contrast, the Rome Statute with its 129 articles has a lot more to say, both substantive-legally and procedurally. In this context, the comparative law coaching would have to be pointed out; without it, Part 3 of the Rome Statute, which is devoted to the "General Principles of Criminal Law", would probably have remained even more rudimentary: After the ICC-draft by the International Law Commission had essentially been limited to more formal aspects of jurisdiction, the preparation of essential elements of criminal liability – for example, as related to intent and error, attempt and participation, self-defence and other grounds for excluding criminal responsibility – only got underway when academic circles took the initiative and put forward alternative drafts.[85]

These different starting conditions became apparent in the content of the procedural rules. While the predominantly, if not even one-sidedly common-law origin is widely assumed in the articles for the ICTY and ICTR, few as there

---

84 Cf. Paul Roberts, 'Comparative Law for International Criminal Justice', in Esin Örücü and David Nelken (eds.), *Comparative Law. A Handbook* (Hart Publishing 2007), pp. 329–370, 340 ff., 354 ff. For details with regard to this development, that had already started with the Versailles Peace Treaty, and in some respect before that, see Kai Ambos, *Treatise on International Criminal Law, Volume I: Foundations and General Part* (Oxford University Press 2013), pp. 1 ff.

85 In view of my own involvement in these endeavours, reference may be made to the so-called Siracusa-Freiburg-Chicago-Draft: cf. Albin Eser, 'Individual Criminal Responsibility', in Antonio Cassese et al. (eds.), *The Rome Statute of the International Criminal Court: A Commentary* (Oxford University Press 2002) vol 1, pp. 767–822, 767 f. = www.freidok.uni-freiburg.de/data/3909.

are, stronger influences from the continental-European criminal law tradition become apparent in the Rome Statute. Similar shifts of emphasis can also be observed in the Rules of Procedure and Evidence (RPE) that complement the Statute. This can already be seen in the different role of the judiciary. After the ICTY and the ICTR had to get to work virtually without procedural directives, the judges were obliged to establish the necessary procedural rules for themselves. In this law-creating task and opportunity, which had to be undertaken in regular plenary sessions, it was inevitable that the rules were initially dominated by the legal ideas of that group of judges which, in using this opportunity, could put the most complete and quickly usable compendium on the negotiating table: and that was, after all, achieved by the then mainly common law-based group of judges – above all in the person of the later ICTY president *Gabrielle Kirk McDonald*.[86] However, later on things changed: The more unsuitable the adversarial procedural structure of the common law turned out to be in its practical application in the ICTY – at least for complex international criminal procedures –, the more instructional elements from modern continental-European procedural law – often polemically discredited as "inquisitorial" – gained entry into the judicial-legal Rules of Procedure and Evidence.[87]

The RPE for the ICC did not have to go through such a process of change. On the one hand, not in a formal sense, because they did not come about through judicial plenary decisions, but were created by the competent bodies of the Rome Statute in a procedure resembling a legislative process, and on the other hand, because the experiences gained from ICTY practice could be taken into consideration when the ICC-RPE were drawn up. This happened on a comparative law basis and with the participation of commission members from different legal circles.[88] In doing so, the participants had to familiarize themselves

---

86 Cf. Albin Eser, 'Procedural Structure and Features of International Criminal Justice: Lessons from the icty', in Bert Swart, Alexander Zahar and Göran Sluiter (eds.), *The Legacy of the International Criminal Tribunal for the former Yugoslavia* (Oxford Univesity Press 2011), pp. 108–148, 119 = www.freidok.uni-freiburg.de/data/9713.

87 For details see Albin Eser, 'Changing Structures: From the ICTY to the ICC', in Bruce Ackerman, Kai Ambos and Hrvoje Sikiric (eds.), *Visions of Justice. Liber Amicorum Mirjan Damaška* (Duncker & Humblot 2016), pp. 213–234, 216 ff.; cf. also Vladimir Tochilovsky, 'The Nature and Evolution of the Rules of Procedure and Evidence', in Karim A.A. Khan, Caroline Buisman and Christopher Gosnell (eds.), *Principles of Evidence in International Criminal Justice* (Oxford University Press 2010), pp. 157–184, 159 ff.

88 Cf. Albin Eser, 'Changing Structures: From the ICTY to the ICC', in Bruce Ackerman, Kai Ambos and Hrvoje Sikiric (eds.), *Visions of Justice. Liber Amicorum Mirjan Damaška* (Duncker & Humblot 2016), pp. 213–234, 225 ff.; Vladimir Tochilovsky, 'The Nature and

with the possibly divergent legal ideas and different styles of thinking of the respective negotiation partners – and put themselves in the others' position as well, because "only the person who knows the cultural preconditions of the other side can negotiate sensibly".[89] This sensitivity, however, cannot be reached without comparative law.

4 Conclusion

There are certainly more instances in which a comparative view beyond borders, on the transnatioanl level between different domestic jurisdictions as well as bottom-up from national to supranational law and vice-versa top-down, can be advisable, if not even necessary. But as can already be concluded from the survey presented before, the important and multi-faceted role of comparative law for transnational criminal justice can hardly be overestimated, both in terms of adjudicative and legislative comparative law.

Regarding *Wolfgang Schomburg,* this contribution is devoted to as a longtime friend and judges colleague at the ICTY, in his capacity as judge in international criminal justice he has distinguished himself as one of the most prominent comparatists in criminal law. For this, amongst his many other achievements, he deserves greatest gratitude and best wishes to his 70th birthday.

Evolution of the Rules of Procedure and Evidence', in Karim A.A. Khan, Caroline Buisman and Christopher Gosnell (eds.), *Principles of Evidence in International Criminal Justice* (Oxford University Press 2010), pp. 157–184, 158.

89 As correctly stated by Eric Hilgendorf, 'Zur Einführung: Globalisierung und Recht. Aufgaben und Methoden der Strafrechtsvergleichung heute', in Susanne Beck, Christoph Burchard and Bijan Fateh-Moghadam (eds.), *Strafrechtsvergleichung als Problem und Lösung* (Nomos 2011), pp. 5–25, 18.

CHAPTER 7

Protecting Human Rights through Exclusionary Rules? Highlights on a Conflict in Criminal Proceedings from a Comparative Perspective

Sabine Gless

Abstract

Do exclusionary rules safeguard respect for human rights in criminal trials? In criminal proceedings individual rights are constantly at risk, starting with the establishment of facts in order to reach a decision on the defendant's guilt or innocence. Respect for human rights however must not cease when the bearer of those rights is suspected of having committed a criminal offence or is needed as a witness. Yet, the means to prevent violations of rights in criminal proceedings are limited. A promising instrument for avoiding certain human rights violations is the practice of excluding illegally obtained evidence from the criminal process. The rationale of so-called exclusionary rules is the expectation that law enforcement officers will refrain from employing methods of evidence-gathering that infringe human rights if they know that tainted evidence cannot be used at trial. The article assesses the impact of exclusionary rules in criminal proceedings by analysing the balancing of interests when deciding on the admissibility of evidence in European as well as in the Chinese and U.S. criminal justice systems.

1 Double Hypothesis

The protection of individual rights and, especially, human rights in criminal proceedings is a matter that is very close to *Wolfgang Schomburg*'s heart. On numerous occasions, he has explained that, no matter what charges are brought against an accused, a defendant's human rights may not be violated and access to a fair trial must be provided – in national, international and transnational

---

* Dr. iur., Chair of Criminal Law and Criminal Procedure, University of Basel. I wish to thank Xinyun Peng who assisted me with her knowledge of Chinese law. My gratitude also goes to the participants of the SNF-project "Fair trial through exclusionary rules", Ho Hock Lai, Laura Macula, Thomas Richter, Jenia Turner, Shih-Fan Wang and Thomas Weigendand and to the Swiss National Science Foundation for funding.

proceedings.[1] He strongly believes that the respect for individual rights is a key factor for the credibility and integrity of a legal system.[2] But he also knows that the means to actually ensure effective protection of human rights in criminal proceedings are rather limited. To many scholars of penal proceedings, one of the most promising instruments for obviating human rights violations is the exclusion of illegally obtained evidence from the criminal process, in order to deter future violations of rules.[3] The assumption is that law enforcement officers will refrain from employing methods of evidence gathering that infringe upon individual rights if they know that any evidence gained in such a manner would be useless because it will not be admitted at trial. The question arises as to whether this reasoning is actually validated by the lawmaker's objectives, legal frameworks, doctrine and case law concerning exclusionary rules that we find on the national level? In a first approach to addressing this question, this article scrutinizes the double hypothesis that exclusionary rules are (a) meant and (b) made to protect individual rights in criminal proceedings against the backdrop of the fundamental conflict of interests in criminal proceedings: the wish for comprehensive fact-finding, on the one hand, and protection of individual rights of defendants and witnesses, on the other. An overview of lawmakers' aspirations in Switzerland, Germany, United States of America (USA), People's Republic of China (PRC) and Taiwan when adopting exclusionary rules illustrates the thrust of the laws. Highlighting the issue of excluding fruits of the poisonous tree provide a first basis to assess whether the relevant laws actually have a potential for protecting human rights in criminal proceedings.

---

1   Wolfgang Schomburg, Otto Lagodny, 'Verteidigung im international-arbeitsteiligen Strafverfahren' (2012) Neue Juristische Wochenschrift, 348.
2   Wolfgang Schomburg, 'The Role of International Criminal Tribunals in Promoting Respect for Fair Trial Rights' (2009) 8 Northwestern Journal of International Human Rights, 1.
3   Hock Lai Ho, 'The Criminal Trial, the Rule of Law and the Exclusion of Unlawfully Obtained Evidence' (2014) Crim. L. & Phil. 4; Walter Pakter, 'Exclusionary Rules in France, Germany, and Italy' (1985) 9 Hastings Int'L & Comp. L. Rev. 1, 56; David Ormerod and Diane Birch, 'The Evolution of the Discretionary Exclusion of Evidence' (2004) Crim. L. Rev. Supp (50th Anniversary Edition), 141; Rosemary Pattenden, 'Admissibility in Criminal Proceedings of Third Party and Real Evidence Obtained by Methods Prohibited by UNCAT' (2006) International Journal of Evidence & Proof, 10(1), 13; Dimitrios Giannoulopoulos, 'The Exclusion of Improperly Obtained Evidence in Greece: Putting Constitutional Rights First' (2007) International Journal of Evidence & Proof, 11(3), 181; Paul Roberts, Jill Hunter, 'Criminal Evidence and Human Rights: Reimaging Common Law Procedural Traditions' (2013) Crim. L. Rev. 2, 176–179; see also arguments provided by Association for the Prevention of Torture <http://www.apt.ch/en/evidence-obtained-through-torture> accessed on 24 March 2017.

2 The Ubiquitous Conflict

In all criminal justice systems, the public has a strong interest in determining the truth, because in a common understanding it is only on the basis of "true facts" that a court can decide whether a suspect is guilty or innocent.[4] The interest in finding the truth has led to procedural rules that expose suspects and witnesses to coercive measures, which frequently interfere with individual rights. The classic conflict of criminal proceedings – between the state's interest in determining the facts relevant to the suspect's guilt and potential sentencing, and the suspect's (and possibly other individuals') interest in maintaining privacy and avoiding conviction leads to a conflict between comprehensive fact-finding and safeguarding individual rights, especially those of defendants, in all criminal justice systems.

The infliction of physical pain in order to obtain evidence is a drastic measure and, generally speaking, torture is an outdated concept in criminal justice. The right to be free from torture is a basic right and, in principle, accepted world-wide, based on the U.N. Convention against Torture and Other Cruel, Inhuman or Degrading Treatment or Punishment (CAT),[5] which itself establishes an obligation to exclude evidence acquired through torture.[6] Recent events, however, have revealed that the line may be crossed quickly, even in states solidly committed to the rule of law, for instance, in the fight against terrorism.[7]

---

4 See for the Swiss legal System: Sabine Gless, 'Art. 139–Art. 141 Beweismittel' in Marcel Alexander Niggli, Marianne Heer and Hans Wiprächtiger (eds.), *Basler Kommentar. Schweizerische Strafprozessordnung* (2nd edn, Helbing Lichtenhahn, Basel 2014), art. 139, note 1; for the German legal system: Carl-Friedrich Stuckenberg, 'Schuldprinzip und Wahrheitserforschung. Bemerkungen zum Verhältnis von materiellem Recht und Prozessrecht' (2016) Goltdammer's Archiv für Strafrecht, 689, 695 et seq.; for the Chinese legal system: FAN Chongyi (樊崇义), 'Views on the Objective Authenticity and Discussion about the Standard of Proof in Criminal Proceedings' (客观真实管见：兼论刑事诉讼证明标准) (2000) Chinese Legal Science (《中国法学》) Vol. 1, 114.

5 Convention against Torture and Other Cruel, Inhuman or Degrading Treatment or Punishment, 10 December 1984, 1465 U.N.T.S. 85; <http://www.ohchr.org/EN/ProfessionalInterest/Pages/CAT.aspx> accessed on 24 March 2017.

6 Art. 15 CAT stipulates "Each State Party shall ensure that any statement which is established to have been made as a result of torture shall not be invoked as evidence in any proceedings, except against a person accused of torture as evidence that the statement was made." For further information, see: Tobias Thienel, 'The Admissibility of Evidence Obtained by Torture under International Law' (2006) The European Journal of International Law Vol. 17 EJIL, 349, at 351–353.

7 See for instance: Brugger, 'May Government Ever Use Torture? Two Responses from German Law' (2000) 48 American J Comparative L 661; David Hope, 'Torture' (2004) 53 ICLQ 807;

Furthermore, different forms of "physical coercion" persist in many places as a means of obtaining evidence.[8] Although physically coerced evidence is controversial since its reliability is disputed, it may lead to derivative evidence that can be viewed as reliable.[9]

As constantly pointed out by *Wolfgang Schomburg*, who has sat on benches judging atrocities and core crimes, respect for fair trial rights must not cease when the bearer of those rights is suspected of having committed a criminal offence or is needed as a witness.[10] The protection of individual rights is an intrinsic feature of criminal procedure codes, which, for Western countries, has been dated by some scholars back to the Magna Charta.[11] In recent decades, human rights have become topical in criminal proceedings, with the emergence of a modern human rights movement.[12] This movement promises the safeguarding of individual rights. Best known, perhaps, is the European Convention of Human Rights[13] (ECHR), because it not only establishes rights but offers a remedy, i.e., access to the European Court of Human Rights (ECtHR).[14] Today, various human rights have an impact on criminal proceedings: the right to have one's human dignity respected, to be free from physical force and torture, the right against self-incrimination, and also the right to have the privacy of one's home and intimate sphere respected. It is these rights, in particular, that tend to inhibit the authorities' quest for the truth. The search for truth is a very strong ambition in criminal proceedings it manifests an ever-present

---

Sanford Levinson, *Torture: a Collection* (OUP, Oxford 2004); Marcy Strauss, 'Torture', (2004) 48 New York Law School L. Rev. 201; Alan M. Dershowitz, 'The Torture Warrant: A Response to Professor Strauss' (2004) 48 New York Law School L. Rev. 275.

8 <https://www.amnesty.org/en/latest/research/2016/02/annual-report-201516/> accessed on 24 March 2017.

9 Sabine Gless in 'Art. 139–Art. 141 Beweismittel' in Marcel Alexander Niggli, Marianne Heer and Hans Wiprächtiger (eds.), *Basler Kommentar. Schweizerische Strafprozessordnung* (2nd edn, Helbing Lichtenhahn, Basel 2014), art. 141, notes 6 and 88–98.

10 Wolfgang Schomburg, 'The Role of International Criminal Tribunals in Promoting Respect for Fair Trial Rights' (2009) 8 Northwestern Journal of International Human Rights, 1.

11 Richard M. Re, 'The Due Process Exclusionary Rule' (2014) 127 Harv. L. Rev. 1885, at 1908. The Magna Carta however said little about criminal procedure, see Vincent R. Johnson, 'The Ancient Magna Carta and the Modern Rule of Law: 1215 to 2015' (2015) 47 Sr. Mary's Law Journal, 1, at 5.

12 Göran Sluiter, 'International Criminal Proceedings and the Protection of Human Rights' (2003) 37 New Eng. L. Rev. 935, 936.

13 <http://www.ECHR.coe.int/Documents/Convention_ENG.pdf> accessed on 24 March 2017.

14 <http://www.ECHR.coe.int> accessed on 24 March 2017.

risk that the relevant human rights will be disregarded in national and international criminal justice systems.

3 Human Rights and Criminal Procedure

There are, however, limited means available to prevent human rights violations. The exclusion of illegally obtained evidence from the criminal process offers a real chance to protect human rights: If, for example, a police officer has the option of unlawfully coercing a suspect and thereby forcing a confession, it would be obvious that he will refrain from such coercion if he knows that any confession *or evidence found on the basis of this confession* will be declared inadmissible and excluded from the criminal proceedings against the suspect. The hope that exclusionary rules protect human rights is thus based on a double hypothesis: (a) that lawmakers intend to protect individual rights with exclusionary rules; and (b) that the legal framework, at least theoretically, provides protection for human rights in national criminal justice systems. As has been pointed out previously, the range of human rights discussed as relevant for criminal proceedings is wide. To focus the discussion, this article looks at evidence gained through torture. The right to be free from physical abuse in a criminal investigation has been firmly established as an individual right worldwide, including countries with quite different legal traditions, such as Switzerland, China, USA and Germany. In defining torture, there is a common legal basis, including the CAT as well as regional legal frameworks such as the ECHR.

The five jurisdictions selected for a brief overview encompass a wide geographical and cultural spread, with two continental European jurisdictions (Switzerland, Germany), the USA, the PRC and Taiwan. They also mark a huge legal spectrum of legal models with two inquisitorial systems (Germany and Switzerland), an adversarial system (USA), and "mixed" systems with legal implants from different models (PRC and Taiwan). Nevertheless, they only represent a cursory sampling of domestic laws governing the exclusion of evidence. Interestingly enough, however, despite the vast differences among the legal systems, as a common feature they all provide options for excluding evidence obtained in breach of certain rules, and all carry a statute that prohibits the infliction of pain in order to receive a statement from an individual.[15]

---

15   For further information on transcendental commonalities: Jenia Turner 'The Exclusionary Rule as a Symbol of the Rule of Law' (2014) 67 Southern Methodist University Law Review, 101 at 105–119.

3.1 Are Exclusionary Rules Meant to Protect Human Rights?

Given the common feature of elimination of information obtained in a certain way, one would expect that there is a common rationale behind exclusionary rules. But a brief look at the ideological background is not very promising.

3.1.1 Protecting Human Rights a Western-Leitmotif?

If states are parties to the CAT or a human rights convention like the ECHR, it might be assumed that they provide for exclusionary rules in order to prohibit physical abuse. Such an approach would fit the Western liberal concept of procedural rules safeguarding the position of individuals exposed to state power. In fact, since the adoption of the "*Déclaration des droits de l'homme et du citoyen*" during the French Revolution at the end of the 18th century, the concept of human rights has gradually generated a sense of identity in Europe, which affects all areas of state power, including penal law and criminal proceedings.[16] In North America, similar libertarian ideals heavily influenced the notion of basic human rights in the independence movement, which led to the adoption of the United States Constitution and its amendments forming the Bill of Rights, which to this day have a profound impact on safeguarding individual rights in criminal proceedings.[17] Based on philosophical views of the Enlightenment and the idealism of the early 19th century, the common Western concept of human rights has emphasized the applicability of such rights to every human being, regardless of the positive laws of the person's state of residence.[18]

East Asian countries, however, do not share this tradition of an *individual* human rights heritage, but have developed different ideas.[19] Based, inter alia,

---

[16] The European Court of Justice (ECJ) has referred to human rights as the value system common to all EU member states, ECJ judgment of 13 December 1979, *Hauer v Land Rheinland-Pfalz*, C-44/79, § 15.

[17] See for further information: Richard M. Re, 'The Due Process Exclusionary Rule' (2014) 127 Harv. L. Rev. 1885.

[18] Kate Parlett, The Individual in the International Legal System: Continuity and Change in International Law (Cambridge University Press, Cambridge 2011); Jan Klabbers, Anne Peters and Geir Ulfstein, The Constitutionalization of International Law (OUP, Oxford 2012); Anne Peters 'Compensatory Constitutionalism. The Function and Potential of Fundamental International Norms and Structures' (2006) Leiden Journal of International Law 19, 579–610.

[19] Jack Donnelly, 'Human Rights and Human Dignity: An Analytic Critique of Non-Western Conceptions of Human Rights' (1982) The American Political Science Review, Vol. 76, 308; Julia Ching, 'Human Rights: A Valid Chinese Concept?' (This paper was presented by Dr. Ching on a panel convened by the Religious Consultation on Population, Reproductive

on Confucian traditions of thinking, the accustomed emphasis is predominantly on the collective (i.e. the family and state), while notions of autonomy and the rights of the individual are less present in the legal heritage.[20] In recent years, Chinese politicians have in fact denounced the Western concept of protecting human rights as an ideological tool for justifying intervention in the internal affairs of East Asian countries.[21] In the PRC, the traditional priority of collective interests was re-enforced by the influence of Marxist political thought, which likewise de-emphasized the importance of individual interests in comparison with those of the collective.[22] Even in an arguably non-Socialist country such as Singapore, politicians proclaim the importance of East Asian values, denouncing a strong emphasis on individual rights.[23] This difference between East and West in the understanding of human rights has long been observed and widely accepted by legal scholars.[24] At the same time, the debate about the universalization of human rights has never ceased and recognized standards for the protection of human rights – including in criminal proceedings – are needed at a global level.[25] As *Wolfgang Schomburg* has

---

Health and Ethics at the NGO Forum of the United Nation's World Summit on Social Development, Copenhagen March 1995); Ann Kent, 'Chinese Values and Human rights' in Leena Avonius, Damien Kingsbury (eds.), *Human Rights in Asia* (Palgrave Macmillan, New York 2008), 83–84.

[20] P. Christopher Earley, 'Social Loafing and Collectivism: A Comparison of the United States and the People's Republic of China' (1989) Administrative Science Quarterly, Vol. 34, No. 4, 569; Wei Wu, Tom Vander Beken, 'Police Torture in China and Its Causes: A Literature Review' (2010) Australian and New Zealand Journal of Criminology, Vol. 43, No. 3, 557.

[21] For the implications on the understanding of human rights in criminal proceedings, see however, e.g., Na Jiang, 'The Presumption of Innocence and Illegally Obtained Evidence: Lessons from Wrongful Convictions in China?' (2013) 43 Hong Kong L. J., 745 et seq.

[22] Information Office of the State or China's Cabinet, White Paper on Progress in China's Human Rights in 2012, Beijing May 2013 <http://news.xinhuanet.com/english/china/2013-05/14/c_132380706.htm> accessed on 24 March 2017.

[23] See Fareed Zakaria, 'A Conversation with Lee Kuan Yew' Foreign Affairs March/April 1994. See also Molly Elgin, 'Asian Values: A New Model for Development?' (2010) Southeast Asia, 135, 138.

[24] See, e.g., Henry J. Steiner, Philip Alston and Ryan Goodman, *International Human Rights in Context: Law, Politics, Morals* (3rd edn, OUP, Oxford 2008).

[25] See Kate Parlett, The Individual in the International Legal System: Continuity and Change in International Law, (Cambridge University Press, Cambridge 2011); Jan Klabbers, Anne Peters and Geir Ulfstein, The Constitutionalization of International Law (OUP, Oxford 2012); Anne Peters 'Compensatory Constitutionalism. The Function and Potential of Fundamental International Norms and Structures' (2006) Leiden Journal of International Law 19, 579–610.

noted, in our globalized society, the importance of a common standard for a fair trial cannot be underestimated.[26]

Today, many Asian states, including the PRC, have joined major international human rights treaties, such as the International Covenant on Civil and Political Rights (ICCPR),[27] which grants important individual rights, and the CAT.[28] The Member States of ASEAN (the Association of Southeast Asian Nations) concluded a regional human rights instrument in 2012.[29] As a consequence of the growing prominence of human rights, the domestic laws of relevant jurisdictions – including Vietnam[30] and Taiwan[31] – have been amended to expressly guarantee such entitlements, including explicit exclusionary rules.[32] The PRC signed the ICCPR but has neither ratified the Covenant nor incorporated it into national law.[33] After long debate, Art. 33 para. 3 of the PRC Constitution was amended in 2004 to read that "the State respects and preserves

---

26 Wolfgang Schomburg, 'The Role of International Criminal Tribunals in Promoting Respect for Fair Trial Rights' (2009) 8 Northwestern Journal of International Human Rights, 1, 28.

27 Ministry of Foreign Affairs of the PRC, <http://www.mfa.gov.cn/chn//pds/ziliao/wjs/2159/t9004.htm> accessed on 24 March 2017.

28 Human Rights in China, <http://www.hrichina.org/en/china-and-cat> accessed on 24 March 2017.

29 The ASEAN Human Rights Declaration was adopted by Brunei, Cambodia, Indonesia, Laos, Malaysia, Myanmar, the Philippines, Singapore, Thailand and Vietnam on 18 November 2012; <http://www.asean.org/news/asean-statement-communiques/item/asean-human-rights-declaration> accessed on 24 March 2017.

30 For Vietnam, see Thi Thuy Nguyen, Criminal Justice Reform in Viet Nam. Achievement and Lesson, ASEAN Law Association 10th General Assembly, 2009 p. 1; http://www.aseanlawassociation.org/10GAdocs/Vietnam5-2.pdf accessed on 24 March 2017.

31 Human rights law in Taiwan is primarily domestic law because the United Nations have decided to recognize the representatives of the Government of the PRC as "the only lawful representatives of China to the UN" (UN Resolution 2758 (XXVI) of 1971) and have thus excluded the ROC from official participation in UN organizations.

32 The Code of Criminal Procedure of the Kingdom of Cambodia, article 321 reads: "Unless it is provided otherwise by law, in criminal cases all evidence is admissible. ...Declaration given under the physical or mental duress shall have no evidentiary value.", available at <http://www.wipo.int/wipolex/fr/details.jsp?id=10629> accessed on 24 March 2017. South Korea's criminal procedure act provides that "Confession of a defendant extracted by torture, violence, threat or after prolonged arrest or detention, or which is suspected to have been made involuntarily by means of fraud or other methods, shall not be admitted as evidence of guilt", 309, available at <http://www.wipo.int/wipolex/en/details.jsp?id=12936> accessed on 24 March 2017.

33 See the news in the journal: *The Economist*, <http://www.economist.com/news/china/21695095-how-chinese-versions-un-covenants-gloss-over-human-rights-suppressed-translation> accessed on 24 March 2017; also see news: *Extradition with China, Human Rights*

human rights".[34] In 2012, a similar reference for the "respect and protection of human rights" was inserted in Art. 2 of the PRC Criminal Procedure Code (PRC-CCP) as one of the purposes of the newly revised Code.[35] But these changes of the law on the books have not had much immediate impact on actual law enforcement in the PRC.[36] Nonetheless, they may be seen as a major shift towards official recognition of individual human rights[37] and perhaps a reversal of the earlier insistence on the sufficiency of "Eastern values".[38] Whether and how they translate in the criminal justice system has yet to be seen.

3.1.2 Rationale for Exclusionary Rules

Against this backdrop, the question arises whether lawmakers in the jurisdictions treated here aspire for exclusionary rules to protect human rights. Even a perfunctory glance reveals great differences.

3.1.2.1 *Europe*

The two European jurisdictions under consideration, Switzerland and Germany, at least envisage a clear role for exclusionary rules in safeguarding individual rights: Switzerland sees its ban on torture evidence as part of the global fight against the physical abuse of individuals by state agents, as prohibited by CAT[39] and Art. 3 ECHR.[40] Germany also adopted the relevant provisions, banning physical coercion after World War II as a reaction to the abuses – including

---

and Parliament's Role, available at <http://thecic.org/2016/10/03/extradition-with-china-human-rights-and-parliaments-role/> accessed on 24 March 2017.

34 Art. 33 (3) Chinese Constitution, see the website: National People's Congress of PRC, <http://www.npc.gov.cn/englishnpc/Constitution/2007-11/15/content_1372964.htm> accessed on 24 March 2017.

35 Art. 2 Chinese Criminal Procedure Code, see the website: National People's Congress of PRC, <http://www.npc.gov.cn/englishnpc/Law/2007-12/13/content_1384067.htm> accessed on 24 March 2017.

36 Margaret K. Lewis, 'Controlling Abuse to Maintain Control: The Exclusionary Rule in China' (2011) 43 New York University Journal of International Law and Politics 629, at 650–652.

37 Congyan Cai, 'New Great Powers and International Law in the 21st Century' (2013) European Journal of International Law, Vol. 24, 794.

38 Sophia Woodman, 'Human Rights as "Foreign Affairs": China's Reporting under Human Rights Treaties' (2005) Hong Kong Law Journal, Vol. 35, 181–182.

39 For Switzerland: Sabine Gless in Marcel Alexander Niggli/Marianne Heer/Hans Wiprächtiger (eds.), *Basler Kommentar Schweizerische Strafprozessordnung* (2nd edn, Helbing Lichtenhahn, Basel 2014), art. 141, no. 15.

40 Sabine Gless in Marcel Alexander Niggli/Marianne Heer/Hans Wiprächtiger (eds.), *Basler Kommentar Schweizerische Strafprozessordnung* (2nd edn, Helbing Lichtenhahn, Basel 2014), art. 141, no. 22.

torture – prevalent in interrogations during the national-socialist era.[41] When the newly founded Federal Republic of Germany joined the ECHR it emphasised its commitment to human rights.[42] Since then, the prohibition of torture and degrading punishment stipulated by Art. 3 ECHR has been directly applied by German courts, which rely on the case law of the ECtHR, referring to international human rights law when necessary,[43] and in doing so have shaped value-based rules for not using certain evidence.[44]

But the references to human rights tell only half the truth: In both states, the exclusion of evidence also aims at safeguarding the reliability of fact-finding and at ensuring justice.[45] When put to a tough test, for instance, Germany's seemingly clear commitment to deterring police abuse during interrogations may waver, as in the cases of *Gäfgen*[46] and *Jalloh*.[47] In both cases, Germany had to answer charges of violating the defendants' rights not to be submitted to torture or degrading treatment or punishment.

3.1.2.2   United States

The meaning and purpose of exclusionary rules in the United States are more difficult to assess than the legal policy framing provisions in continental European jurisdictions, as they are found on the basis of common law, constitutional amendments and more recent case law. Only rarely is an exclusionary rule adopted through an act of parliament, with its legislative policy preferences explicitly revealed. Broadly speaking, however, it is clear that under common law the purpose of exclusionary rules is not the protection of human rights, but

---

41   See Kuk Cho, '"Procedural Weakness" of German Criminal Justice and Its Unique Exclusionary Rules Based on the Right of Personality' (2001) 15 Temp. Int'L & Comp. L.J. 1, at 15.

42   See the notification of 15 December 1953 (Bundesgesetzblatt 1954 II 14). Germany has also ratified the European Convention against Torture and Inhumane and Degrading Treatment of 1987 (Bundesgesetzblatt 1989 II 946).

43   Judgement of the German Bundesgerichtshof of February 21, 2001, 3 StR 372/00.

44   Thomas Weigend, 'Germany' in Craig M. Bradley (ed.), *Criminal Procedure: A Worldwide Study* (2nd edn, Carolina Academic Press, Durham 2007), 243, 251–254.

45   See for Germany: Sabine Gless, '§ 136 Vernehmung des Beschuldigten' in Volker Erb, Robert Esser et al (eds.), *Die Strafprozessordnung und das Gerichtsverfassungsgesetz: Grosskommentar Löwe-Rosenberg*, (26nd edn, De Gruyter Recht, Berlin 2014), § 136a, no. 1 and for Switzerland: Sabine Gless in Marcel Alexander Niggli, Marianne Heer and Hans Wiprächtiger (eds.), *Basler Kommentar Schweizerische Strafprozessordnung* (2nd edn, Helbing Lichtenhahn, Basel 2014), art. 141, no. 6.

46   See ECtHR, *Gäfgen v Germany*, Judgment of June 30, 2008, case no. 22978/05; Judgment (Grand Chamber) of June 1, 2010, §§ 165–166. For a comment, see Thomas Weigend, 'EGMR Nr. 22978/05 G. ./. Deutschland v. 01.06.2010, Folterverbot im Strafverfahren', Strafverteidiger 6/2011, 325.

47   See ECtHR (Grand Chamber), *Jalloh v Germany*, no. 54810/00, Judgment of 11 July 2006.

the safeguarding of reliability.[48] Evidence is to be excluded if its prejudicial effect would outweigh its probative value.[49] Under common law, not only torture has been deemed illegal, but confessions made under torture are inadmissible because they are not voluntary and bear a risk of being unreliable.[50] At the same time, torture infringes on individual rights. The common law rationale is reflected to a certain degree by current United States case law. It, for instance, provides that confessions made under torture must be excluded because of the Fifth Amendment's demand that no person "be compelled in any criminal case to be a witness against himself".[51] If one looks more closely at the development of case law, however, the emphasis appears to be shifting: In the more recent past, not a lack of reliability but the disapproval of certain offensive police practices during interrogation often has been the dominant reason for excluding coerced confessions.[52] Scholars have claimed that it is time for a shift of the focal point from a Fifth Amendment justification for exclusionary rules to a due process rationale, which in itself would put the protection of individual rights at the center.[53] With regard to evidence elicited through torture, such an approach is connected to the United States' obligations following from the CAT and its Torture Act, which bans torture under federal law.[54]

3.1.2.3 *China*
Neither the Criminal Procedure Code of the PRC (PRC-CPC, 中华人民共和国刑事诉讼法), dating back to 1979, nor other statutes or regulations elaborate upon the background of the exclusionary rules adopted in 2012. But the history leading to the adoption of exclusionary rules clearly show that the Chinese law is concerned with reliability of evidence, and not with protecting human

---

48 *R v Leathem* (1861) 8 Cox CC 498, Crompton J at 501, overruling an objection to production of a letter which had been discovered in consequence of an inadmissible statement made by the accused: "It matters not how you get it; if you steal it even, it would be admissible."
49 *Lobban v R* [1995] 1 WLR 877 (Privy Council).
50 *A v Secretary of State for the Home Office* [2005] UKHL 71. See also Danny Friedman, 'Torture and the Common Law' (2006) E.H.R.L.R. Issue 2, 180–199.
51 *Brown v Mississippi*, 297 U.S. 278 (1936).
52 Yale Kamisar, 'On the "Fruits" of Miranda Violations, Coerced Confessions, and Compelled Testimony' (1995) 93 Mich. L. Rev. 929, 939.
53 Richard M. Re, 'The Due Process Exclusionary Rule' (2014) 127 Harv. L. Rev. 1885, at 1912; Jenia Turner 'The Exclusionary Rule as a Symbol of the Rule of Law' (2014) 67 Southern Methodist University Law Review, 101.
54 See David Luban, *Torture, Power, and Law* (Cambridge University Press, Cambridge 2014), 122.

rights.[55] Looking beyond the reliability concern in criminal proceedings, some scholars have argued that the adoption of exclusionary rules aims at a broader policy issue as it intends to pacify public dissatisfaction with severe cases of miscarriage of justice, following news of certain cases of wrongful convictions spreading through social media.[56] They also argue that it represents a policy turning point, denoting the aspirations of the central government to extend its control in criminal justice matters over the provinces,[57] while at the same time showing – with a rather symbolic law – its integrity when it comes to criminal justice.[58]

Such claims are supported by the evolution of exclusionary rules: China has been confronted with frequent international and domestic criticism of illegally coerced confessions and torture in criminal proceedings.[59] In 2010, five institutions – the Supreme People's Court, the Supreme People's Procuratorate, the Ministry of Public Security, the Ministry of State Security and the Ministry of Justice – jointly promulgated "Rules Concerning Questions About Exclusion of Illegal Evidence in Handling Criminal Cases" (2010 Exclusionary Rules) out of concerns about revelations concerning miscarriages of justice.[60] Furthermore, a revision of the PRC-CPC was passed in 2012 and includes several provisions that can be shown – at home and abroad – as protecting certain

---

55 Jiahong He and Ran He, 'Empirical Studies of Wrongful Convictions in Mainland China' (2012) University of Cincinnati L. Rev. Vol. 80, 1289; Jun Feng (冯军), 'The Functional Expectations and the Realization of the New Exclusionary Rules' (非法证据排除规则新规定的功能期待及其实现), (2011) Journal of Henan University, Social Sciences (《河南大学学报》社会科学版), Vol. 51, No. 3, 70–71.

56 See news: <http://news.sina.com.cn/s/2010-06-12/101420465898.shtml> accessed on 24 March 2017; <http://www.xiyuanwang.net/html/gnya_1271_1879.html> accessed on 24 March 2017; <http://www.people.com.cn/GB/news/25064/3300177.html> accessed on 24 March 2017.

57 Margaret K. Lewis, 'Controlling Abuse to Maintain Control: The Exclusionary Rule in China' (2011) 43 New York University Journal of International Law and Politics 629, at 632.

58 Margaret K. Lewis, 'Controlling Abuse to Maintain Control: The Exclusionary Rule in China' (2011) 43 New York University Journal of International Law and Politics 629, at 686.

59 See Jiahong He and Ran He, 'Wrongful convictions and tortured confessions: empirical studies in mainland China', in Mike McConville and Eva Pils (eds.), *Comparative Perspectives on Criminal Justice in China* (Edward Elgar, Cheltenham 2013), p. 73 et seq.

60 Joshua Rosenzweig, Flora Sapio, Jiang Jue, Teng Biao and Eva Pils, The 2012 Revision of the Chinese Criminal Procedure Law: (Mostly) Old Wine in New Bottles, pp. 12–13, CRJ Occasional Paper, available at: https://www.law.cuhk.edu.hk/en/research/crj/download/papers/2012-CRJ-OccasionalPaper-CPL.pdf accessed on 24 March 2017; Na Jiang, 'The Presumption of Innocence and Illegally Obtained Evidence: Lessons from Wrongful Convictions in China?' (2013) Hong Kong Law Journal, Vol. 43, 749.

individual rights of defendants. For instance, Art. 50 PRC-CPC now grants the privilege against self-incrimination,[61] while Art. 54 PRC-CPC excludes statements obtained by illegal means, particularly by torture. Since the turn of the century, the central government strives for more control of criminal justice in the provinces, most visible in the control of death penalty judgements.[62] But, even as the ban of coerced confessions was part of a 2009 National Human Rights Action Plan,[63] the intention was not to protect human rights but to prevent miscarriages by excluding unreliable evidence.[64]

3.1.2.4 Taiwan

Taiwan adopted exclusionary rules during an era of democratic consolidation, after a break with the preceding authoritarian rule, with a profound revision of its Criminal Procedure Code. The push for the exclusionary rule was based on a desire to emphasize the validity of human rights in criminal justice.[65] In 2009, Taiwan adopted the "Act to Implement the International Covenant on Civil and Political Rights and the International Covenant on Economic, Social and Cultural Rights".[66] Art. 2 of this Act stipulates: "Human rights protection provisions in the two Covenants have domestic legal status".[67] The ICCPR is part of national law in Taiwan.[68]

---

61 Na Jiang, 'The Presumption of Innocence and Illegally Obtained Evidence: Lessons from Wrongful Convictions in China?' (2013) Hong Kong Law Journal, Vol. 43, 759.

62 Susan Trevaskes, 'China's Death Penalty: The Supreme People's Court, the Suspended Death Sentence and the Politics of Penal Reform', 53 British Journal of Criminology 482–549 (2013).

63 Margaret K. Lewis, 'Controlling Abuse to Maintain Control: The Exclusionary Rule in China' (2011) 43 New York University Journal of International Law and Politics 629, at 659 and 664.

64 Jianghong He, 'Wrongful Convictions and the Exclusionary Rules in China', Frontiers of Law in China (2014) Vol. 9, No. 3, 505.

65 Supreme Court decision 104 taishangzih No. 3052 (最高法院104年度台上字第3052號判決).; LIAO Fu-Te (廖福特), 批准聯合國兩個人權公約及制訂施行法之評論 (Comments on Ratified Two United Nations Covenants on Human Rights and the Enforcement Act), (Nov. 2009), Vol. 174, The Taiwan Law Review, 223et seq.

66 公民與政治權利國際公約及經濟社會文化權利國際公約施行法. The text is available online at <http://law.moj.gov.tw/Law/LawSearchResult.aspx?p=A&k1=%E5%85%AC%E7%B4%84%E6%96%BD%E8%A1%8C%E6%B3%95&t=E1F1A1&TPage=1>, official English translation at <http://law.moj.gov.tw/Eng/LawClass/LawContent.aspx?PCODE=I0020028>, accessed on 24 March 2017.

67 „兩公約所揭示保障人權之規定,具有國內法律之效力".

68 For more information, see below 7.

3.1.2.5 *Interim Conclusion*

As an interim result, we can conclude: Some, but not all criminal justice systems intend their exclusionary rules to (at least indirectly) protect human rights. Others only wish to exclude unreliable evidence. This result however does not answer the question whether the intention to protect human rights actually translates into the design of legal provisions, that are capable of protecting human rights when it comes to a test in practice.

3.2 *Are Exclusionary Rules Made to Protect Human Rights?*

With respect to individuals exposed to the criminal justice system, it is ultimately for the court to determine whether their individual rights prevail over the interest of comprehensive fact-finding. While the lawmaker sets the course with the legal framework, the details in legal regulations of exclusionary rules determine the chances of human rights being actually protected. A crucial detail for safeguarding individual rights in criminal proceedings is the approach to evidence derived from torture evidence, so-called derivative evidence.[69]

The decision of whether or not to use evidence directly gained through torture is clear-cut: The CAT obligates states to ensure that any statement established to have been made as a result of torture is not invoked as evidence in any proceedings, except against a person accused of torture as evidence that the statement was made.[70] The exclusion of derivative evidence however is highly controversial. In certain cases, torture evidence may lead to "hard evidence", like DNA traces on a victim's body or incriminating documents. If officials can hope for such evidence, they may be tempted to use force in order to gain access to it. From a human rights protection angle, the exclusion of direct torture evidence appears thus to be a necessary but not sufficient condition to effectively protect human rights. Only the exclusion of derivative evidence ultimately promises to deter physical abuse, since there is nothing for the state agent to gain in using torture. Therefore, the assessment of a legal framework for excluding torture evidence must be based not only on its capacity to block coerced confessions from criminal proceedings, but especially on the option to sort out the fruits of the poisonous tree. The latter constitutes the litmus test for exclusionary rules actually functioning as safeguards for human rights.

---

69 Stephen C. Thaman, '"Fruits of the Poisonous Tree" in Comparative Law' (2010) 16 SW J Int'l L 333, at 370.

70 For further information, see: Tobias Thienel, 'The Admissibility of Evidence Obtained by Torture under International Law' (2006) The European Journal of International Law Vol. 17 EJIL 349, at 351–353.

3.2.1 Inquisitorial Systems

The two continental European jurisdictions have both adopted specific statutes which ban undue coercion (including torture), but differ in legislative technique: *Switzerland*, only recently, adopted a blanket provision, which establishes a general screen for all evidence obtained in violation of procedural rules, calling for the exclusion of some (but not all) illegally obtained evidence flanked by a ban for tainted derivative evidence. In contrast *Germany*'s procedural code only contains a few explicit rules and normally leaves the decision on "non-use" of evidence to the courts, which decide on a case-by-case basis, following the maxim that exclusion of relevant evidence must remain an exception.[71]

3.2.1.1 *Switzerland*

Swiss law on the exclusion of torture evidence is clear cut: "The use of coercion, violence, threats, promises, deception and methods that may compromise the ability of the person concerned to think or decide freely are prohibited when taking evidence,"[72] even if the person concerned consents to the use of such methods (Art. 140 of the Swiss Criminal Procedure Code, CH-CPC).[73] Any evidence "obtained in violation of Article 140 is not admissible under any circumstances" (Art. 141 para. 1, 1st sentence CH-CPC). Furthermore, the Swiss lawmaker adopted the fruit of the poisonous tree doctrine: If torture evidence "made it possible to obtain additional evidence, such evidence is not admissible if it would have been impossible to obtain had the previous evidence not been obtained" (Art. 141 para. 4 CH-CPC). According to the wording, the statute – rather paradoxically – does not explicitly exclude indirect evidence based on primary evidence obtained by torture. But the intention of the legislature is clear: to establish a *strict* exclusion of *any* evidence in these cases, also of all indirect evidence.[74] Thus, at first glance, Swiss law has an ideal legal design for the efficient protection of human rights with the elimination not only

---

71 Judgement (Beschluss) of the Bundesverfassungsgericht (1. Kammer des Zweiten Senats) of November 9, 2010, 2 BvR 2101/09.

72 See. Wolfgang Wohlers, in Andreas Donatsch, Christian Schwarzenegger and Wolfgang Wohlers (eds.) *Kommentar zur Schweizerischen Strafprozessordnung* (2nd edn. Schulthess, Zürich 2014), art. 3, no. 22.

73 SR 312.0 <https://www.admin.ch/opc/en/classified-compilation/20052319/index.html> accessed on 24 March 2017.

74 Whether the wording allows for a hypothetical clean path doctrine is subject of a controversial debate, see Sabine Gless in 'Art. 139–Art. 141 Beweismittel' in Marcel Alexander Niggli, Marianne Heer and Hans Wiprächtiger (eds.), *Basler Kommentar. Schweizerische Strafprozessordnung* (2nd edn, Helbing Lichtenhahn, Basel 2014), art. 141, no. 90.

of torture, but also of derivative evidence. However, in the few cases in which Swiss courts had to apply Art. 141 para. 4 CH-CPC (which involved evidence obtained by unauthorized searches and surveillance, no torture cases) the decision was in favor of the admissibility of evidence – based on a hypothetical clean path doctrine.[75]

3.2.1.2 Germany

Germany, by contrast, in general terms follows a case-by case-approach when it comes to deciding whether certain evidence can be used for fact-finding.[76] Different considerations play a role in the decision-making, including the reliability of the evidence and the safeguarding of overriding interests (e.g., a right to privacy[77]). Only in few cases, as when evidence has been obtained under undue coercion – which includes torture[78] – it may never be used,[79] even if the individual later consents to the use (§ 136a Sec. 3, 2nd sentence CCP).[80]

However, this apparently firm stance of the "non-use-rule" does not translate into procedural rules, since "an 'excluded' confession will still be in the file available to the judges at trial, even though they are supposed to ignore it".[81]

---

75 See e.g. Decision of the Swiss Federal Court Bundesgericht Urteil of 12 July 2012 6B_805/2011 (= BGE 138 IV 169).

76 See for an appropriate use of terminology in inquisitorial systems, which do not formally exclude evidence: Thomas Weigend, 'Germany' in Craig M. Bradley (ed.), *Criminal Procedure: A Worldwide Study* (2nd edn, Carolina Academic Press, Durham 2007), p. 243 at 254.

77 The German Basic Law requires a certain protection of a core area of privacy, see § 100a Abs. 4 S. 2, § 100c Abs. 5, Abs. 7 German CPP.

78 § 136a CCP does not employ the term "torture" (*Folter*) among the forbidden means of interrogation. But any case of physical torture is necessarily included in the broader term "physical abuse".

79 Fort he debate on the inadmissibility of coerced statements and its consequences see Sabine Gless, '§ 136 Vernehmung des Beschuldigten' in Volker Erb, Robert Esser et al (eds.), *Die Strafprozessordnung und das Gerichtsverfassungsgesetz: Grosskommentar Löwe-Rosenberg* (26nd edn, De Gruyter Recht, Berlin 2014), § 136a, note 71; Claus Roxin 'Anmerkung zu BGH Beschluss v. 5.8.2008 – 3 StR 45/08 (LG Lüneburg)' (2009) Strafverteidiger, 113; Wolfgang Wohlers 'BGH, Urteil vom 22.12.2011 – 2 StR 509/10' (2012) Juristische Rundschau, 391; Herbert Diemer, in Rolf Hannich et al (eds.), *Karlsruher Kommentar StPO* (hereinafter KK StPO, 7th edn, Verlag C.H. Beck, München 2013), § 136a, note 37; Claus Roxin and Bernd Schünemann, *Strafverfahrensrecht* (28th edn, Verlag C.H. Beck, München 2014), 173.

80 This rule does, of course, not preclude the declarant from making the same statement again in court. Such a statement would be admissible if the suspect has been informed that his prior statement is inadmissible.

81 Thomas Weigend, 'Germany' in Craig M. Bradley (ed.), *Criminal Procedure: A Worldwide Study* (2nd edn, Carolina Academic Press, Durham 2007), p. 243 at 254.

Moreover, German courts do not normally apply the fruits of the poisonous tree doctrine.[82] For example, if a suspect makes a coerced statement in which he refers to other persons who allegedly committed the offense together with him, the exclusion of the statement by § 136a Sec. 3 CCP will not block further police investigation into the identity of these persons, and their statements may be used as evidence against the defendant.[83] The German legal framework is thus not ideal for protecting human rights. Although torture evidence is banned from fact-finding, threatening a defendant with the infliction of pain may still lead to useful clues. The lack of adequate procedural safeguards comes as a surprise, since § 136a Sec. 3 CCP was adopted in reaction to the abuses taking place in interrogations during the national-socialist era (see above 3.1.2.1).

3.2.2 The Adversarial System of the United States

Exclusionary rules owe their prominence in global debate to their importance in the United States' legal system. Contrary to what one would expect, however, the Federal Rules on Evidence contain no explicit rule on excluding torture evidence. Such evidence will all the same be excluded under common law rules as well as constitutional rights (see above 3.1.2.2). The Fifth Amendment's Privilege against Self-Incrimination and the Fourteenth Amendment's Due Process Clause compel the exclusion of torture confessions, since no person should be compelled to be a witness against himself in a criminal case,[84] and no one shall be deprived of life, liberty, or property without due process of law.[85]

But even if under a voluntariness analysis, torture confessions cannot be introduced at trial, the question remains as to whether its fruits can be used, since their exclusion does not follow automatically from the ban of primary evidence.[86] In a nutshell, the Supreme Court has generally extended the Fourth Amendment exclusionary rule to "fruits" of the original violation, with the

---

82 Claus Roxin and Bernd Schünemann, *Strafverfahrensrecht* (28th edn, Verlag C.H. Beck, München 2014), 187.
83 See Judgement of the German Bundesgerichtshof of August 24, 1983, 3 StR 136/83 = BGHSt 32, 68, at 70.
84 James J. Tomkovicz, *Constitutional Exclusion* (Oxford University Press 2011) 64; Mark A. Godsey, 'Rethinking the Involuntary Confession Rule: Toward a Workable Test for Identifying Compelled Self-Incrimination' (2005) 93 Cal. L. Rev. 465, 479–480.
85 *Weeks v United States* 232 U.S. 383 (1914); Thomas S. Schrock and Robert C. Welsh, 'Up from Calandra: The Exclusionary Rule as a Constitutional Requirement' (1974) 59 Minn. L. Rev. 251, 343, 362–364.
86 Richard M. Re, 'The Due Process Exclusionary Rule' (2014) 127 Harv. L. Rev. 1885 at 1895–1898.

reasoning that such exclusion is necessary to deter police misconduct.[87] But the case law has also placed limits on how far the fruit of the poisonous tree doctrine extends. In cases in which the link between the original violation and the derivative evidence is too attenuated (e.g. if an event has broken the chain of causation between the original illegality and the derivative evidence), the derivative evidence may be admitted.[88] Furthermore, if the police would inevitably have discovered the evidence even without the violation of rights the exclusionary rule does not apply.[89] The admission of tainted derivative evidence dilutes the deterrence effect.[90]

Interestingly, the Supreme Court points to the importance of comprehensive fact-finding as a justification for these restrictions on the fruit of the poisonous tree doctrine. The Court also reasons that excluding evidence which could have been discovered independently by lawful means would not deter future police abuse.[91] As far as can be ascertained, in recent case law on exclusionary rules, the courts have not addressed possible human rights protection aspects. In fact, courts rather searches for ways to prevent the loss of evidence at a lesser cost through alternative reactions, which may involve disciplining officers.[92] A promising strategy against such curtailment could be to shift the focal point from a Fourth Amendment justification for exclusionary rules to a due process rationale, more focused on protecting individual rights as such.[93]

3.2.3   Mixed Systems

Both Chinese jurisdictions have certain elements derived from the inquisitorial models. But they also include adversarial aspects as well as their own specific features embedded in the systems. Exclusionary rules have been present in the Taiwanese law for a while, but have been adopted in mainland China only recently.

---

[87] *Herring v United States*, 555 U.S. 135, 141 (2009); *Hudson v Michigan*, 547 U.S. 586, 591 (2006).
[88] *Brown v Illinois*, 422 U.S. 590 (1975); *Murray v United States*, 487 U.S. 533 (1988); McCormick on Evidence § 159, at 875 (2013).
[89] *Nix v Williams*, 467 U.S. 431 (1984).
[90] See Richard M. Re, 'The Due Process Exclusionary Rule' (2014) 127 Harv. L. Rev. 1885 at 1895.
[91] *Nix v Williams*, 467 U.S. 431, 444–445 (1984).
[92] *Hudson*, 547 U.S. at 591, 599.
[93] Richard M. Re, The Due Process Exclusionary Rule, 127 (2014) Harv. L. Rev. 1885, at 1912; Jenia Turner 'The Exclusionary Rule as a Symbol of the Rule of Law' (2014) 67 Southern Methodist University Law Review, 101.

3.2.3.1 PRC

In China, Art. 54 PRC-CPC at present provides for the exclusion of statements obtained by illegal means, particularly by torture. As has been pointed out above, the intention is not to protect human rights but rather to prevent miscarriages of justice by excluding unreliable evidence.[94] Therefore, it is only appropriate that the Chinese law does not acknowledge any fruit of the poisonous tree doctrine and allows derivative evidence obtained through torture or other illegal means in criminal proceedings to be admitted as valid evidence.[95] There are, however, rather broad legal options for excluding evidence: "If physical or documentary evidence is obtained in a manner that clearly violates the law and may have an impact on the fairness of an adjudication, redress or some reasonable explanation should be made, otherwise that physical or documentary evidence may not serve as a basis for conviction."[96]

The practical relevance of exclusionary rules depends on many aspects, ranging from the relationship between the Communist Party and the justice system to the way in which exclusionary rules are supported by other procedural rules. Today, the law gives a defendant the option to challenge incriminating evidence.[97] But the onus is on the defense to allege that a confession was obtained illegally and to offer supporting leads or evidence (though it is unclear how much evidence is needed to trigger a further investigation),[98] with the burden shifting if the court has doubts about the admissibility of evidence after an initial review.[99] Thus the threshold is high, with the government

---

[94] Margaret K. Lewis, 'Controlling Abuse to Maintain Control: The Exclusionary Rule in China' (2011) 43 New York University Journal of International Law and Politics 629, with further information on the Zhao Zhenshang case at 630–631 and other cases at 668–670; Jiahong He and Ran He, 'Empirical Studies of Wrongful Convictions in Mainland China' (2012) University of Cincinnati L. Rev. Vol. 80, 1289.

[95] Na Jiang, 'The Presumption of Innocence and Illegally Obtained Evidence: Lessons from Wrongful Convictions in China?' (2013) 43 Hong Kong L.J., 745, at 746.

[96] Evidence Exclusion Rules, art. 14.

[97] Evidence Exclusion Rules, art. 7. Jeremy Daum, 'Tortuous Progress: Early Cases under China's New Procedures for Excluding Evidence in Criminal Cases' (2011) NYU Journal of International Law and Politics, Vol. 43, 700; Yang Yuguan and Chen Zinan, 'On the Question of Exclusionary Rule in China' (2015) China Legal Science, Vol. 3, No. 1, 8–9.

[98] Evidence Exclusion Rules, art. 6. Criminal Procedure Code, Art. 56 (2); Yang Yuguan and Chen Zinan, 'On the Question of Exclusionary Rule in China' (2015) China Legal Science, Vol. 3, No. 1, 9.

[99] Evidence Exclusion Rules, art. 7. Na Jang, 'The adequacy of China's responses to wrongful convictions' (2013) International Journal of Law, Crime and Justice, Vol. 41, 395; Yang Yuguan and Chen Zinan, 'On the Question of Exclusionary Rule in China' (2015) China Legal Science, Vol. 3, No. 1, 11.

adhering to the view that the Chinese people are still connected to the long history of Chinese criminal justice that emphasizes substantive justice over procedural justice.[100]

3.2.3.2 *Taiwan*

According to art. 156 para. 1 of the Taiwanese Code of Criminal Procedure, information obtained by applying torture or inflicting other coercion on the defendant is to be mandatorily excluded and, accordingly, is inadmissible as evidence in criminal proceedings. The statute enshrines the case law that, for instance, excluded coerced confessions in order to safeguard the human dignity of the defendant and his status as a party to the trial proceedings.[101] Taiwan, however, does not apply a comprehensive fruit of the poisonous tree doctrine. Only in cases in which a secret surveillance investigation gravely violates procedural rules, all evidence, including derivative evidence is banned from presentation in court.[102] The representatives in parliament adopted this statute after they had fallen victim to a bugging scandal themselves.[103]

3.3 *Interim Conclusion*

In a nutshell, only the legal set-ups in Switzerland and the United States provide (theoretically) an ideal design to protect human rights, with their preparedness to exclude not only evidence elicited through torture but also derivative evidence. In practice, however, the situation is ambigious considering the ways in which such tainted evidence might enter via the backdoor, for example, based on a hypothetical clean path-doctrine, it is not even clear whether law enforcement officers would refrain from employing coercive methods of evidence-gathering that infringe human rights in severe and difficult cases, if they have reason to believe that tainted evidence could perhaps be of use after all.

4 Conclusion

The analysis of the rationale behind and the design of exclusionary rules shows that a common standard protecting individual rights in criminal proceedings world-wide, as *Wolfgang Schomburg* rightly calls for, is still wishful thinking.

---

100 See Sida Liu and Terence C. Halliday, 'Recursivity in Legal Change: Lawyers and Reforms of China's Criminal Procedure Law' (2009) 34 L. & Soc. Inquiry 911, 920.

101 Supreme Court decision 104 taishangzih No. 3052 (最高法院104年度台上字第3052號判決).

102 See art. 18-1 of the Communication Security and Surveillance Act.

103 Yang, 2014, at 3–4.

The rather superficial examination of exclusionary rules in five jurisdictions, however, has revealed that exclusionary rules have the theoretical potential of addressing the ubiquitous risk of human rights abuse in criminal proceedings in all countries. But in order to achieve their potential of being an instrument for protecting human rights in criminal proceedings, the legal framework must include the option of a ban on derivative evidence and the courts must make use of it. Up to now, exclusionary rules are often not put to work for a better protection of human rights, because the criminal justice system perceives their primary function as guarding against unreliable evidence, not as protecting human rights. Exclusionary rules are part of the criminal process's inherent struggle for a solution of the conflict arising from the need for comprehensive clarification of facts, in situations where individuals would choose not to disclose information. They have not been created as a genuine bulwark against state power in the liberal spirit.

The lesson that could be learned on the international level – where *Wolfgang Schomburg* adjudicated in an impressive way in many criminal proceedings – can best be articulated on the basis of one of his clear statements. When deciding upon cases, international tribunals today must set an example by ensuring justice is done where impunity used to be the rule, but also by making progress where rights of individuals are likely to be violated in the course of criminal proceedings.[104] Art. 69 para 7 of the Rome Statute merely stipulates, "Evidence obtained by means of a violation of this Statute or internationally recognized human rights shall not be admissible if (a) The violation casts substantial doubt on the reliability of the evidence; or (b) The admission of the evidence would be antithetical to and would seriously damage the integrity of the proceedings.", The International Criminal Court must now enhance its own legitimacy by excluding even tainted derivative evidence. Such respect for human rights in criminal procedure at the international level will pave the way for this trend to continue in national legal frameworks and all judicial systems.

---

104 Wolfgang Schomburg, 'The Role of International Criminal Tribunals in Promoting Respect for Fair Trial Rights' (2009) 8 Northwestern Journal of International Human Rights, 1, at 28 et seq.

CHAPTER 8

Implementing Kampala: The New Crime of Aggression under the German Code of Crimes against International Law

Florian Jeßberger

Abstract

Since 1 January 2017, the crime of aggression is defined as an offence under German law. The paper introduces the new Section 13 of the German Code of Crimes against International Law, explains its basis in international law, constitutional law and criminal policy and identifies differences and similarities compared to article 8bis of ICC Statute. The paper argues that the new offence may serve as an inspiration and model for other states considering the implementation of the Kampala amendments.

---

* Professor of Criminal Law, Universität Hamburg. – This paper is dedicated to *Wolfgang Schomburg*, one of the pioneers of international and transnational criminal law in Germany. As a judge, as a lawyer, and as a scholar, he has always been an uncompromising advocate of the idea of international criminal justice and a powerful voice in defence of the principles of substantive and procedural criminal law. – The author thankfully acknowledges invaluable support in the preparation of this paper by *Swantje Maecker*, LL.M. (King's College London). – The present paper elaborates on previous works. The author had the privilege to participate in the early drafting stages of Section 13 of the GCCIL and has, inter alia, submitted a legal opinion to the Federal Ministry of Justice in September 2013, which was later published as Florian Jeßberger, 'Das Verbrechen der Aggression im deutschen Strafrecht: Überlegungen zur Umsetzung der Beschlüsse von Kampala' (2015) Zeitschrift für Internationale Strafrechtsdogmatik 514. The author was also part of a group of experts presenting their views on the Government Draft in the 111th session of the Parliamentary Committee for Law and Consumer Protection, see Florian Jeßberger, 'Schriftliche Zusammenfassung der Stellungnahme vor dem Ausschuss für Recht und Verbraucherschutz des Deutschen Bundestages vom 26. September 2016', <www.bundestag.de/ausschuesse18/a06/anhoerungen/Archiv/stellungnahmen/461332> accessed 15 May 2017.

1 Introduction

On 1 January 2017, a new Section 13 of the German Code of Crimes against International Law (GCCIL; *Völkerstrafgesetzbuch*) entered into force.[1] By defining the 'crime of aggression' as an offence under German law, this new provision strives to implement the amendments to the Rome Statute of the International Criminal Court (ICC Statute) which were adopted at the Review Conference in Kampala in June 2010. Section 13 of the GCCIL replaces Section 80 of the German Criminal Code (GCC; *Strafgesetzbuch*), which had provided for the crime of 'preparation of a war of aggression' since 1968. The GCCIL entered into force in 2002 and adapted substantive German law to the provisions of the ICC Statute – in particular to articles 6 to 8 which encompass genocide, crimes against humanity, and war crimes – but it did not include the crime of aggression at that time.

This paper introduces the new offence and aims to explain its basis in international law, constitutional law, and criminal policy. Differences between the definitions of the 'crime of aggression' in Section 13 of the GCCIL and article 8bis of the ICC Statute will be highlighted and the legal context, including key issues such as the relevant rules on perpetration and participation, jurisdiction and immunity, will be discussed. In its conclusion, the paper will reflect on whether the new offence can serve as an inspiration and model for other states considering the implementation of the Kampala amendments.

2 Background

The origins and development of international criminal law are closely connected with Germany and German history. The Nuremberg Trial against the major war criminals of World War II was the legal response to the crimes committed by Nazi Germany; 'crimes against peace', the precursor to the 'crime of aggression', played a prominent role at this and other post-World War II trials.

Germany had taken an active part in bringing about the amendments on the crime of aggression to the ICC Statute which were passed during the Kampala

---

1 Bundesgesetzblatt (BGBl., German Federal Law Gazette) 2016 II, 3150. The introduction of the new offence was accompanied by a set of alterations to the GCC and the German Code of Criminal Procedure which were necessitated by the replacement of Section 80 of the GCC by Section 13 of the GCCIL and extended investigative powers, e.g. technical surveillance, to the investigation of crimes of aggression.

Conference.[2] In 2013, Germany was one of the first signatories to ratify the changes adopted in Kampala[3] and made a commitment on that occasion to adapt its national legislation if necessitated by the principle of complementarity.[4] However, it took another four years until this was realized and, unlike the majority of other implementing countries,[5] which have simply copied article 8bis of the ICC Statute into their national laws,[6] the German legislator decided to depart from the definition in article 8 *bis* of the ICC Statute in several respects ('modified incorporation'[7]). The decision whether and how to implement the Kampala amendments was based on the following three factors.

First, the decision was taken on the basis of the understanding that under international law – under the ICC Statute in particular – no state, including the state parties to the ICC Statute, has a duty to incorporate Statute crimes into the domestic legal order. This holds true not only with regard to genocide, crimes against humanity, and war crimes but similarly with regard to the crime of aggression under article 8 *bis* of the ICC Statute: Even those states which have ratified the Kampala amendments are not legally obliged to provide for a definition of the crime of aggression in their domestic law. In addition: Under international law, there is no obligation for states to exercise extraterritorial jurisdiction over the crime of aggression.[8] The principle of complementarity in article 17 of the ICC Statute establishes the admissibility of a case before the ICC if national states do not prosecute, but does *not* impose an obligation to

---

2 Susanne Wasum-Rainer, in Claus Kreß and Stefan Barriga (eds.), *The Crime of Aggression: A Commentary* (CUP 2017) vol 2, 1151 with further references; Noah Weisbord, 'Bargaining Practices: Negotiating the Kampala Compromise for the International Criminal Court' (2013) 76 Law and Contemporary Problems 85, 107.
3 BGBl. 2013 II, 139. As of May 2017, 34 states had ratified the Kampala amendments to the ICC Statute.
4 Bundestags-Drucksache (BT-Drs., official documents of the German Parliament) 17/10975, 6.
5 Austria, Croatia, Czech Republic, Ecuador, Luxembourg, Macedonia, Samoa, Slovenia; for an overview of the ratification and implementation status see <www.crimeofaggression.info> accessed 9 March 2017.
6 Section 321k of the Austrian Criminal Code is an exception, see for details Konrad Bühler and Astrid Reisinger Coracini, 'Die Umsetzung des Römischen Statuts in Österreich' (2015) Zeitschrift für Internationale Strafrechtsdogmatik 505.
7 On the options to implement the substantive provisions of the ICC Statute into domestic legislation see Gerhard Werle and Florian Jeßberger, *Principles of International Criminal Law* (3rd edn, OUP 2014), paras 377–391.
8 Gerhard Werle and Florian Jeßberger, *Principles of International Criminal Law* (3rd edn, OUP 2014), paras 231–236 with further references; concurring Government Draft, BT-Drs. 18/8621, 13.

prosecute crimes, including the crime of aggression, committed abroad.[9] The participants of the Kampala Conference explicitly clarified that the adopted amendments to the ICC Statute do not establish an obligation to prosecute.[10]

Secondly, under German constitutional law, 'acts suitable to and undertaken with the intent to disturb the peaceful relations between nations, especially to prepare for a war of aggression', must be penalized.[11] This constitutional obligation reflects the fact that Germany had waged aggressive wars during the first half of the 20th century and it is deeply rooted in the founding history of the Federal Republic of Germany. The obligation has no counterpart as regards other crimes under international law. To meet this constitutional obligation, Section 80, 'preparation of a war of aggression', was included in the German Criminal Code (GCC; *Strafgesetzbuch*) in 1968.[12] Until its abrogation in 2017, Section 80 of the GCC read:

Section 80. Preparation of a War of Aggression[13]

Whosoever prepares a war of aggression (Article 26(1) of the Basic Law) in which the Federal Republic of Germany is meant to participate and creates a danger of war for the Federal Republic of Germany, shall be liable to imprisonment for life or for not less than ten years.

---

9   Gerhard Werle and Florian Jeßberger, 'International Criminal Law is Coming Home: The New German Code of Crimes Against International Law' (2002) 13 Criminal Law Form 191, 194.
10 Resolution RC/Res.6, Adopted at the 13th plenary meeting, on 11 June 2010, Annex III, understanding no. 5.
11 See article 26(1) of the Basic Law of the Federal Republic of Germany (*Grundgesetz*). Translated by the author. The German original reads: 'Handlungen, die geeignet sind und in der Absicht vorgenommen werden, das friedliche Zusammenleben der Völker zu stören, insbesondere die Führung eines Angriffskrieges vorzubereiten, sind verfassungswidrig. Sie sind unter Strafe zu stellen.'
12 BGBl. 1968 I, 741. However, whether Section 80 of the GCC fulfilled the constitutional requirements completely, in particular because it required a link to Germany, was controversial and predominantly rejected, cf Claus Dieter Classen, in Wolfgang Joecks and Klaus Miebach (eds.), *Münchener Kommentar zum StGB* (3rd edn, C.H. Beck 2017), Section 80, para 7; Andreas Zimmermann and Elisabeth v. Henn, 'Das Aggressionsverbrechen und das deutsche Strafrecht' (2013) Zeitschrift für Rechtspolitik 240, 241. Although a number of cases were referred to the Federal Prosecutor, there were no convictions for preparing a war of aggression based on Section 80 of the GCC.
13 Translation provided by Michael Bohlander for the Federal Ministry of Justice and for Consumer Protection.

Compared with article 8 *bis* of the ICC Statute, Section 80 of the GCC was both narrower and broader. It was narrower, at least on its face, in that only the 'preparation' of wars of aggression was criminalized; furthermore, the creation of 'a danger of war' for Germany was required. The definition did not include other acts of aggression. Nor did it include aggressive wars in which Germany was not involved.[14] At the same time, however, Section 80 of the GCC was broader than article 8 *bis* of the ICC Statute since it was not construed – at least not expressly – as a leadership crime. Thus, from the perspective of constitutional law, the ramifications for the implementation of the Kampala amendments were twofold: The constitutional obligation to penalize acts tending to disturb the peaceful relations between nations, in particular wars of aggression, was to be taken into account. In addition, the preexisting offence in Section 80 of the GCC, which reflected this constitutional obligation and which, to some extent, overlapped with the notion of the 'crime of aggression' under international law in general and in the ICC Statute in particular, formed a starting point for legislative action.

Thirdly, when this background – the obligation to penalize under domestic constitutional law, but not under international law; the preexisting offence in the GCC – is taken into consideration, it becomes clear that the decision *whether* and *how* article 8 *bis* of the ICC Statute would be incorporated into German law was predominantly shaped by considerations of legal policy.

The 'whether' was easily answered in the affirmative: It had been the intention of the German government and parliament to give full effect to the principle of complementarity and to make sure that cases falling under the jurisdiction of the ICC, including cases concerned with the crime of aggression, could be tried in Germany.[15] Even though no formal obligation to create offences reflecting articles 6 to 8 *bis* of the ICC Statute in domestic criminal law exists, it was acknowledged that domestic prosecutions of international crimes, including the crime of aggression, are vital to the international system of criminal justice. The ICC Statute acknowledges the idea of a decentralized administration of justice. In addition, Germany's historical legacy expresses itself, inter alia, in its constitution's commitment to respect international law (*Völkerrechtsfreundlichkeit*), which speaks in favour of giving full effect to treaties Germany has signed and ratified. Ultimately, the decision to implement the Kampala amendments by including a specific offence in the GCCIL was

---

14 Gerhard Werle and Florian Jeßberger, *Principles of International Criminal Law* (3rd edn, OUP 2014), para 420.
15 BT-Drs. 18/8621, 11.

predetermined by the fact that the other three Statute crimes – genocide, crimes against humanity, and war crimes – had already been incorporated into German law.

'How' the Kampala amendments should be implemented was more difficult to decide. Ultimately, the decision was guided by three principles: complementarity (i), consistency (ii), and certainty (iii). (i) In order to make sure that cases falling under the jurisdiction of the ICC, including cases concerned with the crime of aggression, could be tried in Germany, the implementation was supposed to stay as close to the model of article 8 *bis* of the ICC Statute as possible.[16] For this purpose, the existing Section 80 of the GCC, it was argued, was insufficient.[17] (ii) Consistency rendered it obvious to follow the road which had already been taken with regard to the implementation of the other Statute crimes. Therefore the (modified) incorporation into the GCCIL had a lot to commend it. (iii) In addition, far-reaching consequences followed from the principle of legal certainty (*nullum crimen sine lege certa*), which, according to article 103(2) of the German Basic Law (*Grundgesetz*), determines that criminal offences are only punishable if they are laid down in clear and certain domestic legal provisions.[18] This means, on the one hand, that even crimes under customary international law must be written into German law in order to be prosecuted in Germany. But beyond that, the prerequisites of a crime must be outlined so precisely that the significance and scope of every element of the crime are discernible.[19]

3 Elements

The new Section 13 of the GCCIL draws on the elements of the definition of the crime of aggression under article 8 *bis* of the ICC Statute and, to the extent necessary and appropriate according to the principles outlined above, modifies or deletes single elements or adds new elements. The new provision reads as follows:

---

16   BT-Drs. 18/8621, 11.
17   BT-Drs. 18/8621, 12.
18   Eberhard Schmidt-Aßmann, in Theodor Maunz and Günter Dürig, *Grundgesetz Kommentar* (78th update, C.H. Beck 2016), article 103, para 197; Helmut Satzger, 'German Criminal Law and the Rome Statute – A Critical Analysis of the New German Code of Crimes against International Law' (2002) 2 International Criminal Law Review 261, 264.
19   BVerfGE 78, 374, 382.

Section 13. Crime of Aggression[20]

(1) Whosoever wages a war of aggression or commits another act of aggression which by its character, gravity and scale constitutes a manifest violation of the Charter of the United Nations shall be liable to imprisonment for life.

(2) Whosoever plans, prepares or initiates a war of aggression or another act of aggression under subsection 1 shall be liable to imprisonment for life or imprisonment for not less than ten years. The offence in sentence 1 of this subsection is only punishable if
   a. a war of aggression was waged or another act of aggression was committed or
   b. it creates the danger of a war of aggression or another act of aggression for the Federal Republic of Germany.

(3) An act of aggression is the use of armed force by a State against the sovereignty, territorial integrity or political independence of another State, or in any other manner inconsistent with the Charter of the United Nations.

(4) Only a person who is in a position to effectively exercise control over or to direct the political or military action of a State may be subject to criminal liability under subsections (1) and (2).

(5) In less serious cases under subsection (2), the punishment shall be imprisonment for not less than five years.

3.1 *World Peace and State Security as Protected Interests*

When undertaking an analysis of the elements of an offence a starting point is the consideration of the legal interest the provision intends to protect. Determining the protected legal interest of international crimes under German law poses a particular challenge as they differ from domestic criminal provisions. For instance, the introduction of the crime of genocide into German criminal law (article 6 of the GCCIL) launched a debate on its protected legal interest.[21] Similarly, there was no agreement on the question whether Section 80 of the GCC protected only the security of the Federal Republic of Germany or whether it – in addition or exclusively – protected the international peace

---

20   Translation by the author.
21   For an overview in English with further references cf Helmut Gropengießer, 'The Criminal Law of Genocide – The German Perspective' (2005) 5 International Criminal Law Review 329, 333–334.

and security.[22] With regard to the introduction of Section 13 of the GCCIL, the German legislator took the opportunity to state its view: 'In line with an implementation that recognises the commitment to respect international law, the character of the crime of aggression shifts from an offence concerned with state protection to an offence concerned with world peace. Thus, the prohibition of force in order to secure international peace as a protected interest under international law is given due consideration.'[23]

While it is apparent that Section 13 of the GCCIL aims to secure world peace, the question remains whether it, in addition, directly protects the security of the Federal Republic of Germany as a legal interest rather than protecting it indirectly by maintaining world peace. Even though the character of the provision has now clearly shifted towards protecting world peace, this does not automatically exclude a twofold purpose. After all, Section 13 of the GCCIL refers explicitly to the security of the Federal Republic of Germany ('the danger of a war of aggression or another act of aggression for the Federal Republic of Germany') as a factor limiting the criminal responsibility for preparatory acts (see Section 13(2)(2)). Moreover, as will be discussed below in more detail, jurisdiction for prosecuting Section 13 of the GCCIL is restricted to acts of aggression which are either directed against Germany or committed by Germans. Thus, the persisting focus on the security of the Federal Republic of Germany imparts a second protected legal interest behind the crime of aggression.

3.2 *War of Aggression, Act of Aggression, and the Threshold Clause*

Section 13 of the GCCIL, very much in line with article 8 *bis* of the ICC Statute, refers to every act of aggression which constitutes a manifest violation of the Charter of the United Nations. In subsection 3, the act of aggression is defined in accordance with article 8 *bis* of the ICC Statute,[24] even though a number of

---

22   For the (exclusive) protection of the security of Germany see, for example, Claus Dieter Classen, in Wolfgang Joecks and Klaus Miebach (eds.), *Münchener Kommentar zum StGB* (3rd edn, C.H. Beck 2017), Section 80, para 1; for the protection of the security of Germany *and* of international peace with further references see, for example, Detlev Sternberg-Lieben, in Adolf Schönke and Horst Schröder, *Strafgesetzbuch Kommentar* (29th edn, C.H. Beck 2014), Section 80, para 2; for the (exclusive) protection of peaceful relations with neighbouring countries see Hans-Ullrich Paeffgen, in Urs Kindhäuser, Ulfrid Neumann and Hans-Ullrich Paeffgen (eds.), *Nomos Kommentar Strafgesetzbuch* (4th edn, Nomos 2013), Section 80, para 1.

23   BT-Drs. 18/8621, 22 (translation by the author).

24   Article 8 *bis* of the ICC Statute reads:
      For the purpose of this Statute, 'crime of aggression' means the planning, preparation, initiation or execution, by a person in a position effectively to exercise control over or to

differences appear at first sight. These differences are exemplary of the special path Germany has taken with regard to the implementation of the crime of aggression[25] but, arguably, do not establish any substantive deviations.

A 'war of aggression' is explicitly and first and foremost listed as an example of a punishable act of aggression. Without intending to deviate from article 8 *bis* of the ICC Statute, this wording is taken from the former Section 80 of the GCC in order to give full effect to the obligation to penalize wars of aggression under article 26 of the German Basic Law.[26] Moreover, it serves the principle of legal certainty by referring to the historical starting point of the crime of aggression and exemplifying the necessary gravity of an act of aggression.[27]

---

direct the political or military action of a State, of an act of aggression which, by its character, gravity and scale, constitutes a manifest violation of the Charter of the United Nations. For the purpose of paragraph 1, 'act of aggression' means the use of armed force by a State against the sovereignty, territorial integrity or political independence of another State, or in any other manner inconsistent with the Charter of the United Nations. Any of the following acts, regardless of a declaration of war, shall, in accordance with United Nations General Assembly resolution 3314 (XXIX) of 14 December 1974, qualify as an act of aggression:

The invasion or attack by the armed forces of a State of the territory of another State, or any military occupation, however temporary, resulting from such invasion or attack, or any annexation by the use of force of the territory of another State or part thereof;

Bombardment by the armed forces of a State against the territory of another State or the use of any weapons by a State against the territory of another State;

The blockade of the ports or coasts of a State by the armed forces of another State;

An attack by the armed forces of a State on the land, sea or air forces, or marine and air fleets of another State;

The use of armed forces of one State which are within the territory of another State with the agreement of the receiving State, in contravention of the conditions provided for in the agreement or any extension of their presence in such territory beyond the termination of the agreement;

The action of a State in allowing its territory, which it has placed at the disposal of another State, to be used by that other State for perpetrating an act of aggression against a third State;

The sending by or on behalf of a State of armed bands, groups, irregulars or mercenaries, which carry out acts of armed force against another State of such gravity as to amount to the acts listed above, or its substantial involvement therein.

25 See generally for the implementation of the ICC Statute into German law and a discussion of the deviations between article 6 to 8 of the ICC Statute and the GCCIL Gerhard Werle and Florian Jeßberger, 'International Criminal Justice is Coming Home: The New German Code of Crimes against International Law' (2002) 13 Criminal Law Forum 191, 199–208.

26 BT-Drs. 18/8621, 16.

27 BT-Drs. 18/8621, 16; Florian Jeßberger, 'Das Verbrechen der Aggression im deutschen Strafrecht: Überlegungen zur Umsetzung der Beschlüsse von Kampala' (2015) Zeitschrift für Internationale Strafrechtsdogmatik 514, 518.

In addition to wars of aggression the new provision, similar to article 8 *bis* of the ICC Statute, criminalizes other acts of aggression. Again, the principle of legal certainty is the reason why none of the illustrative acts of aggression contained in the United Nations General Assembly resolution 3314 (XXIX) of 14 December 1974 were included in the definition in the GCCIL. This decision was motivated by doubts as to the exemplary or conclusive nature of the list and the wish for a more concise definition of the crime.[28] However, the reference in Section 13(3) of the GCCIL to the incompatibility of the use of force with the UN Charter ('in any other manner inconsistent with the Charter of the United Nations') has the potential to create tension as regards the principle of legal certainty. After all, a vital element of the crime is dependent on an external legal order whose judgement on the matter is not obvious. Nonetheless, Section 13(3) of the GCCIL justifiably kept this reference. An international crime cannot escape its international context, and, arguably, some compromises with regard to the principle of legal certainty are inevitable. Accordingly, other crimes under the GCCIL also contain similar references.[29]

The threshold requirement of article 8 *bis* of the ICC Statute – manifest violation of the UN Charter – was also adopted. Although not expressly mentioned in the former Section 80 of the GCC, it was also interpreted to the effect that only the illegal use of force on a larger scale and with sufficient gravity could constitute a war of aggression.[30] To elucidate the vague term 'manifest violation',[31] the legislative history suggests it is to be interpreted in accordance with number 7 of the 'understandings' arising out of the Review Conference Resolution 6 Annex III, whereby the character, gravity, and scale of the violation must be jointly considered.[32] A war of aggression, which is expressly mentioned, serves as an example for determining when an act of aggression meets the threshold.[33] Although the understandings arising from the Review Conference provide supplementary help, the term 'act of aggression' remains vague; it is certainly one of the borderline cases of legal certainty in the GCCIL.

---

28 BT-Drs. 18/8621, 19.
29 For example, Section 7(1)(4) and (9) of the GCCIL.
30 Claus Dieter Classen, in Wolfgang Joecks and Klaus Miebach (eds.), *Münchener Kommentar zum StGB* (3rd edn, C.H. Beck 2017), Section 80, para 14.
31 Which is not unknown to German criminal law appearing, for instance in Section 3 of the GCCIL with regard to the manifest illegality of a command and in Section 326(6) of the GCC in a criminal offence against the environment.
32 BT-Drs. 18/8621, 16.
33 BT-Drs. 18/8621, 16.

3.3 Modes of Action

Section 13 of the GCCIL basically copies the definition of the ICC Statute in criminalizing the planning, preparation, initiation, and execution of acts of aggression. Planning, preparation, and initiation are covered by Section 13(2), whereas the execution[34] of an act of aggression is dealt with in Section 13(1). This approach permits recourse to the ICC's interpretation of these modes of action. Moreover, the German legal system's commitment to respect international law indicates that Section 13 of the GCCIL should be interpreted in accordance with the ICC Statute. It is a welcome development that the restriction of Section 80 of the GCC to preparatory acts was abandoned. The different modes of action – planning, preparation, initiation, execution – reflect the different stages of the perpetration of a crime[35] and are borrowed from article 6(c) of the (Nuremberg) Statute of the International Military Tribunal of 8 August 1945.[36]

3.3.1 Planning and Preparation

Under specific conditions, preparatory acts, such as planning or preparation, can establish criminal liability for the crime of aggression (Section 13(2)). Planning describes predominantly mental steps regarding a specific but not yet detailed act of aggression and consists only of thoughts and ideas. In contrast, merely pondering a crime of aggression does not reach the level of seriousness required to constitute 'planning'.[37] The preparation of an act of aggression usually entails it becoming visible for the first time (such as when it leaves a circle of conspirators) because concrete steps are taken to realize the plan.[38] Planning and preparation may coincide temporarily.

Penalizing the very early stages of the commission of a crime may be in conflict with the principle of *Rechtsgüterschutz*. This principle is still a

---

34 The mere terminological differences between the German versions of article 8 *bis* and Section 13 – that is 'Ausführen' rather than 'Begehen' – are reflected in the translation of Section 13 for the purpose of this paper ('execute' rather than 'commit').

35 BT-Drs. 18/8621, 17; Florian Jeßberger, 'Das Verbrechen der Aggression im deutschen Strafrecht: Überlegungen zur Umsetzung der Beschlüsse von Kampala' (2015) Zeitschrift für Internationale Strafrechtsdogmatik 514, 516.

36 However, this reference does not provide much assistance with interpreting and delineating the different modes of action since the IMT did not categorize the actions of the accused accordingly; Carrie McDougall, in Claus Kreß and Stefan Barriga (eds.), *The Crime of Aggression: A Commentary* (CUP 2017) vol 1, 85–87.

37 BT-Drs. 18/8621, 18.

38 BT-Drs. 18/8621, 18; Florian Jeßberger, 'Das Verbrechen der Aggression im deutschen Strafrecht: Überlegungen zur Umsetzung der Beschlüsse von Kampala' (2015) Zeitschrift für Internationale Strafrechtsdogmatik 514, 517.

predominant legal doctrine in German criminal law.[39] It stipulates that an action can only be penalized if it endangers a legal interest (*Rechtsgut*). Every criminal provision must protect at least one legal interest and will be interpreted in accordance with this protected legal interest. The application of this principle often leads to a restrictive interpretation of a provision where the action in question fails to endanger the legal interest. With regard to the preparation of crimes, only those actions which pose a concrete enough threat to the protected legal interest may be punished. Mere intentions and plans are not usually considered to pose a sufficiently serious threat: In general, only a concrete attempt to commit a crime would sufficiently threaten the legal interest. Such an attempt requires the intention to commit the crime while also requiring the perpetrator to be on the immediate verge of committing the offence.[40] According to the majority view, certain intentions and plans in earlier stages may only be punished if they establish at least an abstract threat and if there is a close enough link to the endangered legal interest. This link can be established if, for instance, at an early stage, a non-controllable chain reaction is started or there is a group crime with uncontrollable dynamics.

In cases involving Section 13 of the GCCIL, however, the criminalization of mere preparatory acts can be justified in several ways. First, the protected legal interest (or one of the two legal interests) in question – international peace – may already be endangered when plans are made. However, this is only true if the interpretation of 'planning' reflects the link to the threat. Accordingly, plans must be concrete and, in a temporal respect, not too far removed from the envisaged execution of the act of aggression. The German legislator has confirmed this by demanding a restrictive understanding of 'planning'.[41] A further justification is that acts of aggression will seldom be carried out by just one perpetrator: Typically, they are planned and executed by groups and – once started – often continue because of group dynamics. This also constitutes a sufficient link to the protected legal interest.[42]

Finally, the German legislator has addressed remaining reservations with the design of Section 13(2) of the GCCIL. It ensures that the legal interest has

---

39 For an introduction in English cf Michael Bohlander, *Principles of German Criminal Law* (Hart 2009) 18–20. See also Helmut Gropengießer, 'The Criminal Law of Genocide – The German Perspective' (2005) 5 International Criminal Law Review 329, 333–334.

40 For the German concept of attempt cf Michael Bohlander, *Principles of German Criminal Law* (Hart 2009), 139–144.

41 BT-Drs. 18/8621, 17.

42 BT-Drs. 18/8621, 17; Florian Jeßberger, 'Das Verbrechen der Aggression im deutschen Strafrecht: Überlegungen zur Umsetzung der Beschlüsse von Kampala' (2015) Zeitschrift für Internationale Strafrechtsdogmatik 514, 517.

actually been threatened in each individual case of criminalization. Preparatory acts are only punishable if either the act of aggression was subsequently executed (Section 13(2)(1)) or if the preparatory acts caused a specific threat of an act of aggression to the Federal Republic of Germany (Section 13(2)(2)). According to the legislative history, a threat of war or another act of aggression to the Federal Republic of Germany under Section 13(2) of the GCCIL does not only arise when Germany *is attacked*, but also when Germany *is the aggressor*,[43] which makes sense from a legal policy perspective, but stretches the limits of the provision's wording.

The execution of an act of aggression is designed as an objective condition of criminal liability (*objektive Bedingung der Strafbarkeit*) for planning and preparation. According to general doctrine, this means that the element of the crime must have occurred, but the perpetrator need not have had intent with regard to it. Thus, Section 13(2)(1) addresses situations in which the offender participated only in the planning of the act of aggression which was then executed without her or him (otherwise she or he would be liable under subsection (1)).[44] Only if the subsequent act of aggression has no connection with the initially planned crime – for instance because a completely new plan has been devised – is there no link sufficient for the objective condition of criminal liability to be established.[45]

At first glance, Section 13(2) of the GCCIL seems to be a major deviation from article 8 *bis* of the ICC Statute, which does not mention the execution of the act of aggression as a prerequisite for criminal responsibility for planning or preparation. This first impression is rebutted, however, by no. 3, elements of crimes of article 8 *bis* of the ICC Statute: 'The act of aggression – the use of armed force by a State against the sovereignty, territorial integrity or political independence of another State, or in any other manner inconsistent with the Charter of the United Nations – was committed.' Accordingly, it may be argued that the ICC Statute contains a similar element to the objective condition of criminal liability established by Section 13(2).[46]

One difference with the definition in article 8 *bis*, however, remains: According to Section 13 of the GCCIL, preparatory acts may also be criminal if the act

---

43 This conclusion can be drawn from the reference to the former Section 80 of the GCC, BT-Drs. 18/8621, 18.
44 BT-Drs. 18/8621, 18.
45 BT-Drs. 18/8621, 18.
46 BT-Drs. 18/8621, 18; Florian Jeßberger, 'Das Verbrechen der Aggression im deutschen Strafrecht: Überlegungen zur Umsetzung der Beschlüsse von Kampala' (2015) Zeitschrift für Internationale Strafrechtsdogmatik 514, 517.

of aggression has caused a specific danger of an act of aggression to the Federal Republic of Germany. In this case, the execution of the act of aggression is not required; the creation of a mere danger is sufficient. This deviation from the ICC Statute seems acceptable, particularly as it does not limit the criminal responsibility for acts of aggression. Hence, no problem arises as regards the principle of complementarity.

3.3.2 Initiation and Attempt

The initiation of an act of aggression, however, encompasses actions which, while they precede the act of fighting, nevertheless merge directly into it.[47] This interpretation of 'initiation' is equivalent to when an attempt of a crime of aggression under Sections 22 and 3 of the GCC is made.[48]

One may argue that the attempt to execute an act of aggression is criminalized under German law twice, albeit under somewhat different conditions: As it has a minimum sentence of more than one year, the offence under Section 13(1) of the GCCIL qualifies as a serious criminal offence (*Verbrechen*) in terms of Section 12(1) of the GCC and Section 2 of the GCCIL. As a legal consequence of this categorization, attempting the offence (i.e. attempting the execution of an act of aggression) is punishable without express mention in the criminal provision itself – in addition to the initiation of an act of aggression being a punishable offence under Section 13(2) of the GCCIL.[49]

A solution to this perplexing phenomenon would be to see the initiation under Section 13(2) as a special provision for the attempt to execute an act of aggression which would exclude taking recourse to the general provisions.[50] This would be in line with the fact that the modes of action themselves mostly sound like attempts. The legislator has only commented on attempts under Section 13 of the GCCIL by stating that the stage of initiation may coincide

---

47 BT-Drs. 18/8621, 18; Florian Jeßberger, 'Das Verbrechen der Aggression im deutschen Strafrecht: Überlegungen zur Umsetzung der Beschlüsse von Kampala' (2015) Zeitschrift für Internationale Strafrechtsdogmatik 514, 516.

48 BT-Drs. 18/8621, 18.

49 For the ICC Statute, the matter of an attempted crime of aggression was discussed without any conclusive votes taking place. In the end, article 25(3)(f) does apply to the crime of aggression, see Roger S. Clark, in Claus Kreß and Stefan Barriga (eds.), *The Crime of Aggression: A Commentary* (CUP 2017) vol 1, 590 615. An interpretation of Section 13 of the GCCIL in line with the German commitment to respect international law would therefore speak in favour of an attempt under the general principles.

50 Michael Greßmann and Ulrich Staudigl, 'Die Umsetzung der Beschlüsse von Kampala in Deutschland' (2016) Zeitschrift für Internationale Strafrechtsdogmatik 798, 800.

with the attempt of an act of aggression.[51] This lack of comment could either be seen as a tacit vote for a specialized regulation of an attempt,[52] or for the application of the general provisions as they otherwise could have been explicitly excluded.

A consideration of the consequences of double criminalization may render further assistance in evaluating its feasibility: The attempt of Section 13(1) of the GCCIL requires, as stated above, the intention to commit the crime in addition to the perpetrator simultaneously being on the immediate verge of committing the offence. Initiation under Section 13(2) of the GCCIL has, in comparison, more specific requirements: While the initiation may coincide with being on the verge of committing an act of aggression, the act must have been subsequently actually executed or must have caused an imminent threat to the Federal Republic of Germany. Hence, the two different 'attempts' do no cover exactly the same situation.

These differences are important as they would also have to justify the differing penalty ranges applicable to Section 13(1) and Section 13(2) of the GCCIL.[53] Section 23(2) and Section 49(1)(1) of the GCC determine that in cases of an attempt, the court has the discretion to lower the minimum penalty to not less than three years of imprisonment. In contrast, Section 13(2)of the GCCIL stipulates a minimum sentence of ten years, a considerable difference to an attempt under Section 13(1) if the court opts to apply the lower range of penalty.

3.4   *Leadership Clause and Immunity*

Section 13(4) of the GCCIL provides for a leadership clause which is in accordance with article 8 *bis* (1) of the ICC Statute and, arguably, customary international law.[54] It restricts criminal liability to persons in positions of governmental (*sensu lato*) power and is meant to preserve the combatant's privilege of international humanitarian law.[55] The principle protects ordinary soldiers in that they do not incur criminal liability for their participation in hostilities irrespective of the legality of the use of force, as long as they comply with *ius in bello*.

---

51   BT-Drs. 18/8621, 18.
52   Florian Jeßberger, 'Das Verbrechen der Aggression im deutschen Strafrecht: Überlegungen zur Umsetzung der Beschlüsse von Kampala' (2015) Zeitschrift für Internationale Strafrechtsdogmatik 514, 516.
53   For further notes on the penalty ranges see below 3.5.
54   BT-Drs. 18/8621, 19.
55   BT-Drs. 18/8621, 20.

The ability to 'effectively exercise control over or to direct the political or military action of a state' does not necessarily presuppose that the offender is a state organ. The legislative history relating to Section 13 of the GCCIL makes clear that private individuals may fulfil the leadership clause, too, as long as their acts are attributable to the aggressor state under international law.[56] Such private individuals may be business leaders or the ideological or religious elite of a country.[57] However, in most cases, the ability to exercise control or direct a state will necessitate a state organ position.[58]

Section 13(4) of the GCCIL stays further in line with the model provided by the ICC Statute in its article 25(3) *bis* in that all modes of participation, including accessorial criminal liability need to fulfil the requirements of the leadership clause. For instance, an aider and abettor may only be punished under Section 13 of the GCCIL if he or she can exercise control over or direct the political or military action of a State. Therefore, under German criminal law, the crime is considered an 'absolute crime of special qualification' (*absolutes Sonderdelikt*).[59]

It should be noted that, for a number of reasons, the adoption of the ICC Statute's leadership clause was not a matter of course in the drafting of Section 13 of the GCCIL. First, article 26 of the German Basic Law does not mention a restriction of criminal liability to military and political leaders of a state. Secondly, under the principle of legal certainty, the leadership clause might not be precise enough since it does not depend on formal positions of power, but political and military relations, which have to be ascertained in each individual case. However, the German legislator did overcome its reservations – if it had any: The majority view holds, with regard to article 26 of the German Basic Law, that only persons in a leadership position can prepare a war of aggression because only they have the necessary amount of power.[60] Furthermore, the commitment of the German Basic Law to respect international law speaks in favour of such an interpretation.[61] This might have

---

56   BT-Drs. 18/8621, 20.
57   BT-Drs. 18/8621, 20.
58   BT-Drs. 18/8621, 20; Florian Jeßberger, 'Das Verbrechen der Aggression im deutschen Strafrecht: Überlegungen zur Umsetzung der Beschlüsse von Kampala' (2015) Zeitschrift für Internationale Strafrechtsdogmatik 514, 518.
59   It departs from the general rule of Section 28 of the GCC under which there would be a mitigated punishment but no impunity in the case of an accessory not fulfilling the special qualification for perpetrators of the crime.
60   Heinrich Wilhelm Laufhütte and Annette Kuschel, in Heinrich Wilhelm Laufhütte, Ruth Rissing-van Saan and Klaus Tiedemann (eds.), *Strafgesetzbuch, Leipziger Kommentar* (12th edn, De Gruyter Recht 2007) vol 3, Section 80, para 8 with further references.
61   BT-Drs. 18/8621, 20.

also contributed to the acceptance of the wording as precise enough. After all, a far less satisfactory alternative could have been to choose the requirements which have been applied in at least some of the Nuremberg follow-up trials.[62] According to their jurisprudence, anyone who was in a position to 'shape and influence a policy' could commit a crime of aggression, which is less restrictive, but arguably also less precise than the approach of article 8 *bis* of the ICC Statute. Moreover, its recognition under international customary law is doubtful.[63]

Closely related to the question of who can be a perpetrator under Section 13 of the GCCIL is the question of who is exempted from criminal responsibility due to immunity. In light of the already small number of possible perpetrators, the aim of the law could be undermined if immunity is granted too freely. This problem does not arise before international courts: It is understood that there is no immunity *ratione materiae*[64] for international crimes.[65] Moreover, international courts do not recognise immunity *ratione personae*, i.e. the immunity of a selected group of state officials who are particularly important to the functioning of their state for acts committed during their tenure, and which lasts until the end of their tenure.[66] In case of the ICC this is confirmed by article 27(2) of the ICC Statute. However, immunity *ratione personae* remains applicable before national courts, including in the German legal system.[67]

This results in a considerable (but not fatal) reduction of the (potential) efficacy of Section 13 of the GCCIL.[68] In Germany, only the president of the

---

62 For a precise reconstruction of the differing views in the jurisdiction of U.S. Military Tribunals, see the excellent study by Kevin Jon Heller, *The Nuremberg Military Tribunals and the Origins of International Criminal Law* (OUP 2012), 193–194.

63 Florian Jeßberger, 'Das Verbrechen der Aggression im deutschen Strafrecht: Überlegungen zur Umsetzung der Beschlüsse von Kampala' (2015) Zeitschrift für Internationale Strafrechtsdogmatik 514, 519.

64 This immunity refers to acts committed in an official capacity which are attributed to the state.

65 Gerhard Werle and Florian Jeßberger, *Principles of International Criminal Law* (3rd edn, OUP 2014), para 733 with further references. It must be noted, however, that immunity *ratione materiae* can be done away with only to the extent to which Section 13 corresponds with the crime of aggression under (customary) international law. Beyond that, immunity fully applies.

66 Gerhard Werle and Florian Jeßberger, *Principles of International Criminal Law* (3rd edn, OUP 2014), para 725, 734, 736 with further references.

67 Gerhard Werle and Florian Jeßberger, *Principles of International Criminal Law* (3rd edn, OUP 2014), para 739.

68 Florian Jeßberger, 'Das Verbrechen der Aggression im deutschen Strafrecht: Überlegungen zur Umsetzung der Beschlüsse von Kampala' (2015) Zeitschrift für Internationale Strafrechtsdogmatik 514, 518.

country and parliamentarians on a federal and state (*Bundesland*) level are granted immunity *ratione personae*, which can be prematurely suspended by a decision of the respective parliament.[69] Notably, this immunity does not encompass government officials or other state officials. Personal immunity for foreign state officials in German courts – including heads of state, heads of government and diplomats – is, however, more extensive since Sections 18 to 20 of the German Courts Constitution Act (*Gerichtsverfassungsgesetz*) make the standards under international law (outlined above) directly applicable. However, this does not weigh too heavy as the circle of exempted leaders remains small and immunity *ratione personae* is only a temporal bar to proceedings.

3.5 Range of Penalty

Unlike the ICC Statute, where article 77 determines the applicable penalties for all crimes, Section 13 of the GCCIL provides for specific penalty ranges (*Strafrahmen*). The need for specific ranges of penalty arises from the principles of legal certainty, personal guilt,[70] and proportionality under German law.[71] They require the legislator to provide for each crime a specific penalty range which reflects the gravity of the specific offence. This results in the difficult task of determining precise penalty ranges where the ICC Statute gives very little guidance.

The provision assigns different penalty ranges depending on whether the perpetrator *commits* an act of aggression (subsection 1) or simply *plans* or *prepares* an act of aggression (subsection 2). Moreover, there is a special penalty range for less serious cases.

Accordingly, the commission of a crime of aggression is punished with life imprisonment. By contrast (and adopting the penalty range of the former Section 80 of the GCC), preparatory acts under Section 13(2) of the GCCIL can be punished with life imprisonment or with imprisonment for ten to fifteen years. Moreover, in so-called less serious cases (*minder schwere Fälle*), Section 13(5) allows for a reduction of the sentence for preparatory acts up to a mandatory minimum of three years of imprisonment. Whether the option of 'less serious cases' will obtain practical relevance might be doubtful considering that Section 13 of the GCCIL excludes lesser offences with its gravity threshold.[72] However, mitigating circumstances offer flexibility for finding an appropriate

---

69 BT-Drs. 18/8621, 20.
70 For an introduction see Michael Bohlander, *Principles of German Criminal Law* (Hart 2009), 20–22.
71 See, for example, BVerfGE 120, 224 para 37.
72 This was considered by the legislator, BT-Drs. 18/8621, 20.

penalty which might be welcome considering the often manifestations of criminal behaviour.

4 Jurisdiction

Another key issue in the discussion of how to implement 'Kampala' was the question as to the jurisdiction of German courts to rule on the crime of aggression. It should be recalled that the German approach with regard to the other international crimes – genocide, crimes against humanity, and war crimes – is uniquely broad and ambitious.[73] Section 1 of the GCCIL provides for pure universal jurisdiction: German law applies 'even when the offence was committed abroad and bears no relation to Germany'. This reflects the status of customary international law according to which the exercise of universal jurisdiction for genocide, war crimes, and crimes against humanity is permissible.[74]

However, the point of departure for the crime of aggression was different: Exercising extraterritorial jurisdiction presupposes an authorizing norm in International Law.[75] It is, in the view of many, including this author, at least doubtful whether such a norm (authorizing the exercise of universal jurisdiction) is recognized under customary international law regarding the crime of aggression.[76] On the one hand, a sufficiently stable state practice is hard to

---

73 The practical consequences of this far-reaching approach are, however, limited by an accompanying procedural provision: Section 153f of the German Code of Criminal Procedure allows dispensing with prosecution if the offence or the offender has no link to Germany; see for an in-depth analysis Julia Geneuss, *Völkerrechtsverbrechen und Verfolgungsermessen: § 153f StPO im System völkerrechtlicher Strafrechtspflege* (Nomos 2013).

74 Gerhard Werle and Florian Jeßberger, *Principles of International Criminal Law* (3rd edn, OUP 2014), para 218 with further references.

75 See Florian Jeßberger, *Der transnationale Geltungsbereich des deutschen Strafrechts* (Mohr Siebeck 2011), 199 et seq.

76 Cf Gerhard Werle and Florian Jeßberger, in Heinrich Wilhelm Laufhütte, Ruth Rissing-van Saan and Klaus Tiedemann (eds.), *Strafgesetzbuch, Leipziger Kommentar* (12th edn, De Gruyter 2007), Vor § 3, para 240 with further references. For a concurring view see, inter alia, Heike Krieger, 'Die Umsetzung des völkerrechtlichen Aggressionsverbrechens in das deutsche Recht im Lichte von Artikel 26 Abs. 1 GG' (2012) Die Öffentliche Verwaltung 449, 457; Stefan Oeter, 'Das Verbrechen der Aggression, die Konferenz von Kampala und das deutsche Strafrecht' in Florian Jeßberger and Julia Geneuss (eds.), *Zehn Jahre Völkerstrafgesetzbuch: Bilanz und Perspektiven eines „deutschen Völkerstrafrechts"* (Nomos 2013), 101, 120; Christian Tomuschat, 'The Duty to Prosecute International Crimes Commited by Individuals' in Hans-Joachim Cremer, Thomas Giegerich, Dagmar Richter and Andreas Zimmermann (eds.), *Tradition und Weltoffenheit des Rechts: Festschrift für Helmut*

find,[77] even if one takes into account the special characteristics of international criminal law. On the other hand, it may appear contradictory to hold that the principle of universality should not extend to the crime of aggression when it has been extended to all other crimes under international law, especially considering that the crime of aggression is directed against world peace, endangering thereby a fundamental interest of the international community.[78] The German legislator was conscious of this predicament and chose to take a rather cautious approach with regard to the issue of jurisdiction. The (amended) Section 1 of the GCCIL reads as follows:

Section 1. Scope of Application[79]

This Act shall apply to all criminal offences against international law designated under this Act, to serious criminal offences under Section 6 to 12 even when the offence was committed abroad and bears no relation to Germany. *This Act shall apply to offences under Section 13 which were committed abroad, regardless of the law applicable in the locality where they were committed, if the offender was German or the offence was directed against the Federal Republic of Germany.*

As a result, extraterritorial jurisdiction is restricted to situations with a clear link to Germany: It can only be exercised where the alleged offender is

---

Steinberger (Springer 2002), 315, 342. Contra (extending universal jurisdiction to the crime of aggression) see, e.g. Michael P. Scharf, 'Universal jurisdiction and the crime of aggression' (2012) 53 Harvard International Law Journal 357, 368; Thomas Weigend, in Jörg Arnold, Björn Burkhardt, Walter Gropp, Günter Heine, Hans-Georg Koch, Otto Lagodny, Walter Perron and Susanne Walther (eds.), *Menschengerechtes Strafrecht, Festschrift für Albin Eser zum 70. Geburtstag* (C.H. Beck 2005), 955, 972.

77 It is reported that (only) five states have provided for universal jurisdiction over 'crimes against peace', 'aggression' or 'preparation of aggressive war' under their domestic law (Azerbaijan, Bulgaria, Czech Republic, Estonia and Belarus), see Report of the Secretary-General of 29 July 2010 'The scope and application of the principle of universal jurisdiction' (A/65/181).

78 Cf also Gerhard Werle and Florian Jeßberger, *Principles of International Criminal Law* (3rd edn, OUP 2014), para 218.

79 The translation of sentence 1 is based on the non-authoritative proposition of the Max-Planck-Institute for Foreign and International Criminal Law which has not been updated to the current status of legislation <www.mpicc.de/files/pdf1/vstgbleng2.pdf> accessed 9 March 2017. Translation of sentence 2 and emphasis by the author.

German,[80] or where an act of aggression directed against the Federal Republic of Germany has been committed. This solution attempts to forestall an overburdening of the German judiciary in general and the investigative authorities in particular.[81] Instead of relying on the law of criminal procedure (such as Section 153f of the German Code of Criminal Procedure) for this purpose – as has been done with the other crimes under the GCCIL – the legislator restricted the scope of the substantive law to underline its difference to the other crimes.[82] This amendment to Section 1 of the GCCIL will certainly not further an extension of universal jurisdiction to the crime of aggression under customary international law. It is a less dynamic approach than the GCCIL adopts in other areas,[83] but it maintains the precarious balance between the conflicting interests burdening the domestic implementation of international crimes and an effective incorporation of the offence.

5 Conclusion

'July 2002 was a good month for international justice.'[84] This was the first sentence of a paper on the implementation of the ICC Statute in Germany and the (at that time) new German Code of Crimes against International Law co-written by this author in 2002. This optimistic assessment was based on the fact that both the ICC Statute and the GCCIL had entered into force in this same month. In retrospect, and notwithstanding the considerable set-backs the enforcement of international criminal law has since been facing, we may agree that there is no reason to withdraw that judgement. Similarly, perhaps, we may agree that January 2017 was a good month for international justice, too – at least for those who, in general, think it a good idea to have the crime of aggression added to the list of crimes under international law.

---

80   'Offender' encompasses under Section 1 of the GCCIL all modes of commission, see BT-Drs. 18/8621, 15.
81   BT-Drs. 18/8621, 15.
82   BT-Drs. 18/8621, 15.
83   See, for instance, on the implementation of war crimes, Gerhard Werle and Florian Jeßberger, 'International Criminal Justice is Coming Home: The New German Code of Crimes against International Law' (2002) 13 Criminal Law Forum 191, 206, 209–213.
84   Gerhard Werle and Florian Jeßberger, 'International Criminal Justice is Coming Home: The New German Code of Crimes against International Law' (2002) 13 Criminal Law Forum 191.

Over all, the incorporation of the new offence into German law must be applauded. It was wise to implement it directly in the GCCIL. It is not difficult to predict, however, that the new crime under the GCCIL (similar to the crime of aggresssion under the ICC Statute) will share the fate of the other crimes within the jurisdiction of the ICC. It is quite certain that there will be even fewer prosecutions, let alone convictions, for the crime of aggression on all levels, international as well as national. However, non-implementation was not an option.

Defining the crime of aggression under German law has been no easy task. On the one hand, there was a strong resolution to stay close to the model of article 8 *bis* of the ICC Statute and give full effect to the principle of complementarity. On the other hand, article 26 of the German Basic Law and the principles of legal certainty, guilt, and *Rechtsgüterschutz* set limits on an indiscriminate adoption of the definition of the crime. They have led the German legislator to introduce specifications (such as the mention of a war of aggression, additional requirements for preparatory acts, and specific penalty ranges), but also to omit elements of the Statute model (such as the list of the United Nations General Assembly resolution 3314's acts of aggression). Moreover, the spirit of the former Section 80 of the GCC still inhabits Section 13 of the GCCIL with the alternative requirement of a threat to Germany for preparatory acts and the 'war of aggression' still serving as a yardstick for other acts of aggression. The hybrid nature of the offence and the fact that Section 13 aims to protect the security of Germany as a state (as part of the 'twofold purpose'), is also a legacy of Section 80 of the GCC. The German legislator has taken the wise, if controversial, decision not to subject Section 13 of the GCCIL to the principle of universal jurisdiction, making the crime of aggression the only international crime to be excluded from this principle under German law. After all, Section 13 of the GCCIL strikes a balance between copying article 8 *bis* to the extent possible and taking account of the constitutional ramifications.

The German approach to implementing article 8 *bis* of the ICC Statute might not be easily transferable to other domestic legal orders as it has been much influenced by the particularities of the German legal system and the country's legal and political history. However, the provision may set an example for other states to consider their own incorporation of the crime of aggression.

CHAPTER 9

The Serendipitous Nature of the ICC Trial Proceedings Risks the ICC's Credibility

Michael G. Karnavas

Abstract

This chapter considers whether the ad hoc nature of ICC trial proceedings risks undermining the ICC's credibility. The Rome Statute and the ICC Rules of Procedure and Evidence have sufficient constructive ambiguity as to how trials should be conducted such that, depending on the serendipitous composition of the Trial Chamber, trials can be shaped in a more 'adversarial' or more 'inquisitorial' fashion. This malleability, which may have been the result of a diplomatic compromise, has resulted in *ad hoc* trial proceedings at the ICC; no two trials are conducted in the same manner. Since the hallmarks of any good court are uniformity, predictability, and reliability in its proceedings, does this feature, which is unique to the ICC, risk undermining the legitimacy of the ICC's judgments and, inexorably, the ICC itself?

Introduction

Innocuous as the Rome Statute and the Rules of Procedure and Evidence (RPE) of the International Criminal Court (ICC) may seem, they have the capacity of turning the ICC trial proceedings into an unpredictable pendulum, with trials being conducted under the classical judge-controlled civil law procedure to the *laissez-faire* common law procedure to anything in between. Variability, unpredictability, and unreliability are not the hallmarks of a mature judicial institution – not if it wishes the public at large to recognize it as fair

---

* Michael G. Karnavas is an American trained lawyer qualified to appear before various international tribunals. Practicing law for over 35 years, he has appeared before State and Federal Courts in the United States, the ICTY, the ICTR, the ECCC, and the ICC and for over 27 years he has taught trial advocacy skills to lawyers and law students, lectured extensively on international criminal law and procedure, authored trial advocacy practice manuals, articles and book chapters on international criminal law and procedure, and has been engaged in a variety of legal reform and development projects in Europe and Asia.

and unbiased, and to accept its decisions and results. This is especially true at international(ized) tribunals and courts where invariably there are certain political elements at play, as recently seen by efforts of several African states to leave the ICC.[1]

If the few trial proceedings in its 14-year practice is indicative of things to come, it may not be too soon to predict that, indeed, trials at the ICC will to a large extent be conducted based on judicial preferences for how much or how little the judges may wish the proceedings to lean in one direction or another, adversarial or inquisitorial.[2] This would not necessarily or inevitably lead to unfair trials. As long as the proceedings meet the underlying criteria of being fair, expeditious, impartial, and are conducted 'with full respect for the rights of the accused',[3] all is fair game. Nonetheless, the unintended consequences may, if not will, lead to criticism and a loss of confidence in the outcomes of trials, resulting from perceptions of unfairness rising from disparate trial proceedings. Query whether this was considered or appreciated by the drafters of the Rome Statute?

Creating a legal regime for an international court to try mass atrocity crimes (to put it generically) was no easy task, yet the drafters of the Rome Statute had several models from which to draw inspiration: the International Military Tribunal in Nuremberg, the International Military Tribunal for the Far East in Tokyo, the International Criminal Tribunal for the former Yugoslavia (ICTY), and the International Criminal Tribunal for Rwanda (ICTR). The procedures adopted at Nuremberg and Tokyo were heavily influenced by common law

---

[1] The African Union's February 2017 resolution adopted an ICC 'Withdrawal Strategy Document', which seeks to initiate withdrawal of the African States Parties from the Rome Statute unless the ICC adopts the proposed reforms. *See* African Union, *African Union 28th Summit in Addis Ababa*, 30–31 January 2017. *See also* 'Withdrawal Strategy Document Draft 2', Version 12 January 2017, paras. 30, 38, listing the proposed reforms.

[2] I use the terms 'adversarial' and 'inquisitorial' for convenience, to compare and contrast (in the general sense) the truth-seeking nature of the criminal procedure in civil law systems, and the adversarial nature of the criminal procedure in common law systems. As Kai Ambos observed, inquisitorial-adversarial divide has only historic meaning and within modern criminal procedures, be it common law or civil law tradition, there are numerous and distinct variations. *See* Kai Ambos, 'International Criminal Procedure: "Adversarial", "Inquisitorial" or Mixed?' 3 *Int Crim Law Rev* (2003) 1, 3–4.

[3] Rome Statute 1998, art 64(2): 'The Trial Chamber shall ensure that a trial is fair and expeditious and is conducted with full respect for the rights of the accused and due regard for the protection of victims and witnesses'. Rome Statute 1998, art 67(1): '… the accused shall be entitled to a public hearing, having regard to the provisions of this Statute, to a fair hearing conducted impartially, and to the following minimum guarantees, in full equality'.

adversarial proceedings as the United States played a dominant role in shaping the way trials would be conducted. The ICTY, and subsequently the ICTR, drew from the procedures and attendant adversarial modalities of the Nuremberg and Tokyo tribunals, with the judges tweaking several times the RPE, often adopting inquisitorial modalities. Notwithstanding these amendments (tinkering and recalibrating) of their respective RPE, both the ICTY and the ICTR, hybrid as they may be, maintained an adversarial pedigree, this despite making tolerant allowances for the trial chambers to adopt their own trial management directives.[4] For the most part, the trial proceedings at the ICTY and ICTR have been uniform and predictable, although not entirely free of criticism.[5]

While the ICTY and ICTR were established by the United Nations Security Council (UNSC) under Chapter 7 of the United Nations Charter (which included the UNSC drafting their founding documents and respective statutes),[6] the Rome Statute is nothing short of a compromise between States from various legal systems and procedures. It appears that the drafters of the Rome Statute were going for a new frontier – *where no tribunal has gone before*. It also appears that many of the drafters were only acquainted with their own legal and

---

4 The Trial Chambers regulate and manage the trial by adopting the time tables, time-limits for the presentation of evidence, admitting documentary evidence from the bar table, etc. For example, in *Popović et al.,* the Trial Chamber decided not to set a specific limit on the Defence for the cross-examination of Prosecution witnesses. *Prosecutor v. Popović et al.,* IT-05-88, Order Concerning Guidelines on the Presentation of Evidence and the Conduct of Parties During Trial Proceedings, 14 July 2006, para. 3(c). In *Prlić et al.,* the Trial Chamber limited the amount of cross-examination by applying a mathematical one-sixth-solution: the Defence collectively have the same time for cross-examination as the OTP takes for direct examination, and in the absence of an agreement between Defence Counsel, each would have one-sixth of the time allocated to the Prosecution for direct examination. This decision was upheld on appeal. See *Prosecutor v. Prlić et al.* ICTY-04-74-AR73.2, Decision on Joint Defence Interlocutory Appeal against the Trial Chamber's Oral Decision of 8 May 2006 Relating to Cross-Examination By Defence and on Association of Defence Counsel's Request for Leave to File an *Amicus Curiae* Brief, 4 July 2006, 4.
5 Discussing the inefficiencies in trial management *see* Judge O-Gon Kwon, 'The Challenge of an International Criminal Trial as Seen from the Bench' (2007) 5 *Journal of Int Crim Justice* 360; Judge Patricia M. Wald, 'The International Criminal Tribunal for the Former Yugoslavia Comes of Age: Some Observations on Day-To-Day Dilemmas of an International Court' (2001) 5 *Journal of Law & Policy* 87, 104; Lilian A. Barria and Steven D. Roper, 'How Effective are International Criminal Tribunals? An Analysis of the ICTY and ICTR' (2005) 9(3) *Int Journal of Human Rights* 349.
6 UNSC Res 827 (25 May 1993) UN Doc S/RES/827, establishing the ICTY; UNSC Res 925 (1 July 1994) UN Doc S/RES/935, establishing ICTR.

criminal procedure, or were promoting their own legal systems, or were unreceptive to other legal procedures.[7] Many common law and civil law experts and practitioners have an aversion – mainly based on ignorance or bias – towards the other's legal system. The intent was to establish a *sui generis* statute with rules of procedure and evidence that would be detailed, yet flexible enough to accommodate the fancies of the judges, so long as the proceedings adopted by them – based on their interpretation of the Rome Statute and the RPE – ensured fairness and impartiality.[8]

To ensure that the Rome Statute and the RPE represented no particular legal system, neutral terms were adopted to the extent possible. This can be seen in the use of the terms 'examine' and 'have examined', as opposed to 'examine and cross-examine'.[9] 'To have examined' connotes that the opposing party would have the opportunity to confront the witness. Seems appropriate and does in fact avoid the term cross-examination, a term associated with the common law system. But what does 'have examined' really mean? It depends. Those coming from the common law system would axiomatically think that it means having the right to pose leading (suggestive) questions to opposing witnesses. Not necessarily so to those who hail from the civil law system – where

---

[7] As Peter Lewis, a participant in the negotiations of the Rome Statute and the RPE, commented, 'It would be easy to characterize the debate about Rule 140 as a clash of cultures between the civil law and the common law. The delegations of France and the United States certainly championed their respective legal traditions'. Peter Lewis, 'Trial Procedure' in Roy S. Lee (ed), *The International Criminal Court, Elements of Crimes and Rules of Procedure and Evidence* (Transnational Publishers Inc 2001), 550. See *id.*, 547–549 on the history of negotiation of Article 64 and Rule 140. See also Hans-Jorg Behrens, 'The Trial Proceedings' in Roy S. Lee (ed), *The International Criminal Court, The Making of the Rome Statute, Issues, Negotiations* (Oxford University Press, 1999). 239–241, discussing the various proposals of Article 64 during the drafting of the Rome Statute.

[8] See Gilbert Bitti, 'Article 64 Functions and Powers of the Trial Chamber' in Otto Triffterer (ed) *Rome Statute of the International Criminal Court, A Commentary* (C.H. Beck Hart Nomos 2016), 1616: 'What transpires from this debate is that delegations, at least some of them, wanted to reach a greater certainty on how future trials at the ICC would look like. This was obviously a praiseworthy effort although unlikely to succeed. Indeed, uncertainty in how trials are to be conducted was simply unavoidable during the first yeas of the Court: Judges and participants to the proceedings ... have to determine gradually how trials at the ICC are to be conducted according to the unique needs and features of this institution. Of course such a *sui generis* system may take more than just a decade to build itself'.

[9] Rome Statute 1998, art 67(1)(e), providing for the right of the accused '[t]o examine, or have examined, the witnesses against him or her'.

parties are generally forbidden to pose leading questions (judges can ask any sort of questions in whichever mode they think is conducive in assisting them in their truth-seeking quest). This will be discussed further below as one of the examples showing just how divergent the emerging trial proceedings at the ICC are based on its modest history of conducting nine trials.

Having examined the cases that have been tried thus far and from my reading of the Rome Statute and the RPE, I will attempt to show that there appears to be sufficient constructive ambiguity on how trials can be conducted. Depending on the serendipitous composition of the Trial Chamber, trials can be shaped in a more adversarial or more inquisitorial fashion. And although, arguably, this would not necessarily lead to unfair trial results (as already noted), with no two trials being conducted in the same manner due to the inherent malleability of the Rome Statute and the RPE resultant from diplomatic compromises by the drafters, it begs the question just how accepted will the ICC's judgments and legacy be.

Due to space and the narrow focus of this chapter, my analysis will be limited to the Trial Chamber's powers under Article 64 of the Rome Statute and Rule 140 of the RPE to shape the conduct of the proceedings. Other statutory provisions and rules will be discussed where and when relevant to this analysis. Raw analysis of the Rome Statute and the RPE (as has been done by some with remarkable prescience before there were cases from which to draw conclusions on the application of these articles and rules)[10] essential as it may be, remains an academic exercise, unless analyzed in the context of their application as reflected in the ICC trial proceedings. To illustrate the point that the unique procedure of the ICC risks undermining the legitimacy of its judgments and the ICC itself, I will examine the Trial Chambers' practice of ruling on the admissibility of evidence, witness proofing, examination of witnesses, judicial questioning, and trial management.

This chapter is divided in two sections. For contextual purposes, I will first discuss the legal basis for procedural discretion before turning to the examples that may assist in drawing conclusions and identifying possible solutions – if, indeed, solutions are needed.

---

10   See e.g. Claus Kress, 'The Procedural Law of the International Criminal Court in Outline: Anatomy of a Unique Compromise' (2003) 1 *Journal of Int Crim Just* 603; Stefan Kirsch, 'The Trial Proceedings before the ICC' (2006) 6 *Int Crim Law Rev* 275; see Kai Ambos, 'International Criminal Procedure: "Adversarial", "Inquisitorial" or Mixed?' (2003) 3 *Int Crim Law Rev* 1.

The Legal Basis for Procedural Discretion in Directing the Conduct of the Trial Proceedings. What Kind of Procedure is it Anyway?

Similar to what has been adopted by other international(ized) tribunals and courts – save for the Extraordinary Chambers in the Courts of Cambodia (ECCC)[11] and the Special Tribunal for Lebanon (STL),[12] which are predominantly civil law-based – the procedure at the ICC is hybrid, a mixture of common law and civil law modalities.[13] As was noted, the Rome Statute is a product of accommodation, drafted by committee based on haggling and diplomatic

---

11 'Unlike the other United Nations and United Nations-assisted tribunals, the Extraordinary Chambers in the Courts of Cambodia forms part of the national court structure. It is a Cambodian national court, based on the French civil law system, with special jurisdiction, and with United Nations participation. It is an example of a special chamber within a national jurisdiction.... [It] is a national court of Cambodia'. *See* UNSC 'Report of the Secretary-General on possible options to further the aim of prosecuting and imprisoning persons responsible for acts of piracy and armed robbery at sea off the coast of Somalia, including, in particular, options for creating special domestic chambers possibly with international components, a regional tribunal or an international tribunal and corresponding imprisonment arrangements, taking into account the work of the Contact Group on Piracy of the Coast of Somalia, the existing practice in establishing international and mixed tribunals, and the time and resources necessary to achieve and sustain substantive results'. (26 July 2010) UN Doc S/2010/394, 42–43.

12 Unlike the ICTY and ICTR, the STL system provides for other civil law system modalities: the victims can participate in the proceedings through legal representatives (STL RPE Rule 86), the Pre-Trial Judge may question anonymous witnesses at the request of the party (STL Rule 93), the Pre-Trial Judge has to make a report for the Trial Chamber on: (a) arguments set out by the parties and participating victims; (b) points of agreement and disagreement; (c) probative material produced in the proceedings; (d) a summary of decisions and orders rendered; (e) suggestions as to the number/relevance of witnesses; and (f) issues of law the Pre-Trial Judge finds contentious (STL RPE 95). STL RPE Rule 92(C) grants the Pre-Trial Judge the authority to gather the evidence himself '[w]here he considers that the interests of justice, the need for the impartial establishment of truth and the necessity to ensure a fair and expeditious trial, in particular the need to ensure the equality of arms and to preserve evidence, make it imperative'.

13 Analyzing the ICC RPE in 2003, Kai Ambos rightly anticipated: 'In sum, it is fair to say that the rules of evidence adopt, despite the broad powers of the Trial Chamber, a mixed approach combining civil and common law features. The practical application of these rules will ultimately depend on the legal background of the judges who are given sufficient discretion to conduct trials in accordance with their own preferences'. Kai Ambos, 'International Criminal Procedure: "Adversarial", "Inquisitorial" or Mixed?' (2003) 3 *Int Crim Law Rev* 1, 32.

compromises.[14] This is most pronounced in the procedural discretion afforded to the judges in conducting the proceedings.

Effectively, Article 64 of the Rome Statute and Rule 140 give the Presiding Judge wide discretion to adopt trial procedures based on his or her legal culture, experiences, and biases. Article 64(3)(a) provides that, upon assignment, the Trial Chamber must '[c]onfer with the parties and adopt such procedures as are necessary to facilitate the fair and expeditious conduct of the proceedings'. This obligation on the Trial Chamber merely implies that the parties have the right to be heard on the matter, not that the Trial Chamber is obliged to consider the parties' submissions. Having heard the parties, the Trial Chamber has the authority to adopt whichever procedure it sees fit for the fair and expeditious conduct of the proceedings so long as it fulfills its general obligation under Article 64(2) to ensure 'that a trial ... is conducted with full respect for the rights of the accused and due regard for the protection of victims and witnesses'.

Article 64(8)(b) of the Rome Statute permits the Presiding Judge to direct the conduct of the proceedings, ensuring they are fair and impartial. The parties, subject to directions from the Presiding Judge, may submit evidence as provided by the Rome Statute. Corresponding Rule 140(1) provides that should the Presiding Judge not give directions on how the proceedings will be conducted, it is up to the Prosecution and the Defence to agree. If they cannot, the Presiding Judge will issue directions. In principle, Rule 140(2) seems quite democratic and inclusive – *let there be no preference for any one procedural system, let no judge be constrained by procedural modalities inconsistent with their own or disfavored*:

(a) A party that submits evidence ... by way of a witness, has the right to question that witness;
(b) The prosecution and the defence have the right to question that witness about relevant matters related to the witness's testimony and its reliability, the credibility of the witness and other relevant matters;
(c) The Trial Chamber has the right to question a witness before or after a witness is questioned by a participant referred to in sub-rules 2 (a) or (b);
(d) The defence shall have the right to be the last to examine a witness.

While Articles 64(3)(a) and 64(8)(b) and Rule 140 may have been intended 'to favour the development of original or innovative judicial practices..., promote

---

14   See e.g., Cherif M. Bassiouni, 'Negotiating the Treaty of Rome on the Establishment of an International Criminal Court' (1999) 32(3) *Cornell Int Law Journal* 443.

genuine procedural consensus by the judges and parties',[15] and enable the court to 'develop its own rules in the light of its unique experience',[16] this innovative judicial process promotes more disharmony than harmony.[17] This is especially evident when considering that the Trial Chamber can adopt whatever procedure it wishes and feels comfortable with based on the judges' legal traditions and experiences.

In practice, this *by and for all* procedure seems to have been cobbled together by well-intentioned but ill-experienced (from the practical sense) drafters, who were willing to sacrifice clarity and uniformity for inclusivity and flexibility. Where there is action there is reaction. Cherry-picking modalities from disparate procedural systems without clearly appreciating how they are likely to be interpreted – individually and as a whole or with other related modalities – invariably results in contradictions and divergences.

Let's start with the burden of proof. Article 66(2) of the Rome Statute mandates that the Prosecution has the burden of proof.[18] Taken literally, this means that it is the Prosecution's exclusive duty to prove the charges. In other words, the judges should not be engaged in gathering evidence or demanding that evidence be presented that would in any way assist the Prosecution in meeting its burden of proof. This is very much a common law approach. And while in some common law jurisdictions judges are entitled to ask questions during

---

15   Fran[c]k Terrier, 'Powers of the Trial Chamber' in Antonio Cassese, Paola Gaeta, and John R.W.D. Jones (eds) *The Rome Statute of the International Criminal Court: A Commentary*, Volume II (Oxford University Press 2002), 1268.

16   Peter Lewis, 'Trial Procedure' in Roy S. Lee (ed), *The International Criminal Court, Elements of Crimes and Rules of Procedure and Evidence* (Transnational Publishers Inc 2001), 549.

17   In his insightful analysis of the ICC procedure, Kai Ambos concludes that 'Although the existing procedural rules leave enough room for both common and civil lawyers to conduct proceedings in accordance with their national law, the practice of the *Ad Hoc* Tribunals, especially of the ICTY, shows that national boundaries in criminal procedure may be overcome with increasing experience and practice within the framework of a system of international criminal justice which is heading towards a harmonic convergence of both systems'. Kai Ambos, 'International Criminal Procedure: "Adversarial", "Inquisitorial" or Mixed?' (2003) 3 *Int Crim Law Rev* 1, 37. Regrettably, I am not so optimistic as Ambos. While lawyers make the adjustments they must (like it or not), Judges are less flexible or even able (intuitively if not intellectually) to abandon their professional experiences and practices they deem just and best.

18   Rome Statute 1998, art 66(2): 'The onus is on the Prosecutor to prove the guilt of the accused'. Article 67(1)(i) provides that the accused has the right '[n]ot to have imposed on him or her any reversal of the burden of proof or any onus of rebuttal'.

the proceedings, common law judges are generally reticent to do so in order to avoid even the appearance of partiality.[19]

Article 66(2) cannot be read in the abstract. When read in context of the statutory provisions conveying the judges' authority, functions, and obligations, it appears that the burden of proof is not solely an obligation of the Prosecution, but perhaps is shared by the judges.

Under Article 64(6)(d) of the Rome Statute, the Trial Chamber 'may, as necessary ... [o]rder the production of evidence in addition to that already collected prior to the trial or presented during the trial by the parties'. According to Article 69(3), '[t]he Court shall have the authority to request the submission of all evidence that it considers necessary for the determination of the truth'. Rule 140(2)(c) gives the Trial Chamber the 'right to question a witness before or after a witness is questioned by a participant'. Article 64(6)(b), not to be confused with Article 64(6)(d), gives the Trial Chamber an enforcement mechanism – subpoena power – to ensure the attendance and testimony of witnesses and the production of documents and other evidence.[20]

An earlier draft of Article 69(3) introduced by Germany at the 1996 Preparatory Committee stated: 'In order to determine the truth, the court shall, ex officio, extend the taking of evidence to all facts and evidence that are important for the decision. The court will decide on the taking of evidence according to its [free] conviction obtained from the entire trial'.[21] This draft article was amended in 1997, stating in part: 'The Court has the *authority and duty* to call all evidence that it considers necessary for the determination of the truth'.[22] An annotation to this article in the 1997 draft stated:

---

19   Common law judges tend to be overly cautious in attempting to avoid any appearance of favoring one party over the other. Speaking on the issue of seeking the truth in common law trials, Judge Frank starkly observes: 'What influences juries, courts seldom know. Indeed, most courts (including the federal courts) not only do not diligently seek such knowledge but have a general policy of deliberate unwillingness to learn – and usually seal up the only possible sources from which they could learn – what occurred in the jury-room. As we recently said, per Judge Learned Hand, this policy stems from awareness that, were the full truth disclosed, it is doubtful whether more than 1% of verdicts could stand'. *United States v. Farina*, 184 F.2d 18, 21 (2d Cir. 1950), Frank J. dissenting.
20   Rome Statute 1998, art 64(6)(b): The Trial Chamber may, as necessary '[r]equire the attendance and testimony of witnesses and production of documents and other evidence by obtaining, if necessary, the assistance of States as provided in this Statute'.
21   'Report of the Preparatory Committee on the Establishment of an International Criminal Court' Volume II, (New York 1996) UN Doc A/51/22, 207.
22   'Report of the Working Group on Procedural Matters' (11 December 1997) UN Doc A/AC.249/1997/WG.4/CRP.11/Add. 2., 2 (emphasis added).

This provision is meant to indicate that the relevant evidence cannot be determined by the parties alone, but has also to be determined by the Court's evaluation of the necessary depth of investigation and determination of the facts. This is, of course, basically a civil law concept, but delegations should bear in mind the additional historical dimension and truth-finding mission of the Court.[23]

The 'authority and duty' language was dropped in the adopted formulation of Article 69(3), raising the question: to what extent is the Trial Chamber obligated to determine the truth?

At first sight, the language 'it considers necessary' in the adopted formulation of Article 69(3) and 'may, as necessary' in Article 64(6)(d) indicate a discretionary authority, rather than a binding obligation on the judges. Arguably, Articles 64(6)(d) and 69(3) presuppose that the Trial Chamber has sufficient evidence to get to the truth. Put differently, only if the Trial Chamber is satisfied that the parties have presented sufficient evidence for it to determine the truth, it need not exercise its discretionary authority under Articles 69(3) and 64(6)(d) to seek evidence on its own. Any authority would be pointless if the judges do not have an obligation to exercise it when necessary to determine the truth. Thus, the Trial Chamber's authority to: order the production of evidence in addition to the evidence collected by the parties (Article 64(6)(d)); request all evidence considered necessary for the determination of the truth (Article 69(3)); question witnesses (Rule 140(2)(c)); and issue compulsory orders to secure the attendance of witnesses and the production of evidence (Article 64(6)(b)) are the *vehicles* by which the Trial Chamber fulfills its obligation to seek the truth.

Read together, Articles 64(6)(b), 64(6)(d), and 69(3), and Rule 140(2) provide support for an interpretation that the judges have an obligation to ensure that all evidence that may be obtainable and relevant for the decision – irrespective of what is adduced by the parties – should be considered so the truth can emerge. The onus would be on the judges – much like in civil law systems – to be persuaded that they have done all that is necessary, despite the Prosecution having the burden of proof, to prove or disprove the charges.[24]

---

23   *Id.*, fn. 4.
24   Some may disagree, as, for example, in Stefan Kirsch, 'The Trial Proceedings before the ICC' (2006) 6 *Int Crim Law Rev* 275, 292, concluding that 'Although a systematic interpretation of the Statute and the Rules of Procedure and Evidence does not tend to show in this direction on the first sight, it is submitted that the rules would clearly allow adopting such an understanding.... However, up until the day of an Appeals Chamber decision on

One commentator, Stefan Kirsch, argues that the ICC procedure is characterized by the absence of a binding obligation on the part of the Trial Chamber to seek evidence on its own to determine the truth,[25] and that absent such obligation, 'it will remain the sole obligation of the Parties ... to ensure that all relevant pieces of evidence are collected and presented during trial'.[26] Kirsch goes on to argue that the absence of a binding obligation in Article 69(3) is not compensated for by the inclusion of Article 64(6)(d), because the provision 'contains nothing but an authorization and clearly not a legal binding obligation'.[27] He considers that even although the Trial Chamber is not under a binding obligation to seek evidence on its own, it must intervene when it becomes aware that the Prosecution might fail to fulfill its obligation under Article 54(1)(a)[28] to collect and present evidence necessary to establish the truth.[29] Kirsch acknowledges that some (presumably judges) may see it differently. He concludes that although a systematic interpretation of the Rome Statute and RPE does not at first sight show a binding obligation on the part of the Trial Chamber to seek evidence on its own to determine the truth, 'the rules would clearly allow adopting such an understanding of the role of the judges'.[30]

Gilbert Bitti, a member of the French delegation during the ICC negotiations, is less nuanced than Kirsch, concluding that Article 64(6)(d):

> [G]ives an *ex officio* power to the Trial Chamber to order the production of further evidence to that already presented by the parties. That gives a very important role to the judges to ascertain the truth; it was indeed impossible for Civil Law Delegations and especially for France to leave all the power on this point in the hands of the parties.[31]

---

this issue, it will remain the sole obligation of the Parties, i.e. the Prosecution and the Defendant and / or his Counsel to ensure that all relevant pieces of evidence are collected and presented during trial'.

25 *Id.*, 278.
26 *Id.*, 292.
27 *Id.*, 279.
28 Rome Statute 1998, art 54(1)(a): 'In order to establish the truth, [the Prosecutor shall] extend the investigation to cover all facts and evidence relevant to an assessment of whether there is criminal responsibility under this Statute, and, in doing so, investigate incriminating and exonerating circumstances equally'.
29 Stefan Kirsch, 'The Trial Proceedings before the ICC' (2006) 6 *Int Crim Law Rev* 275, 286.
30 *Id.*, 292.
31 Gilbert Bitti, 'Article 64 Functions and Powers of the Trial Chamber' in Otto Triffterer (ed) *Rome Statute of the International Criminal Court, A Commentary* (C.H. Beck Hart Nomos 2016), 1610. Commenting on Article 64, Gilbert Bitti, the French delegate to the

Anne-Maria La Rosa, a Legal Advisor of the International Committee of the Red Cross,[32] posits that the idea behind Article 69(3) was to "stress that it was not only the parties' task to decide to present evidence."[33] According to la Rosa, the second sentence of Article 69(3) "reflects the will of the majority of the delegations which participated in the drafting process of the Rome Statute to assign an active role to the Judges with regard to the presentation of evidence necessary for the establishment of the truth."[34]

Franck Terrier, a French Investigative Judge who later became a Senior Prosecution Trial Attorney at the ICTY[35] commenting on the Trial Chamber's powers under Article 64(6) and 69(3), observed:

> These powers must be employed to bring out the truth, an objective of general interest though not the concern of the parties, which are pursuing only particular objectives. Placing the truth at the centre of the judges' interests and concerns, and giving them powers to bring that truth to the fore, give the trial a quite new meaning; no longer just the organization of a competition between two adversaries.[36]

In their commentary to Article 69(4), Bruno Cotte, the Presiding Judge in *Katanga & Ngudjolo*,[37] and ICC Legal Officer Marianne Saracco remark that:

> Section (d) is an emanation from the Romano-Germanic law as far as it gives the Trial Chamber the possibility to order the production of evidence in addition to the ones already collected by the parties. This provision is to relate to Article 69(3) of the Statute which indicates that the Chamber "shall have the authority to request the submission of all evidence that it considers necessary for the determination of the truth."

Preparatory Committee also noted that '[s]uch a power is essential in order to provide a fair trial to the accused'. *Id.*

32 https://www.icrc.org/en/author/anne-marie-la-rosa000.

33 Anne-Maria La Rosa, 'Preuve' in J. Julian Fernandez and Xavier Pacreau (eds), *Statut de Rome de la Cour pénale internationale, commentaire article par article* (Pedone 2012), 1586 (unofficial translation).

34 *Id.*, 1587.

35 http://www.leclubdesjuristes.com/les-membres/franck-terrier/#Commissions.

36 Frank Terrier, 'Powers of the Trial Chamber' in Antonio Cassese, Paola Gaeta, and John R.W.D. Jones (eds) *The Rome Statute of the International Criminal Court: A Commentary Volume II* (Oxford University Press, 2002), 1273.

37 https://asp.icc-cpi.int/iccdocs/asp_docs/Elections/ACN2015/ICC-ASP-EACN2015-FRA-CV-ENG.pdf.

It remains that the implementation of this provision requires the Trial Chamber to have a more or less profound knowledge of the factual part of the dossier. In this sense, if the judges want to make efficient use of this provision they have to "seize" the facts of the case rapidly in order to be able to truly evaluate the necessity to call one or another supplementary witness and to collect one or another piece of evidence on the basis of Article 64(6)(d) of the Statute.[38]

Bitti's, La Rosa's, Terrier's, Cotte's and Saracco's conclusions are akin to my interpretation of the Rome Statute and RPE advanced in this chapter.

Query whether the Trial Chamber's responsibility to determine the truth can override its obligation under Article 64(2) to ensure a fair trial with full respect for the rights of the accused.[39] Considering the inter-play between Articles 64(2), 64(6)(b), 64(6)(d), 66(2), and 69(3), and Rule 140(2), the dilemma arises: whose burden of proof (or persuasion) is it anyway? How can the judges exercise their authority in determining the truth without effectively commandeering the Prosecution's duty to meet its burden of proof?

In *Lubanga*,[40] the Trial Chamber held that the Court has a general right to request the presentation of all evidence necessary for the determination of the truth under Article 69(3) of the Rome Statute that is not dependent on the cooperation or consent of the parties.[41] It further held that while it 'has a statutory obligation to request the submission of all evidence that is necessary for determining the truth under Article 69(3) of the Statute ... this requirement must not displace the obligation of ensuring the accused receives a fair trial'.[42]

---

38 Bruno Cotte and Marianne Saracco, 'Article 64 – Fonctions et pouvoirs de la Chambre de première instance' in Julian Fernandez and Xavier Pacreau (eds), *Statute de Rome de la Cour pénale internationale, commentaire article par article* (Pedone 2012), 1464 (unofficial translation).

39 Rome Statute 1998, art 64(2): 'The Trial Chamber shall ensure that a trial is fair and expeditious and is conducted with full respect for the rights of the accused and due regard for the protection of victims and witnesses'.

40 The Trial Chamber was composed of Presiding Judge Adrian Fulford, Judge Elizabeth Odio Benito, Judge Rene Blattmann.

41 *Prosecutor v. Lubanga,* ICC-01/04-01/06-1119, Decision on victims' participation, 18 January 2008, para. 108. *See also Prosecutor v. Bemba,* ICC-01/05-01/08-55, Decision on the Evidence Disclosure System and Setting a Timetable for Disclosure between the Parties, 2 August 2008, para. 11, where the Pre-Trial Chamber, referring to its mandate to determine the scope of the charges to be retained if the case is sent to trial (confirmation of charges), 'emphasis[ed] that the search for the truth is the principal goal of the Court as a whole'.

42 *Prosecutor v. Lubanga,* ICC-01/04-01/06-1119, Decision on victims' participation, 18 January 2008, para. 121.

For context, at issue in *Lubanga* was the extent of victims' participation in the trial proceedings, including whether (a) victims are permitted to call and examine witnesses without being restricted to reparations issues;[43] and (b) evidence concerning reparations should be considered during the trial or as a separate procedure after trial.[44] Considering that the right to introduce evidence at trial is not restricted to the parties, the Trial Chamber held that it would not restrict questions by victims to reparations issues.[45] Should evidence relating to reparations introduced at trial be relevant to the determination of the charges, the Trial Chamber held that it would need to determine whether it would be fair for it to consider this evidence when deciding on the accused's guilt or innocence.[46]

Victims' participation issues aside, the *Lubanga* Trial Chamber's pronouncement of its authority under Article 69(3) sends a mixed message. Essentially, the Trial Chamber held that it has an obligation to search for the truth and can use its authority under Article 69(3) to request the submission of additional evidence to fulfill that obligation, but it should not go overboard to the accused's detriment. But what exactly does this mean?

If a Trial Chamber believes that there is evidence within its grasp that would lead it to the truth were it only to request its production under Article 69(3), does this mean it should refrain from doing so if it would interfere with the accused's right to have the Prosecution meet its burden of proof? I think not. While the *Lubanga* Trial Chamber' pronouncement of Article 69(3) seems to suggest that it should not be the Prosecution's midwife in delivering a conviction, it simultaneously recognizes that it has the inherent authority to have evidence produced on its own accord to determine the truth. This could in some instances result in a guilty verdict, while perhaps in others in a not guilty verdict.

Presumably, what the *Lubanga* Trial Chamber meant was that in gathering evidence that would lead it to the truth, the Trial Chamber should be mindful of the Defence's rights to have adequate notice of the evidence presented in support of the charges,[47] an expeditious trial,[48] and to examine the evidence presented against him or her.[49] None of these considerations would necessarily

---

43 *Id.*, paras. 108–111.
44 *Id.*, paras. 119–121.
45 *Id.*, para. 108.
46 *Id.*, para. 121.
47 Rome Statute 1998, art 67(1)(a).
48 *Id.*, art 67(1)(c).
49 *Id.*, art 67(1)(e).

preclude the Trial Chamber from exercising its mandate to determine the truth under Article 69(3).

The only limit on the Trial Chamber's duty to seek evidence that would lead it to the truth appears in Article 69(7)(b), which precludes the admission of evidence obtained in violation of the Rome Statute or international human rights if it 'would be antithetical to and would seriously damage the integrity of the proceedings'. Torture tainted evidence or evidence that otherwise shocks the conscience may lead the Trial Chamber to the truth, but to admit such evidence would impugn the integrity of the ICC proceedings by effectively condoning conduct that violates fundamental human rights.

Arguably, the judges, being professionals, are capable of circumscribing their actions and striking the appropriate balance so as not to transgress into the domain of the parties. Arguably. Common law judges may be more inclined, due to their inherent understanding and practical experience, to curb any new-founded rights to be judicial truth-seekers, thus letting the parties do what is expected of them, and especially holding the Prosecution's feet to the fire to meet the burden of proof. Civil law judges may not be so inclined as their common law brethren to take such a passive role considering the procedural DNA of their systems and their understanding of their judicial function to find the material truth. After all, the Rome Statute does vest them with the authority and, indubitably, with the responsibility (as seen by Articles 64(6)(b), 64(6)(d), and 69(3)) to be active truth-seekers and not mere passive observers and fact assessors.[50] Effectively, these judges can dominate the proceedings, by not only seeking and admitting evidence they think is necessary for the truth, but by intrusively intervening in the questioning of witnesses, soliciting evidence that ensures the guilt of the accused.

Not to overstress the point, while this may be acceptable under the ICC statutory regime, such hyper-engagement by a Trial Chamber in one case, when juxtaposed against a placid and non-interventionist Trial Chamber in another case, should cause concern. For example, at the ICTY some civil law judges

---

50   In his commentary on Article 64 of the Rome Statute, Frank Terrier aptly observes that '[w]ith such an arrangement the judges are no longer only arbiters but also actors. Some witnesses, if appropriate, are no longer witnesses for the parties but called by the Chamber; they are witnesses of the Chamber and cannot in principle meet any of the parties before they appear'. See Frank Terrier, 'Powers of the Trial Chamber' in Antonio Cassese, Paola Gaeta, and John R.W.D. Jones (eds), *The Rome Statute of the International Criminal Court: A Commentary Volume II* (Oxford University Press, 2002), 1272.

compared the common law practice of cross-examination to a game.[51] Other judges suggested that they should commence the questioning and conduct the lion's share of it – even though they had not had access to or acquainted themselves with a common dossier or complete case file.[52] It would be tempting to

---

51   See *Prosecutor v. Prlić et al.* ICTY-04-74-T, Transcript, 7 June 2007, p. 19735, lines 2–11:

The Witness: Your Honour, I'm supposed to answer yes or no on things which I would just like to comment so there's some sort of background to my yes or no. I will be very short.

Judge Trechsel: General, the rules of this – it isn't a game, of course, but it has rules like a game has rules, and one of them is that the witness may be required by the Defence on cross-examination just to answer yes or no, and possibly the Prosecution in redirect can solicit your explanations. Although it is very unpleasant for you, I quite understand this. I think Ms. Alaburic is entitled to have the yes or no answers without the commentary.

See also *Prosecutor v. Prlić et al.*, ICTY-04-74-T, Transcript, 14 January 2010, p. 48371, lines 6–25:

Judge Antonetti: [Interpretation] Colonel, I understand that you want to give us additional information to explain. I understand why you're doing this, but this is a specific procedure. Here the Prosecutor is entitled to put questions, but she needs an answer yes or no. A yes or no answer, and if you don't agree, just say no. And if Ms. West wants to know why you are saying no, then she can press on and put another question to you. As I told you earlier, if she's not pressing on, I will infer from this that you're telling the truth. So it's up to her to conduct the game. She puts questions to you, answer by yes or no, and if she wants to contradict you because she doesn't agree with your answer, negative answer, then she has to provide you with additional information, and then you can develop what you want to say. I know that you want to explain yourself. In my own procedure in my own country, there would be no problem with that, and we would spend hours on all of this. And the trial would have been over ages ago. But this is another type of procedure, it's very lengthy, even though we're supposed to have a quick trial according to the Security Council. So, please, we have to follow the procedure. So answer by yes or no, and if Mrs. West wants to press on, she will. Anyway, I will have a question later on. So please answer.

52   In *Prlić et al.*, during the cross-examination of an expert witness, the judges interrupted and began asking questions on matters that would be covered but only after a proper foundation was laid. The situation became so acute that I reacted, suggesting that the judges schedule a special hearing to allow the Defence and the Prosecution to address the Chamber on how the proceedings are generally conducted, or in the alternative, the judges should consider removing themselves from the case or the tribunal if they were unable or unwilling to follow the proceedings as adopted and applied by other chambers at the ICTY. The Trial Chamber granted the special hearing and both the Defence and the Prosecution effectively lectured to the judges on how the examination of witnesses should be conducted. *Prosecutor v. Prlić et al.*, ICTY-04-74-T. Transcript, 14 March 2007, pp. 15628–15633; *Prosecutor v. Prlić et al.*, ICTY-04-74-T, Transcript, 22 March 2007, pp. 16139–16148.

consider just how these judges, were they at the ICC, would exercise their authority under Article 64 and Rule 140 given their attitudes towards adversarial modalities.

From the Defence perspective, it certainly raises issues of lack of fairness and impartiality. It does not all come out in the wash by touting the refrain that all is well and proper and fair game as long as the Trial Chamber ensures the fairness and impartiality of the proceedings. And it is not just about the optics.

From an equality of arms perspective, the Defence is inherently at a disadvantage, no matter the swing of the procedural pendulum at the ICC. By the time the Defence gets involved in a case, not to mention when it actually comes into possession of all the disclosure material, the Prosecution has been investigating, meeting with witnesses, and gathering evidence for months if not years. The Prosecution has enormous resources and greater access to witnesses and evidence. The Defence has a steep learning curve. While the Defence is playing catch-up with disproportionally meager human and financial resources, the Prosecution is fine-tuning its case. And although, statutorily, the Prosecution is obligated to search for and gather exculpatory evidence with the same zeal as it pursues incriminating evidence,[53] in practice this does not seem to be occurring.[54] If anything, the Prosecution at the ICC – which is also assisted by the Victims Representatives – displays all the attributes of common law prosecutors where the objective is not the truth, but winning: having the accused found guilty of the charges.

Unequivocally, the Prosecution is in no real need of any help from the judges. If diligent and fair-minded, and assuming it has not overreached in charging the accused (no confirmation process is bullet proof; it is easy to snare into the prosecutorial net even the most innocent), the Prosecution should have little difficulty in obtaining guilty verdicts. It is tempting to accept as an article of faith that judges will – because of their authority to have evidence

---

53 Rome Statute 1998, art 54(1): 'The Prosecutor shall: (a) In order to establish the truth, extend the investigation to cover all facts and evidence relevant to an assessment of whether there is criminal responsibility under this Statute, and, in doing so, investigate incriminating and exonerating circumstances equally'.

54 *See* Caroline Buisman, 'The Prosecutor's Obligation to Investigate Incriminating and Exonerating Circumstances Equally: Illusion or Reality?' (2014) 27(1) *Leiden Journal of Int Law* 205, analyzing the ICC practice and concluding that in practice the Prosecution does not make sufficient attempts to look for potentially exonerating witnesses or documents.

produced and to question witnesses – come to the aid of the accused who may lack the resources or legal assistance to ensure that exonerating evidence is given a chance to breathe during the trial proceedings. In reality, this is simply not so. A common refrain for the Defence is that most questions posed by the judges and most of the evidence they seek to have admitted or witnesses they summon, are skewed towards the Prosecution – or more acutely, for the benefit of establishing the guilt of the accused. Even when taken with a pinch of salt, considering the charges that the accused generally face at the ICC, this grievance and the attendant sense of unfairness and lack of impartiality is not without traction.

The differences in practice – disparate proceedings shaped by the serendipitous composition of bench – unintentionally risks creating unfortunate perceptions of a lack of equality. At the ICC, where invariably there are certain political elements at play, the differences in procedure from one courtroom to another lends to a perception that there is a correlation between inconsistent application of the Trial Chamber's discretionary authority and the political, ethnic, or national background of the accused. Albeit just a perception, it could lead to a loss of confidence in the outcomes of trials. If the process is perceived to be unfair by the public and the accused, the results, even if grounded in the evidence, are unlikely to be accepted as legitimate and just.

Vignettes

Ruling on the Admissibility of Evidence

While the admissibility of evidence is not as contentious, the disparate manner in which evidence is admitted and assessed has also been a cause of concern for Defence Counsel. We have seen that under the ICC statutory regime the Trial Chambers are free to adopt whatever procedure they feel is most suited for the expeditiousness of the proceedings. Some Trial Chambers have adopted a more common law approach, where the evidence is screened for admission as it is being introduced either through witnesses or wholesale through bar table motions. Other Trial Chambers prefer the civil law approach, where evidence is admitted, including witness statements, with virtually no screening, or more precisely, without admissibility rulings. This makes sense in the civil law systems, where the truth-seeking judges are actively engaged in and entrusted with pursuing the truth, and where the parties play a relatively passive role. It is only having heard all of the evidence that these judges can properly assess what is relevant and to what extent (the probative value), if they are to meet their judicial obligations. Since the Rome Statute makes allowances for this approach to the admission of evidence, expectedly, many judges, especially civil law judges, are inclined or predisposed to this approach.[55]

The common law approach was adopted in the *Katanga and Ngudjolo* case,[56] where the Trial Chamber held that it 'must determine the probative value of an item of evidence *before* it can be admitted into the proceedings'.[57] The Trial Chamber rejected the Prosecution's argument that the Trial Chamber should simply admit the whole of the evidence and leave any matters of reliability and probative value until the end of the trial, where the Trial Chamber will be in a position to consider the totality of the evidence.[58] The Trial Chamber reasoned that if, at the time of tendering, the party is unable to demonstrate its relevance, probative value, and authenticity, the evidence cannot be admitted.[59] The Trial Chamber explained that since probative value and evidentiary weight are two different concepts (probative value being a key criterion in any determination on admissibility, while evidentiary weight is assessed at the end of the trial), the Trial Chamber must assess the probative value of each item of evidence at the time it is tendered and before it is admitted into evidence.[60]

Most Defence Counsel prefer this approach because it provides certainty and awareness as to the evidence being admitted, thus allowing them to better calibrate their case. Strategic and tactical decisions are made concerning the scope or areas of (cross)examination of adverse witnesses, to what extent they will opt to call witnesses to adduce evidence, and to what extent they will seek to have documentary evidence admitted as part of their case. Also, it is important in not just calibrating the theory of the defence, but in summing up the evidence in their final written and oral submissions where they are expected to provide the Trial Chamber with findings of fact and conclusions of law they wish the Trial Chamber to reach.

---

55   Rome Statute 1998, art 69(4): 'The Court may rule on the relevance or admissibility of any evidence, taking into account, *inter alia*, the probative value of the evidence and any prejudice that such evidence may cause to a fair trial or to a fair evaluation of the testimony of a witness, in accordance with the Rules of Procedure and Evidence'.

56   Presiding Judge Bruno Cotte (France), Judge Fatoumata Dembele Diarra (Mali), Judge Christine Van den Wyngaert (Belgium).

57   *Prosecution v. Katanga and Ngudjolo*, ICC-01/04-01/07-2635, Decision on the Prosecution's Bar Table Motions, ICC-01/04-01/07-2635, 17 December 2010, para. 13 (italics in original).

58   *Id.*

59   *Id.*

60   *Id.*

By contrast, the Trial Chamber in *Bemba*[61] adopted a civil law approach. The Trial Chamber (by Majority)[62] decided that witness statements and related documents (previously disclosed to the Defence and which form part of the Prosecution's list of evidence) were *prima facie* admitted as evidence for the purpose of the trial.[63] The Majority explained that its decision was 'based on making a *prima facie* finding of the admissibility of [the] evidence'[64] and that this finding must be distinguished from the Trial Chamber's future determination of the probative value and appropriate weight to be given to the evidence as a whole.[65] The Majority referred to 'the drafting history and the compromise reached at the Rome Conference as to the governing principles for assessing relevance or admissibility of evidence'.[66] 'The compromise was to eschew generally the technical formalities of the *common law* system of admissibility of evidence in favor of the flexibility of the *civil law* system, provided that the Court has discretion to rule on the relevance or admissibility of any piece of evidence'.[67]

The Trial Chamber also stated that the *prima facie* admission of the evidence 'would be in line with the Chamber's statutory obligation ... to search for the truth, and with the discretionary power of the judges to decide on additional elements as they deem necessary for the Chamber's determination of the truth'.[68] Thus, the Trial Chamber admitted the witness statements and related documents before the start of the presentation of evidence.[69]

---

61   Presiding Judge Sylvia Steiner (Brazil), Judge Joyce Aluoch (Kenya), Judge Kuniko Ozaki (Japan).
62   Judge Ozaki dissented. In her view, 'materials presented to the Court must either be admissible, or not admissible, without the possibility of an interim status such as "prima facie admissible"'. See *Prosecutor v. Bemba*, ICC-01/05-01/08-1028, Dissenting Opinion of Judge Kuniko Ozaki on the Decision on the admission into evidence of materials contained in the prosecution's list of evidence, 24 November 2010, para. 5.
63   *Prosecutor v. Bemba*, ICC-01/05-01/08-1022, Decision on the admission into evidence of materials contained in the Prosecution's list of evidence, 19 November 2010, para. 35.
64   *Id.*, para. 9.
65   *Id.*
66   *Id.*, para. 17.
67   *Id.* (italics in original), *citing* Donald K. Piragoff, 'Evidence' in Roy S. Lee (ed), The International Criminal Court, Elements of Crimes and Rules of Procedure and Evidence (Transnational Publishers New York 2001), 349–401; and Donald K. Piragoff, 'Evidence' in Otto Triffterer (ed), Commentary on the Rome Statute of the International Criminal Court, (C.H. Beck Hart Nomos, München 2008), 1317.
68   *Prosecutor v. Bemba*, ICC-01/05-01/08-1022, Decision on the admission into evidence of materials contained in the prosecution's list of evidence, 19 November 2010, para. 28.
69   *Id.*, para. 8.

Both the Prosecution and the Defence appealed this decision, arguing, *inter alia*, that the legal framework of the Court does not allow for the *prima facie* admission of witnesses' written statements and that such admission violates the principle of orality enshrined in Article 69(2) of the Rome Statute.[70] The Appeals Chamber reversed the Trial Chamber's decision, finding that: (a) by admitting evidence based on a *prima facie* finding of admissibility, without an item-by-item evaluation or reasoning, the Trial Chamber acted outside the legal framework of the Court;[71] and (b) the admission of witnesses' statements without a cautious item-by-item analysis was incompatible with the principle of orality.[72]

The Appeals Chamber first clarified and interpreted the provisions of the Rome Statute providing for the Trial Chamber's discretionary power to rule on admissibility issues. Article 69(4) provides that the Trial Chamber 'may rule on the relevance or admissibility of any evidence....' The Appeals Chamber observed that '[a]s borne out by the use of word "may"..., the Trial Chamber has the power to rule or not on relevance or admissibility when evidence is submitted, ... [or] the Chamber may defer its consideration of these criteria until the end of the proceedings'.[73] The Appeals Chamber held that regardless of the approach the Trial Chamber chooses, it must consider the relevance, probative value, and potential prejudice of each item of evidence at some point in the proceedings.[74]

Turning to the Trial Chamber's decision, the Appeals Chamber reasoned that the Trial Chamber ruled on the admissibility of all items of evidence but failed to provide any reasoning as to how it reached its findings, even though the Trial Chamber stated that it would later consider the probative value and prejudice it may cause at the end of the trial.[75] In other words, the Trial Chamber should have carried out an item-by-item analysis of the admissibility of evidence, and this analysis should have been reflected in the Trial Chamber's

---

70 *Prosecutor v. Bemba*, ICC-01/05-01/08-1191, Defence appeal against the 'Decision on the admission into evidence of materials contained in the prosecution's list of evidence', 7 February 2011, paras. 8–52. *Prosecutor v. Bemba*, ICC-01/05-01/08-1194, Prosecution's Document in Support of the Appeal, 7 February 2011, paras. 18–36, 37–42.

71 *Prosecutor v. Bemba*, ICC-01/05-01/08-1386, Judgment on the appeals of Mr Jean-Pierre Bemba Gombo and the Prosecutor against the decision of Trial Chamber III entitled 'Decision on the admission into evidence of materials contained in the prosecution's list of evidence', 3 May 2011, paras. 2, 57.

72 *Id.*, paras. 2, 81.

73 *Id.*, para. 37.

74 *Id.*

75 *Id.*, para. 39.

reasoning. Similarly, in relation to witnesses' statements, the Appeals Chamber observed that the Trial Chamber admitted into evidence 'indiscriminately *all* the witness statements' without assessing each of the statements.[76]

In the *Bemba Article 70* case, the Trial Chamber adopted a similar approach – postponing admissibility rulings until the end of the trial[77] – even concerning evidence admitted through the bar table, where the chain of custody, reliability, and authenticity (the integrity of the sources from which the evidence was collected) was an issue of concern for the Defence.[78] In fact, save for a few rare exceptions,[79] the Trial Chamber refrained from ruling on substantive motions until its deliberations, including on the issue of the applicable elements of the offences and modes of liability.[80] Here two of the three judges were from a civil law system.[81]

Given the wide latitude provided to it under Article 64(8)(b) and Rule 140, the Trial Chamber was within its right to adopt this approach to admitting evidence and ruling on substantive written submissions. The parties, of course, were afforded full, fair, and timely opportunities to make whatever submissions on the admissibility and probative value of the evidence and other legal challenges, thus, in principle, ensuring the fairness and impartiality of the proceedings. Since this approach to the admissibility of evidence and ruling on submissions applied to all parties equally, seemingly, none of the parties were placed in a more onerous position than any other. Seemingly. But considering: (a) the Prosecution's inherent advantage of having investigated and collected the evidence in building its case; (b) the lack of true equality of arms and the challenges the Defence teams face in coming up to speed in preparing the case for trial; (c) the lack of access to all the disclosure material at the moment it comes into the case; and (d) the certainty required of the Defence teams in

---

76   *Id.*, para. 79 (italics in original).
77   See e.g. *Prosecutor v. Bemba et al.*, ICC-01/05-01/13-1285, Decision on Prosecution Requests for Admission of Documentary Evidence (ICC-01/05-01/13-1013-Red, ICC-01/05-01/13-1113-Red, ICC-01/05-01/13-1170-Conf), 24 September 2015, paras. 10–16.
78   *Prosecutor v. Bemba et al.*, ICC-01/05-01/13-1989-Red, Judgment pursuant to Article 74 of the Statute, 19 October 2016, paras. 190–193.
79   See e.g. *Prosecutor v. Bemba et al.*, ICC-01/05-01/13-1854, Decision on Requests to Exclude Western Union Documents and other Evidence Pursuant to Article 69(7), 29 April 2016; *Prosecutor v. Bemba et al.*, ICC-01/05-01/13-1984, Decision on Request in Response to Two Austrian Decisions, 14 July 2016.
80   *Prosecutor v. Bemba et al.*, ICC-01/05-01/13-1989-Red, Judgment pursuant to Article 74 of the Statute, 19 October 2016, paras. 51–98.
81   Presiding Judge Bertram Schmitt (Germany), Judge Marc Perrin de Brichambaut (France), and Judge Raul C. Pangalangan (Philippines).

formulating their theories of defence and in making strategic and tactical decisions throughout the proceedings, this delay in making rulings on the evidence and submissions does in fact place the Defence at a disadvantage. And not to belabor the point, this disadvantage becomes more pronounced when the Trial Chamber, in exercising its authority, is effectively engaged in a truth-seeking mission, as opposed to taking a more passive role and strictly holding the Prosecution to its burden of proof without any assistance from the Trial Chamber.

Witness Proofing

One of the peskier issues concerns the issue of proofing. A more accurate term, and one used in some common law jurisdictions, is *witness preparation*. Effectively, proofing a witness, when done properly, entails: (a) familiarizing the witness with what happens in court: the witness's function, his or her basic rights such as the right not to answer questions if they are self-incriminating, the role of the parties and judges, and maybe even a walk through the courtroom; and (b) going over the witness's testimony, including any documents that are likely to be shown to the witness from which questions may be asked, and giving the witness an opportunity to refresh his or her memory of statements that he or she may have given in the past.

The familiarization aspect of witness proofing has been separated into a distinct category of witness preparation and, to a large extent, is considered an acceptable if not essential function. At the international(ized) tribunals and courts the familiarization process has been viewed as part and parcel of the general functions carried out by the victims and witnesses units (VWU), which are – from my experience – scrupulously neutral and eminently protective and caring towards all victims and witnesses. In some fora where having any contact with the witness is strictly forbidden, such as at the ECCC, the VWU is also entrusted with providing the civil parties (victims) and witnesses with their statements shortly before giving evidence so they may refresh their memories.[82]

The second component of proofing, that of preparing the witness to give evidence, has been contentious, surprisingly mainly from the Defence (I am very pro-proofing). The argument goes that proofing has been used to

---

82 *Case of* MEAS *Muth*, 003/07-09-2009-ECCC-OCIJ, Decision On Meas Muth's Request for the Co-Investigating Judges to Clarify whether the Defence May Contact Individuals Including [Redacted], 4 December 2015, para. 15, stating that 'the Defence ... may not conduct any investigative action including questioning [REDACTED] for the purpose of gathering general descriptive information, nor approach any other persons beyond the limits set by the previous case law'.

coach witnesses to tailor their evidence, thus obstructing or perverting the course of justice. This is a fair concern, and one about which no party to the proceedings – Prosecution, Defence, or Victims Representatives – can claim with certainty the moral and ethical high-ground. Defence Counsel tend to claim that the Prosecution, because of its ready access to witnesses (particularly in the field), and because of its status as part of the judicial institution, is likely to unduly influence witnesses into skewing their testimony – even when there is no actual intent.

The Prosecution invariably produces more witnesses than the Defence, given the burden of proof it must meet and, in no small measure, its abundance of resources in comparison to what is general allocated to the court-assigned/paid Defence. This places the Defence in significant peril – especially where the Defence may, as part of its theory of the case and its understanding of the evidence prior to the trial proceedings, opt for a sharp, targeted and limited case, where most if not all of its evidence will come from cross-examination. Some call this the *reasonable doubt theory of defence* (the Prosecution cannot prove the charges beyond a reasonable doubt) or *no case to answer defence*.

The Prosecution may have met with the witness numerous times and its questioning process may not be so transparent (providing summary notes or worse yet having the investigator write out the statement and merely read it back to the witness as opposed to tape-recording or videotaping it). The source of the evidence, the witness's independent memory, may be polluted and thus less accessible to the witness without considerable coaxing immediately prior to giving evidence.

The same, of course, can be said for the other parties. However, this seems to be more of an issue of conducting proper interviews of witnesses and victims, as opposed to properly preparing the witness to give focused and cogent answers during the trial proceedings where: (a) the witness is under considerable stress; (b) the witness may lack the sophistication to speak in coherent thoughts; (c) large amounts of documents are expected to be shown to the witness who may be asked only to focus his or her attention and testify about only a single sentence or paragraph as opposed to the entire document; and (d) the witness has given several statements over a period of time, which may contain inaccuracies and contradictions.

When factoring in the size and complexity of the cases that are tried at the international(ized) tribunals and courts, the large number of witnesses that must be called both for historical context and to the relevant events, and the need to have the evidence presented in an efficient and expedited matter, proofing, if done properly, can be highly effective and beneficial to the Trial Chamber laboring to manage the proceedings with efficiency while respecting the right of the parties. As meritorious as this seems, this is only one side of the coin. The other side to the issue of proofing – that of witness/memory-tampering – advances an equally compelling argument.

Judges, especially civil law judges, who are not accustomed to having the parties prepare the witnesses to give evidence, argue that any sort of proofing is deleterious. Indeed, this is anathema to them. It not only can contaminate the source of the evidence – the witness's independent memory – but it also deprives the witness of a certain spontaneity to his or her testimony, thus further depriving the judges of their ability to properly assess the witness's testimony. Presumably, this spontaneity is associated with the judge's obligation to factor in the demeanor of the witness as he or she is testifying. Presumably. This argument has little traction. By the time the judgment is deliberated and drafted, months and years have passed. And there are numerous instances where a judge is called upon to join the Trial Chamber midway through the Trial (*Milošević*)[83] or even during the deliberation stage (*Šešelj*).[84]

The stronger argument is that proofing, if not done correctly, adversely impacts the quality and reliability of a witness's evidence. Suffice it to say, proofing a witness correctly requires not just a healthy appreciation of ethics and professional responsibility, but also skill – skill that comes with proper training and experience. And herein lies the problem on all sides. One cure is to have best practices set in place, and to perhaps require that any proofing session be videotaped. Best practices may alleviate some of the problems. But to require videotaping of proofing when the witness arrives at the location of the tribunal and right before testifying is somewhat unrealistic. The logistics and resources would make this process too cumbersome and taxing, especially when considering how dynamic trial proceedings can be. Also, the person questioning the witness is the most suited to proof the witness, where a witness is likely to recall something not previously provided or may wish to re-calibrate or correct a previously recorded answer – all of which will need to be relayed to the other parties post-haste through what is known as 'proofing notes'; a common occurrence at the ICTY which seemed to work relatively well.[85]

---

83   *Prosecutor v. Milošević*, ICTY-02-54-T, Order Replacing a Judge in a Case Before a Trial Chamber, 10 June 2004, assigning Judge Iain Bonomy to replace Judge Richard May.

84   *Prosecutor v. Šešelj*, ICTY-03-67-T, Order Assigning a Judge Pursuant to Rule 15, 31 October 2013, assigning Judge Mandiaye Niang to replace Judge Frederik Harhoff following his disqualification.

85   After the *Lubanga* decision prohibiting witness proofing came out, Defence teams in *Milutinović et al.* and *Limaj et al.* at the ICTY filed motions to prohibit witness proofing. The Trial Chambers in both cases denied the motions, reasoning that this practice enhances the fairness and expeditiousness of the trial. In *Limaj*, the Trial Chamber explicitly

So, is there a middle ground – proofing that would satisfy both sides of the coin to *proof or not to proof*? Well, that is what the ICC Trial Chambers have attempted, with the pendulum swinging from virtually one end of the argument to the other. Judges disagree as much as the parties and academics, some of whom argue that the Rome Statute does not provide for proofing,[86] while others claim it does – or at least does not affirmatively prohibit proofing.[87]

In *Lubanga*,[88] the ICC's first case, the Pre-Trial and Trial Chambers effectively prohibited witness proofing. The parties were prohibited from allowing witnesses to read their statements, refreshing witnesses' memory in respect to the evidence that they will give, and asking witnesses the same questions in the same order as they will be asked during the testimony.[89] Instead of proofing, the witnesses were allowed to be familiarized by the VWU. Through this process, witnesses can read through their past statement(s) prior to testifying in court, become familiar with the courtroom layout, briefly meet with the party

---

stated that the 'practice of proofing witnesses, by both the Prosecution and Defence, has been in place and accepted since the inception of this Tribunal'. *Prosecutor v. Limaj et al.*, ICTY-03-66-T, Decision on Defence Motion of Prosecution Practice of 'Proofing Witnesses', 10 December 2004, p. 2. See also *Prosecutor v. Milutinović et al.*, ICTY-05-87-T, Decision on Ojdanić Motion to Prohibit Witness Practice, 12 December 2006, paras. 11–16.

86 See Kai Ambos, '"Witness proofing" before the ICC: Neither legally admissible nor necessary' in Carsten Stahn and Göran Sluiter (eds), *The Emerging Practice of the International Criminal Court* (Martinus Nijhoff Publishers 2009), 614, advancing an argument that 'familiarisation is sufficient to guarantee that witnesses fulfil their role at trial, i.e., give evidence in the most impartial and comprehensive manner, always recalling the truth and nothing but the truth'. Advocating against the practice of witness proofing, *see also* Wayne Jordash, 'The Practice of "Witness Proofing" in International Criminal Tribunals: Why the International Criminal Court Should Prohibit the Practice' (2009) 22(3) *Leiden Journal of Int Law* (2009) 501.

87 See Sergei Vasiliev, 'Proofing the Ban on "Witness proofing": Did the ICC Get It Right?' (2009) 20 *Crim Law Forum* 193; Ruben Karemaker, B. Don Taylor, and Thomas W. Pittman, 'Witness Proofing in International Criminal Tribunals: A Critical Analysis of Widening Procedural Divergence' (2008) 21 *Leiden Journal of Int Law* 683.

88 In *Lubanga*, the Pre-Trial Chamber I was composed of Presiding Judge Claude Jorda (France), Judge Akua Kuenyehia (Ghana), and Judge Sylvia Steiner (Brazil). The Trial Chamber I was composed of Presiding Judge Adrian Fulford (England and Wales), Judge Elizabeth Odio Benito (Costa Rica), Judge René Blattmann (Bolivia).

89 *Prosecutor v. Lubanga*, ICC-01/04-01/06-679, Decision on the Practices of Witness Familiarisation and Witness Proofing, 8 November 2006, para. 40; *Prosecutor v. Lubanga*, ICC-01/04-01/06-1049, Decision regarding the Practices used to prepare and Familiarise Witnesses for Giving Testimony at Trial, 30 November 2007, paras. 35–52, 57.

or exchange courtesy calls with the opposing party, and have a psychological assessment.

However, any discussion on the topics to be dealt with in court or any exhibits which may be shown to a witness in court, according to the Trial Chamber, risks distorting the truth and 'may come dangerously close to constituting a rehearsal of in-court testimony'.[90] The Trial Chamber further reasoned that such preparation prior to trial 'may diminish what would otherwise be helpful spontaneity during the giving of evidence by a witness'.[91] The Trial Chamber observed:

> The spontaneous nature of testimony can be of paramount importance to the Court's ability to find the truth, and the Trial Chamber is not willing to lose such an important element in the proceedings. The pro-active role of judges under the Statute and Rules will help to ensure that witnesses are not 'revictimized' by their testimony, whilst also preventing any improper influence being applied to the witness.[92]

In *Katanga and Ngudjolo*,[93] and *Bemba*,[94] the Pre-Trial and Trial Chambers adopted a similar procedure as in *Lubanga*.[95] In *Bemba*, however, Judge Kuniko Ozaki dissented. In her view it was not practical or reasonable to prohibit pre-trial meetings between the parties and their witnesses. She pointed out that witness proofing could be used to clarify witnesses' evidence and 'to ensure the smooth conduct of the proceedings by enabling a more accurate, complete, methodical and efficient presentation of the evidence'.[96]

---

90 *Prosecutor v. Lubanga,* ICC-01/04-01/06-1049, Decision Regarding the Practices used to prepare and Familiarise Witnesses for Giving Testimony at Trial, 30 November 2007, para. 51.
91 *Id.*, para. 52.
92 *Id.*
93 In *Katanga and Ngudjolo*, the Trial Chamber II was composed of Presiding Judge Bruno Cotte (France), Judge Fatoumata Dembele Diarra (Mali), and Judge Hans-Peter Kaul (Germany).
94 In *Bemba et al.*, the Trial Chamber III was composed of Presiding Judge Sylvia Steiner (Brazil), Judge Joyce Aluoch (Kenya), and Judge Kuniko Ozaki (Japan).
95 *Prosecutor v. Katanga and Ngudjolo*, ICC-01/04-01/07-1134, Decision on a Number of Procedural Issues Raised by the Registry, 14 May 2009, para. 18 (implicitly rejecting witness preparation); *Prosecutor v. Bemba*, ICC-01/05-01/08-1016, Decision on the Unified Protocol on the Practices used to Prepare and Familiarize Witnesses for Giving Testimony at Trial, 18 November 2010, paras. 31, 34–35.
96 *See Prosecutor v. Bemba*, ICC-01/05-01/08-1039, Partly Dissenting Opinion of Judge Kuniko Ozaki on the Decision on the Unified Protocol on the practices used to prepare and

Several years later, Judge Ozaki presided over the Trial Chamber assigned to *Ruto and Sang* and *Kenyatta*.[97] The Trial Chamber allowed witness proofing by 'pre-testimony meetings ... aimed at clarifying a witness's evidence' on the basis that it 'is likely to enable a more accurate and complete presentation of the evidence, and so to assist in the Chamber's truth finding function'.[98] In both cases, the Trial Chamber adopted a 'Witness Preparation Protocol', setting out permitted and prohibited conduct and the rules regulating the logistical matters.[99] As 'required and permissible conduct', the calling party was allowed to provide a witness an opportunity to review his or her prior statement, review together with the witness any inconsistencies in his or her prior statement, explain in general terms the topics to be covered during examination and potential topics about which the witness may be questioned during cross-examination, and show the witness exhibits and ask him or her to comment on them to decide whether to use them in court.[100] The Trial Chamber prohibited the calling party from seeking to influence the substance of witness's answers, training or practicing the questions and answers expected from the witness, or informing the witness of the evidence of other witnesses.[101]

Judge Chile Eboe-Osuji issued a partly dissenting opinion in *Ruto and Sang* and *Kenyatta*, making reservations regarding the Majority's prohibition

---

familiarize witnesses for giving testimony at trial, 24 November 2010, para. 22 (internal citations omitted).

[97] The Trial Chamber V assigned to *Ruto and Sang* and *Kenyatta* cases was composed of Presiding Judge Kuniko Ozaki (Japan), Judge Christine Van den Wyngaert (Belgium), and Judge Chile Eboe-Osuji (Nigeria).

[98] See *Prosecutor v. Ruto and Sang*, ICC-01/09-01/11-524, Decision on Witness Preparation, 2 January 2013, para. 50; *Prosecutor v. Muthaura and Kenyatta*, ICC-01/09-02/11-588, Decision on Witness Preparation, 2 January 2013, para. 52. Concerning the inconsistencies in approach to proofing at the ICC, and other tribunals, see IBA ICC Perspectives, '*Witnesses before the International Criminal Court, An International Bar Association International Criminal Court Programme report on the ICC's efforts and challenges to protect, support and ensure the rights of witnesses*' (July 2013), 21–26, <www.ibanet.org/ICC_ICL_Programme/Reports.aspx>, accessed 15 May 2017.

[99] See *Prosecutor v. Ruto and Sang*, ICC-01/09-01/11-524, Decision on Witness Preparation, 2 January 2013, with public Annex 'Witness Preparation Protocol', para. 51; *Prosecutor v. Muthaura and Kenyatta*, ICC-01/09-02/11-588, Decision on Witness Preparation, 2 January 2013, With public Annex 'Witness Preparation Protocol', para. 53.

[100] *Prosecutor v. Ruto and Sang*, ICC-01/09-01/11-524-Anx, Witness Preparation Protocol, 7 February 2013, paras. 17–21, 23. *Prosecutor v. Muthaura and Kenyatta*, ICC-01/09-02/11-588-Anx, Witness Preparation Protocol, 7 February 2013, paras. 17–21, 23.

[101] *Prosecutor v. Ruto and Sang*, ICC-01/09-01/11-524-Anx, Witness Preparation Protocol, 7 February 2013, paras. 27, 29. *Prosecutor v. Muthaura and Kenyatta*, ICC-01/09-02/11-588-Anx, Witness Preparation Protocol, 7 February 2013, paras. 27, 29.

of 'practising' testimonies.[102] Judge Eboe-Osuji disagreed with the Majority that 'practicing' is incompatible with the ethics of witness preparation. In his view, 'practicing' can also be understood as 'rehearsing' and is generally encouraged in jurisdictions that permit witness preparation, such as the United States and Canada.[103] He reasoned that practicing the testimony can be sensible and practical 'to identify and possibly tease out problem spots with delivery for purposes of enhancing efficiency in court-room testimonies'.[104] He listed the benefits of such practicing, or 'rehearsing':

> [T]he witness is enabled with simulated experience as (s)he goes into the witness box; counsel sees where witness may have trouble with the testimony in terms of comprehension, awkwardness or emotional difficulty of the question being asked and the words employed in asking the questions; with specific regard to sexual violence cases, a witness is given an early opportunity to confront or deal with habitual personal or cultural sensitivity or resistance to public reference to body parts or the recall of events that might involve very deep invasions of personal autonomy.[105]

Judge Eboe-Osuji pointed out that 'rehearsing' or 'practicing' testimony is not the same as 'coaching', since it does not involve 'counsel's heavy footprint' in what a witness says and how he or she should say it.[106] In other words, as long as Counsel does not, by speech or hint, suggest to a witness what to say, practicing does not pose a risk of impropriety or ethics.

In *Ntaganda*,[107] the Trial Chamber adopted the identical 'Witness Preparation Protocol' as in *Ruto and Sang* and *Kenyatta*, although the Trial Chamber added that if the non-calling party wished to review the video recording of the

---

102   *Prosecutor v. Ruto and Sang*, ICC-01/09-01/11-524-Anx, Witness Preparation Protocol, 7 February 2013, para. 28: '[Prohibited Conduct:] Undertake to train the witness or practice the questions and answers expected during the witness's in-court testimony so that the witness memorises those questions and answers'. *Prosecutor v. Muthaura and Kenyatta*, ICC-01/09-02/11-588-Anx, Witness Preparation Protocol, 7 February 2013, para. 28.
103   *Prosecutor v. Ruto and Sang*, ICC-01/09-01/11-524, Decision on Witness Preparation, Partly Dissenting Opinion of Judge Eboe-Osuji, 2 January 2013, para. 49.
104   *Id.*, para. 50.
105   *Id.*
106   *Id.*, para. 52.
107   In *Ntaganda*, the Trial Chamber VI was composed of the Presiding Judge Robert Fremr (Czech Republic), Judge Kuniko Ozaki (Japan), and Judge Chang-ho Chung (South Korea).

witness preparation session, it must apply to the Trial Chamber setting out the reasons supporting the request.[108]

In *Gbagbo and Blé Goudé*, the Trial Chamber (by Majority)[109] followed a more civil law approach, allowing witness familiarization, but prohibiting the calling party from preparing witnesses, reasoning that this practice 'could inhibit the entirety of the true extent of an account, and could "diminish what would otherwise be helpful spontaneity during the giving of evidence by a witness"'.[110] The Presiding Judge Geoffrey Henderson dissented, explicitly concurring with Judge Ozaki's reasoning in *Bemba*.[111] Judge Henderson observed that '[a]t the Court, the parties, not the judges, conduct investigations, which include both the interview of witnesses and taking of witness statements, as is done in an adversarial system'.[112] He further reasoned that while 'the exercise of witness preparation itself may lead to "impermissible conduct such as rehearsal, practice and coaching" ... witness preparation is not the genesis of such a risk occurring at the Court'.[113] '[S]uch risks exist before witness preparation, insofar as the parties conduct their own investigations'.[114] In Judge Henderson's view, 'it would seem incongruous to conclude that prohibiting witness preparation is the best approach to preventing "impermissible conduct" generally'.[115] A more appropriate measure would be a protocol with robust safeguards for the conduct of witness preparation. Judge Henderson also pointed that the risk of witness manipulation is addressed both in the domestic rules of professional conduct and the ICC Code of Professional Conduct for Counsel.[116]

---

108 *Prosecutor v. Ntaganda*, ICC-01/04-02/06-652. Decision on Witness Preparation, 16 June 2015, with one public annex, para. 32.

109 The Trial Chamber I was composed of Presiding Judge Geoffrey Henderson (Trinidad and Tobago), Judge Olga Herrera Carbuccia (Dominican Republic), Judge Bertram Schmitt (Germany). Judge Henderson dissented in part.

110 *Prosecutor v. Gbagbo and Blé Goudé*, ICC-02/11-01/15-355, Decision on Witness Preparation and Familiarization, 2 December 2015, para. 17 *quoting Prosecutor v. Lubanga*, ICC-01/04-01/06-1049, Decision Regarding the Practices Used to Prepare and Familiarise Witnesses for Giving Testimony at Trial, 30 November 2007, para. 52.

111 *Prosecutor v. Gbagbo and Blé Goudé*, ICC-02/11-01/15-355-Anx1, Partially Dissenting Opinion of Judge Henderson to Decision on Witness Preparation and Familiarization, 2 December 2015), para. 2.

112 *Id.*, para. 4.

113 *Id.*, para. 8.

114 *Id.*

115 *Id.*, para. 9.

116 *Id.*, para. 12.

In the *Bemba Article 70* case, the Trial Chamber considered that preparation was not necessary since 'a significant number of the witnesses have already testified before the Court in the [*Bemba*] case..., and are therefore familiar with the Court's proceedings and the expected principal issues arising in their testimonies'.[117] The Trial Chamber of the same composition in *Ongwen*[118] considered witness preparation unnecessary and only allowed the witness familiarization by the VWU.[119]

Examination of Witnesses

Another anomaly as procedure goes resulting from the freewheeling judicial discretion on how proceedings can be held is the issue of questioning witnesses. As previously noted, the drafters of the Rome Statute wanted to use neutral terms and, to the extent possible, concoct a unique blend of procedures that effectively would not be identified with either of the two major legal systems, common law and civil law, recognizing that there are variations and significant differences within each system.

The term 'cross-examination' is not be used in the Rome Statute. Rather there is just a generic reference to having the right 'to examine and have examined' under Article 67. It appears that the drafters took this language from Article 14(3)(e) of the International Covenant on Civil and Political Rights (ICCPR).[120] While the General Comment to Article 14(3)(e) of the ICCPR clarifies that '[t]his provision is designed to guarantee to the accused the same legal powers of compelling the attendance of witnesses and examining or cross-examining any witnesses as are available to the prosecution,'[121] no such clarification is provided in the ICC's RPE or Regulations.

---

117   *Prosecutor v. Bemba et al.*, ICC-01/05-01/13-1252, Decision on Witness Preparation and Familiarisation, 15 September 2015, para. 24.

118   The Trial Chamber IX had the same composition of the Trial Chamber as in the *Bemba Article 70* case: Presiding Judge Bertram Schmitt (Germany), Judge Marc Perrin de Brichambaut (France), and Judge Raul C. Pangalangan (Philippines).

119   *Prosecutor v. Ongwen*, ICC-02/04-01/15-504, Decision on Protocols to be Adopted at Trial, 22 July 2016, paras. 16–17, 20–24. The composition of the Trial Chamber changed to: Presiding Judge Bertram Schmitt (Germany), Judge Peter Kovacs (Hungary), and Judge Raul C. Pangalangan (Philippines).

120   ICCPR Article 14(3)(e): 'In the determination of any criminal charge against him, everyone shall be entitled to the following minimum guarantees ... [t]o examine, or have examined, the witness against him and to obtain the attendance and examination of witnesses on his behalf under the same conditions as witnesses against him'.

121   ICCPR General Comment No. 13: Article 14 (Administration of Justice) Equality before the Courts and the Right to a Fair and Public Hearing by an Independent Court Established

'To examine' refers to what is commonly known as 'direct examination', where the questioning party is only permitted to ask open-ended or neutral questions. The objective is to hear the evidence of the witness in an unvarnished and uninfluenced form. There are some exceptions when leading or suggestive questions can be asked, provided permission is granted from the Trial Chamber. The format of direct examination is the acceptable format in most civil law systems, and seems to be the preferred method of questioning by civil law judges. Of course, it bears highlighting that in many of the civil law systems, it is the trial judge that does the questioning. This is significant because the judges are entitled to ask any question in whichever form they wish, since it is their responsibility to get to the truth. Also, the judges have a complete case file (dossier) which is the universe of known evidence gathered during the pre-trial stage and from which the trial judge, having fully acquainted himself with it, will determine which witnesses he or she wishes to hear, in which order, and for what purpose. The parties play a secondary role in this process in that they can seek to have other witnesses called to give evidence in the proceedings, and have the right to ask supplemental questions to those asked by the judge.

Having access to and examining the entire case file before the commencement of the trial proceedings and leading the questioning parade are significant components in civil law proceedings. Considering the role and function of the judges in seeking the truth, it is easily appreciated why this procedural system is characterized as judge-controlled.

The reciprocal or counter-right (if it can be considered as such) 'to have examined', does not specify the type of questions that can be posed by the party not calling the witness. In the civil law context, as noted, all this means is that the parties can ask open-ended (who, what, where, when, why, explain, describe) questions. Since it is a judge-driven system, there is no dilemma; the parties do not have a case to speak of, and all witnesses are considered court witnesses – not affiliated with or in support of any of the parties to the case. However, where the proceedings are adversarial or have an adversarial component to them, such as at the ICC, 'to have examined' should be understood as having the right to confront, which is distinct from merely having the right to ask questions. Confrontation in the adversarial sense means to have the right

---

by Law, adopted at the twenty-first session of the Human Rights Committee on 13 April 1984.

to ask leading questions; questions that suggest the answer, often eliciting a mere 'yes', 'no', or 'I don't know'.[122]

In adversarial proceedings, the parties do in fact have a case of their own. The Prosecution's case is in the form of the charging document. The Defence has its theory of the case. This is despite the notion that once witnesses appear in court they are court witnesses and that there is only the court's case. Each party is eliciting evidence from the witnesses or pressing for the admission of evidence that supports their objective: winning the case. Cross-examination allows for the questioning party to have a certain control over the witness in order to expose inconsistencies or highlight evidence relevant to the party's case. Without this tool, the opposing party risks getting meandering and unhelpful testimony, or worse yet, unwelcomed evidence, while the party calling the witness is able to develop a desired narrative. As noted earlier, most witnesses are called by the Prosecution.

Thus far, common law terms, such as 'examination-in-chief', 'direct examination', 'cross-examination', are being used even if they are not found in the lexicon of the Rome Statute or the RPE.[123] Some Trial Chambers have forbidden the use of leading questions – thus stripping the parties, and in particular the Defence, of one of its most important arsenals at trial. Others have taken a common law approach, allowing the parties to conduct classical direct and cross-examination as generally understood and permitted in places such as the United Kingdom and the United States. And then there is one particular Trial Chamber that has taken a middle ground, or more appropriately, a confusing, muddled, and unorthodox approach. Of course, the result of these disparate

---

122 On the importance of asking leading questions when confronting adverse or hostile witnesses, *see* Larry S. Pozner and Roger J. Dodd, *Cross-Examination Science and Techniques*, (LexisNexis, 2004), 1.02.

123 *See,* for example, Witness Preparation Protocols adopted in *Prosecutor v. Ruto and Sang*, ICC-01/09-01/11-524, Decision on Witness preparation, 2 January 2013, with public Annex 'Witness Preparation Protocol'; *Prosecutor v. Muthaura and Kenyatta*, ICC-01/09-02/11-588, Decision on Witness preparation, 2 January 2013, with public Annex 'Witness Preparation Protocol', using the terms 'examination-in-chief', 'cross-examination'. *See also Prosecutor v. Lubanga*, ICC-01/04-01/06-2127, Decision Public on the Manner of Questioning Witnesses Representatives of Victims, 16 September 2009, para. 22: 'The terms "examination-in-chief", "cross-examination" and "reexamination", which are used in common law and Romano Germanic legal systems, do not appear in the Statute. However ... these expressions have been used as terms of convenience by the parties and the participants when addressing the issue of how witnesses are to be questioned during their evidence before the Trial Chamber'.

approaches to question witnesses is disquieting. While this may not impact so much the Prosecution, it definitely impacts the Defence.

The Defence, if dependent on legal aid, normally has limited resources to conduct lengthy and extensive investigations in search of witnesses. It may, depending on its theory of defence, the formal burden of proof (not judicial truth seeking), and its understanding of the evidence, rely on a *no case to answer* strategy, that is where reasonable doubt is planned to be established through cross-examination. As noted, this sort of theory of defence becomes significantly more difficult to run without control of the witnesses through cross-examination. In any event, denying the Defence the right to cross-examine with leading questions before one Trial Chamber, while allowing it to do so before another, creates the perception that one trial is more judge-driven, while the other more party-driven. And query whether the adoption of the civil law format of questioning of witnesses compels or invites the judges to also be more active in their questioning, thus avoiding having a skewed or unhelpful trial record?

In *Lubanga*, the Trial Chamber addressed the manner of questioning witnesses by the parties in an oral decision during a status conference. It set out the following principles: (a) leading questions should not be used by the party calling a witness when dealing with contentious issues; (b) in its questioning following the examination by the other party, the party calling the witness should avoid leading questions; and (c) if the defence had not called the witness and if it asks questions following re-examination by the calling party, leading questions were to be avoided.[124]

In *Katanga and Ngudjolo*, the Trial Chamber interpreted Rule 140(2) to provide the right to 'cross-examine' the witness and regarded it as a 'principle of fairness'.[125] The Trial Chamber adopted a detailed practice direction governing the scope and mode of conducting cross-examination.[126] The Trial Chamber also allowed both leading and closed questions during cross-examination.[127]

In *Bemba*, the Trial Chamber held that the party not calling the witness could ask questions related to witness credibility, the reliability of the evidence, as well as in relation to mitigating or aggravating circumstances and

---

[124] *Prosecutor v. Lubanga*, ICC-01/04-01/06-T-104-ENG, Transcript, 16 January 2009, p. 37, lines 8–24.

[125] *Prosecutor v. Katanga and Ngudjolo*, ICC-01/04-01/07-1665-Corr, Corrigendum Directions for the Conduct of the Proceedings and Testimony in Accordance with Rule 140, 1 December 2009, para. 68.

[126] *Id.*, paras. 69–81.

[127] *Id.*, para. 74.

reparation issues.[128] However, the Trial Chamber required that all parties and participants ask 'neutral' (non-leading) questions.[129] When the Prosecution requested leave to appeal this decision arguing, *inter alia*, that the Trial Chamber is prohibiting the use of leading questions during cross-examination,[130] the Trial Chamber refused to grant leave. The Trial Chamber found that the Prosecution misrepresented the decision as imposing 'an absolute, indiscriminate "ban" on the use by the parties of leading questions'.[131] In the Trial Chamber's view the preference for 'neutral' questions did not amount to a prohibition of leading questions.[132]

In *Ruto and Sang*, the Trial Chamber adopted an adversarial approach, using the common law terminology ('examination-in-chief', 'cross-examination', and 're-examin[ation]')[133] in its directions for the conduct of the trial.[134] The parties were allowed to confront witnesses and use leading questions during cross-examination. In *Ntaganda*, the Trial Chamber not only allowed leading questions during cross-examination. It also went further by detailing the mode of refreshing the witness's memory and impeaching witnesses' credibility.[135]

In *Gbagbo and Blé Goudé*,[136] Presiding Judge Cuno Tarfusser prohibited the use of questions that can 'pre-determine' the witnesses' answers.[137] Judge Tarfusser explained that it is not considered to be 'leading' to confront witnesses using documents, prior statements, or another person's testimony and

---

128 *Prosecutor v. Bemba*, ICC-01/05-01/08-1023, Decision on the Directions of the Conduct of the proceedings, 19 November 2010, para. 13.

129 *Id.*, para. 15.

130 *Prosecutor v. Bemba*, ICC-01/05-01/08-1086, Decision on the Prosecution's Request for Leave to Appeal the Trial Chamber's Decision on Directions for the Conduct of the Proceedings, 15 December 2010, para. 3. The Defence did not file a response to the Prosecution's request for leave.

131 *Id.*, para. 19.

132 *Id.*

133 The Trial Chamber did not use the common law term 're-direct' but allowed 'the calling party ... to re-examine the witness in relation to matters which were raised for the first time in cross- examination'. *Prosecutor v. Ruto and Sang*, ICC-01/09-01/11-847-Corr, Decision on the Conduct of Trial Proceedings (General Directions), 9 August 2013, para. 15.

134 *Id.*, paras. 13–21.

135 *Prosecutor v. Ntaganda*, ICC-01/04-02/06-619, Decision on the Conduct of Trial Proceedings, 2 June 2015, para. 28.

136 The Trial Chamber's composition changed to Presiding Judge Cuno Tarfusser (Italy), Judge Olga Herrera Carbuccia (Dominican Republic), and Judge Geoffrey Henderson (Trinidad and Tobago).

137 *Prosecutor v. Gbagbo and Blé Goudé*, ICC-02/11-01/15-T-14 ENG, Transcript, 4 February 2016, p. 3, lines 10–12.

statements that contradict the testimony of that witness and cast doubt on his or her credibility. Therefore, he allowed asking questions and clarifications on the contradictory facts or circumstances.[138]

The Defence sought leave to appeal this decision, arguing that without the possibility to use leading questions, it had been deprived of the possibility of confronting witnesses called by other parties or participants.[139] The Prosecution joined the Defence, arguing that a prohibition of leading questions could seriously delay the trial, deprives the parties of an essential tool in eliciting truthful testimony, and negatively affects the parties' abilities to present their cases.[140] Both the Defence and the Prosecution argued that there is a need to unify the conflicting practice on this issue.[141]

The Trial Chamber (by Majority)[142] refused to grant leave to appeal. The Majority reasoned that the Defence misunderstood the Trial Chamber's decision, and that it only established the basis upon which it will control the manner in which the parties are to question the witnesses. Judge Tarfusser further explained that the decision would be implemented on a case-by-case basis to ensure that the rights of the parties and participants would be duly safeguarded at all times.[143]

Judge Henderson dissented, eloquently pointing out that 'the abolition of the right to pose leading questions carries with it the serious potential to hinder the party from advancing his case'.[144] He further explained that in adversarial proceedings a party's failure to confront a witness on every aspect of his or her evidence amounts to an implied acceptance of the evidence. Therefore, the party will not be able to challenge the evidence in closing argument. Judge Henderson reasoned that cross-examination by leading questions ensures fairness to the witness and the fact-finders, since it allows a witness to put his version of the events and have the cross-examining party to test the veracity

---

138 *Id.*, p. 3, lines 15–22.
139 *Id.*, p. 10, lines 21–24; p. 11, lines 1–2; p. 16, lines 18–22.
140 *Prosecutor v. Gbagbo and Blé Goudé*, ICC-02/11-01/15-T-15-Red-ENG, Transcript, 5 February 2016, p. 4, lines 11–20.
141 *Id.*, p. 3, lines 12–15; p. 4, line 21–25. Interestingly, the Legal Representative of Victims submitted that the request for leave to appeal should not be granted and that the challenged decision does not preclude the parties from confronting the witnesses. *See Prosecutor v. Gbagbo and Blé Goudé*, ICC-02/11-01/15-T-14-ENG, Transcript, 4 February 2016, p. 17, lines 16; 18, lines 12–16.
142 *Prosecutor v. Gbagbo and Blé Goudé*, ICC-02/11-01/15-T-15-Red-ENG, Transcript, 5 February 2015, p. 7.
143 *Id.*, p. 6, lines 4–21.
144 *Id.*, p. 11, lines 17–18.

of witness's testimony, pointing out the contradictions in the form of leading questions.[145]

In the *Bemba Article 70* case,[146] the Trial Chamber avoided the terms 'direct' and 'cross-examination' in its directions on the conduct of the trial proceedings. Instead, it used the terms 'presentation of evidence by the Prosecution' and 'presentation of evidence by the Defence'.[147] When the trial began, Presiding Judge Bertram Schmitt explained: 'I wish to make clear at the outset that the Chamber has not set strict regulations on questioning so that appropriate limitations can be set on a case-by-case basis'.[148] Judge Schmitt further elaborated:

> [O]n 2 September 2015, directions on the conduct of proceedings were given to the parties. This decision regulated certain aspects of the conduct of the proceedings, but also, as you may have noticed, intentionally left certain matters unaddressed which would be subject to oral determinations in the course of the trial. The reason for this is the following: A trial hearing is a dynamic process which evolves constantly. If it was not so we could limit ourselves to written procedure. ...The Chamber is of the opinion that trying to regulate in detail the conduct of proceedings beforehand and thus putting the parties and also the Judges in a sort of procedural corset is at least futile.[149]

Judge Schmitt then urged the parties to avoid repetitive questioning, and to make focused, clear, concise, and timely objections. The issue of leading questions was not raised. In practice, the parties used the term 'cross-examination' during the trial, and leading questions during questioning by the opposing party were allowed.[150] Throughout the trial, the Trial Chamber exercised its authority to control the mode of questioning. When an issue of using prior statements for refreshing witnesses' memory and impeachment arose, the Trial Chamber stated:

---

145   *Id.*, p. 11, lines 9–16.

146   Presiding Judge Bertram Schmitt (Germany), Judge Marc Perrin de Brichambaut (France), and Judge Raul C. Pangalangan (The Philippines).

147   *Prosecutor v. Bemba et al.*, ICC-01/05-01/13-1209, Directions on the conduct of the proceedings, 2 September 2015, para. 14.

148   *Prosecutor v. Bemba et al.*, ICC-01/05-01/13-T-10-Red-ENG, Transcript, 29 September 2015, p. 7, lines 13–14.

149   *Id.*, p. 6, line 21 to p. 7, line 10.

150   For example, *see* cross-examination of a witness, *Prosecutor v. Bemba et al.*, ICC-01/05-01/13-T-11-Red-ENG, Transcript, 30 September 2015, p. 75.

> The Chamber would appreciate it if the examining party would first try to elicit the information sought by asking direct questions before seeking to refresh the witness's recollection. However, the Chamber deems it not necessary to ask the witness before such try to recollect his memory if he or she believes his or her memory would be refreshed. The Chamber would also emphasise that when prior statements refresh a witness's recollection, the evidence given is the witness's subsequent testimony and not the contents of the prior statements.... As regards a general guideline for impeaching witnesses, the Chamber does not consider that any such guideline is necessary or appropriate. The Chamber will not abandon or undermine its authority to control the calling party's questioning of its witness. Any improper use of witnesses' prior statements will not be tolerated and non-calling parties are always entitled to object to the way a prior statement is put to a witness.[151]

Similar vague and general directions for the conduct of trial proceedings were adopted in *Ongwen* by the same Trial Chamber.[152]

Judicial Questioning & Power to Call Witnesses

Relevant to some extent, although problematic in and of itself, is the issue of judicial questioning. Unquestionably, judges can ask questions – no holds barred. Nothing seems off limits, even going outside the scope of the charges and eliciting incriminating evidence against the accused. Truth-searching has no limits. While such evidence may not be used to convict – since it is outside the charging document – it can be used to establish aggravating circumstances for sentencing purposes.

This may seem perfectly natural to civil law judges (and most likely welcomed by some common law judges who find themselves chomping at the bit to get into the mix of questioning witnesses), but this is unsettling to the Defence, which not only has to contend with the Prosecution and Victims' Representatives, but also with the Judges. Triple-teamed. Depending on the regularity and systematic intrusiveness in the questioning by judges, the perception shared by the Defence is that the Trial Chamber is no longer judging the case on the basis of whether the Prosecution has met its burden of proof, but on whether the Trial Chamber – after having questioned the witnesses

---

151 *Prosecutor v. Bemba et al.*, ICC-01/05-01/13-T-18-Red2-ENG, Transcript, 12 October 2015, p. 17, line 12 to p. 18, line 7.
152 *Prosecutor v. Ongwen*, ICC-02/04-01/15-497, Initial Directions on the Conduct of the Proceedings, 13 July 2016, paras. 4–5.

without restraint – is endeavoring to find the evidence to convict. This perception is sharpened when the Trial Chamber further exercises its unfettered prerogative to call witnesses to testify or to have evidence admitted that it believes is essential in getting to the truth. It is also worth mentioning that, unlike the Prosecution which has lived with the case for months and years and has (or should have) a clear path in meeting its burden of proof, the judges are less acquainted with the case and do not have access to all the documents or information that the parties have at their disposal, and thus are less able to know the case. Discussing the differences in the trial style adopted by proactive and more passive judges at the ICTY, Judge Patricia M. Wald aptly observed:

> [Judicial] questioning may throw off the rhythm of the prosecution's or the defense's case presented in an adversarial mode, casting the judge in the role of an uninvited guest at the party. The prosecution or the defense may have a carefully selected series of witnesses, called in sequence to build on each other's testimony and with knowledge of just how far to take each witness in questioning. The other side, for its own strategic reasons, may have no desire to press that witness further, but then when the judge steps in and asks the ultimate blunt conclusionary questions the prosecution (or the defense) have been slowly and painstakingly working toward, the lawyer that presented the witness must scramble to get back control of the case. Additionally, judges don't always repeat the witness's testimony precisely when they ask a follow-up question (or, not infrequently, it may be garbled in translation), thereby risking an answer based on an erroneous premise. Counsel are understandably hesitant to correct the judge and, candidly, the judges do not always welcome such interruptions.[153]

Perhaps the drafters of the Rome Statute did not consider that by adopting Articles 64(6)(b), 64(6)(d), and 69(3), and Rule 140(2)(c), they effectively gave free reign to the judges. Not only can they lead and dominate the questioning process, but they can also actively participate, effectively making them – at least perception-wise – into what I call *the fifth prosecutor*, the excessively

---

153 Former Chief Judge of the United States Court of Appeals for the District of Columbia Circuit and former ICTY Judge Patricia M. Wald, 'The International Criminal Tribunal for the Former Yugoslavia Comes of Age: Some Observations on Day-To-Day Dilemmas of an International Court' (2001) 5 *Journal of Law & Policy* 87, 90.

activist judge in adversarial proceedings, doing the Prosecution's handiwork in securing a conviction. These may be mere perceptions, but when the trial proceedings dominated by overly and overtly active judges in taking and producing evidence are compared to the more *laissez-faire* proceedings where the judges are reserved (intervening mostly for clarification purposes to ensure a clear trial record) the differences are stark. A few examples are worth examining.

In *Lubanga*, the Defence raised the issue of the subject and form of judicial questioning. The Defence argued that the subject-matter and the form of a significant number of questions put by the Trial Chamber to the witnesses called by the Prosecution, the Court and the participating victims could 'seriously affect' the 'appearance of impartially' if they are repeated during the examination of Defence witnesses.[154] The Defence provided several examples when judicial questioning was improper in the view of the Defence. The Defence argued that one witness during his testimony never raised the issue of sexual violence, yet Judge Odio Benito asked the following question:

> Could you assist the Court with whatever information you got about sexual violence committed against the PMF during the training period, especially against the young girls recruited?[155]

A similar question was posed to another witness, who, as the Defence submitted, never spoke of the crimes of sexual violence:

> My question, sir, was if, for instance, when you were visiting training camps you were informed about sexual violence against girl soldiers. And when I talk about sexual violence I'm talking about rapes, I'm talking about sexual slavery, I'm talking about forced impregnation. Have you heard about that? Has somebody told you about that?[156]

---

154 *Prosecutor v. Lubanga*, ICC-01/04-01/06-2252, Requête aux fins de détermination des principes applicables aux questions posées aux témoins par les juges, 15 January 2010, para. 1.

155 *Id.*, para. 8; *see also Prosecutor v. Lubanga*, ICC-01/04-01/06-T-191-Red2-ENG, Transcript, p. 15, lines 15–18.

156 *Prosecutor v. Lubanga*, ICC-01/04-01/06-2252, Requête aux fins de détermination des principes applicables aux questions posées aux témoins par les juges, 15 January 2010, para. 9; *see also Prosecutor v. Lubanga*, ICC-01/04-01/06-T-178-ENG WT, Transcript, p. 78, lines 18–23.

The Defence argued that these questions, aside from being suggestive, could lead to introducing new criminal acts outside the facts and circumstances described in the indictment.[157]

Another example related to the form of questioning. The Defence submitted that after one witness described a case of abducting young girls and subjecting them to sexual violence, stating specifically '[w]e would take them from their parents and take them to a place, a place that we would find where we could do those things, and after that we would free them', Judge Benito asked the following: 'Or perhaps you also killed them?'.[158] The Defence argued that this question was not only suggestive, but also risks being interpreted as an expression of the judge's partiality.[159] The Defence did not object to these questions during the hearing. As explained in its written submission, since the ICC legal texts are silent, and following the practice of the main jurisdictions, the Defence 'until now considered that it has no right to object to questions posed by the judges'.[160] However, since the Defence requested the Trial Chamber to clarify the principles of judicial questioning, the Defence also sought to clarify the issue of objecting to judges' questions that contravene any governing principles.[161]

The Trial Chamber held that there was no foundation in the Rome Statute or in the ICC jurisprudence for the suggestion that the Trial Chamber is unable to ask questions about facts and issues that have been 'ignored, or inadequately dealt with, by counsel'.[162] The Trial Chamber reasoned that the general evidence in the case is not restricted to the facts and circumstances described in the indictment.[163] It also reasoned that under Article 69(3) the Trial Chamber is entitled to request the submission of all evidence that it considers necessary for the determination of the truth.[164] As to the form of questions, the Trial Chamber stated that whether it is appropriate to ask a leading question

---

157 *Prosecutor v. Lubanga*, ICC-01/04-01/06-2252, Requête aux fins de détermination des principes applicables aux questions posées aux témoins par les juges, 15 January 2010, para. 10.
158 *Id.*, para. 20; *see also Prosecutor v. Lubanga*, ICC-01/04-01/06-T-138-ENG, Transcript, p. 21, lines 19–22.
159 *Prosecutor v. Lubanga*, ICC-01/04-01/06-2252, Requête aux fins de détermination des principes applicables aux questions posées aux témoins par les juges, 15 January 2010, paras. 21–22.
160 *Id.*, para. 25 (unofficial translation).
161 *Id.*, paras. 25–28.
162 *Prosecutor v. Lubanga*, ICC-01/04-01/06-2360, Decision on Judicial Questioning, 18 March 2010, para. 41.
163 *Id.*
164 *Id.*

depends on the circumstances, which is 'quintessentially a matter for judicial determination'.[165] The Trial Chamber also held that there is nothing in the Rome Statute or jurisprudence to allow the parties to challenge questions put by the judges.[166] The parties can, however, bring to the attention of the judges a question that is 'clearly put on the basis of a mistake'.[167]

This example shows that the judges' power to ask questions has been interpreted broadly, placing virtually no limits on judges in questioning witnesses.

The judges' power to intervene goes further than questioning witnesses. The Trial Chambers have used their power to call witnesses in addition to the evidence submitted by the parties; a civil-law feature that would be, at a minimum, controversial in common law adversarial systems, if not impossible.

In *Katanga and Ngudjolo*, the Trial Chamber exercised its power to call a witness before the parties' presentation of evidence even though neither the Defence teams nor the Prosecution requested it to do so. Before the trial, the Defence teams objected to the Prosecution's narrow interpretation of its duty to search for potentially exculpatory evidence. Ngudjolo argued that the Trial Chamber should exercise its authority under Article 64 to instruct the Prosecution to produce a table of its evidence so that the trial could proceed fairly and expeditiously.[168] Katanga requested that the Trial Chamber order the Prosecution to: (a) provide a full and complete description of the nature and scope of the exculpatory part of its investigations; (b) provide a detailed description of its review process in identifying exculpatory material; (c) organize the material so that the Defence can focus its resources; (d) disclose exculpatory material; and (e) identify to what aspect of the case the disclosed material is potentially relevant.[169] Neither team specifically requested that a Prosecution investigator testify. The Trial Chamber considered 'it necessary to order the appearance of the person in the Office of the Prosecutor in charge of investigations in this case ("the Lead Investigator"), in addition to the Prosecution witnesses already due to testify'.[170] The Lead Investigator was called to explain: (a) how

---

165 *Id.*, para. 43.
166 *Id.*, para. 48.
167 *Id.*
168 *Prosecutor v. Katanga and Ngudjolo*, ICC-01/04-01/07-863, Defence Response to the Prosecution' Submissions regarding paragraph 8 of the Order of 10 December 2008, 2 February 2009, para. 8.
169 *Id.*, para. 16.
170 *Prosecutor v. Katanga and Ngudjolo*, ICC-01/04-01/07-1603-tENG, Second Decision on issues related to the closing of the case, 5 November 2009, para. 17.

the investigation was conducted; (b) how the statements were taken; and (c) what methods were used to investigate and identify exculpatory evidence.[171]

In *Bemba*, the Trial Chamber also used its power to call witnesses, but only after the Defence concluded its case.[172] The details as to the identity of the witnesses are redacted, although it appears that their 'role ... at the time of the events has been extensively discussed at trial' and their 'names have been repeatedly mentioned by both prosecution and defence witnesses'.[173] The witnesses were first questioned by the Trial Chamber, then by the Prosecution, the Victim Representatives, and finally by the Defence.[174]

Trial Management

Less contentious and less obvious are trial management practices that vary among the Trial Chambers. These practices vary to some extent because not all cases are alike, and thus adopting boutique practices to meet the challenges and needs of the case so that the proceedings are fair, impartial, efficient and expeditious is sound. Here too, however, a perceived or real disparity in the quality of justice afforded to the parties can result when practices adopted are ill-conceived, inflexible, or ill-suited. This criticism is virtually universal at all the international(ized) tribunals and courts. It would be grossly unfair to suggest that the practices that have been adopted by the various Trial Chambers at the ICC deserve special attention as contributing factors to the overarching argument that the proceedings at the ICC vary from trial to trial based on the serendipitous composition of the Trial Chamber, and in particular the Presiding Judge.

One example merits examining: requiring the Prosecution to produce an analytical chart of the evidence disclosed for admission and how each item relates to one another.

In *Lubanga*, no detailed chart or table linking all incriminatory evidence was required of the Prosecution because they were neither ordered nor requested

---

171   *Id.*

172   *Prosecutor v. Bemba*, ICC-01/05-01/08-2837, Second Decision on issues related to the closing of the case, 18 October 2013, para. 20; *Prosecutor v. Bemba*, ICC-01/05-01/08-2731, Decision on the timeline for the completion of the defence's presentation of evidence and issues related to the closing of the case, 16 July 2013, para. 26.

173   *Prosecutor v. Bemba*, ICC-01/05-01/08-2837-Red, Second Decision on Issues related to the Closing of the Case, 18 October 2013, para. 20.

174   *Prosecutor v. Bemba*, ICC-01/05-01/08-2863-Red, Decision on the Presentation of Additional Testimony Pursuant to Articles 64(6)(b) and (d) and 69(3) of the Rome Statute, 6 November 2013, paras. 4–7.

to do so.[175] In *Katanga and Ngudjolo*, the Trial Chamber ordered the Prosecution to submit not only a detailed table linking incriminating evidence, but also indicate where evidence related to more than one factual allegation.[176] The Trial Chamber reasoned that while this task 'might entail an additional administrative burden on the Prosecution ... at this late stage of the proceedings, the Prosecution must know its case in full detail and be able to present it in the format requested by the Chamber'.[177] It further reasoned that such a table 'will facilitate the subsequent work of the accused and the Chamber and thereby expedite the proceedings as a whole'.[178] The *Bemba* Trial Chamber adopted the same approach, requesting the Prosecution to provide in advance 'an in-depth analysis chart' illustrating a clear linkage between each piece of evidence and the allegations in the indictment.[179] However, in *Kenyatta* and *Ruto and Sang*, the Trial Chamber considered such a chart unnecessary and requested the Prosecution to submit an updated indictment and a pre-trial brief.[180] In *Ruto and Sang*, the Defence did not request an in-depth analysis chart and in issuing the decision on the schedule leading up to trial, the Trial Chamber stated that 'these two documents [updated indictment and pre-trial brief] will ensure that the accused are informed of the charges against them and are not prejudiced in their preparation for trial'.[181]

In *Kenyatta*, both Defence teams requested they be provided with an in-depth analysis chart.[182] The Prosecution objected, arguing that such a chart would be of limited usefulness and that a pre-trial brief is a better guide to the

---

175 See *Prosecutor v. Bemba*, ICC-01/05-01/08-656, Prosecution's Submissions on the Trial Chamber's 8 December 2009 Oral Order Requesting Updating of the In-Depth-Analysis Charter, 15 December 2009, para. 7. The Prosecution in *Bemba* argued that a detailed analytical chart was 'not a necessary component of a fair trial, as it was not required in the case of *The Prosecutor v. Thomas Lubanga Dyilo*'.
176 *Prosecutor v. Katanga and Ngudjolo*, ICC-01/04-01/07-956, Order concerning the Presentation of Incriminating Evidence and the E-Court Protocol, 13 March 2009, paras. 13–14.
177 *Id.*, para. 15.
178 *Id.*
179 *Prosecutor v. Bemba*, ICC-01/05-01/08-682, Decision on the 'Prosecution's Submissions on the Trial Chamber's 8 December 2009 Oral Order Requesting Updating of the In-Depth-Analysis Chart', 29 January 2010, paras. 26–31.
180 *Prosecutor v. Kenyatta*, ICC-01/09-02/11-451, Decision on the Schedule Leading up to Trial, 9 July 2012, para. 11.
181 *Prosecutor v. Ruto and Sang*, ICC-01/09-01/11-440, Decision on the Schedule Leading up to Trial, 9 July 2012, para. 6.
182 *Prosecutor v. Kenyatta*, ICC-01/09-02/11-451, Decision on the Schedule Leading up to Trial, 9 July 2012, para. 2.

Prosecution's case at trial.[183] The Trial Chamber reasoned that '[a]lthough both defence teams submit that the [in-depth analysis chart] would be a useful tool, there is no reference to this document in the core legal texts if the Court'.[184] The Trial Chamber further considered that such a chart would be unnecessary if the Prosecution provides an updated indictment and a pre-trial brief.[185]

The practice of providing an analytical chart, which appears very civil law-centered, has been adopted by other tribunals.[186] It is nothing unique. A well-prepared Prosecution case would have utilized such a chart as a road map and check-list for meeting its burden of proof for each element of each charge. Thus, it is not necessarily unduly taxing to require the Prosecution to produce an analytical chart at the commencement of the trial proceedings. It certainly assists the judges in understanding what the Prosecution's case is and how it intends to prove the charges. More importantly, it provides significant assistance to the Defence. Being handed the proverbial needle instead of the haystack, the Defence, with its limited resources and seemingly less appreciable understanding of the evidence, is placed on a more equal footing during the trial proceedings. This practice is consistent with and in furtherance of the Trial Chamber's obligation to ensure that the proceedings are fair and unbiased. And when considering that the Prosecution has an affirmative duty to ensure that justice is done (as reflected in its mandate to search for both exculpatory and inculpatory evidence with equal zeal), this practice is sound and equitable. Yet even in relation to this issue there is no consistent practice at the ICC.

---

183   *Id.*, para. 4.
184   *Id.*, para. 11.
185   *Id.*
186   At the ICTY, the Prosecution must specify in its witnesses list 'the points in the indictment as to which each witness will testify, including specific references to counts and relevant paragraphs in the indictment'. Rule 65 *ter* (E) of the ICTY Rules of Procedure and Evidence. Several Trial Chambers at the ICTY, ICTR, and the Special Court for Sierra Leone (SCSL) have ordered the Prosecution to prepare, in addition to the pre-trial brief, a chart linking witnesses and exhibits to counts of the indictment and to the accused. See e.g., *Prosecutor v. Prlic et al.*, ICTY-04-74-PT, Revised Version of the Decision Adopting Guidelines on Conduct of Trial Proceedings, 28 April 2006, para. 9: 'chart linking witnesses and exhibits to counts of the indictment and to the Accused'; *Gacumbitsi v. Prosecutor* ICTR-2001-64-A, Judgement, 7 July 2006, para. 56: 'chart that shows the charges to which each witness's testimony was expected to correspond'; *Prosecutor v. Brima*, SCSL-2004-16, Transcript, 30 April 2004, p. 24, lines 23–37, p. 25, line 1: 'proofing-chart ... to focus on the count system indicating specifically for every count, paragraph, the testimonial or primary documentary evidence that supports those counts'.

Concluding Observations and Recommendations

The serendipitous composition of the Trial Chamber and the judges' broad discretion in determining procedural modalities leads to stark differences in the conduct of the trial proceedings from one case to another. As shown and discussed through the vignettes in this chapter, this inconsistent practice goes to the fundamentals of the procedure as opposed to minor technical trial-management issues. Such diversity among the Trial Chambers of a single court appears undesirable and counterproductive. While the ICC procedure does not inevitably lead to unfair trials, its flexible and fragmented nature makes it unforeseeable to the accused. The disparate treatment of the accused between different Trial Chambers risks undermining the perceived fairness and the right of all accused to equal treatment. This in turn, risks undermining the legitimacy of the ICC proceedings, and the ICC itself. Query whether the outcomes of the trials – however well-grounded in the weight of the evidence – will be accepted as legitimate and just, if the process is perceived to be unfair? It seems that the results of such trials, regrettably, are likely to be viewed with skepticism, detracting from the legacy and legitimacy of the ICC and undermining its credibility.

Far-reaching procedural reform may be the optimal way to address these problems. However, considering the difficulties in reaching consensus among the States Parties in negotiating and drafting the legal framework of the ICC, it is questionable how realistic the possibility of amending the Rome Statute or the RPE is. Less radical yet effective solutions are available. Regular mandatory training may prove effective in overcoming the lack of a shared legal culture among judges. Developing guidelines and directives harmonizing the Court's practice is another effective solution, which does not involve the States Parties. Similarly, drafting an official commentary to the Rome Statute and RPE may be an option to consider. The 14-year practice of the ICC could serve as a basis for comprehensive appraisal and indicate the contours of possible amendments.

CHAPTER 10

Vom eingeschränkten Nutzen strafrechtlicher Urteile für die Historiographie: Ein Beitrag zum Zustandekommen des ersten deutschen Urteils wegen Völkermordes in Ruanda

Stefan Kirsch

Abstract

While it is an elementary precondition for a just verdict that it is based on a truthful set of facts, judicial proceedings are surprisingly limited in their capability to discover the truth. In spite of various hopes articulated in the transitional justice arena a criminal trial is not well equipped to establish a truthful historical record. After briefly outlining the reasons for this limited capability the following article portrays and analyses the judicial proceedings that lead to the first conviction by a German court for genocide in the context of the atrocities that occurred in Rwanda in 1994. Although the accused was finally convicted as a perpetrator the facts of the case do not support such a finding. A closer look at the procedural history of the case, however, demonstrates how special features of the procedure aided to come up with such a result.

Geht es um die Zwecke und Funktionen des Völkerstrafrechts, wird neben der Befriedigung von Opferinteressen vor allem die Feststellung und Dokumentation historischer Fakten genannt. Überraschend ist das nicht, da strafgerichtliche Entscheidungen in aller Regel dem Anspruch genügen wollen, dass der ihnen zugrundeliegende Sachverhalt der Wahrheit entspricht.[1] Gleichwohl darf diese Annahme nicht zu dem gegenteiligen Fehlschluss verleiten, dass das Strafrecht auch geeignet sei, historische Wahrheiten festzustellen und

---

* Rechtsanwalt in Frankfurt am Main.
1 Vgl. Karl Peters, Strafprozess, 4. Aufl., 1985, 287 („Nur ein Sachverhalt kann dem wirklichen Geschehen entsprechen"). Instruktiv insoweit auch Herbert Landau, *Verfassungsrecht und Strafrecht,* in Europäische Grundrechtezeitschrift 2016, 505 (506); Ulfrid Neumann, *Materiale und prozedurale Gerechtigkeit im Strafverfahren,* Zeitschrift für die gesamte Strafrechtswissenschaft 101 (1989), 52.

zu dokumentieren. Denn auch wenn sich die moderne Historiographie wohl nicht mehr darauf beschränkt aufzuzeigen, „wie es eigentlich gewesen ist"[2], so erfolgt die Sachverhaltsermittlung im Strafverfahren unter Voraussetzungen, die sich wesentlich von denen historischer Forschung unterscheiden. Der insbesondere aus dem Bereich der transitional justice geltend gemachte Anspruch an justizielle Verfahren, historische Wahrheiten festzustellen, birgt daher die Gefahr einer Überforderung der entsprechenden Verfahren wie auch von Missverständnissen im Hinblick auf deren Ergebnisse.

Am Beispiel der ersten Verurteilung durch deutsche Gerichte im Zusammenhang mit dem Völkermord in Ruanda versucht der nachfolgende Beitrag zu veranschaulichen, welche Eigentümlichkeiten die strafrechtliche Sachverhaltsfeststellung prägen, und damit vor einer unkritischen Übernahme entsprechender Feststellungen als historische Wahrheit zu warnen. Dabei eignet sich das zu der Verurteilung führende Verfahren, das erst nach zwei Entscheidungen sowohl des Oberlandesgerichts Frankfurt am Main als auch des Bundesgerichtshofs sein Ende gefunden hat, aus zwei Gründen ganz besonders für eine vertiefte Befassung. Zum einen wird die Verurteilung wegen Völkermords durch das Oberlandesgericht Frankfurt nicht nur als Beweis der Praxistauglichkeit des deutschen Strafrechts im Hinblick auf die Schaffung globaler Gerechtigkeit gefeiert[3], sondern fügt sich mit der Feststellung eines „von staatlicher Seite realistisch formulierten Zerstörungsziels"[4] bruchlos in das Narrativ eines staatlich angeordneten und gelenkten Völkermordes an der Volksgruppe der Tutsi.[5] Zum anderen zeigt die Verfahrensgeschichte, die zu der Verurteilung geführt hat, zwei Besonderheiten, die die Beschränkungen justizförmiger Wahrheitssuche besonders deutlich machen. So belegt das Verfahren nicht nur eindrucksvoll, wie materiell-rechtliche Überlegungen die Sachverhaltsfeststellung determinieren, sondern auch, wie die besonderen Strukturen des Rechtsmittelrechts auf diese einwirken.

Bevor aber die einzelnen Stationen dieses Verfahrens nachgezeichnet werden, sollen zunächst noch einmal die Besonderheiten der strafjuristischen Wahrheitssuche vorgestellt werden. Damit knüpft der nachfolgende Beitrag an Gedanken und Diskussionen auf einem Kolloquium im April 2012 an der Universität Durham an, auf dem Wolfgang Schomburg sich – wie bei vielen

---

2 Leopold von Ranke, Sämtliche Werke Bd. 33/34, Leipzig 1885, 7.
3 Vgl. etwa Gerhard Werle und Moritz Vormbaum, *Völkerstrafverfahren in Deutschland*, in Juristenzeitung 2017, 12.
4 Oberlandesgericht Frankfurt, Urteil vom 29.12.2015 – 4-3 StE 4/10 – 1/15, III.A.3.
5 Kritisch Gerd Hankel, Ruanda: Leben und Neuaufbau nach dem Völkermord. Wie Geschichte gemacht und zur offiziellen Wahrheit wird, 2016.

anderen Gelegenheiten seither auch – kritisch mit den Beschränkungen der Wahrheitsermittlung an internationalen Strafgerichten auseinandergesetzt hat.

Wahrheitsermittlung im Strafverfahren

Wahrheitsermittlung im Strafverfahren erfolgt nicht um ihrer selbst willen[6], sondern dient dem Zweck der Überprüfung eines jeweils individuellen Schuldvorwurfs. Der auf diese Weise beschränkte Gegenstand der Wahrheitsfindung im Strafverfahren zeigt sich vor allem darin, dass allein der in der Anklageschrift formulierte Vorwurf den Umfang der Beweisaufnahme bestimmt und Tatsachen, denen im Hinblick auf diesen nicht nur zeitlich und örtlich, sondern auch personell und sachlich konkretisierten Vorwurf keine Relevanz zukommt, unberücksichtigt bleiben müssen.

So ist es entgegen einer anfänglich weit verbreiteten Übung am Ruandastrafgerichtshof[7] für die Beurteilung eines individuellen Vorwurfs des Völkermordes für sich genommen vollkommen irrelevant, ob in Ruanda „ein Völkermord" stattgefunden hat oder nicht. Denn eine solche allgemeine Feststellung, wäre allenfalls dann von Bedeutung, wenn die Handlung des Täters sich in irgendeiner Art und Weise als Teil einer solchen Gesamttat darstellt und sich zumindest im subjektiven Tatbestand hierauf bezieht.[8] Dann aber bedarf es keiner isolierten Feststellung mehr, die allenfalls Missverständnisse im Hinblick auf den Gegenstand des Verfahrens aufkommen lässt.

Die Wahrheitsfindung im Strafverfahren ist aber nicht nur hinsichtlich ihres Gegenstandes beschränkt, sondern auch hinsichtlich ihrer Mittel. So soll die Erforschung des Sachverhaltes in rechtsförmiger Weise erfolgen und damit die Rechte der vom Verfahren Betroffenen wahren. Dementsprechend sichern Beweiserhebungs- und Beweisverwertungsverbote, dass die Wahrheit nicht um jeden Preis erforscht wird.[9]

---

6 Henning Radtke, *Wahrheitsermittlung im Strafverfahren*, in Goltdammer's Archiv für Strafrecht 2012, 187.

7 So bspw. *Prosecutor v Karemera et al.* ICTR -98-44-AR 73(C), Decision on Prosecutor's Interlocutry Appeal of Decision on Judicial Notice, 16.6.2006.

8 Vgl. Stefan Kirsch, *The social and the legal concept of genocide*, in: Behrens/Henham (eds.), Elements of Genocide, 2013, 7 (18).

9 Bundesgerichtshof, Urteil vom 14.6.1960 – 1 StR 683/59 = Entscheidungen des Bundesgerichtshofes in Strafsachen, 14. Band, 365.

So ist der Beschuldigte nicht zur Mitwirkung an der Sachverhaltsermittlung verpflichtet (*nemo tenetur se ipsum accusare*) und genießt dementsprechend ein Recht, zu den ihm gegenüber erhobenen Vorwürfen zu schweigen. In der Strafprozessordnung ist insoweit ausdrücklich geregelt, dass die Freiheit der Willensentschließung und -betätigung des Beschuldigten nicht durch Misshandlung, durch Ermüdung, durch körperlichen Eingriff, durch Verabreichung von Mitteln, durch Quälerei, durch Täuschung oder durch Hypnose beeinträchtigt werden darf, und auch die Drohung mit einer nach den Vorschriften des Strafverfahrensrechts unzulässigen Maßnahme oder das Versprechen eines gesetzlich nicht vorgesehenen Vorteils sind verboten (§ 136a Abs. 1 StPO). Aussagen, die unter Verletzung eines dieser Verbote zustande gekommen sind, dürfen selbst dann nicht verwertet werden, wenn der Beschuldigte einer solchen Verwertung zustimmt (§ 136a Abs. 3 StPO). Die frühere Rechtsprechung hatte unter Bezug hierauf sogar die Anwendung eines vom Beschuldigten gewünschten Polygraphentests für unzulässig erklärt.[10]

Aber nicht nur der Beschuldigte, sondern auch Dritte sind von der Verpflichtung zur Mitwirkung an der Sachverhaltsfeststellung entbunden, sofern es sich um nahe Angehörige des Beschuldigten handelt (§ 52 StPO) oder sie als Berufsgeheimnisträger zur Verschwiegenheit berechtigt sind (§ 53 StPO). Als wäre dieser Verzicht auf mitunter hervorragende Quellen der Wahrheitserforschung noch nicht genug, erlaubt das Strafverfahrensrecht jedem Zeugen, die Auskunft auf solche Fragen zu verweigern, deren Beantwortung ihn selbst oder einen nahen Angehörigen in die Gefahr bringen würde, wegen einer Straftat oder auch nur einer Ordnungswidrigkeit verfolgt zu werden (§ 55 StPO).

Das Strafverfahrensrecht verzichtet aber nicht nur insoweit auf eine Inpflichtnahme zu aktiver Mitwirkung, sondern beschränkt bei Eingriffen in den Kernbereich privater Lebensgestaltung sogar die Verpflichtung zur Hinnahme von Ermittlungsmaßnahmen. Betroffen ist dieser Kernbereich etwa im Falle intimer Tagebuchaufzeichnungen oder bei Selbstgesprächen.[11]

Darüber hinaus sind auch Maßnahmen des Schutzes verletzter oder gefährdeter Zeugen regelmäßig geeignet, die Qualität der Wahrheitserforschung zu beeinträchtigen. Zwar kennt das deutsche Strafverfahren – anders als etwa

---

10 Bundesgerichtshof, Urteil vom 16.2.1954 – 1 StR 578/53 = Entscheidungen des Bundesgerichtshofes in Strafsachen, 5. Band, 332 (335) („Ein solcher Einblick in die Seele des Beschuldigten und ihre unbewußten Regungen verletzt die Freiheit der Willensentschließung und – betätigung (§ 136a StPO) und ist im Strafverfahren unzulässig. Zur Erhaltung und Entwicklung der Persönlichkeit gehört ein lebensnotwendiger und unverzichtbarer seelischer Eigenraum, der auch im Strafverfahren unangetastet bleiben muß").
11 Vgl. Claus Roxin und Bernd Schünemann, Strafverfahrensrecht, 28. Aufl. 2014, 184.

Regel 96 der Verfahrens- und Beweisregeln des Jugoslawienstrafgerichtshofes oder Regeln 70 und 71 der Verfahrens- und Beweisregeln des Internationalen Strafgerichtshofes – keine besonderen Beweisregeln in Fällen sexuellen Missbrauchs, doch liegt auf der Hand, dass auch jede andere Maßnahme des Zeugenschutzes, wie etwa die Anordnung einer „nur" audiovisuellen Vernehmung (§ 247a StPO) oder die Aufnahme in ein Zeugenschutzprogramm[12], die Gefahr einer Beeinträchtigung der Wahrheitserforschung mit sich bringt. Dies gilt umso mehr, wenn die Identität eines verdeckten Ermittlers oder V-Mannes geheim gehalten wird.

Schließlich führen auch strukturelle Besonderheiten des Strafverfahrens jenseits des Beweisrechts zu möglichen Einschränkungen der Wahrheitsfindung. So müssen alle Beweise in einer öffentlichen Hauptverhandlung erhoben werden. Die Gerichtssprache ist deutsch. Es liegt auf der Hand, dass diese Erfordernisse gerade bei Verfahren, die Geschehnisse im Ausland zum Gegenstand haben, zu mitunter erheblichen Problemen führen.[13]

Das Urteil des Oberlandesgerichts Frankfurt vom 18.2.2014

Am 18.2.2014 hat der 5. Strafsenat des Oberlandesgerichts Frankfurt den ruandischen Staatsbürger O.R. wegen Beihilfe zum Völkermord zu einer Freiheitsstrafe von 14 Jahren verurteilt.[14] Die vom Senat aufgrund des Tatzeitpunktes im Jahr 1994 angewandte Vorschrift des § 220a Abs. 1 Nr. 1 StGB aF entspricht – ungeachtet kleinerer Abweichungen in der Formulierung[15] – der am 30.6.2002 in Kraft getretenen Vorschrift in § 6 VStGB. Der Tatzeitpunkt erklärt insoweit auch, warum sich das Oberlandesgericht nicht veranlasst sehen musste, Verbrechen gegen die Menschlichkeit zu untersuchen.

Zu der Verhandlung, die 120 Hauptverhandlungstage in Anspruch genommen hat, war es gekommen, nachdem das Oberlandesgericht Frankfurt durch

---

12 Kritisch etwa Ulrich Eisenberg, *Zeugenschutzprogramme und Wahrheitsermittlung im Strafprozeß*, in: Weßlau/Wohlers (Hrsg.), Festschrift für Gerhard Fezer zum 70. Geburtstag, 2008, 193; Fredrik Roggan, *Der polizeiliche Zeugenschutz in der Hauptverhandlung*, in: Goltdammer's Archiv für Strafrecht 2012, 434.

13 Hierzu Natalie von Wistinghausen, *VStGB und Strafverfahren: Beweisaufnahme und Angeklagtenrechte*, in Safferling/Kirsch (Hrsg.), Völkerstrafrechtspolitik, 2013, 199.

14 Oberlandesgericht Frankfurt am Main, Urteil vom 18.2.2014 – 5-3 StE 4/10 – 4 – 3/10.

15 Vgl. hierzu Claus Kreß, in Münchner Kommentar zum Strafgesetzbuch, 2. Aufl. 2013, § 6 VStGB, Rn. 27.

Beschluss vom 6.11.2008[16] die Auslieferung des im Jahr 1957 in Byumba / Kiyombe in Ruanda geborenen Beschuldigten, der seit 2002 in Deutschland lebte, nach Ruanda für unzulässig erklärt hatte, da dort ein faires Strafverfahren nicht gewährleistet sei. Aufgrund dieser Entscheidung wurde der Beschuldigte zunächst aus der Auslieferungshaft entlassen, in der er sich seit seiner ersten Festnahme im März 2008 befunden hatte. Die Ablehnung der Auslieferung führte allerdings zur Aufnahme von Ermittlungen in Deutschland[17], aufgrund derer der Beschuldigte am 22.12.2008 auf Basis eines Haftbefehls des Ermittlungsrichters des Bundesgerichtshofes vom 18.12.2008 erneut festgenommen wurde und sich bis zur Aufhebung dieses Haftbefehls durch Beschluss des Bundesgerichtshofes vom 14.5.2009 in Untersuchungshaft befand. Abermals festgenommen wurde der Beschuldigte dann am 26.7.2010 aufgrund eines Haftbefehls des Ermittlungsrichters des Bundesgerichtshofs vom 21.7.2010.

Der nicht vorbestrafte Angeklagte, welcher der Volksgruppe der Hutu angehört, war seit 1988 Bürgermeister der ca. 65.000 Einwohner zählenden, im Norden Ruandas gelegenen Gemeinde Muvumba. Nachdem am 1. 10. 1990 die Front Patriotique Rwandais (FPR), der mehrheitlich Tutsi angehörten, von Uganda aus Ruanda angegriffen hatte, flohen die Bürger Muvumbas in Richtung Süden und erreichten im Jahr 1993 die Gemeinde Murambi, wo sie unter der Verwaltung des Angeklagten in drei Flüchtlingslagern lebten.

Nach den Urteilsfeststellungen griffen am 11.4.1994 Soldaten, Gendarmen, Gemeindepolizisten, Angehörige der Interahamwe-Milizen sowie Bürger Murambis und Muvumbas mindestens 450 Menschen, von denen die allermeisten der Volksgruppe der Tutsi angehörten und die auf dem Gelände der Kirche des in der Gemeinde Murambi gelegenen Ortes Kiziguro Schutz vor Gewalttaten gesucht hatten, mit dem Ziel an, sie zu töten. Der Angriff sei, wie am Vortage bei einer Zusammenkunft im Beisein des Angeklagten besprochen, vom ehemaligen Bürgermeister der Gemeinde Murambi, Jean-Baptiste Gatete, und anderen Autoritätspersonen befehligt worden, zu denen auch der Angeklagte gehörte. Die Angreifer hätten mindestens etwa 400 der auf dem Kirchengelände befindlichen Menschen überwiegend mit Macheten, Lanzen, Knüppeln, Äxten, Beilen und Hacken zumeist auf sehr qualvolle und grausame Weise umgebracht. Viele der Getöteten und einige noch Lebende hätten die Angreifer in eine 350 Meter entfernte tiefe Grube geworfen; außerdem

---

16 Oberlandesgericht Frankfurt, Beschluss vom 6.11.2008 – 2 Ausl. A 175/07 = Neue Zeitschrift für Strafrecht – Rechtsprechung Report Strafrecht 2009, 82.
17 Vgl. Gerhard Werle und Boris Burghardt, *Der Völkermord in Ruanda und die deutsche Strafjustiz*, in: Zeitschrift für Internationale Strafrechtsdogmatik, 2014, 46 (47).

vergewaltigten sie Tutsi-Frauen und -Mädchen. Höchstens 60 Personen überlebten nach den Feststellungen des Oberlandesgerichts das Massaker teilweise deshalb, weil sie in die Grube sprangen und von dort nach etwa einer Woche befreit wurden.

Der Angeklagte habe sich nach Auffassung des Oberlandesgerichts der Beihilfe zum Völkermord schuldig gemacht, da er sowohl dem „starken Mann" Jean-Baptiste Gatete, der aufgrund der bestehenden Hierarchie Tatherrschaft gehabt habe und der mit Blick auf den ihm zur Verfügung stehenden Machtapparat trotz der voll deliktisch handelnden unmittelbaren Täter als „Täter hinter dem Täter" anzusehen sei, als auch den übrigen Angreifern Hilfe geleistet habe. Er habe um die näheren Tatumstände und die Motivation Gatetes und der übrigen Angreifer gewusst, welche mit dem Ziel handelten, jedenfalls die in Ruanda lebenden Tutsi auszurotten. Dagegen habe der Angeklagte selbst nicht in der Absicht gehandelt, die Gruppe der Tutsi ganz oder teilweise zu zerstören. Vielmehr habe er gegenüber den Tutsi eine ambivalente Haltung eingenommen: Einerseits sei ihm die Verfolgung und Vernichtung dieser Gruppe kein besonderes Anliegen gewesen und er sei auch am Wohlergehen derjenigen Bürger Muvumbas interessiert gewesen, die Tutsi waren. Andererseits habe er aber auch Reden gehalten, in denen er die offizielle gegen die Tutsi gerichtete Propaganda verkündete, welche er auch in die Tat umzusetzen bereit gewesen sei, wenn es ihm aufgrund der jeweiligen Situation opportun erschien, um seiner Stellung als Funktionsträger des Regimes zu genügen und diese zu erhalten. Konkret hat das Oberlandesgericht festgestellt:

> Die Verfolgung und Vernichtung der Volksgruppe der Tutsi war dem Angeklagten selbst kein besonderes eigenes Anliegen, er war vielmehr – auch wegen der Erfahrungen während seines Studiums in Deutschland – in dem Sinne fortschrittlich eingestellt, dass er auch am Wohlergehen derjenigen der ihm unterstehenden Bürger Muvumbas interessiert war, die Tutsi waren. Da er aber auch seine Stellung als Bürgermeister innehalten und dieses Amt zur Zufriedenheit der ihm übergeordneten Personen ausüben wollte und in diesem Sinne obrigkeitsergeben war, musste er als dem MRND angehörender, das Regime repräsentierender Bürgermeister auch die staatliche Doktrin, der zufolge die Tutsi Staatsfeinde waren, die sowohl körperlich als auch als soziale Gruppe vernichtet werden müssen, jedenfalls insoweit vertreten, dass er bei der Obrigkeit – insbesondere bei dem die auf die körperliche und soziale Vernichtung der Volksgruppe der Tutsi als solcher gerichtete Propaganda extrem vertretenden Gatete keinen Anstoß erregte.[18]

---

18 Oberlandesgericht Frankfurt, Urteil vom 29.12.2015 – 4-3 StE 4/10 – 1/15, I.B.3.

Ein Schuldspruch wegen einer durch die zur Verurteilung gelangten Tat möglicherweise verwirklichten tateinheitlichen Beihilfe zum Mord (§§ 211, 27 StGB) bzw. der Beihilfe zum Totschlag (§§ 212, 27 StGB) musste unterbleiben, da der Senat die Verfolgung mit Beschluss vom 14.12.2011 gemäß § 154a StPO mit Zustimmung des Generalbundesanwalts auf die Strafbarkeit gemäß § 220a Abs. 1 StGB aF beschränkt hatte.[19] Ebenfalls durch Beschluss vom 14.12.2011 hat das Oberlandesgericht Frankfurt das Verfahren auf Antrag des Generalbundesanwalts gemäß § 154 StPO im Hinblick auf die zur Verurteilung gelangte Tat vorläufig eingestellt, soweit dem Angeklagten mit der unverändert zur Hauptverhandlung zugelassenen Anklage vom 29.7.2010 weitere Taten – darunter die Beteiligung an zwei weiteren Massakern, die am 13.4.1994 in der Kirche von Kabarondo und am 15.4.1994 im Economat von Kibungo stattgefunden haben sollen – vorgeworfen worden waren.

Das Urteil des Bundesgerichtshofs vom 21.5.2015

Auf die Revisionen des Generalbundesanwalts und der Nebenkläger hob der BGH das Urteil des Oberlandesgerichts unter Aufrechterhaltung der Feststellungen zum objektiven Tatgeschehen auf.[20] Nach Auffassung des mit der Sache befassten 3. Strafsenats belegten die getroffenen Feststellungen entgegen der Ansicht des Oberlandesgerichts die Voraussetzungen des objektiven Tatbestands eines mittäterschaftlich vom Angeklagten begangenen Völkermordes (§ 25 Abs. 2, § 220a Abs. 1 Nr. 1 StGB aF).

An einer Umstellung des Schuldspruchs auf täterschaftlich begangenen Völkermord und der Verhängung einer lebenslangen Freiheitsstrafe sah sich der Senat allerdings gehindert, da den Urteilsgründen die nach § 220a Abs. 1 StGB aF erforderliche Völkermordabsicht nicht positiv zu entnehmen sei. Gleichwohl beanstandete der BGH die der Feststellung des OLG Frankfurt, der Angeklagte habe nicht in Völkermordabsicht gehandelt, zugrunde liegende Beweiswürdigung auch mit Blick auf den insoweit im Revisionsverfahren geltenden eingeschränkten Prüfungsmaßstab als rechtsfehlerhaft.

So habe das Oberlandesgericht im Zusammenhang mit dem ambivalenten Verhalten des Angeklagten gegenüber den Tutsi festgestellt, der Angeklagte habe Reden gehalten, in denen er die offizielle gegen die Volksgruppe der Tutsi gerichtete Propaganda verkündete, welche er auch in die Tat umzusetzen bereit gewesen sei, wenn es ihm aufgrund der jeweiligen Situation opportun

---

19 Eine entsprechende Beschränkung mit Zustimmung nunmehr auch der Nebenkläger wiederholte der Bundesgerichtshof durch Beschluss vom 21.5.2015.
20 Bundesgerichtshof, Urteil vom 21.5.2015 – 3 StR 575/14.

erschienen sei, um seiner Stellung als Funktionsträger des Regimes zu genügen und diese zu erhalten. Diese ausdrückliche Feststellung, so der 3. Strafsenat, hätte Anlass gegeben zu erwägen, ob die Zerstörung zumindest eines Teils der Volksgruppe der Tutsi sich für den Angeklagten als notwendiges Mittel für einen dahinter liegenden weiteren Zweck – die Erhaltung seiner Stellung im staatlichen System Ruandas – darstellte. Denn es genüge, wenn die ganze oder teilweise Zerstörung der Gruppe das Zwischenziel des Täters bilde; sie müsse ebenso wie bei den sonstigen Delikten mit einer durch eine besondere Absicht geprägten überschießenden Innentendenz nicht Triebfeder bzw. Endziel, Beweggrund oder Motiv des Täters sein.

Während die Überlegungen des 3. Senats zur Mittäterschaft in den Reaktionen auf die Entscheidung Zustimmung gefunden haben, sind die Ausführungen zur Völkermordabsicht zu Recht überwiegend kritisch aufgenommen worden.[21] Denn das von der Entscheidung in Anspruch genommene Verständnis des Absichtserfordernisses missachtet eine wichtige Differenzierung im Hinblick auf Zwischenziele und Nebenfolgen, die auf eine Entscheidung des Bundesgerichtshofes aus dem Jahr 1961[22] zurückgeht und auch von dem vom 3. Strafsenat zum Nachweis einer ständigen Rechtsprechung angeführten Urteil vom 11. 12. 2014[23] nicht in Frage gestellt wird.

Zugrunde lag der Entscheidung aus dem Jahr 1961 ein wenig aufsehenerregender Fall, der im Jahr 2017 eher Schmunzeln auslösen dürfte als die Vermutung einer Befassung durch den Bundesgerichtshof. Der Angeklagte in dem dort entschiedenen Fall benutzte regelmäßig den Zug von seinem Wohnort Bochum nach Dortmund, um beim dortigen Finanzamt Süd als Anwärter für den gehobenen Finanzdienst an einem dort wöchentlich einmal stattfindenden Kurs teilzunehmen. Als er am Tattag kurz vor Abfahrt des Zuges in Bochum die Bahnsperre passieren wollte, konnte er allerdings seine zu Beginn des Monats gelöste Mehrfachfahrkarte nicht finden und löste, um die Abfahrt des Zuges nicht zu verpassen, eine Bahnsteigkarte, die ihm das Besteigen des Zuges ermöglichte. Nachdem der Angeklagte auch während der Fahrt seine Mehrfachkarte nicht finden konnte und auch nicht genügend Geld bei sich

---

21 Vgl. Kai Ambos und Christopher Penkuhn, *Beteiligung am Genozid in Ruanda und Zerstörungsabsicht*, in Strafverteidiger 2016, 760; Lars Berster, Entscheidungsanmerkung zu BGH, Urteil vom 21.5.2015 – 3 StR 575/14, in Zeitschrift für Internationale Strafrechtsdogmatik 2016, 72; Christoph Safferling und Johanna Grzywotz, *Die Völkermordabsicht nach Karlsruher Meinung*, in Juristische Rundschau 2016, 186.

22 Bundesgerichtshof, Beschluss vom 23.2.1961 – 4 StR 7/61 = Entscheidungen des Bundesgerichtshofes in Strafsachen, 16. Band, 1.

23 Bundesgerichtshof, Urteil vom 11. 12. 2014 – 3 StR 265/14, Rn. 66 = Entscheidungen des Bundesgerichtshofes in Strafsachen, 60. Band, 94.

hatte, eine Fahrkarte nachzulösen, entschloss er sich, die Ausgangssperre in Dortmund ohne Fahrausweis zu passieren. Von einer Meldung wollte er gleichwohl absehen, da er fürchtete, sonst infolge der Besprechung und Regelung seines Falles zu viel Zeit zu verlieren und den Kursbeginn zu versäumen. Der Angeklagte fiel jedoch dem Bahnbediensteten an der Sperre am Bahnhof in Dortmund auf, der ihn zurückrief und an den Aufsichtsbeamten verwies. Während sowohl das Amts- als auch das Landgericht Bochum den Angeklagten wegen Betruges verurteilten, da dieser in der Absicht gehandelt habe, sich rechtswidrig um den Fahrpreis (1,50 DM) zu bereichern, ging das Oberlandesgericht Hamm davon aus, dass die Feststellungen die Annahme einer Bereicherungsabsicht nicht rechtfertigten. An einer entsprechenden Entscheidung sah es sich jedoch durch Entscheidungen der Oberlandesgerichte Braunschweig und Oldenburg gehindert und legte dem Bundesgerichtshof die Frage vor, ob die Bereicherungsabsicht beim Betrug zwar nicht das alleinige und ausschließliche Handlungsmotiv, aber jedenfalls als „nächstes und unmittelbares Ziel maßgebend für die Willensbestimmung des Täters gewesen sein müsse", wenn gegen ihn der begründete Vorwurf erhoben werden solle, er habe in der in § 263 StGB vorausgesetzten Absicht gehandelt.

Zwar folgte der 4. Strafsenat dem vorlegenden Oberlandesgericht Hamm nicht und entschied, dass auch Zwischenerfolge vom zielgerichteten Streben des Täters umfasst sein könnten. Doch gelte dies nur, wenn der Vermögensvorteil erwünscht sei, nicht aber, wenn der Täter den Bereicherungserfolg als peinliche oder lästige Folge seines Handelns, das auf ein anderes Ziel oder mehrere andere Ziele gerichtet ist, nur hinnehme, weil er glaube, sonst sein Ziel zu verfehlen. In ähnlicher Weise hat der 3. Strafsenat im Jahr 1962 entschieden, dass es für die Annahme einer Untergrabungsabsicht im Sinne des damaligen § 91 StGB (Zersetzung) nicht genüge, wenn der Täter den Taterfolg – die pflichtgemäße Dienstbereitschaft etwa eines Angehörigen der Bundeswehr zu untergraben – zwar wolle, diesem aber gleichgültig oder sogar ablehnend gegenüberstehe.[24] Sowohl auf die Entscheidung des 4. Strafsenats aus dem Jahr 1961 als auch auf seine eigene Entscheidung vom 28.11.1962 nahm der 3. Strafsenat Bezug, als er im Jahr 1963 entschied, dass nicht in verfassungsfeindlicher Absicht im Sinne der Delikte des Staatsgefährdungsrechts handele, wer dem Erfolg des eigenen Handelns gleichgültig oder ablehnend gegenüberstehe.[25] In gleicher Weise auf die Billigung des Zwischenzieles abgestellt hat auch noch

---

24   Bundesgerichtshof, Urteil vom 28.11.1962 – 3 StR 39/62 = Entscheidungen des Bundesgerichtshofes in Strafsachen, 18. Band, 151 (155).
25   Bundesgerichtshof, Urteil vom 6.2.1963 – 3 StR 58/62 = Entscheidungen des Bundesgerichtshofes in Strafsachen, 18. Band, 246 (251).

der 5. Strafsenat in einer Entscheidung aus dem Jahr 2009, in der er ausführte, dass es für die Annahme einer Bereicherungsabsicht genüge, wenn es dem Täuschenden auf den Vermögensvorteil als sichere und „erwünschte Folge" seines Handelns ankomme.[26]

Die Aufgabe der in der bisherigen Rechtsprechung beachteten Differenzierung im Hinblick auf Zwischenziele und Nebenfolgen durch den 3. Strafsenat vermag schon deswegen nicht zu überzeugen, weil sie das kognitive mit dem voluntativen Absichtselement vermengt, indem sie von der Kenntnis der Nebenfolge auf das „Darauf-Ankommen" dieses Erfolges schließt, und damit dem Phänomen der Absicht nicht gerecht wird.[27] Eine solche Gleichsetzung ist allenfalls dann möglich, wenn der Täter den notwendigen Zwischenerfolg auch anstrebt, sich also wünscht. Soweit der Zwischenerfolg dem Täter aber explizit unerwünscht ist, handelt er – worauf Ambos und Penkuhn in ihrer Anmerkung zu Recht hinweisen – nicht „absichtlich".[28]

Entscheidungserheblich war die unterlassene Differenzierung, da das oberlandesgerichtliche Urteil die Tötung der Tutsi zwar aus der Sicht des Angeklagten als notwendig beurteilt, aber keine Feststellungen zur voluntativen Seite getroffen und insbesondere nicht festgestellt hat, ob dieser Zwischenerfolg dem Angeklagten erwünscht oder unerwünscht war. Nach den Feststellungen des oberlandesgerichtlichen Urteils lag dies eher fern.

Ganz entscheidend gegen die Rechtsauffassung des 3. Strafsenates, die Annahme einer Völkermordabsicht sei schon im Hinblick auf ein vom Täter unerwünschtes Zwischenziel gerechtfertigt, spricht nicht zuletzt aber vor allem die hierdurch bewirkte Auflösung des Unrechtskerns des Völkermordtatbestandes[29]. Denn auch ein nur flüchtiger Blick auf die eher dürftigen Voraussetzungen des objektiven Tatbestandes des Völkermordes zeigt, dass das besondere Unrecht, das dem Tatbestand seine internationale Dimension verleiht[30] und zu seiner Charakterisierung als „crime of all crimes"[31] geführt hat, im subjektiven Tatbestand und dort im zusätzlichen Erfordernis einer besonderen Völkermordabsicht aufgehoben ist. Denn nur die besondere Absicht, eine nationale,

---

26 Bundesgerichtshof, Beschluss vom 9.6.2009 – 5 StR 394/08 = Neue Zeitschrift für Strafrecht 2009, 506 (508).
27 Vgl. Dirk von Selle, *Absicht und intentionaler Gehalt der Handlung*, in Juristische Rundschau 1999, 309 (310).
28 Kai Ambos und Christopher Penkuhn, *Beteiligung am Genozid in Ruanda und Zerstörungsabsicht*, in Strafverteidiger 2016, 760 (764).
29 So auch Christoph Safferling und Johanna Grzywotz, *Die Völkermordabsicht nach Karlsruher Meinung*, in Juristische Rundschau 2016, 186 (188).
30 Gerhard Werle, Völkerstrafrecht, 4. Aufl. 2016, Rn. 756.
31 Vgl. Christoph Safferling, Internationales Strafrecht, 2011, 155 (mwN).

rassische, religiöse oder ethnische Gruppe als solche ganz oder teilweise zu zerstören, charakterisiert das besondere Unrecht des Völkermordes und unterscheidet dieses etwa vom Unrecht eines Mordes aus niedrigen Beweggründen. Nur folgerichtig erscheint es daher, das Erfordernis einer besonderen Absicht im deutschen Wortlaut der Vorschrift[32] ernst zu nehmen und in Einklang mit der hergebrachten Dogmatik zu fordern, dass es dem Täter im Sinne eines zielgerichteten Wollens auf die Zerstörung einer geschützten (Teil-)Gruppe ankommen muss. Nicht ausreichend ist es dagegen, wenn – wie in der Literatur vertreten – der Täter (nur) in dem Wissen darum handelt, einen Beitrag zu einem kollektiven Angriff zu leisten, der auf die Zerstörung einer geschützten (Teil-)Gruppe gerichtet ist.[33] Prägt aber die Völkermordabsicht auf diese Weise das Unrecht des Völkermordtatbestandes, so kann es ersichtlich nicht ausreichen, wenn diese „nur" ein möglicherweise unerwünschtes Zwischenziel des Täters darstellt.[34] Die besondere Deliktsstruktur des Völkermordtatbestandes verbietet vielmehr eine Annäherung an die Absichtsdogmatik bei „gewöhnlichen" Delikten mit überschießender Innentendenz.

Dementsprechend finden sich weder in der deutschen[35], noch in der Rechtsprechung internationaler Strafgerichtshöfe zum Völkermord Belege, die zur Unterstützung der Rechtsauffassung des 3. Strafsenats herangezogen werden können, nach der die Völkermordabsicht auch im Hinblick auf ein vom Täter möglicherweise unerwünschtes Zwischenziel des Täters zu bejahen sei. So hat der 3. Strafsenat bereits in seinem Urteil vom 30.4.1999 in der Sache *Jorgic* ausdrücklich klargestellt, dass die Tathandlungen des Völkermordes ihren besonderen Unrechtsgehalt, der sie von gemeinen Tötungsverbrechen oder Körperverletzungsdelikten abhebe, erst durch die von § 220a Abs. 1 StGB vorausgesetzte Absicht erhalten.[36] Konkretisiert wird diese Absicht in späteren Entscheidungen des Bundesgerichtshofes als „erstrebter Erfolg"[37] oder

---

32 Der Wortlaut des § 6 VStGB folgt nicht nur insoweit – wie auch der Wortlaut des früheren § 220a StGB – der Regelung in Art. 2 der Völkermordkonvention vom 9.12.1948 („... committed with intent to destroy...").

33 Vgl. Claus Kreß, in Münchner Kommentar zum Strafgesetzbuch, 2. Aufl. 2013, § 6 VStGB, Rn. 79 (mwN).

34 So auch Christoph Safferling und Johanna Grzywotz, *Die Völkermordabsicht nach Karlsruher Meinung*, in Juristische Rundschau 2016, 186 (189).

35 Vgl. Jürgen Schäfer, Die Rechtsprechung des Bundesgerichtshofs zum Völkerstrafrecht, in Safferling/Kirsch (Hrsg.), Völkerstrafrechtspolitik, 2013, 237.

36 Bundesgerichtshof, Urteil vom 30.4.1999 – 3 StR 215/98 = Entscheidungen des Bundesgerichtshofes in Strafsachen, 45. Band, 64 (86).

37 Bundesgerichtshof, Urteil vom 21.2.2001 – 3 StR 372/00 = Entscheidungen des Bundesgerichtshofes in Strafsachen, 46. Band, 292.

„zielgerichtetes Wollen"[38], die damit in Einklang stehen mit Entscheidungen internationaler Strafgerichtshöfe, die die Völkermordabsicht ebenfalls im Sinne eines „zielgerichteten Wollens" versteht.[39]

Vermag nach alldem schon der pauschale Verweis auf ein Zwischenziel als Gegenstand der Völkermordabsicht im Urteil vom 21.5.2015 nicht zu überzeugen, so begegnet die Entscheidung aus einem weiteren Grund, auf den *Berster*[40] zu Recht hingewiesen hat, durchgreifenden Bedenken. Denn die Absicht des Täters eines Völkermordes muss darauf gerichtet sein, eine geschützte Gruppe ganz „oder teilweise" zu zerstören. Zwar werden insoweit sowohl in der deutschen als auch in der internationalen Rechtsprechung geographische Teilgruppen als Bezugspunkt der Völkermordabsicht anerkannt, doch muss es sich auch bei einer solchen Teilgruppe um einen erheblichen, zahlenmäßig bedeutsamen Teil der Gruppe handeln.[41] Von einer tauglichen Zerstörungsabsicht könnte man also auch im vorliegenden Fall nur ausgehen, wenn der Gruppenteil, dessen Tötung der Angeklagte zum Erreichen seines Endzieles für erforderlich gehalten hat, einen erheblichen Teil der Gesamtgruppe der Tutsi ausgemacht hätte. Dies war aber nicht der Fall. Denn selbst unter Zugrundelegung der insoweit „expansiven Tendenz"[42] der deutschen Rechtsprechung handelte es sich bei den etwa 450 Menschen, die auf dem Kirchengelände in *Kiziguro* Schutz gesucht hatten, nicht um einen erheblichen Teil der zu diesem Zeitpunkt in Ruanda lebenden Tutsi.[43]

Trotz erheblicher Bedenken im Hinblick auf die zur Teilaufhebung der Entscheidung des Oberlandesgerichts Frankfurt vom 18.2.2014 führenden Überlegungen des 3. Strafsenats lag es daher nun in den Händen eines anderen Strafsenats des Oberlandesgerichts Frankfurt, rechtsfehlerfreie Feststellungen

---

38   Bundesgerichtshof, Urteil vom 21.2.2001 – 3 StR 244/00 = Neue Juristische Wochenschrift 2001, 2732 (2733).

39   Vgl. Claus Kreß, in Münchner Kommentar zum Strafgesetzbuch, 2. Aufl. 2013, § 6 VStGB, Rn. 80 (mwNachw); Christoph Safferling und Johanna Grzywotz, *Die Völkermordabsicht nach Karlsruher Meinung*, in Juristische Rundschau 2016, 186 (189).

40   Lars Berster, Entscheidungsanmerkung zu BGH, Urteil vom 21.5.2015 – 3 StR 575/14, in Zeitschrift für Internationale Strafrechtsdogmatik 2016, 72.

41   Vgl. Claus Kreß, in Münchner Kommentar zum Strafgesetzbuch, 2. Aufl. 2013, § 6 VStGB, Rn. Rn. 77 (mwN).

42   Claus Kreß, in Münchner Kommentar zum Strafgesetzbuch, 2. Aufl. 2013, § 6 VStGB, Rn. 77.

43   So auch Lars Berster, Entscheidungsanmerkung zu BGH, Urteil vom 21.5.2015 – 3 StR 575/14, in Zeitschrift für Internationale Strafrechtsdogmatik 2016, 72 (74). Kritisch insoweit auch Christoph Safferling und Johanna Grzywotz, *Die Völkermordabsicht nach Karlsruher Meinung*, in Juristische Rundschau 2016, 190.

zum subjektiven Tatbestand zu treffen. Schon bei oberflächlicher Betrachtung wird erkennbar, dass der zur Neuverhandlung berufene Senat dieser Aufgabe nicht gerecht geworden ist.

Das Urteil des Oberlandesgerichts Frankfurt am Main vom 29.12.2015

So hat der 4. Strafsenat des OLG Frankfurt den Angeklagten am 29.12.2015 wegen Völkermordes zu einer lebenslangen Freiheitsstrafe verurteilt und die besondere Schwere der Schuld festgestellt[44], ohne eine nennenswerte Beweisaufnahme durchzuführen. Vielmehr hat der Senat sich neben der Verlesung des ersten tatrichterlichen Urteils vom 18.2.2014 auf eine Befragung des Angeklagten zu seinen persönlichen Verhältnissen beschränkt und auf eine weitergehende Beweisaufnahme, etwa durch Vernehmung von Zeugen verzichtet. Einen von der Verteidigung gestellten bedingten Beweisantrag, der sich erkennbar gegen die Annahme einer Völkermordabsicht des Angeklagten richtete, hat der Senat zurückgewiesen.

Nicht zuletzt der Umstand, dass der Angeklagte entgegen den nach der Entscheidung des Bundesgerichtshofes bindenden Feststellungen zum objektiven Tatgeschehen geltend gemacht hat, nicht am Tatort anwesend gewesen zu sein, lässt erkennen, vor welche nicht ganz einfache Aufgabe sowohl Gericht als auch Verteidigung mit der Neuverhandlung gestellt waren. Gleichwohl erstaunt es, wenn der Senat in den Gründen seiner Entscheidung den Eindruck zu erwecken versucht, dass das Schweigen des Angeklagten es notwendig gemacht habe, hinsichtlich der subjektiven Tatseite allein auf den Erklärungswert seines bindend festgestellten äußerlich erkennbaren Verhaltens abzustellen, und weitere Beweismittel insoweit offenbar nicht in Betracht kamen. So als ob Feststellungen zum subjektiven Tatbestand allein aufgrund einer Einlassung des Täters oder einer Interpretation seiner Taten möglich seien. Die entsprechende Passage im Urteil lautet wie folgt:

2. Feststellungen zur inneren Tatseite

Der Angeklagte hat die ihm vorgeworfene Tat wie schon in der Hauptverhandlung vor dem 5. Strafsenat vor dem Oberlandesgericht Frankfurt am Main im Rahmen der Hauptverhandlung vor dem erkennenden Senat in Abrede gestellt und dazu geschwiegen, wo er sich am 11. April 1994

---

44 Oberlandesgericht Frankfurt am Main, Urt. vom 29.12.2015 – 4-3 StE 4/10 – 1/15.

aufgehalten hat. Er hat sowohl in seiner – kurzen – Einlassung wie auch im letzten Wort seine Unschuld beteuert und angegeben, dass er am Tatort nicht anwesend gewesen sei. Er hat sich allgemein darauf beschränkt zu sagen, dass ihm die Worte fehlten, um zu beschreiben, welche Katastrophe über sein Land gekommen sei.

Aufgrund dessen kam es hinsichtlich der subjektiven Tatseite auf den Erklärungswert des bindend festgestellten äußerlich erkennbaren Verhaltens des Angeklagten an.

Dass dies nicht überzeugt, liegt auf der Hand. Denn selbstverständlich hätte es dem Senat freigestanden, insoweit eine ergänzende Beweisaufnahme durchzuführen und Zeugen zu vernehmen, die weitergehende Angaben zur Einstellung und dem Verhalten des Angeklagten gegenüber dem Bevölkerungsteil der Tutsi machen konnten. Genau solche hatten etwa die beiden Verteidigerinnen in ihrem Beweisantrag benannt.

Zu einer entsprechenden Beweisaufnahme hätte sich der Senat erkennbar schon deshalb gedrängt sehen müssen, weil der 5. Strafsenat aufgrund der Annahme, der Beschuldigte habe nicht als Täter, sondern nur als Gehilfe gehandelt, keinen Anlass hatte, sich der Frage des Vorliegens einer Völkermordabsicht vertieft zuzuwenden. Vor diesem Hintergrund mehr als fragwürdig erscheint daher die in den Urteilsgründen erkennbare Kunstfertigkeit des Senats, die Feststellungen im ersten tatrichterlichen Urteil vom 18.2.2014 so lange zu drehen und zu wenden, bis sie etwa den Schluss tragen,

> [A]uch vorliegend hat sich der Angeklagte mit seinem Tatbeitrag bewusst in den Dienst des von staatlicher Seite realistisch formulierten Zerstörungsziels gestellt und unter innerer Bejahung dieses Ziels gehandelt.[45]

Im ersten tatrichterlichen Urteil vom 18.2.2014, das aufgrund einer umfassenden Beweisaufnahme ergangen ist, klang das noch ganz anders.[46]

Über die Gründe für den Unwillen des Senats die – auch im Hinblick auf die Schuldschwerefeststellung – gebotene Beweisaufnahme durchzuführen, kann nur spekuliert werden. Angesichts des „kurzen Prozesses", den der 4. Strafsenat mit der Sache gemacht hatte, durfte man aber durchaus gespannt sein, wie der auf die Revision des Angeklagten erneut mit der Sache befasste Bundesgerichtshof mit dieser umgehen würde.

---

45 Oberlandesgericht Frankfurt am Main, Urteil vom 29.12.2015 – 4-3 StE 4/10 – 1/15, III.A.3.
46 Oberlandesgericht Frankfurt am Main, Urteil vom 18.2.2014 – 5-3 StE 4/10 – 4 – 3/10, I.B.3. Die entsprechende Passage ist oben im Text bei Fn. 18 wiedergegeben.

Der Beschluss des Bundesgerichtshofes vom 26.7.2016

Der erneut befasste 3. Strafsenat erachtete die Revision des Angeklagten gegen das Urteil des Oberlandesgerichts Frankfurt vom 29.12.2015 für offensichtlich unbegründet und verwarf sie im Beschlusswege.[47] Die Entscheidung enthält – wie dies bei Beschlussverwerfungen nach § 349 Abs. 2 StPO regelmäßig der Fall ist – keine weitere Begründung.

Mag dieses Ergebnis angesichts der bemerkenswerten Verfahrensweise des 4. Strafsenats des Oberlandesgerichts Frankfurt zunächst erstaunen, so erklärt es sich gleichwohl aus der besonderen Ausgestaltung des Revisionsrechts, das keine umfassende Rechtsprüfung von Amts wegen kennt. Anders als der Tatrichter, der aufgrund der in § 244 Abs. 2 StPO verankerten Amtsaufklärungspflicht dazu berufen ist, „zur Erforschung der Wahrheit die Beweisaufnahme von Amts wegen auf alle Tatsachen und Beweismittel zu erstrecken, die für die Entscheidung von Bedeutung sind", trifft den Revisionsrichter keine vergleichbare Verpflichtung zur umfassenden rechtlichen Prüfung der angefochtenen Entscheidung. Eine solche umfassende Prüfungspflicht besteht allein im Bereich der Sachrüge, während es im Hinblick auf Verfahrensrügen der Entscheidung des Revisionsführers überlassen bleibt, ob und welche Verfahrensbeanstandungen er dem Revisionsgericht zur Prüfung unterbreiten will.

Aufgrund dieser besonderen Struktur des Revisionsrechts finden in gewisser Weise Elemente des Parteiverfahrens Eingang in das deutsche Strafverfahren, das zwar keine unmittelbare Disposition der am Verfahren Beteiligten im Hinblick auf Tatsachenfeststellungen zulässt, mit der Einräumung einer Entscheidungsbefugnis im Hinblick auf Verfahrensbeanstandungen aber gleichwohl hinnimmt, dass die entsprechenden Entscheidungen der am Verfahren Beteiligten sich auch auf die Feststellungen auswirken. So kann der Revisionsführer durch eine erfolgreiche Beanstandung den „Wegfall" eines Beweismittels herbeiführen, wie er umgekehrt durch das Unterlassen einer Beanstandung eine fehlerhafte oder unzureichende Tatsachenfeststellung bestandskräftig werden lassen kann.

Letzteres ist im vorliegenden Verfahren eingetreten, da es die in der Revisionsinstanz personell veränderte Verteidigung aus Gründen, über die ebenfalls nur spekuliert werden kann, offenbar[48] unterlassen hat, die erkennbar unzureichende Sachaufklärung durch den 4. Strafsenat des Oberlandesgerichts

---

47 Bundesgerichtshof, Beschl. vom 26.7.2016 – 3 StR 160/16.
48 Da der Verwerfungsantrag des Generalbundesanwaltes vom 25.4.2016 allein Bezug auf „die mit der Sachrüge begründete Revision" nimmt, darf angenommen werden, dass keine Verfahrensrügen erhoben wurden.

Frankfurt zu rügen. Stattdessen hat sich die Revision darauf beschränkt, die Sachrüge mit einem Verstoß gegen die Bindungswirkung des § 358 Abs. 1 StPO zu begründen, den sie darin gesehen hat, dass der Bundesgerichtshof in seinem aufhebenden Urteil vom 21.5.2015 die für den neuen Tatrichter verbindliche Rechtsauffassung vertreten habe, allein auf Basis der bisherigen Urteilsfeststellungen sei eine eigene Beurteilung des subjektiven Tatbestandes nicht möglich. Tatsächlich aber hat der 3. Strafsenat lediglich entschieden, dass auf der Grundlage der Feststellungen des tatrichterlichen Urteils vom 18.2.2014 ein Durcherkennen – durch eine Berichtigung des Schuldspruchs von einer Beihilfe zu einem täterschaftlich begangenen Völkermord entsprechend § 354 Abs. 1 StPO – nicht möglich war, weil die Urteilsgründe die nach § 220a Abs. 1 StGB erforderliche Völkermordabsicht nicht positiv belegten. Kam es daher allein darauf an, welche Schlussfolgerungen aus den Feststellungen zum objektiven Tatgeschehen auf den subjektiven Tatbestand getroffen werden können, so war dies aufgrund der Aufgabenverteilung zwischen Tat- und Revisionsgericht, die eine eigenständige Beweiswürdigung durch das Revisionsgericht verbietet, notwendige Aufgabe des neuen Tatrichters.

Zusammenfassung

Die nähere Betrachtung des Verfahrens, das zur ersten Verurteilung durch deutsche Gerichte im Zusammenhang mit dem Völkermord in Ruanda geführt hat, zeigt die Besonderheiten und Beschränkungen strafrechtlicher Sachverhaltsfeststellung in eindrücklicher Weise. Denn die Verurteilung des Beschuldigten wegen täterschaftlichen Völkermordes erfolgte letztlich ohne entsprechende Beweisaufnahme.

Die in § 244 Abs. 2 StPO niedergelegte Verpflichtung des Tatrichters, zur Erforschung der Wahrheit die Beweisaufnahme von Amts wegen auf alle Tatsachen und Beweismittel zu erstrecken, die für die Entscheidung von Bedeutung sind, darf also keinesfalls als Garantie dafür missverstanden werden, dass die gerichtliche Wahrheitsermittlung den historischen Sachverhalt zutreffend erfasst. Zwar kennt das deutsche Strafverfahren im Unterschied zum adversarischen Strafverfahren des anglo-amerikanischen Rechts grundsätzlich keine unmittelbare Disposition der am Verfahren Beteiligten im Hinblick auf die Tatsachenfeststellungen, doch unterliegt auch ein vom Grundsatz der Amtsermittlung geprägtes Strafverfahren Bedenken, wenn es um die Feststellung „historischer Tatsachen" geht. Kaum besser lässt sich das ausdrücken, als mit den Worten Hannah Arendts aus Anlass des Eichmann-Prozesses:

The purpose of a trial is to render justice, and nothing else; even the noblest of ulterior purposes – <<the making of a record of the Hitler regime which would withstand the test of history>>, as Robert G. Storey, executive trial counsel at Nuremberg, formulated the supposed higher aims of the Nuremberg Trials – can only detract from the law's main business: to weigh the charges brought against the accused, to render judgment, and to mete out due punishment.[49]

---

[49] Hanna Arendt, Eichmann in Jerusalem, New York, 1964, Epilogue.

CHAPTER 11

Fundamentally Dissenting Judge Schomburg

André Klip

Abstract

This contribution will specifically focus on the Dissenting, Opinion of Judge Wolfgang Schomburg in the Krajišnik case. What are the issues that brought Schomburg to write a separate opinion? What was his approach? What does it say about his view on the law and the way procedures at international criminal tribunals ought to be conducted? How influential was this Dissenting Opinion, was he followed in later majority decisions? The contribution will be a challenging attempt to characterise and to assess the individual contribution of Judge Schomburg to the development of international criminal law.

1   Introduction

In the month that Wolfgang Schomburg turns 70, it is exactly 25 years ago that the two of us published an article together.[1] For him, it was the umpteenth publication, for me, it was the first publication in German. For him, it was one of the many issues of interest in international cooperation in criminal matters, for me, it was an essential part of my PhD research. Rereading the short article again after decades, it brings back to my memory some of the discussions we had on the text and on the positions to take. I got to know Wolfgang Schomburg as somebody who is interested in quality research only, but also dares to take a stand and does not hold back to issue qualitative statements, leaving no doubt as to what is meant and the position taken.[2] This was all several years before he was elected to become a judge at the ICTY (2001–2008). From this

---

*   André Klip is Professor of Criminal Law, Criminal Procedure and them Transnational Aspects of Criminal Law at Maastricht University. He is a member of the Royal Netherlands Academy of Arts and Sciences and a Judge at the 's-Hertogenbosch Court of Appeal.
1   Wolfgang Schomburg und André Klip, Entlastung der Rechtspflege durch weniger Auslandszeugen?, Strafverteidiger April 1993, pp. 208–212.
2   "Es ist eine grobe Irreführung" (p. 209), more or less translated with "this will drive us completely mad"; "tragen auch hier die gefundenen Lösungen den Makel der Untauglichkeit auf der Stirn" (p. 212), which means "also these solutions carry the signs of utter uselessness".

period I selected a remarkable decision: the Fundamentally Dissenting Opinion.[3] The unique character of Wolfgang Schomburg is already expressed by the title he gave to his Dissenting Opinion in the case of Krajišnik.[4] No other judge at the international criminal tribunals ever issued a *Fundamentally Dissenting Opinion*. Wolfgang Schomburg is a rather independent spirit. If he disagrees, or considers something to be unjust or simply wrong, he will make that abundantly clear. That is was he did in the case at hand, which will be analysed in more detail below. Can we, for instance, establish that the warnings of the dissenting judge were later taken seriously and that he was followed, or did the majority's view become the prevailing one? Did the trial on appeal result in "a recipe for disaster" as Judge Schomburg predicted?[5]

The decision on self-representation in the Krajišnik case must be seen in the context of the struggle of the ICTY with accused that simply do not obey the rules of the Tribunal.[6] The accused of the ICTY are of a different character

---

3 ICTY, Fundamentally Dissenting Opinion of Judge Schomburg on the Right to Self-Representation, Decision on Momčilo Krajišnik's Request to Self-Represent, on Counsel's Motions in Relation to Appointment of *Amicus Curiae*, and on the Prosecution Motion of 16 February 2007, *Prosecutor v. Krajišnik*, Case No. IT-00-39-A, A.Ch., 11 May 2007, in: Klip/ Sluiter, Annotated Leading Cases of International Criminal Tribunals XXXIV, p. 102. Commentated by Alexander Zahar as follows: "To say that one dissents 'fundamentally' from something probably has a precise meaning in German, but in English adds no more than the verbal equivalent of thumping one's fist on the table", in: Klip/ Sluiter, Annotated Leading Cases of International Criminal Tribunals XXXIV, p. 190.

4 The procedural follow up to the Fundamentally Dissenting Opinion was as follows: By Order of the President of 16 May 2007, Judge Schomburg was replaced as a judge on the Appeals Chamber in the case of Krajišnik (ICTY, Order Replacing a Judge in a Case Before the Appeals Chamber and Re-assigning a Pre-Appeal Judge, *Prosecutor v. Krajišnik*, Case No. IT-00-39-A, Pres., 16 May 2007.). The Prosecution asked for clarification from the Appeals Chamber, but the Appeals Chamber rejected the request stating it had no jurisdiction (ICTY, Order on Prosecution Request for Clarification of President's Order of 16 May 2007, *Prosecutor v. Krajišnik*, Case No. IT-00-39-A, A.Ch., 22 June 2007.). It referred the request to the President for consideration and determination. President Pocar did so on June 28th, 2007 (ICTY, Decision on Prosecution Request for Clarification of President's Order of 16 May 2007, *Prosecutor v. Krajišnik*, Case No. IT-00-39-A, Pres., 28 June 2007.). In that decision it is revealed that Judge Schomburg had issued a Declaration on May 14th, 2007 stating that he regarded "the continuation of the proceedings, as ordered in decision's disposition, without assigned counsel assisting the Appellant as not feasible. More significantly, as expressed in my opinion, the proceedings now have become unfair." As a consequence, Judge Schomburg recused himself from this case and was replaced.

5 Fundamentally Dissenting Opinion of Judge Schomburg, par. 82.

6 Philipp Ambach, Selbstvertretung im internationalen Strafprozess – Grundlagen, Kritik und ein Lösungsansatz für die prozessuale Handhabe in der Zukunft, Zeitschrift für die

than accused in ordinary criminal cases. They are strongly politically driven, verbally very well equipped, may regard the trial as a continuation of their conflict, be willing to go on a hunger strike[7] and finally may regard the Tribunal as their enemy or at least as not being impartial. The accused and the Tribunal have entirely different battles to fight and neither of them wishes to be lured into the battle of the other. This especially played out in the cases of Milošević and Šešelj and to a lesser extent in the case of Krajišnik.[8] It has resulted in various compromises by the Tribunal and individual accused in order to keep the process going. Especially, the death of Milošević, before the proceedings could be completed did have an impact. The arrangements are not the same for all cases and can be regarded as rather pragmatic approaches to find a compromise that satisfies the accused to such an extent that he more or less abides by the rules of the Tribunal, so that the show can go on and there is a reasonable chance of completing the case.

2 The Dispute in the Krajišnik Case

What was the dispute essentially about? There were basically two questions at stake in the decision. The first was whether the right to self-representation also applies on appeal. The second was whether the appointment of an *amicus curiae* may take place on request of the accused. In addition, the question arose whether the answers to the two questions are interrelated. All of this must be answered in the broader context of the right of the accused to have a fair trial as guaranteed in Article 21 of the ICTY Statute and more specifically with regard to the minimum right of self-representation in paragraph 4 (d) of the same article.

The majority decision is remarkably short and does not give any insight into the fierce debates that must have taken place behind the scenes in deliberation. The first step the Appeals Chamber takes is to acknowledge that self-representation is also a right on appeal. It held that there is no need to

---

Internationale Strafrechtsdogmatik 2009, pp. 286–305. See also Michael Bohlander, "A Fool for a Client" – Remarks on the Freedom of Choice and Assignment of Counsel at the International Criminal Tribunal for the Former Yugoslavia, 16 Criminal Law Forum 2005, pp. 159–173.

7   See in more detail Alexander Zahar, Legal Aid, Self-Representation and the Crisis at The Hague Tribunal, 19 Criminal Law Forum 2008, p. 257.

8   See also Gideon Boas, Self-Representation before the ICTY, 9 Journal of International Criminal Justice 2010, p. 54.

make a distinction between trial stage and on appeal.[9] The Appeals Chamber also stated that obstructive behaviour could give rise to a decision imposing counsel on the accused. In relation to the *amicus curiae*, the Appeals Chamber stated that there is no right to appointment of an *amicus curiae*, but that in this case it would be appropriate to appoint the accused's former counsel as such. In his rather brief Dissenting Opinion, Judge Pocar held that neither the Statute nor the RPE provided for the appointment of *amicus curiae* to act as a *de facto* counsel. The Separate Opinion of Judge Shahabuddeen and the Fundamentally Dissenting Opinion of Judge Schomburg shed more light on the issues that were at stake.

In his Separate Opinion, Judge Shahabuddeen raises the question of how fairness of the proceedings can be achieved.[10] He approaches the concept of fairness via the added impact of separate rights of the defence, such as presence of the accused, and the possibility to collect evidence and have it admitted to the proceedings. Judge Shahabuddeen acknowledges the unique character of the proceedings, and indirectly acknowledges that there are some risks, but expresses that there is no need to be worried as the system of the Tribunal provides for remedies should abuses occur.[11]

In his Fundamentally Dissenting Opinion, Judge Schomburg analyses step by step what is wrong with the majority's decision. The first issue is that it presents a false dichotomy: the right to defend oneself negates the right to be assisted by the court.[12] The second is that an *amicus curiae* is there to assist the Tribunal, not to assist the accused.[13] The third is that the Appeals Chamber wants to have it both ways:[14] self-representation of the accused and assistance

---

9   ICTY, Decision on Momčilo Krajišnik's Request to Self-Represent, on Counsel's Motions in Relation to Appointment of *Amicus Curiae*, and on the Prosecution Motion of 16 February 2007, *Prosecutor v. Krajišnik*, Case No. IT-00-39-A, A.Ch., 11 May 2007, in: Klip/ Sluiter, Annotated Leading Cases of International Criminal Tribunals XXXIV, p. 85, par. 11.

10 ICTY, Separate Opinion of Judge Shahabuddeen, Decision on Momčilo Krajišnik's Request to Self-Represent, on Counsel's Motions in Relation to Appointment of *Amicus Curiae*, and on the Prosecution Motion of 16 February 2007, *Prosecutor v. Krajišnik*, Case No. IT-00-39-A, A.Ch., 11 May 2007, in: Klip/ Sluiter, Annotated Leading Cases of International Criminal Tribunals XXXIV, p. 93, par. 3.

11 Separate Opinion of Judge Shahabuddeen, par. 33.

12 Fundamentally Dissenting Opinion of Judge Schomburg, par. 2.

13 Fundamentally Dissenting Opinion of Judge Schomburg, par. 3.

14 Fundamentally Dissenting Opinion of Judge Schomburg, par. 82. In a later decision, the Appeals Chamber boomerangs this back: "To allow an accused to self-represent and yet also to receive full legal aid funding from the Tribunal, would, as the saying goes, let him have his cake and eat it too." ICTY, Decision on Krajišnik's Request and on Prosecution

by a professional lawyer. In essence, it means that the solution Judge Schomburg would have proposed is that the accused would have been assigned counsel.

Looking at the methodology applied in the Fundamentally Dissenting Opinion, it is interesting to see that Judge Schomburg first identifies a series of unfortunate decisions of Appeals Chambers of which he did not form part.[15] He then embarks on an impressive comparative legal journey, looking at how domestic and international jurisdictions deal with self-representation in general and more specifically with self-representation in the appeal stage.[16] The picture that emerges from this is that, in principle, the right to self-representation can be limited and that further distinctions can be made on this limitation depending on the stage of the proceedings, whether it relates to the trial proceedings or the appeal proceedings. Lastly, the behaviour or conduct of the accused during the proceedings may influence such decisions.[17] An important role in building up the argumentation is foreseen for a quote from the transcripts of the hearing in which Judge Schomburg raises a specific question to the accused on whether he can represent himself in the complex appeal procedure.

Motion, *Prosecutor v. Krajišnik*, Case No. IT-00-39-A, A.Ch., 11 May 2007, in: Klip/ Sluiter, Annotated Leading Cases of International Criminal Tribunals XXXIV, p. 175, par. 41. Boas uses the term "procedural contortion", see Gideon Boas, Self-Representation before the ICTY, 9 Journal of International Criminal Justice 2010, p. 73.

15   Fundamentally Dissenting Opinion of Judge Schomburg, par. 4, especially footnotes 8 and 9. On the history of previous case law: Gideon Boas, Self-Representation before the ICTY, 9 Journal of International Criminal Justice 2010, pp. 53–83. The position of Schomburg may also be explained by the fact that in the Šešelj case he initially presided over the Trial Chamber that assigned counsel to the most disruptive accused: Vojislav Šešelj. see ICTY, Decision on Prosecution's Motion for Order Appointing Counsel to Assist Vojislav Šešelj with his Defence, *Prosecutor v. Šešelj*, Case No. IT-03-67-PT, T. Ch. II, 9 May 2003, in: Klip/ Sluiter, Annotated Leading Cases of International Criminal Tribunals XIV, p. 217. That Trial Chamber decision was subsequently reversed by the Appeals Chamber (ICTY, Decision on appeal against the Trial Chamber's decision on assignment of counsel, *Prosecutor v. Šešelj*, Case No. IT-03-67-AR73.3, A.Ch., 20 October 2006, in: Klip/ Sluiter, Annotated Leading Cases of International Criminal Tribunals XXXIII, p. 159, and Decision on appeal against the Trial Chamber's decision (No.2) on assignment of counsel, *Prosecutor v. Šešelj*, Case No. IT-03-67-AR73.4, A.Ch., 8 December 2006, in: Klip/ Sluiter, Annotated Leading Cases of International Criminal Tribunals XXXIII, p. 181. In addition, the case was reassigned from Schomburg's Trial Chamber II to Trial Chamber III by Order of the President on 3 May 2006. See in more detail Alexander Zahar, Legal Aid, Self-Representation and the Crisis at The Hague Tribunal, 19 Criminal Law Forum 2008, pp. 241–263.

16   Fundamentally Dissenting Opinion of Judge Schomburg, par. 7–63.

17   Fundamentally Dissenting Opinion of Judge Schomburg, par. 64–74.

The answer given by Krajišnik reads: "I am convinced that I can defend myself in a more professional way than the team that I currently have could do, but *I believe that the appeal procedure is specific and I would need counsel's assistance to deal with this appeals procedure.* So when I'm defending myself, *I would like to have a very experienced lawyer as a member of the Defence team.*"[18] In combination with all the complex legal instruments and the extremely large court file, Schomburg's assessment is that this is too difficult and that this affects the fairness of the proceedings. From this overview, I deduct the following main issues for debate that require further analysis: fairness of the proceedings; self-representation and the autonomy to determine defence strategy; the role of amicus curiae; and the interrelation of all of these.

3 The Concept of Fairness of the Proceedings

What is the relation between fairness of the proceedings and the choices that a defendant may make in constructing and planning his defence strategy? This is relevant because one of the building blocks of Schomburg's critique is that the Appeals Chamber gives precedence to self-representation over a fair trial.[19] Is it so, that the fairness is affected when the accused represents himself? Does fairness require that the accused must be protected against himself?[20]

For me this relates quite to an essential question. Does the right to a fair trial and the obligation of the Court to respect the fairness of the proceedings mean that the accused can be forced to adjust the way the defence is conducted?

---

18   Fundamentally Dissenting Opinion of Judge Schomburg, par. 70 (original italics).

19   Fundamentally Dissenting Opinion of Judge Schomburg, par. 73. Wolfgang Schomburg, Some Reflections on the Right to Self-representation Before International Tribunals, ERA Forum 2011, p. 195: "Before International Tribunals, dealing with extraordinary difficult cases only, assistance of a highly qualified counsel is a must". See also Wolfgang Schomburg, The Role of International Criminal Tribunals in Promoting Respect for Fair Trial Rights, 8 Northwestern Journal of International Human Rights 2009, p. 6: "The right to a public hearing has two purposes: it guarantees the protection of the defendant from secret trials, and it protects the right of the public to scrutinize the integrity of the proceedings. However, guarantees cannot be viewed in isolation. They have to be balanced against the interests of the judiciary in protecting the rights of especially vulnerable witnesses, some of whom are alleged victims of the accused."

20   Ambach supports that an objective assessment by the Chamber may lead to such a limitation. See Philipp Ambach, Selbstvertretung im internationalen Strafprozess – Grundlagen, Kritik und ein Lösungsansatz für die prozessuale Handhabe in der Zukunft, Zeitschrift für die Internationale Strafrechtsdogmatik 2009, p. 295.

In other words: does the right to represent oneself find its limits where it is objectively no longer possible to guarantee fair proceedings? The question is whether this is, as Vasiliev has put it, a choice between approaching human rights on the basis of a *fair enough threshold* in which human rights are balanced against each other or on the basis of *over-protection*.[21] The latter expresses a level of fair trial protection that is higher than applicable domestically and accepted as sufficient by the ECtHR. More specifically on self-representation, the consequence of the Appeals Chamber wishing to strengthen the right to defend oneself may be that it "has the opposite effect. Arguably, it strikes the wrong balance between the individual autonomy and the interests of justice, thereby undermining the integrity of the proceedings and creating, rather than averting, the risk of unfairness towards the accused."[22] Vasiliev explains the disadvantages of the over-protection: "Firstly, granting the accused a level of protection that is too generous, over and above sufficient and necessary, might have detrimental effects on the enjoyment of other rights. The 'over-protection' in one area might bring about 'under-protection' in the other. Given that the extent to which some rights may be exercised is subject to the need to guarantee other fundamental rights, hardly any rights are unlimited in scope. The expectation of the 'highest standard' in respect of all rights is unreasonable and a recipe for failure. The different fair trial rights presuppose the delicate balancing exercise to be performed on them to minimize any tensions. The overly lax approach to allowing the accused to represent himself in the proceedings or to granting postponements to enable him to prepare for trial might undermine his own right to be tried without undue delay. In a similar vein, the right to cross-examine witnesses is not boundless but subject to limitations recognized in Rules and in jurisprudence. Second, the 'liberal' approach of allocating over-the-top protections to one participant, e.g. the accused, is bound to trample on the legitimate interests of other actors which should form part of the paradigm of fairness."[23]

Looking at rights from the perspective of ownership, "his trial"[24] in the words of the Trial Chamber in Milošević, one might also take the view that

---

[21] Sergey V. Vasiliev, International criminal trials: A normative theory, dissertation University of Amsterdam 2014, Volume I, Chapter 2, p. 148.

[22] Sergey V. Vasiliev, International criminal trials: A normative theory, dissertation University of Amsterdam 2014, Volume I, Chapter 2, p. 149. See also Chapter 5, p. 354.

[23] Sergey V. Vasiliev, International criminal trials: A normative theory, dissertation University of Amsterdam 2014, Volume I, Chapter 2, p. 149. See also Chapter 5, p. 354.

[24] ICTY, Decision on Interlocutory Appeal of the Trial Chamber's Decision on the Assignment of Defence Counsel, *Prosecutor v. Milošević*, Case No. IT-02-54-AR73.7, A.Ch., 1 November 2004, in: Klip/ Sluiter, Annotated Leading Cases of International Criminal Tribunals XX, p. 194, par. 13.

the Tribunal has an obligation to create all the circumstances to make use of all defence rights. However, when the accused does not want those, or makes choices that are objectively against his own interests, the court should not intervene. The very fact that consecutive chambers did so very much relates to an interest of the Tribunal that is certainly not embraced by the accused: the perception of the Tribunal's legitimacy with the wider public: "To a lay observer, who will see Milosevic playing the principal courtroom role at the hearings, the difference may well be imperceptible."[25]

The Appeals Chamber does not regard the right to self-representation as absolute, it can be limited if self-representation, intentionally or unintentionally "is substantially and persistently obstructing the proper and expeditious conduct of his trial."[26] Could it be that in the Trial Chamber decision that preceded the Appeals Chamber decision, the seed has been planted that self-representation is a fairness of the proceedings issue? The Trial Chamber stated: "The right to represent oneself must therefore yield when it is necessary to ensure that the trial is fair. The primary duty of the Trial Chamber, as reflected in Article 20 of the Statute, must always be to take such steps as are necessary and available to ensure that the trial of the accused is completed fairly and expeditiously. Thus the ordinary meaning of Article 21(4)(d) of the Statute, when read in light of the object and purpose of securing for an accused his right to a defence and to a fair trial, is that an accused has a right to represent himself, but that right may be lost if the effect of its exercise is to obstruct the achievement of that object and purpose. The Trial Chamber is, therefore, entirely satisfied that, on the proper interpretation of Articles 20 and 21, it is competent, in appropriate circumstances, to insist upon an accused being represented by counsel in spite of his wish to represent himself. If the Accused refuses to appoint his own counsel, then it is open to the Trial Chamber to assign counsel to conduct the defence case."[27] Whereas in essence the proper and expeditious conduct of the trial is the norm, this causes limitations or forces amendments on how to conduct his defence. One may question whether speeding

---

25   ICTY, Decision on Interlocutory Appeal of the Trial Chamber's Decision on the Assignment of Defence Counsel, *Prosecutor v. Milošević*, Case No. IT-02-54-AR73.7, A.Ch., 1 November 2004, in: Klip/ Sluiter, Annotated Leading Cases of International Criminal Tribunals XX, p. 196, par. 20.

26   ICTY, Decision on Interlocutory Appeal of the Trial Chamber's Decision on the Assignment of Defence Counsel, *Prosecutor v. Milošević*, Case No. IT-02-54-AR73.7, A.Ch., 1 November 2004, in: Klip/ Sluiter, Annotated Leading Cases of International Criminal Tribunals XX, p. 194, par. 13.

27   ICTY, Reasons for Decision on Assignment of Defence Counsel, *Prosecutor v. Milošević*, Case No. IT-02-54-T, T.Ch. III, 22 September 2004, in: Klip/ Sluiter, Annotated Leading Cases of International Criminal Tribunals XX, p. 172, par. 34.

up proceedings has a link with the fairness of the proceedings. The latter is a concept that determines the conditions offered to the accused. If the accused makes other choices, this cannot have an impact on the fairness. The latter is a right for the accused. One may also find elements of this line of reasoning in the case law of the ICTY. In its Judgement, the Appeals Chamber held: "while a Trial Chamber is required to guarantee a fair and expeditious trial with full respect for the rights of the accused (Article 20(1) of the Statute), it is not for the Trial Chamber to dictate to a party how to conduct its case. If an accused believes that his right to effective assistance is being infringed by the conduct of his counsel, it is his responsibility to draw the Trial Chamber's attention to the problem."[28]

The accused may not be interested at all in playing the game by its rules. He wants to play a completely different game: "To that end, the accused will first and foremost be addressing the public gallery, the mass media, and the audiences back home in an attempt to turn the 'court of public opinion' in his favour. By using the trial as a platform for selfaggrandizement and for presenting himself as a martyr who is being sacrificed for a political cause, the accused will hope to win the war having lost the battle. Thus, his conviction and punishment would merely confirm the court's lack of impartiality and, paradoxically, would amount to a strategic victory over the accusers. The verdict of guilty dovetails into the conspiracy theory of political bias and the non-legal justifications for the political conduct placed on the record might weaken the historical and normative power of any legal condemnation."[29]

This is certainly not what a criminal trial was meant for and may seriously frustrate the efforts of the Tribunal to bring the trial to an end. Once the trial is over, the accused no longer has a platform. These opposing interests make it inevitable that the Tribunal becomes a party in a bilateral conflict with the accused. Whereas the accused did not ask to become a party in criminal proceedings, he will make use of the opportunities it offers once he has become an accused. He does not recognise the legitimacy of the Tribunal. The accused thus creates a new battle field and despite the fact that the Tribunal does not want it, it cannot escape the attacks, because they take place within the proceedings of the Tribunal. The Tribunal is thus forced to respond. See as an example from the Šešelj case what Trial Chamber II stated: "Article 21 of the Statute, and

---

28   ICTY, Judgement, *Prosecutor v. Krajišnik*, Case No. IT-00-39-A, A.Ch., 17 March 2009, in: Klip/ Freeland, Annotated Leading Cases of International Criminal Tribunals XLVIII, p. 222, par. 42.

29   Sergey V. Vasiliev, International criminal trials: A normative theory, dissertation University of Amsterdam 2014, Volume I, Chapter 5, p. 350.

the jurisprudence of this Tribunal and the Rwanda Tribunal, leave open the possibility of assigning counsel to an accused on a case by case basis in the interests of justice. The existence of Rule 45 Quarter of the Rwanda Tribunal's Rules of Procedure and Evidence confirms that the assignment of counsel in the interests of justice to represent the interests of an accused is considered by the Rwanda Tribunal to be in conformity with Article 20 of its Statute which has the same wording as Article 21 of this Tribunal's Statute. In reaching its decision in this case, the Trial Chamber takes the right to self-representation articulated in the Statute as a starting point, but notes that according to international and national jurisprudence, this right is not absolute. The phrase 'in the interests of justice' potentially has a broad scope. It includes the right to a fair trial, which is not only a fundamental right of the Accused, but *also a fundamental interest of the Tribunal related to its own legitimacy*. In the context of the right to a fair trial, the length of the case, its size and complexity need to be taken into account. The complex legal, evidential and procedural issues that arise in a case of this magnitude may fall outside the competence even of a legally qualified accused, especially where that accused is in detention without access to all the facilities he may need. Moreover, the Tribunal has a legitimate interest in ensuring that the trial proceeds in a timely manner without interruptions, adjournments or disruptions."[30] In other words, both the accused and the Tribunal are forced to fight a battle they do not want, for which they are unprepared.

It seems that in the end, the concern with the Tribunals on their perceived legitimacy is what drives them most. This is understandable if one realises that they do not derive their authority from a domestic political sphere.[31] Vasiliev wrote: "But 'doing justice' comes first, lest there would be nothing of it to be shown. The function of truth-finding in accordance with the principles of fairness must of course remain the cornerstone of the proceedings, instead of being reduced to a communicative message that serves to assure the public and affirms the Tribunal's credibility. The legitimacy of a trial forum as a perception is crucial for attaining the broader goals of international criminal justice, but the legitimacy as an objective fact, immeasurable as it may be, remains a core

---

30   ICTY, Decision on Prosecution's Motion for Order Appointing Counsel to Assist Vojislav Šešelj with his Defence, *Prosecutor v. Šešelj*, Case No. IT-03-67-PT, T. Ch. II, 9 May 2003, in: Klip/ Sluiter, Annotated Leading Cases of International Criminal Tribunals XIV, p. 223, par. 21–22 (italics AK).

31   Sergey Vasiliev, Between International Criminal Justice and Injustice: Theorising Legitimacy, in: Nobuo Hayashi and Cecilia M. Bailliet (eds.), The Legitimacy of International Criminal Tribunals, Cambridge University Press 2017, Chapter 3, p. 5.

requirement. The extrovert manifestations of the 'fairness' message are not a primary concern for the judges whose obligation is to guarantee a fair rather than a 'fairish' trial."[32]

4 Self-representation

What does self-presentation mean? There are no guidelines for self-representation.[33] This may explain that the ICTY followed a rather unstable policy and changed it from case to case, from accused to accused and from Trial Chamber to Appeals Chamber.[34] For Schomburg, it is clear that self-representation can be combined with counsel: "The disjunction of "self-representation or counsel" in Article 14(3)(d) of the ICCPR[35] was never meant to be understood as a dichotomy. Instead, "the right to defence ensures that the accused has an active role in the proceedings, the role of a subject rather than an object. Based on a sound interpretation, the word 'or' in Article 14(3)(d) of the ICCPR has to be replaced by the word 'and,' thus reflecting the proper approach to a holistic understanding of 'defence' forming part of the fair trial guarantee.""[36] As the appeal continues, self-representing Krajišnik requests for more funds to finance his legal assistance. The Appeals Chamber reiterates that a denial of such a request is the logical consequence of his choice to represent himself. The Appeals Chamber held: "Article 21(4) (d) gives the accused the right 'to defend himself in person or through legal assistance of his own choosing'. We have held that these two options stand in 'binary opposition'. An accused

---

[32] Sergey V. Vasiliev, International criminal trials: A normative theory, dissertation University of Amsterdam 2014, Volume I, Chapter 5, p. 358.

[33] Fundamentally Dissenting Opinion of Judge Schomburg, par. 77–78. See for an historical overview of the position of the defence, also in the first international criminal tribunals: Albin Eser, Verteidigung in der internationalen Strafgerichtsbarkeit, Eine rechtsvergleichende Analyse, in: Heinz Schöch (Hrsg.): Strafverteidigung, Revision und die gesamten Strafrechtswissenschaften: Festschrift für Gunter Widmaier zum 70. Geburtstag am 28. September 2008, Köln, Heymann 2008, pp. 147–176.

[34] Steven Kay and Gillian Higgins, The Right of Self-Representation – The Lawyers in the Eye of the Storm, International criminal Law Bureau 2010, pp. 1–21.

[35] En français: "à se défendre elle-même *ou* à avoir l'assistance d'un défenseur de son choix."

[36] Wolfgang Schomburg, The Role of International Criminal Tribunals in Promoting Respect for Fair Trial Rights, 8 Northwestern Journal of International Human Rights 2009, p. 17. This view received support from Stefan Trechsel, The Significance of International Human Rights for Criminal Procedure, 6 National Taiwan University Law Review 2011, p. 194.

who chooses to self-represent is not entitled to legal assistance."[37] It regards standby counsel or other counsel assigned to a self-represented accused as an "imposed limitation to an accused's right to self-represent."[38] It may be so that the different approaches one may find in common law and civil law relate rather to their basic origins than to differing views on the concept of fairness. Jalloh expressed this notion as follows: "The judge's authority to impose counsel upon a criminal defendant also seems to stem from the civil law's focus on truth finding over resolution seeking. The resolution seeking court must preserve respect for individual autonomy in order to guarantee confidence from the parties involved that both sides were given a fair chance to present their positions and that the winner was more convincing."[39]

Zahar stated that he does not see a clear winner in the debate. As he puts it: "The right of the accused to put his own case to the court is no weaker, and no stronger, it seems to me, than the rights of the 'state' in an adversarial proceeding to ensure that the prosecution's case is competently answered."[40] Is self-representation factually possible? Schomburg denied this quite recently: "The lawyer who represents himself has a fool as a client. (…) There is no justice without experienced defence counsel in the interests of justice."[41] Ambach states that effective defence through self-representation is not possible.[42] Boas answers this question by quoting Milošević to whom some 1.2 million pages of material were disclosed to by the Prosecutor: "What is the purpose of providing material that nobody has time to read? What occurs to me

---

37 ICTY, Decision on Krajišnik's Request and on Prosecution Motion, *Prosecutor v. Krajišnik*, Case No. IT-00-39-A, A.Ch., 11 September 2007, in: Klip/ Sluiter, Annotated Leading Cases of International Criminal Tribunals XXXIV, p. 175, par. 40.

38 ICTY, Decision on Krajišnik's Request and on Prosecution Motion, *Prosecutor v. Krajišnik*, Case No. IT-00-39-A, A.Ch., 11 September 2007, in: Klip/ Sluiter, Annotated Leading Cases of International Criminal Tribunals XXXIV, p. 175, par. 40, footnote 100. Cockayne describes standby counsel as counsel "mandated to serve as assistant, and not as as master." James Cockayne, Commentary in: Klip/ Sluiter, Annotated Leading Cases of International Criminal Tribunals XIV, p. 298.

39 Charles Chernor Jalloh, Does Living by the Sword Mean Dying by the Sword?, 117 Penn State Law Review 2012–2013, p. 727.

40 Zahar, in: Klip/ Sluiter, Annotated Leading Cases of International Criminal Tribunals XXXIV, p. 191.

41 Wolfgang Schomburg, 23 June 2017, speaking at the ICTY Legacy Dialogues Conference – Sarajevo 2017, http://www.icty.org/en/outreach/legacy-conferences/icty-legacy-dialogues-conference-2017 .

42 Ambach, p. 304.

[is that there is] … no human being able [sic] of handling such a trial."[43] Boas therefore suggests a *presumption against self-representation*.[44] However, it is unclear how much room he would still see for self-representation. The use of the word presumption implies that there could be circumstances in which self-representation would be inappropriate. However, approaching things in this manner means taking the perspective of what would be objectively good for the defence, who wishes to achieve as much as possible according to the rules of the Court in what we normally would understand as such: An accused striving for an acquittal or a more lenient penalty. There is, however another side of the coin and that is the freedom of the accused to determine his own strategy. As Franken has put it: "The freedom of each accused to choose his own line of defence, whether wise or not, collides in these cases with the concept of a proper and expeditious trial."[45]

All in all, it appears to me that the ICTY has yet not been able to clarify what exactly it means when an accused chooses to represent himself. At first, the Appeals Chamber's choice for a binary opposition seemed to give such clarity. However, this was immediately undermined by decisions to allow *amicus curiae* counsel for the accused. The ICTY was seriously divided over the issue. This is expressed by the 3-2 vote and by the inconsistent combination of recognising self-representation and assignment of counsel.

5   Amicus Curiae

What is the role of the *amicus curiae* and especially can he be a *de facto* friend of the accused?[46] For Schomburg, it is clear that the purpose of an *amicus curiae* "is to submit arguments of states or others who do not have standing at trial, but nevertheless want the judges to hear their perspective. *Amici curiae* cannot serve both a pseudo-counsel for an accused pursuant to Article 14(3)(d) of the ICCPR and as pseudo-assistants, to the bench. The conflict of interests in such circumstances is blatantly obvious."[47]

---

43   Boas, p. 78.
44   Boas, p. 82. Whereas the ICTY practices a "presumptive right to self-representation." See Rachel K. Jones, Untangling the Right to Self-Representation in the International Criminal Tribunal for the Former Yugoslavia, 43 Georgia Law Review 2008–2009, p. 1315.
45   Stijn Franken in: Klip/ Sluiter, Annotated Leading Cases of International Criminal Tribunals XXI, p. 405.
46   Fundamentally Dissenting Opinion of Judge Schomburg, par. 79–81.
47   Wolfgang Schomburg, Some Reflections on the Right to Self-representation Before International Tribunals, ERA Forum 2011, p. 192.

Just some months after the initial decision from which Schomburg fundamentally dissented the Appeals Chamber was confronted with the difficulties of having former counsel to the accused now acting as *amicus curiae*, when the latter claimed that there was ineffective assistance of counsel.[48] The Appeals Chamber stated: "Recognizing that Mr. Krajišnik had chosen to self-represent and 'must accept responsibility for the disadvantages that this choice may bring,' the Appeals Chamber did not vest *amicus curiae* with the full responsibilities that the counsel for defendants normally possess. Instead, recognizing that the role of *amicus curiae* was largely to help the Appeals Chamber to assess 'whether the interests of justice requires the Appeals Chamber to consider, *proprio motu*, issues not raised in Mr. Krajišnik's appeal or in his responses to the Prosecutions's appeal,' the Appeals Chamber limited *amicus curiae* to consulting 'the evidence at issue in the trial record' rather than 'conduct[ing] any new factual investigations.' (...) Under this reasoning, *amicus curiae*'s role would become essentially equivalent to that of a defence counsel rather than limited to helping the Appeals Chamber assess whether the Trial Judgement and other relevant rulings of the Trial Chamber are fair to Mr. Krajišnik in light of the evidence at trial and the applicable law."[49]

The ICTY has seriously contributed to the problem itself by conflating various different types of counsel (standby, duty counsel, court-assigned counsel, administrative counsel and *amicus curiae*).[50] Despite the fact that accused did allege that the trial with the assistance of any type of counsel had not been fair, all these appeals were rejected.[51] It is rather significant that Kay and Higgins, counsel with experience in many of the modalities the ICTY has invented, advised to adopt "a strict application of the decision by an accused to represent himself as an 'all or nothing' decision."[52] This seems also to be more in line with

---

48 ICTY, Decision on Motion of *Amicus Curiae* Regarding Appellate Ground of Ineffective Assistance of Counsel, *Prosecutor v. Krajišnik*, Case No. IT-00-39-A, A.Ch., 20 July 2007, in: Klip/ Sluiter, Annotated Leading Cases of International Criminal Tribunals XXXIV, p. 155.

49 ICTY, Decision on Motion of *Amicus Curiae* Regarding Appellate Ground of Ineffective Assistance of Counsel, *Prosecutor v. Krajišnik*, Case No. IT-00-39-A, A.Ch., 20 July 2007, in: Klip/ Sluiter, Annotated Leading Cases of International Criminal Tribunals XXXIV, p. 155, par. 8.

50 See Jalloh, pp. 711–715 and Jarinde Temminck Tuinstra, Commentary in: Klip/ Sluiter, Annotated Leading Cases of International Criminal Tribunals XXXIII, p. 207.

51 See for instance, ICTY, Judgement, *Prosecutor v. Krajišnik*, Case No. IT-00-39-A, A.Ch., 17 March 2009, in: Klip/ Freeland, Annotated Leading Cases of International Criminal Tribunals XLVIII, p. 203.

52 Steven Kay and Gillian Higgins, The Right of Self-Representation – The Lawyers in the Eye of the Storm, International criminal Law Bureau 2010, p. 21.

clearer steps of the Trial Chamber in Sam Hinga Norman, in which disruption and absence of the accused does not interrupt the trial.[53] Likewise, interrupting Mladić was removed from the courtroom of the ICTY.[54]

Why would international criminal tribunals be more hesitant? National courts would not bother to impose counsel in order to contribute to their legitimacy. That is there on a self-evident basis. If ever, national courts will not spend much time on motions contesting their legitimacy or jurisdiction. A national criminal court would never have been tempted to go down the road that the ICTY did, because it would not be bothered at all with the perceived legitimacy of the measures it takes to enforcement the order of the procedure prescribed by law. Whereas national courts may occasionally deal with politically motivated crimes, the international criminal tribunals were established for it. National courts are simply there as part of the system that maintains the rule of law. The *ad hoc* international criminal tribunals were established as a measure to restore and maintain peace,[55] and given a more encompassing and long term function when a subsequent UNSC Resolution noted "that the strengthening of national judicial systems is crucially important to the rule of law in general and to the implementation of the ICTY."[56] The question is whether in its desire to contribute to the legitimacy of the Tribunal and the perception thereof in the situation states concerned, it serves the purpose of making compromises with the accused. What one might win in legitimacy with some, can easily be lost at another side, the opposing faction of the underlying conflict, or the side of those who do not need to be convinced that the normative setting of the ICTY, in terms of substantive criminal law, criminal procedure and jurisdiction are fully justified. One may seriously doubt that trying to obtain a

---

53   SCSL, Ruling on the issue of non-appearance of the first accused Samuel Hinga Norman, the second accused Moinina Fofana, and the third accused, Allieu Kondewa at the trial proceedings, *Prosecutor v. Sam Hinga Norman and others*, Case No. SCSL-04-14-PT, T. Ch. I, 1 October 2004, in: Klip/ Sluiter, Annotated Leading Cases of International Criminal Tribunals XXI, p. 395, par. 23: "The Trial Chamber considers that the exercise of the right to self-representation should not become an obstacle to the achievement of a fair trial. As stated by the Trial Chamber of the ICTY in the Milosevic case, "the right to represent oneself must therefore yield when it is necessary to ensure that the trial is fair". The Trial Chamber therefore concludes that on account of the Accused's deliberate absence from Court, his right to self-representation is revoked, and in accordance with Rule 60 of the Rules, the CDF trial will be continued in the absence of the First Accused and that he will be represented by Court Appointed Counsel".

54   See transcript Mladić Trial Chamber hearing, 4 July 2011.

55   See Preamble of UNSC Resolution 827 (1993).

56   See Preamble of UNSC Resolution 1503 (2003).

perception of legitimacy in all of the constituencies is possible. Whatever the ICTY will do, it will always receive severe criticism from one side or the other.[57] What compromise will deliver the perceived legitimacy in Serbia? Will that come when Šešelj will have unlimited time and resources and means to say what he wants, whether it is related to the indictment or not? It may be, that the thought that a compromise may raise the chance of completing a trial is false. Both Milošević and Šešelj are evidence of that.

6   Concluding Remarks

Back to the beginning, where the question was raised whether it can be established that dissenting judge was later followed? What we can see is that the heydays of a conflict between the accused and the ICTY are over and that at the ICC similar issues did not emerge. This may have various causes. It could be that it was a coincidence in the sense that it was the specific type of accused standing trial simultaneously or consecutively in a rather short period. It could also be that the ICTY and other Tribunals did learn of how not to do it. Rule 45ter was inserted in the RPE ICTY (Assignment of Counsel in the Interests of Justice, adopted 4 November 2008). Since then the Trial Chamber may, if it decides that it is in the interests of justice, instruct the Registrar to assign a counsel to represent the interests of the accused. This rule became effective on 8 November 2008. Schomburg left on 17 November 2008. There can be no doubt that his views contributed strongly to the introduction of Rule 45ter RPE.

There are also signs that the international criminal tribunals have become stricter in enforcing their own rules and combatting disrespect for it. Did the Krajišnik trial on appeal result in "a recipe for disaster" as Judge Schomburg predicted? I do not think so. Not because the Appeals Chamber on appeal said that there was nothing to complain about and the right to a fair trial had not been violated. But because of the fact that, allowing self-representation and *de facto amicus curiae* did allow the case to be completed with the accused having a *de facto* counsel. So, in substance the final practice was much more closely to what Schomburg wanted.

It seems to me that it would have been possible to have the cases completed much earlier, without having violated the right to a fair trial. This relates to my understanding of the right of a fair trial and the consequences of the choices

---

57   Sergey Vasiliev, Between International Criminal Justice and Injustice: Theorising Legitimacy, in: Nobuo Hayashi and Cecilia M. Bailliet (eds.), The Legitimacy of International Criminal Tribunals, Cambridge University Press 2017, Chapter 3, p. 8.

that accused may make. The right to a fair trial with all its sub-rights, such as self-representation, is a right given to the accused to defend himself against the accusation that initiates the criminal proceedings. An accused using procedural rights for other purposes may see these possibilities curtailed.[58] That does not affect his access to a fair trial, but does limit his possibilities to fight any other battle than the criminal proceedings. A court of law is not there to tell an accused how to conduct his case. However, the right to a fair trial does not force a court to allow all kinds of special requests of which it can be said that they do not demonstrate a will to defend oneself against the accusation, but create new battlefields. A criminal trial is not the platform for freedom of speech. In the concrete case of Krajišnik that could have been achieved by accpeting self-representation and counsel at the same time.

It is through their procedures that the international criminal tribunals will achieve their legitimacy, not through their compromises. If Vasiliev is right in stating that "legitimacy is a dynamic, relative, and variable value, and is subject to constant renegotiation,"[59] legitimacy cannot be regarded as something that can be reached overnight. Legitimacy must be earned over time and a court may not become the credits of the generation that lived at the time of the conflict and in the situation state, but may be there to convince younger generations that what has been done laid the basis for a new legal order under the rule of law.

---

58   Moesenthin would allow self-representation but if it does not work consider it as an implied waiver. Michael Moesenthin, Commentary in: Klip/ Sluiter, Annotated Leading Cases of International Criminal Tribunals XX, p. 216.

59   Sergey Vasiliev, Between International Criminal Justice and Injustice: Theorising Legitimacy, in: Nobuo Hayashi and Cecilia M. Bailliet (eds.), The Legitimacy of International Criminal Tribunals, Cambridge University Press 2017, Chapter 3, p. 10.

CHAPTER 12

Combatting Terrorism without Secret Services?

Otto Lagodny

Abstract

Facing terrorist attacks all over the world and every day, not only in "certain regions", I want to argue that cooperation in criminal matters is far from being enough to prevent or combat them. In addition, police cooperation or – in general – cooperation in administrative matters will not suffice. We rather have to accept the idea that most probably only international cooperation of intelligence services provides some kind of protection. This confronts us with the task to adjust this approach to human rights standards.

1 Introduction

The cooperation of secret services is needed in order to prevent and combat acts of terrorism. The aim of my contribution is to prove this statement. Neither criminal and procedure law nor public law and police law nor private law are – *faute de mieux* – satisfying tools in this respect. My analysis will cover the Central European perspective only, more precisely the German and Austrian one. I was not aware of quite different approaches (e.g. in the U.K.) until we

---

*   Otto Lagodny (born 1958) studied law at the University of Tübingen (1982). His dissertation dealt with the legal position of the person to be extradited from the Federal Republic of Germany (1988). He was a senior research fellow at the Max-Planck-Institute for Foreign and International Criminal Law, Freiburg i. Br. (1988–1995). Together with Wolfgang Schomburg he is since 1992 co-author of a commentary on international cooperation in criminal matters covering European Union, German, Austrian and Swiss Law (5th edition 2012). After his habilitation which dealt with substantive criminal law and national basic rights (1995) and participation in a research project in Jerusalem (1994) he became a university professor at the University of Dresden (1996–1999). Since 1999 he has the Chair for Austrian and Foreign Criminal Law and Criminal Procedure and Comparative Criminal Law at the University of Salzburg. From 2001–2003 he was the Vice-Dean of the Law Faculty. The author is particularly grateful to Ms. Mag. Elisabeth Stoeger (Salzburg) for her support in the preparation of this paper.

exchanged our own manuscripts amongst the editors.[1] In Germany or Austria it is almost sacrilege even to raise such questions, whereas in the U.K. they seem to be abundantly discussed.[2]

In my opinion, this originates from German and Austrian history: one of the consequences of Nazism is the so-called "separation principle" (*"Trennungsprinzip"*).[3] Embedded in German constitutional law, this principle stipulates a very strict organizational and functional separation between the police and its organs on the one side and the secret services on the other. Having in mind the atrocities of the Gestapo, the Nazi secret service, it is necessary to handle this topic with great care in order to prevent history from repeating itself.

The reluctance to call secret service methods what they are, becomes obvious when thinking about the role of substantive criminal law and its procedures[4] in combatting terrorism.[5] As will be shown in detail, we are creating – first – more and more substantive criminal law which comes close to the criminalizing of mere thoughts or intentions instead of actions. Secondly, throughout recent years and even over decades, more and more investigation methods which have their origins in the work of the secret services have gained importance in criminal procedure, such as "electronic or other forms of surveillance and undercover operations" or "other special investigative techniques" according to, e.g. Art. 20 of the United Nations Convention of 15 November 2000 against Transnational Organized Crime (UNTOC).

---

1 My footnotes are following the Austrian or German tradition to indicate as precisely as possible the source of the reference. They do not intend to give a more detailed bundle of information around the subject.

2 See for example the many monographs and articles published by Ian Leigh and Helen Fenwick from Durham University <www.dur.ac.uk/law/staff/stafflist/?id=428resp/?id=421> accessed 22 November 2017.

3 Kay Nehm, 'Das nachrichtendienstrechtliche Trennungsgebot und die neue Sicherheitsarchitektur' (2004) Neue Juristische Wochenschrift 3289; as to Switzerland, see Mark Pieth, 'Strafverfolgung in der Dunkelkammer: Eine rechtspolitische Bestandsaufnahme', in Forum Strafverteidigung et al (eds), *Strafverteidigung und Inquisition* (NWV 2017), 9–20, 16 ff.

4 See Ingeborg Zerbes, *Spitzeln, Spähen, Spionieren. Sprengung strafprozessualer Grenzen durch geheime Zugriffe auf Kommunikation* (Verlag Österreich 2010), who delineates the development very clearly in her entire book.

5 Just to highlight at this point is a very recent and basic consideration by Ulrich Sieber, 'Der Paradigmenwechsel vom Strafrecht zum Sicherheitsrecht: Zur neuen Sicherheitsarchitektur der globalen Risikogesellschaft', in Klaus Tiedemann, Ulrich Sieber, Helmut Satzger, Christoph Burchard and Dominik Brodoswki (eds), *Die Verfassung moderner Strafrechtspflege. Erinnerung an Joachim Vogel* (Nomos 2016), 351–372. In Sieber's view, this change from criminal law to security law should serve as a model.

What made me choose the topic of this paper were my own experiences with various aspects of terrorism in everyday life: in 1994, I spent a memorable six months of research as a fellow of the Institute for Advanced Studies at the Hebrew University of Jerusalem. During this time, I realized two things: first how Israel's society has learned to exist with the possibility and presence of imminent terrorist attacks, and secondly how neighbouring states have learned to live with the reaction thereto. When living on French Hill in Jerusalem, my family and I had diverse experiences with acts of terrorism and hatred, be it traces of blood on the pavement of an everyday walk, private citizens with guns in the streets, a rocket-attack on the city which we were to go to the next day, and so on. I realized that, on my daily bus-ride to the Institute, I learned to check every new passenger as soon as they entered the bus: might he or she be dangerous? This was a normal question which vanished from habit only some time after our return to Germany. Meanwhile, I am also quite sure that we were screened by an Israeli intelligence institution in Germany before we came to Israel, even though we had nothing to do with areas sensitive to terrorism. I cannot – of course – prove this. Such experiences clearly showed me that there is no way to avoid the work of the secret services in combatting terrorism. Ignoring this issue altogether does not change anything.

Therefore, the aim of my essay is to reveal that in Germany or Austria today we *are* in need of secret services in combatting terrorism. On this basis only, we may discuss the conditions and absolute limits thereof, i.e. questions on *how* secret services work. The latter obviously is too comprehensive to be discussed in this article.[6] I simply aim to lay the foundation for new discussions on this sensitive topic.

2   The Analytical Approach via "international cooperation"

It goes without saying that the problem of terrorism cannot be challenged by a single state alone. At least more than one or even many states – if not the community of all states – have to work together, to cooperate. The field of international cooperation offers a tool for analyses that are neither too narrow nor too national-minded.

In other words, when analyzing the role of secret services in combatting terrorism it is necessary to start out open-minded. When arguing only from

---

[6] Just to mention a recent example concerning the right to have defence counsel in a terrorism context, see *Ibrahim and others v UK* App no 50541/08, 50571/08, 50573/08 and 40351/09 (ECHR [GC], 13 September 2016).

a criminal law or administrative law point of view, it is tempting to see this area of law as indispensable when combatting terrorism. Only a consideration detached from the traditional branches of law offers a clear view. To do otherwise narrows the scope of search; if we look for an object in a three-storey building, and we merely search the first two floors of said building, we narrow the scope of the search and might never find the object. The field of international cooperation is a good starting point, because we all are aware of the fact that purely national solutions are unlikely to lead to a proper result. As we are able to agree on this, we have to continue by asking: cooperation in which matters?

3 The Matters of Cooperation

To answer this pivotal question, it is necessary to look within national law to determine these different matters. This means that it is necessary to exclude in this respect solutions based only on international public law. The reason is that this field is always linked to national law. Even if the laws forming international cooperation are part of public international law, our starting point still needs to be national law and its different "matters".[7]

Usually these "matters" can be matched to three different fields of law:

– Criminal law
– Public law (including administrative law and other fields which are not purely private law, such as the law of competition or labour law)
– Private law.

This is important because international cooperation requires states to have a common understanding of what the matters concern and comprise. States have to find a common denominator, regardless of whether it is a broad or narrow one. Therefore, it does not matter if one could "place" a certain issue in this or that "matter"-basket. Numerous examples can be found. Consider the case of contraventions of road traffic law and their sanctions: in Austria this is a clear matter of only administrative law, whereas in bordering Germany this branch of law, the *"Ordnungswidrigkeitenrecht"*, is a matter of both administrative and criminal law. This brings about unexpected difficulties in international

---

[7] The term "matters" has to be understood here in a broad sense, not only, for example, in a procedural way.

cooperation.[8] The underlying explanation is a different understanding of the separation of powers.[9] Likewise, "punitive damages" are a well-established institution in U.S. private law, but from a Continental European perspective it is still under debate whether or not to apply principles of criminal law thereto.[10] However, such questions of concrete national classification will not be discussed in substance. They do not matter for my analytical purposes. It is sufficient to understand that states are making use of such categories in order to deal with enormous masses of law. This allows us to focus on issues of central interest and not to argue on those which are not relevant.

3.1 *Criminal Law*

It is beyond debate that criminal law was and is necessary to combat terrorism. However, there are important shortcomings which have to be kept in mind when arguing in favour of solutions based on criminal law. The following deliberations are not meant to abandon criminal law solutions, but to portray them and their limits in a realistic way.

3.1.1 Criminal Law without an Actor or an Action?

Cooperation in criminal matters requires first and foremost a crime. This presupposes either an act or an omission. Above all, an act or an omission requires an actor, a human being.[11] When applied to suicide bombers, this principle leads to a problem. The actor is dead. And a criminal procedure against a deceased person is not possible, at least in Germany or Austria.[12]

---

8   See Wolfgang Schomburg and Otto Lagodny, 'Internationale Rechtshilfe in Verkehrsstrafsachen – insbesondere: Das neue Überstellungsrecht und die Vollstreckungshilfe im Verhältnis zu Österreich' (1992) Deutsches Autorecht 445–448.

9   See Ewald Wiederin, 'In allen Instanzen getrennt' (2001) Österreichische Juristen-Zeitung 352; Christoph Grabenwarter and Brigitte Ohms, *Bundes-Verfassungsgesetz mit Nebenverfassungsrecht* (13th edn, Manz 2014) 184.

10 See Jens M. Schubert, 'Punitive Damages – das englische Recht als Vorbild für das deutsche Schadensrecht' (2008) Juristische Rundschau 138; Andreas Kletečka, 'Punitive damages – Der vergessene Reformpunkt?' (2008) Österreichische Juristen-Zeitung 785; Helmut Koziol, 'Punitive Damages – A European Perspective' (2008) 68 Louisiana Law Rev 741.

11 An exception which is not relevant in our context is the criminal liability of legal persons. According to the German or Austrian rules of the sanctioning of legal persons, this requires an act by natural persons which will be attributed to the legal person. See Section 3 of the Statute on Responsibility of Legal Entities (*Verbandsverantwortlichkeitsgesetz*) (AT) or Section 30 of the Administrative Offence Act (*Ordnungswidrigkeitengesetz*) (FRG).

12 See in Germany: Federal High Court (BGH), (1983) Neue Zeitschrift für Strafrecht 463, with further references; Austria: Supreme Court (OGH) RIS-Justiz RS0097073 (e.g. Case 11 Os 41/87 [OGH, 9 June 1987]).

Of course, there are aiders and abettors in the "background", i.e. those who supplied the suicide bomber with the bomb or who instructed him how to proceed. These persons might be prosecuted. But this is already a detour in fighting acts of terrorism. The main interest is not met, which is to prevent suicide bombings or attacks by a van driving into a crowd, which sadly seems to be one of the new strategies of IS, as shown in the recent past in Europe.

The consequence could be to create law which is applicable already at an earlier stage and think about "endangering actors" (*"Gefährder"*), i.e. persons who intend to commit suicide (in the future) by a bomb attack or – even without suicide – who intend to throw a bomb or drive a van into a crowd without killing themselves. One may conclude that criminal law might not necessarily require an act in the past. As the traditional "preventative measures"[13] (*"vorbeugende Maßnahmen"*) in Austria[14] show, the future dangerousness of persons suffices to "freeze" them by taking them into custody under Section 23 of the Austrian Criminal Code, where the detention of dangerous repeat offenders is possible for a maximum of ten years (in detail: Sec. 25 para. 1 Austrian Criminal Code). During this time, regular court decisions are required in order to check whether that person is still dangerous. Broadly speaking, dangerous people can be "locked away" from others. But this requires the person to have already committed an initial crime. A person cannot be characterized as dangerous in the sense of these provisions until he (or she) has committed a crime.

To declare a person dangerous although he or she never violated a law seems to be illegitimate. Who will judge and decide on the basis of which criteria whether a certain person is dangerous or not if this person has not yet committed a crime? Is it sufficient that a person has travelled to certain countries? Is it sufficient that this person speaks a "suspicious" language? That he or she looks dangerous? Is it necessary that the person had (how long and how intensively?) contact with "suspicious" people? What about living in a stable relationship and having two children or being integrated into a good neighbourhood?

This is exactly where today's deliberations start. Can we create a possibility to apprehend dangerous persons who have *not* yet committed their first crime and put these persons under arrest, take them into custody? In Germany, one

---

13   Translation of Andreas Schloenhardt and Frank Höpfel, *Strafgesetzbuch – Austrian Criminal Code* (NWV 2016) 41 and note 16 (on p. 17).

14   In Germany: "Maßregeln der Besserung und Sicherung" according to Sections 61–72 Criminal Code (Strafgesetzbuch) (FRG) (<www.gesetze-im-internet.de/englisch_stgb/> accessed 22 November 2017).

talks about a length of time between some days and indefinite imprisonment.[15] We could characterize this still as criminal law or as rather excessive police law. However, as the focus of this article is not to draw sharp distinctions, I would simply call this the "Guantanamo approach". What happens in Guantanamo is exactly the same. The only difference is that in Guantanamo people are locked up for an indefinite time without judges sitting on "their" case.

This idea is simple: why wait until the bomb has exploded? On the other hand, this would mean to give up nearly all principles and basic rights guarantees elaborated in Europe.

The suicide bombings also provoke a critical question on the effectiveness of criminal law: to what extent does criminal law have a deterrent or preventive effect at all? Research shows that the augmentation of penalties does not at all deter any people. Rather, it is the probability of being apprehended which has a decisive deterrent effect.[16] But this is especially true – I suppose – with regard to suicide bombers as they do not think about the punishment. Almost no suicide bomber will refrain from his or her plan just because the legislator has (once again) provided for a more severe punishment. It is, however, an act to calm down any populistic tendencies and to reassure people that they can feel safe. Starting from these empirical facts, it would be a logical consequence to make it more probable that a criminal would be apprehended. Thus, the more civilians are monitored, the more terroristic acts are prevented. To achieve blanket coverage, states would need to place microphones everywhere, to install cameras even in people's homes, and to make possible dangerous humans vanish without a trace. This would result in an almost perfect prevention, but it clearly cannot be the solution as we do not want to live in the world of Orwell's *1984*.

In addition, when punishing "evil persons" as such, courts would have to presume their guilt. This contradicts the presumption of innocence and the principle of *in dubio pro reo*, respectively. Therefore, it is not legitimate to convict people of a "thought-crime".

---

15   See <www.zeit.de/politik/deutschland/2017-02/terrorismus-bayern-gefaehrder-inhaftierung-ohne-begrenzung> accessed 22 November 2017. As to the problems of evidence in this respect, see also Stephan Meyer, 'Kriminalwissenschaftliche Prognoseinstrumente im Tatbestand polizeilicher Vorfeldbefugnisse' (2017) Juristenzeitung 429–439.

16   See very recently: Helmut Hirtenlehner, 'Differentielle Abschreckbarkeit – Über den Stand der modernen Abschreckungsforschung' (2017) Journal für Strafrecht 141–154; Wolfgang Joecks, 'Einleitung', in Wolfgang Joecks and Klaus Miebach (eds), *Münchener Kommentar zum Strafgesetzbuch, Band 1 §§ 1–37 StGB* (2nd edn, CH Beck 2011) margin no 67 with further references, as well as Otto Lagodny, *Strafrecht vor den Schranken der Grundrechte* (Mohr Siebeck 1996) 318–321 with further references.

With these considerations, we finally reach the limits of the *"Rechtsstaat"*[17] and of basic rights. In continuing these reflections, they would turn into discussions on *how* secret services work and *how* – e.g. – intelligence information may be introduced into criminal proceedings without colliding with central principles of criminal procedure, like the right of the accused to confrontation with someone whose identity is hidden. As already indicated, this question cannot be dealt with in this article. The reference to the term *"Rechtsstaat"* or to "basic rights" will, thus, serve in this article as a repository for all the questions which will definitively have to be discussed after the central question of my article has been answered. I deliberately make use of such an ambiguous term as these problems would immediately fill whole libraries as we have to deal with questions like those discussed by Bohlander in this book.

3.1.2 Reduction of the "conduct" Requirement as a Feature of Anti-terror Laws

If we cannot focus on the "bad guy" as such, the "endangering actor" (*"Gefährder"*) and, thus, need an act (or omission). The next step would be that we minimize at least the requirements for such an act (or omission). Indeed, in today's criminal law, there is a tendency to minimize the requirement of objective "conduct" as a basis for a crime, especially in relation to terrorist offences.[18] There is a clear trend to strict liability offences. The effects are clear: the less conduct is required, the less has to be proven. This is the philosophy of crimes concerning the mere possession of dangerous objects (e.g. drugs, weapons, etc.). The only objective element which has to be proven is the "possession". If the police apprehend a person, for example while in the possession of drugs, this suffices for the objective element of the crime of possessing drugs.[19] There is neither any effect of this possession required nor any other fact. It is an act (or an omission) which is the only basis for penalization.

Another feature of anti-terrorism criminal laws is to combine an allowed act of everyday life with a specific criminal intent or purpose. An outstanding example is the combination of travelling abroad (this part is as such allowed)

---

17 As to the (im)possibility to translate the notion of *"Rechtsstaat"* see Stephan Kirste, 'Die Rule of Law in der deutschen Rechtsstaatstheorie des 19. Jahrhunderts' (2013) 21 Jahrbuch für Recht und Ethik 23–62; Stephan Kirste, 'Philosophical Foundation of the Principle of the Legal State (Rechtsstaat) and the Rule of Law' in James R. Silkenat, James E. Hickey and Peter D. Barenboim (eds), *The Legal Doctrines of the Rule of Law and the Legal State (Rechtsstaat)* (Springer 2014), 29–44.

18 Mark Zöller, 'Der Terrorist und sein (Straf-)Recht – Wege und Irrwege der neueren Gesetzgebung zur Terrorismusbekämpfung' (2016) Goldtammer's Archiv 90–108.

19 See Art 3 Ic)i) UN Convention of 20 December 1988 against Illicit Traffic in Narcotic Drugs and Psychotropic Substances, 1582 UNTS 95.

with the intent to prepare a terrorist attack. This subjective element turns travelling into a crime, as can be seen in Art. 89a Sec. 2a of the German Criminal Code.[20] This category of crime is called a "preparatory crime" as it is defining the mere preparation of a crime a "crime".[21]

One could argue that this is as legitimate as the criminalization of the sending of a letter (which as such is neutral) which contains a bomb. But this deliberation does not grasp the core of the problem: by doing so, the legislator minimizes, step-by-step, areas of liberties. Liberties are to the human mind what bread is to the human body. Both we consume to live; both we can cut off slice by slice. As we can continue to cut another slice and another one and so on, we still hold a piece of bread in our hands or we still have liberty. But eventually all the bread is eaten or all our liberty is gone.[22]

3.1.3   Consequences for Procedural Law

The consequences of an approach that reduces the requirement of conduct can be seen on a procedural level: the more the legislator minimizes the requirement of conduct, the more he lowers the requirement of *suspicion* which is the basis for any investigation under criminal procedure. No detention, no search and seizure or any other act of investigation can be undertaken without the basis of suspicion.[23] Here the procedural consequences of changes in substantive law become visible.

Here, also, the border between criminal law/criminal procedure law on the one side and police law on the other comes into play. The more we neglect the requirement of probable cause concerning a single situation or a single person or group of persons, the more we get to the central principle of police law: the prevention of imminent danger. In German or Austrian law governing the powers of police law, it is an indispensable requirement that there is some kind of danger for economic or non-economic goods in the future.[24]

---

20 Section 89a sub-s 2a of the Criminal Code (*Strafgesetzbuch*) (FRG) (<www.gesetze-im-internet.de/englisch_stgb/> accessed 22 November 2017).

21 Helmut Fuchs, *Strafrecht Allgemeiner Teil 1, Grundlagen und Lehre von der Straftat* (9th edn, Verlag Österreich 2016), Ch 28, margin no 16.

22 Friedrich Dencker, 'Gefährlichkeitsvermutung statt Tatschuld? – Tendenzen der neuen Strafrechtsentwicklung' (1988) StV 262–266, 266.

23 See especially Mark Pieth, 'Strafverfolgung in der Dunkelkammer: Eine rechtspolitische Bestandsaufnahme', in Forum Strafverteidigung et al (eds), *Strafverteidigung und Inquisition* (NWV 2017), 9–20, 16 f.

24 Andreas Hauer and Rudolf Keplinger, *SPG – Sicherheitspolizeigesetz* (4th edn, Linde 2011), § 21, 223 ff; Theodor Thanner and Mathias Vogl, *SPG – Sicherheitspolizeigesetz* (2nd edn, NWV 2013), § 21, 196 ff.

It is important to be aware of the difference between an individual suspicion which concerns a *certain* person[25] and a general suspicion which concerns persons[26] or groups of persons or situations. A general suspicion in this sense is – roughly speaking – the basis of the work of the secret services according to the practice of the ECJ.[27] This differs significantly from the necessity of an individual suspicion as a prerequisite for action by the police according to German or Austrian law. The difference between a general and an individual suspicion marks the borderline between the law of the secret services and the law of the police. This could be summarized as follows:[28]

1   General suspicion of danger in the future:
    law of the secret services;
2   Individual suspicion of danger in the future:
    law of the police;
3   Individual suspicion of a crime having been committed in the past:
    criminal law prosecution.

It is important to stress that the work of the secret services happens before the work of either the police or the criminal law prosecution has started. Another borderline between these three types of suspicion is not really known to us. There is a grey area in which it is unclear – do we still have to deal with criminal law and procedure, or are we already arguing about police law and the procedures of the police or even about subjects of the secret services? The consequences for the individual are enormous. This is even more valid for Art. 6 para. 3 of the European Convention on Human Rights, which is not applicable to procedures governed by administrative police law. This means there is no right to defence counsel; no right to be informed of one's rights in one's own language, and so on. At this point, problems with regard to the *"Rechtsstaat"* come to light, because we would have to talk about the *"how"* of the work of the secret services and its integration into principles of criminal procedure.

3.1.4 The Remaining Importance of Criminal Law

In spite of the problems just described, we may not abandon criminal law as such when it comes to questions of terrorism. The aforementioned

---

25 This also applies to a group of persons or situations.
26 This also applies to groups of persons or situations which are not yet identified.
27 See Case C–293/11 *Digital Rights Ireland v Minister for Communications* (ECJ [Grand Chamber] 8 April 2014).
28 This does not necessarily reflect national views.

deliberations are only meant to relativize the populistic cry for "more" criminal law. In my view, criminal law serves one main purpose – forcing the natural desire of victims for retaliation[29] to use only means and methods which are acceptable from the view of the *"Rechtsstaat"*, especially from the view of basic rights. But in this paper, I simply want to underline that it is too seductive to seek solutions *only* in criminal law, because a terrorist attack also fosters such desires, particularly when it happens to a person close to oneself. I do not believe in saints who would not have any feelings of revenge when their child is the victim of a terror-attack and they have to hold that dead and bloodied body in their arms. The state and its legal order have to prevent citizens from taking revenge by installing a criminal procedure which safeguards both the suspect(s) and the victim(s). If we see the functioning of criminal law and procedure in this light, it becomes even more clear that criminal law alone is ineffective to combat terrorism.

3.2 *Public Law*

"Public law" has to be distinguished from "private law", but it contains many areas of law which are not considered private law in their entirety, such as certain areas of labour law or competition law. However, administrative law and especially police law definitively belong to public law, as the state acts in a hierarchical manner vis-à-vis its subordinates. In Germany or Austria, police law concerns the direct prevention of concrete, dangerous *situations*. One clear example would be when a public authority issues a written order which obliges the owner of a condemned house to tear it down (and bear the associated costs). This is lawful without the owner being personally responsible for the dangerous condition of the house.

This is – at least in Germany or in Austria – a very clear and simple legal situation: police law does not take the responsibility or culpability of the owner into consideration. He owns it and therefore he has to prevent dangers resulting from his property. The demolition of a house of the family of a terrorist may not be justified in this way, as the terrorist danger does not result from the house as such. The questions of criminal law are much more different because they ask for personal responsibility. It might be surprising for non-Germans or non-Austrians to learn that the questions meet when it comes to preventative measures.

---

29 See especially Stefan Trechsel, 'Die Entwicklung der Mittel und Methoden des Strafrechts' (1974) 90 Schweizerische Zeitschrift für Strafrecht 271–289.

A next step could be to demolish houses owned by families of terrorists. This is current practice in Israel.[30] To classify this as part of criminal law is problematic, because it is unclear against whom this sanction is directed. If it is police law, it is quite an excessive application. In both cases this is not covered by human rights and – for instance – the principle of *"Rechtsstaat"* or guilt; the families of suicide-bombers are held responsible for the acts of their grown-up relatives or room-mates. The "message" of such state-action is very clear: never live together with a suspect person in your house, otherwise your house will be destroyed. But such argumentation would disregard basic principles of police law: it creates no concrete danger just to live in a house and to live together with others.

3.3   Private Law

It may be surprising to mention private law with regard to terrorism. Looking more closely, however, at the anti-terror-lists of the United Nations or the European Union,[31] we realize that these instruments are "anchoring" (or having effect) in the field of private law, even though they are a matter of public administrative law. Suspected terrorists are isolated by actions such as taking away the possibility to conclude treaties; hence they can no longer make any transactions in private law. That means that buying houses or opening a simple bank account is impossible. These persons are unable to act in the legal sphere.

I do not want to argue about the meaningfulness of such lists nor do I want to challenge their being in accordance with national or international human

---

30   See Mordechai Kremnitzer and Lina Saba-Habesch, 'House Demolitions' (2015) 4 Laws 216–228; Mordechai Kremnitzer, '§ 13 Terrorism and Democracy – An Israeli Perspective', in Thomas Würtenberger, Christoph Gusy and Hans-Jürgen Lange (eds), *Innere Sicherheit im Europäischen Vergleich* (LIT 2012), 203–215; Mordechai Kremnitzer and Lina Saba-Habesch, 'Executive measures against the liberties of terrorism suspects', in Genevieve Lennon and Clive Walker (eds), *Routledge Handbook of Law and Terrorism* (Routledge 2015), 222–236.

31   For the implementation of smart sanctions of the UNO (e.g. lists of suspected terrorists) see Case T–315/01 *Kadi v Council and Commission* [2005] OJ C281/17 (CFI, 21 September 2005); Case C–402/05 P, C–415/05 P *Yassin Abdullah Kadi, Al Barakaat International Foundation v Council of the European Union, Commission of the European Communities, United Kingdom of Great Britain and Northern Ireland* [2008] OJ C285/2 (ECJ [Grand Chamber], 3 September 2008); Case T-85/09 *Kadi v Commission* [2010] OJ C317/29 (GC, 30 September 2010); also very instructive, see Frank Meyer, 'Rechtsstaat und Terroristen – Kaltstellung ohne Rechtsschutz' (2010) HRRS [Online-Publication "Höchstrichterliche Rechtsprechung zum Strafrecht"] 74–85; see also Anni Pues, 'Das Vorabentscheidungsverfahren zum EuGH in der strafrechtlichen Praxis' (2011) StrafRechtsReport 140–142.

rights. For this article, it suffices that such an approach requires that we have identified concrete individuals who have to be placed on such a list. The most probable source of such information is from the activities of the secret services.

3.4 Intelligence Services: Neither Suspicion nor Imminent Danger

So far I have not dealt with the secret services as such. This is due to the fact that it would be difficult to place them in one of the areas mentioned above. In my or a Middle-European view, they should be considered as a part of the executive branch governed by public administrative law. But this is not decisive. What makes it hard to match the secret services to either police law or criminal procedure is how these two fields are categorized. Police law on the one hand prevents future but imminent and concrete *"dangers"*. Criminal procedure, on the other hand, deals with the *"suspicion"* of a crime having been committed in the past; it requires the suspicion of a concrete crime. The law of intelligence services – as already mentioned – requires neither a concrete suspicion nor an imminent danger. The secret services act long before police law or criminal law come into play. This is the reason why this area of law offers space for combatting terrorism.

The secret services do not face the traditional thresholds of police law or criminal law procedure. This can be seen in the very recent amendment of two pieces of national legislation on the secret services in Germany and in Austria. The German law on the *"Bundesnachrichtendienst"*, the secret service for information on developments outside Germany,[32] has been changed.[33] This law regulates issues such as the international exchange of data and information on a very large scale. It also allows the *transnational* use of common databases. This is one of the closest forms of cooperation: two states use the same database. The tasks of the *"Bundesnachrichtendienst"* are very broadly defined as gathering information about foreign countries which are of security relevance (Sec. 1).[34]

---

[32] The "Verfassungsschutz" deals with developments within Germany; the "Militärische Abwehrdienst" covers both (foreign and national) areas if it is connected with the army.

[33] See in detail: Kurt Graulich, 'Reform des Gesetzes über den Bundesnachrichtensdienst. Ausland-Ausland-Fernmeldeaufklärung und internationale Datenkooperation' (2017) Kriminalpolitische Zeitschrift 43, 45–49.

[34] See Section 1 of the Federal Intelligence Service Act (*Gesetz über den Bundesnachrichtendienst*) (FRG) Federal Law Gazette (*BGBl* 1990 I, 2954, 2979; 2016 I, 3346). A general overview is given by Kurt Graulich, 'Reform des Gesetzes über den Bundesnachrichtensdienst. Ausland-Ausland-Fernmeldeaufklärung und internationale Datenkooperation' (2017) Kriminalpolitische Zeitschrift 43, 45–49.

In Austria, the term, the "Protection of the State by the Police" (*"Polizeilicher Staatsschutz"*) refers to the general secret service of Austria.[35] It has to deal with the "extended investigation of dangers" (*"erweiterte Gefahrenerforschung"*) according to Sec. 6 of this law. This means that, according to the law, e.g. to observe a group when it is likely that severe criminality will happen. The conditions for action by the secret service are as vague as they are uncertain. At any rate, they are much less precise and less strict than the law for the police and for criminal investigation.

The laws also show the necessity for special control boards as a supplement for the lack of the court's control. This seems a bit odd at first glance because control by a court is an absolute necessity and consequence in a *"Rechtsstaat"*. In Germany, this is guaranteed by Art. 19 para. 4 of the Basic Law. The European Convention on Human Rights does not go that far and only requires, according to Art. 13, "an effective remedy before a national authority". Thus, the laws on secret services provide a protection which probably does not even meet the requirements of Art. 13 of the European Convention. However, this seems to me to be some kind of a judicial "tranquilizer". In such a situation, there is no visible judge sitting as an independent person or institution in a transparent procedure, just a secret board of control, as stipulated in Sec. 16 of the above mentioned German law on the *"Bundesnachrichtendienst"*. The members of this board are high-ranking federal judges and prosecutors. Nevertheless, sessions as well as other activities are held secretly. The board of control gives a report to a parliamentary board of control every six months. This, of course, has nothing to do with a court's control in a certain procedure against the state dealing with the question: was this very procedure lawful?

Another major problem arises when it comes to the exchange of data between secret services and criminal prosecution authorities. To what extent may a prosecutor or court make use of intelligence information?[36] Such information may be the result, for example, of the secret surveillance of private

---

35   See Police State Protection Act (*Polizeiliches Staatsschutzgesetz*) (AT), Federal Law Gazette (*BGBl*) I 2016/5 (as of 4 July 2016); Farsam Salimi, 'Der polizeiliche Staatsschutz – Schutz oder Bedrohung der Freiheit?' (2017) Österreichische Juristen-Zeitung 115–121; Gregor Heißl, 'Polizeiliches Staatsschutzgesetz, Überblick und Besprechung ausgewählter Aspekte' (2016) Österreichische Juristen-Zeitung 719.

36   See Case VGW-102/013/5726/2014 (Regional Administrative Court Vienna, LVwG Wien, 23 January 2014); Alexander Tipold and Ingeborg Zerbes, in Helmut Fuchs and Eckhart Ratz (eds), *Wiener Kommentar zur Strafprozessordnung* (243th suppl, Manz 2016), § 134, margin no 59 ff and Susanne Reindl-Krauskopf, in Helmut Fuchs and Eckhart Ratz (eds), *Wiener Kommentar zur Strafprozessordnung* (243th suppl, Manz 2016), § 140, margin no 30 ff.

communication, secret videos or other secret actions. Is the use of intelligence information gathered by secret methods in a criminal procedure in accordance with human rights, e.g. Art. 6 or 8 of the European Convention on Human Rights? Without going into detail, in order to challenge such an act of prosecution, one first of all needs to know of its existence. Here it becomes decisive that the data are gathered by invisible authorities.

This brings about all the shortcomings which are not to be used in a "*Rechtsstaat*".

4   Conclusion

In sum, the secret services act in an area where there is neither a concrete and imminent danger in the *future*, nor a *concrete suspicion* of a crime which happened in the *past*. Therefore, the conditions of their work are hard to establish. The lack of thresholds makes it very difficult for courts to control their actions. As they operate in a hidden world, always *present* but never visible, they are able to vaporize possible dangers before they even become dangerous. This and the fact that they can hardly be controlled make their work itself dangerous for basic rights and civil liberties.

On the other side, the secret service per se has to be able to work in secret. And this is the dilemma: obviously, we can combat terrorism only with the help of the secret services.

Until now, we have looked only at the national level, namely those measures which are possible if only one single legal order would act. As a result of this analysis, we may conclude that there is a lot of shortcomings on all three levels of law – be it criminal, private or public law. It is quite logical that these shortcomings will not be overcome by international cooperation: we saw problems in the sphere of criminal law, i.e. the lack of prevention by augmenting the sanctions, or the impossibility to create criminal law just for "dangerous" people (= the Guantanamo-principle), in the sphere of private law, i.e. isolating people from any business transaction, and in the sphere of public law (demolition of houses; cooperation of police authorities in a federal state). None of these problems will be solved by international cooperation.

As already mentioned, the current trend is to enlarge substantive and procedural criminal law. We still call it "criminal law" although we have already reached a level of secret service standards. However, we refrain from calling them "secret service methods" because this might cast some doubt on them. In my opinion, we need to discuss them and their limits openly, instead of testing for how long we are able to continue calling them a "criminal law procedure".

Questions such as those dealt with above involve legal problems which challenge Wolfgang Schomburg's principles and values. It has been more than thirty years since Wolfgang and I have vigorously discussed and argued about issues of transnational criminal law and procedure. I have always appreciated his openness to look for unknown legal paths and to explore new ways and methods to resolve basic problems in this area ever since. It has always been an exchange of ideas in which we adopted each other's basic ideas. This turned our discussions and joint work into quite a satisfying experience. Nevertheless, we both certainly knew that there always was the possibility of a better solution. The feeling of knowing that it exists but being unable to grasp it was the driving force behind our talks and our friendship. But this time, I simply hope that this paper proposes new questions and sparks new discussions, not only with Wolfgang. As I do look forward to this, I for now propose a toast to my dear friend: *ad multos annos*!

CHAPTER 13

Judging in International Criminal Cases: Challenges, Aspirations and Duties

Howard Morrison

Abstract

There are many similarities between the tasks facing judges in international criminal and humanitarian law cases, not least the essential requirements of conducting fair trials according to the applicable law.

There are however aspects of international trial judging that raise especial difficulties and tasks.

They include the complexity of some aspects of the law, for instance joint enterprise and co-perpetration, the sheer size of the trials and amount of evidence, the intense social and political interests such cases generate, the variety and scope of the problems arising from a mix of legal and social cultures and, not least, the linguistic and interpretation challenges that arise in both written documents and oral advocacy. There are tensions between civil law and common-law procedures and priorities, different evidential cultures and, as one example, different approaches to the limitations on leading and non-leading questions in examination and cross-examination of witnesses. Witnesses come from a wide variety of cultural, linguistic and social backgrounds and the expectations of affected civil society may be far more obvious and complex than in domestic cases. All this has to be contained and dealt with in a fair, rational and coherent way, often by a panel of judges trying both fact and law but coming from very different legal cultures. How is this managed and what are the issues and problems to be solved? What mechanisms can be put into place to assist and what needs to be done differently better than the last few decades has produced?

---

* The author is Judge at the International Criminal Court. What follows are purely his own views as a fairly long-term legal practitioner and judge. They are not, and not intended to be, any reflection of any policy or view of the International Criminal Court, nor of any other judge of that court.

1 Introduction

Any criminal lawyer from a national jurisdiction would recognize the layout and procedure in any of the established international courts or tribunals without much difficulty, whether he or she came from a civil or common law tradition. The procedures of the international courts or tribunals are generally contained in court-specific rules of evidence and procedure and the fair trial safeguards reflect well-known international norms. There are many similarities between the tasks facing both lawyers and judges in international criminal and humanitarian law cases and domestic or national criminal cases, most notable of which are related to the essential requirements of conducting fair trials according to the applicable law.

There are however, and perhaps inevitably, some aspects of international trials that raise especial and case-specific difficulties and complications. Certain complex questions of law continue to be the subject of debate, in particular those related to different models of individual criminal responsibility applicable to those in most senior positions who did not themselves directly commit the crimes, for instance joint criminal enterprise and co-perpetration and command and superior responsibility. The sheer scale of the subject-matter of the trials poses a challenge as well. Modern day international criminal courts lean towards the civil law system in tending to be light on exclusionary rules of evidence and, the resulting heavy volume of evidence disclosed and relied upon creates technical information management and human resources difficulties that are rarely encountered in domestic trials. Finally, international criminal trials generate intense social and political interest and pressure that, although not entirely unknown in the domestic context, has a different dimension at the international level.

It must be acknowledged that problems are to a certain extent inevitable when practitioners from varied legal backgrounds and social cultures collaborate and interact. There can be tensions, both in culture and in practice, between civil law and common law procedures and priorities. One of the more obvious examples in this regard is the different evidential requirements of both systems. It is easy to imagine the confusion that must be caused by the different disclosure obligations that apply at the international level, especially to those practitioners who come from certain civil law countries that employ the *dossier* system, and by limitations on leading questions in the examination and cross-examination of witnesses to those practitioners who are not accustomed to framing their questions in the required manner. Given that particular legal concepts and terms may mean entirely different things in systems, practitioners of international criminal law also face particular linguistic and interpretative challenges in ensuring that written documents and oral advocacy are clearly understood and unambiguous in their references.

It cannot be forgotten that witnesses too come from a wide variety of cultural, linguistic, educational and social backgrounds. In international cases, a Judge must strive to transcend boundaries of language and culture to understand an explanation or description of events from a witness with different life experiences and different cultural ideas of normal or expected reactions or behaviours in a situation of crisis. Yet this process of understanding the account of a witness and determining whether it is credible and reliable is essential in reaching the truth of the matter at issue. At the same time, witnesses who were victims of the terrible crimes that are prosecuted at the international level have their own personal expectations of the criminal process. These expectations may be linked to the wider expectations of affected civil society at large in a way that is far more obvious and usually far more complex than in domestic cases.

All this has to be contained and dealt with in a fair, rational and coherent way, often by a panel of judges trying both fact and law but coming from different legal cultures and experiences, both from each other and from the accused and witnesses or victims.

Much has been written of the problems and challenges of achieving justice in international criminal trials and criticisms of the recent criminal tribunals and the International Criminal Court are commonplace and frequent. Yet, at times, it is necessary to take a step back and adopt a more holistic view of the system of international justice that we are striving to create and to take stock, not just of the challenges and obstacles, but also of the immense and encouraging progress that has been made over the past century in the fight against impunity. Putting our present-day problems and challenges in their full historical perspective allows us to distil essential lessons from the annals of history and to better understand how to move this painstaking but important project forward. It is a reassuring exercise, if only to remind ourselves that the problems we now face find their forebears in past experience and are by no means novel or unique to the present day.

2 Creation of International Criminal Tribunals Following the Second World War and the Dissenting Opinions of the Tokyo Tribunal

For practical purposes, it is not particularly instructive to venture further back in time than the Nuremberg and Tokyo Tribunals. Both institutions attracted much criticism internally and externally, and the judges were neither immune from nor inactive in formulating and perpetuating the critiques. Both Nuremberg and Tokyo were accused by some of exercising little more than "Victor's Justice". As a matter of practical possibility it will always be the prevailing nation or nations that can hold accused persons to account, but the manner in which they do so is important in terms of fostering acceptance of the outcome in the vanquished nations.

It should be noted, however, that during the Second World War, the Allied Forces did conduct investigations and instigate trials involving members of their own armed forces. They were usually court martial proceedings and the judges were serving officers applying military law. Nevertheless the officers who were judging were bound to comply with the internationally recognised fair trial processes, including the presumption of innocence and the standard and burden of proof. Add to that the "international" aspect of the accusations and the wider societal strictures on everyone in the midst of hostilities and it is easy to see that such trials made huge demands on the participants, not least for those who had had no formal legal training and, especially, no active judicial experience.

The creation of the international criminal tribunals at both Nuremberg and Tokyo generated mixed reactions from both lawyers and judges. One school of thought was that the crimes committed during the Second World War were so widespread and egregious that specialised legal entities were required to punish those responsible and dilute any notions of immunity or impunity, and thereby advance international law. Other lawyers and jurists took a more narrow view, based upon what were perceived to be partisan legal shortcomings, and were critical of any suggestion of retroactive charging of newly formulated international crimes or selective charging against leaders of the defeated nations only.

During the London Conference from 26 June to 2 August 1945, even the allied victors encountered difficulties in reaching an agreement as to how justice should be dispensed by these novel tribunals. As Sellars has noted:

> The Americans threatened to walk out over the question of a definition of aggression, the British fretted over the risk of German counter-charges, the French objected to plans to try crimes against peace, and the Soviets refused to countenance anything other than ad hoc charges. The debates were by turns acrimonious, meandering, portentous, repetitive and disjointed. Until the final day, none of the delegates could be sure that a tribunal would be established at all, let alone that their discussions would provide the conceptual framework for two great assizes, one in

Nuremberg, the other in Tokyo. This was history in the making, and its making was messy and unedifying.[1]

Given the size and diverse composition of the bench of the Tokyo Tribunal, it is perhaps unsurprising that similar differences of opinion were also reflected in the views of its members. Eleven Judges from France, India, the Philippines, Russia, the United States, the Netherlands, China, New Zealand, Australia, Canada and the United Kingdom were responsible for judging 28 Japanese defendants of the highest decision-making level, accused of crimes against peace, conventional war crimes and crimes against humanity.[2] Jurisdiction over crimes against peace was provided for in the International Military Tribunal for the Far East Charter, or the Tokyo Charter as it became known.[3] The majority of the bench accepted this jurisdiction uncritically, finding that they were not empowered to examine the question of whether crimes against peace were recognised under international law at the time of the commission of the offences alleged.[4]

The Dutch Judge at Tokyo, Justice Bert Röling, a respected Professor of law and a domestic criminal law judge, took a different view. He initially aired his opinion that the Tribunal was bound to determine whether the Tokyo Charter was in conformity with international law in the form of a memorandum written during the trial. This brought him into an uncomfortable state of disagreement with his Government, which held a contrary view and exerted pressure on him not to be a dissenting voice. He subsequently stated:

> My government considered the Tribunal to be bound by the provisions of the Charter, and it also considered the crime against peace a crime under existing international law. A small advisory committee of leading experts in international law was even set up in the Netherlands. They gave the advice that the crime against peace was recognized under international

---

[1] K. Sellars, *Crimes against Peace' and International Law* (Cambridge University Press, New York, 2013), p. 84.
[2] F. Hisakazu, 'The Tokyo Trial: Humanity's Justice v Victors' Justice' in Y. Tanaka, T. McCormack and G. Simpson (eds), *Beyond Victor's Justice? The Tokyo War Crimes Trial Revisited* (Martinus Nijhoff Publishers, Leiden/Boston, 2011), pp. 6–7.
[3] Special Proclamation of the Supreme Commander for the Allied Powers Establishing an International Military Tribunal for the Far East and Charter of the Tribunal, available at http://www.legal-tools.org/doc/29f6df/, p. 4.
[4] International Military Tribunal for the Far East, Majority Judgment, available at http://www.legal-tools.org/doc/28ddbd/, pp. 23–28.

law. Well, there was a kind of conflict. I was accustomed to working as an independent judge, guided only by the law, without any interference from outside. So I let it be known that I was prepared to resign, and that I was not willing to be influenced. It was really an awkward situation. I hated the thought that I might have to resign, because the reason would certainly become public knowledge. But I felt it was impossible to participate in a judgement that ran counter to my own well-considered opinion.[5]

The Dutch Government ultimately did not pursue the matter and Judge Röling proceeded to voice his own views with clarity.[6]

Justice Röling considered that, although "[v]ictorious powers may convene a Tribunal, may promulgate rules for its procedure, and may determine which acts or 'omissions' the Tribunal shall have the power to try and punish", the Tribunal itself "is called upon to decide whether those acts or 'omissions' are crimes under international law".[7] He was not persuaded by the argument that the Kellogg-Briand Pact of 1928, which condemned the waging of war and committed the signatories to peace, was evidence that aggression or crimes against peace existed as criminal concepts before the Second World War.[8] He thought it was next to impossible to define the concept of initiating or waging a war of aggression either accurately or comprehensively. He was also adamant that there should not only have been "neutral" participants in the trials, but also Japanese participants, on the basis that they could have assisted by arguing issues of Japanese government policy and cultural imperatives which would be unfamiliar to the allied jurists.

Nevertheless, Justice Röling ultimately concurred with the majority's decision (and that of his Government) and found the prosecution of crimes against peace to be in conformity with international law. He based this view on the thesis that victorious powers following a war have the right "to counteract elements constituting a threat to that newly established order, and are entitled as a means of preventing the recurrence of gravely offensive conduct, to seek and retain the custody of the pertinent persons".[9] On this question, Justice Röling

---

5 B.V.A. Röling and A. Cassese, *The Tokyo Trial and Beyond* (Marston Lindsay Ross International Ltd, Oxfordshire, 1993), p. 63.
6 *Ibid.*, pp. 61–62.
7 International Military Tribunal for the Far East, Opinion of Mr. Justice Röling, Member for the Netherlands, available at http://www.legal-tools.org/doc/fb16ff/, p. 8.
8 *Ibid.*, pp. 26–35.
9 *Ibid.*, p. 46.

arguably ceded to the political imperative to punish those responsible for the initiation and waging of the war in Asia with all the terrible consequences that it entailed. As a result, he was in favour of detaining the accused convicted of crimes against peace to protect the new order from threats to its stability, but he would not have applied the death penalty for these crimes.

In his consideration of the facts too, Justice Röling distinguished himself from his colleagues.[10] His dissenting opinion and subsequent commentaries on the subject of the Tokyo Tribunal demonstrate that he sought genuinely to understand Japanese culture and history and to place the events that led to the war in Asia in their proper national and international context. In so doing, he achieved a remarkably objective view of the events that drew Japan into the Second World War that has come to be more favourably considered with the fullness of time. In consequence of his view that the Japanese conspiracy aimed at the forceful domination of Asia came into being close to the actual outbreak of war, he was in favour of acquitting Kōki Hirota,[11] who served as Japanese Prime Minister from 1936 to 1937, and who resigned from government following a disagreement regarding the military. Hirota was ultimately the sole civilian convicted and sentenced to death by hanging by the International Military Tribunal for the Far East and duly executed.

Justice Röling's partially dissenting opinion was also notable in its sophisticated treatment of responsibility for war crimes through omission to prevent the commission of the crimes.[12] The majority had endorsed the criminal responsibility of members of a cabinet, which is collectively responsible for the care of prisoners, in circumstances where the members know that crimes are being committed and they omit or fail to ensure the prevention of such crimes in the future, but, nevertheless, choose to continue as part of the cabinet.[13] Importantly, the majority found that members of such a cabinet would be criminally responsible even if the department over which they had oversight was not concerned with the care of prisoners.[14] This, in Justice Röling's estimation, represented an overly broad conception of criminal responsibility. He opined that criminal responsibility of officials for acts that they did not order or permit should be limited to those who: (i) knew or should have known of the crimes and lacked knowledge as a result of criminal negligence; (ii) had the

---

10   Ibid., p. 62 et seq.
11   Ibid., pp. 81–84, 123–125.
12   Ibid., p. 54 et seq.
13   International Military Tribunal for the Far East, Majority Judgment, available at http://www.legal-tools.org/doc/28ddbd/, pp. 29–31.
14   Ibid., p. 31.

power to prevent the acts and failed to take all possible steps that were available in the context of his or her official position to do so; and (iii) had the duty to prevent the acts.[15] In the latter regard, Justice Röling would have required a "specific obligation, placed on government officials or military commanders, which makes them criminally responsible for 'omissions'", although he noted with prescience that international law may develop to the point of recognising a duty to prevent the acts when knowledge of and power to prevent the acts are apparent.[16]

The dissenting judgment of the Indian Judge at the Tokyo Tribunal, Justice Radhabinod Pal also demonstrated a high level of independence from the prevailing political context, albeit that it had strong political undertones against the tide of opinion of the victorious allies and was, to a certain extent, legally contradictory in its attempts to absolve the Japanese defendants of all criminal guilt. Justice Pal criticised the prosecution of the Japanese defendants for crimes against peace and crimes against humanity because, in his view, these crimes had no previous existence under international law and were created by the Tokyo Charter for the political ends of the victorious powers.[17] Regarding the charges for conventional war crimes, Justice Pal found that the evidence was "overwhelming that atrocities were perpetrated by the members of the Japanese armed forces against the civilian population of some of the territories occupied by them as also against the prisoners of war".[18] However, he found that the evidence did not establish that the defendants had ordered, authorised or permitted others to commit the acts in question and, accordingly, they could not be held criminally responsible.[19] Justice Pal viewed the alleged aggression of the Japanese forces through the lens of Western colonialism and imperialism, and concluded that "a Japanese apologist might discover precedent [...] in Western post-war as well as pre-war practice".[20] He observed:

---

15   International Military Tribunal for the Far East, Opinion of Mr. Justice Röling, Member for the Netherlands, available at http://www.legal-tools.org/doc/fb16ff/, pp. 59–60.
16   *Ibid.*, p. 60.
17   International Military Tribunal for the Far East, Judgment of The Honorable Justice Pal, Member from India (Part 1), available at http://www.legal-tools.org/doc/712ef9/, pp. 151–152.
18   International Military Tribunal for the Far East, Judgment of The Honorable Justice Pal, Member from India (Part 4), available at: http://www.legal-tools.org/doc/2a6ce2/, p. 1069.
19   *Ibid.*, pp. 1089–1090.
20   International Military Tribunal for the Far East, Judgment of The Honorable Justice Pal, Member from India (Part 2), available at http://www.legal-tools.org/doc/03dc9b/, p. 528.

It is considered probable that it might be attributed in part to an anxiety to imitate Western behaviour – an anxiety which had become an *idee fixe* in Japanese minds since the beginning of the Meiji era. "A candid Western historian" it is said, "cannot ignore this probability when he remembers how painstaking and how literal the Japanese manner of imitating Western fashions was apt to be, and when he considers that the policy of constitutional humbug was just as prominent in the colonial history of the modern Western World as it had been in the domestic history of medieval Japan."

Was it not Western Imperialism that had coined the word 'protectorate' as a euphemism for 'annexation'? And had not this constitutional fiction served its Western inventors in good stead? Was not this the method by which the Government of the French Republic had stepped into the shoes of the Sultan of Morocco, and by which the British Crown had transferred the possession of vast tracts of land in East Africa from native African to adventitious European hands? And if the ex-victors in the General War of 1914–18 should protest that, since the War, they had experienced a conviction of sin and had replaced the tarnished word 'protectorate' by the brand-new word 'mandate', would not the Japanese be able to cite American and Russian, as well as German opinion in support of the view that this latest change of name had introduced a distinction without a difference?[21] [Emphasis in original]

Justice Pal took the view that Japanese leaders had believed that they were acting in self-preservation to defend themselves from Communist expansionism as opposed to acting in aggressive and illegitimate war.[22] In my view, Justice Pal's dissent was not intended to be based upon calculated misunderstanding. Rather it was born, amongst more complex and modernist ideas of legal philosophy, of a steadfast conviction that it was dangerous to apply innovative proceedings in line with the dictates of conscience because certainty and predictability in law required a strict adherence to the letter of the law and not victor's justice cloaked in some abstracted moral application of even well-meaning humanistic conviction. Justice Pal seems to have been of the view that what might be termed "anti-colonial" justice should take precedence over peace, perhaps at any price, rather than peace taking an irreversible precedence over justice.

---

21   *Ibid.*, p. 527.
22   *Ibid.*, pp. 529–558.

Yet his views are difficult to reconcile with the realities of Pearl Harbour. Moreover, his post-war visits to Japan and well-publicised speeches suggest that his adoption of the defence arguments had been conflated with an apparent support for their wider nationalistic cause.

The Tokyo Tribunals also bore witness to the difficulties that judges from different legal systems face in being forced together to develop a procedural and evidentiary trial framework that is coherent, functional and promotes the interests of justice and fairness to the accused. The dissenting opinion of Justice Henri Bernard from France was motivated *inter alia* by a concern for the observance of the procedural rules that would guarantee due process and highlighted his discomfort with the adaptation of common law principles and rules for international proceedings that were largely dominated by the Prosecutors and Judges from the English speaking countries. It must be recognised that the latter had a linguistic advantage as the proceedings were conducted in English and Japanese. Justice Bernard, unable to understand either language, was reliant on a translator.[23]

Justice Bernard was of the view that "[e]ssential principles, violations of which would result in most civilised nations in the nullity of the entire procedure, and the right of the Tribunal to dismiss the case against the Accused, were not respected".[24] Justice Bernard took issue with the premise of the trial, which was that the violation of treaties was criminal and that the burden fell to the accused to establish their innocence.[25] He took issue too with the disclosure process and lamented the fact that the defendants "were directly indicted before the Tribunal and without being given an opportunity to endeavor to obtain and assemble elements for the defense by means of a preliminary inquest conducted equally in favour of the Prosecution as of the Defense by a magistrate independent of them both and in the course of which they would have been benefitted by the assistance of the defense counsel".[26]

---

23 M. Ho Foui Sang, 'Justice Bernard (France)' in Y. Tanaka, T. McCormack and G. Simpson (eds), *Beyond Victor's Justice? The Tokyo War Crimes Trial Revisited* (Martinus Nijhoff Publishers, Leiden/Boston, 2011), p. 96.

24 International Military Tribunal for the Far East, Dissenting Judgment of the Member from France of the International Military Tribunal for the Far East, available at http://www.legal-tools.org/doc/d1ac54/, p. 18.

25 M. Ho Foui Sang, 'Justice Bernard (France)' in Y. Tanaka, T. McCormack and G. Simpson (eds), *Beyond Victor's Justice? The Tokyo War Crimes Trial Revisited* (Martinus Nijhoff Publishers, Leiden/Boston, 2011), pp. 96–97.

26 International Military Tribunal for the Far East, Dissenting Judgment of the Member from France of the International Military Tribunal for the Far East, available at http://www.legal-tools.org/doc/d1ac54/, p. 18.

Justice Röling also struggled with the differences between the common law and civil law and admitted to having "many difficulties and misgivings" regarding the rules of admission of evidence, which, in his view, were applied inconsistently and tended to favour the Prosecution.[27] Nevertheless, Justice Röling ultimately concluded that the trial at Tokyo was fair.[28] He subsequently remarked on Justice Bernard's difficulties with the procedure adopted:

> I think he considered the Anglo-Saxon system unfair. I share his preference for the continental system, but I must confess that it only works as long as judges are impartial and so long as a country has a decent, honest government. One could argue that the Anglo-Saxon system offers fewer guarantees for the real truth in a specific case, but that in adverse political circumstances it provides better guarantees for the rights of the accused.[29]

3 Lessons for International Judges Today

It was thought by many that the Nuremberg and Tokyo Tribunals were institutions which, having completed their mandates, were unlikely to be revived anywhere or in any international format. In time, the *ad hoc* tribunals for the former Yugoslavia and Rwanda put paid to that assumption as the maturing political climate following the fall of the Berlin Wall allowed for a renewed interest in pursuing justice for the international crimes committed in those territories. The tasks of, and challenges facing, the judges for those tribunals mirrored the experiences of their predecessors, although to a certain extent the ground had been broken by those pioneers who went before. The same challenges arose at the Special Court for Sierra Leone, the Special Tribunal for Lebanon, the East Timor Tribunal, the Extraordinary Chambers in the Courts of Cambodia and, no doubt, they will arise at the newly formed Kosovo Tribunal. However, the biggest and more lasting challenges and endeavours are likely to fall to the judges of the International Criminal Court, not least because it is a permanent court with a world-wide mandate.

In approaching these challenges, the dissenting opinions of the Tokyo judgment offer valuable lessons as early portents of the problems that persist today

---

27 B.V.A. Röling and A. Cassese, *The Tokyo Trial and Beyond* (Marston Lindsay Ross International Ltd, Oxfordshire, 1993), pp. 50–54.
28 *Ibid.*, p. 54.
29 *Ibid.*, p. 52.

in international judging. For present purposes and in the interests of brevity, I will focus on and highlight two of these issues below: (i) the necessity of judicial independence in international criminal trials, and (ii) the need to develop a set of coherent procedural rules to deliver justice in the international arena that allows for the adaptation of those elements of common law and civil law procedure that will best serve the aims of achieving a fair trial in the often prejudicial context in which these trials take place.

3.1 *Judicial Independence*
The circumstances surrounding Justice Röling's dissent as described above offer a keen reminder of the difficulties inherent in separating the judicial process of determining the guilt or innocence of an individual from the broader political environment and in insulating the judiciary from the influence of their states' interests or perspectives on the international plane. The impact of post-war politics and its shaping of the law are also abundantly evident in the majority judgement and Justice Pal's dissenting judgment, which was equally, if not more, political than that of the majority. In this sense, the Tokyo Tribunal offers a salient reminder of the many ways in which international judging leads judges into areas they could and would not experience in executing their judicial tasks in a national or domestic institution.

If there were only one essential feature of being a judge in any forum, national or international, it would, for me, be true independence, that is an admixture of independence from any external influences added to an innate internal independence which is far more difficult to define, but no less important. Judicial independence is a vital element of the separation of powers necessary to preserve the integrity of a domestic State. Yet, it is no less important in international courts and is arguably even more so, if that be possible.

At the international level, Judges must carefully insulate and separate their views on the criminal responsibility of an individual (which must be established through the production of the requisite proof in the context of a criminal trial) from the views of the Government and media of the state or states that are concerned with the crimes in question. Given that the tendency at international level has been to prosecute those who bear the greatest responsibility for the alleged crimes, the persons who stand accused in international tribunals generally attract greater notoriety than the direct lower level perpetrators. As a result, the states concerned may maintain a high level of political interest in the conviction or acquittal of accused persons (depending on the relationship of the Government with the parties involved in the commission of the crimes) and the local and international media reports, sometimes vociferously and critically, on the day to day procedural management and substantive developments of the trials. Complex (and often uncertain) issues are parsed in the public sphere, often to various political ends and sometimes with a high degree of inaccuracy, deliberate or accidental.

Other states beyond those directly concerned with the criminal conduct under examination may also be keenly interested in the development of particular aspects of the law, regarding for example superior or command responsibility, or immunity from prosecution of heads of state or the lack thereof. Thus, third party states that may have a neutral stance regarding the substantive issue under examination may have strong views and bring enormous political pressure to bear on interpretations of the law that they regard as setting an erroneous or dangerous precedent for the international community. The Government of South Africa offered one such salient example in its attempted withdrawal from the Rome Statute in 2016 faced with what it perceived to be a diplomatic and legal tension between its cooperation obligations to the International Criminal Court to arrest heads of state for whom arrest warrants have been issued and its obligations to other states to recognise head of state immunity under international law.[30]

Judges in international courts must also exercise care to not act as, or indeed be seen as acting as, representatives of their nominating states and certainly not activists for any home state's policy interests, either in respect of their relationship with the court (fiscal or otherwise) or their wider foreign policy interests.

All of this means that international judges have to cope with pressures far wider than the parameters of just substantive or procedural law, or the pressures of relatively well known domestic social and cultural expectations. Whether it is a dictatorial, or quasi-dictatorial, highly positioned military or political figure seeking to protect his or her position from proper scrutiny or judgement and desperate to retain unjustifiable immunity or impunity, or a more diverse and arcane nationalistic political or cultural movement seeking to attract or divert international attention, the pressures on judges can be immense and unrelenting. There often appears in some quarters to be an expectation of conviction rather than a sober appreciation of fair trials according to the established standards and burden of proof, which inevitably may fairly and properly lead to acquittal in spite of pre-trial adverse publicity surrounding the accused.

---

30   At the time of writing, Pre-Trial Chamber II responsible for the situation in Sudan and the case against Omar Al Bashir continues to deliberate on submissions received on this issue from the South Africa in an oral hearing, which took place on 7 April 2017.

Against this backdrop of often fervent political interest, the international judge must remain immune from external influence and discharge his or her individual responsibility in dispensing justice impartially and objectively to the person who stands accused before him or her. Indeed, the dispassionate application of the law is essential to establishing a credible system of justice that can stand the test of time. As Justice Pal sagely remarked', "[f]ormalized vengeance can bring only an ephemeral satisfaction, with every probability of ultimate regret; but vindication of law through genuine legal process alone may contribute to the re-establishment of order and decency in international relations".[31]

Judging in criminal cases where the underlying facts and possibility of sanctions raise both emotions and tensions is especially difficult and, in the very public arena of international courts and tribunals, even more so. It has found reflection in public reaction to all of the existing and recent international courts and tribunals where partisan movements have been critical of any decision implicating their preferred nationals or institutions and has even raised accusations of deliberate political and racial bias in a sometimes hostile atmosphere with which national judges do not generally have to cope.[32] Those pressures alone call for judicial strength and determination and an even more acute sense of independence. The occasional indication that even national newspaper editors have no real concept of the division of executive and judicial authority is as worrying as it is astonishing.

However, it is fortunate that the nature of the task that befalls criminal case judges tends to harden their attitudes towards both personal and professional criticism. That, in my view, is both welcome and inevitable. The mindset that produces successful judges is one that means they undertake their role out of commitment to the rule of law, both national and international, and a determination that they are going to do their sworn duty to remain independently fair even in the face of sometimes unjustifiable comment or either measured or hysterical criticism.

---

31   International Military Tribunal for the Far East (IMTFE), Judgment of The Honorable Justice Pal, Member from India (Part 1), available at http://www.legal-tools.org/doc/712ef9/, p. 37.

32   A recent and extreme example of when they do occurred in 2016 when the UK's Daily Mail newspaper ran a headline accusing three UK judges of being "Enemies of the People" for determining that it was beyond the role or authority of an executive order to formally indicate the departure of the UK from the European Union but instead required a positive vote in Parliament.

3.2 Rules of Procedure and Evidence of International Trials

The dissenting opinions of the Tokyo trial highlight above also illustrate the real differences between domestic and international cases in terms of procedure. In national courts a trial is conducted in accordance with [usually] well-established laws and tried and tested rules of evidence and procedure. All of these will be of easy familiarity to an experienced trial judge, whether in a common law or civil law jurisdiction. Although national legal systems can also be dynamic, they tend to deal with far more fixed and predictable jurisprudence than international courts or tribunals with less scope for individual judges or even appellate benches to interpret, modify or deviate from established norms.

In contrast, although there is an increasing foundation of customary international law and precedent, mainly from the ICTY at present, international judges are frequently dealing with a far less fixed and predictable body of both substantive and procedural law than their national court counterparts. Although the modern day tribunals and the International Criminal Court have their own Rules of Procedure and Evidence (a luxury that would no doubt have been a considerable source of envy to those civil law judges grappling with the application of an alien common law procedure during the Tokyo trial), the rules therein are broadly articulated and, themselves the result of much discussion and compromise during drafting, are often open to a myriad of different interpretations and contortions to more easily adapt to the vagaries of the common law or civil law perception.

An important distinction may also be made between the training and professional experience of judges appointed to criminal courts at the national level and those who are appointed at the international level. Domestic judges are either specially trained for that purpose or have come from years of active criminal court practice and experience before elevation to the bench.

In contrast, international judges may, and have, come to their courts having never sat as a criminal judge before and, possibly, without any active experience as a defending or prosecuting advocate in serious criminal cases. For example, in relation to the election of judges to the International Criminal Court, article 36 (3) (b) of the Rome Statute provides:

> Every candidate for election to the Court shall:
> (i) Have established competence in criminal law and procedure, and the necessary relevant experience, whether as judge, prosecutor, advocate or in other similar capacity, in criminal proceedings; or
> (ii) Have established competence in relevant areas of international law such as international humanitarian law and the law of human

rights, and extensive experience in a professional legal capacity which is of relevance to the judicial work of the Court.

This means that the background of some judges may have been as administrative judges or academics or diplomats. As such, they are required to make a considerable shift in professional mind-set and face a steep learning curve in order to meet the minimum necessary requirements. That lack of hard criminal trial experience, added to the rather more fluid nature of both international criminal and humanitarian law presents very real challenges that have been met with varying degrees of success.

Particular challenges are encountered in developing the experience required to elaborate effective, and not only efficient, procedures for criminal trials in the International Criminal Court as a result of the continuous rotation of the serving judges. Every three years, the International Criminal Court loses one third of its judicial strength and six new judges have to adapt to and grow into their role. In contrast, the permanent mandate of the *ad hoc* tribunal judges gave far more scope for the institutional continuity of jurisprudence, which was beneficial to the development of the law. In my view, it is imperative that future ICC judges assigned to the trial division are primarily drawn from professional judges who have a strong grasp of international criminal and humanitarian law and long experience of practicing and judging in serious criminal law cases, either in their own jurisdictions or internationally.

Discharging the varied functions of a judge in any court is far from easy. The judge is referee and focal point for all that is deemed successful and, by parity of observation, all that is deemed to be faulty. The judge must conduct the proceedings within the appropriate legal framework and strive to make the entire trial proceedings as fair as possible, and not only to the accused.

4 Conclusion

The experiences of the judges of the Tokyo and the Nuremberg tribunals has paved the way for the establishment of a permanent international criminal court and the international judges of today. Those early pioneers must have noted with irony that some of the acrimonious and nationalistic debates that surrounded the establishment of those tribunals at the London Conference held from June to August 1945 were mirrored and repeated in the debates leading up to the Rome Statute of the International Criminal Court some sixty years later. In both instances, there were frequent misunderstandings between common and civil law delegates and many felt compelled to advocate for their own respective national interests. Issues of contention which dogged the creation of the Nuremberg and Tokyo tribunals, and continue to provide ample fodder for disagreement amongst jurists, scholars and judges alike, include the most appropriate methods for defining individual criminal responsibility and assigning culpability in situations of hierarchy and the definition of the crime of aggression.[33]

While commentators may lament the slow pace of evolution of international criminal law and concerns may be voiced about the repetition of the same discussions and disagreements in different fora, these complaints fail to accord sufficient deference to the requirements of the international environment and the complexity of the system of law that is under development. I have alluded above to the political implications both overt and, at least as often, covert that can be seem to shadow almost every international trial in one form or another. Those require especial judicial skills to manage and can really only be dealt with on a case-by-case basis. Aspects of international criminal procedure that attempt to marry or juxtapose elements from the common law and civil law systems also raise particular complexities. The natural adherence of judges to the familiarity of their own legal system will undoubtedly produce variations in the law and procedure until the repetition of practices at international level creates a well-worn path and in turn acquires its own familiarity.

The exceptional nature of and pressures brought to bear by the international environment has been apparent, at least to some extent, in all of the international courts and tribunals from Nuremberg onwards. In domestic situations it is rare that the existence of a criminal justice mechanism is challenged. While there may be many variables that affect confidence in the workings of a system, or even the outcomes of individual cases, the need for some regulatory system for the state to control a citizen's behaviour, individually or collectively, is rarely rationally contested. The rule of law is accepted as having far greater and more obvious benefits than drawbacks.

In the international arena, judges are forced to trespass outside the familiar national boundaries and enter the contentious and complex interactive territory between the accused, the victims and the global community exacerbated by the friction of elements of sovereignty (real or manufactured) and the fear of broader concepts, such as constitutional constraints or human rights trumping executive power. International criminal law has no access to a universal set

---

33   There is a wealth of literature on the Nuremberg and Tokyo tribunals, more recently including G. Mettraux, *Perspectives on the Nuremberg Trial* (Oxford University Press, 2008), and N. Boister and R. Cryer, *The Tokyo International Military Tribunal: A Reappraisal* (Oxford University Press, 2008).

of pre-determined criteria that render international legal rules as being universally binding; instead it relies upon pronounced moral values and mature international cooperation and agreements for its international social legitimacy, and for its enforcement apparatus.

Against this backdrop, one of the biggest tangible achievements of international criminal justice, aided by properly utilised modern communications, is the dramatic change in the way in which the world community perceives political violence both within and without national boundaries. In contrast to the early days of the creation of the Nuremberg and Tokyo when four victorious powers could scarcely agree on what should be tried by Tribunals set up for the limited purpose of trying their defeated enemies, today there appears to be a great deal of universal consensus about a refusal to tolerate genocide, other crimes against humanity and war crimes, and indeed the dynamic extension of those offences as need arises.

Judge Wolfgang Schomburg, the first German judge at the ICTY and ICTR and a formidable legal scholar, has proved his worth and abilities as an independent international judge on many occasions and, through many of his decisions and legal writings, has contributed ably to the development of the system of international criminal law. I appeared before him as counsel and have shared conferences tables with him over many years and appreciated his qualities at close hand. He has proved to be a brave and decisive judge with a formidable intellect and a capacity of hard and sustained work. The international legal world needs more like him.

CHAPTER 14

25 Years of International Criminal Justice: Ebb and Flow or Rise and Fall?

Jan Christoph Nemitz

Abstract

Taking a pause to look back at about 25 years of a developing system of international criminal justice, one cannot escape to notice a period in which international – and hybrid – courts have been mushrooming on a global level, and a phase in which the initial euphoria and support by the international community appears to have cooled off considerably. This contribution will first set out to examine the root causes for the growth and the rapid development, within less than a decade, of international tribunals such as the ICTY, the ICTR, the ICC, the East Timor Tribunal, the SCSL and, some years later, the ECCC and the STL. In a second step, it will look at the reasons for what seems to be a certain slowing down – or even halt? – in the further development of international criminal tribunals. Finally, the contribution will try to provide an outlook of the near future of international criminal justice.

1   Introduction

Wolfgang Schomburg is a pioneer of international criminal justice. Not only as a co-editor of the first comprehensive bilingual (German-English) commentary on international cooperation in criminal matters, but also as the first German judge to be elected by the United Nations General Assembly to serve at an international criminal tribunal established by the United Nations Security Council (in 2001). This makes him a member of an exclusive group of legal experts whose names will forever be intrinsically connected to the notion of international criminal justice in general, and the work of the International Criminal Tribunals for the former Yugoslavia (ICTY) and for Rwanda (ICTR) in particular.

---

* Dr. iur. (Freiburg i. Br., 2002), Juris Magister (Stockholm, 1996). Desk Officer in the Legal Directorate-General of the German Federal Foreign Service, Berlin. The views of the author do not necessarily represent the views of the Federal Foreign Service.

Wolfgang Schomburg has dedicated seven years of his professional life to both Tribunals, but he has given them much more than this. His tenure as a Judge was characterized by a steadfast devotion to the cause of the Tribunals. He was committed to the cases he was assigned to and demonstrated in an exemplary manner what it meant to swear the oath as a judge at an international tribunal. In doing so, Schomburg can pride himself on having contributed to the strengthening of international criminal law and to the empowering of some of their most prominent enforcement mechanisms, namely the Tribunals.

The purpose of this chapter is to take account of the state of international criminal justice at the time the Rwanda Tribunal and the Yugoslavia Tribunal were established, to describe its development in the years until, and during which, Schomburg served as a Judge at both Tribunals, and to describe where it stands today. This means to pause for a moment and to look back at about 25 years of a developing system of international criminal justice, which started in earnest when the Yugoslavia Tribunal and the Rwanda Tribunal were established in 1993 and 1994, respectively.

Much has been said and written about this early phase and the reasons for the establishment of the first truly international criminal tribunals after World War II, but these tribunals' development was not linear. One cannot escape to notice a period in which international and hybrid courts have been mushrooming on a global level, and a phase in which the initial euphoria and support by the international community appears to have cooled off considerably.

This contribution will first set out to examine the root causes for the growth and the rapid development, within less than a decade, of international and hybrid tribunals such as the Yugoslavia Tribunal, the Rwanda Tribunal, the International Criminal Court, the East Timor Tribunal, the Special Court for Sierra Leone, and some years later, the Extraordinary Chambers in the Courts of Cambodia, the Lebanon Tribunal and the Kosovo Special Chambers. Next, it will look at the reasons for what seems to be a certain slowing down in the further development of international and hybrid criminal tribunals. Finally, the contribution will try to provide an outlook of the near future of international criminal justice.

II   The Early Years of International Criminal Justice – 1993 to 2001

"Rien n'est plus puissant qu'une idée dont l'heure est venue." This quote commonly attributed to Victor Hugo (1802–1885) most accurately illustrates the notion of international criminal justice. On one hand, it shows the strength and impact an idea may have when everyone is convinced that it is the right thing to do. On the other hand, Hugo's *bon mot* describes the weakness of international criminal justice. As of today, its organs and enforcement mechanisms are still not sufficiently established, and they are often weak. To date, it is not yet possible to enforce prosecutorial measures against each national of every state, regardless of which nationality this person may have. Further, in contrast to national justice systems, there is no powerful executive and there are no law enforcement structures that could guarantee that decisions of international tribunals would invariably be complied with. Thus, the biggest strength of an international criminal justice system is its moral backing. In particular, the global conviction that adherence to it is the right thing to do, which translates to backing by governments and civil society worldwide.

However, this international support has suffered some severe setbacks when various African countries recently announced that they would withdraw from the International Criminal Court.[1] These setbacks are dangerous, and not only because they limit the territorial jurisdiction of the Court that may lead to safe havens for criminals. The more severe danger of those potential withdrawals is the detrimental effect that they may have on the moral authority of the International Criminal Court. If states no longer believe that the Court is the solution to the problem of impunity, if they are of the opinion that the Court is biased and yet another form of colonialism by way of legal means, and if such beliefs garner support within states that have been very supportive in the beginning, then the Court risks losing its greatest strength: the conviction that it is imperative to put alleged war criminals worldwide on the docket.

Back in the early 1990s, the member states of the United Nations Security Council were in a predicament, which subsequently gave birth to the Yugoslavia Tribunal. Pressured by civil society to end the bloodshed in the former Yugoslavia and faced with the alternatives to either send troops or to negotiate with the warring parties with no end in sight, they miraculously proposed a third option: an international tribunal for the prosecution of alleged war criminals. It can be safely assumed that part of the reasoning was that such tribunals would effectively prevent and deter criminal acts of potential war criminals. Overall, this hope has not become a reality. Two years following the creation of the Yugoslavia Tribunal, the horrible events in Srebrenica occurred. While it can be argued that this was partly due to the fact that the Tribunal was hardly operational in 1995, the commission of war crimes in Kosovo four years

---

1   See, for instance, Eunice Kilonzo, 'Kenya's formal process to quit ICC yet to begin' *Daily Nation* (24 October 2016) <www.nation.co.ke/news/1056-3427420-5hu8frz> accessed 2 May 2017.

later – while the Tribunal was already working at full capacity – could not be halted either.

Against this background, it is somewhat astonishing that these events did not discourage decision-makers to establish other international tribunals on a global level. In 1994, the Yugoslavia Tribunal's sister tribunal was founded in Arusha, and only four years later, 120 states crowned their seemingly endless negotiation with the adoption of the Rome Statute of the International Criminal Court. This was quickly followed by hybrid tribunals, which are of a mixed national and international nature, including the Special Court for Sierra Leone, the Extraordinary Chambers in the Courts of Cambodia, and the Special Tribunal for Lebanon.[2] These tribunals reaffirmed the global community's trust in international criminal justice. Additionally, they represented the moment in time when there was a global consensus that international tribunals could play an important role in the international endeavor to achieve peace and security through the rule of law. The fact that countries like the United States, Russia, China, India, and Pakistan, to name but a few, did not ratify the Rome Statute does not falsify this statement, as these states did not prevent the establishment of the other above-mentioned tribunals.

It was during this golden time of international criminal justice when Wolfgang Schomburg reported for duty at the Yugoslavia Tribunal in November 2001. This was only two months after the attack on the Twin Towers that sent shockwaves around the globe, subsequently leading to the wars in Afghanistan and Iraq. Consequently, these events ended any hope that the newly established tribunals would be the *fora* where international conflicts would be dealt with in the future. Yet, there was still the desire to believe that the global community would not fall back behind what it had already achieved in terms of international criminal justice. For example, no high-ranking military official, if confronted with crimes committed by soldiers under his authority, could any longer successfully argue in his defence that he did not know what his soldiers did at some other location. This argument suddenly sounded unconvincing in light of comparable accusations against Slobodan Milošević and other high-ranking ex-Yugoslav politicians who were faced with accusations according to which their knowledge comprised of the commission of crimes in distant

---

2   See Ernestine Meijer, 'The Extraordinary Chambers in the Courts of Cambodia for Prosecuting the Crimes Committed by the Khmer Rouge: Jurisdiction, Organization, and the Procedure of an Internationalized Court', in Cesare P R Romano, André Nollkaemper and Jann K Kleffner (eds), *Internationalized Criminal Courts and Tribunals: Sierra Leone, East Timor, Kosovo and Cambodia* (Oxford University Press 2004) 229.

places. This exemplifies the strength of the law. Because even if you do not apply it *vis-à-vis* everyone, the public will demand precisely this.

Wolfgang Schomburg brought a wealth of experience to both the Yugoslavia Tribunal and to the Rwanda Tribunal. He was an experienced national lawyer who worked in various legal professions including as defence counsel, a prosecutor, a Supreme Court judge, and a state secretary in the Land Berlin. In the seven years of service at the Yugoslavia Tribunal and the Rwanda Tribunal, he proved to be a beacon of professionalism. He served as a prime example of a judge who was entrusted by the global community, represented by the General Assembly, to decide the guilt and innocence of those accused of having committed the most serious crimes known to mankind. It is judges like him that international tribunals need in order to fulfill the promise they give to international law, to the victims of an armed conflict, and to the global community at large.

III   The International Criminal Justice System in Its Prime: 2001–2008

So, one is tempted to think that it is no coincidence that the years Schomburg spent at the Yugoslavia and Rwanda Tribunals were the most successful years of international criminal justice! These years saw the establishment of a number of new international criminal courts and tribunals. In 2002, the jurisdiction of the International Criminal Court started and the court began its work in earnest.[3] Shortly thereafter, in 2004, a regional hybrid court followed, the Special Court for Sierra Leone, which started its proceedings in Freetown and later moved to The Hague. This was followed by the Extraordinary Chambers in the Courts of Cambodia in Phnom Penh (2006) and the Special Tribunal for Lebanon in The Hague (2007).[4] These years also saw a significant growth of the Rwanda Tribunal and the Yugoslavia Tribunal. The latter, at one point, spread out over three buildings in The Hague, including the so-called Beach Building at the lighthouse (veterans of the Yugoslavia Tribunal remember the shuttle bus between the Beach Building and the Main Building). However, because the newer tribunals were not established by the United Nations Security Council, it was evident that it would be increasingly difficult to convince all members of this organ that international tribunals are an effective tool to fight global

---

[3] See, for instance, Luis Moreno-Ocampo, 'The International Criminal Court: Seeking Global Justice' (2008) 40 Case Western Reserve Journal of International Law 215.

[4] For a general overview see Philipp Ambach, Eine Rahmenkonvention für die Errichtung hybrider internationaler Strafgerichte (Verlag Dr. Kovač 2009).

impunity. Instead, hybrid tribunals seemed to be more appropriate *fora* to deal with international crimes, as they combined the easy access of a war-torn society to the proceedings with the judicial independence and professionalism of international judges.

When Wolfgang Schomburg left both the Rwanda Tribunal and the Yugoslavia Tribunal in 2008, these courts and tribunals just began to face a powerful threat: the global economic crisis. Like other non-profit organs, the tribunals were particularly vulnerable to the effect of this crisis because they do not offer an immediate return on investment. Their impact on global peace and security cannot be measured in dollars and euros, yet the costs of these tribunals are immense. As a result, member states started paying particular attention to the financial contributions they had to pay to them. Still today, the registrars of tribunals like the Extraordinary Chambers in the Courts of Cambodia, the Lebanon Tribunal, and the Residual Special Court for Sierra Leone (which took over from the Special Court for Sierra Leone after its closure in 2013[5]) need to devote a substantial part of their jobs to flying around the globe in an effort to secure the financial means necessary to keep their judicial institutions alive.

IV The Global Financial Crisis and Other Setbacks to the Tribunals from the Outside (and Inside): 2008

Thus, while the idea of international criminal justice thrived at the time Wolfgang Schomburg joined the Rwanda Tribunal and the Yugoslavia Tribunal and continued to blossom during his years, by the time he left these institutions their radiance started to slightly fade.

However, this was not entirely due to external factors such as the global financial crisis with its ensuing effect that states became increasingly hesitant to spend money on justice projects with no immediate financial gain. Truth requires that it must be mentioned that some of the problems of the tribunals were intrinsic. For instance, no matter how detailed, convincing, and elaborate a judgement may be, it inevitably cannot satisfy everyone who is affected by it. Generally, members of the ethnic group to which the convicted person belonged would criticize the harshness of the sentence. In cases where the accused was acquitted, many of his supporters would hail this result, while claiming the unfairness of having dragged him before the court in the first place.

---

5 Fidelma Donlon, 'The Transition of Responsibilities from the Special Court to the Residual Special Court for Sierra Leone: Challenges and Lessons Learned for Other International Tribunals' (2013) 11 Journal of International Criminal Justice 857.

Obviously, other groups will be disappointed as, in their view, the sentence of the convicted person is too lenient or the acquittal of the accused is scandalous, as the tribunal got the facts and/or the law completely wrong. Such criticism even has the power of thwarting the very mandate of, for instance, the Yugoslavia Tribunal, which is to contribute to peace, security and stability in the region. The acquittals of Vojislav Šešelj[6] by a first-instance judgement and of Ante Gotovina[7] by the Appeals Chamber caused major repercussions in the region, and the tragedy is that such repercussions would most likely have happened regardless of the outcome. Damned if you do, damned if you don't.

Such effects can even be stronger by outspoken dissenting opinions of individual judges. When reading the dissenting views of Judge Pocar in the Appeals Chamber's judgement against Gotovina,[8] those who were already sceptical as to whether or not he should have been convicted acquired the factual and legal arguments necessary to heavily criticize his acquittal. Similarly, Judge Vaz's dissenting opinion in the Trial Chamber's judgement against Vojislav Šešelj leaves no wish unheard by those who are of the opinion that he is indeed guilty of having committed serious violations of humanitarian law. Unlike in German national penal law, the possibility to issue strong individual opinions is provided for in the Rules of Procedure and Evidence of the international and hybrid tribunals. These opinions provide helpful and authoritative arguments to the critics of those judgements that have been issued over the outspoken dissent of one or two judges. In this sense, it is questionable whether it was a good idea to adopt a rule allowing for individual opinions. Not only does it potentially ignite criticism of the tribunals' decisions, but it also effectively reveals secrets of the judges' deliberations, which would otherwise be protected by a rule on confidentiality. Because if a judge publishes a harsh dissenting opinion, the public can safely assume that the deliberations comprised of discussions on exactly those issues referenced in the dissent.

Similarly, assumed political motivations behind the reasoning of the majority in some Yugoslavia Tribunal judgements were the basis of further criticism of the Tribunal's work. For instance, in his dissenting opinion in the Appeal

---

[6] Owen Bowcott, 'Serb nationalist Vojislav Šešelj acquitted of war crimes at The Hague' *The Guardian* (London, 31 March 2016) <www.theguardian.com/law/2016/mar/31/serb-nationalist-vojislav-seselj-acquitted-war-crimes-crimes-against-humanity-icty-the-hague> accessed 3 May 2017.

[7] Bruno Waterfield, 'Croatian hero Ante Gotovina acquitted of war crimes' *Daily Telegraph* (London, 16 November 2012) <www.telegraph.co.uk/news/worldnews/europe/croatia/9682855/Croatian-hero-Ante-Gotovina-acquitted-of-war-crimes.html> accessed 3 May 2017.

[8] *Prosecutor v. Ante Gotovina and Mladen Markač*, Case No. IT-06-90-A, Judgement, 16 November 2012, Sect. x.

Judgement against Ante Gotovina and Mladen Markač, Judge Pocar fundamentally disagreed with the majority's decision to reverse Gotovina's and Markač's convictions for committing, through a joint criminal enterprise whose common purpose was to permanently remove the Serb civilian population from the Krajina region, various crimes against humanity and war crimes. Towards the end of his dissenting opinion, in which he disagreed with the reasoning and any major conclusion of the majority of judges, he insinuated that the majority's decision might not have been based exclusively on legal reasoning: "Finally, even if the Majority wished to acquit Gotovina and Markač entirely [!], one might wonder what the Majority wanted to achieve by quashing the mere existence of the JCE rather than concentrating on Gotovina's and Markač's significant contributions to the JCE. I leave it as an open question."[9] Critics of the judgement who interpreted it as a deliberate means to state that "Operation Storm", the battle launched to restore Croatian control in the Krajina, was not part of a joint criminal enterprise, could feel supported by this individual opinion of an Appeal's Chamber judge.

In a similar vein, public criticism arose when the Yugoslavia Tribunal's Appeals Chamber overturned the convictions of Momčilo Perišić for having aided and abetting jurisdictional crimes. The reversal of his conviction was predicated on the majority of judges' finding that the Trial Chamber erred in holding that the so-called "specific direction" is not a requisite element of the *actus reus* of aiding and abetting liability. As a result, the majority of the Appeals Chamber conducted a *de novo* review of the entirety of the evidence, finding that there was insufficient evidence to establish that the contribution Perišić provided was specifically directed towards the criminal activities of the Army of the Republika Srpska in Sarajevo and Srebrenica. In this judgement, it was Judge Liu's turn to append a dissenting opinion. Yet again, critics saw other than entirely legal motivations behind the majority's decision. They argued that this jurisprudence made it deliberately difficult to convict an accused for aiding and abetting, because the proof that an accused provided his aid with the specific intention to aid and abet a crime is difficult to establish beyond reasonable doubt. Then, only a few months later, the Appeals Chamber in the *Šainović et al.* case decided that the specific intention requirement was *not* an element of the *actus reus* of aiding and abetting. Two blatantly contradictory decisions by the same Appeals Chamber within a few months!

It is hardly surprising that the above-mentioned controversies among the judges at the Yugoslavia Tribunal detrimentally affected the perception of the

---

9 *Prosecutor v. Ante Gotovina and Mladen Markač*, Case No. IT-06-90-A, Judgement, Dissenting Opinion of Judge Fausto Pocar, at para. 30.

Tribunal in the region, in the media and in academic circles. This perception received another blow when the ICTY Trial Chamber acquitted Vojislav Šešelj of all charges in 2016. For Wolfgang Schomburg, this was a special case. It was Schomburg who, on 26 February 2003, held the initial appearance of this accused. From that date on, it took almost 13 years before a first instance judgement was rendered. The reasons for this exceptionally long and cumbersome trial were certainly not grounded in the acts and decisions of Schomburg. He no longer formed part of the bench before which the trial proceedings were held. When the trial judgement was finally pronounced, it was startling to see that its main text contained only just over 100 pages.[10] Thus, after 13 years of proceedings, it was hardly surprising that this acquittal was met with strong opinions from Šešelj's supporters and his opponents alike. A few weeks later, the Office of the Prosecutor filed a notice of appeal against the trial judgement.[11] This appeal is currently being heard before the Appeals Chamber of the Mechanism for International Criminal Tribunals (MICT). This institution is the successor tribunal of the Yugoslavia Tribunal, originally designed to perform the legacy work of the latter. As it turned out, the Mechanism will conduct more proceedings than originally foreseen, including a full re-trial in the case against Stanišić and Simatović.[12] Additionally, it cannot be ruled out that the judgement of the Mechanism's Appeals Chamber against Šešelj will eventually lead to a re-trial as well. Again, there is a forceful dissent attached to the trial judgement. Flavia Lattanzi, the Italian judge on the bench, strongly dissented from the decision of the majority of judges to acquit the accused. Once again, an individual opinion highlighted the deep divides that ran within the trial chamber, providing critics of the court and its work with arguments to question the solidity of its output. However, it must be noted that the trial judgement is not yet final and a comprehensive discussion of the proceedings against Šešelj can only begin following the judgement of the Mechanism's Appeals Chamber.

All these examples exemplify that part of the criticism directed against the Yugoslavia Tribunal was based on the work of the Tribunal itself. However, there were other complications stemming from factors outside the court. For instance, even before the global financial crisis started in 2008, the Tribunal faced cuts in the budget which led to temporary hiring freezes. Similarly,

---

10   *Prosecutor v. Vojislav Šešelj*, Case No. IT-03-67-T, Judgement, Vol. 1, 31 March 2016.
11   *Prosecutor v. Vojislav Šešelj*, Case No. MICT-16-99-A, Prosecution's Notice of Appeal, 2 May 2016.
12   *Prosecutor v. Jovica Stanišić and Franko Simatović*, Case No. MICT-15-96-PT, Order Assigning Judges to a Case Before a Trial Chamber, 17 December 2015.

because a completion strategy was developed according to which all proceedings should be finished by the end of 2010, many staff members left the court in search for a more stable job and other career opportunities. All these factors contributed to a far from ideal working environment for staff members who need to focus on their work.

Further, the situation of tribunals primarily financed by voluntary contributions is even more problematic. For instance, the Extraordinary Chambers in the Courts of Cambodia is dependent on the contributions of both the Kingdom of Cambodia and the voluntary contributions of United Nations member states. In theory, this is a system that should work nicely. However, in practice, the majority of states are unwilling to pay, which proves to be, to put it mildly, problematic for the Extraordinary Chambers. This situation shows that the international community installs the nucleus of potential failure in every tribunal that is improperly funded. The search for financial contributions creates uncertainty not only for staff members who are looking for job security, but also for investigations and proceedings. As early as 2013, the Appeals Chamber of the Extraordinary Chambers held that: "The ECCC's funding crisis affects the judicial institutions as a whole[.] If there is insufficient funding to guarantee a trial driven by law, all ECCC proceedings must be terminated and the court must close down."[13] A strong statement that holds true for any international or hybrid court that is dependent on voluntary contributions.

Tribunals that are funded by regular contributions from the United Nations by its member states are, more or less, on the safe side. Still, there have been instances when, for instance, the United States withheld part of its usual financial contributions, leading to hiring freezes and other forms of spending cuts at the Yugoslavia Tribunal. However, the situation of hybrid courts like the Extraordinary Chambers is even more bleak. These Chambers depend on the goodwill of only some of the states who are asked to pay for the institution on an annual basis. Some states commit themselves to biannual contributions, or even for a four year-period, which provides the court with some stability. On the other hand, other states fail to provide their share, leading to huge holes in the budget. This, in turn, imperils the work and eventual success of the Chambers as gaps in the budget lead to short-term contracts, causing job insecurity. This results in the staff incessantly searching for more stable working arrangements, which means that deadlines may not be accomplished, causing prolonged proceedings and higher costs. The situation is similar at the Special Tribunal for Lebanon and at the Residual Special Court for Sierra Leone.

---

13   Decision on Immediate Appeals Against Trial Chamber's Second Decision on Severance of Case 002 – E284/4/8, at para. 75.

The newest kid on the block, however, will benefit from a more stable financial regime: the Kosovo Special Chambers. It became operational in April 2016, and it is financed by the European Union which committed itself to a five year budget. With the knowledge, however, that criminal proceedings before international or hybrid courts tend to take longer than anticipated, it is fair to assume that after the initial phase of five years, the European Union will be obliged to assess whether another multi-annual budget can be secured. Until then, the organs of the Court profit from a security that most of the other international and hybrid courts do not have.

v A Breath of Fresh Air – New Hybrid Tribunals (2013–2016)

The establishment of the Kosovo Special Chambers represents an example of what can be called a new vague of hybrid Tribunals. As we have seen earlier, several of these tribunals were founded in the beginning of the current century. About ten years later, we can observe several similar tribunals coming to the forefront. For instance, in 2013, the Extraordinary African Chambers were established by way of an agreement between Senegal and the African Union. The mandate of this tribunal covers international crimes committed on the territory of Tchad between June 1982 and December 1990, *i.e.* during the reign of former president Hissène Habré. Financed by voluntary contributions of several states, the Chambers rendered a first instance verdict against Habré in 2016, sentencing him to life imprisonment. The case is currently on appeal, and further proceedings remain possible. Particularly in light of other African states trying to withdraw from the International Criminal Court, the example of these Extraordinary Chambers serves as a successful example of how regional hybrid courts can contribute to the fight against impunity.

Another example of a breath of fresh air in international criminal justice is the establishment of a special tribunal in the Central African Republic.[14] MINUSCA, the stabilization mission of the United Nations, had been incapable of preventing many of the serious crimes committed in a conflict between the Islamic rebel group Séléka and the Christian anti-Balaka groups. Similarly, the national justice system was not in a position to sufficiently address these crimes and to launch the necessary investigations and criminal proceedings against potential perpetrators. After a change of the then ruling Government,

---

14 See Godfrey M. Musila, 'The Special Criminal Court and Other Options of Accountability in the Central African Republic: Legal and Policy Recommendations' (Occasional Paper No. 2. International Nuremberg Principles Academy 2016).

the Central African Republic referred the situation to the International Criminal Court in 2014. However, at that stage, it was understood that the International Criminal Court would only be in a position to deal with a comparatively small number of crimes and perpetrators. As a consequence, the transitory Government and minusca agreed on the establishment of a national special court in Bangui, the capital of the Central African Republic, for the persecution of serious human rights violations committed on the territory of the Central African Republic since 2003. The law required for the establishment of the court was enacted in June 2015. The temporal mandate will be an initial five years with the option of renewal following that initial period. The court's judges will be predominantly nationals of the Central African Republic, while the chief prosecutor must be international. As for its material jurisdiction, the special court will be competent for human rights violations which will neither be prosecuted before the International Criminal Court, nor before any national court. While the financing of the special court is still unclear, the initiative to launch this court is laudable. It is yet another stimulating example of an internationalized national court that can be seen as a second layer in the international criminal system: between truly international courts like the International Criminal Court on the one hand, and the national judicial system on the other.[15]

In a similar vein, Kenya is in the process of establishing a so-called International and Organised Crimes Division at the Kenyan High Court. Its mandate covers the prosecution of alleged perpetrators of crimes committed after the presidential elections in 2007. The Crimes Division will primarily focus on persons whose role was not senior enough to be prosecuted before the International Criminal Court. Because the jurisdictional crimes encompass genocide, crimes against humanity, war crimes, and other transnational crimes, the Division will assume a complementary role *vis-à-vis* the International Criminal Court. Its temporal jurisdiction is not limited to the immediate time after the elections as it was originally intended. Now, there is no fixed period of time limiting the temporal jurisdiction. As to the financing of the Organised Crimes Division, being part of the Kenyan national justice system, they are supported primarily by national sources. It now remains to be seen if the Crimes Division will finally take up its work and start the prosecution of perpetrators of jurisdictional crimes.

---

15   See also United Nations, *Report of the International Commission of Inquiry on Central African Republic* (19 December 2004) <www.un.org/ga/search/view_doc.asp?symbol=S/2014/928> accessed 3 May 2017.

The establishment of several international and hybrid courts may prompt the concern that it weakens the position of the International Criminal Court. After all, it was designed to be THE institution before which international crimes should be prosecuted. This argument, however, misses the important point that one of the International Criminal Court's basic principles is the above-mentioned notion of complementarity. The Court will only find a case admissible if it is not being investigated or prosecuted by a state that has jurisdiction over it. Nonetheless, this principle is of sheer practical necessity. It would be impossible for one court to deal with all of the international crimes committed on a global level. Thus, the founders of the International Criminal Court intended that, in general, national legal systems would investigate and prosecute crimes falling under the jurisdiction of the Court. With this in mind, it should be welcomed that the establishment of hybrid courts, being rather regional in character, creates an additional layer between national and international courts. This additional layer is as much in line with the principle of complementarity as are national courts.[16] Thus, they should not be perceived as a threat to the Court but rather as yet another sign of the strengthening of an effective international criminal justice system. This, however, requires an important precondition: each and every hybrid court needs to manage its proceedings in line with *mutatis mutandis*, the Rome Statute, and the jurisprudence of the International Criminal Court, as well as other international tribunals like the Rwanda Tribunal and the Yugoslavia Tribunal. The diversity of courts prosecuting alleged perpetrators of international crimes must not lead to a diversity of core elements of the jurisprudence of the International Criminal Court. This does not mean that the doctrine of *stare decisis* applies to decisions of the Court in the sense that they are binding on each and every international and hybrid court worldwide. However, for instance, when it comes to the material elements of the jurisdictional crimes, the lack of any immunity for current or former leaders, or the principle that no person shall be tried twice for conduct for which that person has already been convicted or acquitted, then no international or hybrid court should ignore the established jurisprudence of the International Criminal Court. As we have seen earlier, the main power of international criminal law lies in its moral strength and conviction. This could be thwarted if the creation of several courts would fragmentize the very notion of international criminal law to the extent that it becomes unclear, unpersuasive, and ultimately unsuccessful. If, on the other

---

16 On the notion of complementarity and regional courts see Miles Jackson, 'Regional Complementarity: The Rome Statute and Public International Law' (2016) 14 Journal of International Criminal Justice 1061.

hand, national and regional courts follow the major tenets of the International Criminal Court's jurisprudence, then they will make it even stronger and contribute to the success of the Court rather than minimizing it.

VI Other Elements of International Criminal Justice: Commissions of Inquiry

There is yet another type of institution which is aimed at the investigation and prosecution of international crimes, albeit it not, at least not in the immediate future, in a court of law. These institutions are commissions, which have been established to find facts and collect evidence that could later be used in a courtroom. Various tribunals have been preceded by such commissions. For instance, prior to the establishment of the Yugoslavia Tribunal, the then United Nations Secretary-General Boutros Boutros-Ghali established a five-member Commission of Experts chaired by Professor Frits Kalshoven. Following his resignation, it was chaired by Professor Cherif Bassiouni to examine and analyse information gathered to determine whether grave breaches of the Geneva Conventions and other violations of international humanitarian law were committed in the territory of the former Yugoslavia.[17] This Commission performed its task between November 1992 and April 1994, and among other activity, it established a database with a comprehensive record of the reported violations of international humanitarian law.[18] In doing so, the Commission both preceded the establishment of the Yugoslavia Tribunal and worked alongside this court for about a year. It can be safely assumed that its studies, on-site investigations, and reports describing its work as well as providing preliminary conclusions on committed crimes, played an important part in the Security Council's decision to create the Tribunal in May 1993.

About ten years after the Kalshoven Commission saw the light of day, in October 2004, acting upon the request of the Security Council, the United Nations Secretary-General established an international commission of inquiry in order to investigate reports of violations of international humanitarian law and human rights law in Darfur, Sudan.[19] In addition, the Commission was tasked to identify the alleged perpetrators of these violations in order to allow for their

---

17 United Nations Security Council Resolution 780 (1992), 6 October 1992 (S/RES/780 (1992)).
18 United Nations Security Council, Final Report of the Commission of Experts Established Pursuant to Security Council Resolution 780 (1992), 27 May 1994 (S/1994/674).
19 United Nations Security Council Resolution 1564 (2004), 18 September 2004 (S/RES/1564 (2004).

future prosecution in a court of law. Again, it was a five-member Commission, this time chaired by the late Professor Cassese. The Commission was supported by a team of, *inter alia*, legal experts, investigators, forensic experts, and military analysts who were all requested to provide a report within three months. After what seemed to be an extraordinary short period of time for the task that needed to be accomplished, the Commission completed a full report detailing its findings and presented it to the Security Council on 25 January 2005.[20] Not only did it provide an overview of the historical and social background to the Darfur conflict, but it also set out detailed findings on violations of international human rights and humanitarian law by all parties to the conflict. These findings included whether or not the crime of genocide had been committed, the identification of perpetrators, as well as potential accountability mechanisms. As a result, on 31 March 2005, the Security Council referred the situation of Darfur to the International Criminal Court.[21]

This practice continued when only a couple of weeks after the Cassese Commission had presented its final report to the Security Council, on 14 February 2005, former Lebanese Prime Minister Rafik Hariri and 22 other persons were assassinated in a bombing attack. Shortly thereafter, the Security Council established the International Independent Investigation Commission to assist the Lebanese authorities in their endeavour to investigate the attack.[22] The Commission was chaired by Detlev Mehlis, a German national, and it presented altogether eleven reports on the investigation of this crime. Finally, in March 2009, the Commission transitioned into the newly established Special Tribunal for Lebanon, which in turn, benefitted from the leg work performed by the Commission.

Similarly, in 2011, the Independent International Commission of Inquiry was created by the Human Rights Council to investigate alleged violations of international human rights law since March 2011 in Syria.[23] Like its predecessors, the Commission of Inquiry's mandate was to establish the facts and circumstances of such violations as well as to identify, if possible, the alleged perpetrators.

---

20 Report of the International Commission of Inquiry on Darfur to the United Nations Secretary-General Pursuant to Security Council Resolution 1564 (18 September 2004), 25 January 2005; Christine Byron, 'Comment on the Report of the International Commission of Inquiry on Darfur to the United Nations Secretary-General' (2005) 5 Human Rights Law Review 351.
21 United Nations Security Council Resolution 1593 (2005), 31 March 2005 (S/RES/1593 (2005)).
22 United Nations Security Council Resolution 1595 (2005), 7 April 2005 (S7RES/1595 (2005)).
23 Human Rights Council Resolution S-17/1, *Situation of human rights in the Syrian Arab Republic*, 22 August 2011.

The mandate of the Commission has been renewed several times and various reports have been issued. Yet, while the establishment of the Commission of Inquiry appears to share many similarities with the previous commissions, there is an important difference. While the former commissions could start their work in the belief that, depending on their findings, the creation of a court of law possibly awaits at the end of their mission, the situation in Syria was different. At the time of the Commission's establishment, it was generally understood that there would neither be a referral of the Syrian situation to the International Criminal Court, nor would there be another international or hybrid court that would immediately follow up on the Commission's findings. Thus, the other commissions could be seen as a prelude to the subsequent tribunals, as a necessary test to see whether the establishment of a court was justified. The Syrian Commission of Inquiry, however, is rather an action by the international community that refuses to stand idly by in the wake of atrocities merely because there is insufficient political will to create a court. This became apparent most recently in May 2014 when China and Russia vetoed a Security Council Resolution that asked to refer the situation in Syria to the International Criminal Court. Thus, it remains to be seen whether the violations of international humanitarian law committed in Syria will ever be prosecuted before an international or hybrid court. Until then, the Commission's main task is to conduct interviews with witnesses and victims, to review photographs, videos, satellite imagery, forensic reports, academic analysis, and United Nations reports. Overall, this process aims at collecting the facts and securing what could potentially be used as evidence in court.

In addition, and most recently, the United Nations General Assembly established the so-called International, Impartial and Independent Mechanism in December 2016 to assist in the investigation and prosecution of alleged perpetrators of war crimes and crimes against humanity in Syria since March 2011.[24] In cooperation with the above-mentioned Commission of Inquiry, the Mechanism will collect, preserve, and analyse evidence related to violations of international human rights and humanitarian law. It will be of the utmost importance to prevent these institutions from getting in each other's way; instead, they need to work together to reach their common goal of facilitating and preparing criminal proceedings in national, regional, or international courts that already have, or potentially will have, jurisdiction over the crimes that have been committed in Syria over the past years. In order to enable the Mechanism to accomplish this task, all United Nations Member States and civil society stakeholders are called upon to cooperate fully with the Mechanism.

---

24 United Nations General Assembly Resolution, 19 December 2016 (A /71/L.48).

VII Outlook: Will the International Criminal Justice System Remain a Pillar in the Global Order?

The heavy blows to the international criminal justice system – the global financial crisis, criticism of judgements of the Yugoslavia Tribunal, member states threatening to withdraw from the International Criminal Court, unwillingness of the United Nations Security Council to refer the situation of Syria to the ICC – have had a sobering effect on those who thought that the establishment of international and hybrid courts would play a decisive role in international relations. However, the new wave of hybrid courts and commissions as described above offers substantial hope that the notion of international criminal law as a core pillar in the global order is still alive. The fact that a new government in The Gambia renounced the intention of the former government to withdraw from the International Criminal Court[25] is yet another sign that the international criminal justice system has matured over the years and is here to stay.

Yet, it will still be necessary to support this system of international accountability every day. Wolfgang Schomburg has embraced this idea wholeheartedly, which means that he is still a strong voice advocating for international justice.

In an article published in the German daily *Süddeutsche Zeitung* on 2 September 2013, Wolfgang Schomburg argued that the international community's duty to protect the civilian population in Syria required that a gas attack near Damascus should be referred to the International Criminal Court.[26] At that time, he hoped that China and Russia would agree on such an initiative in the Security Council, because it would be an acceptable compromise between the options of military engagement on the one hand and abstention from any action on the other. "Before you take action, you need to establish the facts," stated Schomburg. His initiative was supported by the late foreign policy speaker of the CDU/CSU parliamentary fraction, Philipp Mißfelder, as well as Member of Parliament Peter Gauweiler. In a similar vein, Professor Lagodny at the time argued that the indictment against Slobodan Milošević contributed to his fall. The indictment against Radovan Karadžić caused him to go underground for

---

[25] Mustapha K Darboe, 'Gambia halts ICC withdrawal' *Anadolu Agency* (Banjul, 14 February 2017) <http://aa.com.tr/en/africa/gambia-halts-icc-withdrawal/749751> accessed 3 May 2017.

[26] Stefan Ulrich, 'Strafrechtler fordern Prozess gegen Assad in Den Haag' *Süddeutsche Zeitung* (München, 2 September 2013) <www.sueddeutsche.de/politik/buergerkrieg-in-syrien-strafrechtler-wollen-assad-in-den-haag-den-prozess-machen-1.1759936> accessed 3 May 2017.

years before he was finally brought to The Hague in 2008. Similarly, an indictment against Bashar al-Assad could have a similar effect and be a demonstration of the existence and effectiveness of international criminal justice. As we have seen, however, this initiative was silenced by the Russian and Chinese vetoes in the Security Council about half a year later.

This episode demonstrates that Wolfgang Schomburg is, in the words of the German newspaper *Frankfurter Allgemeine Sonntagszeitung*, a lawyer to the core (*"Jurist durch und durch"*). Right before he started his assignment as a Judge at the Yugoslavia Tribunal on 17 November 2001, Schomburg gave an interview to the paper.[27] His subsequent seven years at the Tribunals, and the years thereafter, proved the characterization made at the time. He was reported by colleagues to be an obsessive worker, he was so much a lawyer that he would even bring along a thick legal commentary to the interview in a café, and he firmly believed that laws must apply to everybody, no matter how high they rank in the political or military hierarchy. We who worked for him at the Tribunal can fully corroborate these character traits. After having worked in the trenches and at the Olympian *Bundesgerichtshof*, he did not see his appointment in The Hague as a comfortable international assignment, which would allow him to take things a bit easier. Very much to the contrary, he threw himself into the work, he became immersed in the cases he was presiding over, and he never shied away from any professional task or debate that would contribute to a high-quality decision or judgement.

He truly did what he had promised to do, namely, to administer justice no matter how difficult it would be. He lived for his work, and everyone at both the Rwanda and the Yugoslavia Tribunal was ready to admire his dedication to the noble mandate of the Tribunals. It is characteristic of Wolfgang Schomburg that, even after his time as a Judge at the Tribunals, he still got involved in questions of international criminal law. He stayed involved on the academic level, which earned him an honorary doctor at the University of Durham, but also on the political level, as the Syria-example has shown. He just cannot stop doing the right thing, namely, acting in pursuit of the maxim which has been the creed of his work in The Hague and Arusha: No peace without justice, and no justice without law.

---

27 Alexander Marguier, 'Bin Ladin gehört vor ein internationales Gericht' *Frankfurter Allgemeine Sonntagszeitung* (Frankfurt, 11 November 2001) <">https://fazarchiv.faz.net/document?id=FAS__SD120011111143877#start> accessed 3 May 2017.

CHAPTER 15

International Criminal Liability for Incitement and Hate Speech

Ines Peterson

Abstract

The ICTR has found that "incitement to genocide", as defined in Article 3(c) of the 1948 Genocide Convention, is punishable regardless of whether or not it was successful (*see, e.g., Akayesu* Trial Judgement, para. 562). International legal instruments on war crimes and crimes against humanity do not contain a similar incitement provision. Consequently, calls for the commission of such crimes will normally have to be considered from the perspective of instigation. For this mode of liability, the ICTY and ICTR require a causal connection between the instigation and the *actus reus* of the underlying crime (*see, e.g., Kvočka et al.* Trial Judgement, para. 252; *Kajelijeli* Trial Judgement, para. 762). The proposed article would aim to address the distinction between incitement and instigation and analyse whether there is a legal basis in international law to conclude that urging the commission of war crimes or crimes against humanity can also be criminal without proof that this conduct led to crimes. The conclusions would be used to address, in particular, some of the factual findings in the *Šešelj* Trial Judgement.

Introduction

Under the current state of international law, there seems to exist a clear distinction between the treatment of hate speech directed towards genocide as opposed to war crimes and crimes against humanity. While incitement to commit genocide is a crime in and of itself, criminal liability in relation to war crimes and crimes against humanity depends on whether the words in question satisfy the elements of the usual modes of participation, such as commission, instigation, ordering or aiding and abetting. This generally requires a link between the conduct of an accused and subsequent crimes.

---

* Former Associate Legal Officer ICTR; Judge, German State of North-Rhine Westphalia, Münster, Germany.

The main aim of the paper is to address the proceedings against Vojislav Šešelj before the International Criminal Tribunal for the Former Yugoslavia (ICTY). This case has the potential to influence future prosecutions of high-level persons of authority based on the allegation that they induced the commission of crimes even by making political speeches. The prosecution's theories advanced in *Šešelj* are compared with previous jurisprudence of the ICTY and the International Criminal Tribunal for Rwanda (ICTR; together: Tribunals); the legal regime applicable before the International Criminal Court (ICC); and customary international law. It is submitted that the prosecution may have adopted an overly broad approach to criminal liability, in particular, by claiming that Šešelj was responsible for committing persecution as a crime against humanity and instigation.

Direct and Public Incitement to Commit Genocide

Direct and public incitement to commit genocide was for the first time expressly declared a crime under international law in Article 3(c) of the *Convention on the Prevention and Punishment of the Crime of Genocide* of 9 December 1948.[1] The provision has been incorporated in the statutes of most modern international criminal courts, including the ICTY and ICTR.[2]

In order to satisfy the *actus reus* of this crime, the accused has to make a direct appeal to commit an act of genocide, which excludes vague or indirect suggestions.[3] The public element is not limited to the use of mass communications, but can also include speeches addressed to smaller audiences in a public space, for example a public meeting.[4] The decisive factor is that the recipients

---

1   Convention on the Prevention and Punishment of the Crime of Genocide (adopted 9 December 1948, entered into force 12 January 1951), 78 UNTS 277 (Genocide Convention).
2   *See* UNSC, Statute of the International Criminal Tribunal for the Former Yugoslavia (25 May 1993), UN Doc S/RES 827 (ICTY Statute), Art. 4(3)(c); UNSC, Statute of the International Criminal Tribunal for Rwanda (8 November 1994), UN S/RES 955 (ICTR Statute), Art. 2(3)(c). *See also* Rome Statute of the International Criminal Court (adopted 17 July 1998, entered into force 1 July 2002), 2187 UNTS 90 (ICC Statute), Art. 25(3)(e).
3   *See, e.g., Prosecutor* v. *Pauline Nyiramasuhuko et al.* (Appeal Judgement), ICTR-98-42-A (14 December 2015), para. 3338; *Prosecutor* v. *Callixte Nzabonimana* (Appeal Judgement), ICTR-98-44D-A (29 September 2014), para. 233; *Prosecutor* v. *Ferdinand Nahimana et al.* (Appeal Judgement), ICTR-99-52-A (28 November 2007), para. 692.
4   *See Nzabonimana* Appeal Judgement, *supra* note 3, paras. 122–128, 231.

of the message belong to the general public, thus requiring an appeal to an indeterminate group of people.[5] As for the *mens rea*, the perpetrator must act with intent to directly and publicly incite others to commit genocide, which presupposes genocidal intent on his part.[6]

The ICTR has consistently held that the crime is inchoate in nature, meaning that it is punishable even if no act of genocide resulted therefrom.[7] In other words, a conviction for direct and public incitement to commit genocide does not require proof of a link between the incitement and any subsequent crime.[8] This interpretation arguably goes beyond what the drafters of the Genocide Convention could agree on. The convention's *travaux préparatoires* demonstrate that initial drafts containing language to the effect that incitement to genocide should be criminalized regardless of whether or not it was successful were eventually dropped after long and controversial discussions.[9] Admittedly, the debate appears to have centred on the need to include incitement as a separate punishable act at all because of a potential overlap with complicity to commit genocide and instigation as well as possible repercussions on the freedom of speech.[10] Nonetheless, the fact that Article 2 of the Genocide

---

5   See ibid., paras. 126, 231, 384; G. Werle and F. Jeßberger, *Völkerstrafrecht*, 4th edn. (Mohr Siebeck, Tübingen, 2016), marginal no. 892. See also *Nahimana et al.* Appeal Judgement, *supra* note 3, para. 862 (finding that supervising individuals at a certain roadblock did not constitute public incitement to genocide because such a group did not represent the general public). *Similarly, Prosecutor v. Callixte Kalimanzira* (Appeal Judgement), ICTR-05-88-A (20 October 2010), paras. 155–165.

6   See, e.g., *Prosecutor v. Augustin Ngirabatware* (Appeal Judgement), MICT-12-29-A (18 December 2014), para. 58; *Nzabonimana* Appeal Judgement, *supra* note 3, para. 121; *Nahimana et al.* Appeal Judgement, *supra* note 3, para. 677.

7   See, e.g., *Nyiramasuhuko et al.* Appeal Judgement, *supra* note 3, para. 2677; *Nzabonimana* Appeal Judgement, *supra* note 3, para. 234; *Prosecutor v. Simon Bikindi* (Appeal Judgement), ICTR-01-72-A (18 March 2010), para. 146; *Nahimana et al.* Appeal Judgement, *supra* note 3, para. 678; *Prosecutor v. George Ruggiu* (Trial Judgement and Sentence), ICTR-97-32-T (1 June 2000), para. 16; *Prosecutor v. Jean-Paul Akayesu* (Trial Judgement), ICTR-96-4-T (2 September 1998), paras. 561–562.

8   The ICTR has been criticized for nonetheless having factually overemphasised a causal link in some cases. See R.A. Wilson, 'Inciting Genocide with Words', 36 *Michigan Journal of International Law* (2015), pp. 277–320 (at pp. 287–299).

9   For a detailed analysis, see W.K. Timmermann, 'Incitement in International Criminal Law', 88 *International Review of the Red Cross* (2006), 823–852 (at pp. 832–838).

10 See ibid. See also W.A. Schabas, *Genocide in International Law*, 2nd edn. (Cambridge University Press, Cambridge, 2009), pp. 319–324 with further references.

Convention was ultimately adopted without the above mentioned addition indicates that there was no clear consensus on this issue among the founding fathers.[11]

Still, the literature largely endorses the ICTR approach and suggests that it has been adopted in Article 25(3)(e) of the ICC Statute.[12] This understanding is supported by the fact that Article 25(3)(b) of the ICC Statute, which covers ordering, soliciting and inducing, expressly mentions that a crime needs to occur or at least be attempted as a result. It would have been easy for the ICC states parties to include a similar phrase in Article 25(3)(e) of the ICC Statute had they wished to deviate from the ICTR jurisprudence.

'Incitement' to War Crimes and Crimes against Humanity

There is no treaty similar to the Genocide Convention declaring incitement to war crimes and crimes against humanity to be, in itself, a crime under international law. Some assert that Julius Streicher's case before the International Military Tribunal at Nuremberg is indicative of such a principle.[13] During World

---

11 See also W.K. Timmermann, 'The Relationship between Hate Propaganda and Incitement to Genocide: A New Trend in International Law Towards Criminalization of Hate Propaganda?', 18 *Leiden Journal of International Law* (2005), 257–282 (at p. 267).

12 See, e.g., K. Ambos, *Der Allgemeine Teil des Völkerstrafrechts: Ansätze einer Dogmatisierung* (Duncker & Humblot, Berlin, 2002), p. 652; K. Ambos, 'Article 25', in O. Triffterer and K. Ambos (eds.), *Rome Statute of the International Criminal Court*, 3rd edn. (Beck, Munich, 2016), marginal no. 38; L. Baig, 'Inchoate Crimes', in A. Cassese et al. (eds.), *Cassese's International Criminal Law*, 3rd edn. (Oxford University Press, Oxford, 2013), p. 203; R. Cryer et al., *An Introduction to International Criminal Law and Procedure*, 3rd edn. (Cambridge University Press, Cambridge, 2014), p. 377; W.A. Schabas, *The International Criminal Court: A Commentary on the Rome Statute*, 2nd edn. (Oxford University Press, Oxford, 2016), pp. 582–583; Werle and Jeßberger, *supra* note 5, marginal no. 888.

13 See Prosecutor v. Ferdinand Nahimana et al. (Trial Judgement), ICTR-99-52-T (3 December 2003), para. 981; *Ruggiu* Trial Judgement, *supra* note 7, para. 19; *Akayesu* Trial Judgement, *supra* note 7, para. 550; G.S. Gordon, 'Formulating a New Atrocity Speech Offense: Incitement to Commit War Crimes', 43 *Loyola University Chicago Law Journal* (2012), 281–316 (at p. 296); Timmermann, *supra* note 9, pp. 827–828; Wilson, *supra* note 8, pp. 283–285. In Art. 2(13)(ii) of its 1954 *Draft Code of Offences against the Peace and Security of Mankind*, the International Law Commission proposed a general provision on incitement, pertaining not only to genocide, but also to aggression, crimes against humanity and war crimes, based on the cursory observation that the notion of incitement was 'found in the Convention on Genocide as well as in certain national enactments on war crimes'. See *Yearbook of the International Law Commission* 1954, Vol. II, p. 137. By contrast, Art. 2(3)(f) of the 1996 *Draft Code of Offences against the Peace and Security of Mankind* states that direct and public

War II, Streicher published the viciously anti-Semitic weekly *Der Stürmer* in Germany. The International Military Tribunal considered that he repeatedly called for the annihilation of Jews in this magazine and thereby 'infected the German mind with the virus of anti-Semitism and incited the German people to active persecution'.[14] Streicher's 'incitement to murder and extermination' was found to constitute persecution as a crime against humanity.[15] While the tribunal observed that these acts took place 'at the time when Jews in the East were being killed under the most horrible conditions',[16] it did not expressly find a direct causal link between Streicher's publications and any specific acts of murder.[17] The condemnation of hate speech in several international human rights instruments has also been invoked in support of a criminal prohibition.[18]

It is rather doubtful whether these sources are sufficient to demonstrate that customary international law acknowledges incitement to war crimes or crimes against humanity as a crime in and of itself, in particular without any link to physical offences. The findings on Streicher's liability in the IMT Judgement are extremely cursory. Moreover, background material reveals that the prosecutors may have consciously avoided addressing the causality requirement at trial despite being aware of a lack of international precedent for a genuine hate

---

incitement would be punishable only if a crime in fact occurred. *See Yearbook of the International Law Commission* 1996, Vol. II, pp. 18, 22.

14   International Military Tribunal at Nuremberg (Judgement of 1 October 1946), in The Trial of German Major War Criminals, Proceedings of the International Military Tribunal Sitting at Nuremberg, Germany, Part 22 (IMT Judgement), p. 501.

15   *See ibid.*, p. 502.

16   *Ibid.*

17   *See also Nahimana et al.* Trial Judgement, *supra* note 13, paras. 981, 1007; Timmermann, *supra* note 9, p. 828. Another defendant at Nuremberg, radio commentator and head of the radio division at Goebbel's 'Ministry of Popular Enlightenment and Propaganda', Hans Fritzsche, was accused of having 'incited and encouraged the commission of war crimes, by deliberately falsifying news to arouse in the German people those passions which led them to the commission of atrocities'. The International Military Tribunal acquitted him on the basis that '[h]is position and official duties were not sufficiently important ... to infer that he took part in originating or formulating propaganda campaigns', his speeches 'did not urge persecution or extermination of Jews', and it was not proved that he knew the falsity of some of the news he disseminated. Ultimately, the tribunal was unable to find that Fritzsche's speeches 'were intended to incite the German people to commit atrocities on conquered peoples'. *See* IMT Judgement, *supra* note 14, p. 526. It has been correctly pointed out that these findings do not reflect any statement on causality. *See* Timmermann, *supra* note 11, pp. 261–262.

18   *See* Timmermann, *supra* note 11, pp. 263–266. *See also Nahimana et al.* Trial Judgement, *supra* note 13, paras. 983–1010.

speech crime at the time.[19] The reliance on international human rights treaties is open to criticism for a number of reasons. First of all, these instruments differ quite significantly in substance, thus making it hard to discern a commonly accepted definition of what constitutes prohibited hate speech.[20] Any suggestion to the contrary would also need to address reservations formulated by state parties to the treaties in question. Moreover, the treaties hardly require penal sanctions. Often times, they merely allow state parties to enact domestic legislation curtailing freedom of speech where it infringes upon the human rights of others by propagating hate and discrimination.[21] Consequently, the content of human rights conventions is far from showing that states generally accept an inchoate crime of incitement under international law.

Of utmost importance is that the issue was addressed in the course of shaping the ICC Statute. A clear majority of delegations to the Rome Conference in 1998 rejected proposals to extend Article 25(3)(e) of the ICC Statute to cover incitement to war crimes and crimes against humanity.[22] This indicates that, regardless of the IMT Judgement and human rights treaties, states are not prepared to elevate such conduct to an international crime.[23] Accordingly,

---

19 For details, see Wilson, supra note 8, pp. 283–285 with further references.

20 See, e.g., Universal Declaration of Human Rights (adopted 10 December 1948), UNGA RES. 217(III), Art. 7 (proclaiming the right to 'equal protection against any discrimination [...] and against any incitement to such discrimination'); International Covenant on Civil and Political Rights (adopted 16 December 1966, entered into force 23 March 1976), 999 UNTS 171, para. 20 (requiring that 'propaganda for war' and 'advocacy of national, racial or religious hatred that constitutes incitement to discrimination, hostility or violence' shall be prohibited by law). For further analysis, see Nahimana et al. Trial Judgement, supra note 13, paras. 983–999.

21 Although an exception can be found in the International Convention on the Elimination of All Forms of Racial Discrimination (adopted 21 December 1965, entered into force 4 January 1969), 660 UNTS 195, this treaty also focuses primarily on domestic criminal law. See ibid., Art. 4, which requires state parties to: (a) '[...] declare an offence punishable by law all dissemination of ideas based on racial superiority or hatred, incitement to racial discrimination, as well as all acts of violence or incitement to such acts against any race or group of persons of another colour or ethnic origin, and also the provision of any assistance to racist activities, including the financing thereof; and (b) '[...] declare illegal and prohibit organizations, and also organized and all other propaganda activities, which promote and incite racial discrimination, and shall recognize participation in such organizations or activities as an offence punishable by law'.

22 See Schabas, supra note 10, p. 325; Schabas, supra note 12, p. 583; Timmermann, supra note 9, p. 843. See also Ambos in Triffterer and Ambos, supra note 12, marginal no. 35.

23 As Schabas points out, similar discussions already took place during deliberations on the Genocide Convention in 1948. The Soviet Union proposed of prohibition of '[a]ll forms of

criminal responsibility depends on the establishment of accepted modes of liability,[24] which will be analysed in the following.

Commission

On several occasions, the Tribunals have addressed whether making incendiary statements could amount to commission, thus turning an accused into a perpetrator of ensuing crimes. In some cases, dissemination of propaganda was found to be a contribution to a 'joint criminal enterprise' (JCE).[25] However, the conduct in question was normally accompanied by other criminal acts of the accused.[26] In *Nyiramasuhuko et al.*, the Appeals Chamber stressed that a conviction for commission requires that the accused's conduct be an 'integral part of the [crimes]'.[27] In this respect, it would be essential whether the accused was present at the crime scene and conducted, supervised, directed, played a leading role or otherwise fully exercised influence over the physical perpetrators.[28] Where this was not the case, 'making a speech days, if not weeks, before the physical perpetration of killings' could not be deemed to constitute direct participation in or an integral part of such killings.[29]

---

public propaganda [...] aimed at inciting racial, national or religious enmities or hatreds or at provoking the commission of acts of genocide'. The majority of other delegations decisively rejected this proposal. See Schabas, *supra* note 10, p. 324 with further references. Cryer *et al.* mention that persecution under Art. 7 of the ICC Statute must be committed in connection with other crimes under the ICC's jurisdiction and that this addition was added because of a fear that 'any practices, more suitably addressed by human rights bodies, would be labelled as "persecution", giving rise to international prosecutions'. See Cryer *et al.*, *supra* note 12, p. 257.

24 See, e.g., ICC Statute, Art. 25(3)(a)–(d); ICTY Statute, Art. 7(1); ICTR Statute, Art. 6(1). These modes of liability may also be relevant in the context of genocide, in particular where the requirements of direct and public incitement to genocide have not been met.

25 See, e.g., *Prosecutor v. Radovan Karadžić* (Trial Judgement), ICTY-95-5/18-T (24 March 2016), paras. 3485–3487, *Prosecutor v. Vujadin Popović et al.* (Trial Judgment), ICTY-05-88-T (10 June 2010), paras. 1812–1822.

26 See, e.g., *Karadžić* Trial Judgement, *supra* note 25, paras. 3475–3505.

27 See *Nyiramasuhuko et al.* Appeal Judgement, *supra* note 3, para. 3322, *referring to Prosecutor v. Yussuf* Munyakazi (Appeal Judgement), ICTR-97-36A-A (28 September 2001), para. 135; *Kalimanzira* Appeal Judgement, *supra* note 5, para. 219; *Prosecutor v. Athanase Seromba* (Appeal Judgment), ICTR-2001-66-A (12 March 2008), para. 161; *Prosecutor v. Sylvestre Gacumbitsi* (Appeal Judgement), ICTR-01-64-A (7 July 2006), para. 60.

28 See *Nyiramasuhuko et al.* Appeal Judgement, *supra* note 3, para. 3322.

29 *Ibid.*, para. 3323.

The prosecution at both the ICTY and ICTR has sought convictions for committing persecution as a crime against humanity by hate speech.[30] In *Kordić and Čerkez*, the trial chamber rejected this proposition, finding that 'encouraging and promoting hatred on political etc. grounds' was neither listed as a crime in the ICTY Statute nor did it rise to the same level of gravity as the other acts enumerated in Article 5 and 'the criminal prohibition of this act has not attained the status of customary international law'.[31] At the ICTR, the prosecution was more successful. George Ruggiu was found guilty of persecution as a crime against humanity based on the allegation – to which he pleaded guilty – that he made broadcasts over *Radio télévision libre des mille collines* (RTLM) calling for the elimination of Tutsis.[32] In *Nahimana et al.*, the trial chamber took this approach to new levels. It convicted Ferdinand Nahimana, Jean-Bosco Barayagwiza and Hassan Ngeze for persecution as a crime against humanity, *inter alia*, because they were responsible for RTLM broadcasts advocating ethnic hatred or inciting violence against the Tutsi population or similar publications in the newspaper *Kangura*.[33] The trial chamber considered that 'hate speech targeting a population on the basis of ethnicity, or other discriminatory

---

30 See, e.g., *Prosecutor v. Vojislav Šešelj* (Third Amended Indictment), ICTY-03-67 (07 December 2007), paras. 5, 15, 17k, 20, 22, 33; *Prosecutor v. Dario Kordić and Mario Čerkez* (Amended Indictment), ICTY-95-14/2 (30 September 1998), para. 37(c) (alleging that Kordić participated in a campaign of widespread or systematic persecutions, which was carried out, *inter alia*, by 'encouraging, instigating and promoting hatred, distrust and strife on political, racial, ethnic or religious grounds, by propaganda, speeches and otherwise'); *Prosecutor v. Jean-Bosco* Barayagwiza (Amended Indictment), ICTR-97-19-I (14 April 2000), paras. 5.1–5.2, 5.9–5.11, 6.1–6.13, 6.15–6.23, Count 7; *Prosecutor v. Ferdinand* Nahimana (Amended Indictment), ICTR-96-11-I (15 November 1999), paras. 5.11–5.12, 5.17, 5.22, 6.7, 6.9–6.10, 6.14, Count 5; *Prosecutor v. Hassan* Ngeze (Amended Indictment), ICTR-97-27-I (10 November 1999), paras. 5.24, 5.26, 6.11, 6.17–6.19, Count 6; *Prosecutor v. George* Ruggiu (Amended Indictment), ICTR-97-32-I (18 December 1998), paras. 5.8–5.10, Count 5.

31 See *Prosecutor v. Dario Kordić and Mario Čerkez* (Trial Judgement), ICTY-95-14/2-T (26 February 2001), para. 209.

32 See *Ruggiu* Trial Judgement, *supra* note 7, paras. 18–24. The trial chamber considered that the accused, 'like [Julius] Streicher, infected peoples' minds with ethnic hatred and persecution' and that his 'acts were direct and public radio broadcasts all aimed at singling out and attacking the Tutsi ethnic group and Belgians on discriminatory grounds, by depriving them of the fundamental rights to life, liberty and basic humanity enjoyed by members of wider society'. See *ibid.*, paras. 19, 22.

33 See *Nahimana et al.* Trial Judgement, *supra* note 13, paras. 1081–1084. For the content of the materials, *see ibid.*, in particular, paras. 1078–1079. Barayagwiza was only convicted as superior under Art. 6(3) of the ICTR Statute. See *ibid.*, para. 1082. For a critical assessment of the factual findings in the *Nahimana et al.* Trial Judgement, see A. Zahar, 'The

grounds' was a 'discriminatory form of aggression that destroys the dignity of those in the group under attack'.[34] It would create 'a lesser status not only in the eyes of the group members themselves but also in the eyes of others who perceive and treat them as less than human'.[35] In particular, the 'denigration of persons on the basis of their ethnic identity or other group membership in and of itself, as well as in its other consequences, can be an irreversible harm'.[36] Consequently, such conduct reached the same level of gravity as the other acts enumerated as crimes against humanity under the ICTR Statute and therefore amounted to persecution.[37] Moreover, since persecution was not a 'provocation to harm', but the harm itself, criminal liability would neither depend on a call to action nor require a link with acts of violence.[38]

On appeal, Nahimana's and Barayagwiza's convictions were largely overturned because they lacked sufficient control over the choice of RTLM contents at the relevant time.[39] Ngeze's conviction was also quashed due to the fact that *Kangura* had not been in circulation when the genocide in Rwanda occurred and there was insufficient evidence to conlude that prior publications substantially contributed to the persecution of Tutsis during that period.[40]

Nonetheless, the *Nahimana et al.* Appeal Judgement contains various findings on persecution by hate speech. At the outset, the Appeals Chamber dismissed the defence submission that hate speech does not constitute a crime under international law by pointing to ICTY jurisprudence that underlying acts of persecution do not have to amount to international crimes.[41] It went on to find that 'hate speech targeting a population on the basis of ethnicity, or any other discriminatory ground' consituted 'actual discrimination' because it

---

ICTR's "Media" Judgement and the Reinvention of Direct and Public Incitement to Commit Genocide', 16 *Criminal Law Forum* (2005), pp. 33–48.

34 *Nahimana et al.* Trial Judgement, *supra* note 13, para. 1072.
35 *Ibid.*
36 *Ibid.*
37 See *ibid.*
38 See *ibid.*, para. 1073.
39 See *Nahimana et al.* Appeal Judgement, *supra* note 3, paras. 588–601, 631–636, 996–997. The majority upheld Nahimana's conviction as a superior under Art. 6(3) of the ICTR Statute because he failed to prevent or punish acts of persecution and instigation committed by RTLM staff after 6 April 1994. See *ibid.*, para. 996. The Appeals Chamber also confirmed Barayagwiza's conviction for instigating persecution by supervising roadblocks where Tutsis were killed. See *ibid.*, para. 1002.
40 See *ibid.*, paras. 516–519, 1013–1014.
41 See *ibid.*, para. 985, *referring to Prosecutor v. Radoslav Brđanin* (Appeal Judgment), ICTY-99-36-A (3 April 2007), para. 296; *Prosecutor v. Milorad Kvočka et al.* (Appeal Judgment), ICTY-98-30/1-A (28 February 2005), para. 323.

violated the targeted group's right to respect for their dignity and, in the case of incitement to violence, also the right to security.[42] However, in deciding whether hate speech was equally grave as other crimes against humanity, the Appeals Chamber stressed that speeches do not directly kill, injure or imprison people; rather, 'other persons need to intervene before such violations can occur'.[43] It implicitly acknowledged that there may be a difference between hate speech not inciting to violence and hate speech that does, but found it unnecessary to decide whether speeches of the former kind could amount to crimes against humanity because it 'is the cumulative effect of all the underlying acts of the crime of persecution which must reach a level of gravity equivalent to that for other crimes against humanity' and 'the context in which these underlying acts take place is particularly important for the purpose of assessing their gravity'.[44] The speeches attributed to the accused were accompanied by other RTLM broadcasts directly calling for genocide against the Tutsi group and 'took place in the context of a massive campaign of persecution directed at the Tutsi population of Rwanda, this campaign being also characterized by acts of violence (killings, torture and ill-treatment, rapes ...) and of destruction of property'.[45] The Appeals Chamber did not expressly adress the trial chamber's conclusion that liability for persecution by hate speech does not require the commission of subsequent crimes. However, it observed that some of the RTLM broadcasts 'did in practice substantially contribute to the commission of other acts of persecution against the Tutsi'.[46]

Some of these comments are not easily reconciled with the outcome of the Rome Conference in 1998. As mentioned above, the ICC state parties clearly rejected a crime of incitement to war crimes and crimes against humanity. That expression of will is certainly circumvented by finding – as the ICTR did in *Ruggiu* and the *Nahimana et al.* Trial Judgement – that hate speech may amount to persecution as a crime against humanity regardless of a proven link with subsequent crimes. In fact, the events at the Rome Conference even raise doubts as to whether hate speech should be considered an underlying act of persecution at all. In any event, for the reasons already provided, a different conclusion cannot be justified solely by referring to Streicher's conviction or international human rights conventions.

---

42   See *Nahimana et al.* Appeal Judgement, *supra* note 3, para. 986.
43   *Ibid.*
44   *Ibid.*, para. 987.
45   *Ibid.*, para. 988.
46   *Ibid.* See also *ibid.*, paras. 514–515, 995.

Instigation

Instigation is expressly mentioned as a mode of liability under both the ICTY and ICTR Statute.[47] Article 25(3)(b) of the ICC Statute punishes, *inter alia*, solicitation or inducement of the commission of crimes, which is generally understood to describe instigation as interpreted by the Tribunals.[48]

According to established Tribunal jurisprudence, the *actus reus* of instigating is to prompt another person to commit an offence.[49] The term 'prompting' means incitement to immediate or concrete action with respect to the commission of a crime.[50] In contrast to public and direct incitement to genocide, instigation can also take place in a private forum.[51] The most important distinction between instigation and incitement to genocide is that the former requires proof of a tangible link with subsequent crimes. For Article 25(3)(b) of the ICC Statute, this already follows from the wording of the provision, which expressly states that a crime has to be committed or at least attempted.[52] Similarly, the Tribunals have consistently held that while it is not necessary to show that a crime would not at all have been committed without the involvement of the instigator, the instigation must have at least substantially contributed to the perpetrator's conduct.[53] The *mens rea* of instigation consists of direct

---

[47] See ICTY Statute, Art. 7(1); ICTR Statute, Art. 6(1).

[48] See Ambos in Triffterer and Ambos, *supra* note 12, marginal no. 19; S. Finnin, *Elements of Accessorial Modes of Liability – Article 25(3b) and (c) of the Rome Statute of the International Criminal Court* (Martinus Nijhoff, Leiden / Boston, 2012), p. 62; Schabas, *supra* note 12, p. 575; Werle and Jeßberger, *supra* note 5, marginal no. 587.

[49] See, e.g., *Prosecutor v. Dario Kordić and Mario Čerkez* (Appeal Judgement), ICTY-95-14/2-A (17 December 2004), para. 27; *Brđanin* Appeal Judgment, *supra* note 41, para. 312; *Nyiramasuhuko et al.* Appeal Judgement, *supra* note 3, para. 3327; *Nzabonimana* Appeal Judgement, *supra* note 3, para. 146; *Nahimana et al.* Appeal Judgement, *supra* note 3, para. 480.

[50] See *Nyiramasuhuko et al.* Appeal Judgement, *supra* note 3, para. 3328, fn. 7619, *referring to* Black's Law Dictionary, 9th edn. (2009) and Oxford English Dictionary 2015. Regarding proof of an act of instigation based on non-explicit conduct, *see Prosecutor v. Ljube Boškoski and Johan Tarčulovski* (Appeal Judgement), ICTY-04-82-A (19 May 2010), para. 157.

[51] See Finnin, *supra* note 49, p. 67 with further references.

[52] See *Prosecutor v. Bosco Ntaganda* (Decision, Pre-Trial Chamber), ICC-01/04-02/06 (June 2014), para. 153 (requiring a 'direct effect' of the inducement on the commission or attempted commission of a crime); *Prosecutor v. Laurent Gbagbo* (Decision, Pre-Trial Chamber), ICC-02/11-01/11 (12 June 2014), paras. 244, 247; Ambos in Triffterer and Ambos, *supra* note 12, marginal no. 19; Schabas, *supra* note 12, p. 576.

[53] See *Kordić and Čerkez* Appeal Judgement, *supra* note 49, para. 27; *Nyiramasuhuko et al.* Appeal Judgement, *supra* note 3, para. 3327; *Nzabonimana* Appeal Judgement, *supra* note 3, para. 146; *Nahimana et al.* Appeal Judgement, *supra* note 3, paras. 480, 660; *Gacumbitsi*

intent to prompt another to commit a crime or awareness of the substantial likelihood that a crime will be committed in execution of the instigation.[54]

Crystallizing a proper connection between a potential act of instigation and crimes in the complex contexts of an armed conflict, widespread attacks against a civilian population or genocide can be extremely difficult. Although it is possible to conceive of instances where someone satisfies the elements of this mode of liability by calling upon an unidentified group of people to commit crimes, the causal link requirement as described above will normally limit criminal liability for instigation to cases in which there is evidence that the instigator induced certain identifiable individuals to engage in particular criminal actions. The larger the addressed audience and the more remote an act of instigation is to the commission of specific crimes, the less likely it will be to successfully demonstrate the requisite nexus between the instigation and such crimes.

The ICTR acknowledged this problem in *Nahimana et al.*, when the Appeals Chamber concluded that RTLM broadcasts denouncing certain Tutsi individuals before the start of the genocide in Rwanda on 6 April 1994 did not amount to instigating their murder because there was no evidence that the killers had heard the specific broadcasts and 'the longer the lapse of time between a broadcast and the killing of a person, the greater the possibility that other events might be the real cause of such killing'.[55] In *Nyiramasuhuko et al.*, the prosecution charged the mayor of a commune in Butare Prefecture, Joseph Kanyabashi, with instigating genocide based on a speech he gave at the swearing-in ceremony for his co-accused Sylvain Nsabimana as Prefect for Butare in April 1994. The trial chamber's acquittal was upheld on appeal. The Appeals Chamber noted that the trial chamber had considered that, at the ceremony, Kanyabashi expressed support for prior speeches made by other government officials, which amounted to direct and public incitement to genocide and contributed to triggering widespread killings in Butare prefecture.[56] However,

---

Appeal Judgement, *supra* note 27, para. 129. See also *Prosecutor v. Momčilo Krajišnik* (Appeal Judgement), ICTY-00-39-A (17 March 2009), para. 662. For an example of the requisite analysis, see *Brđanin* Appeal Judgement, *supra* note 41, paras. 312–319.

54 *See, e.g., Boškoski and Tarčulovski* Appeal Judgement, *supra* note 50, para. 68; *Kordić and Čerkez* Appeal Judgement, *supra* note 49, para. 32; *Prosecutor v. Siméon Nchamihigo* (Appeal Judgement), ICTR-2001-63-A (18 March 2010), para. 61; *Nahimana et al.* Appeal Judgement, *supra* note 3, para. 480.

55 See *Nahimana et al.* Appeal Judgement, *supra* note 3, para. 513.

56 See *Nyiramasuhuko et al.* Appeal Judgement, *supra* note 3, paras. 3314–3315; *Prosecutor v. Pauline Nyiramasuhuko et al.* (Trial Judgement), ICTR-98-42-T (24 June 2011), paras. 890, 898, 911, 925, 932–933, 5671, 5673, 5676, 5738, 5741, 5746, 5753, 5990.

his own speech was not found to be inflammatory.[57] In the Appeals Chamber's opinion, Kanyabashi's mere expression of commitment to implement the directives and instructions given by his previous speakers did not necessarily amount to *prompting* the attendees of the swearing-in ceremony or the people of Butare Prefecture to kill Tutsis.[58] It further stressed that there was no evidence that Kanyabashi's speech had any impact on subsequent killings.[59]

Ordering

Ordering means that a 'person in a position of authority uses it to convince another to commit an offence'.[60] The order needs to have a substantial effect on the commission of a crime.[61]

Aiding and Abetting

Aiding and abetting may encompass encouragement and moral support.[62] However, since this mode of liability also requires that the assistance have a substantial effect on the commission of crimes and encouragement and moral support qualify as 'psychological' assistance, there must be proof that the perpetrator of a crime was aware of the assistant's encouraging acts.[63]

The *Šešelj* Case

During the conflict in the Former Republic of Yugoslavia in the 1990s, Šešelj was a Serbian politician who served as a deputy in the Assembly of the Republic

---

57 See *Nyiramasuhuko et al.* Appeal Judgement, *supra* note 3, para. 3315; *Nyiramasuhuko et al.* Trial Judgement, *supra* note 56, para. 5753.
58 See *Nyiramasuhuko et al.* Appeal Judgement, *supra* note 3, paras. 3314–3315, 3328. See also *Nyiramasuhuko et al.* Trial Judgement, *supra* note 56, paras. 5753, 5993.
59 See *Nyiramasuhuko et al.* Appeal Judgement, *supra* note 3, paras. 3328, 3333.
60 See, e.g., *Prosecutor v. Radoslav Krstić* (Trial Judgement), ICTY-98-33-T (2 August 2001), para. 601; *Akayesu* Trial Judgement, *supra* note 7, para. 483.
61 See, e.g., *Nyiramasuhuko et al.* Appeal Judgement, *supra* note 3, para. 976.
62 See, e.g., *Prosecutor v. Duško Tadić* (Trial Judgement), ICTY-94-1-T (7 May 1999), para. 689 (stating that 'aiding and abetting includes all acts of assistance by words or acts that lend encouragement or support, as long as the requisite intent is present'.); *Brđanin* Appeal Judgement, *supra* note 41, paras. 273, 277; *Kalimanzira* Appeal Judgement, *supra* note 5, para. 74.
63 See, e.g., *Nyiramasuhuko et al.* Appeal Judgement, *supra* note 3, para. 2088; *Brđanin* Appeal Judgement, *supra* note 41, para. 277.

of Serbia and headed first the Serbian Chetnik Movement (sčp) and then the Serbian Radical Party (srs).[64]

On 31 March 2016, Trial Chamber III of the ICTY, by a majority vote of 2 against 1, fully acquitted Šešelj after a trial that by then had lasted almost eight and a half years, with the accused having been detained on remand already since February 2003.[65] The trial proceedings were overshadowed, *inter alia*, by Šešelj's insistence that the Tribunal lacked legitimacy to pass judgement on him and that he should be free to defend himself without assignment of legal counsel, a right which he successfully claimed by such extreme measures as going on an extended hunger strike. In addition, the ICTY was confronted with side-proceedings regarding Šešelj's repeated violations of the prohibition to disclose confidential information, and, finally, the fact that, well after the evidentiary phase and the parties' closing arguments, Judge Harhoff – who had been sitting on the bench since the beginning of trial – was disqualified for potential appearance of bias.[66] Consequently, a new judge had to be instituted who did not have the benefit of observing the trial proceedings in person, but instead was given time to review relevant court records.

The Prosecution's Case at Trial

The prosecution charged Šešelj only with crimes against humanity and war crimes. In the indictment, it alleged that through speeches made in Vukovar (Croatia), Mali Zvornik and Hrtkovci (Serbia) in 1991 and 1992, Šešelj 'physically committed' persecution because of 'direct and public ethnic denigration through "hate speech"',[67] as well as – by virtue of his speech in Hrtkovci – deportation and forcible transfer.[68]

The prosecution further pleaded that Šešelj participated in a JCE, the purpose of which was the permanent forcible removal of a majority of the Croat, Muslim and other non-Serb populations from approximately one-third of the territory of Croatia, large parts of Bosnia and Herzegovina and the Serbian autonomous province Vojvodina, in order to incorporate these areas into a new Serb-dominated state.[69] According to the indictment, Šešelj willingly contributed to the JCE, *inter alia*, by: (i) making inflammatory speeches in the media, during public events and visits to Serbian volunteers connected to the

---

64 See *Prosecutor v. Vojislav Šešelj* (Trial Judgement), ICTY-03-67-T (31 March 2016), para. 2.
65 See *Šešelj* Trial Judgement, *supra* note 64.
66 See *Prosecutor v. Vojislav Šešelj* (Decision, Trial Chamber), ICTY-03-67-T (28 August 2013).
67 See *Šešelj* Third Amended Indictment, *supra* note 30, paras. 5, 15, 17k, 20, 22, 33.
68 See *ibid.*, paras. 5, 15, 17(i), 31–33.
69 See *ibid.*, para. 6.

SRS and/or the SČP units and other Serb forces in Croatia and Bosnia and Herzegovina, thereby 'instigating' them to commit crimes against humanity and war crimes; (ii) espousing and encouraging the creation of a 'Greater Serbia' by violence, thereby participating in 'war propaganda and incitement of hatred towards non-Serb people'; (iii) calling for the expulsion of Croat civilians from the Vojvodina region, thus 'instigating' his followers and local authorities to engage in a persecution campaign against the local Croat population; and (iv) indoctrinating Serbian volunteers connected to the SRS 'with his extreme ethnic rhetoric so that they engaged in the forcible removal of the non-Serb population in the targeted territories through the commission of the crimes [...] with particular violence and brutality'.[70] On this basis, Šešelj was also charged with planning, ordering, instigating and aiding and abetting.[71]

In its closing brief, the prosecution maintained that 'hate speech' constitutes an underlying act of persecution.[72] It submitted that '[t]hroughout Croatia, Bosnia and Vojvodina', Šešelj engaged in a campaign of persecutory speeches that 'denigrated non-Serbs, thereby infringing their right to dignity and security'.[73] Noting that Šešelj undertook this campaign 'in the midst of escalating ethnic mistrust and violence' and that he occupied a position of influence, the prosecution considered that his 'hate speeches were like oil to the flame of ever increasing inter-ethnic strife'. It concluded that 'hate speech and other acts of persecution' reached the level of gravity of other crimes under Article 5 of the ICTY Statute and that 'hate speeches' were thus underlying acts of persecution 'themselves'.[74] In addition, the prosecution asserted that '[a]t least' three of Šešelj's speeches 'were so vitriolic' that they 'each independently' amounted to persecution even without reference to other persecutory acts.[75] In this regard, the prosecution maintained that Šešelj had described Croats in Vukovar and Hrtkovci with the 'offensive, derogatory, and dehumanizing "Ustaša" term', thereby associating all Croats 'with the "Ustašas" from World War II who committed terrible crimes against Serbs' and thus violating their right to dignity.[76]

---

70 See ibid., para. 10.
71 See ibid., para. 11. The charges of 'planning' and 'ordering' appear to have been dropped at some point during trial. They are not mentioned in the prosecution's closing brief. See *Prosecutor v. Vojislav Šešelj* (Prosecution's Closing Brief), ICTY-03-67-T (5 February 2012).
72 See Šešelj Prosecution Closing Brief, *supra* note 71, para. 559.
73 See ibid., para. 561, *referring to Nahimana et al.* Appeal Judgement, *supra* note 3, paras. 985–988, 1078; *Ruggiu* Trial Judgement, *supra* note 7, paras. 18–22.
74 See Šešelj Prosecution Closing Brief, *supra* note 71, para. 561.
75 See ibid., para. 562.
76 See ibid., para. 563.

For these reasons, the prosecution submitted that Šešelj 'physically committed' persecution in Šid (Vojvodina), Vukovar and Hrtkovci as well as deportation and forcible transfer in Hrtkovci.[77] It is interesting to note that, regarding the charge of persecution, the closing brief does not mention any link between Šešelj's speeches and subsequent crimes.[78] By contrast, the indictment is somewhat more forceful in arguing for the existence of such a link.[79]

With respect to instigation, the prosecution submitted in its closing brief that Šešelj had satisfied this mode of liability by: (i) using inflammatory and denigrating propaganda against non-Serbs in speeches, publications and public appearances; (ii) travelling to the frontlines to visit and encourage Serb forces in the fight against non-Serbs; (iii) dispatching high-ranking SRS/SČP members or commanders to spread his message of hate, revenge and ethnic cleansing; and (iv) failing to act against his subordinates who had participated in crimes against non-Serbs.[80]

While the closing brief claims that Šešelj's instigation substantially contributed to the crimes charged in the indictment,[81] it does not refer to any incident in which Šešelj addressed individualized individuals calling for the commission of specific crimes which were then committed by the recipients of his message or persons influenced by them.[82] It is merely suggested that Šešelj 'created a coercive environment where non-Serbs felt compelled to leave their homeland' and 'participated in creating conditions for committing the charged crimes and encouraged and provided moral support to *the perpetrators*';[83] addressed 'thousands in rallies', toured the front, appeared on television and was quoted in newspapers so that his nationalistic pro-Serb propaganda 'held

---

77 See ibid., para. 588. At this point, the prosecution expressly dropped the charge of persecution in relation to Šešelj's speech in Mali Zvornik. See ibid., para. 562 fn. 1715.

78 In this context, the prosecution only mentioned that Šešelj made speeches in Vukovar days before the Serb takeover of the city and shortly before violent crimes were committed by Serb forces and that, after his speech in Hrtkovci, interethnic violence increased. See ibid., para. 564. Regarding the prosecution's arguments in relation to the charges of JCE liability and instigation, see ibid., paras. 580, 583–584, 591–601. With respect to deportation and forcible transfer in Hrtkovci, see ibid., paras. 506–512.

79 See Šešelj Third Amended Indictment, supra note 30, paras. 20, 22, 33.

80 See Šešelj Prosecution Closing Brief, supra note 71, para. 589. With respect to the charge of JCE through the use of inflammatory statements, the closing brief primarily refers to its analysis on instigation. See ibid., para. 580. See also ibid., paras. 50–55.

81 See ibid., para. 590.

82 See ibid., paras. 591–601.

83 See ibid., para. 592 (emphasis added).

resonance with *Serb nationalists and sympathisers*';[84] and 'intended to provoke violent action *by whomever his words inspired*' while understanding the substantial likelihood that crimes would be committed as a consequence of his messages to 'nationalist Serbs', including 'volunteers, his sympathizers and other members of the Serb Forces'.[85] Where the closing brief mentions particular speeches, it refers to public threats of, for example, impending 'bloodshed' issued by Šešelj against Bosnian Muslims[86] or his use of historically-charged and polarising terms such as 'Ustašas', 'Shiptars' and 'Pan-Islamists' in order to promote contempt and hatred against non-Serbs and instigate violence against them.[87]

The Findings of the Trial Chamber

The analysis of the *Šešelj* Trial Judgement is mainly limited to cursory findings, often consisting of ultimate conclusions without setting out the relevant evidence adduced at trial. By a two-to-one majority, the trial chamber dismissed all charges against Šešelj for crimes against humanity already due to a lack of sufficient proof of a widespread and systematic attack against the non-Serb population in Croatia, Bosnia and Herzegovina and Vojvodina at the relevant time.[88] Furthermore, the majority concluded that the prosecution had failed to demonstrate the existence of a JCE because it had not concretely enough defined and proved a common criminal purpose behind Šešelj's acts, which was shared by other alleged JCE members.[89]

Consequently, the trial chamber only addressed *obiter* whether Šešelj could be held liable for having 'physically committed' the crime against humanity of persecution through hate speech. In this regard, the trial judgement notes, without reference to specific evidence, that the prosecution 'often conflated the calls by the Accused aimed at rallying the Serbian forces and fighters in the face of the enemy [...] and the calls that were directed against the non-Serb civilians'.[90] It continues that the mere use of abusive or defamatory terms

---

84 See *ibid.*, para. 593 (emphasis added). *See also ibid.*, para. 594 (stating that Šešelj 'inspired and instigated violence through his use of brutal, vulgar language and boasting about acts of vandalism and violence committed by him and those members of the Serb Forces who perpetrated the crimes charged in the indictment').
85 See *ibid.*, paras. 597–598 (emphasis added).
86 See *ibid.*, paras. 595–596, 599.
87 See *ibid.*, paras. 598, 600.
88 See *Šešelj* Trial Judgement, *supra* note 64, paras. 192–197.
89 See *ibid.*, paras. 227–281.
90 *Ibid.*, para. 283.

would not be sufficient to demonstrate persecution and scolds the prosecution for not having offered any contextual evidence that would have allowed for measuring 'the real significance or impact of the speeches in Hrtkovci and Vukovar'.[91] In particular, it is observed that Šešelj's alleged calls for cleansing the area of Croats were not accepted by the Serbian government at the time, let alone executed.[92]

The findings in the trial judgement on Šešelj's liability for instigation are expressly limited to the charge of war crimes.[93] The trial chamber considered that it was necessary to assess Šešelj's relevant statements and their potential impact on the perpetrators of crimes in light of the cultural, historical and political context.[94] At the outset, the majority decided that it would exclude from review speeches not covered by the indictment period and assign only limited probative value to press articles that did not come from official SČP/SRS newspapers or were published by Šešelj himself where the authors of such pieces had not been heard as witnesses.[95] In addition, the majority stated, again without reference to specific evidence, that it would not consider to Šešelj's detriment speeches, which 'could be assessed as nothing more than support for the war effort, as electoral speeches or as speeches that concerned territories that did not come under the geographic scope of the Indictment'.[96]

In the following, the trial judgement addresses five particular speeches, which had already been pleaded in the indictment.[97] With respect to the first, a speech that Šešelj delivered at a press conference in Šid while on his way to Vukovar on 7 November 1991, a newspaper article quoted him as stating that 'this entire area will soon be cleared of the Ustashas' and that Catholics in the region would have nothing to fear if they did not cooperate with the Ustashas and joined their units.[98] The majority noted that neither had the author of this article testified at trial nor had any other witness provided the context of the speech.[99] Even more importantly, the speech could not be considered instigation to a crime because the context 'rather suggests that these were speeches aimed at reinforcing the Accused's political party'.[100]

---

91 Ibid.
92 See ibid., para. 284.
93 See ibid., para. 293.
94 See ibid., para. 300.
95 See ibid., paras. 301–302.
96 Ibid., para. 303 (internal citation omitted).
97 See Šešelj Third Amended Indictment, *supra* note 30, paras. 20, 22, 33.
98 See Šešelj Trial Judgement, *supra* note 64, para. 306, *referring to* prosecution exhibit 1285.
99 See Šešelj Trial Judgement, *supra* note 64, para. 307.
100 Ibid.

Regarding two speeches given by Šešelj in Vukovar on 12 and 13 November 1991, the majority observed that witnesses had provided contradictory accounts of what Šešelj actually said on these occasions.[101] The witness statements reproduced in this section of the trial judgement range from purported calls in front of high-ranking members of the Serbian forces that 'No *Ustashas* must leave Vukovar alive',[102] to exclamations in the presence of at least fifty volunteers and soldiers to 'fight heroically against them, show no mercy',[103] and public calls, sometimes accompanied by threats, addressing Croat soldiers to surrender.[104] The majority concluded that, 'even if the statements ascribed to the Accused in their most controversial version are accepted', it could not dismiss the reasonable possibility that the speeches were made in a context of conflict and aimed at reinforcing the morale of the troops on his side, rather than being an appeal to commit crimes.[105]

The Trial Chamber further noted evidence that, in March 1992, Šešelj stated during a speech in Mali Zvornik in the presence of almost 1.000 people, including Muslim protesters and large numbers of Serbian policemen:

> Brothers, Chetniks, [...] The times has come for use to give the *balijas* tit for tat. [...] The Drina, the River Drina, is not a boundary between Serbia and Bosnia. It is the backbone of the Serbian state. Every foot of land inhabited by Serbs is Serbian land. Let's rise up, Chetnik brothers, especially you from across the Drina. You are the bravest. [... L]et us show the *balijas*, the Turks and the Muslims [...] the direction tot the east. That's where their place is.[106]

In the majority's opinion, this was not a clear call for 'ethnic cleansing' to be committed against the non-Serbs of Bosnia, since it could not exclude the possibility that Šešelj merely wished to contribute 'to the war effort by galvanising the Serbian forces' and, moreover, there was no evidence that his speech 'had even a limited impact'.[107]

Finally, the trial chamber observed that according to the prosecution, Šešelj gave an 'inflammatory' speech in Hrtkovci on 6 May 1992, as a result of which

---

101   See ibid., para. 318.
102   Ibid., para. 309. See also ibid., para. 314.
103   Ibid., para. 310.
104   See ibid., paras. 310–312, 314–315.
105   See ibid., para. 318.
106   Ibid., paras. 322–323.
107   Ibid., para. 328.

many Croatian inhabitants decided to leave the village.[108] While the trial chamber mentioned 'numerous testimonies and exhibits' describing the circumstances and the content of the speech, it addressed only two exhibits in further detail.[109] According to these exhibits, Šešelj stated, *inter alia*, that there was no room for Croats in Hrtkovci, Croats who had not yet left on their own accord would be escorted to the border by bus and the Serbs would 'promptly get rid of the remaining Croats'.[110] At the end, the crowd chanted slogans such as 'Ustashas out', 'Croats, go to Croatia' and '[t]his is Serbia'.[111] By majority, the trial chamber considered that Šešelj's speech in Hrtkovci clearly constituted a call for the expulsion or forcible transfer of Croats from the village.[112] However, with Judge Lattanzi dissenting, the majority found that the prosecution had failed to prove that this speech 'was the reason for the departure of the Croats or for the campaign of persecution' that was allegedly carried out.[113]

In addition, the trial judgement analyses two speeches given by Šešelj in the Serbian Parliament on 1 and 7 April 1992, which are not mentioned in the indictment. In the majority's view, these speeches also constituted calls for the expulsion and forcible transfer of Croats.[114] However, they were ultimately 'the expression of an alternative political programme that was never implemented' and the prosecution had failed to demonstrate any measurable impact of the speeches on subsequent crimes.[115] The majority voiced the same criticism with respect to other – unspecified – speeches studied in a prosecution expert's report.[116]

As regards the charge of aiding and abetting, the majority briefly concluded that Šešelj's 'nationalist' propaganda was not criminal in itself and that the prosecution had not presented evidence that his speeches substantially contributed to crimes charged in the indictment.[117]

---

108 *See ibid.*, para. 329.
109 *See ibid.*, paras. 330–332.
110 *See ibid.*, para. 331.
111 *See ibid.*, para. 332.
112 *See ibid.*, para. 333.
113 *Ibid.* (internal citation omitted).
114 *See ibid.*, paras. 335–338.
115 *See ibid.*, paras. 338–339, 342–343. *See also ibid.*, para. 341 (stating that the testimonies of witnesses that Šešelj's speeches had a significant impact on volunteers and others who listened to them, 'do not provide any reliable indicia through which the impact of the Accused's speeches could be measured or even remotely discerned in any concrete way').
116 *See ibid.*, para. 340.
117 *See ibid.*, para. 356.

Current Arguments under Appeal

The prosecution has appealed most parts of the *Šešelj* Trial Judgement, including the findings on the *chapeau* elements for crimes against humanity,[118] Šešelj's liability under the JCE-doctrine,[119] his responsibility for instigating,[120] aiding and abetting[121] and 'physically' committing persecution as well as deportation and forcible transfer.[122]

As far as physical commission of persecution by hate speech is concerned, the prosecution's appeal brief cites to findings in the *Nahimana et al.* Trial Judgement, also in support of its now express suggestion that it is irrelevant whether Šešelj's appeals for expulsion were ultimately carried out.[123] Potentially deviant findings in the *Nahimana et al.* Appeal Judgement are only mentioned in an accompanying footnote.[124] It is then claimed that, in any event, evidence admitted at trial shows that, after Šešelj's speech in Hrtkovci on 6 May 1992, Croats were subjected to discrimination, harassment and violence forcing them to leave the village.[125]

With respect to instigation, the prosecution complains that '[o]f the large number of Šešelj's statements admitted into evidence', the trial chamber's analysis was limited to 'only half a dozen speeches'.[126] The prosecution submits that the trial chamber erroneously failed to engage with the argument that Šešelj's 'repeated invocation of past crimes against Serbs, denigration of non-Serbs, fomenting fear of a genocide against Serbs, calls for revenge and overt calls for expulsion of non-Serbs from Serb-claimed areas, *taken together*,

---

118 See *Prosecutor v. Vojislav Šešelj* (Prosecution's Notice of Appeal), MICT-16-99-A (2 May 2016), paras. 11–12; *Prosecutor v. Vojislav Šešelj* (Notice of Filing of Public Redacted Version of Prosecution Appeal Brief), MICT-16-99-A (29 August 2016), paras. 120–121, 139–157.

119 See *Šešelj* Prosecution's Notice of Appeal, *supra* note 118, paras. 11–12; *Šešelj* Prosecution Appeal Brief, *supra* note 118, paras. 37, 158–171.

120 See *Šešelj* Prosecution's Notice of Appeal, *supra* note 118, paras. 11–12; *Šešelj* Prosecution Appeal Brief, *supra* note 118, paras. 109–117; 172–192.

121 See *Šešelj* Prosecution's Notice of Appeal, *supra* note 118, paras. 11–12; *Šešelj* Prosecution Appeal Brief, *supra* note 118, paras. 133–136, 193–195.

122 See *Šešelj* Prosecution's Notice of Appeal, *supra* note 118, paras. 11–12; *Šešelj* Prosecution Appeal Brief, *supra* note 118, paras. 125–131, 196–215.

123 *Šešelj* Prosecution Appeal Brief, *supra* note 118, paras. 128–130.

124 *Ibid.*, para. 130, fn. 348.

125 See *ibid.*, para. 130. For a discussion of the underlying evidence, *see ibid.*, paras. 198–210. With respect to Šešelj's speech in Vukovar on or about 13 November 1991, the prosecution does not mention specific evidence regarding the impact of this speech. *See ibid.*, para. 214.

126 *Ibid.*, para. 111.

amounted to instigation of crimes'.[127] Regarding the substantial contribution requirement for instigation,[128] the prosecution's appeal brief specifically points only to volunteers who repeated Šešelj's phraseology or praised him as supreme commander;[129] volunteers under Šešelj's control who responded to a speech he gave in Vukovar by firing their guns in their air;[130] and findings in the trial judgement that Croat soldiers detained at Velepromet, 'at least some of whom had surrendered in Vukovar', were murdered.[131]

Concluding Observations

There is an evident difference between incitement to genocide and to war crimes and crimes against humanity. The *Šešelj* case squarely addresses the extent to which instigation can be pushed, either by diluting the causal link or by formulating the nature of the harm in non-physical terms.

The prosecution's decision to pursue Šešelj for 'physically' committing persecution through 'hate speech' has obviously been heavily influenced by the *Nahimana et al.* case. Although the prosecution did not clearly state so trial, it appears to have now taken the position, based on findings in the *Nahimana et al.* Trial Judgement, that this form of liability does not require any link between the accused's conduct and subsequent crimes. However, as explained above, the *Nahimana et al.* case essentially ignores the decision of ICC state parties at the Rome Conference in 1998 not to criminalize incitement to war crimes and crimes against humanity as such. In light of these circumstances, it is difficult to conclude that acts of this nature are already punishable under international law, regardless of a causal link with crimes committed by the recipients of the inciting messages. Moreover, attempting to salvage the matter through the backdoor by relying on the crime of persecution means extending this offence to rather intangible harm, which deviates from other acts that have been found to amount to persecution.[132]

---

127 *Ibid.*, para. 110 (emphasis added). See also *ibid.*, paras. 174, 176.
128 *See*, in total, *ibid.*, paras. 177–190.
129 *See ibid.*, para. 179.
130 *See ibid.*, para. 182.
131 *See ibid.*, para. 183, *referring to Šešelj* Trial Judgement, *supra* note 64, para. 207(a). *See ibid.*, fn. 513, for evidence of '[m]any physical perpetrators in Vukovar' who could be placed 'listening to Šešelj's speeches'.
132 For other examples of persecutory acts accepted in the Tribunals' jurisprudence, *see* Cryer *et al.*, *supra* note 12, pp. 258–259.

In faulting the trial chamber for not having addressed more of Šešelj's statements for the purpose of his instigation liability, the prosecution's appeal submissions raise interesting questions regarding the scope of the charges. The indictment only mentions a maximum of five speeches,[133] which are addressed in the trial judgement. It may be argued that, in order to evaluate whether these speeches amounted to instigation, the trial chamber should have taken into account evidence of other speeches, for example by assessing the meaning of the speeches pleaded in the indictment in light of that other evidence. However, it is problematic to suggest that speeches pleaded and not pleaded in the indictment, 'taken together', satisfied the requirements for instigation.[134] Such an argument indicates that the prosecution may seek a conviction also based on speeches not pleaded in the indictment. This would stand in contrast with Tribunal jurisprudence that the indictment has to identify the particular acts or course of conduct on the part of the accused forming the basis for the charges in question.[135]

In any event, the case against Šešelj rests on a very broad notion of instigation. No matter how denigrating and spiteful some of his statements may have been, it is difficult to extract from the speeches mentioned in the indictment and trial judgement a call for immediate and concrete action with respect to the commission of a crime.[136] It seems rather doubtful whether this issue could be overcome by assessing these speeches together with other evidence. In addition, general considerations as to whether Šešelj's conduct was 'the reason for the departure of the Croats',[137] are besides the point. Such statements suggest that instigation liability may attach even where victims decide to leave an area because they feel threatened by inflammatory remarks of the accused. However, instigation is a secondary mode of liability, thus requiring a main perpetrator. Consequently, the focus needs to be on whether the remarks induced others to force victims out or to commit other crimes.

The prosecution has remained rather vague in this respect. It has not even attempted to establish that Šešelj ever addressed certain individuals or at least a specific crowd. It has also adopted an extremely lenient approach to the substantial effect requirement of instigation by only loosely connecting the

---

133 See Šešelj Third Amended Indictment, *supra* note 30, paras. 20, 22, 33.
134 See Šešelj Prosecution Appeal Brief, *supra* note 118, para. 110.
135 See, e.g., *Nyiramasuhuko et al.* Appeal Judgement, *supra* note 3, para. 2757. Similarly, *Prosecutor v. Vujadin Popović et al.* (Appeal Judgement), ICTY-05-88-F (30 January 2015), para. 66.
136 Cf. *Nyiramasuhuko et al.* Appeal Judgement, *supra* note 3, para. 3328.
137 See Šešelj Trial Judgement, *supra* note 64, para. 333.

timing of Šešelj's speeches with crimes charged in the indictment and hardly identifying listeners to these speeches as participants in such crimes.[138] The prosecution submissions further leave open whether Šešelj sparked any decision among members of his audience to commit crimes because they had not been determined to do so before.[139] If there is witness testimony to that effect, the Appeals Chamber will need to take a careful look at whether such evidence is reliable and sufficient. This would arguably require an assessment as to whether the purported perceptions of Šešelj's speeches as reported by the witnesses could have reasonably induced them to commit crimes.

Whether there is evidence of a link between Šešelj's speeches and subsequent crimes should also be relevant to his liability under the JCE doctrine and for aiding and abetting. In sum, the *Šešelj* case provides ample opportunity to revisit the Tribunal jurisprudence on the criminalization of incitement and hate speech. Notably, the contours of liability for instigation and persecution appear to be in need of further refinement. Developing a solution that comports with customary international law is not only required under the ICTY's mandate. It will also assist in establishing a clear guideline both for future prosecutions and potential accused to what extent incitement in relation to war crimes and crimes against humanity may lead to criminal proceedings on the international level.

---

138   See *Šešelj* Third Amended Indictment, *supra* note 30, paras. 20 (stating that, after Šešelj's speeches in Vukovar around 8 and 13 November 1991, Serb forces removed Croats and other non-Serbs from the hospital in Vukovar on or about 20 November 1991, some of whom were then tortured and killed), 22 (stating that, after Šešelj's speech in Mali Zvornik in March 1992, Serb forces committed crimes in various locations in Bosnia and Herzegovina between April and July 1992), 33 (stating that, as a result of Šešelj's speech in Hrtkovci on 6 May 1992, many non-Serbs were harassed, threatened with death and intimidated, forcing them to leave the area during the next three months).

139   See *Prosecutor v. Naser Orić* (Trial Judgement), ICTY-03-68-T (30 June 2006), para. 271 (finding that, where a perpetrator had definitely decided to commit the crime, further encouragement or moral support would not amount to instigation but could qualify as aiding and abetting).

CHAPTER 16

Die Konfliktregion Südosteuropa und das internationale und nationale Strafrecht

Herwig Roggemann

Abstract

Croatia and the other successor states of the Yugoslav Federation are tied to Germany by a common history. At times, more than 630.000 Yugoslav citizens lived in West Germany as so-called "guest workers" (*Gastarbeiter*). Geographical and cultural proximity, as well as personal and economic relations and friendly cooperation notwithstanding, ... occasional conflicts occur and demand a mutually agreed solution. This includes conflicts related to international legal assistance. Behind questions of procedure about who has to provide assistance when and under what conditions lurk historical frictions within domestic and foreign policy constellations, which still exert an effect until the present day. Questions of international legal assistance take on the broader form of coming to terms with the past. Examples for this are the judgments of the State Supreme Court at Munich in the murder case of *Đureković* against *Krunoslav Prates* of 16 July 2008, and against *Josip Perković* and *Zdravko Mustać* of 3 August 2016. The findings of the court and recent Croatian studies show the degree to which the socialist Yugoslav government under Tito, but also later governments until the democratic reform and dissolution of the Federation, were at permanent loggerheads with political opponents especially from Croatia. The Yugoslav government of the day used a two-prong approach against Croatian dissidents and especially leading members of the Croatian exile community: On the one hand by using the tools of the criminal law and international legal assistance, on the other hand through extra-legal violence and assassination orders. From 1946 to 1989, of 68 politically motivated murders of Croatian exiles, 39 were committed in Germany. This "special war" of Socialist Yugoslavia against dissidents in its exile community proved to be a harbinger of the ensuing war in Yugoslavia from 1991 to 1995. This war in 1993 became a major cause for the creation

---

* Dr. iur. Dr. h. c., Univ.-Prof. a. D. am Fachbereich Rechtswissenschaft und am Osteuropa-Institut der Freien Universität Berlin sowie Koordinator im Interuniversitären Zentrum Berlin/Frankfurt/O/Split/Paris, Der Verfasser verdankt Prodekan Doz. Dr. Matko Pajčić, Split, und Ivan Brčić, Berlin, anregende Gespräche und nützliche Hinweise.

of the ICTY. As its first German trial and appellate judge, Wolfgang Schomburg was part of the great international attempt to re-establish "peace through justice" by means of judicial intervention in the conflict area of the Balkans. Without this international tribunal and its 25 years of jurisprudence, the criminal law environment for the subsequent reconciliation in the conflict region could not have come about. A late contribution to addressing this chapter of Yugoslav, Croatian but also of German history, was made by the court at Munich in its judgments of 2008 and 2016. The option of surrendering the suspects from Croatia to Germany for the purpose of trying them there became possible only after Croatia's accession to the EU under the European Arrest Warrant framework, and after controversies between the German and Croatian – and within the Croatian – judicial systems had been put to rest.

1 Vom Anfang zum Ende des ICTY

1.1 Deutsche und kroatische Geschichte

1.1.1 Deutsche und kroatische Geschichte – freundschaftliche Beziehungen und Konflikte

Kroatien und die anderen Nachfolgestaaten der Jugoslawischen Föderation sind ebenso wie Deutschland und Europa insgesamt Subjekte und Objekte einer überaus konfliktreichen Geschichte[1]. Geografische und kulturelle Nähe sowie persönliche und wirtschaftliche Verflechtungen[2] aber auch die Aggression des nationalsozialistischen Deutschland und deren Folgen haben ebenso wie der Zerfall der Sozialistischen Föderativen Republik Jugoslawien und dessen Folgen[3] dazu geführt, daß die deutsche und kroatische Entwicklung, deren Gegenwart durch vielfältige freundschaftliche Zusammenarbeit geprägt ist,

---

1 Vgl. Holm Sundhaussen, Jugoslawien und seine Nachfolgestaaten. Eine ungewöhnliche Geschichte des Gewöhnlichen, Wien-Köln-Weimar 2012.
2 Dazu stellt das Perković/Mustač-Urt., OLG München v. 3. 8. 2016, 7 St 5/14 (2) unveröffentlicht, nicht rechtskräftig, S. 22, fest: „Zu Beginn der achtziger Jahre des vergangenen Jahrhunderts hielten sich in der Bundesrepublik Deutschland neben 632.000 jugoslawischen Staatsbürgern, die mit Billigung des Heimatlandes als Gastarbeiter nach Deutschland gekommen waren, etwa 10.000 Kroaten auf, die der politischen Emigration zuzurechnen waren. Daneben befanden sich etwa 4.000 Serben und 1.000 Angehörige anderer Volksgruppen in der Bundesrepublik Deutschland, die als politische Emigranten anzusehen waren".
3 Dunja Melčić (Hrsg.), Der Jugoslawienkrieg. Handbuch zu Vorgeschichte, Verlauf und Konsequenzen, 2. Aufl., Wiesbaden 2007; Herwig Roggemann, Krieg und Frieden auf dem Balkan, Berlin 1993; ders., Der Internationale Strafgerichtshof der Vereinten Nationen von 1993 und der Krieg auf dem Balkan, Berlin 1994.: ders., Der neue Balkankrieg der 90er Jahre-eine Herausforderung für das internationale Recht, Neue Justiz 1994, S 337 ff.

von Zeit zu Zeit auch die gemeinsame Lösung von Konflikten verlangt. Dazu gehören auch Rechtshilfekonflikte. Dabei zeigt sich immer wieder, daß hinter scheinbar nur verfahrensrechtlichen Fragen, wer wem unter welchen Voraussetzungen Hilfe bei der Strafverfolgung zu leisten habe[4], lange zurückliegende, tiefgehende innen- und außenpolitische Konfliktkonstellationen zum Vorschein kommen, die bis in die Gegenwart nachwirken. Fragen der Strafrechtshilfe weiten sich aus zu Fragen der Vergangenheitsverarbeitung. Beispiele für diesen zeithistorischen und politischen Zusammenhang von Rechtshilfefragen bieten die Urteile des OLG München im Mordfall Đureković gegen Krunoslav Prates v. 16. 7. 2008[5] und gegen Josip Perković und Zdravko Mustač v. 3. 8. 2016[6].

1.1.2   Aufarbeitung von Unrecht oder Schlußstrich?

Ursache für in großer Zahl und über längere Zeiträume begangene Rechtsverletzungen können nichtrechtsstaatliche Regierungssysteme oder innerstaatliche und zwischenstaatliche wirtschaftliche, ethnische, ideologische und militärische Konflikte oder beides sein. Das war in der jüngeren deutschen Geschichte mehrmals der Fall[7]. Es war unter anderen Bedingungen und auf andere Weise auch in der kroatischen und jugoslawischen Geschichte der Fall[8]. Vergangenes Unrecht wirkt nach, umso mehr und umso untergründiger, wenn es nicht aufgeklärt und aufgearbeitet wird. Das lehrt die historische Erfahrung. „Schlußstrich-Lösungen" und Generalamnestien erweisen sich immer wieder

---

4   Grundlegend zur Rechtshilfe das von Wolfgang Schomburg in Zusammenarbeit mit anderen Mitautoren herausgegebene, deutsche und europäische Standardwerk: Wolfgang Schomburg/Michael Bohlander/Otto Lagodny/Sabine Gieß/Thomas Hackner (Hrsg.), Internationale Rechtshilfe in Strafsachen – International cooperation in criminal matters, 5. Aufl., München 2012.

5   OLG München v. 16. 7. 2008, 6 St 005/05 (2), unveröffentlicht, rechtskräftig; im Internet unter dem Suchbegriff: urteil-safaric-safaric (bzw.http://www.safaric safaric.si/udruge/hsk/ 201012%20Urteil%20Uberlandesgericht%20Munchen.pdf [21. 6. 2017]).

6   OLG München v. 3. 8. 2016, 7 St 5/14 (2) unveröffentlicht, nicht rechtskräftig. Zu beiden Urt. weitere Angaben in Teil 2 dieses Beitrags.

7   Das gilt für den nationalsozialistischen Unrechtsstaat im Deutschen Reich von Beginn der Hitler-Herrschaft 1933 bis zur Bedingungslosen Kapitulation und Befreiung 1945 und für den staatssozialistischen Vorrechtsstaat der Deutschen Demokratischen Republik (DDR) von 1945/1949–1990.

8   Das gilt für den faschistischen Ustaša-Staat „Nesavisna Država Hrvatska" (Unabhängiger Staat Kroatien, NDH) von 1941–1944 und für den stalinistischen Vorrechtsstaat der Föderativen Republik Jugoslawien der Jahre unter Tito seit 1944 bis 1953 und in anderer Weise für den autoritären sozialistischen Vorrechtsstaat der Sozialistischen Föderativen Republik Jugoslawien (SFRJ) von 1953 bis zu deren schrittweisem Zerfall, beginnend mit Separation und Unabhängigkeit der Republiken Slowenien und Kroatien 1990/1991.

als Scheinlösungen und schaffen keinen nachhaltigen, ethisch legitimierten Rechtsfrieden[9].

1.1.3 Unverjährbarkeit von Mord und Völkermord

Aus diesen allgemeinen Gründen, aber auch aus dem besonderen deutschen Grund, um Zeit für die verspätet begonnene Strafverfolgung von ns-Straftaten zu gewinnen[10], ist nach deutschem Recht Mord[11] unverjährbar. Für Völkermord gilt dies auch aufgrund internationalen Rechts[12]. Das Völkerstrafgesetzbuch v. 25. 4. 2002 bestimmt und bestätigt dies für Völkermord, Verbrechen gegen die Menschlichkeit und Kriegsverbrechen[13]. Entsprechende Regelungen

---

9   Dies zeigt vor allem das Beispiel Spanien. Die demokratische Transformation nach dem Tode des Diktators Franco 1975 begann auf der Grundlage eines Kompromisses mit einer „Politik des Vergessens" und einer Generalamnestie durch das AmnestieG v. 1976. Nicht nur ein „Aufstand der Opfer", sondern auch die wachsende Forderung der Gesellschaft nach Aufklärung führten zu einem Wandel und dem Beginn einer offenbar unverzichtbaren „Rekonstruktion der Vergangenheit", dazu Walther L. Bernecker, Spaniens Übergang von der Diktatur zur Demokratie, Vierteljahreshefte für Zeitgeschichte 2004/4, S. 710: Lange Zeit war die spanische Gesellschaft bereit, den Preis der Tabuisierung der Repression zu zahlen. „Erst neuerdings, ein Vierteljahrhundert nach der Transition, wird der Schweigekonsens aufgebrochen. Verbunden mit dem Wunsch nach einer historischen Herleitung der Demokratie und einer Uminterpretation der Geschichte artikuliert sich immer stärker das gesellschaftliche Bedürfnis nach Aufarbeitung der dunklen Phasen...". Vgl. auch Julia Macher, Verdrängung um der Versöhnung willen? Die geschichtspolitische Auseinandersetzung mit Bürgerkrieg und Franco-Diktatur in den ersten Jahren des friedlichen Übergangs von der Diktatur zur Demokratie in Spanien (1975–1978), Bonn-Bad Godesberg 2002. Weitere Beispiele bieten die Verjährungsdebatten in Schweden und Frankreich. Der Verjährungsausschluss im deutschen Recht beruht unabhängig von besonderen historischen Verfolgungsanlässen „auf der Erwägung, daß bei solchen Taten das Strafbedürfnis nie entfällt", so Schönke/Schröder/Stree, StGB, 25. Aufl., München 1997, § 78 Rdn. 1.

10 Zur Verjährungsdebatte um die NS-Delikte im Deutschen Bundestag vgl. Anica Sambale, Die Verjährungsdiskussion im Deutschen Bundestag. Ein Beitrag zur juristischen Vergangenheitsbewältigung, Diss. Halle 2002 (Strafrecht in Praxis und Forschung Bd. 9).

11 Vgl. § 78 I StGB BRD.

12 Zur Unverjährbarkeit von Völkerrechtsverbrechen vgl. § 5 Völkerstrafgesetzbuch BRD, Art. 5; Art. 29 IStGH-Statut, dazu Gerhard Werle, Völkerstrafrecht, 2. Aufl., Tübingen 2007, S. 259; Otto Triffterer (ed.), Commentary on the Rome Statute of the International Criminal Court, Baden-Baden 1999, Art. 29; William Schabas, An introduction into the International Criminal Court, 2. Aufl., Cambridge 2004, S. 115. Die gewohnheitsrechtliche Geltung des Grundsatzes ist allerdings zweifelhaft.

13 Dazu Helmut Kreicker, Die völkerstrafrechtliche Unverjährbarkeit und die Regelung im Völkerstrafgesetzbuch, in: Neue Justiz 2002, S. 281 ff.

gelten auch im kroatischen Recht[14]. Insbesondere besteht nunmehr keine Verfolgungsverjährung für die dem Mord vergleichbare "Schwere Tötung" in Kroatien[15], während für diese Tatkategorie zuvor eine 25-jährige Verjährungsfrist galt[16].

Bei der notwendigen justizförmigen Verarbeitung früherer Rechtsverletzungen nach erfolgtem politischem und rechtlichem Systemwechsel und nach dem Ende der militärischen Konflikte kommt die Stunde rechtsstaatlicher Strafgerichtsbarkeit. Dabei spielt neben der nationalen kroatischen, serbischen und bosnisch-herzegowinischen und der deutschen Strafjustiz diese Rolle für Kroatien und seine konfliktbeteiligten Nachbarländer vor allem der Internationale Strafgerichtshof der UN für das ehemalige Jugoslawien (ICTY) von 1993.

So ist es nicht verwunderlich, daß auch *Wolfgang Schomburg*, der sich in seiner Laufbahn als Staatsanwalt, Staatssekretär, Richter hoher und höchster Gerichte und Rechtsanwalt stets der politischen und gesellschaftlichen Relevanz strafrechtlicher Entscheidungen bewußt war und ist wie wenige, mit Kroatien und dessen postjugoslawischen Nachbarländern mehrfach als Richter und als akademischer Lehrer und Berater in Beziehung trat.

Als ihn selbst aber auch die Rechtsprechung dieses ersten internationalen Strafgerichtshofs seit Nürnberg 1945 und Tokyo 1946 prägende Arbeit darf seine Tätigkeit von 2001 bis 2008 als erster deutscher Richter zunächst an der Strafkammer, später an der Revisionskammer des ICTY in Den Haag sowie des ICTR in Arusha angesehen werden.

---

14 Vgl. Art. 81 Kazneni zakon (Strafgesetzbuch) der Republik Kroatien – StGB Kro), Narodne Novine (Gesetzblatt), NN 125/2011 i. d. F. der ÄnderungsG 144/2012, 56/2015 und 61/2015, die u. a. die Regelungen des am 17. 7. 1998 beschlossenen, am 1. 7. 2002 in Kraft getretenen, am 21. 5. 2001 bereits von Kroatien ratifizierten des Rom-Status des IStGH inkorporiert haben; dazu Maja Munivrana Vajda, Međunarodni zločini prema novom kaznenom zakonu (Internationale Straftaten nach dem neuen Strafgesetzbuch) in: Hrvatski ljetopis za kazneno pravo i praksu (Kroatische Zeitschrift für Strafrecht und Praxis), vol. 19 Nr. 2/2012, s. 819 ff.

15 Vgl. Art. 81 StGB Kro von 2011.

16 Vgl. Art. 90 StGB Kro i. d. F. v. 1997. Zur Verjährungsdiskussion in Kroatien vgl. Ana Garačić (Richterin am Obersten Gericht der Republik Kroatien), Zastara Kaznenog Progona (Verjährung von Straftraten – de lege ferenda und de lege lata), unter: www.vsrh.hr/AGa rancic-ZastaraKaznenogProgona, S. 11: „Das bedeutet, daß nach Ablauf einer Frist von 30 Jahren ein Strafverfahren wegen schwerster Straftaten wie Totschlag oder schwerer Totschlag nicht mehr eingeleitet werden kann. Wir können die Frage stellen, ob diese Verjährungsfrist heute lang genug ist, wo wir viele unerledigte Strafsachen dieser Art haben, bei denen seit Tatbegehung schon 20 Jahre vergangen sind".

1.2 Schwierigkeiten internationaler Rechtsprechungstätigkeit und außergerichtlicher wissenschaftlicher Zusammenarbeit

Welchen Schwierigkeiten sich der lange und langwierige – von kritischen Betrachtern in der Konfliktregion immer wieder in Zweifel gezogene – Prozeß der rechtlichen und politischen Rezeption der Strafverfolgung und Rechtsprechung des Haager UN-Tribunals für das ehemalige Jugoslawien in den drei Konfliktstaaten Serbien, Kroatien und Bosnien und Herzegowina – und damit auch die Arbeit Wolfgang Schomburgs – gegenübersah, veranschaulichen einige Beispiele.

1.2.1 Šešelj-Fall[17]

Gleich zu Beginn des durch Provokationen seitens des Angeklagten und am Ende auch durch schwer verständliche Entscheidungen des Gerichts gekennzeichneten, übermäßig langen Verfahrens gegen den ehemaligen serbischen Parlamentspräsidenten und Vorsitzenden der Serbischen Radikalen Partei (SRS), *Vojislav Šešelj*, wies dieser den offenbar ein kroatisch gefärbtes „BosnischKroatischSerbisch" (Kürzel: BKS) sprechenden Gerichtsdolmetscher mit der Begründung zurück, dies sei nicht seine Sprache[18]. Der Angeklagte bezeichnete das Gericht als „illegal" und unzuständig, die Anklagevorwürfe als „völlig haltlos", zudem sei ein Gericht, an dem Richter wie Wolfgang Schomburg aus dem „Nazi-Land" Deutschland tätig seien, gegenüber einem Serben ohnehin befangen[19]. Im späteren Prozeßverlauf bedrohte er Zeugen und machte herabwürdigende Äußerungen gegenüber Tatopfern.

Der Šešelj-Prozeß zog sich wegen des obstruktiven Verhaltens des Angeklagten aber auch infolge der im ICTY-Verfahren aufgrund der Verfahrensordnung vorherrschenden Verfahrensmaximen des angloamerikanischen Parteiverfahrens – die Wolfgang Schomburg nicht müde wurde, mit Recht zu

---

17 Vgl. AZ. IT-03-67.
18 Vgl. dagegen die von 200 Linguisten und Autoren aus den vier Staaten Kroatien, Serbien, Bosnien und Herzegowina und Montenegro unterzeichnete, am 29. 3. 2017 im Portal lupiga.com veröffentlichte Deklaration: „Wir sprechen die gleiche Sprache", dazu Caroline Fetscher, in: Der Tagesspiegel v. 2. 4. 2017. Allerdings ist hierbei zugunsten des Angekl. wie aller anderen Prozeßbeteiligten die besondere Sensibilität der Sprachenfrage in und zwischen den Balkanländern und ihrer multiethnischen Einwohnerschaft zu berücksichtigen, die den prozessualen Anspruch auf serbische bzw. kroatische oder bosnische Gerichtsdolmetscher in jedem Fall als begründet erscheinen läßt, unabhängig davon, ob diese Sprachen zu 90% übereinstimmen und transethnisch verständlich sind.
19 Der Verf. nahm 2003 mit seinen Seminarteilnehmern aus Berlin und Kroatien zunächst an einer Diskussion mit Wolfgang Schomburg und der Staatsanwältin Hildegard Uertz-Retzlaff im ICTY in Den Haag und später als Besucher an dieser Sitzung teil.

kritisieren[20] – mehr als 12 Jahre hin. Schließlich entschied das Tribunal 2014, den Angeklagten Šešelj vor Verfahrensabschluß aus Gesundheitsgründen unter Auflagen vorläufig aus der Haft nach Serbien zu entlassen, um ein dem Milošević-Prozeß vergleichbares Ende durch Todesfall zu vermeiden. Schon bei seiner von großer öffentlicher Aufmerksamkeit begleiteten Ankunft in Serbien gab der Angeklagte unter Bruch der gerichtlichen Auflagen Erklärungen gegen das Tribunal und über seine eigenen künftigen politischen Pläne ab. Die serbische Presse berichtete darüber ausführlich, während die kroatische Presse dies als Bestätigung für das Scheitern des ICTY bei der Wahrnehmung seiner friedenstiftenden Mission mit Mitteln der Rechtsprechung ansah[21].

Der Aufforderung der Revisionskammer, zur Fortsetzung der Verhandlung in Den Haag zu erscheinen, leistete der Angeklagte nicht Folge. Der erstinstanzliche Freispruch in allen neun Anklagepunkten, mit dem die Strafkammer 2016 eine Abkehr von bisher praktizierten Zurechnungs- und Beweisgrundsätzen vornahm, bestärkte die nationalistischen Kritiker des ICTY in Serbien, während er in Kroatien und Bosnien und der Herzegowina empörte Reaktionen

---

[20] U. a. in einer beachtlichen Anzahl Dissenting votes und wohl auch in so mancher nicht nachlesbaren, nichtöffentlichen Beratungssitzung. – Kritisch zur Rolle des Richters im Beweisverfahren bemerkte Schomburg pointiert: „Der Zynismus des angloamerikanischen Systems, einen Prozeß um jeden Preis gewinnen zu wollen und die Suche nach der erreichbaren Wahrheit als unangebrachten Idealismus abzutun, ist bedauerlich. Menschen vor Ort, die Menschen, für die wir arbeiten, fragen sich oft: Warum sind bestimmte Leute „nur deswegen" angeklagt worden, obwohl doch jeder vor Ort „weiß", daß durch den Angeklagten noch andere, sogar schwerere Delikte begangen wurden? Ein informeller Deal über Tatsachen oder rechtliche Bewertungen vor Anklageerhebung wird dem Richter nicht bekannt. Dem Richter sind die Hände gebunden", so in: FAZ.net v. 23. 9. 2009. Ebenso negativ wirkt sich die im Parteiverfahren schwache Position des Richters im Beweisverfahren aus, dessen Inhalt weitgehend durch die Anträge der Parteien bestimmt wird.

[21] Vgl. Ines Sabalić, Smrt Haškog suda (Der Tod des Haager Gerichts), in „Globus" (Zagreb) v. 21. 11. 2014, S. 30 ff. Die Autorin unterzieht die Rechtsprechungstätigkeit des ICTY in der wohl wichtigsten kroatischen Wochenzeitschrift einer zusammenfassenden Analyse und setzt sich kritisch mit der „Marginalisierung" des ICTY auseinander, deren Anfang die Autorin nach dem Tod von Milošević und der Freilassung Šešeljs – unter Berufung auf die ICTY-Kritik von Autoren wie Mirko Klarin, Marko Hoare und Eric Gordy – einsetzen sah. Im Gegensatz zum Nürnberger Kriegsverbrechertribunal, wo es um die eine Ideologie des Nazismus und das eine große Verbrechen des Holocaust gegangen sei, fehle in Den Haag ein gemeinsames Narrativ. Statt dessen verliere sich das Gericht in hunderten von Fällen und mehr oder weniger bewiesenen Straftaten. Dennoch überwiege trotz der Mängel die positive Bedeutung des Gerichts, da „ohne dieses niemand angeklagt und verurteilt worden wäre".

hervorrief. Der kroatische Ministerpräsident Tihomir Orešković bezeichnete das Urteil als „schändlich". Dieses Urteil spaltete nicht nur ein weiteres Mal die öffentliche Meinung in der Konfliktregion, sondern auch im Gericht selbst. Die Begründung steht teilweise in Widerspruch zu Feststellungen im kurz zuvor ergangenen Karadžić-Urteil über die Beteiligung des Angeklagten Šešelj an einem übergreifenden gemeinschaftlichen verbrecherischen Unternehmen (joint criminal enterprise – JCE). Und die Annahme der Kammer, es sei dem Angeklagten der erforderliche subjektive Tatbestand in Bezug auf die Mitwirkung an diesem gemeinschaftlichen Unternehmen nicht nachweisbar; ist bei diesem Angeklagten wenig überzeugend, hatte er doch die Übereinstimmung seiner Ansichten und Absichten mit dem militärischen Vorgehen der serbischen Seite und dem zugrunde liegenden „großserbischen" Konzept, in das er sich unterstützend einbrachte, wiederholt öffentlich kundgetan. Die überstimmte italienische Richterin der Kammer, *Flavia Lattanzi,* kam daher in ihrer von ihren beiden Richterkollegen abweichenden Meinung zu gegenteiligen Schlußfolgerungen für die strafrechtliche Verantwortlichkeit des Angeklagten bei der Vorbereitung und Unterstützung von Kriegsverbrechen[22]. Und der ehemalige Richter *Wolfgang Schomburg* nannte die Entscheidung „ein glattes Fehlurteil".

1.2.2   Blaškić-Fall[23]

Nachdem der kroatische General Tihomir Blaškić im Jahr 2000 in erster Instanz wegen fahrlässig verletzter Vorgesetztenverantwortlichkeit („command responsibility") bei Einsätzen in Bosnien und der Herzegowina zu der unverhältnismäßigen[24] Freiheitsstrafe von 45 Jahren verurteilt worden war, wurde

---

22   Dieses abweichende Votum (vgl. AZ 51/62793 BIS), das an Deutlichkeit in einem internationalen Strafverfahren wohl Seltenheitswert besitzt und ein Licht auf die Probleme des ICTY und der Besetzung seiner Richterschaft wirft, leitete die Richterin wie folgt ein: „I regret that I have to begin my partially dissenting opinion by specifying that the adverb `partially` here is more of an euphemism. In fact, unusually for a dissenting opinion, I disagree on almost everything: the description of the context, the use of the evidence, the flawed or, at best, cursory analysis of the evidence, the disregard for the jurisprudence, and the conclusions". Vgl. dazu nur Hildegard Uertz-Retzlaff, Zur neueren Judikatur des Jugoslawiengerichtshofes, in: Zeitschrift für Internationale Strafrechtsdogmatik (ZIS) 2016, S. 851 ff.
23   AZ: IT-95-14 A v. 29. 7. 2004.
24   Von der damaligen Chefanklägerin Carla Del Ponte unverständlicher Weise mit Befriedigung aufgenommen: „Ich war darüber hocherfreut, schien doch das Urteil gegen Blaškić – 45 Jahre – weitaus angemessener als manche andere Schuldsprüche des Tribunals", so Carla Del Ponte mit Chuck Sudetic, Im Namen der Anklage. Meine Jagd auf

dieses erstinstanzliche Urteil in Bosnien und der Herzegowina als Sieg der Gerechtigkeit gefeiert. In Kroatien dagegen wurde das Urteil mit Entsetzen aufgenommen und als Beweis für die Voreingenommenheit des Tribunals gegenüber dem Aggressionsopfer Kroatien kommentiert.

Als zuständiger Richter in der Revisionskammer begründete *Wolfgang Schomburg* am 29. 7. 2004 die Aufhebung des Ersturteils wegen zahlreicher Verfahrensmängel, insbesondere auch im Beweisverfahren[25]. Das Strafmaß wurde auf 9 Jahre herabgesetzt und die sofortige Freilassung des Verurteilten unter Anrechnung der Untersuchungshaftdauer angeordnet. Den ein Jahr später am 29. 7. 2005 gestellten Antrag der Anklage auf Wiederaufnahme des Verfahrens wies die Revisionskammer am 23. 11. 2006 zurück. Diese Entscheidung

---

Kriegsverbrecher und die Suche nach Gerechtigkeit, Frankfurt/Main 2008, S. 322. Diese Äußerung belegt das spezifische, aus unterschiedlichen Rechtskulturen rührende und bis zum Ende nicht überwundene Dilemma internationaler Strafgerichtsbarkeit und insbesondere des ICTY bei der Strafzumessung.

25 Zu den Besonderheiten dieses Verfahrens gehörte, daß die erstinstanzliche Richterin Kirk McDonald Beweismittelerzwingungsgrundsätze der US-amerikanischen Zivilprozeßpraxis („Subpoena ducis tecum" – subpoena for production of evidence) kurzerhand ins internationale Strafprozeßrecht übertrug und auf Staaten wie Prozeßparteien anzuwenden suchte. Dazu Herwig Roggemann, Problems and Limitations of the Procedure of Evidence Before the International Criminal Tribunal in The Hague, Amicus Curiae Expertise, Accepted by the Appeals Chamber Sept. 19th, 1997; ders., The Problem of Legality and the Limits of a Sub Poena Duces Tecum Decision in the Blaškić-Case, in: Zbornik Radova Pravnog Fakulteta u Splitu, vol. 49–50 (1998), No. 1–2, S. 17 ff. Zu den durch Sicherheitsinteressen der souveränen Staaten gezogenen Rechtsgrenzen des Ermittlungs- und Beweisverfahrens und den aus der Sicht des Verf. in diesem Punkt problematischen Unterscheidungen zwischen Verfahren und Beweiserzwingungsmöglichkeiten vor dem ICTY und dem ICC vgl. die Beiträge in: Herwig Roggemann/Petar Šarčević, (eds.), National Security and International Criminal Justice, The Hague-London-New York (Kluwer) 2002. Erfolgt eine Intervention zur Friedenssicherung auf Grund einer Resolution des Sicherheitsrates in Form einer "juridischen Intervention", so stehen auch dem Ad-Hoc-Gericht nur die gewohnheitsrechtlich gesicherten Formen des gerichtlichen Beweisverfahrens zur Verfügung. Dem Sicherheitsrat kommt keinerlei darüber hinausgehende Gesetzgebungskompetenz im Verfahrensrecht zu. Mit dem Hinweis auf die Differenz zwischen "horizontalem" und "vertikalem" Kooperationsverhältnis läßt sich diese Legitimationsgrenze des Sicherheitsrats als "Verfahrensgesetzgeber" durch die in seinem Auftrag handelnden Richter bei der Selbstschöpfung ihrer Verfahrensordnung nicht erfassen und erst recht nicht überspielen. Zum ICTY als Verfahrensordnungsschöpfer vgl. Christiane Kamardi, Die Ausformung einer Prozeßordnung sui generis durch das ICTY unter Berücksichtigung des Fair-Trial-Prinzips, Berlin 2009, demgegenüber vgl. Davor Krapac, Die Grundsätze des kroatischen Strafprozeßrechts, in: Dirk Fischer (Hg.), Transformation des Rehts in Ost und West, Roggemann-FS, Berliner Wissenschaftsverlag, Berlin 2006, S 283 ff.

wurde in Kroatien als später Sieg der Gerechtigkeit gefeiert, denn nicht nur dort hatte die überlange Verfahrens- und U-Haftdauer – die in diesem wie in anderen ICTY-Fällen mit menschenrechtlichen Standards der EMRK nicht vereinbar ist – berechtigte Kritik hervorgerufen. In Bosnien und Herzegowina und Serbien dagegen sah man in dieser überzeugend begründeten Korrektur der erstinstanzlichen Entscheidung einen Beleg für die Abhängigkeit des Gerichts von Einflußnahmen der internationalen Politik.

1.2.3   Gotovina-Fall[26]

Ähnlich schroff geteilt war die öffentliche Meinung in den verschiedenen Staaten der Konfliktregion auch bei Gelegenheit späterer Entscheidungen des ICTY. Scheinbar unüberbrückbar standen einander die Wahrnehmungen des Gotovina-Verfahrens durch die Öffentlichkeit in Kroatien und Serbien gegenüber. Der vom kroatischen Staatspräsidenten Franjo Tudjman zum General beförderte ehemalige Fremdenlegionär Ante Gotovina war Kommandeur in der legendären „Oluja-Operation" im Sommer 1995. In diesem – ungeachtet des UN-Embargos gegenüber den postjugoslawischen Konfliktparteien mithilfe US-amerikanischer Militärberater und anderer Waffenlieferanten vorbereiteten – Militäreinsatz ging es um die Befreiung und Wiedereingliederung der von einer großen serbischen Minderheit bewohnten kroatischen Region „Lika", im Verfahren „Krajina" genannt, in den kroatischen Staatsverband. Diese Region hatte sich zuvor mit serbischer Unterstützung, und begleitet von Übergriffen und Gewaltmaßnahmen gegen die kroatischen Bewohner, zur von Kroatien unabhängigen „Serbischen Republik Krajina" erklärt und der Republik Serbien angeschlossen[27]. Bei der Wiedereinnahme kam es zu Übergriffen kroatischer Militärs auf serbische Zivilisten. Zahlreiche Zivilpersonen kamen zu Tode und Zehntausende oder mehr serbischer Bewohner flüchteten nach Serbien und Bosnien und Herzegowina[28]. Im erstinstanzlichen Urteil war Gotovina, der dem ICTY erst nach jahrelanger Fahndung und Verhaftung durch die spanische

---

26   AZ: IT-06-90 A v. 16. 11. 2012.
27   Dazu Ante Nazor, Velikosrpska Agresija na Hrvatsku 1990.ih (Die Großserbische Aggression gegen Kroatien in den 1990er Jahren), Zagreb 2011, S. 52 ff.
28   Die Zahlen sind, wie fast alle Verlustzahlen aus dem Jugoslawienkrieg von 1991–1995 umstritten. Entgegen behaupteten höheren Verlustzahlen sah die Strafkammer des ICTY (AZ: IT-06-90 A v. 15. 4. 2011) die Tötung von 44 serbischen Zivilpersonen als erwiesen an. Die Angaben zu den aus der Region geflüchteten serbischen Einwohner schwanken zwischen einigen zehntausend und rund 150 000 oder mehr Personen. Vgl. zu den Kriegsfolgen im Einzelnen die umfassende (998 seitige) Dokumentation: Helsinki Committee for Human Rights in Serbia, Conflict in Numbers. Casualities of the 1990s Wars in the Former Yugoslavia (1991–1999), Belgrade 2009.

Polizei auf Teneriffa zugeführt werden konnte, 2011 u. a. wegen Verletzung seiner Vorgesetztenveranwortlichkeit und Begehung eines gemeinschaftlichen verbrecherischen Unternehmens zu einer Freiheitsstrafe von 24 Jahren verurteilt worden. Die Revisionskammer sprach Gotovina mangels Beweises frei und vollzog in der Urteilsbegründung eine viel diskutierte und kritisierte, teilweise Abkehr von den zuvor vom ICTY entwickelten Zurechnungsgrundsätzen des gemeinschaftlichen verbrecherischen Unternehmens (JCE)[29]. Während die kroatische Presse den Urteilsspruch feierte, Gotovina von der Regierung in Zagreb empfangen und der Oluja-Einsatz in einer Regierungserklärung als legitim und rechtmäßig bezeichnet wurde – als was man ihn durchaus ansehen kann, ohne die dabei geschehenen Übergriffe zu rechtfertigen oder zu entschuldigen – und die Presse in Gotovina schon einen aussichtsreichen Kandidaten für die nächste Präsidentenwahl sah, wertete man das Urteil auf serbischer Seite als Parteinahme des ICTY für menschenrechtswidrige Gewaltanwendung gegen die serbische Minderheit, die angeblich zur Massenflucht geführt habe[30].

Zu den Kritikern dieser Entscheidung gehörte zum Erstaunen auf kroatischer Seite auch der ehemalige ICTY-Richter *Wolfgang Schomburg*. Dessen Kritik richtete sich allerdings gegen die Begründung der Entscheidung und die teilweise Abkehr des Gerichts von seiner früheren Rechtsprechung.

---

29   Zu dieser teilweise umstrittenen Zurechnungsfigur und ihren drei Varianten vgl. die Analyse von Igor Bojanić, Davor Derenčinović, Željko Horvatić, Davor Krapac, Maja Seršić in: Davor Derenčinović, Željko Horvatić (eds.), Theory of Joint Criminal Enterprise and International Criminal Law – Challenges and Controversies, Zagreb 2011. Ihre Untersuchung fassen die Autoren u. a. in der Kritik zusammen, a. a. O., S. 253, daß JCE zur Zeit der Tatbegehung nicht Teil internationalen Gewohnheitsrechts gewesen sei, im Widerspruch zum Schuldprinzip als einem der Grundprinzipien des Strafrechts stehe und sich der Strafbarkeit durch Organisation im Organisationsstrafrecht nähere, das im Statut des ICTY keine Grundlage habe. Zum Problem Kai Ambos, Joint Criminal Enterprise and Command Responsibility, Journal of International Criminal Justice 5 (2007), S. 159–184; ders., Internationales Strafrecht, 2. Aufl., München 2008, S. 142 ff.; Thomas Weigend, Bemerkungen zur Vorgesetztenverantwortlichkeit im Völkerstrafrecht, ZStW 116 (2004), S. 999–1027, Gerhard Werle, Völkerstrafrecht, 2. Aufl., Tübingen 2007, S 172 ff. Zu den politischen Rahmenbedingungen Ivan Brčić, Der ICTY zwischen Recht, Politik und Diplomatie, in: Ost-West Gegeninformation, Nr. 4/2006, S. 7 ff.

30   „Es ist klar", schrieb der serbische Präsident Tomislav Nikolić in einer Erklärung zum Urteil, „daß das Tribunal keine juristische sondern eine politische Entscheidung gefällt hat. Das trägt nicht zur Stabilisierung der Lage in der Region bei. Dieser Spruch der Richter wird alte Wunden wieder aufreißen", dazu www.spiegel.de-Politik-Ausland-Jugoslawien-Tribunal-Ante Gotovina, Spiegel online v. 16. 11. 2012.

1.2.4 ICTY-Richter in Split

Im Rahmen seiner Zusammenarbeit mit dem Interuniversitären Zentrum Berlin – Split[31] referierte und diskutierte Wolfgang Schomburg mehrfach auf internationalen Symposien mit Rechtswissenschaftlern und Studierenden der Juristischen Fakultät Split wie auch mit Richtern des Obersten Gerichts und der örtlichen Gerichte Kroatiens, um diesen *„Aufgaben und Verfahrensregeln des ICTY"* und dessen Bedeutung für die Stabilisierung des Friedens in der Konfliktregion Südosteuropa zu erläutern. Wolfgang Schomburg bewies sich als fesselnder Rechtslehrer und erfuhr bei diesen Gelegenheiten große Aufmerksamkeit und Aufgeschlossenheit, sowohl beim universitären Auditorium als auch in der erweiterten Öffentlichkeit und bei der Presse.

Er wußte mit Stimme und Argument zu überzeugen und ging geduldig auf die Fragen seiner Hörer ein.

Wie schwierig die Einschätzung der Reaktion der universitären und außeruniversitären Öffentlichkeit auf dieses Unternehmen sich damals für die kroatischen Mitveranstalter darstellte, zeigt die Tatsache, daß die zunächst in den Räumen der Fakultät vorbereitete, zweitägige Veranstaltung schließlich unter Beteiligung der Hochschullehrer der Juristischen Fakultät und zahlreicher Teilnehmer in den Räumen des Deutschen Honorarkonsulats mit Amtshilfe des Honorarkonsuls *Karlo Grenc*[32] in Split stattfand[33]. *Wolfgang Schomburg* erschien in Begleitung von fünf Leibwächtern, zwei vom ICTY aus Den Haag entsandten und drei von den kroatischen Sicherheitsbehörden gestellten. Dieser erste Auftritt eines ICTY-Richters in Kroatien wurde dennoch zu einem Erfolg – für *Wolfgang Schomburg* und die schrittweise Akzeptanz des ICTY in Kroatien.

1.2.5 Exkurs: Deutsch-französische Rechtshilfeprobleme

Nicht nur im Südosten Europas und im Verhältnis zwischen Deutschland und Kroatien am Vorabend der Aufnahme Kroatiens am 1. 7. 2013 als 28. –

---

31 Vgl. die Angaben in: Das Interuniversitäre Zentrum Berlin/Split – 10 Jahre internationale wissenschaftliche Zusammenarbeit Berlin – Südosteuropa, Heft 8/2010, 2. Aufl., S. 11 ff. (www.das interuniversitäre zentrum berlin-split).

32 Einem für seine Arbeit mit dem Bundesverdienstkreuz ausgezeichneten und im Deutschen Bundestag empfangenen Promotor der deutsch-kroatischen Zusammenarbeit und Gründer der Karlo Grenc Stiftung „Forum Diocletianum" in Split.

33 Dazu Herwig Roggemann/Anita Kurtović/Petar Novoselec (Hrsg.), Rechtsfragen der Zusammenarbeit mit der Internationalen Strafgerichtsbarkeit – Pravna pitanja suradnje s međunarodnim kaznenim sudovima, Arbeitspapiere des Interuniversitären Zentrums für deutsches, kroatisches, europäisches Recht und Rechtsvergleichung Berlin/Split, Heft 6/2004, Berlin/Split 2004, dazu näher Ivan Brcic, Kroatien und das ICTY-Tribunal in Den Haag oder wie Vergangenheit eine schwierige Frage sein kann, in: Tranformation des Rechts a. a. O. (Anm. 25), S. 431 ff.

nach dem Brexit 27. – Mitgliedsland der Europäischen Union, sondern auch im Zentrum Europas und im Verhältnis zwischen den EU-Gründungsstaaten Deutschland und Frankreich gestaltet sich die Durchsetzung allgemein anerkannter Rechtsgrundsätze im internationalen Rechtsverkehr bisweilen konfliktreich. Im folgenden Fall wiederum unter Mitwirkung *Wolfgang Schomburgs* als Anwalt- und Tatbeteiligter aus der Balkanregion.

Auf einem weiteren Symposion des Interuniversitären Zentrums in Split erörterten zwei der deutschen Referenten, *Wolfgang Schomburg*[34] und *Helmut Grothe*[35], Fragen der internationalen Rechtshilfe im Straf- und im Zivilverfahren – beide am Beispiel des „Falles Krombach". In dieser deutsch-französischen Familien- und Justiztragödie[36] hatte die Frau in zweiter Ehe den Deutschen Krombach geheiratet, in dessen Wohnung unter ungeklärten Umständen ihre minderjährige Tochter aus erster Ehe ums Leben kam. Der deutsche Stiefvater war daraufhin von einem französischen Gericht in Abwesenheit zu 15 Jahren Gefängnis verurteilt worden, hatte gegen dieses Abwesenheitsurteil aber erfolgreich Beschwerde beim EGMR in Straßburg eingelegt[37]. Ermittlungen in Deutschland gegen ihn wurden mangels Beweises rechtskräftig eingestellt, ein Rechtshilfeersuchen der französischen Justiz mit internationalem Haftbefehl daher abgelehnt. Daraufhin ließ der französische Vater der toten Tochter, André Bamberski, den gesuchten Krombach von albanischen Helfern in Deutschland zusammenschlagen, über die Grenze nach Frankreich schaffen und gefesselt nahe dem Gerichtsgebäude in Mühlhausen im Elsaß ablegen.

Wolfgang Schomburg als Anwalt berichtete den kroatischen und deutschen Teilnehmern der Veranstaltung in Split anschaulich von seinem vergeblichen Versuch, den französischen Richter davon zu überzeugen, daß Verfahren und Verurteilung Krombachs gegen europäische Rechtsgrundsätze (ne bis in idem, faires Verfahren) verstießen. Der französische Richter, so *Schomburg*, sei mit ihm im ans Fenster getreten und habe auf die Flagge der Republik Frankreich vor dem Gerichtsgebäude mit den Worten gewiesen: Hier wird französisches Recht gesprochen. Krombach wurde 2009 erneut zu 15 Jahren Haft verurteilt und dem Strafvollzug in Frankreich zugeführt. Sein Antrag auf Erlaß der noch nicht verbüßten Reststrafe wurde später abgelehnt. Gegen Bamberski und seine albanischen Helfer wurden Verfahren wegen Entführung eingeleitet,

---

34 Seit 2009 Honorarprofessor und Inhaber des Chair of the Centre for Criminal Law and Criminal Justice an der Durham University in England.

35 Inhaber des Lehrstuhls für Bürgerliches Recht, Internationales Privatrecht und Rechtsvergleichung am Fachbereich Rechtswissenschaft der Freien Universität Berlin.

36 Dazu näher Felix Netzer, Krimi – Tragödie und Lehrbuch-Klassiker – Der Fall Krombach, ZJS 2009, S. 752 ff.

37 Vgl. EGMR v. 13. 2. 2001, NJW 2001, S. 2387 ff.

Bamberski erhielt 2014 eine einjährige Bewährungsstrafe. Rechtsstaatliches Rechtshilfeverfahren ist, wie dieser Fall zeigt, auch innerhalb des Rechtsraums der EU nicht garantiert, sondern eine immer wieder neu zu erarbeitende Aufgabe.

1.3 Zur Wirkungsmöglichkeit der Rechtsprechungstätigkeit des ICTY
1.3.1   Internationale Strafgerichtsbarkeit – Versöhnung durch Gerechtigkeit

Ungeachtet der Rezeptionsprobleme bei der Konfliktbewältigung mithilfe der internationalen Strafgerichtsbarkeit und entgegen negativer Sicht kritischer Betrachter insbesondere von serbischer, aber auch von kroatischer und bosnischer Seite auf den ICTY ist der Ansicht *Wolfgang Schomburgs* zuzustimmen: *„Beim Völkermord beginnt die Strafbarkeit schon dann, wenn unmittelbar und öffentlich zu seiner Begehung aufgefordert wird". – „Schon die Begehung von Straftaten auch mit juristischen Mitteln zu verhindern ist das Beste, was in Menschenhand liegt. Existierende Gesetze müssen nur genutzt werden. Es gilt, ein wenig mehr Gerechtigkeit zu schaffen und damit den Frieden zu schützen*[38]*".*

Dies trifft zu und bestätigt sich immer wieder in politisch, ideologisch und auch religiös und ethnisch begründeten militärischen Großkonflikten, hinter denen oft auch wirtschaftliche Interessen stehen, wie im neuen Jugoslawienkrieg oder in Ruanda oder andernorts.

Außerdem zeigt die Erfahrung aus fast allen zurückliegenden oder noch andauernden Konflikten: Die unmittelbaren Konfliktbeteiligten, das gilt für Täter wie für Opfer, nicht zuletzt für aussagebereite Zeugen, aber auch für das Strafverfolgungs- und Justizpersonal selbst, sind zumeist infolge ihrer physischen und psychischen Nähe zur Tat und deren Umfeld, ihrer Angst um eigene und Anderer Sicherheit und Ansehen oder einfach aus persönlichem oder beruflichem Karriereinteresse oft zur Mitwirkung an einer rechtlichen Aufarbeitung begangenen Unrechts nicht bereit oder nicht in der Lage[39].

Ohne die Arbeit des ICTY und Richter wie *Wolfgang Schomburg* hätte daher dieser Teil der neueren Konfliktgeschichte und mühsamen, bis heute nicht abgeschlossenen Befriedung Südosteuropas mit den Mitteln des Rechts nicht geschrieben und hätten erste Schritte zur Versöhnung[40] durch Aufklärung und

---

38 So FAZ.net v. 23. 9. 2009.
39 Ein Beispiel hierfür bietet das anfängliche und langdauernde Versagen der deutschen Justiz bei der strafrechtlichen Aufarbeitung nationalsozialistischen Unrechts, dem zum Teil erst nach Jahrzehnten angemessene Ermittlungsmaßnahmen und Verurteilungen folgten.
40 Vgl. Herwig Roggemann (Hrsg.), Versöhnung auf dem Balkan – rechtliche und politische Fragen, Arbeitspapiere des Zentrums für deutsches, kroatisches, europäisches Recht

Urteilsspruch kaum getan werden können. Inzwischen hat in Kroatien, aber auch in der Rechtsdiskussion der anderen postjugoslawischen Länder, die wissenschaftliche Arbeit zur Rezeption des ICTY begonnen[41].
Der Rezeptionsprozeß gestaltet sich schwierig. Und dies nicht nur in der ehemaligen Konfliktregion Südosteuropa. Die Glaubwürdigkeit des

---

und Rechtsvergleichung Split/Berlin, Heft 10/2012, S. 48 f.; ferner Michael Bongardt/Ralf K. Wüstenberg (Hrsg.), Versöhnung, Strafe und Gerechtigkeit. Das schwere Erbe von Unrechtsstaaten, Göttingen 2012; Simone Schuller, Versöhnung durch strafrechtliche Aufarbeitung? Die Verfolgung von Kriegsverbrechen in Bosnien und Herzegowina, Frankfurt/Main, 2010; Axel Montenbruck, Zivilreligion. Eine Rechtsphilosophie II. Grundelemente: Versöhnung und Mediation, Strafe und Geständnis, Gerechtigkeit und Humanität aus juristischen Perspektiven, Berlin – Freie Universität, 2011; Friedrich-Christian Schroeder/Herbert Küpper (Hrsg.), Die rechtliche Aufarbeitung der kommunistischen Vergangenheit in Osteuropa, Frankfurt/Main-Berlin-Bern usw., 2010 (Studien des Instituts für Ostrecht Bd. 63); Angelika Nussberger/Caroline von Gall (Hrsg.), Bewußtes Erinnern und bewußtes Vergessen – Der juristische Umgang mit der Vergangenheit in den Ländern Mittel- und Osteuropas, Tübingen 2011, Otto Lagodny, Wirklichkeit und Perspektiven der internationalen Strafgerichtsbarkeit, in: Transformation des Rechts, a. a. O. (Anm. 25), S. 453 ff.

41   Vgl. dazu die erste ausführliche Untersuchung von Marin Bonačić, Nasljeđe Međunarodnoga Kaznenog Suda Za Bivšu Jugoslaviju (Das Erbe des Internationalen Strafgerichtshofs für das ehemalige Jugoslawien), Doktorski Rad (Diss. Jur.), Gutachter: Prof. dr. dc. Ivo Josipović,, Zagreb, 2015.

Zum internationalen Straf- und Prozeßrecht aus kroatischer Sicht vgl. im übrigen Davor Krapac, Međunarodni sud za ratne zločine na područje bivše Jugoslavije (Das Internationale Gericht für Kriegsverbrechen auf dem Gebiet des ehemaligen Jugoslawien), Hrvatski Helsinški odbor za ljudska prava i Hrvatski pravni centar, Zagreb 1995; Josipović, Ivo/Krapac, Davor/ Novoselec, Petar, Stalni međunarodni kazneni sud (Der Standige Internationale Strafgerichtshof). Zagreb (Narodne novine, Hrvatski pravni centar) 2001; Pavišić, Berislav/Bubalović, Tadija, Međunarodno kazneno pravo (Internationales Strafrecht). Pravni fakultet Sveučilišta u Rijeci 2013. Den aktuellen internationalen Diskussionsstand präsentiert und reflektiert zuletzt: Davor Krapac unter Mitarbeit von Matko Pajčić, Međunarodno procesno pravo. Oris postupka pred međunarodnim kaznenim sudovima (Internationales Strafprozessrecht. Grundzüge des Verfahrens vor den internationalen Strafgerichten), Narodne Novine, Zagreb 2012.

Veröffentlichungen zum Thema in Bosnien und Herzegowina und Serbien: Petrović, Borislav/Jovašević, Dragan, Međunarodno krivično pravo (Internationales Strafrecht), Sarajevo (Pravni fakultet) 2010; Petrović, Boris/Bisić, M./Perić, Violeta, Međunarodno kazneno sudovanje (Internationale Strafgerichtsbarkeit). Sarajevo (Privredna štampa) 2011; Degan, Vladimir Đuro/Pavišić, Berislav/ Beširević, Violeta, Međunarodno i transnacionalno krivično pravo (Internationales und transnationales Strafrecht), Beograd (Pravni fakultet Univerziteta Union, Službeni glasnik) 2011; Kaseze, Antonio, Međunarodno krivično pravo (Internationales Strafrecht), Beogradski centar za ljudska prava (Belgrader Zentrum für Menschenrechte) 2005.

transnationalen Anspruchs internationaler Strafjustiz: „Frieden durch Gerechtigkeit" zu schaffen, wurde und wird beeinträchtigt durch in der Begründung von Rechtswidrigkeit und Schuldvorwurf aber auch im Strafmaß schwankende bis widersprüchliche Entscheidungen des ICTY. Zu einem Glaubwürdigkeitsproblem wegen fehlender Gleichheit vor Gesetz und Richter wird aber vor allem die Tatsache, daß fünf der größten Länder der Erde[42], allen voran die USA, ihre politischen und militärischen Aktivitäten nach wie vor dem Urteil einer unabhängigen internationalen Strafgerichtsbarkeit in Gestalt des ICC entziehen[43]. Solange das so ist, und dieser Zustand wird sich in absehbarer Zeit kaum ändern, sehen sich Kritiker einer nur selektiven internationalen Strafgerichtsbarkeit in Südosteuropa, vor allem in Serbien[44], in ihrer skeptischen Haltung bestätigt.

Umso wichtiger bleibt die Unterrichtung der akademischen Eliten über die materiellen und prozessualen Grundsätze internationaler Suche nach Gerechtigkeit. In den postjugoslawischen Staaten ging Kroatien in dieser Richtung voran. Mit der Aufnahme von Fragen des internationalen Straf- und Prozeßrechts in das Veröffentlichungs- und Veranstaltungsprogramm der Juristischen

---

42 USA, China, Russland, Indien, Japan.

43 Die USA Die USA haben ihre unter der Regierung Clinton zunächst gegebene Unterschrift zur Einrichtung eines Ständigen Internationalen Strafgerichtshofs unter der Regierung Bush wieder zurückgezogen. Russland, das großen Einfluß auf Serbien ausübt, ist diesem – negativen – Beispiel 2016 gefolgt. In einer großen internationalen Kampagne haben die USA seither auch mehr als 100 andere, darunter insbesondere wirtschaftlich abhängige Staaten Ost- und Südosteuropas veranlaßt, sich durch bilaterale Verträge der Zusammenarbeit mit dem Internationalen Strafgerichtshof jedenfalls dann zu entziehen, wenn es um die potentielle Überstellung eigener und US-amerikanischer Soldaten an dieses Gericht geht, näher hierzu Susen Wahl, Osteuropa und die Zusammenarbeit mit Internationalen Strafgerichtshöfen, Berlin 2014.

44 Im Sammelband von Jovan Ćirić (ed.), The Hague Tribunal between Law and Politics, Belgrade 2013, kommen die Verfasser zu durchweg kritischeren Einschätzungen als die Mehrzahl ihrer deutschen Kollegen: „As a matter of fact the legality of the establishment of the International Criminal Tribunal for the former Yugoslavia is disputable, to say the least and may be contested by strong legal arguments", so Milan Škulić, A View of ICTY and its Place in History a. a. O., S. 56 ff.; Boris Krivokapis, A somewhat different view of International Criminal Courts, a. a. O., p. 7 ff., 38, meint: „After all, even if one would assume that all persons convicted by the international criminal courts are in fact guilty for the crimes imputed to them, some dilemmas still remain. First of all selected justice is not justice at all. That is one of the worst forms of injustice". "Die Legitimität und Legalität stellt niemand mehr ernsthaft in Zweifel". Diese Feststellung Lagodnys, a. a. O. (Anm. 25), S. 453, gilt daher für den Konfliktraum Südosteuropa nur mit Einschränkungen. Das gilt auch für den Anspruch, es handele sich beim ICTY-Statut „beyond any doubt" um Völkergewohnheitsrecht; dazu Werle, a. a. O. (Anm. 29), S. 19.

Fakultäten in Zagreb, Split, Rijeka, später auch in Sarajevo und Belgrad ist trotz mancher kritischer Vorbehalte, denen die Tätigkeit des ICTY nach wie vor in Serbien, aber auch in den anderen postjugoslawischen Ländern begegnet, ein wichtiger Schritt in eine am Ende nachhaltige Rezeption getan worden.

Zum internationalen Symposion „Versöhnung auf dem Balkan – rechtliche und politische Fragen[45], auf dem im Jahre 2012 am Osteuropa-Institut der Freien Universität Berlin erstmals die wichtigsten, an der Aufarbeitung des Jugoslawienkrieges 1991–1995 arbeitenden Nichtregierungsorganisationen aus Kroatien, Serbien, Bosnien und Herzegowina an einem Tisch zusammen kamen, schrieb *Wolfgang Schomburg*:

> Wie sähe es heute nicht nur im früheren Jugoslawien aus, wären nicht wesentliche mutmaßlich für Kriegsverbrechen verantwortliche Persönlichkeiten aus Politik, Militär, der Gesellschaft insgesamt individuell strafrechtlich zur Verantwortung gezogen worden? Wie sähe Jugoslawien heute aus mit den bekannten Größen im Gesamtstaat aber auch in den Munizipalitäten noch immer an der Macht? Haben nicht allein die lange nicht vollstreckten Haftbefehle für Befriedung gesorgt? – Haben nicht die vielen Anhörungen von Opfern, ihren Angehörigen, Überlebenden vor dem Tribunal eine friedensstiftende Wirkung gehabt? – Kurz: Durch Wahrheitsfindung und Gerechtigkeitssuche ist man einem dauerhaften Frieden näher gekommen. Wir wissen um die Fragilität dieses Friedens in einigen Regionen. Die Suche nach dem Recht muß daher vor Ort weitergehen.

1.3.2 Das Ende des ICTY und die Überleitung auf die nationale Strafgerichtsbarkeit

Damit wurde der Weg für die Strafverfolgung durch nationale Gerichte mit oder ohne internationale Beteiligung in Südosteuropa geebnet[46]. Eine eigens

---

45 Dazu Arbeitsheft des Interuniversitären Zentrums Berlin-Split 10/2012, S. 15 m. w. A. zur Aufklärungsarbeit der einzelnen Nichtregierungsorganisationen.

46 Zum Abschlußverfahren (Completion strategy) und zur Zusammenarbeit des ICTY mit den nationalen Gerichten und dem Einfluß auf materielles und Verfahrensrecht sowie Rechtskenntnis und Rechtsbewußtsein sowie den hindernisreichen Versöhnungsprozeß vgl. die gründliche Untersuchung von Marin Bonačić , a. a. O. (Anm. 42) , S. 34 ff., 44 ff., 129 ff., 165 ff.; ferner vgl. den Überblick bei Gerhard Werle, Völkerstrafrecht, 2. Aufl., Tübingen 2007, S. 110 ff., 122 ff.; zur Bewertung: Dominic Raab, Evaluating the ICTY and its Completion Strategy: Efforts to Achieve Accountability for War Crimes and their Tribunals, Journal of International Criminal Law, vol. 3/1, 2005, S. 82 ff.; Kim Kung/James Meernik, Assessing the Impact of the International Criminal Tribunal for the Former Yugoslavia:

für die Abgabe von Verfahren an die Justizbehörden des Tatortstaats, des Verhaftungsstaats oder des Staates, dessen Gerichtsbarkeit zur Durchführung eines Strafverfahrens bereit ist, vom Präsidenten des ICTY gebildete Abgabekammer[47] hat bis zur definitiven Schließung des ICTY am 31. 12. 2017 über die Erledigung durch Abgabe an die nationalen Justizbehörden zu entscheiden[48].

1.3.2.1 Bosnien und Herzegowina

Zur strafrechtlichen Aufarbeitung durch die nationale Gerichtsbarkeit in Zusammenarbeit mit dem ICTY wurde 2005 am Staatsgerichtshof von Bosnien und der Herzegowina in Sarajevo eine Kammer für Kriegsverbrechen eingerichtet[49]. Diese hatte bis 2009 39 rechtskräftige Entscheidungen erlassen. Als das Parlament von Bosnien und Herzegowina die Mandatsverlängerung der internationalen Staatsanwälte und Richter ablehnte – zu denen zeitweise auch der Vorsitzende Richter des im Verfahren Perković/Mustač entscheidenden Staatsschutzsenats des OLG München, Dr. Manfred Dauster, gehörte –, machte der Hohe Repräsentant der Internationalen Gemeinschaft in Sarajevo von seinem Überstimmungsrecht Gebrauch und ordnete im Interesse der Rechtspflege die Verlängerung des internationalen Mandats an. Um die Einhaltung rechtsstaatlicher Verfahrensgarantien bei nationaler Strafverfolgung durch bosnische Organe zu sichern, überprüfte die Anklagebehörde des ICTY zeitweise das Beweisverfahren, überließ diese Kontrollfunktion jedoch seit 2004 den bosnischen Justizbehörden.

Neben „ICTY Legacy Dialogues" sind in Bosnien und der Herzegowina zwei Informationszentren in Sarajevo und in Srebrenica/Potočari, dem Ort eines der größten Massenverbrechen von serbischer Seite, eingerichtet worden[50].

Balancing International and Local Interests While Doing Justice, in: Bert Swart/ Alexander Zahar/Göran Sluiter (eds.), The Legacy of the International Criminal Tribunal for the Former Yugoslavia, Oxford 2011, S. 7–54.

47 Gem. Regel 11bis VerfO ICTY i. d. F. v. 8. 7. 2015, RPE IT/32/Rev. 50.

48 Zu den Einzelheiten vgl. den Rechenschaftsbericht zur Abwicklung (Completion strategy report) des Präsidenten des ICTY, Carnel Agius, an den UN-Sicherheitsrat v. 17. 11. 2016.

49 Aufgrund SR-Resolution 1503 v. 28. 8. 2003 sowie Zakon o izmjenama indopunama Zakona o Sudu Bosne i Hercegovine v. 14. 12. 2004. Dazu Bogdan Ivanišević, The War Crimes Chamber in Bosna i Hercegovina: From Hybrid to Domestic Court, International Center for Transitional Justice, 2008, S. 6; Organisation for Security and Co-operation in Europe, Report May 2011, S. 13: Delivering justice in Bosna and Hercegovina: An Overview of War Crime Processing from 2005 to 2010.

50 Vgl. Report a. a. O. (Anm. 49) Ziff. IX.

1.3.2.2 Kroatien

In Kroatien wurden mit der Ratifizierung des IStGH-Statuts und Erlaß des Verfassungsgesetzes über die Zusammenarbeit mit dem IStGH von 2003[51] die Zuständigkeit nationaler Spruchkörper für Kriegsverbrechen[52] in Gestalt von Kammern für Kriegsverbrechen bei den Bezirksgerichten in Osijek, Rijeka, Split, Zagreb und falls angebracht auch an anderen Gerichten begründet[53]. Für die Zeit von 1991 bis 2005 wird von rund 1700 in Kroatien angeklagten und 800 verurteilten Personen berichtet[54]. In ihrem Bericht von Oktober 2012 bestätigte die EU-Kommission die Umsetzung der Strategie zur Verfolgung von Kriegsverbrechern durch die kroatische Justiz. Seit Kriegsende 1995 wurden demnach in Kroatien 490 Kriegsverbrechen registriert und führten bis Ende 2012 zur Einleitung von 1090 Ermittlungsverfahren. In 316 Fällen konnten Täter identifiziert werden. 849 Strafverfahren führten zu 112 Verurteilungen[55]. Kritisiert wird, daß viele der mutmaßlich von Angehörigen der kroatischen Armee und Polizei an Serben und anderen Angehörigen von Minderheiten begangene Straftaten ungeahndet geblieben seien. Die örtlichen Widerstände aber auch die Entschlossenheit der kroatischen Justiz belegt der „Fall Mihajlo Hrastov", der erstmals 1992 wegen Tötung einer Gruppe von Serben in Karlovac angeklagt und vom Strafgericht in Karlovac freigesprochen worden war. Das

---

51   NN 75/2003, 29/2004, 55/2011, 125/2011.
52   Odjel za ratne zločine (Kammer für Kriegsverbrechen).
53   Dazu Ivo Josipović, Novo hrvatsko implementacijsko međunarodno kazneno pravo: procesupravni i orgasnizacijski aspekti (Neue kroatische Implementierung internationalen Strafrechts: prozessuale und organisatorische Aspekte), Hrvatski Ljetopis za kazneno pravo i praksu, vol. 10, 2003, br. 2, S. 843–876, 858; ders. , Odgovornost za ratne zločine pred sudovima u Hrvatskoj, Knjiga I Izvori prava s uvodnom studijom: Odgovornost za ratne zločine – povijesni korijeni, međunarodna iskustva i hrvatska praksa, ABA-CEELI Hrvatska i fakultet Sveučilišta u Zagrebu (Verantwortlichkeit für Kriegsverbrechen vor den kroatischen Gerichten, Buch I Rechtsquellen mit einer einführenden Studie: Verantwortlichkeit für Kriegsverbrechen – geschichtliche wurzeln, internationale Erfahrungen und kroatische Praxis), Zagreb 2006, S. 92–97.
54   Dazu Gerhard Werle, Völkerstrafrecht, a. a. O. (Anm. 12), S. 123 und Anm. 626 unter Bezugnahme auf Ivo Josipović, International Review of the Red Cross 88 (2006), S. 145, 152 ff.
55   Nach Amnesty International, Report 2013 Kroatien. Nach Angaben der Kroatischen Staatsanwaltschaft DORH wurden in Kroatien von 1991 bis 31. 12. 2013 Ermittlungsverfahren wegen Kriegsverbrechen gegen 3599 Personen eingeleitet. In 112 Fällen wurde in diesem Zeitraum gegen Angehörige der kroatischen Streitkräfte ermittelt, davon 44 durch Urteil abgeschlossen, vgl. Državno Odvjetništvo Republike Hrvatske. Ažurirano izvješće o kaznenim postupcima zbog kaznenih djela ratnih zločina (Staatsanwaltschaft der Republik Kroatien. Aktualisierter Bericht über Strafverfahren wegen Kriegsverbrechen) v. 27. 2. 2014, http://www.dorh.hr/DrzavnoOdvjetnistvoRepublikeHrvatskeAzurirano.

Oberste Gericht in Zagreb hob den in drei Verfahren erfolgten Freispruch jedesmal wieder auf und verwies zurück.

1.3.2.3 Serbien

In Serbien wurden ebenfalls im Jahre 2003 spezielle Justizorgane – Ermittlungsorgane, Staatsanwaltschaft und eine Sonderkammer bei Bezirksgericht Belgrad, jetzt Oberstes Gericht Serbiens – zur Verfolgung von Kriegsverbrechen eingerichtet[56]. Ebenso wie in Kroatien und anders als in Bosnien und Herzegowina war in Serbien eine (Mit)Zuständigkeit internationaler Richter an diesem speziellen Spruchorgan nicht vorgesehen.

2005 und 2006, rund ein Jahrzehnt nach Beendigung der Kriegshandlungen fanden sich die Strafverfolgungsbehörden von Kroatien, Bosnien und Herzegowina, Serbien und Montenegro bereit zum Abschluß von Kooperationsvereinbarungen über Rechtshilfe bei der Verfolgung von Kriegsverbrechen[57]. Dieser Schritt leitete eine neue Qualität der justiziellen Zusammenarbeit zwischen den postjugoslawischen Staaten ein. Im Ergebnis dieser Zusammenarbeit der ehemaligen Konfliktparteien übermittelte Kroatien den serbischen Strafverfolgungsbehörden bis 2014 Angaben über 41 Straftaten, woraufhin 18 Personen verurteilt wurden. An Montenegro wurden Angaben über 3 Straftatkomplexe übermittelt, die zu 4 Verurteilungen führten. Bosnien und Herzegowina lieferte an Kroatien Angaben über 5 Straftaten, woraufhin es in Kroatien zu einer Anklageerhebung und zwei Ermittlungsverfahren kam. In Anbetracht der hohen Verluste des Jugoslawienkrieges von 1991 bis 1995 und der großen Zahl nicht geahndeter Kriegs- und Menschlichkeitsverbrechen mutet dieses Ergebnis erneuerter justizieller Zusammenarbeit bescheiden an. Dennoch ist es ein wichtiger Schritt auf dem mühsamen Weg zur Befriedung durch Recht. Konflikte ergeben sich bis heute aus der von den serbischen Strafverfolgungsbehörden seit 2003 in Anspruch genommenen Zuständigkeit für auf dem gesamten Territorium der ehemaligen Jugoslawischen Föderation (SFRJ) begangene Kriegsverbrechen unabhängig von der Staatsangehörigkeit der mutmaßlichen Täter.

1.3.2.4 Friedenswirkung durch Strafrecht

Die bisherigen Ergebnisse internationaler und – ab 1. 1. 2018 wieder ausschließlich -nationaler Strafverfolgung in der Konfliktregion gelten nicht durchweg als überzeugend. Kritiker sehen in der nationalen Strafverfolgung

---

56 Durch Zakon o organizaciji i nadležnosti državnih organa u postupku za ratne zločine (Gesetz über die Organisation und Zuständigkeit staatlicher Organe im Verfahren wegen Kriegsverbrechen), SG RS br. 67/2003, 135/2004, 61/2015, 101/2007, 107/2009.

57 Dazu näher Marin Bonačić, a. a. O. (Anm. 42), S. 177 ff.

eine Tendenz, vorzugsweise Angehörige des jeweils anderen, nicht aber des eigenen Staates zu Adressaten von Verfolgungsmaßnahmen zu machen. Auch fehlen, in dieser Region von besonderer Wichtigkeit, Zeugenschutzstandards und entsprechend wirksame Sicherungsmaßnahmen. Wichtig ist gleichwohl, daß inzwischen Verfahren vor nationalen Gerichten überhaupt, und auch gegen eigene Staatsangehörige, stattfinden.

Die Grundlage für diese schrittweise Wiedergewinnung der „Herrschaft des Rechts" in der Konfliktregion hat die fast 25-jährige Rechtsprechungstätigkeit des ICTY mit in vielfältiger Weise fortwirkenden positiven Einflüssen[58] auf Gerichtsorganisation, Rechtsdenken, materielles Straf- und Verfahrensrecht, Gesetzgebung, Rechtsprechung, nicht zuletzt auf die akademische Rechtslehre[59] gelegt. Und ein Argument von besonderem Gewicht: Rund 58% der Bevölkerung Bosniens und der Herzegowina, des Landes, das unter den Kriegsfolgen am meisten gelitten hat, sehen in der Rechtsprechungstätigkeit des ICTY einen Beitrag zur Versöhnung[60]. Zu dieser Einschätzung kann beitragen, dass die Strafkammer des ICTY in ihrem letzten großen Urteil am 22.11.2017 (IT-09-92) den Befehlshaber der Armee der Bosnischen Serben (VRS), General Ratko Mladic, einen der Hauptverantwortlichen für den Massenmord von Srebrenica, bei dem 1995 mindestens 7000 muslimische Männer und Jugendliche ihr Leben verloren, wegen Völkermords, Kriegs- und Menschlichkeitsverbrechen zu lebenslanger Gefängnisstrafe verurteilt hat.

1.3.3   Vom Balkankrieg über den ICTY zum ICC

Vor allem aber bereitete der ICTY den Weg zum ständigen Internationalen Strafgerichtshof. In diesem Sinne lieferte der Jugoslawienkrieg der Jahre 1991–1995[61] den Anstoß sowohl für die Gründung des Ad-Hoc-Strafgerichtshofs

---

58   Zu den verschiedenen Aspekten der Fortwirkung Marin Bonačić, S. 177; skeptisch zur Versöhnungswirkung durch Strafrecht bei Makroverbrechen Oliver Diggelmann, International Criminal Tribunals and Reconciliation: Reflections on the Role of Remorse and Apology, Journal of International Criminal Justice, 14 (2016), S. 1073: „Positive effects of remorse and apology in the context of macro crimes tend to be overestimated". Eyal Benvenisti/Sarah M.H. Nouwen, Leaving Legacies Open-Ended: An Invitation for an Inclusive Debate on International Criminal Justice, American Journal of International Law, 110 (2016) S. 205–208.

59   Ein Beispiel: Wolfgang Schomburg, Jurisprudence on JCE – revisiting a never ending story about a judge made mode of criminal liability before some international criminal tribunals, in: Godišnjak Akademije pravnih znanosti Hrvatske, 3 (2012) br. 1, S. 59–92.

60   So Bonačić, a. a. O. (Anm. 42), S. 189 ff.

61   Dazu Herwig Roggemann, Der neue Balkankrieg – eine Herausforderung für das internationale Recht, in: Neue Justiz 1994, S. 337 ff.; ders., Der Internationale Strafgerichtshof der

als auch für den ohne diesen kaum denkbaren Ständigen Internationalen Strafgerichtshofs ICC auf der Grundlage des 2002 in Kraft getretenen Rom-Statuts von 1998.

Zu den Geburtshelfern des ICTY von 1994 und damit auch des ICC gehörten zwei Gleichgesinnte ägyptischer Herkunft: Der langjährige Präsident der International Association of Penal Law (AIDP), Direktor des International Institute of Higher Studies in Criminal Sciences (ISISC) in Siracusa, Lehrstuhlinhaber an der De-Paul-University in Chicago und Promotor des Gedankens einer internationalen Strafgerichtsbarkeit, *Cherif Bassiouni*[62], und der damalige Generalsekretär der UN, *Boutros Boutros-Ghali*. An einer der von *Cherif Bassiouni* veranstalteten Sircusa-Konferenzen, die angesichts sich ausweitender Kampfhandlungen, Kriegsverbrechen und ihrer Opfer auf dem Balkan einen Aufruf zur Friedenssicherung durch Wiederherstellung des Rechts und Errichtung eines Internationalen Strafgerichtshofs an den damaligen UN-Generalsekretär *Boutros-Ghali* richtete, nahm auch *Wolfgang Schomburg* teil.

2 Vom Deutsch-Jugoslawischen zum Deutsch-Kroatischen Auslieferungskonflikt

2.1 *Vorgeschichte und Entwicklung der deutsch-Jugoslawischen und deutsch-kroatischen Rechtshilfebeziehungen*

2.1.1 Zwischen justizförmiger und außerrechtlicher Durchsetzung von Staatssicherheits- und Strafverfolgungsinteressen

Der Auslieferungskonflikt zwischen Kroatien und Deutschland, der den Verfahren gegen Prates 2008[63] sowie gegen Perković und Mustač[64] 2013–2016 vor dem OLG München vorausging, hat eine lange Vorgeschichte. Und auch in dieser spielte das OLG München eine Rolle. Der Konflikt kulminierte im Auslieferungsstreit zwischen Jugoslawien und Deutschland von 1978. Als der Verfasser dieses Beitrags sich vor mehr als 25 Jahren der Untersuchung der

---

Vereinten Nationen von 1993 und die Balkankriegsverbrechen in: Zeitschrift für Rechtspolitik 1994, S. 297 ff; ders. Die Internationalen Strafgerichtshöfe, 2. Aufl. Berlin 1998.

62 Zu dieser Entwicklung grundlegend M. Cherif Bassiouni, From Versailles to Rwanda in Seventy-Five Years: The Need to Establish a Permanent International Criminal Court, 10 Harvard Human Rights Journal 11 (1997); ders., The Sources and Content of International Criminal Law: A Theoretical Framework in: Bassiouni (ed.), International Criminal Law, vol. I–III, Crimes, 2nd ed., Leiden (2008).

63 OLG München v. 16. 7. 2008, 6 St 005/05 (2), unveröffentlicht, rechtskräftig, s. o. Anm. 5 und 6.

64 OLG München v. 3. 8. 2016, 7 St 5/14 (2) unveröffentlicht, nicht rechtskräftig.

Rechtshilfebeziehungen zwischen beiden Staaten widmete[65], waren ihm wie wohl vielen anderen wissenschaftlichen, rechtsvergleichenden Betrachtern und womöglich auch Historikern die Dimensionen dieses sich neben der Normalform justizförmiger Durchsetzung von Strafverfolgungsansprüchen beider Staaten jenseits von Recht und Gesetz vollziehenden Kampfes des jugoslawischen Staates mit seinen politischen Gegnern nicht nur in Jugoslawien selbst sondern auch auf deutschem Staatsgebiet in ihrem vollen Umfang nicht bekannt.

Das Gewicht und damit die historische Dimension der hier angesprochenen Fälle wird anhand der Zahlenangaben des OLG München im Prates-Urteil[66] sowie neuerer Angaben in der kroatischen Presse[67] und Publizistik[68] deutlich.

Dazu führt das OLG München im Prates-Urteil aus:

> Der Sachverständige Ro.[69] erläuterte, seine Recherchen hätten ergeben, dass von 1945 bis 1989 in der Bundesrepublik Deutschland 67 Tötungsdelikte an Kroaten verübt worden seien, für die lediglich ein politisches Motiv erkennbar sei. Allein von 1970 bis 1989 gebe es in Deutschland 22 kroatische Opfer, für die, da andere Motive ausgeschlossen werden könnten, vermutlich der jugoslawische Sicherheitsapparat verantwortlich sei. Dabei habe es sich in einigen Fällen um ausgesprochen militante Gegner des jugoslawischen Staates gehandelt, aber auch Publizisten seien das Ziel von Anschlägen gewesen."

---

65   Vgl. dazu Herwig Roggemann, Der Auslieferungsverkehr zwischen der Bundesrepublik Deutschland und Jugoslawien – Grundlagen, Entwicklung, Rechtsprechung, Goltdammer's Archiv für Strafrecht (GA) 1989, S. 98 ff. Aus einem Vortrag an der Juristischen Fakultät der Universität Belgrad ging 1988 die serbokroatische Fassung hervor: Ekstradicija u krivičnim stvarima između Savezne Republike Nemačke i Jugoslvije – Osnovi, razvoj, sudska praksa, in: Jugoslovenska revija za međunarodno pravo, Beograd 1988/XXXV (2), S. 212–233.

66   A. a. O. (Anm. 64), S. 15, 81.

67   Vgl. Zdravka Soldić-Arar zu den geheimen Enthüllungen im Arbeitsbericht über die siebenjährige Arbeit des Viječa za utvrđivanje poratnih žrtava komunističkog sustava ubijenih u inozemstvu (Rates zur Feststellung der im Ausland getöteten Nachkriegsopfer der kommunistischen Ordnung), in: Slobodna Dalmacija (SL) Dossier v. 23. 9. 2013, S. 23–25.

68   Vgl. die umfangreiche Dokumentation von Bože Vukošić, Tajni rat Udbe protiv Hrvatskog iseljeništva (Der geheime Krieg des Udba gegen die kroatische Emigration) sowie ders.: Tajni rat Udbe protiv hrvatskih iseljenika iz Bosne i Herzegovina (Der geheime Krieg des Udba gegen die kroatischen Emigranten aus Bosnien und der Herzegowina), Zagreb 2002. Udba = Uprava državne bezbednosti (Verwaltung der Staatssicherheit). Dazu näher Matica Hrvatska (Hrsg.), Represija i zločini komunističkog režima u Hrvatskoj (Repression und Verbrechen des kommunistischen Regimes in Kroatien), Zagreb 2012.

69   Zur Klarstellung: Hierbei handelt es sich nicht um den Verfasser dieses Beitrags.

Diese Zahlenangaben finden ihre Bestätigung und Ergänzung durch neuere Angaben in der kroatischen Presse. Die anhand eines dort genannten Arbeitsberichts eines *Rates zur Feststellung von Opfern des Kommunismus* wiedergegebenen Opferzahlen weichen teilweise von den im Prates-Urteil[70]. und auch im Perković-Urteil[71] angegebenen Zahlen ab, bestätigen aber deren etwaigen Gesamtumfang und gehen für neuere versuchte Taten teilweise darüber hinaus..

Das Gericht nennt im Perković-Urt. 11 in der Zeit von 1968 bis 1982 von unbekannten, im Zeitraum von 1968 bis 1980 vier von bekannten Tätern begangene und im Zeitraum von 1969 bis 1989 acht von unbekannten Tätern versuchte politische Morde in Deutschland.

Der Bericht von *Soldić-Arar* in Slobodna Dalmacija[72] spricht dagegen für den Zeitraum von 1946 bis 1989 von 68 vollendeten Mordtaten an kroatischen Emigranten, davon 36 in Deutschland, darunter zwei noch in den Jahren 1987 und 1989, also geraume Zeit nach Titos Tod und kurz vor dem Zerfall der Jugoslawischen Föderation und der Unabhängigkeit Kroatiens. Für den Zeitraum von 1948 bis 1988 wird von 19 versuchten Taten, davon 12 in Deutschland begangenen Taten berichtet. Drei Personen aus Emigrantenkreisen wurden entführt und fünf verschwanden spurlos. Zu den weiteren Tatortländern neben Deutschland gehörten Italien, Österreich, Frankreich, England, Belgien, Argentinien, Australien, Kanada und die USA.

Vukušić[73] berichtet von 37 in den Jahren von 1976 bis 1989 in Deutschland begangenen Mordtaten und 16 versuchten Taten.

Der eindeutige Tatschwerpunkt liegt in Deutschland. Auch dies zeigt die in jeder Hinsicht besonderen Verflechtungen Kroatiens und seiner Nachbarländer mit Deutschland – und begründet die gemeinsame Verpflichtung beider Länder zur Aufdeckung und Aufarbeitung dieses Teils ihrer gemeinsamen Geschichte auf dem Weg Südosteuropas in eine europäische Friedensordnung, die nicht mehr durch politische Instrumentalisierung nicht aufgearbeiteter Rechtsverletzungen in Frage gestellt werden kann.

Das Ausmaß der Taten, die damit verbundenen Verletzungen der individuellen Grund- und Menschenrechte der Opfer und ihrer Angehörigen aber auch der Grundsätze des internationalen Rechts und zwischenstaatlichen Rechtsverkehrs erlauben es weder in Deutschland noch in Kroatien und den anderen

---

70 A. a. O. (Anm. 64), S. 81.
71 A. a. O. (Anm. 65). 91–97.
72 A. a. O. (Anm. 68), S. 24, 25.
73 A. a. O (Anm. 69), S. 461 ff.

Nachfolgestaaten der Jugoslawischen Föderation, darüber einfach hinwegzusehen und hinwegzugehen.

Dies ist der Hintergrund, vor dem sich der deutsch-jugoslawische Rechtshilfekonflikt vor rund vier Jahrzehnten abspielte und der bis in den jüngsten Rechtshilfekonflikt fortwirkt und ihm seine politische Relevanz verleiht.

2.1.2 Die besonderen Rechtshilfe- und Auslieferungsbeziehungen zwischen Deutschland und Jugoslawien

Ebenso wie die politischen, wirtschaftlichen und personellen Beziehungen zwischen Deutschland und Jugoslawien von besonderer Art waren – und zwischen den Nachfolgestaaten der SFRJ, insbesondere Kroatien und Deutschland nach wie vor sind – gilt dies auch für die Rechtshilfebeziehungen. In der Zeit des „Kalten Krieges" und der Spaltung Europas beschränkten sich vertragliche Rechtshilfebeziehungen in der Regel auf Staaten gleicher oder ähnlicher politischer und rechtlicher Ordnung. Eine Ausnahme bildeten frühzeitig der Vertrag zwischen der Bundesrepublik Deutschland und der Sozialistischen Föderativen Republik Jugoslawien über die Auslieferung v. 26. 11. 1970[74] und der Vertrag zwischen der Bundesrepublik Deutschland und der Sozialistischen Föderativen Republik Jugoslawien über die Rechtshilfe in Strafsachen vom 1. 10. 1971[75].

Beide Verträge wurden von Kroatien nach der Unabhängigkeit übernommen und galten weiter[76].

Jugoslawien war das erste und lange auch das einzige sozialistische Land, mit dem die Bundesrepublik Deutschland entsprechende Abkommen geschlossen hatte. Die Abhängigkeit praktizierter Rechtshilfe und Auslieferung vom politischen „Klima" läßt ein sprunghafter Anstieg der Zahl von Ersuchen und Bewilligungen unmittelbar nach Abschluß der Abkommen im Jahr 1971 und ein Absinken der Zahlen nach dem deutsch-jugoslawischen Auslieferungskonflikt von 1978 erkennen. Doch bis dahin konnte von einer insgesamt rechtshilfe- und bewilligungsfreundlichen Situation auch bei den zuständigen deutschen Gerichten ausgegangen werden. Dies galt bemerkenswerter Weise auch, obwohl die in den Münchner OLG-Urteilen berichteten Rechtsverletzungen seitens der jugoslawischen Regierung und ihrer Sicherheitsdienste der Justiz in Deutschland zumindest teilweise bekannt waren. Von 1964 bis 1985 sind im Auslieferungsverkehr zwischen BRD und SFRJ, eingeleitet durch

---

74   BGBl. 1974 II S. 1257.
75   BGBl. 1974 II S. 1167; 1975 II S. 228.
76   Vgl. Davor Krapac, Zakon o kaznenom postupku (Strafprozeßordnung), Zagreb 2003, S. 725, 727.

jugoslawische Ersuchen, 287 Auslieferungsverfahren gezählt worden. Setzt man diese Zahl zur oben genannten Zahl der im gleichen Zeitraum versuchten und vollendeten gewaltsamen Konfliktaustragung jenseits der Rechtsordnung in Beziehung, so stellt sich die Frage, ob und inwieweit eine aus Rechtsgründen verweigerte Rechtshilfe zur gewaltsamen „Konflikterledigung" führen konnte. Doch in der ganz überwiegenden Zahl von Strafrechtskonflikten suchten beide Staaten offenbar eine Lösung auf dem zwischenstaatlichen Rechtsweg.

2.1.3 Das Auslieferungsverfahren nach IRG – auslieferungsfreundliche Rechtsprechung in Deutschland

Das zweistufige Auslieferungsverfahren mit der unabhängigen gerichtlichen Zulässigkeitsprüfung vor Eintritt ins behördliche Bewilligungsverfahren – das in besonders bedeutsamen und streitigen Einzelfällen wie dem Auslieferungsstreit von 1978 mit Jugoslawien bis ins Bundeskabinett führen konnte – verlangte auf der Grundlage des IRG und lange vor den Vereinfachungen durch das Europäische Haftbefehlsverfahren das herkömmliche gesetzliche Prüfungsverfahren[77] zu beiderseitiger Strafbarkeit, Auslieferungshindernissen, politischem Delikt sowie Spezialitätszusagen. Aus teilweise abweichenden Prüfungsmaßstäben der einzelnen Oberlandesgerichte ergaben sich immer wieder unterschiedliche Ergebnisse in der Auslieferungspraxis. So hielten einzelne Gerichte es für angebracht und sich auch für berechtigt, anhand der Unterlagen des Ersuchens zu prüfen, ob ein Verfolgter überhaupt tatverdächtig sei, während andere Gerichte diese Prüfung für unzulässig hielten. Zur Ermittlung beiderseitiger Strafbarkeit sollte die *Feststellung korrespondierender Strafbarkeit* ausreichen und bei Anlegung eines nur formellen Prüfungsmaßstabs wurde die Nachprüfung von Tatverdacht und Schuldverdacht im Einzelnen für nicht erforderlich gehalten. Das OLG München erklärte die Auslieferung wegen Verjährung für unzulässig, da eine Verjährungsunterbrechung durch deutsche Strafverfolgungsmaßnahmen nicht erfolgt sei und berücksichtigte dabei, unrichtiger Weise, nicht die Verfolgungshandlungen des ersuchenden Staates. Zum Prinzip der Gegenseitigkeit führte das BVerfG trotz vorangegangener Auslieferungskrise aus, daß die Erfüllung der Gegenseitigkeitserwartung im deutsch-jugoslawischen Rechtshilfeverkehr nach wie vor anzunehmen sei:

> Schließlich zwingt auch die Weigerung Jugoslawiens, eine dort festgehaltene Terroristengruppe auszuliefern, zu keiner anderen Beurteilung. Es handelt sich dabei offenbar um einen politisch brisanten Sonder-

---

77 Zu den folgenden Einzelfragen und der Rspr. näher Herwig Roggemann, GA 1989, S. 104 ff. m. w. N.

fall. Bisher spricht jedoch nichts dafür, daß sich Jugoslawien auch in Fällen wie den vorliegenden nicht an seine Pflichten aus dem deutsch-jugoslawischen Auslieferungsvertrag halten werde[78].

Als Auslieferungshindernis sah der BGH die Verweigerung des Waffendienstes durch einen Gesuchten an und verlangte zu Recht eine förmliche Spezialitätszusage der jugoslawischen Seite, um die Einberufung nach Strafverbüßung auszuschließen[79].

2.1.4 Auslieferungsverfahren und Asylverfahren

Daß die damalige auslieferungsfreundliche Rechtsprechung der Strafgerichte zur Schwächung der Asylrechtsgarantien für betroffene jugoslawische, insbesondere kroatische Emigranten führen konnte, liegt nach den Erkenntnissen des OLG München von 2008 und 2016 auf der Hand, war aber auch damals schon ersichtlich. Mit Hinweis auf die Verläßlichkeit jugoslawischer Spezialitätszusagen waren Rechtsprechung und Bewilligungspraxis in Deutschland offenbar bereit, dieses Risiko bis zu einem gewissen Grade in Kauf zu nehmen. Der Streit entzündete sich dabei an der Auslegung des die Auslieferung grundsätzlich ausschließenden politischen Delikts. Denn in zahlreichen Fällen beantragten von Auslieferungsersuchen betroffene Kroaten als jugoslawische Staatsbürger wegen ihrer Gegnerschaft zum sozialistischen Jugoslawien zugleich Asylrecht als politisch Verfolgte. Das stellte die deutschen Strafgerichte in jugoslawischer Zeit vor schwierige Fragen, deren Beantwortung auch eine Befassung mit der neueren politischen Entwicklung im Jugoslawien der 70er und 80er Jahre verlangte.

Hinzu kam damals und kommt bis heute der Entscheidungskonflikt, der sich daraus ergeben kann, daß Asylentscheidungen im Verwaltungsverfahren für das Auslieferungsverfahren nicht als bindend anzusehen sind[80].

---

78   BVerfGE 64, 46 ff. = NJW 1983, 1721 ff.
79   BGHSt 27, 191 ff. = NJW 1977, 1599 f.
80   Vgl. § 4 S. 2 AsylVerfG. Zum Verhältnis beider Verfahren vgl. Albrecht Randelzhofer in: Maunz/Dürig, GG-Komm, Art. 16a GG, Rdn. 150, 78. EL 2016, unter Hinweis auf Kai Hailbronner/Volker Olbrich, Asylrecht und Auslieferung, NVwZ 1985, 297 ff.; Otto Lagodny, Die Rechtsstellung des Auszuliefernden in der Bundesrepublik Deutschland, Freiburg/Breisgau 1987, S. 164 ff.; Volker Olbrich, Die Auslieferungsausnahme bei politischer Verfolgung, 1987, S. 41 ff., 286 ff. Zur älteren Rechtslage Herwig Roggemann, a. a. O. (Anm. S. 110 f. Ferner BVerfGE 52, 391, 400 = NJW 1980, 516; BVerfGE 60, 348, 358 = NJW 1982, 2728, wo das BVerfG diese Auswirkung der Trennung beider Verfahren für verfassungsrechtlich unbedenklich erklärte. Vgl. auch BVerfGE 62, 46 ff. = NJW 1983, 1721 ff. Im Wesentlichen gleichlautend § 18 des 1982 geänderten (BGBl I, S. 946) AsylVerfG.

Dies hat immer wieder zu für die Betroffenen belastenden und mit den Verfassungsgarantien des Asyls schwer zu vereinbarenden Ergebnissen geführt. So hat das BVerfG[81] die Auslieferung eines jugoslawischen Staatsangehörigen an Jugoslawien für zulässig gehalten, obwohl dieser zuvor in Frankreich aufgrund der Genfer Konvention als politischer Flüchtling anerkannt worden war und das zuständige französische Gericht die Auslieferung an Jugoslawien abgelehnt hatte. Dieses gegenüber Jugoslawien auslieferungsfreundliche Vorgehen der deutschen Gerichte hatte zu einem Protest des Vertreters des Hohen Flüchtlingskommissars beim Bundesjustizminister in Bonn geführt[82].

Hier hat sich in neuerer Zeit eine veränderte Sichtweise insofern entwickelt, als gegenüber dem „formellen Vorrang des Auslieferungsverfahrens" vor den Oberlandesgerichten der „materielle Vorrang des Asylrechts"[83] stärkere Berücksichtigung verlangt und Strafgerichte sowie Exekutive im Auslieferungsverfahren zu einer vollständigen inhaltlichen Prüfung und Bewertung etwaiger Asylgründe verpflichtet[84]. Es ist anzunehmen, daß eine solche Sichtweise auch Auswirkungen auf die Auslieferungspraxis gegenüber dem ehemaligen Jugoslawien gehabt hätte. Was das womöglich für die damalige kriminelle „Verfolgungspraxis" der jugoslawischen Seite jenseits von Rechtshilfe und Rechtsordnung bedeutet hätte, bleibt eine offene Frage.

2.1.5 Der deutsch-jugoslawische Auslieferungskonflikt von 1978 und der deutsch-kroatische Auslieferungskonflikt von 2013 – Wirkungen und Nachwirkungen desselben innerjugoslawischen Konflikts

Die Einhaltung des Spezialitätsgrundsatzes war im deutsch-jugoslawischen Auslieferungsverkehr nur einmal grundsätzlich in Zweifel geraten. 1978 war von jugoslawischer Seite um Auslieferung von sechs Kroaten, einen Serben und einen Albaner ersucht worden, denen die Beteiligung an terroristischen Aktivitäten und kriminellen Organisationen vorgeworfen wurde. Die

---

81 In BVerfG v. 14. 11. 1979, NJW 1980, 516 ff.

82 Ebenso hatte auch das OLG Karlsruhe (Beschl. v. 5. 12. 1985, GA 1986, S. 278 f.) die Auslieferung für zulässig gehalten, obwohl auch in diesem Fall in Frankreich zuvor politisches Asyl anerkannt und die Auslieferung abgelehnt worden war.

83 So Randelzhofer, a. a. O. (Anm. 81).

84 „Für Auslieferungssachen folgt daraus eine Verpflichtung der zuständigen Stellen, soweit Anhaltspunkte für eine politische Verfolgung des Auszuliefernden bestehen ... auch bei der Prüfung von § 6 II IRG oder entsprechender auslieferungsvertraglicher Regelungen (z.B. Art. 3 Nr. 2 EuAlÜbK) eigenständig zu prüfen, ob dem Betroffenen im Fall seiner Auslieferung politische Verfolgung droht". Diese Verpflichtung zur „eigenständigen Prüfung des Asylanspruchs durch das OLG" sieht das BVerfG nicht nur in § 6 II IRG sondern auch in den „norminternen Direktiven von Art. 16 a I GG begründet, dazu BVerfG v. 9. 4. 2015 – 2 BvR 221/15, NVwZ 2015, S. 1204, 1205, m. Anm. Bertold Huber.

Bundesregierung hatte im Gegenzug Jugoslawien um Auslieferung von vier mutmaßlichen RAF-Terroristen ersucht. Die deutschen Oberlandesgerichte erklärten die Auslieferung in vier Fällen für unzulässig, im übrigen für zulässig und die Gesuchten wurden in Haft genommen. Die Bundesregierung erklärte daraufhin als oberste Bewilligungsbehörde die Auslieferung mit der Begründung für unzulässig, sie werde die Strafverfolgung nach dem Territorialitätsprinzip selbst in Anspruch nehmen. Daraufhin ließ die jugoslawische Seite die vier gesuchten mutmaßlichen deutschen Terroristen ihrerseits frei, ohne die deutsche Bundesregierung zu informieren. Der Fall führte zu einer diplomatischen Krise und zeitweiligem Rückruf der Botschafter beider Länder.

2.2 Der Auslieferungskonflikt um Perković/Mustač von 2013

2.2.1   Nichtbeantwortung des ersten deutschen Rechtshilfeersuchens
Dem Senat war es nicht möglich, Zdravko Mustač und Josip Perković als Zeugen zu vernehmen oder im Rahmen der Rechtshilfe vernehmen zu lassen". – „Das Rechtshilfeersuchen des Senats um richterliche Vernehmung beider Zeugen in Zagreb vom 18. März 2008 ist bis zur Urteilsverkündung am 16. Juli 2008 nicht beantwortet worden[85].

Mit dieser Feststellung umschreibt das OLG München die Tatsache, daß die kroatische Regierung auch während der Regierungszeit des konservativen Ministerpräsidenten Ivo Sanader eine Rechtshilfe bereits im Fall Prates, in dem die beiden späteren Angeklagten als Zeugen geladen waren, stillschweigend ablehnte.

2.2.2   Neue Rechtslage: EU-Beitritt Kroatiens und Europäischer Haftbefehl
Eine grundlegende Änderung der Rechtslage ergab sich aus dem Beitritt Kroatiens zur EU am 1. 7. 2013 und der Übernahme des Europäischen Haftbefehlsverfahrens, das in Deutschland bereits aufgrund des zum 2. 8. 2006 in Kraft getretenen 2. Europäischen Haftbefehlsgesetzes (EuHBG) v. 20. 7. 2006[86] zur Anwendung kam. Dieses vereinfachte Haftbefehlsverfahren war von Kroatien

---

85   So im Prates-Urt, OLG München v. 16. 7. 2008, a. a. O. (Anm. 64 und 5). OLG München v. 3. 8. 2016, 7 St 5/14 (2) unveröffentlicht, nicht rechtskräftig.
86   BGBl I 2006, 1721. Zur Verfassungswidrigkeit der Vorfassung BVerfGE 113, 273 = NJW 2005, S. 2289; zur 2. Fassung vgl. den Überblick bei Thomas Hackner/Wolfgang Schomburg/Otto Lagodny/Sabine Gless, Das 2. Europäische Haftbefehlsgesetz, NStZ 2006, S. 663 ff.; Klaus Michael Böhm, Das neue Europäische Haftbefehlsgesetz, NJW 2005, S. 2289; zur Vereinbarkeit des Rahmenbeschl. 2002/584/JI des Rates v. 13. 6. 2002 über den EuHB mit dem EUV vgl. EuGH v. 3. 5. 2007, JuS 2007, S. 854 ff.; zu Vereinfachungsfolgen des EuHBG und weiterhin zu prüfenden Voraussetzungen vgl. z. B. OLG Karlsruhe v. 10. 8. 2006, NStZ

im Zuge seines EU-Beitritts-Verfahrens ebenfalls übernommen worden[87] und sollte dort mit dem Beitritt zum 1. 7. 2013 zur Anwendung kommen. Am 25. 5. 2013 stellte die GenStA beim OLG München daraufhin den Haftbefehl gegen Perković erneut ins Netz.

Aus dem Europäischen Haftbefehlsverfahren ergeben sich Vereinfachungseffekte und weitergehende Kooperationspflichten für das Auslieferungsverfahren zwischen den Mitgliedstaaten. Dies gilt insbesondere für den Direktverkehr der Justizorgane, die grundsätzliche Anerkennung der formalen Wirksamkeit justizförmiger Ersuchen, die Pflicht zur Auslieferung eigener Staatsangehöriger des ersuchten Staates, den Wegfall der Voraussetzung beiderseitiger Strafbarkeit für die Katalogtaten (gem. Art. 2 II)[88]. Diese Rechtsvereinfachung betraf im Verhältnis der Mitgliedsländer Deutschland und Kroatien auch den am 12. 6. 2009 vom BKA gegen Perković und Mustač erlassenen und auf der Internetseite des BKA veröffentlichten Haftbefehl, dem die kroatische Seite zunächst nicht Folge leistete.

2.2.3 Das Gesetz zur Änderung des Gesetzes zur Übernahme des Europäischen Haftbefehls – „Lex Perković" und Konflikt mit Deutschland und der EU-Kommission

Am 28. 6. 2013, dem letzten Sitzungstag des Sabor vor dem Tag des Beitritts Kroatiens zur EU am 1. 7. 2013, nahm das kroatische Parlament ein Gesetz zur Änderung des Gesetzes über die gerichtliche Zusammenarbeit in Strafsachen mit den Mitgliedstaaten der Europäischen Union an[89], das in seinem Art. 81 einen neuen Art. 132 a zur Übernahme des EuHB in das ÜbernahmeG von 2010 einfügte, dessen Abs. 3 bestimmte: *„Der Europäische Haftbefehl wird angewandt auf Straftaten, die nach dem 7. 8. 2002 begangen worden sind."*

Mit dieser vielfach als *„Lex Perković"* bezeichneten Novelle sollten die Erstreckung des zunächst unbeschränkten zeitlichen Geltungsbereichs des Europäischen Haftbefehls in Kroatien nachträglich auf Taten nach dem Inkrafttreten des EuHB in Kroatien aufgrund der Erstfassung des ÜbernahmeG

2007, S. 111 ff.; KG v. 14. 8. 2006, NStZ 2007, S. 110 ff.; OLG Zweibrücken v. 7. 8. 2006, NStZ 2007, S. 109 ff.; OLG Karlsruhe v. 18. 6. 2007, BeckRS 2007, 10862.

87 Durch Zakon o pravosudnoj suradnji u kaznenim stvarima s držama članicama Europske Unije (Gesetz über die gerichtliche Zusammenarbeit in Strafsachen mit den Mitgliedstaaten der Europäischen Union) v. 9. 7. 2010, Narodne Novine (NN) 91/10, dessen Art. 1 Ziff. 1 die uneingeschränkte Übernahme des EuHB durch Kroatien vorsieht.

88 Dazu zusammenfassend Klaus Michael Böhm, Das neue Europäische Haftbefehlsgesetz, NJW 2006, S. 2592; Thomas Hacker/Wolfgang Schomburg/Otto Lagodny/Sabine Gless, Das 2. Europäische Haftbefehlsgesetz, NStZ 2006, S. 663 ff.

89 NN 81/13.

v. 2010 beschränkt und damit die Täter von Alttaten wie im Fall Perković von der Auslieferung im Europäischen Haftbefehlsverfahren ausgeschlossen werden.

Diese nachträgliche Veränderung der Rechtslage mit dem offensichtlichen Ziel, die Durchführung eines laufenden Auslieferungsverfahrens und insbesondere die Weiterverfolgung eines besonderes Aufsehen erregenden Falles aus der Serie politischer Geheimdienst-Morde vonseiten des kommunistischen Jugoslawiens in Deutschland zu verhindern, führte zu schweren Konflikten mit der deutschen Bundesregierung und zur Absage der Teilnahme von Bundeskanzlerin Angela Merkel an der Beitrittsfeier in Zagreb am 1. 7. 2013.

Die Justizkommissarin der EU-Kommission, Viviane Reding, bezeichnete das kroatische Vorgehen als einen „elementaren Rechtsverstoß", drohte dem Neumitglied Kroatien mit rechtlichen und finanziellen Folgen und setzte der kroatischen Regierung eine Frist bis zum 13. 8. 2013 zur Aufhebung dieses Gesetzes und damit zur Rückkehr der Erstfassung des Übernahmegesetzes mit der Folge der vollen Anwendung des Europäischen Haftbefehlsverfahrens auf alle auslieferungsfähigen Täter und Taten ohne Rücksicht auf ihr Begehungsdatum.

Nach weiteren ergebnislosen Gesprächen drohte die EU mit der Sperrung von 80 Mio. € zur finanziellen Unterstützung des Schengen-Beitritts Kroatiens und setzte am 6. 10. 2013 eine neue Frist von 10 Tagen für den Erlaß eines Gesetzes zur Rücknahme des Änderungsgesetzes mit der Maßgabe, daß dieses Änderungs-Änderungsgesetz zum 1. 1. 2014 in Kraft trete.

2.2.4 Die Änderung des Änderungsgesetzes – Verhaftung der Gesuchten – innenpolitische Auseinandersetzung und der Rechtsweg in Kroatien

Dieser Vorgabe der EU-Kommission kam die kroatische Regierung nach heftigen Debatten im Parlament und in den Medien nach. Ministerpräsident Zoran Milanović hatte erklärt, er werde es nicht länger zulassen, daß Kroatien von der EU „wie ein Wischlappen" behandelt werde. Diese Debatte wurde von der deutschen und europäischen wie auch von der kroatischen Öffentlichkeit mit großer Aufmerksamkeit verfolgt. Sie stellt der kritischen demokratischen Öffentlichkeit Kroatiens 25 Jahre nach dem Ende des Einparteisystems insgesamt ein gutes Zeugnis aus:[90] Der demokratische kroatische Rechtsstaat erwies sich als funktionsfähig.

---

90 Zur Aufarbeitung in Kroatien vgl. Josip Jurčević, Spašavanje Zločinačke Budućnosti (Rettung einer verbrecherischen Zukunft), Zagreb 2013; ferner die umfangreiche Chronologie in: Dnevnik hr v. 3. 8. 2016.

Am 1. 1. 2014 trat die Rücknahme der „Lex Perković" durch das von der kroatischen Regierung am 30. 10. 2013 eingebrachte Gesetz zur Änderung des Gesetzes zur Änderung des Gesetzes über die gerichtliche Zusammenarbeit mit den EU-Mitgliedstaaten[91] in Kraft.

Der Gesuchte Perković wurde noch am Tage des Inkrafttretens des 2. ÄnderungsG am 1. 1. 2014 von der Polizei in Zagreb verhaftet und wegen Fluchtgefahr in Untersuchungshaft genommen.

Doch damit ging der „Kroatische Krimi"[92] weiter und verlagerte sich in die politische und Pressedebatte sowie auf den Rechtsweg innerhalb Kroatiens. Die Schärfe dieser innenpolitischen Auseinandersetzung in Kroatien, hinter der gegensätzliche politische Interessen an der (Nicht)Aufarbeitung der vordemokratischen sozialistischen Vergangenheit Kroatiens und Jugoslawiens standen und wohl bis heute stehen, veranschaulicht eine außergewöhnliche Presseerklärung des Präsidenten des Obersten Gerichts Kroatiens v. 9. 1. 2014[93]. Darin weist das Gericht eine zuvor in der größten kroatischen Tageszeitung Jutarnji List berichtete Äußerung aus „hoher Quelle aus der Regierung" zurück, worin es hieß: „Skandalöser Beschluß! Die kroatischen Gerichte wollen die kroatischen Gesetze nicht anwenden! Das ist ein Staatsstreich mit einem Schuß ins Wasser". Das Oberste Gericht erklärte dazu:

> Ein solcher Kommentar in Bezug auf einen nicht rechtskräftigen Gerichtsbeschluß stellt einen verfassungswidrigen und gesetzwidrigen Versuch der Exekutive in der eindeutigen Absicht dar, auf das weitere Verfahren und die Entscheidungsbildung in einem konkreten Fall vor dem Obersten Gericht der Republik Kroatien Einfluß zu nehmen. – Das Oberste Gericht weist daher warnend auf die Unzulässigkeit solcher und ähnlicher Äußerungen und Kommentare hin, die die Unabhängigkeit des Richters berühren.

Nachdem das Bezirksgericht Zagreb am 8. 1. 2014[94] die Auslieferung für zulässig erklärt hatte, wies das Oberste Gericht Kroatiens am 17. 1. 2014 die Beschwerde dagegen zurück[95]. Die dagegen wegen Verletzung von Menschenrechten und in der Verfassung garantierten Grundrechten durch diese Entscheidung und die vorangegangene Entscheidung des Bezirksgerichts eingelegte

---

91 Vgl. NN 81/ und 124/13.
92 Der Tagesspiegel (Berlin) v. 3. 1. 2014.
93 AZ Su-IV-41/14.
94 AZ KV-EUN-2/14.
95 AZ Kz-eum 214–5.

Verfassungsbeschwerde des inhaftierten Perković wies das Verfassungsgericht der Republik Kroatien mit Beschl. v. 24. 1. 2014[96] ebenfalls zurück. Daraufhin erfolgte die Auslieferung von Josip Perković am 24. 1. 2014. Die von Zdravko Mustač folgte im April 2014 nach ebenfalls erfolglosem Gang durch die Instanzen. Anders als im Fall Perković hatte allerdings im Fall Mustač das Bezirksgericht Velika Gorica in seinem später aufgehobenen Beschl. v. 9. 1. 2014[97] dessen Auslieferung mit der Begründung abgelehnt, daß die absolute Verjährung bereits am 28. 7. 2008 eingetreten sei und die Auslieferung auch nach dem Europäischen Haftbefehlsverfahren ausschließe.

2.2.5   Vermeintliche oder tatsächliche Auslieferungshindernisse?
Der Verteidiger von Perković, Ante Nobilo, hatte die Unzulässigkeit der Auslieferung mit zwei durchaus gewichtigen Argumenten begründet: Schon 1997 und 1999 seien Ermittlungsverfahren gegen Perković von der Generalstaatsanwaltschaft In Zagreb mangels hinreichenden Tatverdachts rechtskräftig eingestellt worden. In der Zwischenzeit sei nach kroatischem Recht die absolute Verjährung eingetreten. Dem auch von Regierungs- und Parlamentsmitgliedern und in der Presse Kroatiens vorgetragenen Verjährungsargument[98] begegnete der führende kroatische Strafprozeßrechtler und Verfassungsrichter Davor Krapac mit dem Gegenargument:[99] Bei konkurrierenden Verfolgungszuständigkeiten

---

96   AZ U-III-351/2014.
97   U. 4 KV-EUN-1/14-7.
98   „Das kroatische Gesetz ist klar: Die Verjährung ist im Fall Perković noch 1998 eingetreten, denn es sind volle 15 Jahre seit Begehung dieser Straftat verstrichen. Die Generalstaatsanwaltschaft Kroatiens hat 1997 ein Strafverfahren gegen Perković aus Mangel an Beweisen als unbegründet eingestellt. – Was bedeutsamer ist: Perković kann nach allgemeinem Urteil selbst dann nicht ausgeliefert werden, wenn der Sabor die Verfassung ändern und eine Vorschrift über die Unverjährbarkeit schwerer Tötung aus politischen Motiven einführen würde. Auch in der Strafgesetzgebung und Praxis der Europäischen Gerichte kann Verjährung nicht verlängert werden, nachdem sie schon einmal eingetreten ist", so Marina Karlović-Sabolić in: Slobodna Dalmacija (SD) v. 16. 8. 2013.
99   Im Einleitungsbeitrag zu der von ihm gegründeten wichtigsten kroatischen Strafrechtszeitschrift Hrvatsko Kazneno Pravo i Praksa (Kroatisches Strafrecht und Praxis), Vol. 2/2013 schreibt – der leider zwischenzeitlich verstorbene – Davor Krapac: „Bei einer Kollision der Regeln über die Verfolgungsverjährung müssen die EU-Staaten diejenige Regelung wählen, die die Durchführung (des Europäischen Haftbefehls) begünstigt und nicht dessen Ablehnung, denn die gesuchte Person hat kein Recht auf Nichtauslieferung, wenn das Recht (auf Verfolgung) in einem Land erloschen ist, jedoch im um Auslieferung ersuchenden oder sogar in mehreren Ländern weiterbesteht".
Im anschließenden Verfahren vor dem Kroatischen Verfassungsgericht hatte Krapac sich selbst für befangen erklärt, obwohl das Gericht im Beschlußwege klargestellt hatte,

und unterschiedlichen Verjährungsvorschriften sei zur Durchsetzung des EuHB diejenige Verjährungsregelung des ersuchenden Staates maßgeblich, die Rechtshilfe ermögliche. Anders als das genannte BezG Velika Gorica sahen die oberen Gerichte Kroatiens in ihren Entscheidungsbegründungen in der streitigen Verjährung im ersuchten Staat jedoch kein i. S. des kroatischen ÜbernahmeG des EuHB-Verfahrens zwingendes Auslieferungshindernis.

Ob im Falle einer entsprechenden hypothetischen Umstellung des Rechtssachverhalts die deutsche Strafgerichtsbarkeit ebenso entschieden hätte, erscheint allerdings nicht sicher. Im Falle konkurrierender Gerichtsbarkeit, wie sie hier gegeben ist, wird die Auslieferung für zulässig gehalten, wenn die Tat im deutschen Inland wegen Verfolgungsverjährung nicht mehr geahndet werden kann, die Strafverfolgungsbehörden des ersuchenden Staates jedoch Handlungen vorgenommen haben, die auch nach deutschem Rechts geeignet wären, die Verjährung zu unterbrechen[100].

Das BVerfG[101] hat diesen Grundsatz im Interesse des Vertrauensschutzes eines von Auslieferung betroffenen deutschen Staatsangehörigen auf die Voraussehbarkeit von Rechtsfolgen durch eine „verfassungskonforme Auslegung von § 9 Nr. 2 IRG" jedoch dahin gehend eingeschränkt, daß lediglich inländische Unterbrechungstatbestände anerkannt werden könnten.

Ausschlaggebend bliebe dann als Argument für die erst nach erheblichem politischen Druck auf die kroatische Regierung erfolgte Rückgängigmachung des Änderungsgesetzes mit der anschließenden Auslieferung die Tatsache der nachträglichen Änderung der Rechtslage Kroatiens im Verhältnis zu den anderen Mitgliedsstaaten der EU. Dies Verfahren kann als unzulässige, rückwirkende Verschlechterung vorher vereinbarter Beitrittsbedingungen angesehen werden, wie vonseiten der EU-Justizkommissarin auch vorgetragen. Sieht man jedoch im Verjährungsgrundsatz eine inhaltliche Beschränkung des staatlichen Strafanspruchs, der im Sinne der verfassungsmäßigen Freiheitsvermutung zugunsten jedes Rechtsgenossen auch eine menschenrechtliche Qualität zukommt, so ließe sich fragen, ob das europarechtliche Argument diesen Grundsatz des Vertrauensschutzes, so unangenehm seine Auswirkungen im

---

daß eine Besorgnis der Befangenheit in derartigen Fällen wissenschaftlicher Stellungnahme zu streitgegenständlichen Problemen nicht zu besorgen sei.

100 So Otto Lagodny in: Schomburg/Bohlander/Lagodny/Gieß/Hackner (Fn. 4), § 9 IRG Rdn. 20 unter Hinweis auf BGHSt 33, 26 = NJW 1985, S. 570.

101 BVerfG v. 3. 9. 2009 – 2 BvR 1826/09, EuGRZ 2009, S. 686 = StV 2010, S. 315; zur Unzulässigkeit der Auslieferung wegen Verfolgungsverjährung in Deutschland auch OLG Hamm v. 13. 6. 2013 – 2 Ausl 47/13.

Einzelfall – wie auch in den hier vorgestellten Fällen – sich auswirken mögen, entkräften kann.

Der Grundsatz des erneuten Verfolgungsverbots wegen vorangegangener rechtskräftiger Einstellungsentscheidungen der kroatischen Justizbehörden – insofern weisen die hier erörterten Fälle eine Parallele zu dem von *Wolfgang Schomburg* in Split vorgetragenen „Fall Krombach" auf[102] – spielte in der weiteren rechtlichen und politischen Auseinandersetzung keine Rolle mehr.

2.3 Schluß: Rechtshilfe zur Rechtshilfe zur Aufarbeitung der gemeinsamen deutschen und kroatischen Vergangenheit

Diese dramatische Entwicklung eröffnete eine „Rechthilfe zur Rechtshilfe":

> Kroatien und seine demokratisch legitimierte, rechtsstaatliche Justiz leistete Deutschland Rechtshilfe bei der Strafverfolgung zweier gesuchter Straftäter, die nach den – noch nicht rechtskräftigen – Feststellungen des OLG München Verantwortung für zahlreiche in Deutschland begangene politische Mordtaten gegen kroatische Emigranten tragen.

Deutschland leistete Kroatien mit dem Münchner Strafurteil von 2008 und mehr noch mit dem Urteil von 2016 durch die Verurteilung zweier prominenter Mitarbeiter des Geheimdienstes des sozialistischen Jugoslawien „Rechtshilfe" in einem übertragenen Sinne: bei der notwendigen Aufarbeitung früherer jugoslawisch-kroatischer „Regierungskriminalität" und damit eines schwierigen Kapitels seiner eigenen und der gemeinsamen kroatischen und deutschen Geschichte.

3 Zusammenfassung

Kroatien und die anderen Nachfolgestaaten der Jugoslawischen Föderation sind mit Deutschland durch eine gemeinsame Geschichte verbunden. Zeitweilig lebten in der Bundesrepublik Deutschland mehr als 630.000 jugoslawische Staatsbürger als Gastarbeiter in Deutschland. Geografische und kulturelle Nähe sowie persönliche und wirtschaftliche Verflechtungen und freundschaftliche Zusammenarbeit schließen gelegentliche Konflikte nicht aus und verlangen deren gemeinsame Lösung. Dazu gehören auch Rechtshilfekonflikte. Hinter verfahrensrechtlichen Fragen, wer wem unter welchen Voraussetzungen Hilfe bei der Strafverfolgung zu leisten habe, kommen innen- und

---

102 S. o. unter 1.2.

außenpolitische Konfliktkonstellationen zum Vorschein, die bis in die Gegenwart nachwirken. Fragen der Strafrechtshilfe weiten sich aus zu Fragen der Vergangenheitsverarbeitung. Beispiele für diese Zusammenhänge bieten die Urteile des OLG München im Mordfall Đureković gegen Krunoslav Prates v. 16. 7. 2008 und gegen Josip Perković und Zdravko Mustać v. 3. 8. 2016. Aus den Feststellungen des Gerichts und neueren kroatischen Untersuchungen ergibt sich, in welchem Maße sich die Regierung des sozialistischen Jugoslawien unter Tito und auch danach bis zur demokratischen Wende und dem Zerfall der Jugoslawischen Föderation in ständigem Konflikt mit politischen Gegnern insbesondere aus Kroatien befand. Gegen diese kroatischen Systemgegner und vor allem gegen führende Vertreter der Exilkroaten in Deutschland ging die damalige jugoslawische Regierung zweigleisig vor: Mit den Mitteln des Strafrechts und der internationalen Rechtshilfe in Strafsachen und mit den außerrechtlichen Mitteln der Gewaltanwendung durch politische Mordaufträge. So wurden in den Jahren von 1946 bis 1989 , soweit bisher aus unterschiedlichen Quellen bekannt geworden, von 68 politisch motivierten Morden an Exilkroaten 39 in Deutschland begannen. Dieser „Sonderkrieg" des sozialistischen Jugoslawiens mit seinen exilkroatischen Gegnern stellt sich als Vorbote des späteren Jugoslawienkrieges von 1991 bis 1995 dar. Dieser Jugoslawienkrieg wurde 1993 zu einem wesentlichen Anstoß für die Errichtung UN-Strafgerichtshofs für das ehemalige Jugoslawien. Als erster deutscher Richter an einer Strafkammer und an der Berufungskammer des ICTY nahm Wolfgang Schomburg an diesem großen internationalen Versuch teil, „Frieden durch Gerechtigkeit" mit den Mitteln juridischer Intervention im Konfliktraum des Balkan wieder herzustellen. Ohne dieses internationale Tribunal und seine rund 25-jährige Rechtsprechungstätigkeit wären die strafrechtlichen Voraussetzungen für eine spätere Versöhnung in der Konfliktregion nicht geschaffen worden. Einen späten Beitrag zur Aufarbeitung dieses Kapitels der jugoslawischen, kroatischen und auch der deutschen Geschichte leistete das OLG München mit seinen Entscheidungen 2008 und 2016. Rechtshilfe durch Auslieferung der Tatverdächtigten von Kroatien an Deutschland zur Verhandlung vor diesem Gericht wurde erst nach dem EU-Beitritt Kroatiens ihm Rahmen des Europäischen Haftbefehlsverfahrens und nach Beilegung von Kontroversen zwischen der deutschen und kroatischen und innerhalb der kroatischen Justiz möglich.

CHAPTER 17

International Prosecution of Sexual and Gender-Based Crimes Perpetrated during the First World War

William A. Schabas

Abstract

Sexual and gender based violence has become a focus of modern-day international criminal justice. It is widely believed that the issue was ignored in previous efforts at international prosecution. Yet during and after the First World War there were serious and credible efforts to address allegations of sexual and gender-based violence. Feminist organizations took up the matter, submitting petitions to the Paris Peace Conference insisting that rape and forced prosecution not be neglected by the Commission on Responsibilities, which was charged with organizing the prosecutions. Ultimately, only a few trials took place at Leipzig and they did not address crimes against women.

There is no doubt that '[r]ape and other forms of sexual violence have long been prohibited by international humanitarian law', as a Trial Chamber of the International Criminal Court confirmed in January 2017.[1] But writing in the *Oxford Companion to International Criminal Justice*, Katrina Gustafson said that until the establishment of the *ad hoc* tribunals for the former Yugoslavia and Rwanda, 'rape was largely ignored as an international crime'.[2] There is certainly no question, as Wolfgang Schomburg and Ines Peterson noted, that

---

* William Schabas is professor of international law at Middlesex University London and professor of international criminal law and human rights at Leiden University.
1 *Prosecutor v. Ntaganda* (ICC-01/04-02/06), Second decision on the Defence's challenge to the jurisdiction of the Court in respect of Counts 6 and 9, 4 January 2017, para. 46. Also: Theodor Meron, 'Rape as a Crime Under International Humanitarian Law' (1993) 87 *American Journal of International Law* 424, at p. 424.
2 Katrina Gustafson, 'Rape' in Antonio Cassese (ed.), *The Oxford Companion to International Criminal Justice* (Oxford, Oxford University Press 2009), pp. 477–179. See also Theodor Meron,

'[t]he ad hoc Tribunals are the first to have dealt extensively with crimes of sexual violence in times of armed conflict'.[3]

In the post-Second World War prosecutions, the term 'rape' was generally used in another context: 'the rape of Nanking',[4] 'the rape of Czechoslovakia',[5] 'the rape of Prague',[6] 'the rape of the gallant Netherlands and of Belgium'.[7] There are only isolated references in the Nuremberg proceedings to rape perpetrated by German soldiers in occupied France[8] and the Soviet Union.[9] Some writers have criticized a tendency to overlook the attention given to sexual violence by the International Military Tribunal for the Far East.[10]

The significant efforts that were made to prosecute sexual and gender-based violence perpetrated during the First World War have not been studied in any depth. At the time, violent crimes against women attracted considerable attention from the feminist movement. Notably, during the Paris Peace Conference of 1919 women's organizations intervened to insist that rape be addressed within the framework of post-war prosecutions. The post-First World War period was very much the dawn of the modern system of international criminal justice. The Hague Conventions of 1899 and 1907 did not expressly provide for individual criminal liability but they began a period of international lawmaking inspired, according to the famous Martens clause, by 'the principles of the law of nations, as they result from the usages established among civilized peoples, from the laws of humanity, and the dictates of the public conscience'.

'Rape as a Crime under International Humanitarian Law' (1993) 87 *American Journal of International Law* 424, at pp. 425–426.

3   Wolfgang Schomburg and Ines Peterson, 'Genuine Consent to Sexual Violence under International Criminal Law' (2007) 101 *American Journal of International Law* 121, at p. 122.

4   *United States et al. v. Araki* et al., Judgment of the International Military Tribunal for the Far East, 4 November 1948, paras. 49,240, 49,605–49,612.

5   'Eleventh Day, Monday, 3 December 1945, Morning Session', (1947) 3 IMT 35; 'Thirteenth Day, Wednesday, 5 December 1945, Morning Session', (1947) 3 IMT 173; 'One Hundred and Eighty-eighth Day. Saturday, 27 July 1946, Morning Session', (1948) 19 IMT 496.

6   'Twenty-ninth Day, Tuesday, 8 January 1946, Afternoon Session', (1947) 4 IMT 566, 568.

7   'One Hundred and Eighty-seventh Day. Friday. 26 July 1946, Afternoon Session', (1948) 19 IMT 457.

8   'Forty-third Day, Friday, 25 January 1946, Afternoon Session', (1947) 6 IMT 178; 'Forty-seventy Day, Thursday, 31 January 1946, Afternoon Session', (1947) 6 IMT 404–406.

9   'Fifty-fourth Day, Friday, 8 February 1946, Afternoon Session', (1947) 7 IMT 179; 'Fifty-ninth Day, Thursday, 14 February 1946, Afternoon Session', (1947) 7 IMT 440, 442, 455–457; 'Sixtieth Day, Friday, 15 February 1946, Morning Session', (1947) 7 IMT 467, 494.

10 David Cohen, 'Prosecuting Sexual Violence from Tokyo to the ICC' in Morten Bergsmo, Alf Butenschøn Skre and Elisabeth J. Wood (eds.), *Understanding and Proving International Sex Crimes* (Beijing, Torkel Opsahl Academic EPublisher 2012), pp. 13–63, at pp. 14–15.

Article 46 of the Regulations annexed to the fourth Hague Convention of 1907 declared: 'Family honour and rights, the lives of persons, and private property, as well as religious convictions and practice, must be respected.' The Commission of Inquiry established by the Carnegie Foundation that investigated allegations of war crimes committed during the Balkan wars of 1912 and 1913 considered the crime of rape within the framework of article 46 of the Hague Regulations. 'En réalité, le viol n'étonne plus personne, et on oublie même de le considérer comme un crime', wrote the Commission in the chapter of the report dealing with war and international law. 'Les Bulgares, sous ce rapport, sont probablement, moins coupables que les autres. Plus patriarcaux ou plus primitifs, ils conservent en pays ennemi l'esprit du terroir et sont beaucoup plus disciplinés que les autres.'[11]

1   Official Reports on Atrocities in France and Belgium

The outbreak of the First World War in August 1914 was accompanied by allegations of a range of atrocities, including sexual and gender-based violence, perpetrated by German combatants in the occupied portions of Belgium and France. These charges figured in general discussions about war crimes. The official British inquiry, whose report was published in 1915, and that is known as the Bryce Committee, concluded that 'there is evidence of offences committed against women and children by individual soldiers, or by small groups of soldiers, both in the advance through Belgium and France as in the retreat from the Marne'. Referring specifically to northeast France, the Bryce Committee spoke of 'acts of cruelty, including aggravated cases of rape, carried out under threat of death, and sometimes actually followed by murder of the victim, were committed by some of the German troops'.[12] The offical French inquiry, also published in 1915 reported: 'Les attentats contres les femmes et les jeunes filles ont été d'une fréquence inouïe. Nous en avons établi un grand nombre, qui ne représente qu'une quantité infime auprès de ceux que nous aurions pu relever; mais, par un sentiment très respectable, les victimes de ces actes odieux se refusent généralement de se révéler.'[13] Referring to Belgium, the British inquiry

---

11   *Enquête dans les Balkans, Rapport présenté aux directeurs de la dotation par les Membres de la Commission d'enquête* (Paris, Centre européen de la dotation Carnegie 1914), p. 223.
12   *Report of the Committee on Alleged German Outrages* (London, HMSO 1915).
13   *Rapports et procès-verbaux d'enquête de la commission instituée en vue de constater les actes commis par l'ennemi en violation du droit des gens (décret du 23 septembre 1914)* (Paris, Imprimerie Nationale 1915) vol I, p. 8.

said that '[m]urder, rape, arson, and pillage began from the moment when the German army crossed the frontier.' It continued: 'Individual acts of brutality treatment of civilians, rape, plunder, and the like – were very widely committed. These are more numerous and more shocking than would be expected in warfare between civilised Powers, but they differ rather in extent than in kind from what has happened in previous though not recent wars.'[14]

Some of the more outrageous charges were subsequently discounted. At one point, the Bryce Committee Report referred to a massacre of 32 civilians in the Place de l'Université in Liège, adding that 'a witness states that this was followed by the rape in open day of 15 or 20 women on tables in the square itself'.[15] Elsewhere in the Report, but apparently with reference to the same incident, it said: 'A witness gives a story, very circumstantial in its details, of how women were publicly raped in the market-place of the city, five young German officers assisting.'[16] The Committee Report presented this allegation in a somewhat qualified way, citing the evidence of a single witness. But the mere reference to such a notorious act with such little substantiation was rather sensationalist. It seems the allegation was subsequently discredited.

With respect to the sexual and gender-based violence, the British and French reports described these as acts of individual soldiers rather than conduct that was driven by official policy. The Bryce Committee stated that 'the maltreatment of women was no part of the military scheme of the invaders, however much it may appear to have been the inevitable result of the system of terror deliberately adopted in certain regions'.[17] The French report depicted the sexual and gender-based violence as 'actes individuels et spontanés de brutes déchaînés'.[18] The Bryce Committee also noted that the German military authorities could be quite harsh in punishing their own soldiers for these crimes: 'One witness reports that a young girl, who was being pursued by a drunken soldier at Louvain appealed to a German officer, and that the offender was then and there shot; another describes how an officer of the 32nd Regiment of the Line was led out to execution for the violation of two young girls, but reprieved at the request or with the consent of the girls' mother.'[19] Later in

---

14   *Report of the Committee on Alleged German Outrages* (London, HMSO 1915).
15   Ibid.
16   Ibid.
17   Ibid.
18   *Rapports et procès-verbaux d'enquête de la commission instituée en vue de constater les actes commis par l'ennemi en violation du droit des gens (décret du 23 septembre 1914)* (Paris, Imprimerie Nationale 1915) vol I, p. 8.
19   *Report of the Committee on Alleged German Outrages* (London, HMSO 1915).

the war, the United States executed its own soldiers for the crime of rape,[20] and it seems likely that this was also the case with the British and French armies.

According to historians John Horne and Alan Kramer, 'it would be improper to assume that rapes were a dominant feature of German behaviour'.[21] Nevertheless, they concluded that 'while there was no official toleration of rape by the German army, and rape thus was not part of a reprisal policy against supposed francs-tireurs, sexual menace was ubiquitous in the violence of the German invasion'.[22] There is some basis for believing that many victims of rape as well as members of their families did not report the crimes.[23] There was much scepticism about the validity of the reports of atrocities, particularly during the 1920s and 1930s, when it was suggested that these were exaggerations of Allied propagandists. But more recently, historians have tended to attribute more credence to the allegations and to judge those who made them, like the British Lord Bryce, as persons of integrity.[24]

Almost immediately, these reports of sexual and gender-based violence attracted attention from the women's movement. Late in April 1915, the International Congress of Women convened in The Hague. The delegates – more than 1,000 women – came from the parties to the conflict, including Britain, Belgium, Austria and Germany, as well as neutral powers like the United States. Although the movement behind the Congress was focussed on universal suffrage, the agenda took up much broader themes, namely bringing an end to the war and defining the new international legal order that should emerge following the conflict. Specifically, attention was devoted to 'women's sufferings in war'. According to Freya Baetens, the records of the Congress make clear that this was a reference to 'the use of mass rape both as a strategy and a crime of war under international law'.[25] Resolution 2 adopted by the Congress

---

20 *United States Army in the World War, 1917–1919* (Washington, Centre for Military History 1948) vol 15, p. 362.

21 John Horne and Alan Kramer, *German Atrocities, 1914, A History of Denial* (New Haven and London, Yale University Press 2001), p. 196. Also: Stéphane Audoin-Rouzeau, *L'enfant de l'ennemi (1914–1918), Viol, avortement, infanticide pendant la grande guerre* (Paris, Aubier 2009).

22 John Horne and Alan Kramer, *German Atrocities, 1914, A History of Denial* (New Haven and London, Yale University Press 2001), p. 71.

23 *Ibid.*, pp. 197–198.

24 *Ibid.*, pp. 232–237; Ruth Harris, 'The "Child of the Barbarian": Rape, Race and Nationalism in France during the First World War' (1993) 141 *Past & Present* 170.

25 Freya Baetens, 'International Congress of Women (1915)' in Rüdiger Wolfrum (ed.), *The Max Planck Encyclopedia of Public International Law* (Oxford, Oxford University Press 2012) vol V, pp. 455–459, at p. 456.

'oppose[d] the assumption that women can be protected under the conditions of modern warfare. It protests vehemently against the odious wrongs of which women are the victims in time of war and especially against the horrible violation of women which attends all war.'

2 Organising Post-War Prosecutions

From the earliest days of the war there were trials of captured enemy combatants for various violations of the laws and customs of war. For example, on 5 October 1914, the newspaper *Échos de Paris* reported that two German soldiers had been sentenced to death for pillage. But as the war wore on, the parties to the conflict came to appreciate the vulnerability of their own nationals who were prisoners, and the danger of escalating reprisals should one side insist upon trying and punishing the combatants of the other side. They reached agreements whereby sentences imposed upon prisoners would not be carried out until after the war. This practice of reciprocity no doubt saved the lives of many prisoners of war. Eventually, restrictions on the punishment of prisoners of war were codified in the Geneva Conventions, but that would have to wait until 1929 and 1949.[26]

In October 1918, when German defeat seemed inevitable, the governments of Britain and France revived the discussions about punishment. On 1 November 1918, the British Attorney General, Sir Frederick Smith (later Lord Birkenhead), acting under the authority of the War Cabinet, appointed a Committee of Enquiry into Breaches of the Law of War. The Committee was to enquire into and report upon the fact as to 'breaches of the laws and customs of war, affecting members of the British armed forces or other British subjects, committed by the forces of the German Empire and their allies on land, on sea, and in the air during the present war'. It was also to consider issues concerning the creation of an appropriate tribunal for such offences. The British Committee of Inquiry produced its first report on 19 December 1919. It provided two lists of war crimes, the first of a general nature to be used in prosecution of enemy combatants and the second for the trial of Kaiser Wilhelm II. In both cases, the lists were intended to define the subject-matter jurisdiction of an international criminal tribunal. The two lists were not identical, although both included a category labelled 'systematic terrorism in Belgium, France and elsewhere' that

---

26   International Convention Relative to the Treatment of Prisoners of War, (1932–33) 118 LNTS 343, arts. 65, 66; Geneva Convention of August 12, 1949 Relative to the Treatment of Prisoners of War, (1949) 75 UNTS 287, arts. 100, 101.

could well comprise sexual and gender-based violence.[27] There was, however, no direct reference to rape.

The issue of sexual and gender-based violence was explicitly mentioned in a report prepared by two distinguished members of the Faculty of Law of the University of Paris, Ferdinand Larnaude and Albert Geouffre de Lapradelle. The French document listed nine categories of war crimes, among them 'deliberate violations of the honour of young girls'. The two French academics concluded that '[i]n all of them the Emperor, during more than four years, took a supreme part, openly or tacitly, either by ordering them or abstaining from forbidding them'.[28] The French prime minister, Georges Clemenceau, spoke of the report by the French professors when he addressed the first meeting of the Preliminary Peace Conference, on 18 January 1919. Clemenceau insisted on the importance of punishing 'the authors of the abominable crimes committed during the war'.

The task of preparing the prosecutions was assigned by the Bureau of the Preliminary Peace Conference to the Commission on the Responsibility of the Authors of the War and on the Enforcement of Penalties. The reports of the French experts and of the British Committee, in particular the specific offences enumerated in those documents, provided a basis for the discussions. At its second meeting, the Commission divided into three sub-commissions, the first with responsibility for establishing the facts, the second assigned to consider legal liability for the outbreak of the war, and the third to report on legal liability for violations of the laws and customs of war. The first sub-commission held only perfunctory meetings, gathering materials from the Allied governments and then compiling them. In its report it provided a list of violations that included '(5.) Rape' and '(6.) Abduction of girls and women for the purpose of enforced prostitution'.[29] Details of specific allegations with respect to Belgium, Greece, and Serbia were provided in annexed tables, complete with references to documentary materials. The third sub-commission

---

27 'First interim report' in *First, Second and Third Interim Reports of the Committee of Inquiry into Breaches of the Laws of War with Appendices*, 26 February 1920, TNA CAB 24/11/13, pp. 17, 98.

28 'Inquiry into the Penal Liabilities of the Emperor Wilhelm II' in *Report on the Responsibility of the Authors of the War and on the Enforcement of Penalties, Minutes of the Commission*, USNA F.W. 181.1201/16, pp. 39–41, pp. 4–18, at p. 5.

29 'Report of Sub-Commission I on Criminal Acts' in *Report on the Responsibility of the Authors of the War and on the Enforcement of Penalties, Minutes of the Commission*, USNA F.W. 181.1201/16, pp. 39–41; 'Rapport de la 1ere sous-commission' in *Conférence de Paix 1919–1920, Recueil des Actes de la Conférence*, Partie IV(B)(2) (Paris, Imprimerie nationale, 1922), pp. 59–66.

also produced a list of possible crimes. It referred to 'honour of women', citing article 46 of the Hague Convention, noting that detailed information would be provided in the report of the first sub-commission.[30] The information and allegations in the report of the first sub-commission were subsequently incorporated, without modification, into the final report of the Commission, produced at the end of March 1919.[31]

The report referred to rapes perpertrated by German troops in August 1914 in three Belgian municipalities, Louvain, Korbeek-Lo, and Nimy. For Greece, it listed multiple cases of rape of women and girls in eastern Macedonia, carried out from 1916 to 1918 and attributed to 'Bulgarian authorities'. The list also referred to a large number of Greek victims of rape in Ayvalık (Aivali) and Goumisi, Asia Minor, in 1915, attributable to Turkish officials. With respect to Serbia, the report stated that in many villages few women were spared from rape, committed by officers and policemen but also by ordinary soldiers. It said there were many cases where women were abused in the presence of their daughters and vice versa. Often, victims were beaten before the rape and subsequently mutilated. Bulgarian soldiers with venereal diseases were ordered to rape girls. A woman was 'given up to officer's dog' by Bulgarian soldiers. There was a general allegation of rape perpetrated by Austrian soldiers against Serb women. These crimes were alleged to have been committed throughout the war and in Serbia generally. The only specific allegations concerned the locality of Požarevac (Pojarevatz).[32]

Only Greece was listed with respect to the crime of abduction of girls and women for the purpose of enforced prostitution. The report spoke of Greek women sent to Bulgaria as prostitutes, and more than 2,000 Greek children under 14 years of age sent to Bulgaria. It also referred to numerous cases of Greek

---

30 'Report of Sub-Commission III on the Violation of the Laws of War', 8 March 1919, USNA F.W. 181.12302/3; 'Rapport de la 3eme sous-commission' in Conférence de Paix 1919–1920, *Recueil des Actes de la Conférence*, Partie IV(B)(2) (Paris, Imprimerie nationale 1922), pp. 71–81, at p. 75. Also: 'Draft report of Sub-Commission III (Prepared by the Drafting Sub-Committee and submitted to the Sub-Commission, 4 March 1919', USNA F.W. 181/12302/2; 'Final draft prepared by the Drafting Committee, and submitted to the Sub-Commission', 8 March 1919, USNA F.W. 181/12302/3.

31 'Report presented to the Preliminary Peace Conference by the Commission on the Responsibility of the Authors of the War and on the Enforcement of Penalties' in *Report on the Responsibility of the Authors of the War and on the Enforcement of Penalties, Minutes of the Commission*, USNA F.W. 181.1201/16, pp. 113–176; 'Rapport de la Commission à la Conférence des Préliminaires de Paix (29 mars 1919)' in Conférence de Paix 1919–1920, *Recueil des Actes de la Conférence*, Partie IV(B)(2) (Paris, Imprimerie nationale 1922), pp. 162–234.

32 *Ibid.*

girls and women who were abused and detained in Turkish harems, as well as Greek children who were abducted and placed in Turkish houses. Under the heading 'Greece', the report also referred to a large number of Armenian women, girls and children who were confined to harems and converted by force to Islam.[33]

3 Women Petition the Peace Conference

In February 1919, the British delegation forwarded correspondence from the Council of Scotch Electors, a suffragist organization, concerning sexual and gender-based violence perpetrated during the war to the distribution to delegates. A covering letter from the Council, addressed to the British Minister of Foreign Affairs, asked that 'you use your influence' with the Peace Conference so as to 'give the commission of violation of rights and customs of war the necessary authority to make this question of extreme importance a vital part of this work'. It was signed by Louisa Innes Lumsden, who was president of the Council, and Alexia B. Jack, its secretary.[34]

Louisa Lumsden, later Dame Louisa Lumsden, was a native of Aberdeen in Scotland. She had been one of the first students at Girton College in Hitchen, a college for women located about 50 km north of London. After graduating, she became a lecturer at the college and, somewhat later, headmistress at St Leonards School in Fife. She is credited with introducing the sport of lacrosse to girls' schools in Britain. Lumsden had seen the sport played in Montreal by Caughnawaga Indians, describing it as 'a wonderful game, beautiful and graceful'.[35] In retirement, she became an active suffragist. During the First World War, she campaigned actively to recruit soldiers.[36]

---

33 *Ibid.* See also: 'Notes sur les auteurs responsables des massacres d'Arménie (Mémoire de la délégation arménienne), 14 mars 1919, Conférence de Paix 1919–1920, *Recueil des Actes de la Conférence*, Partie IV(B)(2) (Paris, Imprimerie nationale 1922), pp. 511–514.

34 Letter from Louisa Lumsden to Foreign Secretary and annexed documents, 7 February 1919, USNA F.W. 185.118/23. See also: Council of Scotch Electors, 6 March 1919, TNA FO 608/161.

35 Louisa Innes Lumsden, *Yellow Leaves, Memories of a Long Life* (Edinburgh and London, William Blackwood and Sons 1933), p. 81.

36 Elizabeth J. Morse, 'Lumsden, Dame Louisa Innes (1840–1935)' in *Oxford Dictionary of National Biography* (Oxford, Oxford University Press 2004) [http://www.oxforddnb.com/view/article/48571, accessed 26 Jan 2017].

The Secretariat of the Peace Conference organized the translation of the materials into French and on 4 March 1919 the documents were distributed:[37]

ELECTORS COUNCIL (NON POLITICAL)
Edinburgh Group   7 February 1919

To the Representatives of the Allied Powers assembled in conference.

Sirs:

The Council of Scotch Electors, Society composed of men and women, have noted with profound pity the lot of women and young girls of Allied countries who have been subject of brutal treatment or who have been taken into slavery by enemy troops and would like to bring this question to the attention of the powers assembled at the Peace Conference.

We want to insist that the Governments of the Allied Nations should without delay try and hunt for and find and return to their homes men as well as the women who have been taken, deported or sold by the Germans and their Allies, and to assure the punishment of all those who are found to be connected with these atrocities.

The Council of Scotch Electors would also like to call to the attention of the conference the fact that the Greek military mission is occupying itself at present and trying to find the women and young girls who were violated and taken away by Bulgars and Turks. It would be well to include this question which is of the greatest improtance in the work of the Commission constituted by the conference to occupy itself with the "violations of the laws and customs of war" and that also this question might fall under the fifth article of the resolutions that have been adopted by the conference.

Civilized women can no longer stand that violations committed on women should be neglected under pretext of being regrettable incidents of war.

Please accept sir the expression of our deepest respect.

Signed: Louisa Innes Lumsden. President
Alexia B. Jack. Secretary.[38]

---

37   Letter from Secretariat General to US delegation, 4 March 1919, USNA F.W. 185.118/23.
38   Letter from Louisa Lumsden to Foreign Secretary and annexed documents, 7 February 1919, USNA F.W. 185.118/23.

In mid-April, the Secretariat of the Conference distributed two other submissions along similar lines, one from women in the United States of America and the other from those in France. The document from the United States was the resolution of a body named the 'Committee on the Protection of Women under International Law'. The Secretariat distributed the resolution, translated into French, noting that it had been signed by 'cinq millions de Femmes Américaines, désireuses de protester contre les outrages dont les troupes des Puissances ennemies se sont rendues coupables à l'égard des Femmes des pays alliés'.[39] The claim that it was signed by 5 million American women must surely be inaccurate. At the time, the population of the United States was about 100 million. That would mean that one in every ten female Americans signed the petition, which seems unlikely. The text read as follows:

RESOLUTION

WHEREAS there is overwhelming evidence that in the present war the armies of the Central European Powers and of their Allies have been permitted and encouraged to commit and, officers and men en masse, have actually committed every form of sexual offence against the women of every country they have entered.

WHEREAS such offences are crimes as well under the laws of war as under the laws of peace, as well under the common law of nations as under the municipal law of every nation which is even superficially civilized; and under the Hague Conventions.

WHEREAS such crimes, besides their monstrous insult to the dignity of womenhood strike at the heart of society, the home. And the deliverate, wholesale, authorized commission of them by the Germans and their Allies confronts Society, accordingly, with the alternatives EITHER, acquiescing in its own destruction to allow the violation, the mutilation, the enslavement and compulsory prostitution of womena nd girls to become established by foerce of precedent as a permitted custom under the laws of war; Or unmistakbly to destroy that precedent;

AND INASMUCH AS more than a million French women have unitedly appealed to the women of all countries to join them in denouncing this infamous and sinister attack on the common life of humanity through its womankind;

---

39   Letter from Secretariat of Peace Conference to US delegation, 19 April 1919, USNA F.W. 185.118/62.

THEREFORE we, women of the United States, hereby

1. Associate ourselves with the women of France in their Protest and Appeal, which is annexed hereto.
2. Demand that any officers, solders or civilian of the Central Powers of their Allies who have been Guilty of any sexual offence against a woman or girl of France or her allies, in the course of the present war, be punished if possible, especially in flagrant and notable cases, and that measures be taken by the nations in Conference, that in any further war, the Commission of these dangerous and degenerate villianies be absolutely forbidden and denounced, and adequate pealties with proper methods of enforcing them be carefully provided and promulgated.
3. Declare our own deliberate feeling, judment and position to be that all women so injured by a despicable enemy ought to be treated and regarded, not as shamed, but as wounded in war. And we implore our Allies to confer that status on them, both officially and in the public mind.

FURTHERMORE, we directuly our Committee in charge to deliver these RESOLUTIONS duly authenticated, to each of the Government, (including our own Government) allied against any or all of the said Central Powers and their Allies in the present war, and to each of the Societies associated in the Appeal of the French Women, and to arrange so far as possible, for their publication in every allied country.[40]

To the same effect, a French organization, the Alliance Universitaire Française, presented a petition to the Peace Conference. According to the Alliance, the petition had been signed by 15,000 people, a number that seems rather more plausible than the figure of 5 million claimed for the American petition. The text of the petition was translated into English and circulated to delegates at the Peace Conference on 22 April 1919:

Petition to members of the Peace Conference

In contravention of the most elemental laws of humanity thousands of women, young girls, and even children in the north of France and in Belgium, of all social conditions, have been systematically dragged from their families, contaminated by order, submitted to worse promiscuousness, treated like slaves.

---

40   *Ibid.* The numerous typographical and grammatical errors have not been identified using [sic].

> Our hearts broken and bleeding, we the women of France ask of the Allied Nations, come before the Peace Conference to ask for justice in the name of our martyred sisters.
>
> To prevent forever the recurrence of such atrocities, we ask that those who have ordered them and those who have carried them out be condemned like criminals under common law.
>
> We count on your firmness to ensure that Germany and her Allies, who have armed the hands of these executioners be placed under the ban of humanity.[41]

Accounts by historians about the women's movement at the time do not mention this campaign to promote prosecutions of rapes committed by German combatants. Indeed, the author has found no references whatsoever to the documents on sexual and gender-based violence that were circulated at the Paris Peace Conference in either the writings of historians or those of legal academics interested in the subject of post-war prosecutions. The central issue in the feminist movement at this time was obtaining the right to vote, although that does not mean that it was indifferent to a broad range of matters falling generally under the rubric of women's equality. Women's organisations had been sharply divided in their attitude towards the war, with a large number campaigning for peace while many of their sisters, like Louisa Lumsden, fell into step with wartime patriotism and nationalism.[42] It may be that those campaigning for prosecution of Germans for war crimes, including rape and other sexual and gender-based violence, were linked to the more militarist part of the movement. Women who had been associated with pacifism would also, following the war, have tended to align themselves with those who were critical of the Treaty of Versailles and other measures directed at Germany and Austria. This explains why the International Congress of Women, meeting in Zurich in May 1919, did not adopt any resolutions about the post-war prosecutions. Indeed, there is no record of the issue even being discussed.[43]

---

41   Letter from Secretariat of Peace Conference to US delegation, 22 April 1919, USNA F.W. 185.118/62; Letter from Secretariat of Peace Conference to British delegation, 22 April 1919, TNA FO 608/247/12.

42   Alison S. Fell and Ingrid Sharp, 'Introduction: The Women's Movement and the First World War' in Alison S. Fell and Ingrid Sharp (eds.), *The Women's Movement in Wartime, International Perspectives, 1914–19* (Basingstoke and New York, Palgrave 2007), pp. 1–17.

43   Anne Wiltsher, *Most Dangerous Women* (London, Boston and Henley, Pandora 1985), pp. 200–211; Gertrude Bussey and Margaret Tims, *Pioneers for Peace, Women's International League for Peace and Freedom* (London, George Allen & Unwin 1965), pp. 24–33; Erika Kuhlman, 'The "Women's International League for Peace and Freedom" and Reconciliation after the Great War' in Alison S. Fell and Ingrid Sharp (eds.), *The Women's Movement*

The International Congress of Women was the successor of the 1915 Congress in The Hague where violence against women had been protested, but essentially from a pacifist perspective.

4 Plans for Prosecution of Sexual and Gender-Based Violence

The Commission on Responsibilities concluded its work at the end of March 1919. The members of the Commission would by then have received the statement from the Council of Scotch Electors but they would yet not have obtained the petitions from the American and French organizations. There is no reference in the debates of the Commission to the petition from the Scottish women. For that matter, the minutes of the Commission and its sub-commissions do not indicate any discussion whatsoever about the issue of rape and enforced prostitution.

The recommendations of the Commission on Responsibilities were only partly followed by the Council of Four when it prepared the text of the Treaty of Versailles, in April and early May 1919. Woodrow Wilson and Emanuele Orlando would probably have been happy enough to drop the matter of prosecution altogether. But faced with the insistence of Georges Clemenceau and David Lloyd George they agreed to incorporate provisions in the text of the Treaty of Versailles. The clauses themselves, eventually numbered articles 227 to 230 of the Treaty, were crafted by Wilson personally in an effort at consensus and then approved by the three other leaders as well as the Japanese representative.[44]

After the Treaty was signed, on 28 June 1919, the Allies hastily prepared lists of prisoners to be surrendered by Germany in accordance with article 228. Following protracted negotiations, a compromise was reached whereby the trials were to take place before German courts in Leipzig, based upon a limited selection from the original list of wanted men. Only 45 candidates for prosecution were identified. Most of these concerned the actual conduct of hostilities on land and at sea, as well as abuses directed at prisoners of war.[45] A few dealt with atrocities against the civilian population. However, none of the charges referred to sexual and gender-based violence.

---

in Wartime, International Perspectives, 1914–19 (Basingstoke and New York, Palgrave 2007), pp. 227–243.

44   Wilson to Lansing, 9 April 1919, USNA F.W. 185.118/59.
45   Gerd Hankel, *Die Leipziger Prozesse: Deutsche Kriegsverbrechen und ihre strafrechtliche Verfolgung nach dem Ersten Weltkrieg* (Hamburg, Hamburger Edition 2003); James F. Willis, *Prologue to Nuremberg: The Politics and Diplomacy of Punishing War Criminals of the First World War* (Westport, CT, Greenwood Press 1982).

Pursuant to article 227 of the Treaty, the former Kaiser Wilhelm II was arraigned for 'a supreme offence against international morality and the sanctity of treaties'. The unusual wording was proposed by Wilson based on language used in a letter from his Secretary of State, Robert Lansing. Lansing was himself quite vehemently opposed to prosecution of the Kaiser and almost certainly had not intended for his words to be used in defining a crime under international law.[46] Be that as it may, the four leaders agreed on the formulation. Today, the offence defined in article 227 is generally understood as being directed to the illegality of the war, the *jus ad bellum*, rather than to the violations of the laws and customs of war commited in the conduct of hostilities and in occupied territories. But it does not seem that this was the view adopted by the British when they made their initial preparations for the trial of the Kaiser.

In July 1919, R.W. Woods was assigned by the Solicitor General to prepare the case against the Kaiser. He relied very largely on published sources, including the Bryce Committee report and similar materials prepared by other countries. His detailed memorandum, consisting of more than 200 pages, devoted considerable attention to the violations of the laws and customs of war. Woods wrote: 'Of the violation of women, there is unfortunately a surfeit of evidence In all the reports, instances will be found of loathsome debauchery on the part of Officers and men of the German Army. It may be obserbed that it was by no means unknown for the women to be dragged before a Belgian Priest and violated in his presence.'[47] Woods concluded that the Kaiser might be held responsible in a general sense for German atrocities, as he either condoned them or ignored them, but he made no specific reference in his report to liability of the former emperor the sexual and gender-based violence.[48]

The Treaty of Versailles entered into force on 10 January 1920. Immediately, a demand was made by France, Italy and the United Kingdom for his surrender, but the Netherlands refused extradition.[49] The Dutch government reacted to Allied pressure by agreeing to confine the Kaiser to his new residence in Doorn, near Utrecht, and to prevent him from engaging in political activity. By this point, the thirst for justice had decline considerably from its paroxysm in late 1918. The principal concern of the victorious powers was royalist intrigue

---

46   Lansing to Wilson, 8 April 1919, F.W.181/1202/7.
47   The Arraignment of William II of Hohenzollern, Memorandum on the Responsibility of William II of Hohenzollern for Acts Committed in Breach of the Laws of War, TNA TS 26/1, p. 201.
48   *Ibid.*, pp. 211–213.
49   'Note to the Queen of Holland demanding the Delivery of the Kaiser for Trial' in Rohan Butler and J.P.T. Bury, *Documents on British Foreign Policy 1919–1939* (1st series, London, His Majesty's Stationery Office 1958) vol II, pp. 912–913.

in an unstable Germany. After a few more belated requests for extradition, the Allies dropped the matter.[50]

5 By Way of Conclusion

The project of international criminal justice as we know it today really began with the efforts to prosecute combatants and officials of the countries that were defeated during the First World War, principally Germany. The sexual and gender-based violence perpetrated during the conflict did not result in any trials or convictions, at least to the extent that this was mandated by international law. But much the same can be said of the other violations of the laws and customs of war, with the exception of the handful of cases dealt with at Leipzig. Rape and enforced prostitution were addressed by the Commission on Responsibilities as part of its overall examination of violations. The codification adopted by the Commission that includes these two crimes was influential when international justice was revived during the Second World War. For example, René Cassin, the vice-president of the London International Assembly, reproduced the Commission's list of crimes in a report on Nazi war crimes.[51] The list was also considered by the United Nations War Crimes Commission in 1944 as it examined the specific acts to be included in the concept of laws and customs of war.[52]

Of particular interest is the engagement of women's organizations at the time with the issue of prosecution. The debate within the feminist movement may have been influenced by the position taken towards the war itself, with those on the pacifist side of the fence being less enthusiastic not because they were indifferent to violence against women but out of concern that a focus on prosecution might obstruct efforts at reconciliation.

---

50 'Reply to the Dutch Government, as approved by the Conference of Ambassadors and Foreign Ministers on March 24, 1920' in Rohan Butler and J.P.T. Bury, *Documents on British Foreign Policy 1919–1939* (1st series, London, His Majesty's Stationery Office 1958) vol VII, pp. 616–617.

51 René Cassin, 'Note of violations of the laws and customs of war perpetrated by the Germans since September 1939' in London International Assembly, *Reports on Punishment of War Criminals* (1943), pp. 42–55, at p. 50. Also: M. De Baer, 'Scope and Meaning of the concept of war crimes' in London International Assembly, *Reports on Punishment of War Criminals* (1943), pp. 156–162, at p. 159.

52 Draft Convention on the Trial and Punishment of War Criminals, 14 April 1944, art. I, UNWCC II/11; Article I of Draft Convention on the Trial and Punishment of War Criminals, 12 June 1944, UNWCC II/17.

CHAPTER 18

The ICTY's *Šešelj* Trial: Taking Stock of a Disaster

Matthias Schuster

Abstract

The ICTY's trial proceedings against Serb politician and demagogue extraordinaire Vojislav Šešelj, which took more than ten years of proceedings in the Hague, can be described as nothing short of a disaster. This is not because the Trial Chamber decided to acquit the accused (even though its reasoning is shockingly thin) but what happened along the way to the judgment. From the initial appearance, held before Judge Wolfgang Schomburg, the accused had made clear his intention to 'destroy' the Tribunal. While he did not succeed in doing so, the Tribunal's credibility was severely undermined and its authority put in question by the way the proceedings were handled. This paper examines what went wrong (e.g., permitting an accused to lead his own defense even when convicted for brazen contempt of court), whether the trial is symptomatic for the weaknesses of international criminal procedure (e.g. by allowing proceedings to continue for years on end) and what can be done to avoid similar failures in the future (e.g. installing tight oversight mechanisms).

1 Introduction

The International Criminal Tribunal for the former Yugoslavia (ICTY), established in 1993 as the first international criminal court since the Nuremberg and Tokyo trials after World War II, will close its doors at the end of 2017. By then, it will have indicted 161 individuals, the majority of whom was convicted and sentenced for charges such as genocide, war crimes and crimes against humanity, all crimes committed in the wake of the breakup of the former Yugoslavia in the 1990s.[1] While the Tribunal will cease to exist, its work will continue in the framework of the Mechanism for International Criminal Tribunals (MICT),

---

* Matthias Schuster, LLM (Sussex) is a Legal Officer with the United Nations. The views expressed in this article are those of the author alone and do not necessarily reflect the views of the United Nations.

1 See the latest statistic, at <http://www.icty.org/en/content/infographic-icty-facts-figures> accessed 14 June 2017. 19 persons were acquitted. In the remainder of the cases, the accused were either transferred to another jurisdiction or their proceedings were terminated or the indictments were withdrawn for other reasons.

which was set up to take over a number of residual functions of the ICTY and the International Criminal Tribunal for Rwanda (ICTR).[2] This includes conducting a full re-trial of an ICTY case which was remanded by the ICTY Appeals Chamber[3] and hearing two appeals arising from ICTY trial judgments.[4]

One of these appeals was lodged by the Prosecution against the Trial Chamber's acquittal of Vojislav Šešelj, Serbian politician and ultranationalist. The trial against Šešelj before the ICTY can be described as nothing but a disaster. This is not because the majority of the Trial Chamber decided to acquit the Accused – although its reasoning is shockingly thin – but because of what happened in the thirteen years of proceedings leading up to the judgment.

Even before his initial appearance in The Hague, held before Judge Schomburg, the Accused made it clear that he intended to 'destroy' the Tribunal.[5] While he ultimately did not succeed in doing so, the Tribunal's credibility was severely undermined and its authority put in question by the way the proceedings, which at times bordered on the farcical, were handled.

This article examines what went wrong (*e.g.*, permitting an accused to lead his own defence even when convicted for brazen contempt of court) and whether the trial is symptomatic for the weaknesses of international criminal justice (*e.g.*, allowing proceedings to continue for years on end).

2   What Went Wrong?

A friend once compared the workings of international criminal justice to the operation of an airplane. There are a number of built-in redundancies allowing the plane to fly without accident and to arrive safely at its destination. This is ensured by the pilots, the flight attendants, the ground-crew and many other staff who are together responsible for the plane and its cargo. The same system of shared responsibility applies in international trials – it is the joint task of the Judges, the Prosecution, the Defence and the Registry to safeguard that the proceedings are fair, expeditious and respectful of the rights of the accused and the interest of the international community as a whole to see that justice is done in a particular case. At the end of the process, there is either a conviction of the accused if the charges are proven beyond reasonable doubt,

---

2   The ICTR completed its mandate on 31 December 2015.
3   The *Stanišić & Simatović* case.
4   The *Karadžić* and *Šešelj* cases. It can also be expected that one of the parties will appeal the last judgment to be handed down by the ICTY in the *Mladić* case.
5   See *Šešelj Case* (Trial Chamber, Decision on Prosecution's Motion for Order Appointing Counsel to Assist Vojislav Šešelj with his Defence) ICTY-03-67-PT (9 May 2003) para 22.

or an acquittal if not. In the *Šešelj* trial, the proverbial plane crashed, with multiple failures by all sides involved in the handling of the case.

The *Šešelj* case had its origins in the conflicts taking place in the former Yugoslavia in the early 1990s. In its indictment, the Prosecution alleged that Vojislav Šešelj, founder of the banned Serbian National Renewal Party and later leader of the Serb Radical Party, had propagated a policy of a "Greater Serbia", which would unite all Serbs in one country comprised of Serbia, Montenegro, Macedonia and substantial parts of Croatia and Bosnia and Herzegovina. Acting in the framework of a joint criminal enterprise aimed at forcibly and permanently removing a majority of the Croat, Muslim and other non-Serb civilian populations from parts of Croatia, Bosnia and Herzegovina and from the province of Vojvodina in the Serbia, Šešelj was alleged to be responsible for the recruitment and direction of volunteer fighters connected to the Serb Radical Party and the so-called "Serbian Chetnik Movement", for participating in the planning and preparation of the take-over of towns and villages in Croatia and in a number of municipalities in Bosnia and Herzegovina, and the subsequent forcible removal of the majority of the non-Serb population from those areas, which were accompanied by other crimes of high brutality. In addition, Šešelj was accused of having delivered inflammatory hate speeches, in which he denigrated non-Serbs and called for their deportation. The Prosecution charged Šešelj with war crimes (including murder and torture) and crimes against humanity (including persecutions and deportation).[6]

After the confirmation of the initial indictment[7] and the issuing of an arrest warrant in early 2003, Šešelj surrendered to the Tribunal voluntarily. At his initial appearance, Judge Schomburg ensured that Šešelj was informed of his rights and read out the charges in the indictment. Šešelj was defiant and laid the foundations of what would become a large part of his strategy of obstruction throughout the proceedings. He disputed the terms used in the indictment by insisting that he receive documents in the Serb language (as opposed to the Bosnian/Serb/Croat language used by the Tribunal);[8] complained about the attire worn by the Judges and counsel ('This associates me with the inquisition of the Roman Catholic Church');[9] and made clear from the outset that he would refuse any assignment of counsel, insisting on his right to defend himself.[10] Šešelj also declined to enter a plea or to seek provisional release, given

---

6 *Šešelj Case* (Indictment) ICTY-03-67-I (15 January 2003).
7 *Šešelj Case* (Third Amended Indictment) ICTY-03-67-T (7 December 2007).
8 *Šešelj Case* (Transcript) ICTY-03-67-PT (26 February 2003) 44–45.
9 Ibid 54.
10 Ibid 55.

that he had surrendered voluntarily and that there was 'no government that could provide guarantees for [him]'.[11]

In the months following the initial appearance, the Prosecution became concerned with Šešelj's conduct and requested that the Trial Chamber assign counsel to him, based among other factors on Šešelj's public statements to cause harm to the Tribunal and his apparent intent to use the proceedings as political forum, which would result in a disorderly trial. The Trial Chamber, with Judge Schomburg presiding, carefully considered an accused's right to self-represent in the proceedings before the court – as enshrined in the Tribunal's Statute – but noted that this right was not absolute and that it could be restricted, also to the accused's benefit, when the 'interests of justice' so demanded. The Chamber outlined specific examples of behaviour by Šešelj that could be qualified as obstructive – including filing handwritten documents, repeatedly exceeding the appropriate word limits, and pretending not to understand the B/C/S language. However, it determined that a balance could be struck by assigning standby counsel, who would receive all documents, would be present in court and could be asked by Šešelj for assistance. At the same time, standby counsel would be prepared to take over from Šešelj if the Accused behaved in an obstructionist fashion or in other narrowly prescribed circumstances.[12]

A few months later, the Trial Chamber was recomposed with different judges.[13] Notably, one of the features of the *Šešelj* trial was the astounding number of replacements of the Judges hearing the case. Including the Judge confirming the indictment, 14 Judges of the Tribunal participated in the pre-trial or trial proceedings.[14] The same revolving-door policy seemingly applied at the Prosecution, with a series of lead attorneys taking charge of the case only to leave at a later stage. It can be argued that this lack of continuity had a negative impact on the trial, given the fact that each new jurist, be it on the bench or for the

---

11   Ibid 49.

12   *Šešelj Case* (Trial Chamber, Decision on Prosecution's Motion for Order Appointing Counsel to Assist Vojislav Šešelj with his Defence) ICTY-03-67-PT (9 May 2003). In many ways, the decision was a first expression of Judge Schomburg's position on the issue of self-representation, namely, that an accused's right to defend himself was not absolute and that it could be limited by assigning counsel when the circumstances so demanded, not only in the interests of an orderly trial but also to further an accused's rights to have the best defence possible.

13   Judge Schomburg had been assigned to the Appeals Chamber where he would remain for the next six years.

14   See the (incomplete) list in *Šešelj Case* (Trial Chamber, Judgement, vol 1) ICTY-03-67-T (31 March 2016) (*"Šešelj Judgment"*) Annex II, paras 17–28. This was certainly unusual, even in the context of the Tribunal with its long-running cases.

Prosecution, had to familiarize him- or herself with the details of what was an exceedingly complex case, both substantively and procedurally.

Adding to the complexity was the fact that the Prosecution had to amend the indictment several times (including after the trial had commenced), repeatedly clarifying ambiguities and at one point – upon the invitation of the Chamber – significantly reducing the counts in the indictment.[15]

Meanwhile, during the pre-trial proceedings, Šešelj filed a flurry of motions before the Chamber, the Appeals Chamber, the President and the Registrar. These filings were often trivial and at times offensive, berating officials of the Tribunal[16] and containing outlandish requests.[17] They also exceeded the word limits set by the Tribunal's practice directions and straining the resources of the Translation Unit. At some point, and after having given several warnings to the Accused, the Trial Chamber ordered that filings from him that failed to comply with the rules were to be returned.[18] Nevertheless, until the end of the trial Šešelj continued to test the boundaries of what was permissible.[19] Šešelj's actions also led to the adoption of a new regulation allowing the Tribunal to reject submissions that contain 'obscene or otherwise offensive language'.[20] The filing party would be informed of the rejection and the reasons for it and given a chance to refile. In Šešelj's case, the Trial Chamber directed the Registrar on numerous occasions to return submissions to the Accused on the basis of their offensive substance matter.[21] These filings are not on the record of the Tribunal but choice examples of their rather extreme content were provided by the Trial Chamber in later decisions.[22]

From the earliest stages of the pre-trial proceedings, Šešelj also attempted to seek the disqualification of various Judges of the Tribunal in an aggressive

---

15 *Šešelj Judgment* (n 14) Annex II, paras 11–15; see Rules of Procedure and Evidence of the International Criminal Tribunal for the former Yugoslavia ("ICTY RPE") Rule 73 *bis* (D).
16 See e.g. *Šešelj Case* (Decision on Request to Exclude the Prosecutor of the International Tribunal Carla Del Ponte) ICTY-03-67-PT (2 December 2004).
17 See e.g. *Šešelj Case* (Decision on Motion to Change Seat of the Tribunal) ICTY-03-67-PT (3 May 2005).
18 *Šešelj Case* (Decision on Filing of Motions) ICTY-03-67-PT (19 June 2006).
19 The Trial Chamber decision was later effectively rescinded when the new Presiding Judge Antonetti stated that he would 'never' dismiss a filing because of its size (*Šešelj Case* [Transcript] ICTY-03-67-PT [4 July 2007] 1346–47). This undoubtedly added a huge burden to the Tribunal's translation services, at great cost.
20 Practice Direction on the Procedure for the Review of Written Submissions Which Contain Obscene or Otherwise Offensive Language, ICTY-IT/240 (14 November 2005, last amended on 7 April 2017).
21 See e.g. *Šešelj Case* (Decision Re Submission No 153) ICTY-03-67-PT (19 June 2006).
22 See e.g. *Šešelj Case* (Decision on Assignment of Counsel) ICTY-03-67-PT (21 August 2006) ("*Šešelj Assignment of Counsel Decision*") paras 45–52.

manner. Under the Rules, a party can seek such disqualification 'in any case in which the Judge has a personal interest or concerning which the Judge has or has had any association which might affect his or her impartiality'.[23] Until shortly before the end of the trial, all of Šešelj's requests were rejected. Many of them were regarded as frivolous given that they were either manifestly baseless and/or highly offensive. For instance, Šešelj's first request seeking the disqualification of the Judges of the Trial Chamber was based on Judge Schomburg's nationality ('the smell of crematoriums and gas chambers comes into the Hague courtroom with him') and Judge Mumba's and Judge Agius' religion ('ardent and zealous Catholics').[24] The ICTY Bureau dismissed the motion, noting that the 'nationalities and religions of Judges of this Tribunal are, and must be, irrelevant to their ability to hear the cases before them impartially'.[25] It also reminded Šešelj – obviously to no avail – that '[i]nsults are not arguments and insults based on group identities, such as nationality, religion, and ethnicity, are particularly offensive'.[26] Subsequent requests for disqualification of other Judges – including the President of the Tribunal and the whole Appeals Chamber hearing interlocutory appeals – were rejected because Šešelj persistently refused to adhere to the special procedure applying to such requests,[27] or had failed to show any bias, actual or perceived, on the part of the Judges he sought to have removed.[28] However, as we will see later, Šešelj's final attempt in this regard did succeed, at a crucial moment in the proceedings and with great damage to both the credibility of the trial and the ICTY as a whole.

Another key problematic issue existed in the question of Šešelj's insistence on representing himself in all proceedings and his refusal to accept any counsel assigned by the court. In Šešelj's case, the issue of proper representation – or lack thereof – was perceived even by the initial Judges hearing the case as a central problem that needed to be resolved both in Šešelj's interest and in the broader context of holding trial proceedings that were not held hostage by the Accused. Much has been written about this particular feature of the *Šešelj* case and the issue of self-representation at the ICTY in general.[29] Virtually all

23 ICTY RPE (n 15) Rule 15 (A).
24 *Šešelj Case* (Submission No 13) ICTY-03-67-PT (21 May 2003).
25 *Šešelj Case* (Decision on Motion for Disqualification) ICTY-03-67-PT (10 June 2003) para 3.
26 ibid para 5.
27 See e.g. *Šešelj Case* (Decision on Request for Disqualification of the President of the International Tribunal) ICTY-03-67-PT (11 January 2005).
28 See e.g. *Šešelj Case* (Decision on Motion for Disqualification) ICTY-03-67-PT (16 February 2007).
29 See e.g. Gideon Boas, 'Self-Representation before the ICTY – A Case for Reform' (2011) 9 JICJ 53; see also Gideon Boas, *The Milošević Trial – Lessons for the Conduct of Complex International Criminal Proceedings* (Cambridge University Press 2007).

observers are critical of how the Tribunal ultimately addressed the problem of balancing an accused's right to represent himself with the interest of the court to hold an orderly trial.[30] However, it is worth recounting here how Šešelj managed to put pressure on the court – some would refer to blackmail[31] – in order to have his way and assessing what were the practical consequences of the court's caving in to the pressure, leading to a situation that bordered on the absurd.

Despite the original Trial Chamber's decision to assign standby counsel, which he did not appeal, Šešelj refused to cooperate with the lawyer appointed by the Registry for this purpose and actively yet unsuccessfully sought to have him removed.[32] When the opening of the trial approached, the Prosecution requested the Trial Chamber to assign full-time counsel to Šešelj and order that only counsel had the right to file written submissions. The Trial Chamber, after hearing Šešelj and the Registry, issued a detailed decision, describing Šešelj's unacceptable conduct in connection with the proceedings – including his publications of books with titles such as 'In the Jaws of the Whore Del Ponte'[33] – and how he had behaved obstructively, for instance by filing offensive submissions, deliberately disrespecting procedural rules, disrupting the proceedings and intimidating witnesses.[34] The Chamber also considered Šešelj's ability to defend himself and expressed its 'concern that as a result of his ongoing disruptive conduct and unwillingness to follow the ground rules, the Accused [was] undermining his intention to present his defence'.[35] The Chamber concluded that in light of these findings and taking into account the Appeals Chamber's relevant case-law, in particular its seminal decision in *Milošević*, there was justification in assigning counsel to Šešelj.[36] Indeed, in *Milošević*, the Appeals Chamber had clearly stated that the right to self-representation was not absolute and could be restricted 'on the grounds that

---

30 See e.g. Göran Sluiter, 'Compromising the Authority of International Criminal Justice – How Vojislav Šešelj Runs His Trial' (2007) 5 JICJ 529; Alexander Zahar, 'Legal Aid, Self-Representation, and the Crisis at the Hague Tribunal' (2008) 19 CLF 241; Gideon Boas, 'Self-Representation before the ICTY – A Case for Reform' (2011) 9 JICJ 53.
31 See Sluiter (n 30) 534; Zahar (n 30) 244.
32 *Šešelj Case* (Decision on the Accused's Motion to Re-Examine the Decision to Assign Standby Counsel) ICTY-03-67-PT (1 March 2005).
33 *Šešelj Assignment of Counsel Decision* (n 22) paras 27–34, referring to the then Prosecutor of the Tribunal.
34 Šešelj Assignment of Counsel Decision (n 22) paras 27–65.
35 Šešelj Assignment of Counsel Decision (n 22) para 66.
36 Šešelj Assignment of Counsel Decision (n 22) paras 72–81.

a defendant's self-representation is substantially and persistently obstructing the proper and expeditious conduct of his trial'.[37]

On appeal, the Appeals Chamber confirmed that the right to self-representation was not absolute and could be limited. In that respect, '[a]ll that the Trial Chamber was required to do was to find that appropriate circumstances, rising to the level of substantial and persistent obstruction to the proper and expeditious conduct of the trial exist'.[38] Nevertheless, the Appeals Chamber reversed the Trial Chamber's decision because it had failed to give explicit warnings to Šešelj before removing his right to self-representation.[39]

Following the decision, the Trial Chamber proceeded to reassign standby counsel, that is, return to the previous status of the proceedings, a move that was immediately and vociferously opposed by Šešelj, who for this and other reasons decided to commence a hunger strike.[40]

With Šešelj's health rapidly declining, two different tracks of action were set in motion. On the one hand, the Trial Chamber had to contemplate how to address the hunger strike. Given that Šešelj now refused to appear in court, the Trial Chamber warned him explicitly that it considered his behaviour substantially obstructive and, after giving him the right to be heard, imposed counsel on Šešelj.[41] At the same time, the Trial Chamber was 'primarily and deeply concerned about the impact of the Accused's hunger strike on his health and welfare'.[42] It ordered the Netherlands – as the host state responsible for maintaining the regime in the Detention Unit – to provide medical services 'with the aim of protecting the health and welfare of the Accused and avoiding loss of life, to the extent that such services are not contrary to compelling internationally accepted standards of medical ethics or binding rules

---

37   *Milošević Case* (Decision on Interlocutory Appeal of the Trial Chamber's Decision on the Assignment of Counsel) ICTY-02-54-AR73.7 (1 November 2004) para 13.

38   *Šešelj Case* (Decision on Appeal Against the Trial Chamber's Decision on Assignment of Counsel) ICTY-03-67-AR73.3 (20 October 2006) para 21.

39   Ibid para 52. Ironically, Šešelj's appeal was filed by assigned counsel, an English lawyer who Šešelj had derided as 'this man with a bird's nest on his head' (referring to the wig traditionally worn by English counsel), see *Šešelj Case* (Transcript) ICTY-03-67 (12 September 2006) 570. Šešelj himself had refused to appeal himself and indeed petitioned the Appeals Chamber to reject the appeal submitted by assigned counsel.

40   *Šešelj Case* (Transcript) ICTY-03-67 (22 November 2006) 780–782.

41   See *Šešelj Case* (Reasons for Decision [No 2] on Assignment of Counsel) ICTY-03-67-T (27 November 2006).

42   *Šešelj Case* (Urgent Order to the Dutch Authorities Regarding Health and Welfare of the Accused) ICTY-03-67-T (6 December 2006) ("*Šešelj Order*") para 2.

of international law'.[43] The Dutch authorities were thus left with considerable discretion and it is unclear which course, including the possibility of 'force-feeding', they would have ultimately taken.

In the end, no action was necessary because the Appeals Chamber came to Šešelj's rescue. In a decision on an 'appeal' filed by Šešelj against the Trial Chamber's imposition of counsel, the Appeals Chamber stretched the law and the facts of the case beyond recognition.

Ruling only a day after receiving Šešelj's submission, the Chamber not only accepted his filing even though it failed to meet the formal requirements but it also did so expressly because of the 'extraordinary circumstances' of the situation, *i.e.* Šešelj's hunger strike.[44] While the Appeals Chamber noted that the acceptance of the appeal 'should in no way be construed as evidence of the Appeals Chamber rewarding Šešelj's behaviour',[45] it is difficult to perceive its decision in a different light given the otherwise strict standards applicable to the filing of appeals.[46]

Reasoning equally unpersuasively on the merits, the Appeals Chamber also granted Šešelj's appeal in substance and reversed the Trial Chamber's decision. As the Appeals Chamber recognized itself, there was no error in the Trial Chamber's decision to assign counsel that would give the Appeals Chamber grounds to overturn it.[47] Instead, the Appeals Chamber leaped to an assessment of the Trial Chamber's preceding decision to re-assign standby counsel – a decision that had not been certified for appeal by the Trial Chamber and therefore was not properly before the Appeals Chamber. Nevertheless, the Appeals Chamber stated that this prior decision was 'inextricably linked' to the decision under appeal because it was Šešelj's rejection of the assignment of standby counsel

---

43   *Šešelj Order* (n 42) para 15. Interestingly, even though this is not reflected in the disposition, the Trial Chamber seemed to have based its order not only on the welfare of the Accused but also on 'a prevailing interest in continuing with the trial of the Accused in order to serve the ends of justice', considering that the trial 'should not be undermined by the Accused's manipulative behaviour' (ibid para 11). It is debatable whether such reasoning would comply with international human rights standards.

44   *Šešelj Case* (Decision on Appeal Against the Trial Chamber's Decision [No 2] on Assignment of Counsel) ICTY-03-67-AR73.4 (8 December 2006) (*"Šešelj Appeal Decision"*) para 14.

45   Ibid para 15.

46   See Practice Direction on Procedure for the Filing of Written Submissions in Appeal Proceedings Before the International Tribunal, ICTY-IT/155 (1 October 1999, last amended on 4 April 2012).

47   Šešelj Appeal Decision para 25.

and his refusal to appear in court that consequently resulted in the imposition of counsel by the Trial Chamber.[48]

In what could be perceived as a somewhat disingenuous feat of retroactively reinterpreting its own previous decision, the Appeals Chamber declared that its first decision had supposedly given Šešelj a 'clean slate'[49] in the sense that the Appeals Chamber's prior reversal of the imposition of counsel for lack of explicit warnings had also implied that the Trial Chamber could not go back to the status quo ante, i.e. with Šešelj having been assigned a standby counsel.[50] Of course, no such reasoning can be found in the first appeal decision; and indeed, the issue of standby counsel had not been raised before the Appeals Chamber at that stage. Almost cynically, the Appeals Chamber noted that:

> By so doing [assigning standby counsel], the Trial Chamber failed to give Šešelj a real opportunity to show the Trial Chamber that despite his conduct pre-trial, and the conduct leading up to the imposition of assigned counsel, he now understood that in order to be permitted to conduct his defence, he would have to comply with the Rules of Procedure and Evidence of the Tribunal and that he was willing to do so.[51]

In other words, because the Trial Chamber had failed to implement non-explicit directions by the Appeals Chamber, Šešelj had been entitled to his disruptive behaviour in reaction to a 'provocative move' by the Trial Chamber,[52] which therefore did not permit the Trial Chamber to impose counsel.

In addition to the reversal, the Appeals Chamber also nullified the opening of the proceedings, which had taken place earlier, and ordered a restart of the trial at such a time when Šešelj would be fully able to participate in the proceedings as a self-represented accused.[53] With this victory at hand, Šešelj immediately ended his hunger strike – his pressure on the Tribunal had worked.

The Appeals Chamber's decision will remain a major blight on the legacy of the Tribunal. Undoubtedly, the Judges were in a difficult position, given the human and political ramifications of Šešelj's potential death as a result of his hunger strike. They would have also had on their mind the sudden demise of Slobodan Milošević in the Tribunal's Detention Unit earlier that year, which

---

48   Ibid 20.
49   Ibid para 24.
50   Ibid paras 26–27.
51   Ibid para 27.
52   Ibid para 23.
53   Ibid para 29.

had exposed the Tribunal to criticism even though an inquiry had established that Milošević had died of natural causes.[54] Nevertheless, one may ask whether other options existed permitting the Appeals Chamber to resolve the issue in ways that would have not exposed the Tribunal to criticism that it took a decision 'under psychological restraint not reasonably based on legal standards'.[55]

Following the Appeals Chamber's decision, the proceedings did not move forward for some time. A few months later, the case was assigned to yet another Chamber with Judge Antonetti appointed as the new Pre-Trial Judge.[56] Matters were thus in flux once again, in particular since Judge Antonetti took a different approach. While the previous Trial Chamber had attempted to rein in the Accused's most extreme behaviour, Judge Antonetti on the contrary appeared to indulge him as much as possible. In the first status conference held before him, he made it very clear that he completely disagreed with the previous Trial Chamber's approach vis-à-vis the issue of self-representation and stated that 'as far as [he was] concerned, we will never be conceiving the idea of imposing *amicus curiae* or counsel on Mr. Šešelj'.[57] He also indicated that he would look favourably at any of Šešelj's requests and that he was fully committed to 're-establishing [the] dialogue between the parties'.[58] Even the Accused was caught by surprise: 'Mr. Antonetti, I am sincerely astonished that for the first time in the past four years I hear from the seat of the Presiding Judge a reasonable, mature, legal thinking. I have never heard such thinking from that position before.'[59]

In one of his first decisions, Judge Antonetti ordered that Šešelj was to receive financial aid, despite the fact that he was self-represented and therefore did not fall under the Tribunal's legal aid scheme.[60] Even so, Šešelj did not accept the conditions under which this aid was to be granted, for instance by demonstrating that he was indigent. After a protracted back and forth, the Trial Chamber ultimately ordered the Registry to pay for 50 % of the funds

---

54 See Report to the President – Death of Slobodan Milošević, May 2006 (available at <http://www.icty.org/x/cases/slobodan_milosevic/custom2/en/parkerreport.pdf> accessed 14 June 2017).
55 Sluiter (n 30) 535.
56 *Šešelj Case* (Order Reassigning a Case to a Trial Chamber) ICTY-03-67-PT (20 February 2007); *Šešelj Case* (Order Designating a Pre-Trial Judge) ICTY-03-67-PT (22 February 2007). The other two Judges were only designated at a later point (see *Šešelj Case* [Order Assigning Judges to a Case Before a Trial Chamber] ICTY-03-67-PT [26 October 2007]).
57 *Šešelj Case* (Transcript) ICTY-03-67-PT (13 March 2007) 928.
58 Ibid 931.
59 Ibid 935.
60 *Šešelj Case* (Decision on the Financing [of] the Defence) ICTY-03-67-T (30 July 2007).

normally allocated to a totally indigent accused, 'to the defence team for the Accused consisting of three privileged associates, a case manager and an investigator'.[61] This decision was upheld by the Appeals Chamber, albeit by a narrow majority.[62] One of the dissenting Judges noted that unlike an accused represented by counsel, Šešelj was now receiving financing in the absence of established indigence. 'This reverses the burden of proof, clearly sets a very dangerous precedent and will not provide any incentive or motivation for the Tribunal's accused to prove their indigence, ultimately resulting in a waste and mismanagement of public funds'.[63] Indeed, the issue of financing showed best the absurdities of the system of self-representation at the Tribunal: An accused who nominally claims his right to self-representation still avails himself of 'legal associates' who do substantial part of the work and are paid by the Tribunal – how this can be squared with the 'binary opposition'[64] of the right to counsel and the right to self-representation postulated by the Appeals Chamber remains entirely unclear.[65]

In *Šešelj*, the Prosecution made one final request to have counsel imposed on the Accused, alleging that Šešelj had intimidated witnesses – the trial had finally started in November 2007 – and published confidential material in violation of court orders. The Trial Chamber nevertheless dismissed the request, despite the fact that Šešelj had been convicted for contempt of court by another Trial Chamber in separate proceedings for revealing confidential witness

---

61 *Šešelj Case* (Redacted Version of Decision on Financing of Defence, Filed on 29 October 2010) ICTY-03-67-T (2 November 2010), Disposition.

62 *Šešelj Case* (Public Redacted Version of the "Decision on the Registry Submissions Pursuant to Rule 33(B) Regarding the Trial Chamber's Decision on Financing of Defence") ICTY-03-67-R33B (Rendered on 8 April 2011).

63 Ibid, Dissenting Opinion of Judge Pocar, para 11.

64 See *Krajišnik Case* (Decision on Krajišnik Request and on Prosecution Motion) ICTY-00-39-A (11 September 2007) para 40 ('An accused who chooses to self-represent is not entitled to legal assistance. Hence he is not entitled to the subsidiary right [...] to have legal assistance paid for the Tribunal if he is indigent.'). The Appeals Chamber noted however that 'it would be appropriate for the Tribunal to provide some funding for [legal] associates' but that 'such funding should not be comparable to that paid to counsel for represented accused (particularly since work such as the drafting of written filings should be considered the responsibility of the self-representing accused)' (ibid para 42). The Registry subsequently enacted specific guidelines determining the remuneration of persons assisting self-represented accused; see also *Karadžić Case* (Decision on Interlocutory Appeal of the Trial Chamber's Decision on Adequate Facilities) ICTY-95-5/18-AR73.2 (7 May 2009).

65 For an in-depth analysis of the issue, see Zahar (n 30).

information.[66] Indeed, Šešelj would be convicted two more times for contempt of court[67] and sentenced to substantial prison terms (which he served while in pre-trial detention for the main trial).[68] Judge Antonetti's reasoning in his separate opinion appended to the Trial Chamber decision made clear that the Trial Chamber's interest was primarily to let the proceedings continue without upsetting the relationship it had built with Šešelj.[69] The Accused was thus given carte blanche – whatever he might have done, the Trial Chamber would not impose counsel on him. One may question whether this was in compliance with the Appeals Chamber's original decision on the right of self-representation in *Milošević*, which had clearly spelled out that this right was not absolute and subject to restrictions.

The Trial Chamber did halt the proceedings for almost a year, pending the first contempt case against the Accused and other allegations of witness intimidation by Šešelj and his associates.[70] After the trial had commenced again and the Chamber had heard the last witnesses, Šešelj filed a motion for acquittal pursuant to Rule 98 *bis* of the ICTY's Rules of Procedure and Evidence, arguing that the Prosecution evidence that had been adduced to this point was not sufficiently strong to support a conviction. He also requested compensation in the amount of 10 million Euros ('I'm a very modest person') and threatened to sue

---

66   *Šešelj Case* (Public Version of the "Consolidated Decision on Assignment of Counsel, Adjournment and Prosecution Motion for Additional Time with Separate Opinion of Presiding Judge Antonetti in Annex") ICTY-00-67-T (24 November 2009).

67   These trials had their own farcical moments, for instance when Šešelj, who had complained about the prison food, offered to the presiding Judge to remove confidential material from his website if the Judge in turn would taste the food that Šešelj had surreptitiously brought into the courtroom; see *Šešelj Case* (Transcript) ICTY-03-67-R77.4 (11 November 2011) 39 ('Now, Mr. Hall, here's the deal: Can you please take this, just taste it a bit, and in return I will remove three of my books and five documents listed here from my web site. I think it will make things simple and easy, but please be so kind and receive it from me.' The Judge declined.).

68   See *Šešelj Case* (Judgement) ICTY-03-67-R77.3-A (28 November 2012) para 24. Unfortunately, the Appeals Chamber in this contempt case did not elaborate how an accused could serve his sentence for contempt while at the same time spending time in pre-trial detention in the main case.

69   See *Šešelj Case* (Consolidated Decision [n 66] Separate Opinion of Judge Antonetti) 35–36.

70   *Šešelj Case* (Decision on Prosecution Motion for Adjournment with Dissenting Opinion of Judge Antonetti and Annex) ICTY-00-67-T (11 February 2009). In his Dissenting Opinion, Judge Antonetti expressed his disagreement, stating that the 'main trial must be given priority over secondary contingencies'; ibid (Dissenting Opinion of Presiding Judge Jean-Claude Antonetti) 6.

the Judges and prosecutors.[71] The Trial Chamber by majority – Judge Antonetti dissenting in part – dismissed the motion.[72] When the Trial Chamber did not accept a number of conditions set out by Šešelj, he declined to present a defence case, and the Trial Chamber scheduled closing briefs and arguments,[73] following which it withdrew for its deliberations on the judgment. At this point Šešelj had been in pre-trial detention for more than nine years.

Then, the trial derailed again. Upon an application of the Accused, Judge Harhoff, one of the other two Judges on the *Šešelj* bench, was disqualified by a panel of the Tribunal from sitting on the case.[74] Much has been written about the circumstances that led to Judge Harhoff's disqualification and its aftermath.[75] Suffice it to say that Judge Harhoff's conduct – he had written a 'frank' letter to 56 of his closest friends, in which he complained about the development of the Tribunal's case-law, which allegedly made it impossible to convict certain high-ranking leaders – was ill-considered and inappropriate. Whether it actually rose to a level that warranted his disqualification is debatable; indeed, the Appeals Chamber in a different case where this issue arose, held the contrary.[76] In any event, the Tribunal was in a conundrum – Šešelj's trial had been heard by three Judges only; for reasons not explained and unlike in other long-running cases, the President had not assigned a reserve Judge who could have stepped in once one of these three could not continue to sit on the case.[77]

---

71 *Šešelj Case* (Transcript) ICTY-00-67-T (9 March 2011) 16820. Šešelj stated that the figure of 10 million Euros (as opposed to 100 million Euros) was a 'final expression of goodwill'. He also told the court that 'the beautiful lady guard [had] made [his] day in the courtroom so much nicer' and that he 'prefer[red] her any day to male guards, who [were] not nearly as pretty'. (ibid).

72 *Šešelj Case* (Transcript) ICTY-00-67-T (4 and 5 May 2011) 16826–16991.

73 *Šešelj Case* (Scheduling Order [Final Briefs, Prosecution and Defence Closing Arguments]) ICTY-03-67-T (31 October 2011).

74 *Šešelj Case* (Decision on Defence Motion for Disqualification of Judge Frederik Harhoff and Report to Vice-President) ICTY-03-67-T (28 August 2013) (Judge Liu dissenting); *Šešelj Case* (Decision on Prosecution Motion for Reconsideration of Decision on Disqualification, Requests for Clarification, and Motion on Behalf of Stanišić and Župljanin) ICTY-03-67-T (7 October 2013) (Judge Liu dissenting).

75 See e.g. Matthias Schuster, 'Das ICTY in der Krise? – Der Fall Harhoff im Kontext' (2015) ZIS 248 (Part 1), 283 (Part 2), 323 (Part 3).

76 *Stanišić & Župljanin Case* (Judgement) ICTY-08-91-A (30 June 2016) paras 42–58.

77 See Rule 15 *bis* (G) ICTY RPE (n 15) ('If, in a trial where a reserve Judge has been assigned in accordance with Rule 15 *ter*, a Judge is unable to continue sitting and a substitute Judge is not assigned pursuant to paragraphs (C) or (D), the trial shall continue with the reserve Judge replacing the Judge who is unable to continue sitting.'); see also Rule 15 *ter* ICTY RPE (n 15).

The President ultimately assigned another Judge to the case, even though that Judge had not heard a single piece of witness testimony and required a long period of time to familiarize himself with the case record. When Šešelj argued that his trial had now become unfair and requested his immediate release, the Trial Chamber decided that there was no obstacle to the continuation of proceedings:

> Considering the *sui generis* nature of the present situation caused by the replacement of a Judge of the Chamber two months before the rendering of the Judgement, the Chamber deems that in the interest of justice, and especially of a fair trial, it [is] necessary to resume proceedings from the close of the hearings.[78]

Šešelj appealed the decision. The Appeals Chamber – despite the urgent nature of the matter – took more than five months to render its decision, dismissing the appeal. It concluded that the Tribunal's Rules of Procedure and Evidence permitted the replacement of a Judge even at a late stage of the trial proceedings.[79] With respect to Šešelj's argument that this would result in undue delay – Judge Niang, the replacement Judge, had indicated that he would need six months to familiarize himself with the case – the Appeals Chamber held that the time required could not be considered 'indicative of undue delay' given that the Rules explicitly foresee the need for such familiarization.[80] It also called Šešelj's argument that Judge Niang would in fact require more time 'speculative'.[81] Merely a week after the Appeals Chamber had rendered its decision, the Trial Chamber issued an order in which it stated that Judge Niang needed additional time,[82] which in the end, would turn out to be another year.[83]

---

78 *Šešelj Case* (Decision on Continuation of Proceedings) ICTY-03-67-T (13 December 2013) para 61.

79 *Šešelj Case* (Decision on Appeal Against Decision on Continuation of the Proceedings) ICTY-03-67-AR15bis (6 June 2014) para 41.

80 *Šešelj Case* (Decision on Appeal Against Decision on Continuation of the Proceedings) ICTY-03-67-AR15bis (6 June 2014) para 67. But see ibid Dissenting Opinion of Judge Afande, arguing that the Rules did not provide for the continuation of the case at the deliberation stage with a replacement Judge once a Judge had been disqualified from the proceedings.

81 Ibid.

82 *Šešelj Case* (Order Inviting the Parties to Make Submissions on Possible Provisional Release of the Accused *Proprio Motu*) ICTY-03-67-T (13 June 2014).

83 *Šešelj Judgment* (n 14) Annex II, para 31.

While Judge Niang was familiarizing himself with the case, the last act of what now looked like a tragicomedy unfolded. The Trial Chamber, concerned about the delays, offered Šešelj the possibility of provisional release, as long as he accepted certain restrictions, such as remaining under home confinement in Serbia and not contacting victims or witnesses. When Šešelj refused to accept these terms – which were in line with usual practice – the Trial Chamber terminated the procedure.[84] However, a few months later, and based on apparent but unexplained concerns for the Accused's health,[85] the Trial Chamber by majority suddenly decided *proprio motu* to release Šešelj anyway, ostensibly to 'avoid a worst-case scenario', and without any guarantees but 'satisfied' that the Accused would return to the Tribunal when ordered to do so and that he would comply with the condition of not influencing victims and witnesses.[86] The absurdity of this proposition, when the Accused had just refused to give any assurances in this regard, was pointed out by Judge Niang in his dissent.[87] Even more inexplicably, the Prosecution did not appeal the decision,[88] and consequently, Šešelj was released to Serbia. Upon arrival, Šešelj immediately gave public speeches to large and enthusiastic crowds in which he called for the creation of a Greater Serbia and announced that he would not return to the Tribunal even if ordered.[89]

The Prosecution now requested the Trial Chamber to revoke Šešelj's provisional release. The Trial Chamber refused, noting that it had not yet ordered

---

84   *Šešelj Case* (Order Terminating the Process for Provisional Release of the Accused Proprio Motu) ICTY-03-67-T (10 July 2014).
85   Šešelj had refused to share any information on his health with the Trial Chamber; see *Šešelj Judgment* (n 14) Annex II, paras 77–78.
86   *Šešelj Case* (Order on the Provisional Release of the Accused Proprio Motu) ICTY-03-67-T (6 November 2014).
87   *Šešelj Case* (Dissenting Opinion of Judge Mandiye Niang to the Order on the Provisional Release of the Accused Proprio Motu) ICTY-03-67-T (11 November 2014) ('Perhaps we should just hope that the certainty of the majority 'that the Accused will comply with the [ordered] requirements' will be confirmed. Hope, however, seems to me fairly derisory comfort for the witnesses in a case which has the distinctive characteristic of having seen several allegations of interference with witnesses and even judgements convicting the Accused of having compromised the safety of protected witnesses.').
88   The Prosecution later argued that it did not have access to the medical information on which the Chamber had relied when granting provisional release (see *Šešelj Case* [Prosecution Motion to Revoke Provisional Release] ICTY-03-67-T [28 November 2014] para 3). However, this begs the question of why it did not request this information in the first place.
89   *See* European Parliament resolution of 27 November 2014 on Serbia: the case of accused war criminal Šešelj [2016] OJ C289/06.

Šešelj's return to the Tribunal and that Šešelj's statements were therefore not in breach of any conditions.[90] The Appeals Chamber disagreed, noting that a Trial Chamber had to be satisfied that an accused would comply with any conditions imposed on him during the duration of a provisional release. Given Šešelj's uncontested statement that he would not return to the Tribunal even if ordered, no reasonable Trial Chamber could have remained satisfied that Šešelj complied with the conditions of the provisional release.[91] The Appeals Chamber consequently ordered the Trial Chamber to revoke Šešelj's release and order his return to the Detention Unit in The Hague.[92] When the Trial Chamber failed to do so, the Prosecution requested the Appeals Chamber to enforce its decision. The Appeals Chamber issued an arrest warrant, which however was not enforced by the Serbian authorities.[93] A few months later, the Appeals Chamber suspended the arrest warrant and permitted Šešelj to stay in Serbia either until the end of his medical treatment, the delivery of the judgment or if otherwise ordered to return by the Trial Chamber.[94]

When the delivery of the judgment approached – Judge Niang had finally concluded his familiarization with the case – the Trial Chamber ordered the Serbian authorities 'to take all the necessary measures to ensure the Accused's appearance' on that date.[95] However, having received a report that Šešelj's treatment in Serbia could not be interrupted or continued in the Hague, the Trial Chamber by majority laconically noted 'that, under these conditions, the transfer of the Accused to the Hague is not required by the Trial Chamber'.[96] Judge Niang forcefully dissented from this reasoning, calling a spade a spade:

> It seems to me that the exemption from having to appear is a position that poorly disguises the triumphant defiance by an Accused who has always maintained his refusal to return after his provisional release.

---

90 *Šešelj Case* (Decision on Prosecution Motion to Revoke Provisional Release) ICTY-03-67-T (13 January 2015).
91 *Šešelj Case* (Decision on Prosecution Appeal Against the Decision on the Prosecution Motion to Revoke the Provisional Release of the Accused) ICTY-03-67-AR65.1 (30 March 2015) para 19.
92 Ibid para 22.
93 There is no explanation why the Serbian authorities did not enforce the arrest warrant. The relevant decisions of the Appeals Chamber were taken confidentially and have not been made publicly available.
94 *Šešelj Judgement* (n 14) Annex II, paras 83–84.
95 *Šešelj Case* (Scheduling Order) ICTY-03-67-T (12 February 2016).
96 *Šešelj Case* (Order on Arrangements for Delivery of Judgement) ICTY-03-67-T (16 March 2016).

> [...]
> The Accused is, of course, ill and receiving treatment but his activities in Serbia certainly attract considerable attention. It is ironic that the Tribunal is excusing the Accused at a moment when he is readily attending a hearing at a Belgrade court – a hearing that is nothing more than an offshoot of our procedure here.
>
> In short, faced with someone thumbing their nose at us, we look away to avoid seeing the affront and in the process use the Accused's treatment as a convenient excuse. I prefer to acknowledge the obstacles that are in the way and have everyone honour their responsibilities.
>
> I would indeed hold the hearing on 31 March to deliver the judgement; I would hold it despite the Accused's absence, not because his presence would not be required, but because he refuses to appear and the Serbian authorities would not use the means available to them to force him to appear.[97]

When the Trial Chamber finally issued its judgment on 31 March 2016 – more than 13 years after Šešelj's initial appearance before the Tribunal in The Hague – it found Šešelj not guilty under all counts. The decision, at about 100 pages, was taken by majority, comprising Judges Antonetti and Niang.[98] The majority concluded that there was not sufficient evidence to prove that there had been an attack against a civilian population, a fundamental requirement for any conviction for crimes against humanity;[99] that it was not proven that there had been a joint criminal enterprise;[100] and that Šešelj's speeches did not constitute incitement to commit crimes.[101] Consequently, it acquitted Šešelj.

In a dissenting opinion, Judge Lattanzi noted her disagreement with most of the majority's findings, criticized the majority's lack of reasoning and deplored its failure to take into account the climate of witness intimidation when assessing the witness evidence.[102] She also lamented the majority's narrow focus on the Defence arguments, which for instance allowed the majority to characterize the forceful displacement of individuals as a humanitarian aid operation, despite overwhelming evidence to the contrary.[103] In her view, the

---

97 Ibid (Separate Opinion of Judge Mandiaye Niang) paras 1, 3–4.
98 Šešelj Judgement (n 14) 109.
99 Ibid para 198.
100 Ibid para 281.
101 Ibid para 350.
102 *Šešelj Judgement* (n 14) (Partially Dissenting Opinion of Judge Flavia Lattanzi – Amended Version ['Lattanzi Dissent']).
103 *Šešelj Case* (Summary of Partially Dissenting Opinion of Judge Lattanzi) <http://www.icty.org/x/cases/seselj/tjug/en/160331_summary_of_the_partially_dissenting_opinion.pdf>

evidence was sufficiently strong to convict Šešelj for his actions as a participant in a joint criminal enterprise to rid certain parts of the former Yugoslavia of all non-Serbs. Moreover, Šešelj's inflammatory speeches constituted incitement to most of the crimes set out in the indictment.[104] Judge Lattanzi expressly rejected the majority's strong criticism of the Prosecution:[105]

> It is true that the Prosecutor should have done better. However, in my opinion, it is above all the Chamber – in its former, as well as present composition – that should have done better, despite the complexity of the case and the difficulties we encountered, especially regarding the Accused's behaviour with the witnesses and his obstruction of the proceedings.[106]

In a separate opinion, Judge Niang stated the difficulties of familiarizing himself with the case after the witnesses had been heard and pointed to a number of flaws in the procedure, including the liberal admission of written evidence, which in his view did not comply with the relevant standards. He also pointed to the conduct of the Accused whose behaviour had gone unchecked – 'he did what he pleased'.[107]

Judge Antonetti also appended a separate opinion,[108] which ran into more than 500 pages and, in typically meandering fashion, contained a blistering critique of the way the Tribunal worked, which in his view had contributed to the length of the proceedings.[109] The opinion – which one observer called 'profoundly dilettantish'[110] – also revisited at length a number of procedural issues at trial, such as the Accused's right to self-representation, the disqualification of Judge Harhoff and the granting of Šešelj's provisional release. A common

---

accessed 14 June 2017. See *Šešelj Judgement* (n 14) para 193. Interestingly, even though this example is contained in the summary of her dissent, the full version of the dissent makes no reference to it.

104 Ibid.
105 See *Šešelj Judgement* (n 14) paras 15–19.
106 Lattanzi Dissent (n 102) para 3.
107 *Šešelj Judgement* (n 14) (Individual Statement of Judge Mandiaye Niang ['Niang Opinion']) para 7.
108 *Šešelj Judgement* (n 14) (Concurring Opinion of Presiding Judge Jean-Claude Antonetti Attached to the Judgement ['Antonetti Opinion']).
109 It also included a somewhat convoluted diagram juxtaposing the 'usual functioning' of the ICTY with a proposal for its 'effective functioning'.
110 Marko Milanović, 'The Sorry Acquittal of Vojislav Šešelj' (*EJIL Talk*, 4 April 2016) at <www.ejiltalk.org/the-sorry-acquittal-of-vojislav-seselj/> accessed 14 June 2017.

thread in all those areas was the allocation of blame for the failures of the case to others – the Prosecution, the Registry, other Judges, and the legal staff.[111]

This article is not about the merits of the judgment, aspects of which have been thoroughly analysed elsewhere.[112] However, it is noteworthy that Judge Lattanzi felt it necessary to express herself strongly not only in her dissent[113] but also in an interview given shortly after the verdict, in which she characterized the judgment as a 'nullity', which 'amount[ed] to nothing'. She also noted that that she had 'suffered a lot'.[114]

The Prosecution has appealed the judgment before the MICT Appeals Chamber, arguing that 'the most troubling aspect of the Judgement is the uniquely inadequate adjudication of the case'[115] and that '[a]llowing the erroneous acquittals in this case to stand would be an affront to the victims of the crimes at issue and would jeopardise the integrity of the ICTY and MICT.'[116] At the time of writing, the Appeals Chamber has yet to schedule an oral hearing and it is unclear when it will render a judgment.

3   Is the Šešelj Trial Symptomatic of the Problems of International Criminal Justice?

Almost 25 years after the establishment of the ICTY and the ICTR and 15 years after the entry into force of the Rome Statute of an International Criminal Court, international criminal justice has finally come of age. It is now a

---

111   This is not surprising, given the Judge's previous assurances in another case that he never makes mistakes; see e.g. *Prlić et al.* Case (Transcript) ICTY-04-74-T (11 May 2009) 7881 ('Je peux me tromper mais en réalité je ne me trompe jamais.').

112   See Wibke K. Timmerman, 'Inciting Speech in the former Yugoslavia: The Šešelj Trial Chamber Judgment' (2017) 15 JICJ 133; see also Ines Peterson 'International Criminal Liability for Incitement and Hate Speech' in this volume.

113   'I will conclude this opinion by saying that with this Judgement we have been thrown back centuries into the past, to a period in human history when we used to say – and it was the Romans who used to say this to justify their bloody conquests and the assassinations of their political enemies during civil wars: "Silent enim leges inter arma."' (Lattanzi Dissent [n 102] para 150).

114   Andrea Oskari Rossini, 'Šešelj Verdict: The Dissenting Judge' (*Osservatori balcani e caucaso*, 8 April 2016) <www.balcanicaucaso.org/eng/Areas/Serbia/Seselj-verdict-the-dissenting-judge-169740> accessed 14 June 2017.

115   MICT, *Šešelj Case* (Notice of Filing of Public Redacted Version of Prosecution Appeal Brief) ICTY-16-99-A (29 August 2016) para 1.

116   MICT, *Šešelj Case* (Prosecution Reply Brief) ICTY-16-99-A (22 February 2017) para 4.

permanent fixture among the tools employed by the international community to create an improved world legal order. There are few voices that question its raison d'être. However, criticism rightly continues to be raised with respect to its deficiencies and failures. The *Šešelj* trial is certainly emblematic in this regard, and, among its many difficulties, it is possible to highlight three problematic issues that became apparent throughout its run: the length of the trials and their bureaucratic nature; the inability or unwillingness of some judges to exercise control over the proceedings; and the still unsolved dilemma of the tension between an accused's right to self-representation and the overall interest in conducting an orderly and fair trial.

It took more than 13 years from Šešelj's initial appearance to his acquittal by the Trial Chamber. Šešelj spent more than 11 years in detention. Even considering the time he served for contempt of court during this period, Šešelj was held for a considerable amount of time. In this, he was not alone. The length of the proceedings against him was certainly unprecedented for a single accused but was frequently exceeded in multi-accused trials held before the ad-hoc tribunals. For instance, in the *Butare* case before the ICTR, more than 20 years passed between the arrest of some of the accused and the final judgment of the Appeals Chamber.[117] The Appeals Chamber, which in other long-running cases had found that there had not been undue delay based on their complexity, held in that case that such complexity could not be the only factor relevant to the assessment of an undue delay. It found that the conduct of the Prosecution and the simultaneous participation of the Judges in other proceedings significantly contributed to the delays, which could not be reasonably justified and caused prejudice to the convicted persons.[118] As a remedy, it reduced their sentences.[119] However, such delays are typical and not limited to the ad-hoc tribunals. The first proceedings at the ICC have also been excessively long. In the *Lubanga* case, more than eight years passed between the arrest of the accused and the Appeals Chamber's judgment; in *Bemba*, it took almost eight years between the arrest of the accused and the Trial Chamber's judgment, with no indication when the appeals proceeding will be concluded. Even more worrying is the fact that unlike at the ICTY and the ICTR, the charges in those cases were limited to only a few counts.

There are many reasons for the long duration of international criminal proceedings, including the specific environment in which they take place, which are difficult to remedy. These include delays on account of required

---

117 See *Nyiramasuhuko et al. Case* (Judgement) ICTR-98-42-A (14 December 2005) paras 6–7.
118 Ibid paras 342–399.
119 Ibid paras 3521–3538.

translations/interpretation, the sheer complexity of cases that address serious violations of international law in a multitude of crime sites, and procedural rules that are of a hybrid nature and do not necessarily encapsulate best practices elsewhere. However, some of the delays are entirely avoidable. Many times, investigations have not fully concluded before indictments are submitted, resulting in subsequent amendments, complicating efforts to streamline cases. There is also the bureaucratization of trials, in which the parties file countless submissions and Chambers issue lengthy decisions on arcane procedural matters that could otherwise be disposed of much more concisely and expeditiously.[120] This in turn is facilitated by the courts' internal working structures, which has teams of legal officers working for Judges, who depending on background and experience, may adjust their level of involvement in any given case. Indeed, it is clear from Judge Antonetti's individual opinions that he was not satisfied with the way the Trial Chamber was supported. However, in his reading, the Judges were the 'prisoners of a system where their only role is to wait for drafts from legal officers who fall under the Registrar's, not the Judges', administrative authority.'[121] This is a somewhat astonishing remark by a presiding Judge with the status of an Under-Secretary-General whose primary responsibility it is to author the decisions of the Chamber.

Another aspect is the failure on the part of some Chambers to exercise sufficient control over the proceedings, making it much easier for them to get off track. The required strict supervision of course applies to all parties in the trial but specifically to an accused who is unrepresented and unbound by any professional or legal constraints. In his separate opinion to the *Šešelj* judgment, Judge Niang expressed his shock about how the trial had been conducted:

> The Accused spared no one. He bullied and ridiculed witnesses well beyond any acceptable level of tolerance, even for a vigorous cross-examination. He was not always admonished. And when he was, he frequently turned a deaf ear to the Chamber's injunctions. He did what he pleased. [...] Several hearings were the setting of a surreal performance on the part of the Accused who, while not testifying, managed to steal

---

120   See e.g. *Bemba et al. Case* (Decision on requests for an extension of the time limit for the filing of the documents in support of the appeal) ICC-01/05-01/13 (23 November 2016) (running at eight pages and 56 footnotes for a simple decision on whether to grant an extension of time for the filing of an appeal brief).

121   See *Šešelj Case* (Judge Antonetti's Concurring Opinion on Decision Inviting the Parties to Make Submissions on the Continuation of the Proceedings) ICTY-03-67-T (13 November 2013) 3; see also Antonetti Opinion (n 108) 19–21.

the floor and lecture the Prosecution, the witnesses and the Judges. And, strange as it may seem, this unusual approach often proved successful. On each occasion, the Accused was able to "shed light" on the facts, although how these oral statements, made outside procedural rules, would be treated was a matter that was never clarified. The Prosecution's objections, sometimes relayed by one of the members of the bench in the form of a timid reminder of more orthodox practices, were to no avail.[122]

Many times, the predominantly adversarial procedural rules are blamed for such lack of control; however, even in those tribunals that allow for a much stricter handling of cases, including a more judge-focused presentation of evidence, Judges have chosen to take a more passive role.[123]

Finally, the practicalities of an accused's right to self-representation remain essentially unresolved. While the theoretic underpinnings of the right are settled in the case-law of the ad-hoc tribunals, the courts have not managed to develop a comprehensive system that appropriately addresses and balance an accused's statutory right to represent himself with the exigencies of massively complex cases, or how to deal with an accused who abuses the right by being obstructive or by intimidating victims and witnesses.

In this context, and given that Judge Schomburg is the honouree of this *Festschrift*, it is more than appropriate to make reference to his position on the matter of self-representation, which he not only expressed in the first *Šešelj* decision but also in his famously titled 'Fundamentally Dissenting Opinion' appended to the Appeals Chamber's decision in the *Krajišnik* case that allowed the Accused to represent himself in the appeal proceedings before the Tribunal.[124] Judge Schomburg's view is driven by an accused-centered approach. Self-representation in his opinion is detrimental to the fair trial rights of an accused, arguing that 'there is no fair procedure before international tribunals

---

122 Niang Opinion (n 107) paras 8–9.
123 See e.g. the Statute and the Rules of Procedure and Evidence of the Special Tribunal for Lebanon, which not only permit but in fact require the Trial Chamber to conduct the presentation of evidence along a more inquisitorial model. However, this model has not been applied, in favour of the more traditional adversarial approach.
124 *Krajišnik Case* (Decision on Momčilo Krajišnik's Request to Self-Represent, On Counsel's Motions in Relation to the Appointment of *Amicus Curiae*, and On the Prosecution Motion of 16 February 2007, Fundamentally Dissenting Opinion of Judge Schomburg on the Right to Self-Representation) ICTY-00-39-A (11 May 2007) (*'Krajišnik Dissent'*). While the opinion is limited to self-representation on appeal, Judge Schomburg made no secret of the fact that he disagreed with the *Milošević* and *Šešelj* decisions on the matter in general.

without public legal assistance'.[125] To Judge Schomburg, given the complexity of 'mega trials', self-representation would ultimately result in an unfair trial: 'When it conflicts with the overarching right to a fair, public and expeditious trial, the right to self-representation must yield. [...] [A] waiver of the right to a fair trial is not possible under any circumstances.'[126] Indeed, the continuation of the proceedings in the *Krajišnik* case – without the participation of Judge Schomburg who had recused himself from the bench after the issuing of the decision[127] – proved to be difficult. Once again, the Tribunal permitted self-representation yet also appointed an '*amicus curiae*' who could file his own appeal, and subsequently allowed the appellant to be represented by yet another counsel on a specific legal issue.[128] This was neither self-representation nor representation by counsel, a hybrid that fit in nowhere.

4 Conclusion

While the *Šešelj* case was extreme, it was certainly not unique in many of its aspects. It would therefore be too easy to dismiss it as an anomaly, caused by a belligerent accused with no boundaries and a Tribunal unwilling or unable to control his behaviour. Indeed, efforts by accused persons to sabotage the proceedings continue, most recently in a contempt case held before the Special Tribunal for Lebanon.[129]

How to best address such situations must probably be decided on a case-by-case basis. The tribunals have developed different models, none of which has proven to be perfect – representation by counsel to the exclusion of the accused, self-representation, mostly modified by permitting legal assistance, and standby counsel. A compromise approach has been advocated by Judge Schomburg, that is, to find ways that would allow the accused person to be represented by qualified counsel but at the same time permit him to take charge

---

125 Ibid para 2.
126 Ibid para 83.
127 See *Krajišnik Case* (Decision on Prosecution Request for Clarification of President's Order of 16 May 2007) ICTY-00-39-A (28 June 2007).
128 See *Krajišnik Case* (Decision on Momčilo Krajišnik's Motion to Reschedule Status Conference and Permit Alan Dershowitz to Appear) ICTY-00-39-A (28 February 2008) para 8.
129 In that case, when the accused person (who had not been arrested) refused to appear before the Tribunal and participate in the trial, the Judge presiding over the case ordered that counsel be imposed (see *Al-Amin Case* [Reasons for Decision on Assignment of Counsel] STL-14-06 [5 June 2014]).

of his case to the greatest extent possible.[130] However, as the *Šešelj* trial proves, a strategy that fails to control an accused who openly disregards all rules, is doomed to failure. This conclusion is not new; it was advanced more than ten years ago by an observer after the sudden end of the *Milošević* trial:

> The lesson to be learnt [...] is that senior accused in complex international criminal trials should not be allowed to continue to represent themselves where there is sufficient evidence that self-representation will threaten the fairness of the trial or its reasonable expedition. [...] A clear message to accused prone to such manipulation that the court will not tolerate interference with the forensic trial process in such a way that it threatens fairness and expedition will better serve the cause of justice and fairness.[131]

At the same time, the courts need to take steps to further streamline their internal procedures and manage cases better. Given the volume of material before the Judges and the parties, this is not an easy task. However, at the least, efforts need to be made to exercise tighter control over the proceedings, with Judges playing a more proactive role in order to minimize the parties' tendencies to overwhelm the court with evidence or to discuss tangential issues of no relevance to the case. The *Šešelj* case has demonstrated that failing to take control will have serious consequences not only for any specific proceedings but also for the credibility of international criminal justice in general.

---

130   See *Krajišnik Dissent* (n 124) para 2 ('[T]he Appeals Chamber's jurisprudence is based on a false dichotomy which assumes that the right to defend oneself negates the right to be assisted by counsel. This fundamental understanding that both rights are mutually exclusive adversely affects the fairness of the proceedings.'); see also Boas (n 29) Self-Representation, 55.
131   Boas (n 29) Milošević Trial, 268.

CHAPTER 19

Aut iustitita aut pax? Enforcement of International Prison Sentences in (Former) Conflict Areas

Michael Stiel and Carl-Friedrich Stuckenberg

Abstract

In a 2007 decision concerning the Strugar case, the Appeals Chamber of the International Criminal Tribunal for the former Yugoslavia (ICTY), Judge Wolfgang Schomburg dissenting, seemed to accept the view that States belonging to the former conflict area were barred from being designated to enforce a prison sentence of the Tribunal, even if the sentenced person himself wished to be transferred to that State.

Our article will first give a brief introduction to the enforcement regimes of international criminal courts. In a second step, we will take the majority's decision and Judge Schomburg's long and passionate dissent as an opportunity to analyze the practice of international criminal tribunals with regard to the issue mentioned above. A discussion under which circumstances enforcement of sentences in the former conflict area may be appropriate will conclude the contribution.

1 Introduction

The work of international criminal justice attracts public attention usually only when a high-ranking suspect is arrested, when a trial starts or ends with an acquittal or conviction. The enforcement stage rarely comes into focus, although, given the seriousness of the crimes, the length of the sentences will by far exceed the already lengthy trials. This is particularly unfortunate as the execution of the sentence has considerable implications for the legitimacy of the whole project of international criminal law and thus has appropriately been described as the 'backbone of the international penal system'.[1]

---

* Michael Stiel is a PhD candidate and research assistant at the chair of Carl-Friedrich Stuckenberg who is professor of German and international criminal law and criminal procedure, comparative criminal law, and criminal law history at the University of Bonn, Germany.

1 Claus Kreß and Göran Sluiter, 'Preliminary Remarks' in Antonio Cassese, Paolo Gaeta and John RWD Jones (eds), *The Rome Statute of the International Criminal Court* (OUP 2002) vol II, 1752 f.

In a 2007 decision concerning the Strugar case,[2] the Appeals Chamber of the ICTY seemed to accept the view that States belonging to the former conflict area were barred from being designated to enforce a prison sentence of the Tribunal, even if the sentenced person himself wished to be transferred to that State. In a long and passionate dissent, Wolfgang Schomburg, then a Judge of the Appeals Chamber of the ICTY, delved into fundamental questions of this field of the law. After a brief introduction to the enforcement regimes of international criminal courts, we will take the majority's decision and Judge Schomburg's dissent as an opportunity to analyze the practice of international criminal tribunals and discuss under which circumstances enforcement of sentences in the former conflict area may be appropriate.

2 The First Steps – Enforcement of Sentences of the Nuremberg and Tokyo Tribunals

The International Military Tribunal (IMT) at Nuremberg, established by Agreement between the four occupying powers in Germany,[3] tried leading figures of the former Nazi regime between 14 November 1945 and 1 October 1946. The majority of those convicted were sentenced to capital punishment, while six accused received prison sentences from 10 years to life imprisonment.[4] Sentences were served at Spandau prison in Berlin operated by the four occupying powers. As the political climate changed, decision-making with regard to the prison administration proved to be burdensome and ineffective.[5] The last inmate, Rudolf Hess, died in 1987, having served over 40 years of his life sentence.

The International Military Tribunal for the Far East (IMTFE) was established on 19 January 1946 by special proclamation by the Supreme Commander for the Allied Powers (SCAP) in Japan, General Douglas MacArthur, to try leading Japanese military and governmental officials for crimes committed during the war in the Pacific.[6] Those receiving prison sentences were imprisoned in

---

2 *Prosecutor v Strugar*, Decision on Strugar's Request to reopen Appeal Proceedings, IT-01-42-Misc. 1, AC, ICTY, 7 June 2007.
3 Agreement for the prosecution and punishment of the major war criminals of the European Axis ('London Agreement'), 8 August 1945, 82 UNTS 280.
4 See Trial of the Major War Criminals before the International Military Tribunal (Nuremberg 1948) vol I, 365 f.
5 For a detailed study cf Norman JW Goda, *Tales from Spandau. Nazi Criminals and the Cold War* (CUP 2007).
6 Special Proclamation by the SCAP – Establishment of an International Military Tribunal for the Far East, 19 January 1946, TIAS 1589.

Sugamo Prison, Tokyo, which was initially administered by the American occupation force. Any review or pardon was the SCAP's responsibility according to Art. 17 IMTFE Charter. As the political tide turned quickly,[7] in 1952 the prison's administration was handed over to the Japanese, while Art. 11 of the 1951 San Francisco Peace Treaty[8] reserved the right to any form of early release to the States represented at the IMTFE. However, there seems to have been little resistance against the Japanese efforts to reach early release for the prisoners, as the last of them left Sugamo in 1958.[9] Arguably, as the People's Republic of China and the Soviet Union were not parties to the Peace Treaty, no other State was interested in openly opposing the clemency policy intended by the United States.

The enforcement of the sentences of IMT and IMTFE illustrates the two extreme situations which may occur when enforcement of international sentences is completely left to the political will of one or a group of States: Either there is complete inflexibility (IMT) or inappropriate use of early release that calls into question the whole trial (IMTFE).

3 The Contemporary Enforcement Regime of International Criminal Tribunals

3.1 ICTY

Confronted with the grave breaches of international humanitarian law in the conflicts following the dissolution of the former Yugoslavia in the 1990s, the United Nations Security Council (UN SC) established the ICTY[10] to try the persons responsible for these atrocities as a means to counter this threat to international peace and security. There was a general sentiment that sentences of the Court should be enforced in States prepared to act on behalf of the international community so that the 'not very persuasive'[11] precedent of international enforcement in Nuremberg would not be repeated. Most proposals

---

7   Judge Röling later argued that this would already have been the case at the time of the verdict; cf Bernard VA Röling and Antonio Cassese, *The Tokyo trial and beyond* (Polity Press 1993) 81 ff.
8   Treaty of Peace with Japan, 136 UNTS 1832.
9   Cf Kreß and Sluiter (n 1) 1763 f; Philipp Osten, *Der Tokioter Kriegsverbrecherprozeß und die japanische Rechtswissenschaft* (Berliner Wissenschafts-Verlag 2003) 32 f and 121 ff.
10 UN SC, Resolution 827 (1993) (25 May 1993) UN Doc S/RES/827 (1993).
11 Cf UN SC, Letter dated 10 February 1993 from the permanent representative of France to the United Nations (10 February 1993) UN Doc S/25266, para 155.

submitted to the UN SC for a draft statute did not discuss any preferences or restrictions on the number of possible States of enforcement.[12] However, after the Rapporteurs appointed by the Commission on Security and Cooperation in Europe (CSCE) had published their report arguing that sentences of imprisonment should be served in the former Yugoslavia,[13] Italy,[14] and a few weeks later Russia[15] emphasized in their proposals that the sentence should primarily be enforced in the *locus commissi delicti*, unless the Court should decide otherwise to guarantee the due enforcement of the sentence. Notwithstanding that, the UN Secretary-General (UN SG) adopted the contrary position in his report to the UN SC. He argued that 'given the nature of the crimes in question and the international character of the tribunal, the enforcement of sentences should take place outside the former Yugoslavia'.[16] Yet, the wording of Art. 27 ICTY Statute and of Rule 103(a) ICTY Rules of Procedure and Evidence (RPE) seem to be open to every 'State designated' without restriction.

The first final sentence was handed down by the ICTY in the case *Prosecutor v Erdemović* based on a guilty plea. The sentencing judgment of 29 November 1996 approved the view of the UN SG regarding the enforcement in the States of the former Yugoslavia, and emphasized that the 'situation prevailing in that region' would either endanger the convicted person's security or the proper execution of the sentence.[17]

3.2 *ICTR and MICT*

The International Criminal Tribunal for Rwanda (ICTR), established only a year later by the UN SC after the 1994 genocidal atrocities in Rwanda,[18] follows

---

12 Cf UN Doc S/25266, paras 154 ff; UN SC, Letter dated 5 April 1993 from the permanent representative of the United States of America to the United Nations Addressed to the Secretary-General (12 April 1993) UN Doc S/25575, 10.

13 Hans Corell, Helmut Türk and Hillestad Thune, Proposal for an International War Crimes Tribunal for the former Yugoslavia (9 February 1993), quoted from Virginia Morris and Michael P Scharf, *An Insider's Guide to The International Criminal Tribunal for the Former Yugoslavia* (Transnational Publishers 1995) vol II, 211 ff, 264 f and 293 (Art 46).

14 UN SC, Letter dated 16 February 1993 from the permanent representative of Italy to the United Nations (17 February 1993) UN Doc S/25300, 7 f (Art 14).

15 UN SC, Letter dated 5 April 1993 from the permanent representative of the Russian Federation to the United Nations (6 April 1993) UN Doc S/25537, 11 (Art 27).

16 UN SC, Report of the Secretary-General pursuant to paragraph 2 of Security Council Resolution 808 (1993) (3 May 1993) UN Doc S/25704, para 121.

17 *Prosecutor v Erdemović*, Sentencing Judgment, IT-96-22-T, TC, ICTY, 29 November 1996, para 70.

18 UN SC, Resolution 955 (1994) (8 November 1994) UN Doc. S/Res/955 (1994).

a very similar 'indirect' enforcement model. However, Art. 26 ICTR Statute and Rule 103(a) ICTR RPE list Rwanda as an example for the State of enforcement, thereby not only not excluding but seemingly preferring Rwanda. The relevant report of the UN SG explicitly highlights the contrast to the ICTY, yet without any explanation for this different assessment.[19]

In 2010, the UN SC created the United Nations Mechanism for International Criminal Tribunals (UN MICT)[20] *inter alia* to oversee the enforcement of the sentences of both ICTY and ICTR after the completion of the remaining trials. The relevant provisions, namely Art. 25(1) MICT Statute and Rule 127(a) MICT RPE, are silent on restrictions or preferences on the group of States of enforcement.

3.3 ICC

The discussion about the potential exclusion of the State of commission resurfaced in the negotiation process of the Rome Statute for the International Criminal Court (ICC).

Art. 59 of the 1994 ILC draft[21] contemplated enforcement in any State 'designated by the Court from a list of States which have indicated to the Tribunal their willingness to accept convicted persons' without restriction. The 1995 Ad Hoc Committee Report, however, referred to a proposal to exclude the State of nationality and the State where the crime was committed from a potential obligation to enforce.[22] The Report of the 1996 Preparatory Committee listed various proposals: A broad 'The Court cannot designate an interested State of a given case as the place of imprisonment' as well as an exclusion of the State on the soil of which the crimes had been committed or of the nationality State of either convicted person or victims.[23] It was further discussed to enable the Court to decide otherwise for overriding reasons of social rehabilitation in

---

19 UN SG, Report of the Secretary-General pursuant to paragraph 5 of Security Council Resolution 955 (1994) (13 February 1995) UN Doc S/1995/134, para 19.

20 UN SC, Resolution 1966 (2010) (22 December 2010) UN Doc S/RES/1966 (2010), especially Art 25 of the annexed MICT Statute.

21 Report of the International Law Commission on the work of its forty-sixth session (2 May–22 July 1994) UN Doc A/49/10, 66 (Art 59).

22 Report of the Ad Hoc Committee on the Establishment of an International Criminal Court (6 September 1995) UN Doc A/50/22, para 239.

23 Report of the Preparatory Committee on the Establishment of an International Criminal Court Volume II (Compilation of Proposals) (13 September 1996) UN Doc A/51/22, 289, 291, 293.

individual cases.[24] These proposals formed Art. 59 Option 1*bis*(a) in the subsequent drafts.[25]

The issue remained contentious during the Rome Conference.[26] In a working paper on then Article 94 issued during the course of the Conference, the exclusionary proposals appear to have been dropped.[27] It may have been at this point that delegations decided not to deprive the Court of the 'adequate flexibility'[28] to give prevalence to reasons of social rehabilitation, as the case may be. As one of the criteria for the determination of the State of enforcement, Art. 103(3)(d) of the Rome Statute[29] lists 'the nationality of the sentenced person'. In the case law of the ad hoc tribunals, the State where the crimes had been committed usually coincided with the State of nationality of the perpetrators with the rare exception of the case of Georges Ruggiu, an Italian-Belgian national involved in the Rwandan genocide.[30] Another example may be the case of Jean-Pierre Bemba Gombo,[31] a national of the Democratic Republic of the Congo (DRC) who is being tried before the ICC for crimes his troops committed during the 2002/2003 civil war in the Central African Republic (CAR).[32]

---

24   Report of the Preparatory Committee on the Establishment of an International Criminal Court Volume II (Compilation of Proposals) (13 September 1996) UN Doc A/51/22, 293.

25   Decisions taken by the Preparatory Committee at its session held from 1 to 12 December 1997 – Annex IV Report of the Working Group on International Cooperation and Judicial Assistance (18 December 1997) UN Doc A/AC.249/1997/L.9/Rev.1, 60; Report of the Inter-Sessional Meeting from 19 to 30 January 1998 in Zutphen, The Netherlands (4 February 1998) UN Doc A/AC.249/1998/L.13, 162 (Art 86(59) Option 2, 1bis(a)); Report of the Preparatory Committee on the Establishment of an International Criminal Court (14 April 1998) UN Doc A/CONF.183/2/Add.1, 152 (Art 94(2)(a)).

26   William A Schabas, *The International Criminal Court – A Commentary on the Rome Statute* (2nd edn, OUP 2016) 1377 and 1382.

27   Working paper on article 94 (2 July 1998), UN Doc A/CONF.183/C.1/WEG/L.8, reprinted in Official Records Volume III – Reports and other documents, UN Doc A/CONF.183/13 (Vol. III), 339.

28   Term borrowed from Gerard AM Strijards and Robert O Harmsen, 'Art. 103' in Otto Triffterer and Kai Ambos (eds), *The Rome Statute of the International Criminal Court – A Commentary* (3rd edn, C.H. Beck/Hart/Nomos 2016) mn 26, who, however, would favor a rigid approach, cf fn 94.

29   Rome Statute of the International Criminal Court (1 July 2002), 2187 UNTS 90.

30   *Prosecutor v Georges Ruggiu*, ICTR-97-32.

31   *Prosecutor v Jean-Pierre Bemba Gombo*, ICC-01/05-01/08.

32   It may be doubted whether 'the conduct in question' actually 'occurred' in the CAR in the sense of Art. 12(2)(a) Rome Statute. The accused directed his troops from his

It is for this close interrelation between 'nationality' and 'locus commissi delicti' that commentators have stressed the ambiguity of the 'nationality' criterion with reference to the considerations of the 1993 UN SG Report and concerns of rehabilitation.[33]

3.4 SCSL and RSCSL

The Special Court for Sierra Leone (SCSL) was created pursuant to an Agreement between the United Nations and the Government of Sierra Leone.[34] Art. 22 SCSL Statute as well as Rule 103(A) SCSL RPE declare that primarily 'imprisonment shall be served in Sierra Leone', thus even establishing preference for the former conflict area. This has been explained by some with the strong position of Sierra Leone vis à vis the SCSL as party to an Agreement with the UN.[35] Yet, 'if circumstances so require', the sentence may also be enforced in another State. The respective UN SG Report[36] elaborates on this issue and lays down that such circumstances might be security risks entailed by the enforcement in Sierra Leone. Even in the event of the designation of another State of Enforcement, the UN SG argues, the wishes of the government of Sierra Leone should be respected.

By another agreement between the UN and Sierra Leone,[37] the Residual Special Court for Sierra Leone (RSCSL) was created *inter alia* to supervise the enforcement of sentences handed down by the SCSL (Art. 1 RSCSL Statute). Interestingly, the wording of Art. 23 RSCSL Statute and Rule 103(A) RSCSL RPE does not accord Sierra Leone the same primacy as place of enforcement as in the SCSL provisions, but resembles the more open approach of Art. 26 ICTR Statute and Rule 103(A) ICTR RPE.

---

headquarters in the DRC and only the consequences of his conduct materialized in the CAR; cf on this question Schabas (n 26) 353.

33   Kreß and Sluiter (n 1) 1788 f. Also cf Christoph JM Safferling, *Towards an International Criminal Procedure* (OUP 2001) 351 ff.

34   Agreement between the United Nations and the government of Sierra Leone on the establishment of a Special Court for Sierra Leone (16 January 2002), 2178 UNTS 138.

35   Kreß and Sluiter (n 1) 1783.

36   UN SG, Report of the Secretary-General on the establishment of a Special Court for Sierra Leone (4 October 2000) UN Doc S/2000/915, paras 49 f.

37   Agreement between the United Nations and the Government of Sierra Leone on the establishment of a Residual Special Court for Sierra Leone (11 August 2010), 2871 UNTS 333, Reg No I-50125.

3.5 Other Tribunals

The Special Tribunal for Lebanon[38] shows no preference for a specific State of enforcement, neither in Art. 29 STL Statute nor in Rule 174 of its RPE nor does the respective Report of the Secretary-General[39] contain explanations to this effect.

Other tribunals with international components (Extraordinary Chambers in the Courts of Cambodia, Iraqi High Tribunal) will remain unconsidered, as their sentences are enforced in the national prison system of the respective State without the possibility of sending the prisoner to an external State of enforcement.

The Kosovo Specialist Chambers act as organs of the State of Kosovo to prosecute, *inter alia,* perpetrators of crimes against humanity and war crimes committed in Kosovo between 1998 and 2000. They are supported with international funding and staff, namely by the European Union. One unique feature that distinguishes them from the other hybrid institutions mentioned above is that Art. 50(1) of their founding law[40] provides that imprisonment shall be served in 'a State designated by the President of the Specialist Chambers from among States that have indicated their willingness to accept persons convicted by the Specialist Chambers'. It is not entirely clear up to now, whether this wording from the point of view of a formally Kosovar institution must be read as 'shall be served in a [foreign] State', thereby excluding imprisonment in Kosovo.

4 The Strugar Decision

On 31 January 2005, Pavle Strugar was found guilty of war crimes committed in connection with the attack by the Yugoslav Peoples' Army on the Old Town of Dubrovnik in December 1991 and sentenced to eight years' imprisonment.[41] Both Prosecution and Defence appealed the decision. In several conferences between Judge Schomburg (acting as Pre-Appeals Judge), the Prosecution, the

---

38 Established by UN SC, Resolution 1757 (2007) (30 May 2007) UN Doc S/RES/1757 (2007).
39 UN SG, Report of the Secretary-General on the establishment of a special tribunal for Lebanon (15 November 2006) UN Doc S/2006/893.
40 Republic of Kosovo, Law on Specialist Chambers and Specialist Prosecutor's Office, Law No. 05/L-053 (3 August 2015); cf also Art. 162(8)(2) of the amended Constitution of the Republic of Kosovo: 'persons may be transferred to serve their sentence in a third country'.
41 *Prosecutor v Strugar,* Judgment, IT-01-42-T, TC, ICTY, 31 January 2005, para 481.

Defence, and the Accused, the conclusion was reached that there would 'exist no legal impediments which could prevent him from serving the remainder of his prison sentence in Montenegro'.[42] Following this, both parties withdrew their appeals; the Defence made explicit reference to the results reached before[43] and the Prosecution acknowledged the withdrawal by the Defence.[44] The Appeals Chamber consequently terminated the proceedings against Strugar.[45] However, a few months later, the Registrar notified the Defence that, after verifications with the UN Headquarters, the Republic of Montenegro was excluded as a possible State of Enforcement.[46] The Defence then requested the re-opening of the appeal proceedings on the ground that Strugar's withdrawal was not 'informed'.[47]

The majority of the Appeals Chamber agreed that Strugar's withdrawal was indeed not an 'informed' one, because he was unaware of the fact that it was legally impossible for the President to designate the Republic of Montenegro as State of Enforcement in this case. The Appeals Chamber apparently accepted the Registrar's opinion without any discussion.[48] In contrast, Judge Schomburg arrived at the conclusion in his dissent that Strugar did make an informed decision because he was well aware that a transfer to Montenegro met with a number of legal and other obstacles which would have to be removed and that the outcome was uncertain.[49]

On 17 July 2008, the Appeals Chamber replaced Strugar's original sentence with one of seven and a half years.[50] After having rejected a prior request,

---

42 This statement was qualified by Judge Schomburg as being a matter for the President to decide, but the possibility was never clearly ruled out: *Prosecutor v Strugar*, Transcript Status Conference, IT-01-42-A, AC, ICTY, 31 August 2006, p. 61 line 1 to p. 63 line 4. See generally *Strugar* (n 2), paras 7 ff.

43 *Prosecutor v Strugar*, Defence Notice of Withdrawing Appeal, IT-01-42-A, AC, ICTY, 15 September 2006, paras 10 ff.

44 *Prosecutor v Strugar*, Withdrawal of Prosecution's Appeal against the Judgement of Trial Chamber II Dated 31 January 2005, IT-01-42-A, AC, ICTY, 15 September 2006, para 2.

45 *Prosecutor v Strugar*, Final Decision on 'Defence Notice of Withdrawing Appeal' and 'Withdrawal of Prosecution's Appeal against the Judgement of Trial Chamber II Dated 31 January 2005', IT-01-42-A, AC, ICTY, 20 September 2006.

46 Letter from Hans Holthuis, Registrar, to Goran Rodić, Counsel for Strugar, 15 March 2007, cited in *Strugar* (n 2), para 15.

47 See *Strugar* (n 2), para 16.

48 *Strugar* (n 2) para 28 at fn 70; Johannes Rochner, *Strafvollstreckung und Strafvollzug im internationalen Strafrecht* (Verlag Dr. Kovač 2014) 163 f, stating that the Appeals Chamber at least implicitly followed this line of argument.

49 *Strugar* (n 2), Dissenting Opinion of Judge Schomburg, paras 35 ff.

50 *Prosecutor v Strugar*, Judgment, IT-01-42-A, AC, ICTY, 17 July 2008, para 393.

ICTY President Robinson now granted Strugar's request for early release on 16 January 2009, apparently also because of his deteriorating overall health condition.[51]

5 The Taylor Decision

On 30 May 2012, Charles Gankay Taylor was sentenced to 50 years' imprisonment for serious crimes committed as sitting head of state[52] during the Sierra Leone civil war.

The United Kingdom was designated as State of enforcement of this sentence.[53] After having been transferred there on 15 October 2013, Taylor filed a motion with the RSCSL in order to end the enforcement of his sentence in Europe and to transfer him to Rwanda, arguing that the continued enforcement of his sentence in Europe violated his human rights, because, *inter alia*, he was isolated from his home and family in Africa.[54]

The President of the RSCSL, competent to decide on the motion according to Art. 23(3) RSCSL Statute, composed a special Trial Chamber to assess the validity of Taylor's arguments under Art. 13(1) RSCSL Statute, 'unless the President otherwise decides for good reason'.[55] The Chamber found that, to a great extent, Taylor raised the same matters that had already been decided by the President in the designation decision and found this part of his application inadmissible.[56] It further noted that Taylor and his family were responsible for the denial of visiting visas by the UK authorities since they failed to

---

51 *Prosecutor v Strugar*, Decision of the President on the Application for Pardon or Commutation of Sentence of Pavle Strugar, IT-01-42-ES, President, ICTY, 16 January 2009, paras 12 f. Relevant parts of the decision are redacted, but the decision notes that Strugar's health state 'raises valid concerns about the potential effect of any transfer to a different environment to serve the remainder of his sentence'.
52 *Prosecutor v Taylor*, Sentencing Judgement, SCSL-03-01-T, TC, SCSL, 30 May 2012, p. 40.
53 *Prosecutor v Taylor*, Order Designating State in which Charles Ghankay Taylor is to serve his sentence, SCSL-03-01-ES, President, SCSL, 4 October 2013.
54 *Prosecutor v Taylor*, Motion for Termination of Enforcement of Sentence in the United Kingdom and for Transfer to Rwanda, SCSL-03-01-ES, Defence, 24 June 2014, paras 32 ff.
55 *Prosecutor v Taylor*, Order Convening Trial Chamber, SCSL-03-01-ES, President, RSCSL, 21 July 2014, p. 2.
56 *Prosecutor v Taylor*, Decision on Public with Public and Confidential Annexes Charles Ghankay Taylor's Motion for Termination of Enforcement of Sentence in the United Kingdom and for Transfer to Rwanda, RSCSL-03-01-ES, TC, RSCSL, 30 January 2015, paras 71 ff.

provide necessary documents.[57] The President of the RSCSL later confirmed this decision.[58]

6 Discussion

The first question which arises here is whether the ICTY was legally barred from designating a State of the former conflict area (6.1). Having established that this is not the case, we will discuss whether such enforcement is appropriate (6.2). Finally, we will try to assess the nature of the designation decision (6.3).

6.1 Was the ICTY Bound by the Secretary-General's Report?

The ICTY is bound to apply international law and its operation and procedure is governed by its Statute, being an annex to a UN SC resolution. The ICTY Statute therefore belongs to the class of secondary sources of international law, here derived from a law-making treaty (the UN Charter). The adoption of the ICTY RPE is provided for in the ICTY Statute (Art. 15) and thus amounts to 'tertiary legislation'.[59] As set out above, nothing in the wording of the ICTY Statute (Art. 27) or the ICTY RPE (Rule 103(A)) places a restriction on the choice of possible enforcement states.

A restriction is expressed only in the Secretary-General's report which recommends that 'the enforcement of sentences should take place outside the territory of the former Yugoslavia'.[60] Whether this recommendation is legally binding, as the Registrar assumed, depends on the legal nature of the report. The report was made upon request from the Security Council[61] and subsequently explicitly approved,[62] but was not incorporated into the ICTY Statute and thus is itself not a legislative product. Rather, it resembles the preparatory work of an international convention, since it outlines the normative framework of the

---

57 *Taylor* (n 56) paras 75 ff.
58 *Prosecutor v Taylor*, Decision on Charles Ghankay Taylor's Motion for Termination of Enforcement of Sentence in the United Kingdom and for Transfer to Rwanda AND ON Defence Application for Leave to Appeal Decision for Termination of Enforcement of Sentence in the United Kingdom and for Transfer to Rwanda, RSCSL-03-01-ES, President, RSCSL, 21 May 2015.
59 Cassese et al, *Cassese's International Criminal Law* (3rd edn, OUP 2013) 12.
60 See above n 16.
61 UN SC, Resolution 808 (1993) (22 February 1993) UN Doc S/RES/808 (1993), para 2.
62 UN SC, Resolution 827 (1993) (25 May 1993) UN Doc S/RES/827 (1993), para 1.

Tribunal and contains a draft statute. Yet assimilating the Secretary-General's report to *travaux préparatoires* or circumstances of the conclusion of a treaty would restrict recourse to it to cases of ambiguity or obscurity of the wording, cf. Art. 32 Vienna Convention on the Law of Treaties (VCLT)[63] on supplementary means of interpretation – and the relevant wording here could not be clearer. The ICTY, which has treated its Statute and RPE like treaty provisions and applied the VCLT to their interpretation,[64] has taken a slightly different approach and regarded the Secretary-General's report as 'context' in the sense of Art. 31(1) of the VCLT[65] and even as 'authoritative interpretation' of the Statute unless there is manifest contradiction between Statute and Report.[66] According to this well-settled view, Art. 27 ICTY Statute and Rule 103(A) ICTY RPE have to be read in light of para. 121 of the report so that the enforcement of Strugar's sentence 'should take place outside' Montenegro as well.

But the SG's report formulates only a recommendation which does not – and could not – alter the unqualified wording of Art. 26 ICTY Statute. Recommendations rest on certain grounds and want to achieve certain aims. If these grounds become obsolete or are outweighed by opposing considerations, the recommendation may lose its aptitude to guide the interpretation of the Statute.

The motivation for the recommendation refers laconically to the 'nature of the crimes in question and the international character of the tribunal' which is obviously insufficient because, as shown above, the recommended policy towards the exclusion is the exception rather than the rule as regards other international criminal tribunals dealing with these types of crimes and does not

---

63 Of 23 May 1969, 1155 UNTS 331.
64 *Prosecutor v Tadić*, Decision on the Prosecutor's Motion Requesting Protective Measures for Victims and Witnesses, Case No IT-94-1-T, TC, ICTY, 10 August 1995, para 18; *Prosecutor v Erdemović*, Judgement, Separate Opinion of Judge McDonald and Judge Vohrah, Case No IT-96-22-A, AC, ICTY, 7 October 1997, paras 3–5; *Prosecutor v Delalić et al*, Judgement, IT-96-1-21-T, TC, ICTY, 16 November 1998, para 1161; see also *Prosecutor v Théoneste Bagosora and 28 Others*, Decision on the Admissibility of the Prosecutor's Appeal from the Decision of a Confirming Judge Dismissing an Indictment against Théoneste Bagasora and 28 others, ICTR-98-37-A, AC, ICTR, 8 June 1998, paras 28–29; William A Schabas, 'Interpreting the Statutes of the Ad Hoc Tribunals', in LC Vohrah (ed), *Man's Inhumanity to Man: Essays on International Law in Honour of Antonio Cassese* (Brill 2003) at 847, 849–852.
65 *Tadić* (n 64) para 18 *in fine*.
66 *Prosecutor v Tadić*, Judgement, IT-94-1-A, AC, ICTY, 15 July 1999, para 295; accord *Strugar* (n 2), Separate Opinion of Judge Shahabuddeen, paras 6 f, 9; Mohamed Shahabuddeen, *International Criminal Justice at the Yugoslav Tribunal – A Judge's Recollection* (OUP 2012) 114 f.

reflect a common understanding of states in 1993.[67] Therefore, one might consider the particular situation at the time the report was written. In his dissent, Judge Schomburg argued that the restriction on countries outside the former Yugoslavia had to be seen before the background of the still ongoing conflict in Yugoslavia at the time the ICTY-Statute was enacted. In his view, after more than a decade the situation had changed and the rigid exception that even was not common sense in 1993 was therefore outdated.[68] This understanding of the report as being an expression of contemporary circumstances can already be found in the decision in the *Erdemović* case.[69] Because of these different factual situations, Shahabuddeen's *argumentum e contrario* Art. 26 ICTR-Statute, contrasting the explicit reference to the locus of the conflict in the ICTR Statute with the silence of the ICTY Statute,[70] is not convincing.

Applying Art. 31(3)(b) VCLT *mutatis mutandis*, there shall be taken into account, together with the context, any subsequent practice. It would arguably be outside the competence of the ICTY to review the security situation in the former Yugoslavia on its own,[71] as such findings are the prerogative of the UN SC under Art. 24, 25, 39 UN-Charter. In fact, later developments show that the UN SC might have implicitly changed its risk assessment. In 2002, Rule 11*bis* was introduced in both ICTY RPE and ICTR RPE, that explicitly permitted the referral of cases to be tried by the authorities of a 'State (i) in whose territory the crime was committed'. The UN SC urged the ICTY and ICTR to make use of these provisions to refer 'cases involving intermediate and lower rank accused' to the competent national jurisdictions and favorably noted the newly established Bosnia War Crimes Chamber in Sarajevo.[72] Yet, a strictly logical

---

67   See the proposals above at n 13 ff.
68   *Strugar* (n 2), Dissenting Opinion of Judge Schomburg, paras 13 at fn 16, 25 ff and fn 34.
69   *Erdemović* (n 17) para 70: 'because of the situation prevailing in that region'.
70   *Strugar* (n 2), Separate Opinion of Judge Shahabuddeen, para 10.
71   *Strugar* (n 2), Separate Opinion of Judge Shahabuddeen, paras 11, 15. See in general on the competence of the ICTY to review its own creation: *Prosecutor v Tadić*, Decision on the Defence Motion on Jurisdiction, IT-94-T, TC, ICTY, 10 August 1995, paras 23 ff. It should be noted that the Trial Chamber, without prejudice to these determinations, conducted an inquiry into the merits of the Defence Submission.
72   UN SC, Resolution 1534 (2004) (26 March 2004) UN Doc S/RES/1534 (2004), preamble and op cl 6. Cf also *Strugar* (n 2), Dissenting Opinion of Judge Schomburg, para 26. Extensively on the Bosnian War Crimes Chamber: Avril McDonald, 'Bosnia's War Crimes Chambers and the Challenges of an Opening and Closure' in José Doria, Hans-Peter Gasser and M Cherif Bassiouni (eds), *The Legal Regime of the International Criminal Court* (Brill Nijhoff 2009) 297 ff.

a maiore ad minus-argument[73] is not possible here, as the enforcement of the sentences of those most responsible could create considerably more unrest and political tensions than the complete trial of those accused the UN SC mentioned[74]. Despite this, the later endorsement of Rule 11*bis* referrals by the UN SC, in particular for both ICTY and ICTR without differentiation, may be seen as outweighing the persuasive authority of the outdated UN SG Report.

Art. 31(3)(c) VCLT requires to take into account any relevant rules of international law. In this sense, Judge Schomburg argued that the ICTY could not operate completely detached from international human rights law by depriving prisoners of their rights codified namely in various Prisoner Exchange Treaties (namely the Council of Europe's Convention on the Transfer of Sentenced Persons[75] or the UN Convention against Transnational Organized Crime[76]).[77] In light of the prominence rehabilitation is given in international[78] and national jurisdictions[79], it does not seem untenable to argue that rehabilitation as an aim of punishment has already reached the status of a principle accepted as international custom.[80]

In conclusion, it is argued here that the ICTY was able to assess the possibility of enforcement in the former Yugoslavia in 2007. For ongoing cases, this conclusion seems inevitable as the 2010 MICT Statute has independent enforcement provisions and the respective UN SC Resolution makes no reference to the 1993 UN SG Report.

---

73 *Strugar* (n 2), Dissenting Opinion of Judge Schomburg, para 27; cf Rochner (n 48) 159 f.
74 In the same vein: Róisín Mulgrew, *Towards the Development of the International Penal System* (CUP 2013) 164; *ICTY Manual on Developed Practices* (ICTY – UNICRI 2009) Chapter XII mn 25. Cf also *Strugar* (n 2), Separate Opinion of Judge Shahabuddeen, para 12.
75 Convention on the Transfer of Sentenced Persons (21 March 1983) CETS 112, Preamble and Art 2. Cf also Council of Europe Committee of Ministers, Recommendation No R (92) 18 Concerning the Practical Application of the Convention on the Transfer of Sentenced Persons (19 October 1992).
76 United Nations Convention against Transnational Organized Crime (entered into force 29 September 2003) 2225 UNTS 209, Art 17.
77 *Strugar* (n 2), Dissenting Opinion of Judge Schomburg, paras 14 ff.
78 Cf International Covenant on Civil and Political Rights (19 December 1966) 999 UNTS 171, Art 10(3); UNHRC 'General Comment 21' in 'Compilation of General Comments and General Recommendations adopted by Human Rights Treaty Bodies' (1994) UN Doc HRI/GEN/1/Rev.1, p. 34 para 10; *Vinter and others v United Kingdom*, Applications 66069/09, 130/10 and 3896/10, Judgment, ECtHR, 9 July 2013, paras 114 ff.
79 Constitution of Mexico (Constitución Política de los Estados Unidos Mexicanos), Art 18(2); German Constitutional Court (Bundesverfassungsgericht), Decision of 18 June 1997, BVerfGE 96, 100, 115.
80 Contra *Strugar* (n 2), Separate Opinion of Judge Shahabuddeen, para 13.

6.2 Is it Appropriate to Enforce Sentences in Former Conflict Areas?

As mentioned, rehabilitation of the convicted person is a generally accepted principle in international instruments dealing with the status of prisoners. Evidently, the purpose of rehabilitation is usually best served when the prisoner is able to maintain contact with persons close to him. Experience shows that there is hardly any meaningful rehabilitative effort for prisoners hosted in States of Enforcement far away from their home.[81] If the penal character of a custodial sentence consists in the deprivation of liberty, sending the prisoner to a foreign place with ensuing loss of family ties and communication problems (if he does not understand the local language) would amount to a form of banishment from society and represent a considerable aggravation of the penalty.[82] In *Erdemović*, the ICTY boldly argued that the *nulla poena sine lege* principle required that the accused be cognizant not only of the possible consequences of criminal behavior but also of the conditions under which the penalty would be executed![83]

The need to enforce in the home country is even more pressing, as the ad hoc tribunals and the ICC at present do not, unlike the RSCSL, have a system of release on parole at their disposal.[84] It is doubtful, as is argued by some,[85] whether Rule 119 ICC RPE[86] can be applied by analogy because it is hardly conceivable that the need for provisions on the enforcement stage had been overlooked by the drafters of the Statute.

Judge Schomburg acknowledged that the absence of a prison meeting the UN standards or a sham prison could be an obstacle to designation.[87] In this context, it must be assessed whether the views expressed by the 1993

---

81   Barbora Hóla and Joris van Wijk, 'Life after Conviction at International Criminal Tribunals' (2014) 12 JICJ 109, 121 f; Göran Sluiter, 'State cooperation in the enforcement of sentences' in Róisín Mulgrew and Denis Abels (eds), *Research handbook on the international penal system* (Edward Elgar 2016) 229 ff, 241.

82   *Erdemović* (n 17) paras 74 f. Also cf Virginia Morris and Michael P Scharf, *An Insider's Guide to The International Criminal Tribunal for the Former Yugoslavia*, (Transnational Publishers 1995) vol I, 304, who also see 'hardships' for the prisoner by serving in a foreign country.

83   *Erdemović* (n 17) para 70.

84   Sluiter (n 81) 229 ff, 244 f.

85   Kai Ambos, *Treatise on International Criminal Law – Volume III: International Criminal Procedure* (OUP 2016) 647.

86   The ad hoc tribunals have imposed similar conditions as those listed in Rule 119 ICC RPE absent such an elaborate provision.

87   *Strugar* (n 2), Dissenting Opinion of Judge Schomburg, paras 13, 9, 32 ff.

Secretary-General's Report, although arguably not legally binding on the ICTY (see above), might indeed still be correct, as Judge Shahabuddeen argued.[88]

In the case before him, Judge Schomburg could refer to the fact that Strugar and the authorities in the Republic of Montenegro had already proven their reliability to abide by restrictions imposed by the ICTY.[89] Despite initial reluctance,[90] a Defence motion filed during the appeals proceedings for provisional release to have hip surgery and ensuing rehabilitation in the Republic of Montenegro had been granted with detailed conditions.[91] Strugar complied and re-appeared in The Hague for his hearing in time. Further, due to the deplorable health condition of his brother and sister in Belgrade, he was granted a short period of provisional release to travel to the Republic of Serbia and see them alive,[92] and again complied with the conditions imposed. Therefore, the surveillance of the enforcement by the ICTY was sufficient to hinder any abuses.[93]

But generally speaking, there is indeed an abstract danger of intolerable conditions in the State of enforcement.[94] Being aware that he had a unique case before him,[95] Judge Schomburg also referred to the law of ICTR, SCSL and ICC and even to the IMT and IMTFE as precedents for enforcement in the home country of the perpetrators.[96] However, the practice of the contemporary tribunals shows something else. For the ICTR, authors had early on suggested that Rwanda was practically unable to execute sentences[97] and that the 'same

---

88 *Strugar* (n 2), Separate Opinion of Judge Shahabuddeen, para 11.
89 *Strugar* (n 2), Dissenting Opinion of Judge Schomburg, para 9 at fn 13.
90 *Prosecutor v Strugar*, Decision on 'Defence Motion: Request for Providing Medical Aid in the Republic of Montenegro in Detention Conditions', IT-01-42-A, AC, ICTY, 8 December 2005.
91 *Prosecutor v Strugar*, Decision on 'Defence Motion: Request for Provisional Release for Providing Medical Aid in the Republic of Montenegro', IT-01-42-A, AC, ICTY, 16 December 2005.
92 *Prosecutor v Strugar*, Decision on 'Decision on the renewed Defence Request Seeking Provisional Release on Compassionate Grounds', IT-01-42-A, AC, ICTY, 15 April 2008.
93 *Strugar* (n 2), Dissenting Opinion of Judge Schomburg, para 34.
94 Strijards and Harmsen (n 28), mn 23 and 26 apparently favour a rigid exclusion of the *locus delicti commissi* for enforcement as they fear the detrimental effect of a 'foreseeable' sham imprisonment ('custodia honesta') on the victims. In the same vein: Safferling (n 33) 351 ff.
95 Underlined in *Strugar* (n 2), Dissenting Opinion of Judge Schomburg, para 32 f 'a humanitarian solution tailor-made for this case'.
96 *Strugar* (n 2), Dissenting Opinion of Judge Schomburg, paras 20 ff.
97 Mary Margaret Penrose, 'Spandau Revisited: The Question of Detention for International War Crimes' (1999) 16 New York Law School Journal of Human Rights 553, 566 f. Cf Kreß

concerns' that existed regarding Yugoslavia would 'certainly exist in relation to Rwanda'[98]. These concerns may also have been triggered by the behaviour of the Rwandese government, namely its protest[99] against the inapplicability of the death sentence at the ICTR and that the ICTR Statute did offer the possibility of enforcement outside Rwanda at all.[100] It is thus not surprising that the ICTR was still sceptical to transfer convicted persons back for enforcement to the country. Rule 11*bis* procedures did not achieve a quick improvement of the national justice system,[101] but a cautious approach to referrals might in the long run have brought considerable improvements.[102] Interestingly, the newly built Mpanga prison in Rwanda has been chosen for some SCSL prisoners, thereby showing the progress that was reached in the Rwandese judicial system.[103]

Despite the preference expressed in the SCSL Statute, no one convicted by the SCSL for mass atrocities has been transferred to Sierra Leone to serve his sentence, the designation decisions almost routinely point to the unavailability of Sierra Leone in this respect.[104] In the case of Taylor, even the UN SC noted in Resolution 1688 (2006) that Taylor's presence in the Western African region constituted an impediment to stability and a threat to the peace of Liberia and

---

and Sluiter (n 1) 1773 arguing that the 'difficult situation in Rwandese prisons' would make it unlikely that the ICTR would enforce sentences in the country 'at this moment'. For a compilation of NGO reports on the devastating conditions in Rwandese prisons shortly after the genocide cf Virginia Morris and Michael P Scharf, *The International Criminal Tribunal for Rwanda* (Transnational Publishers 1998) 618 at fn 2020.

98 Penrose (n 97) 567. Cf Rochner (n 48) 270.
99 Cf UN SC, Provisional Record of the 3453rd Meeting (8 November 1994) UN Doc S/PV.3453, 15 f.
100 Kreß and Sluiter (n 1) 1773 at fn 101.
101 For a compilation of serious incidents after ICTY referrals cf Mulgrew (n 74) 160 ff; *Rodić and Others v Bosnia and Herzegovina*, Application 22893/05, Judgment, ECtHR, 27 May 2008. Cf also the escape of Radovan Stanković, *Prosecutor v Stanković*, Prosecutor's Seventh Progress Report, IT-96-23/2-PT, Ref Bench (27 June 2007). Cf also Klaus Hoffmann, 'Some Remarks on the Enforcement of International Sentences in Light of the Galic case at the ICTY' (2011) 8 ZIS 838, 839 at fn 9.
102 Cf Olympia Bekou, 'Rule 11*bis*: exploring the penal aspects of transferring cases to national courts by the *ad hoc* Tribunals' in Doria, Gasser, and Bassiouni (n 72) 211 ff, 225. This fact seems to be conceded for Rwanda by Mulgrew (n 74) 167 ff.
103 Hóla and van Wijk (n 81) 113 f.
104 Cf *Prosecutor v Fofana*, Order Designating State in which Moinina Fofana is to serve his Sentence, SCSL-04-14-ES, President, SCSL, 12 August 2009, p. 2; *Prosecutor v Kondewa*, Order Designating State in which Allieu Kondewa is to serve his Sentence, SCSL-04-14-ES, President, SCSL, 12 August 2009, p. 2.

of Sierra Leone,[105] and expressed its wish that the trial be conducted elsewhere. The abstract danger to the proper enforcement of a sentence of imprisonment or even to peace and stability in the region might in such cases become so concrete that enforcement even in the proximity of the former conflict area is out of question. The continuing emotional and, depending on the person of the accused, either cheerful or hateful reactions of the public to decisions of the ICTY in major cases[106] might indeed strongly advise against the designation of such places.[107] In our view, however, the risk of destabilization must be assessed in each case individually.[108] Even in those cases which initially cannot be enforced in the State of commission, the length of international sentences may give the opportunity to reconsider if prisoner and circumstances (especially by careful capacity building with regard to the judicial infrastructure in the affected States) have changed.[109]

6.3 Is There a Way to Appeal the Designation Decision?

In the Strugar case, Judge Shahabuddeen mentioned the possibility in an *obiter dictum* that the designation decision of the President could be subject to reconsideration by the Appeals Chamber.[110] So far, judicial control of designation decisions has neither been recognized in the statutes of international criminal tribunals nor in their case law.

Although Charles Taylor's motion has been heard by judges of the RSCSL, it is important to recognize that the special Trial Chamber was convened only (as a quasi sub-organ) to prepare the decision of the President and did not act as a reviewing judicial body. In his initial decision, the President (arguably incorrectly) referred to Art. 13(1) RSCSL Statute giving him the authority to convene a Trial Chamber 'in the event that the need arises for a trial or to review a judgment', a provision requiring a judicial purpose for the creation of a Chamber.[111] However, the President made it clear that he reserved the final say on the

---

105 UN SC, Resolution 1688 (2006) (16 June 2006) UN Doc S/RES/1688 (2006), Preamble.
106 Latest examples after the release of former Croatian generals Gotovina and Marcaz, cf Janine N Clark, 'Courting Controversy' (2013) 11 JICJ 399, 419 ff.
107 Rochner (n 48) 160 f.
108 Cf the recent ICC OTP Policy Paper on Case Selection and Prioritisation (15 September 2016) para 42, highlighting the willingness also to prosecute mid- and low-level perpetrators, as the case may be.
109 As is illustrated by the conditional release of Fofana to Sierra Leone, cf *Prosecutor v Fofana*, Disposition on the Matter of Moinina Fofana's Violations of the Terms of his Conditional Early Release, RSCSL-04-14-ES, Single Judge, RSCSL, 25 April 2016.
110 *Strugar* (n 2), Separate Opinion of Judge Shahabuddeen, para 8.
111 *Taylor* (n 55) p. 2.

review of the designation decision for himself in his affirmative decision.[112] Thus, the considerations that 'the circumstances [...] have not changed'[113] as the President of the RSCSL took into account issues now raised by Taylor during the preparation of the designation decision do not mean that the RSCSL has set a precedent for the review of a designation decision by its judiciary.

In his affirmative decision, the President of the RSCSL reasoned that the Rules, Practice Direction and the Enforcement Agreements (concluded by himself) supported the conclusion that the nature of his designation decision is an administrative one.[114] Since the entire sub-statutory legal framework has to be in accordance with the Statute, this argument is of limited scope. The reference to a decision in the *Sesay* case, where the SCSL Appeals Chamber declared itself incompetent to review a decision of the Registrar that prisoners would be transferred at seven days' notice,[115] does not preclude a different assessment for the designation decision as such. Finally, the President referred to the legal framework of common law jurisdictions that accord a certain leeway to prison authorities.[116] The European Court of Human Rights appears to achieve similar results in its jurisprudence under Art. 6 European Convention on Human Rights (ECHR) that requires access to a 'court'. While it seems that Art. 6 ECHR may be applicable to enforcement measures after a sentence has become final,[117] the ECtHR has recently confirmed that for the transfer of a sentenced person serving his or her sentence in the State where the crimes were committed to his State of nationality, even against his will, no issue under Art. 6 ECHR arises.[118] The underlying rationale seems to be the involvement of foreign policy considerations at the international level.[119] It remains dubious whether this rationale applies in the case of international tribunals despite

---

112   *Taylor* (n 58) paras 27, 37. Cf also the official title of the decision.
113   *Taylor* (n 56) paras 71, 73.
114   *Taylor* (n 58) para 22 f.
115   *Taylor* (n 58) para 24.
116   *Taylor* (n 58) para 25.
117   Cf *Enea v Italy*, Application 74912/01, Judgment, ECtHR, 17 September 2009.
118   *Czoszánski v Sweden*, Application 22318/02, Judgment, ECtHR, 27 June 2006; *Szabó v Sweden*, Application 28578/03, Judgment, ECtHR, 27 June 2006. Cf *Smith v Germany*, Application 27801/05, Judgment, ECtHR, 1 April 2010, paras 39 ff, arguing that only the specific circumstances of the case required a different result (the applicant voluntarily appeared for trial and confessed after having been assured that his prison sentence could be enforced in the Netherlands). See however *Veermae v Finland*, Application 38704/03, Judgment, ECtHR, 15 March 2005, arguing that a possible conversion procedure in the receiving State would be heard in front of a court meeting the requirements of article 6.
119   Cf *Smith* (n 118) para 42.

the differences between the 'horizontal' inter-state practice with regard to the prisoner exchange and the 'vertical' enforcement of international sentences (mainly the necessity of a transfer).[120] In light of the enormous importance of the choice between several States of Enforcement potentially situated all over the world,[121] it seems desirable to allow for some judicial control whether the President has properly exercised his or her discretion,[122] as it is the case in other jurisdictions[123]. In a comparable context, this has been demanded by the ICC Appeals Chamber ruling on the admissibility of an appeal against the Presidency's decision[124] under Art. 108 Rome Statute to allow the prosecution of Germain Katanga for additional conduct by his State of enforcement, the DRC.[125] Further elaboration on the nature, organization and concrete depth of scrutiny of such a reviewing body would however exceed the limits of this contribution.

7 Conclusion

It is not the purpose of this contribution to elaborate in detail on the complex relationship between justice, accountability and peace. But even if one does not overload the enforcement stage with expectations, in particular regarding restorative and reconciliatory aims,[126] the successful enforcement of sentences by the impacted society might have a value of its own. In the words of the 1993 CSCE Rapporteurs: 'unless they [States of the former conflict area]

---

120 See in detail Kreß and Sluiter (n 1) 1765 ff.
121 Cf *Erdemović* (n 17) para 70.
122 Cf Denis Abels, *Prisoners of the International Community – The Legal Position of Persons Detained at International Criminal Tribunals* (Springer 2012) 503 f, who proposes an external adjudicator, apparently with full scrutinizing powers.
123 BVerfG, Decision of 11 December 2013 – 2 BvR 1373/12. Cf also *Meachum et al v Fano*, 427 U.S. 215, 229 (1976) highlighting the discretion of States to introduce some form of judicial process with regard to prisoner transfer.
124 *Prosecutor v Katanga*, Decision pursuant to article 108(1) of the Rome Statute, ICC-01/04-01/07-3679, Presidency, ICC, 7 April 2016.
125 *Prosecutor v Katanga*, Decision on the admissibility of Mr Katanga's appeal against the 'Decision pursuant to article 108(1) of the Rome Statute', ICC-01/04-01/07-3697, AC, ICC, 9 June 2016, paras 16 f. The issue does not seem to have been discussed during the 2016 Session of the Assembly of States Parties (ASP), judging from the Official Records of the conference.
126 Cf Denis Abels, 'Limiting the objectives of the enforcement of international punishment' in Mulgrew and Abels (n 81) 272.

are prepared to take upon themselves to accept enforcement, the Rapporteurs foresee little possibility that justice can be done'.[127]

It is one of the lasting achievements of Judge Schomburg to have challenged a rigid and somewhat simplistic interpretation of the ICTY Statute in the sense of 'pax' where 'iustitia' may have demanded a more cautious assessment of the case.

---

127   Corell, Türk, and Thune (n 13) 264 f.